ROMANCING
THE STARS

An excellent book . . . which will
have appeal for everyone who is a
romantic at heart. — *Prediction*

By the same author
DIVINE ENCOUNTERS
THE FORCES OF DESTINY
SYNASTRY

ROMANCING THE STARS

The Astrology of Love and Relationships

PENNY THORNTON

The Aquarian Press
An Imprint of HarperCollins*Publishers*

The Aquarian Press
An Imprint of HarperCollins*Publishers*
77-85 Fulham Palace Road,
Hammersmith, London W6 8JB

First published by The Aquarian Press
as *Suns & Lovers* 1986
This edition 1988

7 9 10 8 6

A catalogue record for this book
is available from the British Library

ISBN 0 85030 750 3

Printed in Great Britain by
Woolnough Bookbinding Limited,
Irthlingborough, Northamptonshire

CONTENTS

To my 'slap-happy Cappy'

FOREWORD

WHEN I wrote my first book, **Synastry**, many of my family and non-astrologer friends complained that they could only understand a third of it—if that. A pity, they thought, since astrology appeared to lend itself very well to the understanding of relationships. Their comments did not fall on stony ground and I quickly became fired with the idea of writing a book about the astrology of relationships that the layman could understand. Yet because of my 'classical' astrological background I did not want to fall into the trap of Sun-sign banalities; and I also wished to address myself to both the fledgling and the professional astrologer. Not an easy task.

My biggest problem lay in the fact that 'the man in street' only sees astrology in Sun-sign terms and only thinks of 'himself' as a Virgo or a Leo. Real astrology isn't just about Sun signs. For a start, astrology involves all the ten known planetary bodies and their positions around the zodiacal circle, not to mention the four major angles (Ascendant, Descendant, Midheaven, and I.C.) of the horoscope itself. Perhaps more importantly, astrology is a rich symbolic language. Sadly, all too often the study of the 'stars' is dismissed as a parlour game, a rather suspect form of fortune-telling, when in truth it is a vivid and meaningful system that enables us to contemplate the deeper significance of our lives in psychological and spiritual terms. However, in order to reach the layman I have had to divide the book into the twelve familiar zodiac categories since they represent the only form of reference to which 'he' could relate. Yet at the same time I have tried to encourage the idea of the signs as themes, not merely Sun signs, and thus broaden the generally held narrow view of astrology. Now, with the increasing availability of computerized charts anyone can discover his or her major astrological themes.

The twelve signs of the zodiac and their ruling planets embody the gamut of human traits and potential; in the introductory sections, I have traced the mythological roots of the signs, searching where possible for less familiar myths and tales. These stories serve as a reflective process, rather like the 'I Ching', and if approached in this spirit the reader should find the themes strike a note in 'his' consciousness, and the insights to be gained will unfold for themselves. In the sections on sexuality and the male and female of each sign, I have deliberately shown the 'warts' as well as the 'beauty spots' since only through the whole view can understanding and acceptance begin—first of the individual, then of his partners.

Astrology is a marvellous 'tool' for 'digging away' at relationships. It never ceases to fascinate me the way the patterns in individual charts and those of relationships work out in real life. And while it is infinitely preferable to have the whole astrological picture, the themes discussed through this book should nevertheless shed considerable light on everyone's weaknesses and strengths and relationship potential.

Relationships are the medium through which the individual grows and changes most. It is as if each partner acts as a mirror for the other—and also frequently as a dustbin for all his or her unacknowledged flaws! Within an intimate relationship each individual is at his most exposed and therefore at his most vulnerable—where he has most to gain and most to lose. We place our highest expectations in relationships and thus receive our biggest disappointments. There is a common need in almost everyone to find their other 'half'. It is as though each individual senses he is not complete and thus he seeks a partner to provide that sense of wholeness and completion. All too often, therefore, the individual is drawn to a partner who possesses qualities he feels he lacks. While the whole chart maps out these individual needs and deficiencies, broadly speaking fiery and airy people—the Arians, the Leos and the Sagittarians (fire) and the Geminians, the Librans and the Aquarians (air)—are far more likely to enter relationships with their antipathies in the earth and water signs—Taurus, Virgo and Capricorn (earth) and Cancer, Scorpio and Pisces (water)—than they are with their complementary signs. Of course what first attracts often repels and the struggle to resolve these differences begins!

Where astrology becomes so valuable is that it provides a basis for understanding how each partner is 'programmed'; it can show what each individual is looking for in a relationship and in a partner and what each one needs (not always the same thing). With such understanding each partner should be able to accept the other for what he is rather than what he wants him or her to be; and this is more than half the way towards easier relationships. Furthermore, in allowing for each other's differences and recognizing one's own foibles harmony will not only reign in the relationship but within each individual.

While fate may seem to propel us into destined relationships that cause us great happiness or dire misery, there is an equally strong argument for each man getting the relationships he deserves; and glass houses simply won't stand up to a surfeit of stone-throwing! Leaving fate on one side for the moment, a little more self-reflection—with the aid of an astrological microscope—would improve all our relationships by leaps and bounds; and it's always worth remembering, 'if there's something wrong with society, there's something wrong with the individual. And if there's something wrong with the individual, there is something wrong with me'!

For my own part, the two and a half years spent preparing the manuscript became a journey of discovery. The hours of research especially into the myths and symbols lead me into many unexplored areas and inspired many new illuminations. My meetings with almost all the celebrities proved equally fascinating, and in the process I learned much about diplomacy! Also interesting were the synchronicities that occurred as I was working on the various signs. While exploring Pisces and the Graiae sisters in Poseidon's realm, I was confronted in my local high street by three of the ugliest old women I had ever seen in my life; one was blind and another lame. During the Gemini section my computer broke down, and throughout the Aries chapter, Arthur Scargill lead his striking miners into some of the fiercest clashes with the police Britain had ever seen.

When I arrived at the final page, it seemed like the end of a gruelling marathon race: I felt a mixture of elation that it was done and sadness because I had lost a constant companion—a companion I had both loved and hated with fierce Aries-Scorpio passion. It was thus the ideal moment to reflect on the words of Robert Louis Stevenson. 'To travel hopefully is a better thing than to arrive. and the true success is to labour.'

Bon Voyage!

ACKNOWLEDGEMENTS

THE Oscar Awards ceremony never goes past without someone misty-eyed saying, 'This could never have been achieved without the help of ...', and now I find myself in the same position! I have many people to thank for their time and efforts in the protracted birth of this book. Thus (in order of appearance) my thanks go out to Judy Freeman, Philippa Galloway, Joan Coward, and Lynne Jackson all of whom nearly went blind knitting the various pieces of my manuscript together on their typewriters until my word-processor arrived. Stephen Callender for his inspiration for the title. My heroic editor, Michael Cox, who almost developed an ulcer in the latter stages of the book. I wish also to thank all the celebrities who allowed me access to their inner 'vaults': Clare Francis, Jeffrey Archer, David Shepherd, Suzi Quatro, Bob Champion, Barbara Cartland (who also gave me a slap-up tea), Colin Wilson, my dear friend, Georgina Hale, David Essex, Twiggy, Jeremy Irons, HRH the Duchess of York (at the time, Sarah Ferguson), Christopher Reeve, Fenella Fielding (with whom I enjoyed an unforgettable cream tea in the sumptuous surroundings of Claridges), Uri Geller, Sarah Miles, my jet-propelled friend, Kathy Ford, Martin Shaw, and Jilly Cooper (who in Piscean style was excessively kind and helpful.) Last but not least, my stalwart husband, Simon, who ploughed through much of the manuscript and kept my Arian ego down to size by periodically falling asleep over the contents. Yet another labour of love!

ARIES

21 March — 20 April

HEROES, HEROINES, AND KNIGHTS IN SHINING ARMOUR

ARIES
HEROES, HEROINES AND KNIGHTS
IN SHINING ARMOUR

ASTROLOGERS say it is easy to spot Aries Rams. They have a highly distinctive way of moving—intensely purposeful and very fast, forehead or chin, sometimes both, jutting forward, body poised at an angle of thirty degrees, and frequently a staccato, almost Chaplinesque gait (Chaplin coincidentally was a Sun Aries). Arians, of course, take themselves exceedingly seriously and see nothing remotely amusing in their demeanour or characteristic forcefulness. Indeed, most consider the only way to get from A to B is in a direct line regardless of obstacles and at the speed of knots—an attitude reflected in all aspects of their lives. Unlike their dreamy, directionless, preceding sign, Pisces, Arians have little difficulty in deciding what they want: their needs, like babies', require instantaneous gratification otherwise huge firework displays usually erupt. Aries' desires and objectives are rarely impeded by forethought or consideration for others and their plans frequently suffer from the lack of crucial, elementary detail. Thus Arians all too often come to grief on the burning hot coals of their ambitions.

I look forward to consulting sessions with my Aries clients: their honesty and lack of subtlety or deviousness is refreshing, their humour lively and stimulating, and, for the most part, I can settle down for an hour or so and let them talk happily and confidently about themselves, their lives, and their grandiose plans. If I do manage to slip in the odd negative comment, the point usually provokes a strong denial accompanied by much bluster, then a pause as some 'ego-gas' escapes from their balloon.

An Aries client of mine had an extremely difficult chart with many tense angles between some of the more powerful planets—Pluto, Saturn, and Uranus. She prattled on cheerfully throughout the consultation, responding with disdain and blatant disregard for any comments or helpful suggestions I had to make about the nature of the darker, more complex planetary patterns. She was six months pregnant at the time, unmarried, and with a business, by the sounds of it, on the verge of bankruptcy. She had obviously come for help, or at least some assurance that things would sort themselves out, yet at the same time she could neither bring herself to acknowledge any personal weakness nor face the spectre of failure. In fact Aries rarely entertains the thought of failure at all and in the event of any disaster prefers to walk away unseen with a mere shrug of the shoulders. Aries also hates to take advice and learns only from direct experience. Fortunately Arians, like fiery Sagittarius, are blessed with blind optimism and belief in their superhuman powers; and like babies and drunks, they survive miraculous falls from the heights of their great expectations.

At the Spring Equinox the Sun enters the sign of Aries, marking the point where the long dark night of winter gives way to the lush verdant bright green of spring. No doubt those readers in the southern hemisphere will loudly complain that for them 21 March marks the beginning of *their* Autumn; but like it or not, the signs symbolically reflect the subtle changing of the seasons from a distinctly northern bias. Thus at the end of March and during most of April the countryside is full of fluffy white lambs innocently frolicking in the spring sunshine with nerry a dark thought in their perky little heads. And of course in many ways in the morning of their lives Aries joyfully hurl themselves with vigour and excited anticipation into every fresh experience –pioneers to a lamb–relying on their agility and ingenuous charm to bail them out of any difficulties. It is as Aries matures that the many paths to their goals and ambitions seem littered with the debris of their good intentions.

Aries is considered by many to be an uncomplicated sign, which is in fact untrue. No sign of the zodiac can be treated as uncomplicated. Perhaps it would be fairer to say all signs are complex but some are more complex than others! In which case Aries, as the thunderbolt of energy to emerge from the primordial waters of Pisces, is a relatively straightforward idea compared to the inexorable power of Scorpio, for instance, or the bizarre genius of Aquarius.

A variety of mythological figures can be related to Aries. First, Greek Ares himself–a very bloodthirsty god indeed who revelled in the glory of war yet, despite his brute strength, often fell victim to his own lack of judgment. Indeed this is a fatal flaw of Aries individuals who are off on an expedition at the first crack of the whip, only to be thwarted half-way through because they forgot to bring a map or ran out of fuel. Greek Ares also fought valiantly in the Trojan Wars–on both sides, a quirk perhaps more worthy of accommodating Libra, Aries' opposite number. However, although Arians are great crusaders, it is the spirit of the crusade (or rather the experience and exhilaration of the fight) that is important to them, not necessarily the cause itself.

A female version of Ares can be found in Artemis, the huntress-goddess who could be decidedly prickly when offended or her wrath provoked. Arians certainly have a short fuse where their temper is concerned (particularly those females who have their Moon in Aries) and many regret their impulsive gestures of anger as they survey the shattered remains of the glass cabinet.

Prometheus himself displayed many heroic Arian traits. In Greek mythology Prometheus stood up for the rights of downtrodden mankind; on one occasion he managed to outwit Zeus who, in revenge, withheld fire from humanity. Undaunted, Prometheus courageously and arrogantly stole some sparks from the 'wheel of the sun' and brought them back to earth. Thus fire, previously sacred and sacrosanct to the gods, came into man's possession. (Aries, of course, is the first fire sign in the Zodiac.) Prometheus was ultimately punished by Zeus but fortunately saved from a grizzly fate through his own immortality and his friend Hercules. Aries individuals rarely lack courage and their valiant deeds are often performed for the benefit of society's underdogs. Indeed, of all the signs of the zodiac, Aries emerges as the original knight in shining armour.

I am not the first astrologer to draw parallels between the Aries' fighting spirit and the kind of heroics and sometimes foolhardy behaviour displayed by many knights during the Middle Ages–the Age of Chivalry. Although brave and fearless to a man, knights tended to be individuals first and foremost and members of a 'team' only as an afterthought. They found subservience a bitter pill to swallow and had little regard for their superiors or their orders; they were also fervently committed to their own personal battles, which produced considerable lack of order and discipline on the battlefield and much in-fighting between the knights themselves. Even in the great myth of King Arthur and the Knights of the Round Table, the stories revolve around individual knights' triumphs and exploits rather than tales of united effort and glory on the battlefield.

Of all King Arthur's knights, Sir Launcelot was perhaps the most Arian. No other knight could equal his strength and valour, yet he had a tragic flaw: he was blinded by desire for Guinevere, his noble king's wife. This strongly Martian desire was to stand in the way of his quest for the Holy Grail; for though Launcelot had achieved glory on the battlefield his most ardent wish was for spiritual fulfilment. This is perhaps the loftiest dimension to Aries, yet at the same time its most fundamental: Aries embodies the principle of spiritual fire and in the more highly motivated Arians, the quest for spiritual understanding becomes the driving force in their lives. Yet all too often, like Launcelot, they encounter obstacles in the form of their earthly passions and attachments.

One tale in particular describes Launcelot's demise and is full of suitable symbolic details. One night Launcelot, weary from travelling, came across a parting of two ways. At the intersection there was a cross and a slab of white marble. Uncertain which path to take, he approached a faintly lit chapel almost hidden under a thick cloak of ivy. Through the window he saw an altar covered in a silk shroud on which stood a silver candlestick with seven branches—all brightly lit. Unable to force his way in, he returned to his horse and fell asleep. Half-waking, half-sleeping he was dimly aware of the arrival of two white horses bearing a sick knight. Then the chapel door opened and the ancient hermit, Nacius, emerged bearing the candlestick which he placed on the marble slab. Suddenly the Holy Grail appeared gliding on a pure moonbeam and paused by the candles. The sick knight touched the Grail and was cured. The knight then turned to Nacius and enquired why the sleeping Launcelot had not awoken although the Grail had brushed passed him. Nacius replied that Launcelot was held to earth by his sins, whereupon he gave the knight Launcelot's sword, his helmet and his horse. Launcelot, unable to move throughout the spectacle, descended once more into a deep sleep. On awakening he thought he must have dreamed it all, but when he found his horse and his armour gone he knew it had been no illusion. Launcelot spent some time with Nacius telling him that all the great deeds he had done were for the love of Guinevere yet he had never stopped to consider if his motives were right or wrong. Thus the realization dawned upon him that his 'forbidden' love for Guinevere was the great sin that kept him from the Holy Grail.

Yet even with this knowledge, temptation proved too great for Launcelot. On the brink of consummating his love for Guinevere the evil Sir Mordred broke into the bedchamber and denounced them both to Arthur. Guinevere was duly sent to the stake. But in an act of daring Aries heroism, Launcelot rescued her, hacking down his opponents on the way—and tragically two of his friends into the bargain. Launcelot's story did not have a happy ending.

Although he ultimately returned Guinevere to Arthur and received his forgiveness, his life that at one time had shone like a bright star dwindled into insignificance.

While the Arthurian legends as a whole are rich in symbolism of all kinds, astrologically it is interesting to note that the two major themes of the legends—the Holy Grail, with its Christian associations (Pisces), and chivalry and combat (Aries)—are the 'end' and the 'beginning' of the zodiac respectively. Launcelot himself is characteristic of the Arian who, blinded by desire, tramples over all in his path to reach his objectives. The Aries individual also tends to use brute force to overcome obstacles, and often confuses physical bravery with inner strength. Launcelot, of course, was never satisfied—another Arian failing. He found the challenge of the unattainable irresistible, and ultimately this proved to be his downfall. Sadly, many an Aries who embarks on a life full of promise, ends it in disappointed ignominity.

The tarot card of the Fool is another symbolic portrayal of the Arian as a spiritual pioneer rather than a soldier of fortune. The youth, clearly a traveller with a knapsack on one shoulder, is about to step over the precipice: like many Arians, he's too busy looking ever onward and upward to see a potential hazard underfoot! Yet the Fool is not blindly ignorant, but in the flower of innocence. He is a pilgrim and thus a figurative representation of the great myth of the celestial origin of man—of his 'fall' and his conscious return to the celestial realm.

Of course there are plenty of modern-day knights who display the Arian single-minded pursuit of ambition and personal glory. Yet, despite the Arian's natural ability to lead and inspire others, all too often his ardour and enthusiasm lead to short-sighted campaigns that lack the benefit of a comprehensive perspective. Their energy is frequently short-lived and many fall victim to the burden of their over-sized egos. Here the Argentinian general Galtieri (Mars in Aries) springs to mind. Galtieri completely misinterpreted Britain's procrastination over the sovereignty of the Falkland Islands as proof of indifference. Thus in a bid to gain support and popularity for his junta's bloodthirsty and faltering regime, an invasion of the Islands was launched. Galtieri and his band of generals all displayed a distinctly Arian talent for issuing their own orders without conferring with any of their colleagues, so that the Army, the Navy, and the Air Force each worked independently of one another. This naturally caused untold confusion, many blunders, and some disastrous moves. The ultimate defeat and humiliation of the Argentinian forces is now history and Galtieri's name rests in their Hall of Infamy, not as a great hero of the people, but as one who was disgraced, dishonoured, and disowned.

Despite these descriptions of misdirected Aries potential there are many Aries individuals who have achieved distinction and honour in various walks of life through their courage, inspiration, and talents. Bismarck, the founder of modern Germany, William Booth, the inspiration of the Salvation Army, Raphael, one of the greatest painters of all time, and the poet William Wordsworth are four such examples. The British political stage carries many an Arian figure—James Callaghan (former Leader of the Labour Party), Neil Kinnock (present Leader of the Labour Party), David Steel (Liberal Party

Leader), Norman Tebbit, and Michael Heseltine. It must also be emphasized that Arians can express their fiery pioneering spirit in many areas of life, not just in warmongering or troubleshooting, and strange as it may seem this sign seems to emerge frequently in the charts of writers, musicians and artists.

Aries is often said to be an aggressive sign, an adjective that is barely acceptable in the male of the species nowadays and is a downright insult to female Rams: assertive is a more suitable word. Certainly, Arians of both sexes can show their displeasure in verbal and physical aggression on occasion, but such displays carry little weight and are usually short-lived. Arians rarely smoulder for long before launching into the attack, which is why, as we have seen, they can be easily deflected and deterred. Aries' explosions, like most fireworks, erupt with a loud bang but are soon over (Scorpio is the sign for devastating long-term effects). Also Aries individuals hardly ever bear grudges; life is too short, or perhaps like Ares the god, they tend to forget what the fight was all about after a while.

Arians like to think of themselves as winners, and competition and challenge provide constant fuel for their fire. They hate obstruction or delay to their plans whether by circumstance or human intervention and will blast huge holes and slice their way through any amount of red tape to reach their objectives. Arians also like to be in the forefront of almost anything—they cannot bear to hide their light, no matter how dim, under a bushel—and in any group or association they will bulldoze their way to the top ranks where their trouble-shooting behaviour often causes endless consternation. This sign thinks no one can do the job as well as they can and impatience and intolerance for those slower or more reticent than themselves pushes them to intervene and attempt some Herculean tasks. Sadly Aries' stunts do not always come off successfully, nor do they themselves emerge totally unscathed from their experiences.

Male and female Rams are seldom wishy-washy creatures; not for them the soft pastel tones of life, rather the vivid primary colours. Everything they do is announced by loud-hailer and when they arrive it is usually with great impact! In many ways the smallest event in their lives becomes a front-page story for Aries and to many onlookers this fire sign's life seems full of glamorous and eventful chapters. One of the explanations is Aries' ability to hurl himself headlong at life, chomping at the bit to try every fresh and novel experience. Some—in my experience many actors—will even claim experiences they have never had. Not only do Arians have plenty of courage and conviction in their abilities (tried or untried) but almost all firmly believe the *only* place to aim for is the top. Aries also hate menial tasks and subservient positions and they especially loathe carrying out other people's orders. As a result Aries tend to chop and change jobs frequently searching for the niche that will guarantee them the success and power they desire. Yet despite their often bossy and autocratic behaviour most Aries individuals can drive themselves very hard, becoming equally invaluable to organisations as well as successful in their own enterprises.

Several years ago, at the request of the managing director of a small company, I prepared an analysis for one of his executives who had four planets in Aries, Aries rising, and the Moon in ambitious Capricorn. During the course of the analysis I mentioned that the executive no doubt nurtured ambitions to have his own business one day. Some time later I asked the managing director if his executive had found the analysis of interest. 'I haven't given it to him yet,' he confessed somewhat sheepishly. 'You see, I know he'd like to launch out on his own but I need him—I thought your comments might spur him into leaving . . . so I upped his salary instead!'

Few people entertain mixed feelings about Aries individuals—they either like them enormously or detest them. This is mainly because Arians find pretence and artifice of any kind cumbersome and awkward; indeed most find it well nigh impossible to disguise their feelings at all, especially about people. They also never suffer fools gladly. When Aries individuals find people they like they exude intense warmth and friendship toward them; conversely they treat those who fail to appeal with indifference verging on the disdainful.

Aries does not like the long drawn-out preamble—it is a sign that comes directly to the point. Indeed, to say Aries is frank is a considerable understatement. A friend of mine with her Moon in Aries telephoned one day to invite my husband and I to a dinner party the following evening. 'Unfortunately,' she volunteered, 'you were the only people I could think of who would be free!' In one fell swoop we had been informed that (a) we were unlikely to be socially in demand, and (b) that we hadn't been considered in the first place!

Since antiquity each sign of the zodiac has been linked to a particular part of the body: in Aries' case it is the head, which is why astrologers love to use such apt and descriptive terms for this sign as headstrong, head-first, and even, perhaps, hedonistic! Not only do strongly Aries individuals suffer from more than their fair share of headaches, teething troubles, and cuts and bruises to noses and chins, but on a psychological level Arians have a tendency to be extremely big-headed. Consequently, Aries Rams are sometimes labelled the ego-maniacs of the zodiac. Although this statement is rather sweeping, in the main it unfortunately rings true. Aries' greatest weakness—his Achilles heel, so to speak—is his large and fragile ego.

However, despite Aries' show of bravado and his preoccupation with his own unstoppable progress to the top, his confidence is only born of the moment, a sort of impulsive exuberance. Once Aries has time to consider his actions—almost always in retrospect—a dark and uneasy cloud of inadequacy looms menacingly over the horizon. Thus Aries will fish for compliments and assurances that he did well, that he is loved and appreciated, handsome—whatever. While Aries' bubble of his own omnipotence is intact and buoyant all will be well, but once burst Aries is vulnerable to attack and defeat and consequently likely to become very angry indeed. Aries is also renowned for his ability to make enthusiastic beginnings, yet has a patent inability to arrive at the finishing line (Arians are not the marathon runners of the zodiac). One of the reasons for this is that Aries individuals become easily bored and need plenty of challenge and stimulation to keep them on their toes—hence their preference for attempting several tasks at the same time. Another reason for their failure to keep doggedly on course is that unless their egos are constantly boosted through flattery and praise, they are unable to sustain their initial enthusiasm and confidence.

All signs have their weak points and their strong ones, and while most

Arians could do with a diplomatic bag to smooth their precarious and eventful progress through life they are not without their winning ways. Despite their sometimes strident and abrasive personalities Aries Rams are unerringly warm-hearted, generous, and spontaneous; their optimism and infectious good humour will turn the most funereal event into a veritable wake. Although some find their behaviour the most irritating and insufferable of the zodiac, others find their ardour and spirited approach to life as welcome and attractive as a blazing beacon on a lonely headland.

RELATIONSHIPS

Some astrology books put forward the idea that Arians are loners. In many ways nothing could be farther from the truth. Aries does not take easily to solitude at the best of times and a hermit's life holds little appeal for them. Aries Rams love company and their strong and warm-hearted personalities usually attract a swarm of friends and lovers. However, occasionally some Aries individuals remain utterly immune to the needs and feelings of others; in consequence, over the years partners and friends become less prepared to tolerate their often selfish and inconsiderate ways and gradually drift away. Thus, in middle to later life some Arians find themselves in a sad, self-imposed, yet basically unwanted bachelor existence.

In the main, however, Aries, as in everything else, likes to enter the arena of romantic relationships as soon as possible—falling in love (and out again) often and leaving a trail of broken hearts and bruised egos in their wake. Aries, like the other two fire signs, Leo and Sagittarius, finds the excitement and exhilaration of a **grande passion** the greatest energy boost of all. In fact life without love is bleak and immensely dull for most Aries natives, and as in many aspects of their lives, if excitement or challenge is thin on the ground they will generate a major crisis to liven things up. Thus, even long-term, basically satisfactory relationships for Aries tend to be peppered with many hiatuses, separations, and reconciliations. Yet, difficult as it may seem to associate loyalty with this impulsive fire sign, strongly Arian individuals can remain deeply attached and entirely committed to another person, provided that person commands their respect and interest and remains a continuous source of challenge and stimulation—a tall order for most individuals perhaps.

Earlier on I mentioned that some astrologers consider Aries to be an uncomplicated sign by dint of its open and impelling nature. Yet the range of emotional highs and lows Arian individuals experience in the pursuit of love and the amazingly intricate patterns of human involvement they encounter throughout their lives give them an enormously rich and varied pool of experience from which to draw. Indeed it is probably Aries' artless and ingenuous approach to love and sex that propels many of them into more human drama in a lifetime than most of the other signs can conjure up in their dreams.

Arians learn best from experience—bitter experience—which means that no matter how much good advice is lavished upon them they simply have to find out the truth of a situation for themselves. Furthermore, no matter what immense trials and tribulations have been encountered in one relationship, Aries Rams charge valiantly into the throes of yet another affair. In Aries' eyes each person is a new experience and should be met on his or her own terms. Once bitten, twice shy is not one of Aries' favourite proverbs. Indeed, as my own mother said to me while discussing arrangements for my second wedding (and perhaps reflecting sagely on my rocky path to love and holy matrimony), 'Will your father be taking you down the aisle as usual, dear?'

THE FEMALE ARIES

Aries of both sexes tend to suffer from the 'knight-in-shining-armour' syndrome, which means that in pursuit of an irresistable challenge any interference from an outside source—no matter how well meaning—is unwanted and ignored. Obviously, female knights tend not to clang about in so much noisy armour as their male counterparts or make such a song and dance about their courting behaviour, but nevertheless they show the same spirit of conquest. The female of the species, of course, may well have her Moon or Venus in one of the more subtle and sensitive signs, like Cancer, Scorpio, or Pisces, in which case her behaviour in courtship and romantic partnerships is infinitely more artful and has less of the cave-man about it.

There is something utterly fascinating about the way most Aries women catapult in and out of romantic interludes—all fire and passion one moment, cool and detached the next. Of all the fire signs it is Ms Aries who likes to have her relationships permanently running on all cylinders; if the passion and high intensity level of the contact cannot be sustained, Aries is likely to move on. Needless to say, one is never in any doubt when a relationship is over with an Aries lady; the once warm and hectic steam that seems perpetually to surround her departs like Concorde, leaving an icy blast and an uncharacteristic silence.

One of the insights I gained while studying relationships in the context of astrology was that contrary to astrological lore people tend to be more attracted to their antipathies than their affinities. In keeping with this principle Aries women seem rarely drawn towards men whose temperaments are as volatile and extravagant as their own but to those who are more taciturn and phlegmatic. (I am of course referring to the earth and water signs.) Once these high-octane women have touched the lives of such men few ever really recover from the experience; Aries females have a way of overtoppling a life that was previously unruffled by intense emotion, or indeed intense activity of any kind!

No doubt it is already apparent that Aries women do not wait like blushing violets for Mr Right (or Mr Wrong for that matter) to waft along their path; they are poised like panthers for him and once in sight pursue him by fair means or foul. A female with Venus and Mars in Aries who responded to my questionnaire wrote, 'When I see a man I want I don't hesitate to pursue him. When I was 14 years old I stuck posters on my school bag proclaiming that I loved so-and-so, just to be sure he'd get the message. In most of my relationships including my marriage I've made the first move. I once went for a job interview where my future husband worked just so that I could bump into him "by accident". This is exactly what happened.' And another with Venus in Aries confessed, 'I am a fairly aggressive woman. I asked my husband to marry me, then made the wedding arrangements. All he had to do was turn up on the day!'

Male and female Rams alike prefer to pursue the object of their desires than be chased themselves; indeed sometimes they hold a pursuer in positive contempt for having the audacity to enter the chase uninvited. Another female with her Venus in Aries wrote on her questionnaire, 'I abhor sexual overtures being made toward me if the person hasn't taken the time to suss out whether I want him or not.' This is one of the reasons why men of a similar temperament rarely appeal to Aries women as much as the proverbial strong and silent types who are usually in a state of shock and thus incapable of showing any emotion at all. It is this apparent indifference that presents an irresistible challenge to Aries women and drives them into a veritable frenzy of desire.

The Aries woman in her Martian element is the perfect prototype of the Bitch Goddess*—the type of female portrayed by Joan Collins (Alexis) in the American soap-opera **Dynasty**. She is the kind of woman men love to hate! The Aries Bitch Goddess is selfish, autocratic, and prone to cutting her men down to size with the alacrity and efficaciousness of a meat cleaver. Hollywood in the 1930s was a veritable hot bed of Bitch Goddesses, many of whom were strongly Arian—film stars like Joan Crawford and Tallulah Bankhead. Joan Crawford expected her lovers to walk in her wake carrying her knitting and her dog. If they didn't do as she bade them, or if they were seen talking to another woman, she'd fly into a fit and hurl the nearest missile at the offender. Of course Miss Crawford was a film star, and her temperamental aberrations could just have been attributed to the pressures of star status! Yet Bitch Goddesses are to be found everywhere, from semi-detached houses in East Cheam to mud huts in Africa. Strangely enough, many an Aries woman fails to recognize the Bitch Goddess in herself. It is her natural inclination to boss everyone in sight, including or more specifically her husband or lover, and she never perceives how fearsome, cringe-making, and demoralizing she can be. Why her partners put up with such behaviour is another story, though it would seem some men find her dominant, sometimes sadistic behaviour sexually exciting.

It is a failing in Arians generally that they can never see themselves as others see them; in the Bitch Goddess's case she may go on for years embarrassing all and sundry with her open abuse of her partner and her monumental put-downs of him, never realizing how in the process she only diminishes herself. While the Bitch Goddess's capricious self-gratifying behaviour may fascinate and hold a partner for some time, if ever he finds the courage to retaliate (in kind), or simply leaves, she is devastated and crumples like an Ascot hat in a downpour.

By contrast, while Ms Aries is as vastly different from her Piscean sister as Germaine Greer is to Zsa Zsa Gabor, both these signs can make terrible fools of themselves in relationships by becoming hopelessly miscast as saviours and martyrs! In Pisces' case the impulse is one of sacrifice and the unconscious desire to become a victim; for Aries it is the need for challenge that propels them into relationships with complex and difficult men who submit them to emotional, psychological and sometimes physical distress. This is a familiar story to many of my female Aries friends and clients and

*Penny Vincenzi first discussed the Bitch Goddess in an article in **YOU** magazine (May 1986).

one that never ceases to amaze observers. Arians are usually considered—rightly or wrongly—to be so much in command of their lives that such turmoil seems anomalous to say the least. Fortunately, Aries women usually have the courage to extricate themselves from such destructive relationships, unlike Pisces, who often suffer and withstand all kinds of hardship and distress—for life!

There are other factors besides the constant challenge that are involved in Aries' inclination to become attached to difficult partners in the first place and then to remain with them. Ms Aries has a sneaking, sometimes completely unconscious, regard for men who give her a hard time and, caught up in a relationship where she never knows from one moment to the next quite what the next drama will be, she feels a certain compulsion to hang on. Often this is seen by others as a misguided sense of loyalty. However, whereas the Piscean or Neptunian female will recoil from confrontation, Aries fairly thrives on it. So even though she may remain unhappily in a difficult and traumatic relationship, she will not suffer in silence. Eventually, of course, the Aries woman recognizes that enough is enough and moves on, often sporting a couple of black eyes! This tendency to have an almost masochistic approach to relationships is even more marked by the Aries female who has personal planets (like the Moon, Mars, or Venus) in Pisces or a strong Neptunian theme.

Doris Day is a classic example of the Aries woman who believes that if at first you don't succeed, try, try again. Miss Day, the bubbly, all-American film star has made four marriages to date—two of which were monumental disasters: her first husband was a psychotic who beat her during pregnancy and another squandered her entire fortune and left her half a million dollars in debt on his death!*

Jealousy is a frequent handmaid to Aries passion. It is almost impossible for an Aries woman to remain cool, calm, and collected (at least for long) when confronted by any threat, real or imagined, to her exclusive rights on a husband or lover. It could be argued that all individuals, male, female, Aries, whoever, are prone to pangs of jealousy when deeply in love; however, it is the way in which they handle their jealousy that separates the sheep from the goats. I have known Aries women to leave no stone unturned to find out if their worst suspicions were grounded. But unlike Ms Scorpio, who can handle the situation like a professional, armed with her icy calm and (temporary) dispassion, Arians are frequently premature in their conclusions or completely lose control once faced with a denouement.

One of my closest friends (a Sun Aries) had the misfortune to be married to a brilliant but erratic and philandering solicitor who had a prestige practice in central London. On the whiff of a notion that her husband was engaged in sweeping his new secretary off her feet, she summoned all her wits and energy to 'stake them out'. She spent several days sleuthing, which involved many abortive forays into various pubs, hostelries and restaurants, and

*Astrologers may like to note that Miss Day has Pisces on the cusp of the house of relationships and the Sun (in Aries) in the 7th house, forming a grand trine with Mars and Neptune and intersected by an opposition to Jupiter!

eventually tracked them down to a picturesque haunt on the Thames. After secretly observing a nauseating display of billing and cooing she left the scene to go to her husband's chambers. On arriving she walked single-mindedly to his office and let herself in, watched with a degree of consternation by partners and switchboard operators alike who clearly sensed the drum-beat of crisis in her every step. Two hours later her husband, complete with secretary, walked in. Flower-pot at the ready, my friend aimed an accurate shot at the startled secretary, laying her flat out on the carpet, whereupon she left without uttering a word to the amazed gasps and suppressed giggles of the rest of the staff. Needless to say the secretary and the affair dematerialized overnight.

Paradoxically, Aries females find little morally wrong in experimenting with the odd extra-marital fling themselves, especially if their lives are lacking sparkle or excitement. However, given the chance to consider their actions and the likely consequences, most Aries women would probably prefer to avoid the ensuing complications of an affair outside a long-term relationship. The problem with this fire sign is that it is exceedingly impulsive and often at the mercy of its strong desires; thus Aries women often fall head over heels into an affair simply on the spur of a passionate moment. Furthermore, living a double life becomes too complicated for Ms Aries after a while; basically she is an all-or-nothing individual and not at all adept at telling lies—no matter how white. Within a few weeks the lustre of secret meetings and stolen afternoons wears off and is increasingly accompanied by the bitter aftertaste of betrayal. At heart the Aries woman is exceedingly loyal to her mate and unless something is badly wrong with the relationship she will usually return to the fold after an illicit sexual hiccup a little sadder, probably not any wiser, but certainly with renewed appreciation and resolve.

In much the same way the single Aries female also gets a little out of her depth if she tries to handle more than one relationship at the same time. It is also worth noting that the Aries female (particularly those with their Moon in Aries) are frequently slow to mature emotionally and her passage from one relationship to the next is a way of ultimately finding herself. This is why fire (and air) sign women should wait until their late twenties before marriage in order to have time to flex their emotional muscles.

Astrology books are often quick to point out that Aries women are extremely independent; by the same token this leads many people to assume they must therefore balk at marriage or long-term relationships. The Aries woman needs romantic relationships every bit as much as the next Libran or Piscean, but she needs to retain aspects of her independence within a relationship. Thus it is often the Aries wife and mother who juggles a career with the Women's Institute, the tennis club, the P.T.A., and the husband and three children. Several years ago I came across the statement in an astrology book that I have never forgotten because it always strikes me as so true, 'children of Aries mothers have to get used to their frequent absences from home . . .'. An Aries woman tied by the apron strings to a life sentence of housework and coffee mornings is not a pretty sight.

Aries females are not exempt from an over-sized, paper-thin ego like their male counterparts; most also have an extremely competitive streak.

Consequently, much of the friction generated in relationships stems from the Aries woman competing (consciously or unconsciously) with her mate for ascendancy. The Aries female also manages to project all the feminine aspects of a woman while frequently thinking and acting like a man, a weapon with which she can strip a man and his ego down to size. And whether or not she's a fully-fledged Bitch Goddess, with her redoubtable temper ignited, the Aries female is quick to resort to physical displays of aggressive superiority and—flower-pots notwithstanding—the Aries woman can wield a frying pan like a broadsword.

Aries women are strong-minded and capable but they nevertheless have extremely soft centres. Thus the men in their lives have to be mature enough to recognize their need for a creative and independent platform on which to strut about and also their equally strong desire to be demonstrably loved, appreciated, and cherished. Ms Aries may not be the best person to manage a budget or deal diplomatically with the in-laws or the boss, and her disarmingly honest—or shall we say brutal—opinions of her partner may tear his self-esteem to shreds, but she will stand up and fight for the man she loves and shower him (regularly) with expensive gifts and a love as fierce as a forest fire.

THE MALE ARIES

'It's not the men in your life, but the life in your men . . .' quipped the infamous Mae West. She could well have been speaking on behalf of all Aries women or about Aries men. The Aries man is all man; in childhood he was brought up on a literary diet of Biggles or Bat Man and for the rest of his life continues to carry a fantasy hero figure within himself. Whatever heady and bellicose qualities the Aries female displays, the male Ram possesses in triplicate. Where love and conquest are concerned he believes that no other male could possibly fulfil the dreams and needs of a beloved nearly as well as himself, and no matter how much the object of his affections may try to deter him, he will blindly insist on taking over every aspect of her life and changing it for the better—regardless.

Aries men are ruled by their emotions and their desires, rarely by logic and rationale. True to form, when away from the heat of the fire many frequently regret their impulsive moments of ardour. Male Rams usually storm their way into a woman's life with all the razzmatazz and verve of an SAS mission—in fact they don't just sweep their women off their feet, they blast them off! Needless to say, the male Arian is not the strong and silent type and no matter how he may try to acquire a suave and aloof persona, his impetuous and ardent spirit shines through the most sophisticated veneer.

Even the great are not immune from occasional displays of grossly insensitive and bloody-minded behaviour. Herbert von Karajan, arguably the world's finest conductor (a Sun Aries), was involved in a bitter feud with his orchestra, the Berlin Philharmonic, from the January of 1983 until mid 1984. The saga began when von Karajan engaged an attractive female clarinettist (only the second woman in the orchestra's history), much against the orchestra's wishes. The Berlin Philharmonic, admittedly displaying considerable chauvinism, claimed the clarinettist did not 'integrate' but were ultimately forced to accept the situation when von Karajan threatened to end their lucrative TV and recording sessions. Relationships between the maestro and his 'men' remained strained, to say the least, for many months and when in June 1984 von Karajan walked out of a concert he was due to conduct with them and took to the rostrum of the rival Vienna Philharmonic, their patience snapped and all 118 musicians tore up their contracts with him. Divorce soon followed.

Politician Michael Heseltine is certainly one of Britain's most notable Arians, displaying many of the valiant aspects of this sign as well as some of its blunderbuss, attention-seeking tactics. In January of 1986 Mr Heseltine, the then Minister of Defence, walked out of a cabinet meeting, resigned his position, and publicly accused the Prime Minister, Margaret Thatcher, of sabotaging an Anglo-European rescue attempt of the Westland helicopter company. It was an unprecedented and dramatic exposure of the workings of modern cabinet government and revealed the cracks in the inter-relationships between Mrs Thatcher and her ministers. But it was behaviour entirely characteristic of the pugilistic Mr Heseltine.

Mr Heseltine had already been dubbed 'Tarzan' after seizing the mace in the House of Commons and shaking it at Labour MPs who were singing 'The Red Flag. He was renowned for his low flash point and his regard for confrontation. In his post as Secretary of State for Defence—the ultimate in cabinet posts for the Aries man—he was in his element helicoptering in to some beleaguered outpost, like the Falklands. As with many Aries men, his pugnacious, flamboyant behaviour made him a figure of amusement at times, as on the occasion he stormed into Molesworth—a quiet English village bordering on a base for US nuclear missiles—wearing a military flak jacket for the eviction of a handful of CND protestors! He is thought to be a fiercely ambitious man, with his sights firmly set on Number 10, Downing Street; and many of his colleagues considered his blazing departure from the cabinet on a point of honour as part of a ploy to take over the leadership of the Tory Party if and when Margaret Thatcher decides to go. In a sense he laid down a single-handed challenge to the one-woman style of Thatcher Government. It remains to be seen if, as in the case of many an Aries man, combat over, or in this case with, a woman proves to be the catalyst of his downfall. But while Mr Heseltine may periodically be down on his luck with politics, he has been fortunate in love, and he has remained happily married to his wife, Anne, for over twenty years.

All the fire signs believe in love and Aries Rams are no exception. Although their strong physical desires may lead them to encounter relationships purely of the physical kind, in reality they are looking for love. And for this they will leave no stone unturned.

Rather like his Leo brother, Mr Aries needs to be worshipped and adored, never criticized or ridiculed. Although initially he may be drawn to females whose gentle supportive demeanour reflects his knightly image, he tends to become rather restless without a challenge or a few skirmishes to liven things up along the way; indeed he may lose respect for, and certainly interest in, women who cannot stand up to him. He also needs continual approval and praise to keep his enthusiasm buoyant, and if his partner fails to demonstrate a high degree of appreciation in either him or his endeavours his naturally itchy feet may carry him off to pastures new.

On a more serious note, the sustaining of the male Aries ego is so essential to his emotional well-being that without a steady diet of flattery and approbation it atrophies—sometimes physically, but more usually psychologically. In fact the male Aries is a far more complicated individual than one would at first suspect. In some cases, particularly where the Sun or Mars in Aries aspects Saturn or Neptune, he may have secret doubts about his masculinity and his ability to fulfil his hero myth. Indeed some of the more obviously macho-Aries men are in fact the most likely to have some conflict about their malehood. Hence their need to devote a great deal of time and energy to proving how manly they can be, not only to everyone else but to themselves. This sign frequently marries early; thus the single Aries man in his mid-thirties onwards who has a string of attractive and willing girlfriends is also likely to have a deep-seated problem with his masculinity. Conversely, the Aries man who is not so intent on maintaining a 'he-man' image and seems able to express vulnerability and sensitivity is likely to be at home with all dimensions of his manhood and therefore more able to sustain long-term relationships. Casanova was a Sun Aries and although his fabled adventures and sexual conquests appear to exemplify the quintessential romantic, swashbuckling hero, his behaviour has attracted comments from more than one modern psychologist. Arian Warren Beatty—the actor/producer—could be considered a kind of twentieth-century Casanova; although he has had many live-in relationships with some of the most beautiful women in the world, he remains apparently allergic to marriage.*

I have known several men, both friends and clients, who suffer from this Don Juan syndrome and who have a strong Aries theme in their charts. Many have experienced difficult or non-existent relationships with their fathers and thus have no realistic male-model to relate to in their formative years. Some who over-identify with macho-man and suppress any natural weakness may overcompensate with ruthless behaviour in the board room and the boudoir. Since Aries is the archetypal warrior-hero of the zodiac it is the antithesis of all things quintessentially feminine. While Aries women can express their femininity through their Moon and Venus signs (hopefully contrasting ones), leaving their Aries Sun to shine out in the world, the Aries man invariably encounters problems in relating to his feminine side—his anima. He cannot successfully accept gentleness and tenderness in his own nature for he sees such qualities as weak; he finds difficulty in yielding and acquiescing to another's needs and feelings. The overly macho Aries man is psychologically uncomfortable with the feminine principle in himself thus his insensitive and ruthless behaviour is a defence against the threat of vulnerability. This kind of Aries man usually resents successful, confident women. Yet if the over-zealous macho Arian can learn to accept his inner 'woman' many of his relationship problems and certainly his bullying tactics will disappear. Like their female counterparts, Aries men have enormously soft centres and once they take off their noisy armour and shiny regalia this sign can be exceedingly gentle and loving.

Another facet of Mr Aries' behaviour is his ability to be long on enthusiasm

---

*Astrologers please note: Beatty has Saturn conjunct his descendant in Pisces and square his MC/IC axis.

and short on tenacity. Aries is at his best at the start of a relationship when all his senses are on fire and he is at his most generous and keen to please his new love. As the relationship progresses, however, his enthusiasm wanes, his generosity dries up and his desire to please becomes more focused on himself. I was once engaged (for a month I might add) to a man with the Sun and Mars in Aries. He was charming, dynamic, witty, and immensely attractive to the opposite sex—certainly one whom Mae West would have had no complaints about! During the length of our relationship he was earning a phenomenal salary while I was practically on the bread-line. One day he complained that whenever we went out (which was often) I always seemed to wear the same trousers which had seen better days and were somewhat shiny at the knees. It never occurred to him that he himself had the power to rectify the situation. However, he continued to deck himself out with new suits, shirts, expensive camera equipment, and watches, not to mention maintaining the upkeep of a four-litre Jaguar and a life-style to match. Like many Aries men, the extent of his feelings was in direct proportion to his spirit of generosity.

The male Aries tends to be very impressed by appearances both in himself and others. In his own case the Aries Ram is quick to display the trappings of success in the latest 'gear' and trendy car. But perhaps more seriously Arians are notoriously bad judges of character (both male and female alike); consequently they are often taken to the proverbial cleaners by gold-diggers in the shape of damsels in distress.

Like the female of the species, male Rams are far more attracted to the more subtle and mysterious members of the opposite sex (especially the water and earth signs) who frequently lead them a merry dance all the way to the altar—and beyond. In keeping with their innate gullibility and disarming openness, Aries Rams fail to spot any devious manoeuvres performed by their women and so, despite their apparent show of strength and dominance in a relationship, they are all too often subtly manipulated and at the mercy of their more passive partners who run emotional and psychological rings around them.

Aries men often find themselves innocently entangled in the most complex webs of romantic intrigue from which their only escape is to affect a little boy lost stance and eject themselves, often forcibly and usually acrimoniously, from the scene. The Aries husband (Paul) of a client of mine (Anne) became thoroughly emmeshed in a triangle of his own making. When Anne initially consulted me the marriage, although strained and Anne by no means fulfilled, was still 'intact'. In fact, like so many couples, the relationship, like a train, was set doggedly on its tracks—domestic and family routine papering over the emotional and psychological cracks. Some months later I was consulted by the husband's girlfriend (Karen) who worked as his personal assistant and virtually ran the company. Apparently Anne knew of Paul's involvement with Karen but was not overly concerned by the relationship—in fact it was she who had suggested that Karen should also see me. During our discussion it became apparent that Karen was not entirely happy in her role as mistress but could see no way out of the vicious circle—she was emotionally and financially dependent on Paul and to leave him meant a severe drop in salary which she could ill afford as she had a daughter from a previous marriage to support and put through boarding school. Almost two years later Anne and Paul decided on an amicable divorce, whereupon Karen moved into the marital home with her daughter. Anne's and Paul's three children remained with Paul. The arrangements seemed satisfactory to all, although relationships between the children and Karen were extremely difficult. Anne, happy to be single and pursuing a new career and life-style with verve and optimism, remained on good terms with Paul and was entirely pleased when he came round to inform her that he was remarrying . . . Fiona!

During the domestic reshuffle and ensuing emotional trauma Paul frequently visited Anne, upon whose shoulder he cried copiously and often, bemoaning the fact that they had divorced and wishing he could turn back the clock. Why had it happened to him? How could fate have dealt him such a poor hand? Fortunately for Paul the women took matters into their own hands, which saved him from having to leave town. After the initial shock, Karen, although emotionally battered, decided not to put up a fight for him, and in many ways was thoroughly relieved to be out of it all. Paul, who was an enormously generous Aries, made a large financial settlement on Karen, which certainly helped soften the emotional blow for her. Fiona, although an apparently unassuming, placid character, stood her ground amidst the emotional furore, but made sure he kept to his word. Fiona and Paul eventually married, although according to Anne, Paul was hardly the picture of the blushing bridegroom and she sensed he had merely exchanged one set of troubles for another.

For all his flaws, his blunderings and his king-size opinion of himself, Mr Aries usually manages to endear himself to women. Indeed he often encounters as much trouble fighting off the opposite sex as he does battling with them once he gets into a relationship. Even the more introverted Arian is a conquering hero at heart. While the Aries man may have to learn the gentle art of persuasion, he's hard to ignore when his emotions have been fired. Since he's often out of touch with his more sensitive Lunar and Venusian qualities the only way he can develop his gentleness and compassion is through his women. But despite his Tarzanesque aura, once committed and captured by Ms Right, the Aries man can become a thoroughly domesticated household pet. Even if he does exceed his financial limitations on occasion or stray off the beaten sexual track, life with the Ram is seldom dull and boring.

SUMMARY

Perhaps the most important abilities Aries of both sexes need to acquire are those of compromise, sharing, and humility. Arians tend to put their their own wishes first and to ride roughshod over their partners, leaving them to follow in their blazing trail.

In marriage the Arian individual needs to stand back and consider his actions on others and realize that other people do not always feel exactly as Aries about everything. With maturity Arians can acquire some of their opposite sign Libra's more diplomatic and considerate ways, but their partners need much patience and courage to stand up to them. Without developing self-awareness and the ability to acquiesce to another's needs and wishes. Aries individuals may always find their marital bed of roses somewhat prickly with thorns.

ARIES PARTNERSHIPS

Traditionally, Aries individuals are said to find their best partners in the air and fire signs, but they are usually attracted to more powerful and problematic relationships with earthy and watery people.

Aries

Aries with **Aries** is a combustible formula to say the least. Certainly this relationship is unlikely to be dull, but in much the same way as with a Leo partner, there is a tendency for both people to want to occupy the driver's seat—an impossible feat unless they allow each other individual vehicles to drive! Also, two Arians in a relationship cannot balance each other's spendthrift tendencies, and thus they frequently over-extend themselves financially, which definitely impedes their happiness! Sex between these two usually gets off to an intense and frequent start, but flags in the long term.

Taurus

Aries and **Taurus** sometimes manage a very workable partnership, for the same reason as do Aries and Pisces—they may have planets in each other's Sun sign. However, Aries tends to find Taurus far too stubborn, reluctant to change and intractable; but on the other hand he gains plenty of security and the good things of life he so appreciates. In return Taurus broadens his horizons and learns how to spend his money! Sex between Aries and Taurus can be stimulating and long lasting.

Gemini

Gemini is probably the best air sign for Aries since the resultant merger is largely stimulating and fun for both. Aries finds Gemini's cool perspective on emotional issues prevents him from making mountains out of molehills and keeps his blood pressure down. Gemini, on the other hand, enjoys Aries' equally quick-witted nature and benefits from the way Aries puts his ideas into action. Variety is the spice of life where sex is concerned for the Arian and the Geminian, and this couple is prone to extra-'marital' relationships.

Cancer

Cancer is the most difficult water sign for Aries. Cancer is far too complex for Aries; the protective armour of the Crab's moods and silences and his tendency to whine and carp drive Aries to distraction, while Aries continually treads on Cancer's sensitive extremities. Only when this couple share the same, or compatible, Moon signs can they be truly happy. While sex can be mutually exciting at first, these two are prone to sexual indifference towards each other as the relationship progresses. Uncommunicated resentments take their toll in the bedroom!

Leo

Aries and **Leo** together reinforce the battle for ego-worship and tend to think it is the other who is overbearing and insufferable, but this combination can nevertheless be a lively and loving one. Both place a great deal of importance on the physical side of the relationship, and when this is going well they display much generosity towards each other!

Virgo

Virgos are often highly attractive to Aries—their discerning and detached personalities harbour the very qualities Aries secretly wants to emulate. Ultimately, however, Virgo's pernickety, nit-picking ways irritate and exasperate Aries, while Virgo finds Aries too pushy and self-centred. Nevertheless, sexual attraction between these two can be extremely powerful, and with compatible Moon signs and/or harmonious Mars and Venus inter-aspects they can sustain a blissful sex life.

Libra

Aries and Libra are zodiac opposites and have the usual trouble with glass-houses and stones but nevertheless both partners can learn much of value about themselves from such a relationship. Of course Libra's indecisiveness irritates Aries beyond measure, consequently he is forever taking the initiative in the relationship which annoys Libra intensely. Libra wishes Aries wasn't quite so bossy but gradually learns how to create harmony in the relationship by agreeing with Aries, but doing as he thinks fit! The Libran makes an inventive and sensual partner for Aries, although their sexual relationship frequently lacks emotional depth.

Scorpio

Aries and Scorpio are quickly locked in mortal emotional combat. This relationship seethes with passion from its first impact; both signs have affiliations with sexy, bellicose Mars, although Scorpio usually retains the upper hand, being naturally more subtle and devious. This is a combination of extremes; at its best the relationship soars, when difficult it devastates both people's lives.

Sagittarius

Aries and Sagittarius are better suited to friendship than a romantic partnership since Aries likes to be the one who holds the copyright on independence; thus he tends to feel thwarted and even insecure with a partner who is ultimately the most foot-loose and fancy-free in the Zodiac. For his part, Sagittarius takes life in a far more relaxed fashion and finds it difficult to become as intense as Aries over anything. Occasionally this combination encounters sexual problems, although in the beginning sex is usually marvellous.

Capricorn

Aries and Capricorn relationships rarely run smoothly. Both signs are enormously strong-willed and ambitious and their bossy and dominating characters create much friction in a relationship as they each struggle for ascendancy over the other. However, these signs frequently experience strong sexual attraction for each other (like Aries and Scorpio) and providing Aries admits Capricorn is the boss—especially in public—and Capricorn remembers to massage Aries' tender ego, the relationship can scale some elevated heights.

Aquarius

Aquarians are far too unpredictable and argumentative for Aries and perhaps a little too stubborn, but again this can be a provocative combination. On the plus side, Aries never finds Aquarius dull and postively relishes his zany sense of humour and excellent mind. Aquarius finds Aries a little too physical on occasion but appreciates the way Aries handles his unorthodox behaviour. He may also wish that Aries didn't lose his temper so often, but at least he forgives and forgets easily. Even if this couple have a good sexual relationship both tend to need extra erotic stimulation after a while—often in the form of a romantic fling!

Pisces

The Aries/**Pisces** combination can work reasonably well, probably because Pisces lets Aries walk all over him yet secretly admires his dominance; also because these signs are found next to each other in the Zodiac, both may have planets in each other's Sun sign. Aries finds tenderness a difficult quality to express and consequently is much drawn towards Pisces' sensitivity and romantic attitude to life. If the Arian and the Piscean share harmonious moon signs and Venus-Mars inter-aspects, their sexual relationship can be sensational.

SEXUALITY

Aries is a sign ruled by Mars—**the** planet of desire—so it is hardly surprising that this fire sign has a reputation for extremely lusty and bawdy behaviour. Libido usually runs high in Arians of both sexes and an active, stimulating sex life enables Aries to invest even more energy and enthusiasm in other areas of his life; an apathetic or lethargic Aries is often one who is temporarily sexually 'on-ice'. In most individuals loss of libido is considered one of the primary indicators of depression; for Aries the lack of an outlet for their libido frequently triggers depression.

In keeping with their impetuous, ardent personalities Aries individuals waste little time in coming to the point sexually. Long drawn-out courtship or protracted foreplay is usually wasted on Aries. Once strongly Arian individuals find someone sexually attractive their passions quickly ignite and, like a plane on take-off, as soon as V.1. is reached there can be no turning back. Indeed, right timing is crucial to Aries' sexual satisfaction and response; if the sexual fire, once alight, is not allowed to take hold it tends to die out—permanently. Also, if sexually frustrated, Arians of both sexes throw major tantrums or sink into an angry silence; their frustrations can in an extreme form lead to violent behaviour and certainly the female of the species will vent her frustration in sarcasm, insults, and general bitchiness. Arians do not like to be blocked or denied, especially when the blood is coursing through their veins. Now, not later, is their maxim.

It has always seemed slightly unfair that while it is considered **de rigueur** for a man to sow his wild oats before marriage, if a woman adopts the same policy she is looked upon as a trollop. Indeed it is traditional that the female remains in mint condition until her wedding night. Even though the 1960s did much to change and free sexual attitudes so that by the late 1970s nearly every women's magazine carried a token article on woman's sexual rights, old traditional views refused to die and be buried. Paradoxically, in the light of the immense sexual freedom actively encouraged in the 1960s and 1970s, today's teenagers seem to be at the spearhead of a romantic revival, upholding sexual monogamy and virginity. Thus, strongly-sexed women, typified by Aries, experience many conflicts during their sexually formative years as their instincts pull them one way and their conditioning another. However, by their mid-twenties most Aries women rally to the call of their independent spirit and recognize they are in sole charge of their lives and cannot be restricted to a set of moral values that do not suit their instincts. Thus they gaily abandon their protective sexual armour and allow their passionate natures to propel them into all kinds of experiences. Their hit and miss approach to sexual relationships generates a fair degree of trauma for them, but once an affair is over Aries women rarely remain in the doldrums for long; their approach resembles that of a motorist who feels he must clamber back into the driver's seat after an accident—in coming to grips with a new relationship memories of the old easily fade.

The male Aries seldom encounters the same hurdles of guilt in his formative sexual years. He is usually an early starter in the sexual race and while he believes in love he is not averse to a sexual skirmish or five along the way.

Arians of both sexes are rarely coy in declaring their desires for another. In turn they expect their feelings to be reciprocated just as vehemently. A rebuttal, even a contrived one, usually fails to boost their interest or desire; in fact such an action frequently acts like a bucket of water on their fire (remember the fragile Aries ego). Aries is also hopeless at the delicate art of sexual innuendo and finds it almost impossible to weave an aura of mystery around their intentions. It could be said that Aries of both sexes carry the lure of the cave-man about them.

Although this sign has a reputation for dominating others and displaying fairly aggressive behaviour on occasion, the same tendencies do not necessarily emerge in the sexual arena. Sex is an enormously rich and subtle area of life and therefore practically impossible to contain within such broad astrological categories as the signs of the Zodiac. Nevertheless, whatever events shape an individual's formative life, whatever the emotional, social, and cultural conditioning he receives, the basic personality comes into play at every level of experience. Thus, loosely speaking, an Aries theme in a chart will make its forceful presence felt in the bedroom equally as well as anywhere else.

First, however, I think the myth that the Aries woman is always the dominant sexual partner needs exploding. Certainly dominance is an issue that Aries of both sexes encounter, but just because the Aries woman tends to command her domestic or career ship like Captain Bligh, she does not necessarily wield the same power in the bedroom. In fact the reverse is more likely to be the case. The obviously dominant and bossy Aries woman is frequently a pussy cat under the sheets and tends to prefer a passive role where sex is concerned. Of course there are Aries women who initiate each and every move in sexual interplay and place their satisfaction over and above (sometimes literally) their partner; but these are usually the Aries souls who soft-pedal their naturally assertive tendencies in everyday life.

In many ways the Aries woman, like her fire-sign sisters, Leo and Sagittarius, has much to offer her partners sexually, since she is a spirited soul at heart and thoroughly hedonistic: she hardly ever has to lie back and think of England! Much depends on the overall content of the chart, but if Ms Aries has her Mars, Venus, or the Moon in a water sign or contacts from the Moon or Venus to Neptune or Pluto, she brings a highly sensitive and richly imaginative element to her love-making.

In the section on Aries relationships, the complexity of the male's attitude to his masculinity was discussed. Not surprisingly it is often in the sexual arena that any anomalies emerge. At the beginning of a relationship nearly all Aries men will tend to play their macho-part, initiating, indeed dominating, sexual interchange. But given a long-term sexual relationship, those individuals who are less at home with the burden of their ultra-masculine image will seem to need more and more encouragement to be aroused so that it is ultimately they who are taking the more passive role. Here the more subtle aspects of astrology come into play, as it is the Saturnian and Neptunian content of the chart, particularly in regard to Mars, that tends to indicate these tendencies rather than the plain and simple placing of the Sun or Mars in Aries.

One of my clients who had his Sun in Aries was to outer appearances a typical bowler-hatted, city 'gent'; he played squash, belonged to the Rotary Club, and was married with three children. However, periodically he felt the urge to dress in female clothes. In my client's case his Mars in Pisces was held in a tense configuration with Neptune and the Moon, thus his ingrained sensitivity and basic confusion over the 'feminine' clashed dramatically with his macho-Aries spirit.

It is worth pointing out here that all of us have both masculine and feminine dimensions to our being* and most experience no great conflict between the two, but in some individuals one function is over-expressed to the detriment of the other and it is then that problems emerge.

Putting aside these complexities, the more typical Aries male is adventurous and exceptionally keen and adept in his love-making. Given the opportunity, this sign will try absolutely anything (at least once) and although he may ultimately prefer the conventional *pas de deux* the Aries man is open to and highly stimulated by threesomes and group sex. Mirrors, blue films, and orgies also often play an important part in the sex life of the Aries male, although the latter usually emerges only in fantasy. Indeed, strongly Aries men frequently fall into the stud category, needing little stimulation to become aroused and accepting all in the spirit of challenge and conquest.

There is, unfortunately, a major 'but' to Aries' sexual prowess which is again linked to their super-sensitive egos. Aries men have a tendency to consider their performance so wonderful that it is inconceivable that their partner could be left in any way unimpressed or dissatisfied. If their partner is

*The psychologist and analyst Carl Jung names these the animus and anima.

as easily aroused and sexually forward as themselves she is unlikely to be left in dissatisfied limbo, but any woman who needs gentle coercion to become fully aroused is likely to be left high but often dry and sans orgasm, with a nagging feeling that she has been involved in an energetic fertility rite! Admittedly this is taking an extreme view of the Aries somewhat insensitive performance in bed, but developing awareness to another's sexual needs does not come instinctively to this sign. As a rule the Aries man should aim to encounter a sexual relationship with an older more experienced lover, or at least one who refuses to be totally overpowered by his somewhat selfish attitude to sexual satisfaction; the sort of woman who will subtly show him *how* to please *her* without sapping his sexual confidence. Aries is keen to excel in this area of life and once he has been made aware of how much more exciting intercourse for two can be, he can become one of the most superb lovers in the Zodiac.

Aries of both sexes like to take immediate advantage of rising passion which is probably why sex for this sign is rarely confined just to the bedroom. Indeed sex in unusual places has a definite fascination for Aries, perhaps because of the accompanying element of danger. Two friends of mine, the husband with a strong Mars and the wife with several planets in Aries were overcome with lust for one another on a long car journey. It was mid-summer and extremely hot—especially for England. They decided to drive off the main road to see if they could find a suitably quiet and overgrown spot. So engrossed were they in their search, moving haltingly along the unfamiliar country lanes that they were somewhat alarmed suddenly to find a police car following close behind and then waving them down. Unfortunately both were in a state of semi-undress at the time and had to quickly gather decorum around themselves as a policeman approached the window. The husband smiled confidently and said they were looking for a quiet spot to picnic, to which the policeman raised a wry eyebrow and after examining the car's tax disc pointed them in a suitable direction.

A word, too, about power. Aries females find power enormously sexually attractive in men. They also admire intellectual brilliance. Thus the mind and status of a partner is ultimately far more attractive to them than physical appearance. Of course there are Aries women who prefer to acquire power only for themselves, in which case such types will tend to be attracted by passivity and lack of ambition in a partner. However, as a general rule of thumb Ms Aries needs to look up to her man for him to gain a sexual hold on her. Conversely Aries men seldom seek power in their female partners; they prefer obviously feminine and passive characteristics in their women. In fact, most Aries men are sexually unimpressed by and often actually dislike strong ambitious women.

Both male and female Arians sustain an enormous appetite for pleasure in general and sex in particular. While their enthusiasms and delight is sexually attractive in itself, this tendency gives rise to a preference for quantity rather than quality. Aries **per se** is not a sensuous sign, thus Arian individuals, especially the men, have to discover and develop their sexual sensitivity. Provided this is achieved, Aries lovers can be some of the most exciting and sought-after in the zodiac.

PROFILE OF AN ARIES WOMAN

CLARE FRANCIS

If the specifications to be a fully paid-up member of the Aries Society include, courage, daring, the single-minded pursuit of objectives, unflinching honesty, a sense of humour verging on the absurd, and an openness that is all-embracing, Clare Francis more than qualifies. Indeed, she should be the patron. Clare has never ducked a challenge. In true Aries fashion she rarely takes a retrogressive step: if she reaches the end of one peninsula, she'll launch herself into open waters and head chin-first towards a distant outpost. 'To me, life is a voyage . . . one should always be progressing . . . moving on.'

Although now, by the late-1980s, Clare is a highly successful, well-established writer, it was her voyages of discovery on the high seas that first brought her to fame. Yet this too provides a sharp contrast to her early aspirations in the world of ballet. While these three career avenues appear as far apart as the chalk Cliffs of Dover and Wensleydale cheese, astrologically they all belong to one theme: Mercury-Neptune. In Clare's chart her Mercury in the powerful first degree of Aries was the first planet to cross the horizon at birth and leads all the others around the horoscopic circle. Mercury, the planet of movement and communication, is placed in the ninth house of long distance journeys, as much of the imagination as of the body; and Mercury forms an opposition aspect to Neptune, a planet associated (among many ideas) with the sea, inspiration and artistic merit.

Clare was brought up in a middle-class home in Surrey. She had no clear ambitions as a young girl but her ballet teacher considered her talented enough to audition for the Royal Ballet School. She did, was accepted, and spent the next five years of her life sweating to become a ballerina. But this was not to be, and after leaving the upper school at seventeen, she went to University College, London, and obtained a degree in economics. Four years in marketing

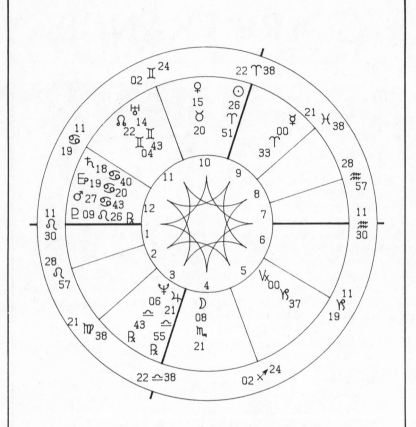

CLARE FRANCIS

17 4 1946   11h 45m 0s GMT

PLACIDUS 51N24 0W19

followed university, and then, almost accidentally, she slipped into her sailing career.

Like many Arian women, Clare is strong minded, self willed, and very independent. Her foray into the commercial world of marketing taught her one important thing: that she was not a 'corporation person'. She required a more creative outlet, one that would give her freedom and allow her talents and abilities full rein. She needed the proverbial Aries challenge. While Clare is a highly intelligent, extremely articulate lady, you need a touch of the Aries blind optimism and blinkered determination to take on the Atlantic single-handed with only a rudimentary knowledge of sailing! It was just this spirit of adventure and the desire to pit her wits against fate and a force 8 gale that not only inspired her to cross the Big Pond, but to make the trip twice, the second time taking part in the **Observer** Single-Handed race where she was the first woman to cross the finishing line—thirteenth out of 120. And not satisfied with a mere 6000 miles to her credit, she took part in the **Whitbread** Round The World Yacht race—this time with the help of a crew—finishing fifth.

Yet although these feats alone were enough to make her a household name, what firmly established her as a popular personality, almost a folk hero, was the televising of a film she herself had made while crossing the Atlantic. The film, which was a fascinating visual log of her journey, did not merely contain the flag-waving high spots, but the moments of stark loneliness, hopeless desperation, and sheer misery. It was this absolute honesty, this portrayal of the successful voyageur as an ordinary human being that drew her to the public's heart. People identified with her weakness and her suffering: 'It was this revelation that created a bridge between me and people . . . here was someone who was not afraid to expose her darkest moments. I've never been one to hide my feelings. Almost too honest. People seem to find this refreshing.'

It is Clare's Aries Sun that shines through these comments; it is her Aries spirit that reveres honesty and feels hopelessly inadequate fabricating false edifices; it is the Arian spark that reaches out for challenge and welcomes innovation and change. But the ability to confront life and death situations, to test to the limit the physical body and the inner spirit, is a distinctly Plutonic affair.

Pluto is associated with transformation: and since this planet is placed within two degrees of her Leo Ascendant this process of 'coming through', both on an inner and an outer level, is an integral part of her life. Clare could relate to this idea, but added that as far as she was concerned nothing in her life had ever matched the rigours and demands of ballet,* a sentiment with which, as a former dancer,

*In my experience, most professional ballet dancers have Pluto prominent in their charts.

I wholeheartedly concur. She went on to say that training in classical dance was 'all about perseverence'—something she found easy: 'I never get there through any brilliance. I get there through persistence and tenacity', qualities no doubt gleaned from her Mars-Saturn conjunction in Cancer. While writing could never be deemed a physical activity in the same way as ballet, Clare finds her career as a writer equally as arduous and all-consuming—if not more so.

Pluto is a key factor involved in her feelings about 'being different' as a child. Although Clare came from a happy home, she felt unhappy within (or perhaps ill-matched to) the family: unconnected. 'I marched to a different drum', she revealed. 'The world seemed to be a very strange place. I was like an observer watching a strange scene. Communications on certain levels did not break through. I felt as though I was a child of the gods—a child made up of an unusual mix. I had to learn the rules. It seemed very difficult for me to slot into the humdrum aspects of family life. But I loved my family very much.' In my experience Clare's comments are consistent with many people who have one of the outer planets (Pluto, Neptune, or Uranus) rising at birth. Some of them feel, quite literally, that they come from another planet!

Pluto increases its 'influence' in Clare's chart by forming the apex of a 'T'-square between the Moon in Scorpio and Venus in Taurus. Some of Clare's feeling of alienation as a child stem from the tie-up between her rising Pluto and the Moon in the fourth 'house' of home and family. More specifically, this aspect suggests that there was difficulty in the relationship between Clare and her mother. While Clare and her mother love each other, during her childhood emotional mis-communications were a mutual obstacle in their relationship. Moon-Pluto squares are notorious astrological 'bogies' where emotions are concerned. This combination implies powerful emotions that are blocked or suppressed: sometimes the mother withdraws her warmth and feelings for the child; then as the child grows up, his or her feelings are in turn controlled. Sometimes the mother is manipulative and possessive. Although Clare is without doubt an 'open' person, someone who can give out great warmth and love to those she cares about, there are times when she seals off her emotions, if only because they threaten to become too powerful or painful, a factor that is both a strength in times of crisis and a weakness in times of intimacy. Since Venus is also involved in the tense configuration with the Moon and Pluto it is the arena of one-to-one relationships where much of the inherent astrological drama is played out.

Sadly Clare and her husband separated in 1982, and although no divorce can be said to be truly amicable, some four years later Clare and Jacques remain good friends and share the common concern and love for their seven-year-old son, Tom. The combination of Moon-Venus-Pluto and a volatile Uranian seventh house of relationships is hardly a recipe for marital harmony, at least not at first. But just how much the outcome of relationships depends on the individual's psychological and emotional conditioning and just how much is down to fate is difficult to tell. In my experience, people like Clare who have hard Venus-Pluto contacts often find an element of fate—and sometimes, although not always, tragedy—operating in their relationships. In Clare's case, she experienced a tragic love affair in her mid-twenties: a love affair she is reluctant to discuss. Marriage to Jacques proved to be yet another severed contact, although of a different variety. While an astrologer might hazard a guess that someone with such a planetary set-up might be the sort to create many of her own problems by projecting unconscious patterns of rejection and emotional upheaval onto her relationships (or simply of exerting poor judgement), to me Clare's set of circumstances seem to have a distinct ring of fate about them.

Clare is not the only woman trying to juggle a need for personal freedom and individuality with an equally strong desire for secure relationships. Since her divorce she has lived with her son and a nanny in a large house in central London. While a single life offers her a sense of liberty, a liberty that allows her time to devote to her writing and the space to develop an exclusive relationship with the son she adores, she doesn't want to be partnerless for life! 'When I was younger, I wanted a knight on a white charger. But I find that all a bit draining at 39. What I'm looking for now is a great adventure of two minds, not passion.' Yet her Scorpio Moon shows her to be a woman for whom intense feelings are practically a prerequisite in a relationship. At the same time, Clare admits to valuing fidelity (an absolute must for Moon Scorpios) and acknowledges that she is a 'faithful animal'. She considers that women can separate sex from love, but as far as she is concerned, it would be extremely difficult for her not to express tenderness, warmth, and affection towards a man with whom she had a physical relationship. Clare also spoke of the telepathic nature of attraction—the 'seeing someone across a crowded room' syndrome: 'There is enormous power in the unsaid. The unspoken. The most important relationship of my life was like that—just one look was all it took. Bang. The thunderbolt, I think the Italians call it.'

In many ways Clare is a fascinating mass of contradictions. On the one hand, there is the Clare who functions supremely well in the real world—successful, popular, and financially very solvent indeed: a Clare who is creatively fulfilled, relishes motherhood, and leads an altogether full life. On the other, there is the Clare who, as a child, took refuge in the Mercury-Neptune world of fantasy and even created her own language; a child who can still be glimpsed in the occasional faraway look and the odd throwaway line. Paradoxically, Clare maintains that she is not a believer in the paranormal and she insists that she has never had a religious experience of any sort: 'I can't believe anything is beyond a rational explanation.' Yet her feelings of being a 'Martian' and her overwhelming sense of beauty that could move her to tears place her firmly in the bracket of the extrasensory person—one step away from the mystic. Like many people who make a fortress of the intellect, Clare has blocked off most of her psychic avenues except the ones that allow her access to the vivid world of her imagination. Clare admits to finding no difficulty in 'becoming' her characters and recreating scenes in a time before she was born, an ability that brings her stories to life.

Clare's chart undoubtedly shows the promise of fame and fortune in life, but they are prizes not easily won. Her Aries Sun is placed on the Midheaven and opposes Jupiter; these in turn are squared by Mars and Saturn. Opportunities abound with Sun-Jupiter aspects: this coupling indicates a 'larger than life' personality, one that will go far—in Clare's case, quite literally. Mars inserts plenty of action and courage into the picture; and in the water sign of Cancer. But Mars is close to harsh taskmaster Saturn, which in turn frustrates the expansive nature of Jupiter and the Sun. Clare's early setbacks as a dancer were the first casualties of this configuration; but like many people who experience failure early on in life, this gave her a strong foundation to build on ('Nothing has ever been as hard as ballet!') This configuration also encapsulates Clare's approach to her writing. She writes big books that sell in their millions. And it's all achieved by hard 'graft'.

Aries women believe in the maxim 'off with the old and on with the new.' And Clare is no exception. She wants to put her sailing career firmly behind her and to concentrate on her writing. However, in times to come, I suspect she will look back fondly on her pioneering days on the briny and wish to be remembered just as much for those heroic journeys as her literary ones. Indeed Clare made a comment about sailing that seems an entirely fitting epigram: 'I never think of sailing as a sport. It is an aesthetic experience. A heightening of awareness . . . an adventure of the spirit. I don't think of myself so much as a pioneer, but a searcher. I think a discovery of one's inner self is vastly more important than reaching Cape Cod!'

Postscript: In 1987, Clare was found to be suffering from myalgic encephalo-myelitis (M.E.), also known as post viral fatigue syndrome—an illness that produces excessive muscle fatigue, speech difficulties and problems with concentration and memory. During this time, transiting Pluto squared radical Pluto while transiting Neptune squared radical Neptune. Clare commented 'I have been to hell and back with this disease. I lost a year of my life. It has been the greatest challenge I have ever faced'.

Note for Astrologers: Relevant progressions and transits in Clare's life are as follows: Summer 1973—her first trip across the Atlantic, progressed Mars was conjunct Pluto, progressed Ascendant was quincunx Mercury and trine the Vertex; transiting Jupiter opposed Pluto, transiting Saturn sextiled the Sun, transiting Uranus squared Saturn, and transiting Pluto opposed the Sun. In July '73, transiting Mars was in Aries, and transiting Venus was in Leo.

In July 1977—the time of Clare's marriage and her successful finish in the **Observer** Single-Handed; transiting Saturn squared Venus (!), transiting Uranus was conjunct the Moon (!), transiting Jupiter was sextile the MC. Progressions for '77 (which also saw the start of the 'Whitbread Round the World') include: progressed Sun sextile Mars, progressed Venus conjunct the North node.

In 1981—the year prior to the separation, progressed Sun moved into Gemini, the progressed MC sextiled Mars, transiting Pluto was conjunct the IC and by December opposed the Sun while Saturn conjoined the IC, transiting Uranus trined Mars.

In 1983—the year her first, best-selling novel, **Night Sky** was published, progressed Venus moved into Cancer and opposed the Vertex, progressed Mars squared Venus, the progressed MC moved into Gemini, sextiled Mercury and quincunxed the Vertex. In September, the month of publication, transiting Neptune trined the Sun, transiting Saturn quincunxed Mercury and sextiled the Vertex, transiting Jupiter trined Mercury and later, Pluto and the Ascendant.

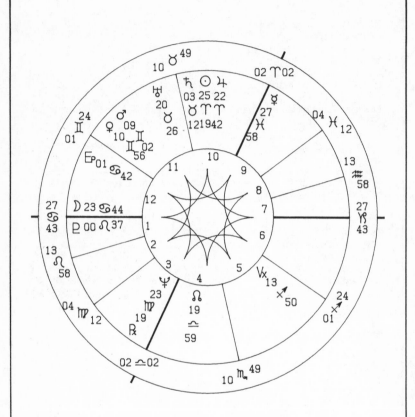

JEFFREY ARCHER

15 4 1940 10h 45m 0s GMT

PLACIDUS 51N14 2W50

PROFILE OF AN ARIES MAN

JEFFREY ARCHER

Jeffrey Archer is all Ram. And like all Aries true-blues, bounding from peak to peak among the Himalayas of success, he hasn't a moment to lose in pursuit of the Possible Dream. Mr Archer isn't the easiest man to meet: his daily timetable reads like a race-meeting, and if you pause too long between sentences, you'll qualify as a non-starter. I was in luck. Jeffrey could spare me fifteen minutes. In the event I stayed the course and was awarded extra time —presumably for good behaviour!

Jeffrey leaves one in little doubt as to his astrological bearing. 'I want the book quickly. I want the picture quickly. And I want to see it the moment I'm allowed to see it in the flesh!' were the orders issued to a retreating figure as we sat down to talk. No self-respecting Aries would live in a basement, thus Jeffrey's London flat is situated at the top of a skyscraper overlooking the Houses of Parliament where he is at present (April 1986) Deputy Chairman of the Tory Party. He is better known, however, as one of the world's best-selling authors with five block-buster successes on his hands to date. But it was not always thus.

Jeffrey was the only child of an army officer. His father died from war wounds when when Jeffrey was fifteen, and his mother remarried a few years later. 'I had a tremendous relationship with my parents—particularly my mother . . . yes, it was a dreadful blow when my father died.' Jeffrey was educated at a local prep school, then went on to Wellington (public school) in Somerset. 'No, I wasn't a high-flier at school.' Indeed, Jeffrey showed not a germ of his future literary prowess when he was young, and all his early ambitions were aimed at sport (particularly athletics and gymnastics)—at which he excelled. But while he may not have lived up to his academic potential at public school he went on to obtain a Diploma of

Education at Headington Polytechnic, which was affiliated to Brasenose College, Oxford. He became president of the University athletics club and in 1966 represented Great Britain in the 100 metres.

Only-children and first-born children tend to become high-achievers. If they also happen to have a Sun-Jupiter conjunction in Aries in the tenth 'house' the tendency becomes a certainty. While Jeffrey's fiery Aries Sun is given even more of a boost by 'larger than life' Jupiter, it is simultaneously restrained by remorseless Saturn.* The effects of this 'package' have been manifold in Jeffrey's life, as I shall gradually reveal. The tenth 'house' is also associated with one of the parents (usually mother) and because this 'house' is heavily occupied it is clear Jeffrey's mother has been a huge influence on his life and his direction. This influence could have been strong simply because she had to take on a joint parental role. But I suspect that, even had his father reached a ripe old age, Jeffrey's mother would still have been the parent to whom he felt closest. The importance of mother in Jeffrey's life is also shown by the Moon-Pluto conjunction on his Ascendant in Cancer—a sign synonymous with mother and the feminine. While some areas of the chart support Jeffrey's 'tremendous relationship' with his parents,† other factors indicate some difficulty.

Individuals with a Sun-Saturn conjunction rarely have an 'easy ride' through life even as a child. This combination suggests the father was not the warmest of individuals and may have been emotionally or physically distant. That Jeffrey was separated from his father by death is one logical interpretation of this aspect; yet there is just a hint in Jeffrey's comments that his father may have been rather heavy-handed with the discipline: 'Yes, my father was strict. He was a soldier. But that's been a great benefit through life. I couldn't perceive it as a child, but I can now.' Clearly many boys require a firm hand, and Jeffrey, with his ebullient Aries nature, was no doubt among them; but with Saturn and Pluto forming hard contacts to the Sun there is an indication that his father's tough line may have come near to crushing Jeffrey's independent spirit at times. And whether through his father's attitude or his own perception, Jeffrey learned to associate winning with being manly and strong and losing with weakness and inadequacy—an observation that could have bred intolerance to failure in himself. Planets involved with the tenth 'house' usually have more to say about mother than father. While Jeffrey cites his father as the heavy hand of discipline, the astrology points also to mother in this capacity. The tenth 'house' positioning

*The Sun is the midpoint of Saturn-Jupiter.

†Venus, the ruler of the fourth 'house'; Mars the ruler of the 10th conjunct Venus.

of Jupiter and the Sun suggest Jeffrey admired his parents (especially mother) and wished to please them and win their approval by doing well. Later this desire prompted greater aspirations as Jeffrey sought public recognition.

Jupiter's conjunction to the Sun is a wonderful bonus and certainly mitigates Saturn's crushing tendencies. However, the combination of these three 'planets' would have a frustrating effect on Jeffrey's life. No matter what successes Jupiter brings, Saturn always puts a spanner in the works. Jeffrey never has a clear home run. For instance, the placing of this trio in one of the key areas of parental influence could have meant that his father's death put severe financial strain on the family; this in turn affected Jeffrey's future plans and made the attainment of his goals that much more difficult. This planetary combination is also a very competitive one, especially since the Sun and Jupiter are both in 'go-getting' Aries. While Jeffrey's athletic build makes him a natural sportsman—he still fits in four games of squash a week—it was his burning desire to win that contributed to his earlier success in sport. This same driving quality is behind everything he aims for in life. And while his charm and sense of humour win him many friends, he has a ruthless streak.

Oxford, with its great political tradition, inspired a new passion in Jeffrey. 'Gradually I became interested in politics at university. It seemed so fascinating compared with any other job ... I didn't go into politics right away. I worked on the GLC [Greater London Council], which I suppose is politics, but it was an unpaid position.' Indeed at twenty-six, Jeffrey was the youngest ever member of the GLC. Jeffrey's twenty-sixth year was also important since he married the girl he had met and fallen in love with at university, Mary.

By twenty-nine, when Saturn returned to its original position, and Jupiter boosted all his Aries planets, Jeffrey attained one of his greatest ambitions. In 1969, by winning the by-election at Louth, he became the youngest Member of Parliament; and for five years he made a considerable name for himself on the back benches and looked set for a golden political future. But what Saturn had given with one hand, 'he' was about to withdraw with the other.

In 1974, a Canadian company called Aquablast went into liquidation. Eight million dollars went down the drain and so nearly did Jeffrey. On the advice of the Bank of Boston he had invested heavily in the company—three of the Bank's directors later went to jail for fraud. 'Bad? I lost a million dollars in one week. What do you call bad?!' Jeffrey's brilliant career plummeted overnight. On the brink of bankruptcy, with debts of almost £500,000, he was compelled to resign from the House of Commons. 'My first reaction was, what a stupid idiot I'd been. I blamed myself—no one else.' For two weeks following the crash, Jeffrey went into an uncharacteristic but predictable trough. And even though he had the immense moral and emotional support of his wife, he felt the problem was his alone. 'Mary was very supportive, but we didn't work it out together. I worked it out on my own. No disrespect to Mary; but what could she say. I'd lost all my money. I'd lost my job. I'd lost my career. I'd lost everything. Even the house had to go. No, you've got to get yourself up. No one else can do it for you.' Fortunately, Mary—a Cambridge don—was able to keep the family afloat with her salary. 'We survived. But it took seven years three months before all the debts were paid.'

At thirty-four and jobless, the future looked bleak for Jeffrey. Surfacing from his temporary slump, writing appeared to be his only option. Within a year he had written his first best-seller, **Not a Penny More, Not a Penny Less**—a story about four young men who are swindled out of a million dollars and how they retrieve it. Clearly Jeffrey decided to follow the author's favourite maxin, write about what you know, and turned a crisis into a saga! The rest is, as they say, history. Every book he has written to date has sold hundreds of thousands of copies, some in their millions. And he has the well-deserved reputation of being one of the world's most accomplished story-tellers.

Astrologically, several factors contribute to the fall and rise in his affairs. As I have already discussed, the Saturn-Sun-Jupiter conjunction depicts a major stop-go pattern in his life, and suggests that success comes at a cost. More appositely, Jeffrey's collapse and resurrection, and his radical life changes, can be linked to the presence of Pluto on the Ascendant and this planet's 90° square aspects to Saturn, Sun, and Jupiter. Pluto symbolizes death and rebirth, and its placing on a highly sensitive area of the birth chart indicates that this process is an integral part of his life.* Some astrologers maintain that individuals with a rising Pluto† have a powerful destiny—greatness may well be thrust upon them. However, with or without greatness, Pluto-rising people tend to encounter periods of crisis in their life during which they are forced to draw upon their innermost emotional, psychological, and physical resources. Jeffrey's attitude that it was his task alone to extricate himself from his demise is typical of the way a strongly Aries character would react to such a traumatic set of circumstances—it became an almighty personal challenge. And while Jeffrey has been

*By strange coincidence, Arian Clare Francis also has Pluto on her Ascendant. In Clare's case, she encountered life and death situations at sea, and became transformed through them. She too has experienced radical changes in career direction.

†And Pluto conjunct the Midheaven.

the butt of some adverse criticism from time to time, the way he handled this life crisis shows him to be a man of considerable guts and determination.

Any reasonably adequate astrologer would have been able to point Jeffrey in the direction of a writing career. Mercury in the imaginative sign of Pisces on the Midheaven, trine the Moon, Pluto and the Ascendant, is a near-perfect—and certainly a winning—combination for a writer. Not only this, but Jeffrey's Venus-Mars conjunction in loquacious Gemini forms a gifted quintile aspect to Mercury. His talent for communication also stands him in good stead in his political career—although his susceptibility to Aries' 'foot and mouth' syndrome occasionally interferes with his oratorical skills. While his Sun-Jupiter conjunction has earned him a fortune through his books, in typical Sun-Saturn fashion he is a hard and tireless worker. 'I'd say writing was 90 per cent hard work and 10 per cent inspiration. It takes me two years to write a novel. I do roughly a year's research, then about ten drafts—all of them hand written.' With the Moon rising in Cancer—a sign much concerned with the past—Jeffrey might well have set one of his novels in the distant past. 'No, I'm not interested in history. I'm a fiction writer.' Perhaps a rollicking tale involving such political figures as Baldwin or Churchill is yet to come?

With the strong Cancerian influence in his chart, marriage and family life are immensely important to Jeffrey. He has two sons, William born in 1972 and Jamie in 1974. 'We waited five years to have children. We wanted to establish our careers first—more so Mary, because when you're a new young don it's not clever to leave immediately to have two children!' Jeffrey has Capricorn on the cusp of his seventh 'house' of relationships, which presents a strong, stable and well-structured view of marriage. Mary is herself a Sun Capricorn and she provides a good anchor for Jeffrey's more volatile personality. 'We have a good and happy relationship—have had for twenty years. I'm better educated because of her. She walks in a quiet gentle academic world—she's very reserved—while I'm a politician who is by nature in the centre of the stage. She doesn't want to do what I'm doing and vice versa. She has immense common sense—painfully honest. She wouldn't have made a good politician!' The Aries-Capricorn relationship is what I call 'the steam-roller': after a noisy uphill beginning it gathers great momentum, felling all obstacles in its path! When this relationship works well, it's marvellous. When it doesn't, it can be disastrous—the couple rarely see eye to eye on any one issue. Perhaps more seriously, there is a tendency for individuals with Saturn or Capricorn linked to partnerships to maintain the outer structure of marriage while becoming emotionally isolated within it. Jeffrey has clearly tapped the higher level of Capricorn with Mary, although I suspect the going has been hard at times. Also with his Mars-Venus conjunction in variety-seeking Gemini and his emotionally complex Moon-Pluto combination, there is just a suggestion that without the freedom to pursue many and various challenges in life Jeffrey would find marriage as much a constraint as a haven.

The seventh 'house' of partnerships is also known as the 'house' of open enemies, and covers working relationships as well as intimate ones. Thus as far as political life is concerned, the Saturnian influence in this area may well indicate difficulties and hostilities in Jeffrey's relationships with colleagues and constituents. 'You can't be the youngest Member of Parliment, the youngest ever member of the GLC, and have dared to write a book that millions have bought, without having people who automatically resent you. There's nothing you can do about it.' The British invariably view overt success as vulgar, and prefer to pigeon-hole personalities; thus perhaps Jeffrey's popularity as a writer might stand in his way as a successful politician? 'No, not now that I'm doing no writing at all . . . It's a great weakness to consider that people can only do one thing. I mean if it was suddenly announced tomorrow that Norman Tebbit was a fine violinist, people would doubt it.' While there are plenty of astrological pointers to Jeffrey's leadership abilities, and he has more than proved his strength of character and his capacity to win, there is also a divisive quality shown in his chart that indicates he may alienate as many people as he attracts. And this could prove the biggest obstacle in the way of his political ambitions.

In September 1985, after eleven years of political exile, Jeffrey returned to Westminster as the Conservative Party Deputy Chairman. It is clear that the political arena is where he is at his most fulfilled. His Aries side likes the cut and thrust of political manoeuvring—as well as the power and influence—while his Gemini side revels in debate and logical argument; his rising Moon in Cancer adds a caring and concerned touch and strategic ability—Cancer rising individuals can also move in mysterious ways! 'Yes, I do see my way ahead in politics. It's the only thing that really interests me, the thing that keeps me going. It excites me.' With the passage of Jupiter through Aries during 1987-8, Jeffrey looks set for more career successes, and with many lessons learned from the past, none of them should be short-lived.

During the course of our meeting, I mentioned to Jeffrey that there was a plethora of Aries politicians in all three parties. He replied jokingly, 'We're a dangerous group, aren't we!' With Michael Heseltine, Norman Tebbit, Neil Kinnock, and Tony Benn among them, he just could be right.

Postscript: I interviewed Jeffrey in the spring of 1986. As I was leaving he jokingly asked. 'Well. will I be Prime Minister one day?' Not wanting to crush his Arian optimism I replied that I could not guarantee the Premiership but I thought he'd do extremely well. I then added that October 1986 looked extremely important for his future. and that that period was also a crucial one for Margaret Thatcher.

In late October 1986. a huge furore broke out over Jeffrey's alleged involvement with a prostitute. Monica Coghlan, and in the process Jeffrey's tenuous foothold on the political ladder collapsed. Margaret Thatcher was forced to suffer the embarrassment of the resignation of one of her blue-eyed boys amid a technicolour scandal.

In July 1987. after some of the most sensational court scenes of the decade. Jeffrey was completely exonerated and the *Star* newspaper was ordered to pay him half a million pounds plus costs. At the same time Jeffrey's first play. *Beyond Reasonable Doubt.* opened in the West End of London and became a smash hit.

Note for Astrologers: Relevant progressions and transits include: 1966– Election to the GLC and marriage: progressed Sun conjunct Uranus, progressed Venus sextile Saturn. progressed Mars sextile Sun. transiting Saturn conjunct Mercury, transiting Jupiter conjunct Ascendant. 1969—entry to the House of Commons: the Saturn Return, transiting Uranus conjunct the IC. transiting Jupiter in Libra opposing all Aries planets. 1974—the crash: progressed Mars square MC-IC axis. transiting Neptune opposing Mars, transiting Uranus opposing Sun and transiting Saturn square the MC-IC. 1975—the publication of his successful first novel: transiting Jupiter in Aries. 1985—return to the House of Commons: progressed Sun conjunct Mars, transiting Neptune square the MC-IC. transiting Jupiter trine Mars and transiting Pluto quincunx the MC.

In the October of 1986. there were two eclipses: a solar eclipse on the 3rd at 10° Libra and a lunar eclipse on the 17th at 24° Libra—the latter straddling his natal Sun and squaring natal Moon. (Margaret Thatcher's radical Mercury is 23° Libra while her Sun at 19° Libra is conjunct Jeffrey's north node.) Also during October. transiting Saturn was applying to an opposition of Radical Mars and Venus. and Jupiter squared his vertex.

In the July of 1987 transiting Jupiter conjuncted Jeffrey's Sun. These events occured 12 years after 'the crash' and the publication of his first novel—a complete Jupiterian cycle.

TAURUS

21 April – 20 May

III

GOLD DIGGERS AND
EARTH MOVERS

TAURUS
GOLD DIGGERS AND EARTH MOVERS

T A U R U S has the enviable reputation of being one of the most gentle, placid, and affectionate signs of the zodiac. All the more surprising therefore, when one considers its symbol, the bull—an animal of awesome power and potency and hardly the most friendly and accommodating beast at the best of times. But Taurus the cow doesn't have quite the same ring to it, does it? Although in many ways the archetypal Taurean has far more in common with this benign, pastoral creature.

In his series of paintings of the zodiac, the artist Johfra captured to perfection the quintessential peace and harmony of Taurus: Europa sits decoratively on a white bull amidst a landscape of lush verdancy, all of which is surrounded by a charming rococo frame. The rejoicing of Nature, the sense of the earth and her riches, and the overall serenity of the composition depict the luxuriant and fertile aspect of this sensual earth sign. Yet this picture is not wholly accurate. There is a piece missing; for in Taurus' Garden of Eden there's always a snake in the grass! And like most of the signs that appear deceptively simple and straightforward, beneath the bovine extremities of Taurus there is some murkier undergrowth.

In keeping with the harmonious theme to this sign, Taureans are often extremely good-looking, and even if Mother Nature hasn't endowed them with perfect features, most of them have a serenity and gentleness about them that is highly appealing. Like the other fixed signs—Leo, Scorpio, and Aquarius—there is a tendency towards a square jaw, and pronounced nostrils; the neck can be on the short side and sometimes rather thick. Since Taurus is said to 'rule' the throat, this area of the body is particularly vulnerable to infection, although many Taureans have beautiful voices. Weight problems are all too familiar to this earth sign, often generated by a love of good food. Yet despite their tendency towards a stocky frame these individuals can be some of the most graceful movers in the zodiac.

Many astrologers have commented that they have fewer Taurean clients than those of any other sign; no doubt because Taureans, like their Scorpio opposites, are some of the most sceptical people in the zodiac. But unlike Scorpios, who are powerfully drawn to the hidden and the mysterious dimensions of life through their watery, feeling natures, Taureans, in the main, prefer to keep their two sturdy feet planted resolutely on terra firma—very much in the realm of the corporeal and the palpable. One of my few Taurean clients, the owner of a building firm, originally consulted me to prove to his wife that—and excuse the excrutiating pun—astrology was nothing but a load of bull! But by the end of the consultation he felt compelled to admit that I had been 86 per cent accurate. When pressed to account for the faulty 14 per cent he upped his assessment to 92 per cent. He unfailingly returns every year a week before his birthday (Taureans love routine) and he now possesses several books on the subject. Like many Taureans, once convinced of the value and use of something he was prepared to pursue it further—not that he'd admit to anyone that he'd changed his mind.

Consecutive signs of the zodiac always present sharply contrasting themes. Aries, a cardinal fire sign, rockets into experience—the impulsive, racy pioneer of the zodiac. Thus Taurus follows somewhat sedately—a cautious, conservative cultivator. During the time of Aries, at least in the northern hemisphere, nature awakes from its sleep, flora begin to sprout, and fauna become frisky. As the sun moves through Taurus the earth celebrates the return of her glory and shimmers in fecund opulence. In the southern hemisphere this enriching process is largely an underground event. Yet since astrology is much concerned with polarities of every sort, the burgeoning growth process on an emotional and psychological level (symbolized by nature's cycle) is as much a part of Taurus as it is of Scorpio.

Many astrologers underestimate Taurus' depths, focusing largely on its green and pleasant aspect and its rather materialistic tendencies. But a voyage among the mythical roots of Taurus shows it to be a sign concerned with riches on all levels, not merely the material.

The bull is an ancient and significant symbol. In 'primitive' cultures the world over bull worship was common and the sacrifice of a bull formed an important part of religious rituals. In Mithraism (Persia-Iran) Mithra's most illustrious act was the capture and slaughter of a wild bull. The slaying of the bull was thought to release fertile blessings on the earth. The ancient Egyptians also associated the bull with fertility, and their greatest god, Osiris, a deity of vegetation, was often depicted with a bull's head.

The bull is also a deeply complex symbol, both from an historical point of view and a psychological one. Its complexity stems from a dilemma as to the interpretation of the bull as a masculine or a feminine idea. On the one hand, the bull and its companion symbols the cow and the ox represent the earth, fertility, and mother; yet on the other hand, the bull also symbolizes heaven and the father. The very appearance of the bull is terribly masculine, yet its horns suggest the 'horned moon'; and all things lunar are synonymous with the feminine. One explanation for this incongruity is that the bull was considered feminine during the time lunar cults flourished, but became a masculine symbol as solar societies replaced cults of the moon (see Cancer, pp. 149–50). Indeed, the ritual slaughter of the bull in so many cultures may have had just as much to do with the death of the lunar cult (and by association the sublimation of feminine power) as with fertility.

Before the introduction of lunar gods and later goddesses, the bull was one of the various animals used to represent the moon. The three-headed hound pre-dated Hecate, the bear was the fore-runner of Artemis, and Hathor, the cow goddess, was later fused with Isis. The animal representations of the moon depicted the fierce, unrefined power of the feminine instinct. The Egyptian goddess Hathor is perhaps the closest relative of the Taurean bull. Hathor was above all else a good and helpful goddess; she was the protectress of infants in arms and the patron of music, dancing, and love. As such, she bears a close resemblance to Greek Aphrodite and Roman Venus—of whom we shall hear more later. Venus was also known as the daughter of the moon. In astrological terms, Venus-ruled Taurus is the first of the 'feminine' signs, and the hornèd moon with all its lunar feminine overtones is clearly represented in its glyph ♉.

To a certain extent all the 'feminine' signs of the zodiac, but particularly

Taurus, Cancer, and Virgo, contain some aspect of lunar symbolism within them. This is because the goddess figures associated with these signs, like all goddesses, spring from the one Great (mother) Goddess herself. Thus each sign reflects aspects of her creative-destroying nature. As far as Taurus is concerned, black and white bulls permeate all myths; the former more usually identified with the violent and destructive dimension of the lunar goddess, the latter with her bright side. The hornèd moon depicts the moon prior to its three-day disappearance when it is a mere slither of a crescent. This dark time of the moon was considered to be the period of the black goddess in her various forms as Hecate, Lilith, Astarte, and Kali. Taurus, like Cancer, is a sign that presents the very best in lunar qualities—gentleness, protectiveness, creativity, and nurture; yet there is also a dark and treacherous side.

The murkier aspect of Taurus is a theme worked through many myths and legends associated with this sign: King Midas and his lust for gold, and Pasiphae and her lust for a bull (which resulted in the ghastly Minotaur) are probably the most well known. Interwoven into these myths are two wildly contrasting figures: Dionysus and Daedalus.

Dionysus (sometimes depicted as a bull) was a numen of nature and a mad, bad, and dangerous god. He had a traumatic start in life since his mother (Semele) was killed while he was in utero and the rest of his gestation was spent in his father's (Zeus) thigh. As a child he was abducted, abandoned, sent mad, and was witness to events of extreme violence. Not surprisingly his cult was an orgiastic and very violent one indeed; he drove others to madness by inducing a kind of mystic delirium in them. One only has to consider the mass hypnotic effect Taureans Adolf Hitler and Jim Jones exerted on their followers, their fanaticism, and their destructive excesses to see the Dionysian force let loose on a grand scale. On a less traumatic level, Taurus, despite its reputation as a sign of peace and serenity, is nonetheless an extreme sign. Many Taureans are capable of extreme self-indulgence and push themselves to the very limits of sensory experience.

By contrast, Daedalus is a thoroughly sober figure. Daedalus was one of the great artisans of myth, a mixture of universal inventor, sculptor, architect, and mechanic. It was Daedalus who built the labyrinthine palace in which to conceal the Minotaur, and Daedalus who fashioned the wooden cow for Pasiphae. Taurus is the zodiac's artisan: this sign is noted for its ability to work with practical and useful ideas. And the Taurus individual, like Daedalus, is eminently capable of finding simple solutions to apparently insuperable problems.

Many myths pertaining to Taurus contain a theme of death and rebirth, often involving a journey to the Underworld: in part this is an allegory of the revivification of Nature, but in psychological terms journeys underground symbolize the inner path the individual must take in order to find the true Self. For Taurus the path involves the stripping away of face values to find inner truth.

The legend of Psyche and Eros is full of fascinating and sometimes obscure symbolism along these lines. Psyche was the (mortal) daughter of a great king. She was very beautiful and hailed by some as the 'new Aphrodite', yet she had no suitors. After consulting an oracle about his daughter's lack of a husband, Psyche's father was told to dress her as a bride and leave her alone at the top of a mountain. There she was to be claimed by a fearful monster. Reluctantly, Psyche's parents complied with the oracle, but unbeknown to them, Aphrodite's hand was behind it all. The goddess, jealous of Psyche's beauty and all the attentions paid her, commanded her son, Eros, to inspire in Psyche irrational love for some ugly creature. However, Aphrodite's plans were foiled since Eros fell madly in love with Psyche and determined to have her for himself.

To cut a longish story short, the West Wind carried Psyche off to a beautiful palace where all her needs were attended to by invisible servants and where each night she was visited by her lover-husband, Eros, under cover of total darkness. (Eros forbade Psyche ever to look upon him.) At first Psyche complied, but taunted by the idea that her husband was a monster bent only on fattening her up to ultimately devour her, her curiosity got the better of her. One night Psyche concealed a lamp beneath her bed so that once her lover had fallen asleep she could see to kill him. But instead of a monster, the lamp revealed Eros in his youthful beauty. In her surprise Psyche dropped some burning oil on Eros, whereupon he awoke and disappeared—apparently forever.

However, Psyche was a stubborn and tenacious mortal. She loved Eros and decided to get him back. But since none of the gods would help her for fear of igniting Aphrodite's wrath, Psyche had no recourse but to confront the goddess herself. Aphrodite first tortured Psyche then set her several daunting tasks, including descending to the Underworld to obtain a small box containing precious ointment. Aphrodite forbade Psyche to open the box. But for the second time curiosity got the better of her; when she opened the box a vapour of sleep escaped and she was plunged into unconsciousness. Happily for Pysche, her tribulations had not been in vain. Eros awakened her, carried her up to Olympus, and asked Zeus to marry them. Zeus agreed, Psyche and Aphrodite were reconciled, and they all lived happily ever after.

Alepius, the creator of this myth, used as its basis an old folk tale, Beauty and the Beast. He considered the tale to represent the journey of the soul. To Alepius, the soul was a reflection of pure beauty chained to the earth by its low passions, especially curiosity. Only when the soul had undergone the necessary preparations, aided by a series of tests, could it perceive real beauty. Love was an essential part of this process.

Beauty and love have much to do with Taurus. So do appearances and values. The tale of Psyche and Eros underlines the frailty of appearances and the weakness of human nature in regard to both.

Astrologically, Venus, Taurus' ruler, represents the principle of beauty and love, which is why Aphrodite, and her various counterparts, like Sumerian Inana, Egyptian Hathor (the Cow-goddess) and Scandinavian Freya, are integral parts of myths and legends linked to Taurus. Yet many astrologers feel deeply uneasy about Venus' association with this earth sign and consider her courtesan ways and capricious nature more suited to airy Libra. Certainly sensuality and love of the arts—all good Venusian attributes—are as much the province of Taurus as Libra, but Taurus demands something more substantial of Venus. To a certain extent, this 'substance' is provided by Aphrodite's husband, the ugly lame god Hephaestos, who like his Roman equivalent,

Vulcan, was the divine smith to the gods. Hephaestos, like Daedalus, emphasizes the practical and useful side of Taurus.

Beautiful Aphrodite and ugly Hephaestos are another rendition of Beauty and the Beast—a recurrent theme of Taurus. This dichotomy can be seen operating through Taurus on various levels. On the one hand, the gentle patient Taurean is often at the mercy of the unpleasant 'beast' lurking in his depths; a monster that can take the form of greed, rampant self-indulgence, avarice, and even violence. On the other, blocks and frustrations are the 'beasts' that stand in the way of the peace and harmony Taureans crave in their lives. In many ways this myth was externalized by Hitler. In order to create a perfect world in which only the beautiful Aryan race could live, his first task was to eliminate the hideous 'beast'—to him the entire Jewish nation.

It is also worth noting that the beast in many myths and fairy tales turns out to be a handsome prince after all. But in order for the transformation to occur the beast must be loved for what he is—the beauty of the soul as opposed to that of the body. One of Taurus' great failings is the tendency to rely on the appearance of things and to give greater credence to the material and the tangible. In so doing he undervalues the feeling side of life and all things ephemeral. Thus Taureans often find out to their cost that beauty is only skin deep. Indeed one of the most crucial issues for Taurus is the recognition that his worth is not so much a matter of how much money he has in the bank or what valuable and beautiful possessions he has, but the sum total of his own self-worth.

The Taurean individual also faces a dichotomy between the practical, realistic side of his nature (earth) and the luxuriant, self-indulgent side (Venus). And by and large, Taureans tend to fall into one camp or another. Yet Taurean men and women are rarely the here-today, gone-tomorrow types: Taurus is after all a 'fixed' earth sign, which is about as rigid as you can find anywhere in the zodiac! Obstinate, dogmatic, and insistent are other adjectives synonymous with this sign; as are dependable, tolerant, stoical, and tenacious.

From childhood, frenetic activity of any sort seems antithetical to the Taurean. And even if any of them eventually opt for energetic careers, like dancing, which many of them do—Fred Astaire (Sun Taurus), Arthur Murray (Venus in Taurus), Dame Margot Fonteyn (Sun, Mars, Mercury in Taurus), Ann Margret (Sun, Moon, Venus, Jupiter, Saturn and Uranus in Taurus!)—they never waste any unnecessary energy. Indeed, sometimes members of this sign can be extremely lazy, and even the Taurean workaholic has periods of slothfulness.

Perhaps because of its lunar association Taurus shares many characteristics with the water sign Cancer. The Bull usually loves his home: it's his greatest security 'blanket', and he's deeply attached to his family, whatever the nature of the inter-relationships. And as soon as he's attended to his insurance policy and his pension, he'll want to have four square walls of his own. Not surprisingly many Taureans find their way into the real estate business or look to careers in building or interior decorating. And the idea of buying up old properties and 'doing them up' (for profit) appeals to almost all of them—the one problem being that they invariably become too attached to the properties to let them go! The Bull, like the Crab, is also a great collector, although he's motivated less by sentiment and more by plain and simple acquisitiveness. His home tends to be less cluttered than the Cancerian's since it's not so packed with memorabilia, and he tends to keep the décor to a similar style or period throughout. The Taurean favours the opulent look or the farmhouse-natural effect. Indeed with its mythical roots deep in the soil, the farmhouse is quintessentially Taurean. So too are green fingers; and most Taureans feel more at home in the bosom of the countryside than the hurly-burly and artificiality of the city.

Taureans are not only great cultivators of the land but great cultivators of people. Mr and Ms Taurus, like the other Venusians, the Librans, can be dreadful snobs and social climbers. While Taurean men and women like to be liked by everyone, they tend to foster relationships with people who can be useful to them or with those who come from the same 'bracket'—or above. In their defence, Taurus is also a very loyal sign and few of them forget their old school chums or those firm friendships forged along the ways to affluence! However, the Bull can be a poor judge of character since he is easily influenced by appearance, so he is often used by others. And because the Taurean lacks the lightness and superficiality of the real social butterfly (he tends to take the whole business too seriously) he can become as paranoid as the Scorpio about his invitations—or his lack of them.

Indeed for all their sweetness and light, Taureans are prone to projecting a rather large Scorpionic shadow. Control is just as much an issue for Taurus as it is for Scorpio. These individuals revere self-restraint and can be relied upon to keep nodding and smiling under the most dire provocation. But their outer calm often acts as a door to a blast furnace; and given enough time and pressure the lid inevitably blows.

Taureans also like to keep their fears to themselves. On the one hand, because they know everyone is relying upon them they cannot run the risk of shattering anyone's faith in them; and on the other, Taureans tend to think that if they don't acknowledge something, it will simply fade away. Thus Mr and Ms Taurus are prone to developing all manner of stress-related conditions as they get older.

Taurus can be just as much of an extremist as Scorpio; and nearly every Bull has a bee in his or her bonnet about something. My family has learned never to mention the Americans and the Battle of Britain in the same breath in the certain knowledge that my father (with his Mars in Taurus) will subject everyone in earshot to an interminable fist-banging tirade. Sadly, Taureans can be some of the most bigoted people in the zodiac. Their opinions once formed set like cement and it takes more than a bulldozer to shift them. While their refusal to swallow anything unpalatable blocks their own growth, their criticism and abnegation of those whose ideas conflict with theirs can sometimes be extremely destructive. In particular, the Taurean mistrusts anything of a dubious 'spiritual' nature and his need to base everything on fact can take him to some absurd lengths. One well-known scientist had the misfortune to undergo a mystical experience; and because he could find no scientific criteria to explain it, he simply had to deny that anything had occurred!

Bulls tend to be very private individuals. While they may present a warm and pleasant front, they'll rarely volunteer any personal information about themselves or their family; in part, because they want to sustain a good image, but also because 'it's nobody else's damned business'! In some cases their refusal to divulge information reaches heroic proportions, as in the case of Odette Sanson (Sun and Saturn in Taurus) who withstood a red-hot iron and two years in solitary confinement under the hands of the Gestapo rather than betray the Resistance movement.

Although Taurus has its secret depths and its darker shadows it is nevertheless a sign that likes the straightforward approach. The Bull tends to say what he thinks, which can make him as blunt as the Aries Ram at times. He's also the type who believes in practice rather than theories. The Bull treats anything revolutionary or iconoclastic with the greatest suspicion (he is a diehard traditionalist) and change of any sort is deeply resented. This fixity permeates the Bull's life on all levels from his eating habits to his clothes and his world view. In consequence, he often gets stuck in ruts of his own making, which can make progress to his goals extremely slow.

Not that Taurus is a tremendously ambitious sign. Male and female Bulls are rarely driven by the desire for success, but they do like a comfortable, if not luxurious, life style. Money in the bank for Taurus does not represent power, but security and happiness. In keeping with their earthy natures, most of them keep a careful check on their credits and debits and make a point of shopping around for bargains. But since they're also a Venusian sign, they're not mean and stingy, and they like to have their 'little indulgences'. Perhaps also because of their Venus rulership, Taureans rarely go in for cut and thrust tactics on their way to their goals and they don't relish competition. Bluff and bluster are the weapons usually wielded by Taurus to weaken an 'aggressor'; if not, their stubborn persistence will eventually wear away any resistance.

Finally a word about the all-important Taurean sensuousness. Almost all Taureans are deeply affected by beauty in one form or another—one of the greatest artists of all time, Leonardo da Vinci has Sun and Venus in Taurus. Yet this finer side to their nature is often suppressed for more practical consideration or kept to themselves as a private pleasure. One Taurean client of mine spent years building up a successful electronics business, then in the aftermath of a divorce he sold up and went to college to study music. Now he earns much less as a musician but he's a totally fulfilled man.

Taureans are not the greatest trail-blazers in the zodiac, nor the greatest innovators or conceptualists. These individuals are like the stuff of earth itself, solid, sure, and palpable, but also creative, sensual, and sometimes blessed with riches! Most of them face the awkward task of blending the two sides of their nature—the realist and the builder with the artist and muse—and sometimes the muse has considerable trouble releasing itself from its earthly bonds. But don't be mislead by the Bull's sedate measured pace through life; he may appear laid back to the point of supineness, but flash a red cape in front of his nose too often and, well—just make sure you're nowhere near a china shop!

RELATIONSHIPS

Finding someone to have and to hold is one of life's priorities for Taurus. Like their Venusian cousins, the Librans, Mr and Ms Taurus need a partner with whom to share their lives to feel complete. And indeed, Mr and Ms Taurus have much to offer their partners with their loyal, trusting natures and their indefatigable faith in those they love.

The Bull, despite its earth-bound, practical nature, is a highly sensuous creature: both male and female Taureans fall in love easily and with great passion. Yet they only commit themselves when they are convinced they've found Mr or Ms Right. Of course they aren't infallible and Bulls are just as capable as the more impulsive fire signs of charging into relationships with Mr and Ms Absolutely Wrong! And to a certain extent relationships tend to veer to extremes for Taureans. Yet, good or bad, where relationships are concerned, Taureans never throw in the towel without considerable soul-searching and after years of tribulation. Divorce is like an amputation for Mr and Ms Taurus: these individuals believe you are theirs for life.

THE FEMALE TAURUS

Are you a man of your word? Are your life insurance payments up to date and your pension organized? And do you have prospects? If you can honestly answer yes to these questions, then you can present yourself to Ms Taurus. If not, think again. Where the flame of romance is concerned, the Taurean Lady is not for scorching. Like the Cancerian, this Venusian female looks meltingly feminine and appealingly submissive, yet emotionally and psychologically she's as strong as an ox. She doesn't like being messed around by anyone, and because she's very straightforward herself she expects absolute honesty from her man. Ms Taurus is never in much doubt as to what she truly wants, and she'll usually get her own way no matter how long it takes. This woman has patience as well as an iron will. Of all the signs, the Taurean woman is the most deceptively easygoing: and the old cliché about still waters applies just as well to the female Bull as it does to her opposite number, Ms Scorpio.

Almost all Taurean women have practised the art of passive resistance from their high-chair days—sometimes to devastating effect. While at the tender age of two Ms Taurus may throw a tantrum or twelve to get her own way, by the time she's twenty-two she's acquired the perfect knack of appearing sweetly co-operative while remaining firmly entrenched in her position. Since Taurean little girls are often very pretty indeed, grown-ups tend to indulge them and give way to their desires all too easily (it's less frustrating than a war of attrition). In consequence, many Taurean women grow up expecting to be pampered and fussed over in their adult relationships—a factor which often leads to much trauma and disappointment for them.

The Taurean girl is usually very attached to her home and family. In this respect she is again very similar to the Cancerian. And like Ms Cancer, as a child she needs plenty of security and demonstrable love to enable her to form intimate relationships without fear later. While her relationships with both parents form the basis of her expectations in marriage, Ms Taurus' mother is usually a far more influential figure in her life.

As an earth sign the Taurean female is normally responsible and obedient, if not rather duty-bound: so much so, that in some cases Ms Taurus can find herself living her life as her parents would wish it, rather than as she would choose to do herself. It is for this reason that the Taurean girl experiences one of the most stormy adolescences in the zodiac. As Ms Taurus' individuality struggles to emerge, if her ideas radically differ from those of her parents, either she must suppress them in order to maintain the peace, or rebel and risk anger and rejection. If the Taurean has plenty of fire and air in her chart, and/or a strong Uranian influence, she will probably break free of any parental restraint and carve her own definitive path; if not, Ms Taurus will try to live up to everyone else's expectations, leaving the conflict to rage within. Sometimes, of course, Ms Taurus emerges into womanhood without any apparent crisis. But as a general rule of thumb, one of the facets of Ms Taurus' character is her overriding desire for a life free from conflict and unpleasantness; and she will sacrifice much, if not much of her own individuality, to those ends.

Indeed, the desire for a pleasurable, unsullied life—preferably with enough money to ensure a comfortable passage—is one of Ms Taurus' principal priorities. Other factors in her chart may urge her to scale ambitious career heights or lead a life of risk and adventure, but in truth she is a lady who requires consistency and a degree of predictability in her life. She also tends to be a creature of habit. Almost all Taurean women observe their 'little rituals': these can be anything from the regular Sunday 'phone call to mother or the children, the morning 'soak', or the weekly bake. Routine supplies the scaffolding around which the rest of her life can be built. Familiar objects and coveted possessions (especially people) form the bricks and mortar. Taurean Audrey Hepburn used to transport the entire contents of her china cabinet around the world with her wherever she went on location. And on royal tours, HM Queen Elizabeth is never without her favourite bottled Malvern water.

Almost all Taurean women respond at some level to their Mother Earth roots. This sign is synonymous with nurture and provision. Like Ms Virgo and Ms Cancer, the Taurean woman usually feels entirely fulfilled in the role of wife and mother. She hardly ever puts her husband and children in second place to a career. Even those Taureans who carry on a full-time career while simulataneously caring for a home and family feel their primary role is that of wife and mother. In my experience, the Taurean who bemoans the lack of a stimulating career and feels frustrated by her family ties is definitely in the minority.

Ms Taurus has a strong procreative urge. She is an immensely physical and sensual female who tends to feel unfulfilled as a woman without giving birth and caring for a child. As a mother she is affectionate but firm, attentive but not over-indulgent. Her primary concern is not to establish a good mental rapport with her children, but to provide them with oodles of physical and emotional nourishment. As the children grow up and demonstrate their independence, Ms Taurus inevitably feels pangs of rejection. Instead of encouraging her fledglings' flight from the nest, however, she tends to reinforce her hold on them by refusing to tolerate any defiant or contradictory behaviour. Like the Cancerian, her emotional and psychological hold on the children is immensely strong: such that her children often resent her 'chains' as adults.

Whether the Taurean female has children or not, she still carries the 'great nurturer' instinct within her. Thus the single, childless Taurean endeavours to create a warm and plentiful aura in her home, and she invariably spoils her nephews and nieces and her friends' children.

Most Taureans are friends of the earth and they like to be close to nature. This can manifest as a preference for everything that is natural and pure, from the food they eat to the way they look: women of this sign often favour hypo-allergenic make-up and the sort untested on animals, or even no make-up at all. The really earthy Taurean believes she should be left as nature intended—unadorned and with every bodily hair intact. The Taurean woman's affinity with animals and plants is also exceptional; and the home that resembles the Palm House at Kew Gardens is sure to belong to Ms Taurus.

If you like your food, Taurus the Earth Mother will oblige. This woman has an instinct for **haute** (or **bas**) **cuisine**, and the appetite to go with it! Like the male of the species, it's often Ms Taurus' love of food, or to be honest, her voracity, that encourages her to develop her gastronomic skills. Since there is a great deal of truth in the old adage about the best way to a man's heart, the Taurean woman is rarely short of lovers.

Of course she has plenty of other attributes, not least her practicality, her organizational skills and her efficiency. Ms Taurus may look as if she wouldn't know one end of a screwdriver from the other, but she can turn her two capable hands to wallpapering and tree felling as easily as dressmaking and oil painting. And while she may not be the speediest lady in town, in her methodical way she can achieve just as much as the fire signs, and at least whatever she does is thorough and guaranteed to stand the test of time.

Daring and initiative are qualities more usually associated with Aries, but stout-headed Ms Taurus has her own brand of courage. A Taurean friend of mine who had left school with an inglorious academic record took it upon herself to single-handedly educate her two sons at home. (She and her husband—a Capricorn—had withdrawn the boys from their public school, considering it a poor moral and Christian influence.) Since at the outset she knew little more than the boys themselves, all three of them pooled their ideas over the syllabus, with staggering success. The elder boy gained 8 'O' levels, the younger 6, and she herself is well underway in a maths degree course. In so doing she also exploded another Taurean myth, that the female Bull is an intellectual dud. The Taurean woman has just as much potential for brilliance as any other sign, but because she has an orderly mind and she's not the type to take huge, intuitive leaps or concern herself with abstractions, she often appears a bit of a slow-coach.

In keeping with her need for stability and permanence in life, the Taurean is extremely loyal and faithful. She's also very possessive. Ms Taurus will stand by her man in sickness and in health, for richer and (if she really loves him) for poorer. On the one hand, she is too honest, conscientious, and caring to give up on a relationship at the first hairpin bend; on the other, she'd rather remain with the 'devil' she knows. Ms Taurus is not a great lover of risk and change; and she'll often stay in a desperately difficult relationship for the security of the familiar. The Taurean is also a great stickler for appearances. She can barely bring herself to admit that her marriage has flaws, let alone allow anyone to see it's heading for the rocks. The Taurean wife will relentlessly paper over the cracks in her marriage, ensuring the children, her relatives, and her friends never see any collapsing struts.

Josie, a client of mine, refused to admit to anyone that her husband Geoffrey, was more than just a lush, or that his outrageous and violent behaviour was not merely a symptom of stress. She would telephone his office to inform his secretary of his recurrent migraine attacks when he was too hung-over to go to work; and when he was to be seen semi-conscious at ten in the morning leaning like the Tower of Pisa she would earnestly explain that he was suffering from exhaustion. Only when he'd been relieved of his important, well-paid job and he was so deep in debt that the house had to be sold and the children recalled from their independent schools did she unburden her fears. Not to anyone close, of course, but to an anonymous astrologer.

During the year Josie consulted me, her husband (a Pisces with Scorpio rising) slipped ignominiously down the hill, sometimes disappearing for days on 'benders'; from time to time he was to be found on waste-tips slugging cheap sherry—or worse—with the other alcoholic flotsam. Josie eventually found a small flat and worked practically around the clock to support herself and the children. Now, some three years later, there is another man in her life, although as yet she feels unable to commit herself to marriage.

It could be argued that many women would have responded to such a set of circumstances in a similar way to Josie, whatever their Sun sign. But what made Josie's behaviour so 'classically' Taurean was her constant fear over what other people would think. Josie was obsessed with the idea that she had failed. All through her life she had wanted people to think well of her. Approval mattered. She had wanted to please her parents by making a good marriage to the right kind of man, and for almost ten years she managed to sustain the picture of the ideal marriage. After Geoffrey's departure and in the process of rebuilding her life, she encountered many black holes. These came in the form of financial and material deprivation and periods of isolation and hopelessness. Josie also discovered who her real friends were and who now crossed to the other side of the road when they saw her. This extremely painful process gave birth to a new set of values for Josie. Stripped of the ease and support of her safe, affluent life style, she found out what really mattered in life. Since she had never 'struck out' on her own terms, having gone straight from home into marriage at eighteen, she had little confidence in her own abilities. Without Geoffrey she had to find self-reliance in order to survive. She also realized how deceptive and meaningless appearances were. But perhaps most important of all, she discovered the value of her own self-worth.

Josie's story also touches on another taboo area for Taurus—anger. Josie, like many Taureans, cannot treat anger as a valid form of emotional expression. Ms Taurus considers self-control essential if she is to sustain a life of peace and harmony. On the one hand the desirability of 'counting to ten' was probably instilled in her as a girl; on the other, anger is antithetical to her sweet and tolerant self-image. The refusal to acknowledge the unacceptable face of anger has several possible outcomes for Ms Taurus. First, since she cannot spontaneously voice her anger or dissension she is habitually forced to accept 'goods' she doesn't want or considers inferior; consequently she is easily taken advantage of. Second, because she refuses to give vent to her own anger she can incite fury and sometimes violence in others: in this way she vicariously experiences anger while remaining entirely in control of herself. Finally, suppressed anger always finds an outlet somewhere—eventually: in consequence, the Taurean female is a prime candidate for tension-related disorders.

Dignity goes hand in glove with self-control for Ms Taurus. Women of this sign, perhaps because of their steel backbone and their high standards, seem almost regal at times. Occasionally Ms Taurus can be rather authoritarian, but when she bosses everyone around (unless there's some Aries in the chart) she always does it nicely! Of course, some Taureans have every right to be regal. Both Queen Elizabeth and Queen Juliana of the Netherlands are Sun Taureans. Queen Juliana was enormously popular during the time she reigned. She was very much a queen of the people: strong and disciplined but enormously warm: like most of the Dutch, she finds her bicycle the most functional and favoured form of transport and sees no reason why her position should bar her from riding it on the streets. Queen Elizabeth also 'runs' a no-frills style of monarchy. Yet she is firmly in control. And despite the galloping disintegration of the British Empire, the Royal Family itself has never been so popular. Her Majesty admits to being happiest in the countryside amid horses and dogs, and she has never been one to spearhead fashion or espouse a current craze. In true Taurean style she maintains her composure magnificently (often while all about her are losing theirs), but the slightly curled lip, the taut smile, and the withering gaze soon put an offender in his place.

In contrast to the earthy side of Taurus femininity, there is the more luxuriant, Venusian dimension. It is the Venusian element in Taurus women that makes them some of the best 'clothes horses' in the world. These women sometimes find as much difficulty in curbing their appetite for clothes as they do for good food. They are rarely leaders in fashion, however: they like to adapt the current vogue to suit themselves. The Taurean woman goes for quality (although she doesn't mind quantity as well). This is the lady who carefully chooses two or three garments of the best material (silk, pure wool, and cashmere are usually favourites) which she can mix and match with less expensive items. She hoards her clothes like her other collectables and is often to be found gazing misty-eyed at her wedding-dress—not daring to put it on for fear it won't fit!

Sensuality is another of Venus' offerings to the Taurean woman. Ms Taurus relishes being feminine. She likes to be pampered and spoiled and she can wield her femininity like the Aries woman her blunderbuss. She knows when to comfort and when to rebuke, and like the Libran she finds it second nature to put her partner first. If he is happy, so is she. Yet sometimes their Venusian streak encourages Taurean women to marry a man for the material comforts and the security he can provide rather than for the love of him. The mercenary gold-digger is no stranger in Taurus territory.

The Taurean lady, whether she's prompted by her Venusian muse or her Earth Mother nature needs a stable, dependable, and loving partner. But what she needs and what she wants are not necessarily the same; nor is what she likes and what she gets! Ms Taurus usually encounters one relationship with an unpredictable, unreliable 'bastard' of the airy or fiery variety. This is without doubt a relationship where the irresistible force meets the immovable object. Ms Taurus tends to be grossly used and abused by this kind of lover, although she learns much in the process—if only never to fall in love again! Since Ms Taurus sticks to a man like super-glue, separation—even from Mr Mean—is an immensely painful experience.

Certainly if you are looking for a lasting relationship with a strong, supportive, and loving woman, Ms Taurus is for you. And your intentions had better be strictly honourable. The Taurean female might flirt delightfully and convince you she's as light-hearted as a mayfly; but she's a mayfly with lead-lined wings, and she needs commitment and permanence rather than flights of fancy. She also has no intention of letting freedom and independence enter the arrangement—on either side. While in principle she's not against her partner pursuing his own interests (provided she knows where he is) she can become rather poker-faced over evenings spent alone while her other half props up the bar at the Conservative club. Infidelity shatters this woman. Since she places all her trust in her partner, her confidence is completely undermined if he has an affair. But unless she has plenty of fire in her chart, she is unlikely to do anything rash. Ms Taurus will bide her time, and dependent upon her partner's continuing fidelity and his acts of contrition, she will forgive him. Ms Taurus is not the perfidious type, but nor is she beyond getting her own back on an unfaithful partner—in kind.

In many respects, Ms Taurus is the ideal woman. She is feminine from the tip of her pretty head to her dainty toe—even when she's swathed in oilskins, bailing water out of the tent during the family 'hols'. And no matter how refined she is or whatever avenue she channels her practical and creative gifts, she is really an Earth Mother through and through. Don't expect her to jump at the idea of moving home; she can't bear to leave her friends, the garden she's carefully tended, the butcher she's cultivated . . . But given no alternative—and she'll try to find one—she'll steer herself in the new direction and get on with the job of planting new roots. This woman may not be easy to move, and never in a hurry. But as the years pass, her implacability will appear less like an obstructive boulder and more like an irreplaceable rock of strength. And why 'fight it' when you could simply lie back and enjoy the peace and serenity of the pasture with your very own earth goddess.

THE MALE TAURUS

I once had a Taurean boyfriend whose attitude toward astrology was derisory to say the least. 'You won't find me in any of those hocus-pocus books of your's,' he'd guffaw, 'because I was born under the sign of Porcus the Pig. Tee hee!' While I didn't find his mockery particularly funny at the time, I can now see there was a grain of truth in his little quip. For although the Bull has many fine qualities he is probably the zodiac's biggest chauvinist pig!

Mr Taurus is almost always the strong and silent type; or at least strong. This individual cares greatly about his manly image, which he cultivates either by engaging in macho activities and behaving in a generally hearty manner or by felling the opposite sex like a lumberjack! He is usually extremely attractive to women, yet for all his sensuality he's often emotionally rather wooden.

Even as a youngster, Mr Taurus may have been spared the usual childish emotional ups and downs. His disposition was probably pleasant and unflappable (he never liked to be rushed into anything, even then) and unless he was forced to do something he didn't want to do, or someone attempted to take away one of his possessions, he was quite contented. There is a story, which I expect is somewhat apocryphal, about a little boy—clearly a Taurean—who never uttered a word until the age of five, when suddenly he informed his mother in perfect English that he didn't like his pudding. Flabbergasted, she asked him why he hadn't spoken until then; to which he replied that he had seen no reason to do so, since everything had been entirely satisfactory up until that point. While this may be a rather extreme illustration of Taurean stoicism, Bulls tend to be emotionally and verbally reticent, tendencies that rarely diminish as they grow older.

Where his emotions are concerned, the Taurus man never goes over the top. He becomes thoroughly embarrassed by emotional displays and considers those who tell their worries to the world or who canoodle in public beyond the pale. Yet he is not without feelings. In fact Mr Taurus often has extremely deep feelings; so deep they may never come up for air. Like Mr Capricorn and Mr Virgo, Mr Taurus is more at ease with his physical senses. He prefers to demonstrate his feelings in tangible ways. This man is far more likely to show his love for a partner by organizing a joint life insurance policy or building her a set of shelves (to last a lifetime). The only time he is likely to be verbally ecstatic about his feelings is at the start of a relationship when he is sexually enthralled; then his passion bursts the lid off his normal self-control. Once he has returned to his normal, balanced state, while he may sustain deep feelings of love for his partner, she may only hear about them on anniversaries. Indeed some Taurean men develop an irritating way of treating their women like much-loved pets—patting them on the head and referring to them in moments of affections as 'old girl'.

The Taurus man is a curious mixture of the poet and the pragmatist. Half the time he's steeped in the business of building a safe and secure life for himself and his loved ones, denigrating anything without practical application or purpose, and abnegating any ideas that threaten his logical and ordered **Weltanschauung**. Yet there is a side of him that can be enormously sensitive and responsive. Sometimes the earthy, practical side of his nature is the only one in view, but almost all Taurean men have a finer dimension. Indeed, like the Capricornian, many Taurean men have a yearning to escape their earthly bonds and find their way to the transcendental. Some achieve this by immersing themselves in creative or artistic pursuits, like music, painting, and sculpture—usually as a hobby unless they're convinced they can make a living from their talent. Others take up daring activities, especially those involving speed and skill.

This finer side of Taurus is also aired in romance. The Bull can be exceedingly romantic—he is Aphrodite's man after all: flowers, chocolates (even if you're on a diet, he isn't), and scent will be liberally showered on his lady in the pursuit of love. And because he's quite the gourmet, there will be plenty of candlelight dinners for two—some prepared by his own fair hand. The Bull often cooks superbly well, although if he feels he is undermining his manhood by tossing a pancake instead of the caber, he'll never develop his culinary talents. Also, he may suspect that if he puts on too good a show in the kitchen, he may be lumbered with a permanent job.

Mr Taurus is a straightforward kind of chap. There's rarely any mystery about his feelings. He's also very persistent; and in the pursuit of fair lady he will plod on regardless of any amount of feminine guile or any number of refusals. He knows it only takes a crisis or two for the lady in question to realize how much she needs his steadfast, reassuring, and capable presence. A Taurean man I know was due to be Best Man at a friend's wedding. A month before the marriage, the bridegroom-to-be called the 'whole thing' off. The Taurean immediately offered support to the jilted bride. He took her out every night, listened to her anguished rantings, calmed her fevered brow and gave her self-esteem a badly needed boost. Six months later, the Taurean and my friend were married, and have been blissfully happy for the past fifteen years. According to my friend, he eventually admitted that he'd been in love with her even during her ill-fated engagement, but he couldn't betray his friend's trust. On the other hand, he had had a sneaking suspicion that he'd get her in the end.

The Taurus man is usually a very moral individual. He never goes back on his word. And since he takes his commitments seriously, he's often excruciatingly slow at making decisions. Like all the earth signs, he likes to calculate the probable outcome of his actions before he makes a move. Impulsive this man is not. By playing safe, however, Mr Taurus tends to miss many glittering opportunities in life; and while he may reach old age indelibly secure, he's sometimes rather embittered. Since marriage is one of the biggest decisions he'll make in life, this, like any other, is not to be rushed.

Because Mr Taurus has a touch of Venus in his nature, he places love at the top of the list of priorities for a wife; suitability and stock come next. Appearances matter to the Taurus man—not merely in the way of a pretty face. Mr Taurus likes a 'lady' and he wants his partner to be an asset: he's used to viewing life as a series of investments, and marriage is no exception. The Bull's ideal woman is virtually a mirror image of himself: sweet and pliable, gracious and composed, efficient and sensible, and OBEDIENT. Mr Taurus, no matter how quiet and patient he seems, does not like to be contradicted, especially in public. When his opinions or actions are questioned he feels his authority threatened. And he cannot abide being humiliated or looking weak and ineffectual. Thus the stars rapidly fade from his eyes if his lady stands up for her own views or countermands his orders—especially when he implemented them so pleasantly. Mr Taurus is definitely not a feminist's man. He's an out and out conventionalist and believes that men should be the breadwinners. And like the Aries man, he has a rather 'me Tarzan, you Jane' approach to relationships. Not that his wife will have too many complaints, since the Taurean will work like an ox to provide for his family. If he's very generous and has confidence in his wife, he'll agree to a joint bank account (or even one in her own name.), but for preference he'd rather let her have an allowance. He's quite prepared to hand over his hard-earned money provided she can tell him precisely where it's going. He doesn't like to see his wife in 'rags' because it reflects badly on him, so he won't hit the roof over expenditure on clothes, hair, or any other life-enhancing item. But he does worry about money; and he's likely to anguish over the monthly credit card and bank statements. Don't ever lie to this man about money: he likes to know exactly where he is to his last penny. And if he discovers you've been fiddling the housekeeping, he'll take over all the purse strings, and have you making daily accounts.

Mr Taurus also likes to own things wholly—he's not a great believer in hire purchase unless it's absolutely necessary: and if he can he'll pay outright for his house and his car. Like the female of the species, he tends to furnish his home tastefully, if not ostentatiously: and if the house escapes his attentions, his garden will glory in the fruits of his labours. Appearances matter to this man.

So far so good: but what about his faults?

There is a difference between Mr Taurus as a suitor and Mr Taurus as a husband. While this man's loyalty and reliability are rarely in question, his rock-like strength can become as immovable as the Matterhorn once he's taken his marriage vows and become The Provider. Mr Taurus feels his responsibilities keenly. Even if his wife opted not to promise to obey, he feels that the 'ship' cannot have two captains and he ought to be the one in charge of the 'wheel'. While the motives behind his autocracy may be entirely laudable, unless his wife is the archetypal doormat she is bound to resent his constraints more and more.

The Bull has a tendency to see the roles of husband and wife as stereotypes. He's the sort who expects his wife to attend to the domestic side of the marriage while he goes out into the big wide world. And sometimes he treats his wife as a kind of batman. This is not the husband who takes on the dish washing and the hoovering while his wife attends her sociology class: nor does he see why he should contribute to any baby chores when he's been 'at the office' all day. Even though he may love his role as a father he doesn't relish wheeling an overloaded trolley with a loudly protesting infant perched in front around the supermarket while the three-year-old runs amok in the biscuit display.

The Taurean man who becomes welded to the tram-lines of his stereotype as a father-provider cannot adapt to a new order or accommodate changes and shifts in the relationship. His fixed attitude not only prevents his wife from becoming an equal partner in the marriage and being an individual in her own right, but crushes the growth of the relationship in emotional and psychological terms. In extreme cases, the Bull may prevent his wife from pursuing any interests or activities of her own without his approval, or from introducing any domestic changes. He may even vet her friends. While his protectiveness and care is not to be faulted, his iron grip on the marriage can turn it into a cage. Indeed the Bull who becomes a veritable dictator in his marriage has all the makings of a Right Man (see Aquarius, pp.460–1).

The Taurean husband can slip into the most dreadful ruts of routine: arriving home at a set time, expecting his slippers to be laid out, the tea on the table/his whisky at the ready, and his domestic empire generally shipshape. And once his blood-sugar level is raised he's prepared to discuss the day and attend to any problems—just as long as they're strictly practical. Mr Taurus is not the best husband to steer you through a psychological crisis. He simply won't understand what all the fuss and tears are all about. Mr Taurus married a companion, a housekeeper, and a mother: he knows nothing whatsoever about an inner woman. And unless he has a strong

Neptunian content in his chart or plenty of watery planets, he won't be able to relate to any ideas about growth and expansion unless it's to do with the economy. Since he spends most of his time working to keep a roof over his wife's head and maintaining her in the style he can afford, he cannot understand why she should be unsatisfied. And if there hasn't been a death in the family he cannot comprehend why she should be depressed. In his strictly practical fashion, he'll see the solution to any of his wife's mystifying troughs as a holiday—to 'take her out of herself'. Thus like many a wife and girlfriend involved with the Taurean man, while she may be extremely secure and stable, she may never feel understood or responded to at a gut level. At the risk of repeating myself, the Taurean man, while being a good listener and a concerned and caring partner, is nonetheless rather emotionally myopic.

In keeping with his fixed temperament, Mr Taurus has a tendency to block his anger. He sets great store by appearing in command of situations and by maintaining a gentlemanly presence at all times. He wants his relationships, like everything else in his life, to run smoothly, or perhaps more importantly, to be *seen* to run smoothly. The Bull would like the rest of the world to believe that never a harsh word comes between himself and his partner and that their life together is one of harmony and contentment. His marriage, like a well-constructed ivory tower, must not be seen to have the slightest fissure. To this end, the Taurean man applies the utmost control, not only of his own feelings of frustration and anger but to the rest of the family's as well. Mr Taurus will not stand for any mutiny on his marital boat, and he'll suppress anything that threatens to sully the wholesome and united image of his marriage.

Of course, Mr Taurus isn't superhuman, or completely bland; he cannot always successfully conceal his rage. But unlike some of the other signs who block their anger, the Taurean's wrath doesn't emerge as vitriol and sarcasm (unless he has his Mercury in Gemini). Since his is an extremely physical sign, Mr Taurus is inclined to use brute force to push his point home although, like his Scorpionic opposite, he also has strong self-destructive tendecies. This man can be a dreadful bully, but usually only when he's been pushed beyond his cast-iron boundaries of patience— or if he's lost his self-esteem.

The Taurean man's self-worth normally goes in tandem with his status and his financial standing. Whether the Taurean is a bank manager, an artist, or a brick-layer, he likes to be admired for his abilities and he takes enormous pride over his work. If he is no longer highly regarded for his work or he is slipping deeper and deeper into debt, the fabric of his self-esteem will disintegrate and a self-destruct button will be pressed.

The late, vastly talented Orson Welles never sustained his early years of brilliance. After great successes writing, directing, and acting in such films as **Citizen Kane** and **The Third Man**, his work was increasingly received with distinct uncritical acclaim and some of his films were never given their deserved publicity or promotion. From middle age he made appearances in films and commercials that belied his stature as an actor and paid poor service to his gigantic intellect. Disappointment and frustration took their toll over the years. With his self-esteem in tatters, his self-indulgence ran riot, and it is probably true to say that he ate and drank himself to a premature death.

Of course the Taurean man is about as likely to admit to anxieties and fears as he is to give anyone a blank cheque. Like all the earth signs, he is a stiff upper lip man. Yet ironically, for all his common sense and his yearning for stability and continuity, he's prone to take at least one blind nose dive into a relationship with a volatile and capricious fiery or airy lady. Since Mr Taurus is a sucker for appearances, he often ends up with third degree burns or his stabilizers blown to smithereens! While the Taurean is attracted to glamorous, sophisticated women, he usually settles down with a safe, bankable proposition. But whatever kind of partner he decides to share his life with, she'll find it is well and truly a binding agreement. The Taurus man is not the live and let live type. He takes a pretty dim view of infidelity. Unless he has indications to the contrary in his chart, he is unerringly faithful. Like all the earth signs, he won't head for the nearest solicitor at the first hint of betrayal; but like the fixed signs, given enough provocation he'll end the relationship—a decision that is irrevocable.

Breaking up the home and family is a desperately difficult and unhappy experience for most men, regardless of their astrological make-up, but it traumatizes Taurus—his very roots are sundered. But although he misses family life as a whole, he tends to be more affected by the severed bond between himself and his wife. This man needs the companionship and physical closeness of a partner.

This is not to say that the Taurus man is an unenthusiastic father, for men of this sign normally have strong paternal instincts. They may not relish the early damp days of babyhood but they like to be seen as family men and take pride in their offspring's progress. Discipline there will be in abundance, usually balanced by plenty of love and affection.

Indeed, none of the Bull's family will go short on love and affection, especially his wife. Mr Taurus' love is like the Rock of Ages, dependable, solid, and indestructible—just like himself, although sometimes he can seem more like an immovable blot on the landscape. He may not be the most spontaneous and original of men, he may even drive you into a frenzy with his self-possessed equanimity, his smugness and his infamous bull-headedness. But think carefully before you pack your bags—you may never get in through the front door again. This man expects loyalty: after all he pays the bills. Also, Taureans have a way of cushioning their loved ones from the harsh realities of life, and you may find the outside colder than you thought!

Never underrate his simple, straightforward reasoning. While he may not astound you with his philosophical breakthroughs or dazzle you with his colourful polemics, he has the sort of simplicity that stems from deep wisdom and clear, practical vision.

Unearthing your Taurus man is probably your biggest problem: this individual isn't the greatest self-promoter. He also has decidedly set ideas about what he wants, and unless you fit the blueprint he won't place a foot in your direction. Of course if you dangle your ICI shares certificate in front of him, show him your collection of nineteenth-century water-colours, or hum some strands of Beethoven's 'Pastoral' symphony, he could be persuaded. Better still, invite him home, settle him in the most comfortable chair—preferably by an open log fire—and present him with a delicious home-cooked meal. (Don't forget the deep-pile rug in front of the fire—you may need it later . . .) After that, you should be home and dry, and safe and secure. You may even live happily ever after.

SUMMARY

One of the Taurean's greatest weaknesses is his or her reliance on appearances. On the one hand, Mr and Ms Taurus tend to take people at face value and after they have given their all to a relationship discover they have been misled, misused, and completely mistaken. On the other, many Taureans are so concerned about keeping up appearances that they suppress any unacceptable feelings, like anger, resentment, and hostility. In so doing they block the growth of their relationships and indeed themselves. Peeling away veneers and discovering the true value of something, be it a situation, an individual or a relationship, is an essential and enriching process for Taurus.

In keeping with the other fixed signs of the zodiac, Leo, Scorpio, and Aquarius, the Taurean individual feels intimidated by change. But to find the happiness and contentment he or she seeks in relationships Mr and Ms Taurus must not only be prepared to make and accept changes in the pattern of their relationships, but also in themselves.

TAURUS PARTNERSHIPS

Taureans like to be liked and even more, love to be loved. Although they can make a go of a relationship with almost every sign of the Zodiac, they tend to find their fellow earth signs and the water signs easier to live with on a long term basis than fiery or airy individuals. Yet since 'opposites' habitually attract, Mr and Ms Taurus seem to find their 'antipathies' in the fire and air signs irresistible.

Aries

The **Aries** individual is the antithesis of the Taurean. Life moves at a hectic pace for Aries, invariably permeated with plenty of risk taking and much conflict. Nevertheless, if the Taurean has some personal planets in Aries and vice versa, these two can find some common ground—albeit rather stoney. For real success, however, the middle way has to be struck between the Aries partner's need for novelty and challenge and the Taurean's desire for constancy and security. Also, the Taurean must communicate his grievances to Aries, otherwise the Ram will ride roughshod over his feelings and his territory. The Arian is an exciting, but unsettling partner for the Bull. However, good sex irons out many of their difficulties.

Taurus

Two **Taureans** usually get on famously with each other. Until they both encounter the other's obstinate streak! Most of the time their relationship is mutually supportive and harmonious, but occasionally they hit a rut that creates much tension and hostility (often suppressed) between them. These two are very giving towards each other in all departments of life. Family life means much to them and lack of children is a severe blow to this couple. Their physical relationship is usually strong, mutually fulfilling, and durable.

As they grow older two Bulls tend to become very set in their ways and their relationship rather prosaic.

Gemini

Gemini tends to be a bit of a featherweight for Taurus—captivating at first, but elusive and maddeningly inconsistent in the long term. Taurus resents the Geminian's attitude that he (the Bull) is boring and dull, simply because he thinks everything out slowly and maintains a serious and responsible attitude! This relationship stands a better chance of success if each partner has planets in the other's Sun sign. By and large, the Geminian needs to respect the Bull's desire for stability and continuity while the Taurean must give the Geminian air to breathe. Although these two are not ideal sexual partners, their differences can create some exciting sparks.

Cancer

This could be a relationship made in heaven! **Cancer** is probably Taurus' ideal partner—yielding, nurturing, gentle, and comforting, but also cautious, sensible, and thorough. Both these signs love SECURITY and the comfort of their own home and family. Sometimes the Cancerian is a mite too moody for the Bull whereas the Crab is prone to complain that the Taurean isn't sensitive or fluid enough. However, sex is usually a powerful experience for these two and guaranteed to unite them in times of marital stress. And unless there are planetary indications to the contrary, theirs is a stable and mutually supportive relationship.

Leo

Leo is often highly attractive to Taurus—and vice versa. The Lion has warmth, exuberance, and style: he's also just as fixed and obstinate as the Bull, which makes for some major blocks along their route to happiness. If these two survive their early head-on collisions, they can make a lasting partnership. But life will run a great deal smoother if the Taurean appears to let the Leonine have his own way most of the time. Both these two normally share a love of the arts, entertainment, and the good life. Passion also runs high between Taurus and Leo, and sex—both for quality and quantity—is a major feature of their relationship.

Virgo

Virgo and Taurus make the best of friends—in or out of love. This is a very workable relationship; indeed, sometimes it may seem a case of all work and no play! While these two can make beautiful music where sex is concerned, unless both of them have plenty of watery planets they may never reach a really deep level of emotional interchange. And both tend to keep their worries to themselves. Sometimes the Virgoan seems a little fussy and overfastidious to the Bull, while the Taurean irritates Virgo with his constant concern over appearances. But by and large, this is a highly durable partnership.

Libra

This can be a real relationship of give and take. Taurus is extremely attracted to the **Libran's** charm, his easygoing nature, and his eloquence, while the

Libran is drawn to Taurus' down to earth approach to life and his sensuality. However, their relationship cannot stand severe financial shortages. Libra and Taurus cannot live on prana! Usually, these two pool their talents and energies to create a comfortable life style for themselves—one that reflects their joint good taste. Differing emotional values and needs sometimes spoil their harmony, and in the long run, the Libran can seem rather shallow to the Bull while the Taurean can appear too set in his ways for Libra.

Scorpio

This is never an easy or light-hearted relationship. It has some ecstatic highs and some grizzly lows. **Scorpio** is just as passionate as the Taurean but his emotions are far more overpowering. Thus the Bull tends to feel emotionally pulled apart by his Scorpionic partner. Also, although both of them are equally security-oriented and possessive, the Scorpion is prone to playing games with the Bull in order to be reassured of the Bull's undying devotion—games that sometimes go over the Taurean's head. Sex is a powerful force between these two, and if their sexual life cools, their relationship is usually in deep trouble.

Sagittarius

Sagittarius loves going places, which in a relationship with Taurus he is usually forced to do alone! These two are often extremely attracted to one another, chemistry notwithstanding, invariably because they are so completely different. The Sagittarian can seem like an irresponsible child to the Taurean, while the Bull feels like a mother to the Archer: ideal perhaps at first, but stultifying in the long run. Freedom versus security are issues that dominate their partnership —and sometimes divide them, permanently. Sex between the Sagittarian and the Taurean does not always fulfil its early promise.

Capricorn

Capricorn is a safe, strong, and dependable partner for Taurus. The Goat has his two feet just as firmly on the ground as the Bull, so they rarely encounter insuperable difficulties in the material and financial areas of life. However, their relationship may never soar. Unless these two have some fiery or watery content in their charts, while they might never have major bust-ups, they may be unable to stretch each other emotionally. However, these two are usually sexually in tune and they rarely tire of each other—even in the rest home!

Aquarius

While Taurus and **Aquarius** might be compellingly attracted to each other, they have many temperamental differences to overcome in order to achieve a happy, durable relationship. At first the Bull is fascinated by the sometimes quirky, cool, and often extremely bright and humorous Aquarian. The Waterbearer is impressed by Taurus' dignity, his honesty, and his gentle charm. However, once the honeymoon is over they discover just how bloody-minded they both can be. This relationship certainly takes work: the Taurean must recognize the Aquarian's need for space, while the Aquarian should respect the Bull's need for constancy. Sex between Aquarius and Taurus can be marvellous in the beginning.

Pisces

A relationship between Taurus and **Pisces** is usually a gentle affair. Pisces is a pliable, sympathetic partner who appreciates the Bull's strength and firmness of purpose. Sexual attraction between them is often potent and they may be inseparable during the early stages of their relationship! As the partnership progresses, passionate moments are balanced by tender ones, and unless there are many conflicting aspects between their charts, Pisces and Taurus rarely have major showdowns or serious temperamental clashes. While the Fish can become the doormat in this relationship, he has a way of getting his own back on the Bull and undermining his authority—sometimes by 'being forgetful' and sometimes by being fickle.

SEXUALITY

Bawdy can be sane and wholesome,
in fact a little bawdy is necessary in every life
to keep it sane and wholesome.

These few lines have a lot to say about Taurean sexuality: and although strictly speaking, bawdy connotes obscenity, the general gist of Lawrence's stanza—that sex is a natural function of life and even a little does a lot of good—would appeal to most Taureans, though perhaps a 'little bawdy' is not quite enough for many members of this sign! Indeed some Taureans can develop as keen an appetite for sex as they do for three square meals a day, a tendency which may throw an entirely new light on why Taureans tend to be such even-tempered, contented people.

Sex might only be a part of life, but as far as astrology is concerned, to perceive an individual's sexual life the whole chart must be taken into consideration. With this in mind, the following themes will apply more directly to those men with their Sun and Mars in Taurus and those women with their Moon, Venus, and Mars in this sign.

Taurus, like its Scorpio opposite, can be an all or nothing sign in many areas of life. Sex is a tremendously powerful force for most Taureans, but because of the fixity of this sign and the control associated with this Quality, some Bulls attempt (and sometimes succeed) in stemming the flood of their sexual desires. The present Pope, John Paul II* (Sun, Moon, Mercury, and Venus in Taurus), has clearly had to suppress any such physical impulses in pursuit of his vocation. Yet at the opposite end of the extreme, Sigmund Freud (Sun, Mercury, Uranus, Pluto conjunct the descendant in Taurus) based his whole psychoanalytic theory on libido!

Since Taurean girls tend to develop physically comparatively early, they're often sexually aware sooner than many of the other signs. But like Ms Libra, the Taurean can run smack into a dilemma between her strong sexual drive and the preservation of her pure and wholesome image. Much depends on the rest of the chart as to which end of the scales eventually tips! Much also

---

*Astrologers may like to note that Pope John Paul II was born on a solar eclipse: 18th May 1920, 06.30 a.m. (GMT) 49N54: 19E29.

depends on Ms Taurus' experience of her mother. If the Taurean girl has been encouraged to develop along her own lines while retaining a close relationship with her mother, come the time S.E.X. rears its tantalizing head, she'll have a strong emotional foundation upon which to either obey or deny her instincts. On the other hand, if the Taurean girl has been too firmly brought up, she'll either hold onto her virginity until it becomes a white elephant, or make a rebellious gesture by breaking all her mother's strictest rules of feminine conduct! There is yet another possibility. If the Taurean girl has had a tense relationship with her mother and there has been little demonstrative affection between the family, she may take the first opportunity that presents itself to leap into bed with a man, simply to experience physical love and closeness. Yet because she hasn't the emotional stability to cope with the experience, she may encounter subsequent difficulties—sexual and emotional—in her relationships.

Since the Taurean female wants to be liked and well thought of, she tends to be a prime candidate for post-coital regrets: not because she wasn't able to enjoy the experience, but because once the afterglow has subsided she fears that her lover may have lost his 'respect' for her. This usually happens when Ms Taurus has just crossed the Rubicon of her maidenhood, but sometimes this conflict occurs time and time again. To a certain extent, this dilemma is one many women experience, whatever their Sun sign; but because self-worth is a major issue for this sign, Taurean females, in particular, find themselves faced with a schism between their rosy-cheeked image and their sexuality.

Usually, however, the Taurus woman's confidence in her sexuality increases with age. Like the Cancerians, women of this sign have a fluid, instinctive sexuality that is enormously attractive to men: a sexuality evoked superbly, both on and off screen, by the late, Simone Signoret (Ascendant, Venus, and Mars in Taurus). The Taurean woman's sexuality, like the Cancerian's, is closely linked to her menstrual cycle. Ms Taurus invariably experiences powerful sexual peaks at ovulation and before and during her period. Even when she is pregnant, the Taurean female may still respond to the same rhythm. Where the Taurean differs from her Cancerian cousin is that when Ms Taurus is pregnant, she rarely loses her normal sex drive. Indeed sometimes pregnancy and childbirth encourage the Taurean woman to become more in touch with her womanhood, and she experiences an increase in her sex drive: other Taurean women who initially may have been sexually inhibited, blossom after childbirth.

Certainly Taurean females have a reputation for being some of the most stunningly sexual in the zodiac. They may not have quite the mysterious allure of the Scorpio—nor any of the accompanying emotional complexities—but they have a genuinely earthy sexuality. Whatever the Taurean's actual dimensions, she has a voluptuousness about her: she is rooted, sensual, receptive, and bounteous. And of all the signs she has the innate ability to be both bawdy and wholesome at the same time. However, since security is also ultra important for this woman, she may not exploit the full range of her sexuality until she feels contained in a stable relationship. But whether she is the sort who finds sex intensely pleasurable without a guarantee that the relationship will be a permanent one, or whether she can only let herself go when she knows she won't be loved and left, once aroused, her passion is usually boundless and her appetite seemingly insatiable.

The Taurean woman loves to please her partner in bed. Although her demeanour may be extremely ladylike, even shy, her inhibitions fade as her ardour increases. And the older she gets, the more adventurous and demanding she becomes. While in the early days of her sexual life she may wince at the idea of oral sex or a rear (vaginal) entry, by her mid-30s she's probably an enthusiastic partaker of both—and many other diversions. With her earthy nature she hardly ever requires any fantasy play to excite her: she is enormously responsive to touch, smell, and sight. Unlike the Virgoan, the Taurean woman doesn't race to the shower immediately after sex (or before) and she often likes to keep the aroma of sex about her for as long as possible. The more nature-minded Taurean frequently detests the use of deodorants or strongly scented soaps since they interfere with the pheromones. The more Venusian type, on the other hand, enhances nature by an artful dab of scent in all the right places: she also appreciates the feel of soft, sensual fabrics close to her skin—and their effect upon her partner. This kind of Taurean usually loves French underwear. However, the Taurean woman is never such a slave to her appearance as the Libran. Ms Taurus doesn't have to feel decorative in order to make love; and even if she's not on speaking terms with her lover, she can be persuaded to forget her grievances with a loving caress. And although the Taurean is not the most argumentative or moody female in the zodiac, making up after a row can be a lengthy and exciting business with this woman.

Unlike some of the other Zodiac ladies, Ms Taurus isn't usually attracted to a man for his intellect. In fact the Taurean can be quite a connoisseur of male beauty—and she likes to touch statues of nude 'Greek gods' in museums and art galleries, especially the buttocks. Ms Taurus is hardly ever attracted to the effete kind of man, and she often prefers her men young and vigorous!

Occasionally the Taurus female will use her sexuality for material gain. Since the Taurus female has a tendency to place material values and security above anything else she may well marry a man who can provide her with the good things of life even if she's not physically attracted to him. One Taurus woman told me that during her marriage she had had a number of affairs with 'exciting men' who satisfied her physical needs, but she had never been tempted to leave her husband for any of them. 'I met my husband when I was sixteen. I knew he was going where I wanted my life to go. He was good-looking, good background, promising career, excellent taste and equable temperament. I was fond of him.' Another with her Moon and Venus in Taurus admitted, 'I had one or two passionate affairs before marrying my husband. But I felt love wouldn't pay the bills. Although I wasn't "mad" about my husband (and our sex life isn't exactly marvellous) I don't regret my decision. I have everything I want in life and over the years I have grown to love my husband dearly.'

The Taurean woman can separate sex from love—at least as she matures. As a sexual novice, her strong physical feelings convince her that she is in love, but as she gains in experience she learns to recognize the difference. Thus sometimes, Ms Taurus lives to regret an early marriage.

A phrase from one of the first (popular) astrology books I read remains indelibly printed on my mind, 'The Taurus man likes to eat, drink and screw and not necessarily in that order'! Certainly Mr Taurus likes to gratify his physical needs and indulge his senses, which may make him seem like a nyphomaniac's dream; yet while his physical performance is usually excellent, he sometimes lacks a certain finesse.

Even with his strong sexual drive, Mr Taurus can be somewhat slow off the mark to lose his virginity. A debilitating shyness (at least for the more earthy Taurean) is nearly always the reason. But with encouragement from a more forward partner, he soon gets into his stride. Mr Taurus, even when he is young and apparently sowing his wild oats, is rarely the 'love 'em and leave 'em' type. Only if he has strong Uranus aspects or plenty of fire and air planets will he treat a sexual relationship lightly. This man, like the Capricornian, is entirely responsible. Also, Mr Taurus doesn't like to look like a 'rotter'. In consequence, the Taurean hardly ever gets enough sexual variety to do his appetite justice.

The more earthy Taurean tends to be on the reticent side with women because he doesn't understand them. To him females are too irrational and too illogical for his comprehension. In their company he feels slightly ill at ease, uncertain what topic of conversation to embark upon, or whether he ought to crack a joke. Somehow his wit that goes down so well at the squash club takes on the lightness of a cement mixer when he's faced with a pretty girl. While his chatting-up technique improves with confidence, he may never feel truly at ease with a woman unless he's making love to her. The more Venusian type, however, has a far easier manner with women—he doesn't necessarily comprehend them more, but he can string them a better line. The Venusian hardly ever suffers from a shortage of women.

But Mr Taurus, with or without the ease and charm of Venus, is an earthy, physical man. He can handle the mechanics of making love superbly well. This man doesn't need erotic suggestion or fantasy to get in the mood—the glimpse of a bare shoulder, the touch of a soft thigh will send the blood racing to its destination! Mr Taurus can take any amount of sensual delight and he has the self-control not to bring the proceedings to an abrupt end. Also unlike the other earth signs, he doesn't place his lovemaking on one side until he has completed his heavy work load. Mr Taurus is easily tempted away from the grindstone. He's not the most experimental of lovers, however, and like his female counterpart, he needs time to get used to some of the more fancy techniques. Also, he's not a 'group' man—intimacy means precisely that to Mr Taurus. And unless he has some of the more sexually problematic combinations in his horoscope, he's not the most complex of sexual beings. His physical response nearly always overcomes any emotional qualms he may have. However, very occasionally the Taurus man picks up some of the cruder, more violent sexual tendencies of his opposite sign. The urge to dominate and control which characterizes the shadow-side of Taurus can emerge in full force in the sexual arena. When this happens, the Taurean man will get more pleasure out of pain than love.

The Taurus man is normally a very giving lover. He wants to satisfy his partner and will try everything in his power to bring her to orgasm. Yet with all his patience and skill, he can sometimes lack tenderness. Like many of the macho men of the zodiac. Mr Taurus equates tenderness with weakness, and it may take a long time and a persuasive woman to prove to him otherwise. Expressing emotions is also something the Taurus man frequently considers weak, which means that the emotional content of the sexual act is often distinctly low-key, if non-existent, on his part. For this reason, even though he may rate as an excellent lover where time, energy, and skill are concerned, the thin emotional exchange may prevent his lovemaking from being a supremely fulfilling experience. This lack of emotional texture in the act of love can occur even when the Taurean loves his partner deeply. The earth signs as a whole tend to be emotionally inarticulate and most of them avoid communicating their feelings verbally at all costs. Thus the Taurean, like the Capricornian and the Virgoan, intensely dislikes a post-coital post mortem. 'My wife says I don't tell her how I feel enough . . . the physical thing says it all for me', wrote one man with Mercury and Mars in Taurus.

Yet the Taurean man who can draw on his emotions as well as his other senses has more to offer a partner in the way of love and sex than almost any man in the zodiac. Indeed, the real expression and understanding of sexual love is accessible to the Taurean man and woman, and because many Taureans (particularly the men) find verbalizing their feelings or admitting their need for their partner so awkward, it is only through the intensity and power of their sexual response that they are able to communicate their love. Also, it is through the medium of sexual interchange, where the Taurean is at his or her most open to give and receive, that personal change—usually so difficult for this sign—can be effected.

Sex is the greatest sensory experience of all for Taurus. Share it, and you may find that the earth has really moved.

PROFILE OF A TAURUS WOMAN

SHIRLEY MACLAINE

'I travel a great deal. I think now it is more than a hobby. It has become my avocation. I think I make movies just to pay for the plane tickets . . . I've always felt that I would never develop into a really fine actress because I cared more about life beyond the camera than life in front of it . . . I was a professional, but basically I was more interested in the people I played than the movies I played them in.'

As we say in the Business (astrology, that is) people always 'speak their charts'. With Mercury, the super-communicator, ruling her horoscope and placed in the pioneering sign of Aries, Shirley MacLaine –internationally famous actress, dancer and singer–is also an inveterate explorer. She has crossed forbidden frontiers with the ease of a perfectly executed **glissade** and in the process has forged indelible links with people of all races, hues and religions. Now, as the best known 'high-priestess' of the New Age, she is conquering inner space too.

All of this is a far cry from her earliest beginnings–as the eldest and only daughter of middle-class Baptist parents in Richmond, Virginia. At the age of three 'a companion in adjustment and rebellion' entered her life. To the family, he was affectionately known as Little Henry (after the comic strip character). He grew up to be Warren Beatty.* Shirley and Warren were friends from the beginning. They weighed up their parents with a perspicacity that belied their years and learned early on how to play them and their parts. 'In the house we were exemplary citizens. Outside we really lived. We emptied garbage cans on other people's

*See **Note for Astrologers** (1).

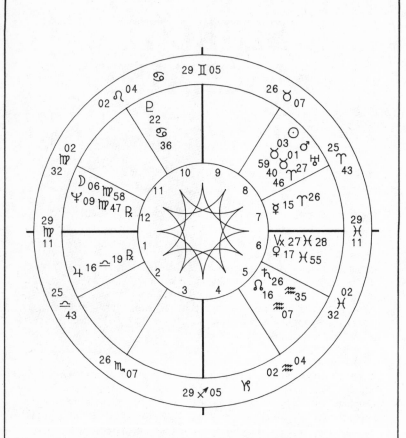

SHIRLEY MACLAINE

24 4 1934   15h 57m 0s EST

PLACIDUS 37N33 77W27

front porches, punched holes in tires, set off fire alarms . . . and crossed busy boulevards with fake limps sometimes pretending to drop dead in the middle . . .'

Shirley describes her father as 'the autocratic head of the family, well educated, with a portly build moving towards rotundity . . . he was sometimes terrifying . . . His sensitivity was bottomless, but the fear of his own feelings was sometimes too painful to witness'. Of her mother she says, '. . . a tall, thin almost ethereal creature with a romantic nature, who found even the most insignificant unpleasantness difficult to accept—nothing unpleasant existed; it was a mistake or a mistaken interpretation'.

The fourth house (related to family and, more specifically, father) accurately depicts Shirley's comments. Both Jupiter and Saturn rule this area of the chart—Jupiter indicating an exuberant, comfortably-off experience of childhood, and father as a portly philosopher. Saturn strikes a harsher note and suggests childhood was a learning experience in more ways than one: 'My father . . . was a stern man, the censor of all he surveyed, and the guardian of our safety. He sat in judgement on our actions and behaviour.' Mercury, as ruler of the 10th house, initially describes mother as a critical, pragmatic figure, yet the Moon also rules this area and, with its conjunction to Neptune, bears out the ethereal, romantic quality Shirley describes; and since the Moon is in Virgo, the fastidious side too. Pluto also enters the maternal picture which implies mother had a Scorpionic flavour to her nature—a powerful, possibly manipulative individual, yet one who was resourceful and determined.

In almost every one of her five books (to date) Shirley's parents play conspicuous parts and she clearly involves them fully in her life. What has enriched her understanding of—and relationship with—her parents in recent years (and in turn added a whole new dimension to the astrology here) is the insight she has gained through her journeys into the 'unconscious' and her forays back through the mists of time. Shirley often refers to her parents' argumentativeness and sees them as two extremely contrasting and not always complementary people. 'It [their relationship] had been a polarity dance of refined and colourful extremes . . . they were hopelessly and profoundly committed to the dramatic comedy of playing opposite each other . . . Now as I watched them closely, two loving, spritely, compassionate human beings . . . I was seeing them through ancient eyes in a long-forgotten time . . . I was reminded once again that I had chosen these two as parental figures this time around **because** they always moved me so deeply, **because** they were the source of much of my learning and knowing myself.'

What emerged most strongly through Shirley's exploration of lives past was the powerful, disturbing and violent nature of her relationship with her mother. A tenth house Pluto well and truly reinforces this theme, especially as this planet forges a hard 90° aspect to Mercury (ruler of the 10th). As Howard Sasportas puts it* '. . . those with Pluto here may see her [mother] as dark, threatening and possessing the ability to destroy them'—albeit on an unconscious level.

In a vivid past-life recall as a Mongolian nomad, Shirley saw herself abducted and treated as a possession by a bandit (her present life mother). Later she was raped by a jealous suiter who cut her throat to avoid his own death. Her bandit/mother left her to a grizzly death under the merciless heat of the desert sun. 'The past life conflicts with my parents flashed in front of my mind . . . There had been violence involved. Violence that was difficult for me to admit that had been perpetrated by my mother . . . I allowed the images of those past life experiences to flow through my emotions while attempting to integrate my feelings for them today. Each of us had been abused by power and were abusers of power ourselves.'

For Shirley, these regression experiences enabled her to resolve some underlying conflicts with her mother, hidden conflicts that might otherwise have given rise to inexplicable but intense feelings of mistrust, fear, and even alienation—the hallmarks of the more negative side of Pluto. With the help of a psychic therapist, Shirley was able to view her mother in a new light: 'Your mother has taught you to love without judgment and reminded you that each of us has been a tyrant at one time or another . . . your mother was your chosen one to learn through . . .' 'What rang so true, in terms of myself, was my observation of my mother's apparent powerlessness in this present lifetime . . . So even though she drew a great deal of frustrated helplessness to her this time around, she served as a lesson to me to avoid the same fate.'

Of course, Pluto shows another face in the 10th house as the significator for life direction, aims and the idealized self. Pluto here describes the nature of the individual's goals and/or career—an intense, deep and meaningful challenge could be sought in such apparently diverse areas as psychology, the occult, crime, prostitution, even nuclear physics. Sometimes Pluto here indicates fame or the ability to exert one's influence on a large stage—guru potential, perhaps. Shirley took her first ballet steps at the age of three. She had exceedingly weak ankles and dancing provided an ideal activity to strengthen them, but 'What started as therapy became my life. And I had an outlet for expression'.

From an early age Shirley pushed herself to the limits of her abilities. She joined an amateur ballet company which entailed frequently working into the small hours of the morning. 'It was a lonely life, for a teenager especially, but I had a purpose—a good reason for being. And I learned something about myself that still holds true: I cannot enjoy anything unless I work hard at it.' Another important discovery she made in her teens was that mind could triumph over matter. Moments before

*The Twelve Houses (The Aquarian Press, 1985).

a performance of **Cinderella** she fell and broke her ankle. She went on to dance the performance seeming to soar above herself and the pain. After the curtain calls she didn't walk again for four months.

Shirley's proverbial big-break came in the Spring of 1954* when she was just 20. She joined the chorus line of a new musical, **The Pyjama Game**; she also became understudy to the star, Carol Haney. In the stuff of Hollywood productions, a few nights into the New York run, Carol broke her ankle and Shirley was on—with no rehearsal. And in true Tinsel Town style she was an overnight sensation. Offers, agents, movie moguls and impressarios fell at her feet, and of course she made some mistakes. Fortunately, she was not alone to bear the brunt of success.

Two years earlier Shirley had met the actor-director, Steve Parker. It was a case of love at first sight for both of them; within five hours of meeting, Steve proposed, though it took them some time to actually get married. 'Steve and I met in 1952, but so intense was our relationship, we forgot to get married until 1954.' Shirley doesn't mention Steve's astrological bearing, but he emerges as an Aries-Pisces individual with Mercury-Pluto overtones—a talented, committed idealist with itchy feet, a man with a deep affection for and identification with Japan and its inscrutably fascinating culture. 'He seemed to be an extension of what I wanted to be myself,* and the more dependent I became on him, the more independent I seemed to become in my own life.' While Shirley talks affectionately and proudly about Steve in her first book, he completely disappears from the pages of the following four. Certainly Shirley and Steve had a curious marriage by orthodox standards—but then these are two highly unorthodox individuals.

Within a year or so of their marriage, Steve's increasing frustration with his role as a Hollywood husband reached its zenith. He was a gifted artist in his own right and he didn't want to be known merely as Mr MacLaine. As he saw it, the resolution of this problem was to return to the Japan he had grown to love in his youth and involve himself in theatre there leaving Shirley to pursue her brilliant career in the States. The thought of separation was devastating to Shirley but none the less she agreed. For some years following this decision, even after the birth of their adored daughter, Satchi, they continued to live on opposite sides of the world for much of the time. It was an arrangement that ultimately came to suit them both, though I suspect at some considerable emotional cost to Shirley.

Although after her debut in **The Pyjama Game** Shirley's career looked full of startling promise, it was some time and a few inglorious film parts later before she really emerged as a star to be reckoned with. Alfred

*See **Note for Astrologers** (2).

*The 7th House of relationships is an area par excellence for projection. Thus Steve was the 'extension' and personification of Shirley's Mercury in Aries.

Hitchcock's **Some Come Running** (1959) turned out to be her springboard and won her an Academy Award nomination. This was to be followed by many memorable performances in films like **The Apartment, The Children's Hour, Irma La Douce**, and **Sweet Charity**. Curiously, Shirley has played a happy hooker in 14 films which can be viewed on the one hand as fulfilling the promise of her natal chart* and, on the other, a fondness to revivify past-life careers—this time for art!

Shirley's attitude to her work is well reflected in the chart: her feelings about not being able to enjoy anything without first working at it are entirely typical of a fifth house Saturn.* With her Taurean Sun and Virgoan Moon, Shirley has a strong practical streak. The money she earned from her first film, **The Trouble With Harry**, was invested carefully in an apartment building. She is also meticulous and painstaking in her research for a part—again a reflection of Saturn in the fifth, Pluto in the 10th and the strong Virgoan emphasis in her chart. The Sun-Mars conjunction in the 8th house also indicates energy and self-expression are released through deep analysis. Indeed, some of the hardest and most hair-raising research she undertook was in preparation for her role as Irma La Douce when she spent several weeks in the infamous Les Halles area of Paris observing prostitutes at work and mixing with them at play. As she commented when she accepted her Golden Globe award. 'I enjoyed the research so much I nearly gave up acting'.

However, at first glance, Shirley's chart does not present the picture of a world-famous film star. One has to look for it. Yes, there is Pluto in the 10th house and it is square a first house Jupiter (in brief, suggesting large scale benefits linked to personality and profession); a Moon-Neptune conjunction is both glamorous and film-oriented; so too is Venus in Pisces in the 6th house of work which in turn trines Pluto—a very dancey combination. Ideally, considering her film career, one would have expected to see the Moon-Neptune combination closer to the Ascendant, or Jupiter on the Ascendant in Libra, perhaps. It's only when you consider Shirley's words at the beginning of this profile that you see her film career, though invaluable, has only played a supporting part to her true vocation.

'Having adjusted reasonably well to fame, affluence and power, I reached for something more . . . My life expanded and opened up on all levels when I began to travel. The money I made enabled me to go anywhere in the world and my fame opened the doors when I arrived.'

*Sun-Mars-Uranus conjunction in the 8th house of, among many themes, sex: and her Moon. Neptune conjunction in Virgo in the 12th house—the latter combination implying love could involve hard work performed in secret.

*Saturn in the 5th is often coincident with someone who finds difficulty in self-expression and creativity—not so Shirley.

As a true daughter of Mercury,* Shirley's thirst to travel has taken her to the four corners of the earth–and beyond. In Africa she became a blood sister of the great Masai tribe (after delivering a baby to a terminally ill syphilitic mother); she became involved in a Himalayan coup d'état while in the kingdom of Bhutan, and in 1972 she led the first woman's delegation to China. These are just three of many extraordinary journeys. She has also attempted to cross political frontiers, at one time involving herself deeply with the ideals of black activists, and in 1972 she campaigned for George McGovern against Richard Nixon. Her travels and crusades have not only broadened her intellectual horizons but enriched her spiritual and emotional sights.

With her open and giving attitude to humanity as a whole Shirley has attracted many friends who have supported, guided and helped her with her searching. Apart from Steve, Shirley mentions two men who have powerfully touched her life and with whom she has experienced a high level of emotional, romantic, and sexual attunement. In Out on a Limb, Shirley recounts her affair with an English politician, 'Gerry', and in Dancing in the Light she tells of her tumultuous relationship with a Russian film director, Vassy. It is through these painfully honest portrayals that the horoscope (in this regard) reveals itself.

Her relationship with 'Gerry' was conducted in secret–passionate meetings in anonymous hotel rooms across the world whose plaster-board walls formed the background to an exchange of feelings that transformed them both. Since 'Gerry's' political career depended on a blemish-free marital record, Shirley, with her banner for truth and honesty, had to balance the inherent deceptiveness of the relationship against its enriching intellectual, emotional and spiritual content. One sad little phrase is redolent with meaning. 'We never undressed. We made love just as we were leading our lives, the pleasure of it hidden from view.'

While 'Gerry' was a pragmatic and rational individual who found reincarnation as difficult to swallow as horse-manure (with a January birthday he could have been a Capricorn or an Aquarian!), Vassy was a much more theatrical event, a Russian with all the Slav intensity and poetry of soul. 'From the very beginning, Vassy and I both believed we had known each other in at least one previous lifetime. For that reason as well as many others, we were spiritually compatible . . . Yet our relationship was colourfully embattled because our personalities were diametrically opposed . . . So, for example, we believed each love affair we experience has its purpose–its reasons for occurring . . . The chemistry that draws us to someone is really the memory of having

---

*Mercury rules her Ascendant and her M.C. and is bound up in a cardinal 'T'-square! Jupiter opposition Mercury square Pluto. See Note for Astrologers (4).

experienced them before, and, understanding that there are unresolved areas that need to be concluded.'

Of course, the understanding of all this was one thing, the mechanics of their relationship in the raw was quite another: ultimately their stormy but loving union drove them apart, though once the dust had settled they were able to remain friends. During the course of the relationship Shirley was constantly forced to view polarities, whether in the sense of religions, race, taste, emotions, whatever, and allow for their mutual coexistence instead of fighting for one at the expense of another. She also had to confront violence through Vassy—her own: it was the act of striking Vassy that precipitated his departure. 'Now when I reflect on the violence Vassy provoked in me, I bless him for it. He put me in touch with it so I could begin to resolve it. He provided me with the gift of understanding myself better.'

In their different ways both these relationships left a residue of pain for Shirley as well as their harvest of self-understanding and soul progress.* One can only assume from a comment she makes in **Dancing in the Light** that Steve had also left an emotional scar or two: 'The break up of my marriage was something I didn't want to discuss with anyone. And hadn't. He had been an integral and long-lasting part of my life. I needed to sort it out and it was taking some time.'

Uranus in the eighth house of emotional and sexual exchange is often coincident with breaks and separations in relationships and this planet certainly presents, as it does in the 7th house, a pattern of attraction towards unusual, iconoclastic individuals. The Sun-Mars conjunction in this area also shows a strong urge to encounter passionate and transformative experiences in intimate unions; and since these two planets hook up to the Moon-Neptune conjunction in the secretive 12th house, a high level of emotional and spiritual compatibility is sought—though some liaisons may well have to remain undercover. As a sensuous Sun in Taurus and romantically idealistic Venus in Pisces, Shirley clearly throws herself hook, line and sinker into love affairs: 'He certainly enjoyed himself, savouring the food with total commitment. He was clearly not a man who did things by halves. The food on his plate seemed symbolic of life to him, and if life, or food, or love, presented itself—he partook wholeheartedly. It was a quality I could revel in, because I was that way myself, even if it had drawbacks.'

This same desire to go out on a limb for all that life offered propelled her towards a spiritual path. Stride by stride from Thailand to Bhutan, Sweden to Peru, Shirley has offered herself up to diverse cultural and emotional experience while treading the path of the initiate to the inner mysteries of Life. From her fledgling steps in **Don't Fall off the Mountain**, she has stoically grappled with complex principles of

*See **Note for Astrologers** (4).

astrophysics, absorbed intricate Bhuddist philosophies, and courageously put herself through severe physical extremes in search of truth and enlightenment; by **It's All in the Playing**, she had experienced the Christ-consciousness itself. Her associations with trance-mediums enabled her to contact her spiritual guides and these same entities patiently encouraged her to see the many dimensions to her being and the many mansions within the cosmic-spiritual framework. In keeping with her fiesty Sun-Mars conjunction, she has gone where many angels might fear to tread. Yet with the strong earth content in her chart, she needs a solid sense of proportion to sustain her leaps of faith. 'The sense of knowing that the great unfathomable mystery isn't really such a mystery was a practical, contributive, earth-plane support system for me.'

It would no doubt have been easier to keep these spiritual explorations and revelations to herself, since for most people such experiences are intensely personal and invariably devalued in the dissemination. But Shirley has opted to tell of her experiences and, though in the main the response has been enthusiastic, in some quarters she is seen to be dancing in the light of serious derision. While the cynic might assume she has merely capitalized on the current trend for mystical pursuits, those on the path view her as the light at the end of a dismal, over-materialistic tunnel.

Certainly Shirley's books have revolutionized many people's attitudes, and I am convinced her experiences are genuine and have delighted in her enthralling exegeses. If there is a criticism, it is in her evangelical approach to it all. Thus despite the infectious enthusiasm and laudable frankness of her dialogue one sometimes feels in imminent danger of spiritual indigestion. Also, in forging headlong through the veil, the ability to stand back and objectify her experience in light of established paths of knowledge is for the most part sadly missing. This, to my mind, prevents her from being the great and respected teacher she could be. Then again, one can only praise her for her accessibility to each and every one of us.

The sheer amount of experience Shirley has absorbed in half a century or so is staggering. Yet I suspect she still feels poised on the threshold of something better than this. She has not only enchanted audiences with her artistic talent and warmed them with her effervescent personality but she has shared her enlightenment with the world and so made it a brighter place. In fact, she's made us all believe we can really get there from here.

References: Don't Fall Off The Mountain; You Can Get There From Here; Out on a Limb; Dancing in the Light; It's All In the Playing (all Bantam Books).

Note for Astrologers: (1) Warren Beatty shares exactly the same Ascendant/Descendant and MC/IC axis as Shirley; his Mercury occupies the same degrees of Aries as Shirley's and his Venus is on her Sun.

(2) From **Don't Fall Off The Mountain;** I worked out that Shirley's unexpected debut in **The Pyjama Game** occurred on 19 May 1954 when transiting Jupiter was conjunct her MC. Significant progressions that year include P. Sun sextile Pluto. PMC square Jupiter and P. Asc. conjunct Jupiter. Since she also met her future husband Steve the same year. it's interesting to note P. Asc. opposition Mercury and PMC trine Venus.

(3) The emotional pain and loss at the demise of relationships can be traced. aside from the fifth house Saturn. to the square aspect between Mercury (in the 7th) and Pluto. and the semi-square between Moon and Pluto. However. in true Plutonic fashion. Shirley has used the pleasure and the pain of love to explore the deeper layers of her consciousness. and thus move on to greater heights of self-awareness.

(4) The Mercury-Pluto square forms part of a 'T'-square also involving Jupiter. There is tremendous cardinal energy caught up in this configuration which. in the cardinal houses. has permeated the most crucial life areas—personality. relationships and life-direction. The expansive. sometimes over-the-top principles of Jupiter have melded with Mercury. the questor. and Pluto. the transformer. to propel her on a voyage of physical. emotional. psychological and transcendental discovery.

PROFILE OF A TAURUS MAN

DAVID SHEPHERD

'You've obviously got no talent or the Slade would have noticed it ... but if you want me to confirm your work is bloody awful, come up to my studio and I will!' So spake the gifted marine and portrait painter Robin Goodwin on meeting the now world-famous artist David Shepherd at a cocktail party in 1950. These were hardly the most encouraging words for an aspiring young artist to hear, especially one who had just been turned down by the Slade and deemed untrainable. But then, when your back is against the wall, like all true British Bulldogs, what else do you do but offer yourself up for more punishment. Thus, the following day, David nervously presented himself at Goodwin's studio armed with six plaster-board paintings of birds, 'of unspeakable awfulness', only to find the wind had changed and instead of being demolished by an avalanche of critical abuse, Mr Goodwin agreed to take him on.

Yet if David Shepherd was to become one of the world's finest and certainly most popular artists, he showed scant promise of greatness in his childhood.

David was born in North London, the second of three children. His father was in advertising, although after the Second World War he went into catering and bought a hotel in Camberley, Surrey. David's childhood was happy, and he had a close relationship with both parents: indeed, the only misery to marr his childhood years was his time at prep school. 'I was a weekly boarder and I hated it. I went through hell every Monday morning. In fact I ran away once because I was terrified of the gym master.' Fortunately, he fared better at his public school, Stowe. 'Public school did an awful lot for me,

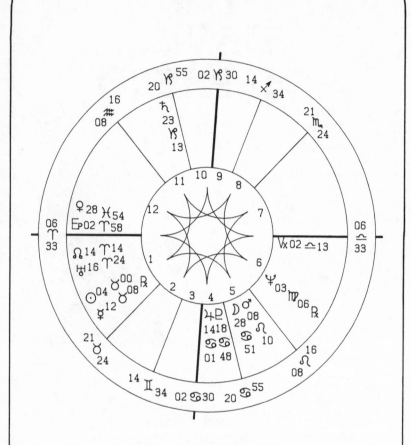

DAVID SHEPHERD

25 4 1931   4h 3m 0s GMT

PLACIDUS 51N35 0W14

although I didn't appreciate it at the time (he has since sent his youngest daughter, Wendy, there). It was very spartan, but then I think that's good. I was bullied rather a lot because I was physically immature for my age ... I didn't distinguish myself at anything except art, I suppose; but then I only fled into the art room to get off the rugby field. I was terrified of playing rugger!' David left Stowe with Higher School Certificate in English, Geography and French, 'none of which did me any good'. But then David was not the slightest bit interested in academic honours. Not for him the hallowed cloisters of Lincoln's Inn or the dusty labyrinthine world of the accountant. He wanted adventure and excitement; 'No, it was a game warden or nothing!' From an early age David had been enthralled by Africa; he bought books by big game hunters telling thrilling tales of adventure in the African Bush and of confrontations with ferocious wild animals. 'I'd never been abroad except across the English Channel to Boulogne in a paddle boat. But I had this conviction that I was God's gift to Africa; and I had to get there! . . . My parents were wonderful about the whole thing: my father said "Well, if that's what you want to do, old chap (he didn't know any more about it than I did) off you go".' His father funded his passage and arranged for David to stay with a friend of a friend in Kenya. So, in late 1949, our young hero set sail from Portsmouth, with all his worldly goods in a crate—including a bicycle and a lion-skin rug! It was to prove a journey of discovery, but not quite in the way he had anticipated.

While David's gentle Taurean Sun and security-oriented Moon in Cancer reflect his sensitivity and his love of home and family, it is his courageous Aries Ascendant that imbues him with a sense of adventure. The strength of the family bond is portrayed in David's chart by the presence of Capricorn and Cancer on the parental MC/IC axis; Saturn is strong in its own sign (Capricorn) and similarly, the Moon is found in its natural habitat, Cancer. Big-hearted Jupiter is placed in the fourth 'house' of family and home, indicating an expansive and philosophical family atmosphere. However, all is not roses in regard to this area of life. With the Moon placed at the opposite end of the chart to Saturn, a degree of emotional hardship and constraint is indicated. While initially an astrologer might assume that David was given a highly disciplined upbringing—one a little short on unconditional love, especially from mother—this aspect may well have more to do with his early anguish over separation from his family and the harshness of life at prep school.

Certainly disabling bouts of homesickness were to dog David throughout his school years and even as a young adult. 'When I arrived in Kenya I became ill—physically ill—with homesickness . . . I remember standing alone on this coffee farm miles from anywhere and it just hit me like a sledge hammer . . . all the romance had vanished.' David's immediate response was to ask his parents to get him home, but his father wisely refused: he didn't want to see David or the lion skin until his son had made tracks into big game! With less than buoyant confidence David applied for a job as a game warden at the Nairobi National Park. Needless to say, he was turned down—after all, one moth-eaten rug and a crate of adventure stories wasn't the most impressive of CVs. So there was little left for David to do but to take any old job to earn enough for his passage back to England. The job he found was as a receptionist at the Sinbad hotel in Malindi; and within minutes of accepting the post he found himself taking a party of Americans scuba diving—total inexperience being the only common denominator. David bluffed it out and from that point his luck seemed to change. He started to paint in Malindi and managed to sell six 'absolutely horrible' bird paintings to gullible tourists for the princely sum of ten pounds each, which paid for his return trip home. However, despite his lacklustre entrée into African life, he came home with a vivid image etched on his memory. 'I spent two gloriously happy days at Amboseli (now a fully-fledged National Park) . . . I will never forget the sight of seeing two hundred elephants browsing completely free . . . over all this hung, almost like magic, the breathtakingly beautiful snowcap of Kilimanjaro . . . I had been hooked by the incurable disease of Africa.'

Once back in England, the problem of David's career loomed as large as Kilimanjaro itself. With no qualifications at all, David saw that he had only two choices: either he could become a bus driver or an artist. Once again David's family were right behind him, 'artist or nothing!' Yet, of course, this too had an unpromising start; and it was only the chance meeting with Robin Goodwin that prevented David from entering the Aldershot and District Traction Company.

Robin was to teach David everything about painting. 'I had no talent whatsoever. The man was a genius—he could have taught a goat' (and certainly a Bull). Robin was also to pass on his practical philosophy to David: 'creative people are no different from anyone else: if you wait for inspiration, you'll starve. Being a painter means getting into your studio on a cold November morning . . . you'll paint for your family and the Inland Revenue!' So, as much as David learned his craft from Robin—how to see colours within colours and to practice the subtlest of techniques—he also learned to treat his art as a job, '99 per cent hard work and 1 per cent inspiration'. David remained with Robin for three years, then he set out on his own.

As a youngster, David's other great passion in life had been aircraft. He was eight and a half when the Second World War broke out, and like many boys at that time plane spotting and collecting 'souvenirs' from crashed German aircraft was an absorbing hobby. Thus, 'It

seemed a natural progression (once he had left Robin) to specialize in
aviation.' David was given permission by the CAA to wander all over
Heathrow Airport, which was then merely a large collection of huts,
and paint anything he wanted. David's technique lends itself well to
painting machinery—he has a precise, almost photographic
style—thus his paintings of Comets and scenes of airport life were
well received, although he gave most of them away. But all that was
to change in 1960.

On the basis of an article about his work in a Shell in-house
magazine David was invited by the Royal Air Force to paint for the
service in Aden. His stay there might have been just a pleasant
working holiday had he not been delayed a further week. 'I can't sit
still for five minutes, let alone a week; so I decided to explore Aden
behind the scenes. I found a place called Slave Island where they
built all the old Arab fishing dhous. I was so staggered by the place, I
put down my easel and canvas—the only one I had and a big
one—and painted for five solid days.' This painting was to bring him
in forty-eight commissions in one night and an extra six weeks flying
all over the Arabian Peninsula, and down to Nairobi. This period in
his life marked the beginning of his enormously successful career as a
painter (he painted his first wild life pictures in Nairobi), but perhaps
more importantly it was the prelude to his consuming passion for
wildlife and its preservation. 'After I'd finished my work for the RAF,
I spent some time with a game warden in the Serengeti National Park
(Tanzania): one morning we came across 255 dead zebra by a watering
hole—they'd been poisoned by a poacher for their skins. I'll never
forget it.' As a result of that sight, as David found increasing success
with his wildlife paintings, he decided in return to pour his efforts
into ensuring the survival of these animals in the wild. 'From these
small beginnings (twenty-five years ago) conservation has taken over
to the point that I practically have no time to paint!'

While Taurus is a sign noted for its artistic sensibilities, time and
again it is David's strong Aries-Mars influence that permeates his life
and work: 'I fight my paintings.' Aries is the sign of the pioneer, and
David has certainly proved himself a frontier fighter for conservation.
It is often the strongly Aries little boy who carries into adult life the
image of himself as a hero—in David's case as a brave and fearless
game hunter. And although he quickly changed his ideas about the
slaughter of animals, David still wields a certain Tarzanesque aura
about him, even amidst the peace and tranquillity of his idyllic
Surrey home. Aries is also a battle-glorious sign; and though David
has never taken part in war *per se*, he has had major connections
through his painting with the armed forces. Since the planet Uranus
is placed in Aries (and rising to the Ascendant) his love of aircraft and
his countless flying visits are typical of this influence. Uranus, of

course, is a highly volatile idea; and by temperament David is far from being the archetypal placid Taurean. There are far too many bees buzzing around David's pasture. 'I'm an emotional painter. I get totally involved with the things I paint. When everything's going badly or I'm exposed to incompetence, I blow my top—I go completely off the deep end. I'm always slamming the door to my studio and breaking the frame. The man who comes to mend it says, "Oh no, David, not again!" The same with the 'phone: British Telecom have to come and repair it at about the same rate.'

Fortunately, David is blessed with a wonderfully patient and understanding wife, Avril (a Sun Aries, with her Moon and Venus in Taurus). David met Avril in the early 1950s at a party in Camberley. 'I first saw Avril, standing rather forlornly, overdressed, by the fireplace. Her life seemed a bit sheltered—she hadn't even heard of Glen Miller! We hit it off. The courting was slow but sure over several years . . .' David and Avril married in February 1957, and their first daughter, Melinda, was born in November 1958. Three more daughters were to follow over the next four years. 'Avril and I are perfect partners. She's placid and I'm not. We're still blissfully happy after twenty-eight years. A couple of years ago, the **Daily Express** wanted to do a feature on my love life. When I told them I'd never slept with anyone else, they were dumbfounded—said they had nothing to write about.' While David's love for Avril and his enthusiasm for their marriage is boundless and obvious, this is not to say they have escaped their troubled times. Contentment and tranquillity are not necessarily synonymous. 'I'm an absolute swine to live with. Being creative is a very lonely business, and at times I'm completely unapproachable. If five or six paintings are going disastrously wrong—which happens often—I tend to take it out on whoever's nearest. Avril's ability to weather my storms is the secret of her staying power—she just switches off. She did once threaten to leave me, but I'd like to think in my arrogance that she didn't mean it. And she's still here, of course.' One of the most testing times for their marriage occurred in 1975. 'I almost went under financially. We nearly had to sell the house. But Avril stood by me. Without her help I would have sunk.' The crisis came about over another of David's great enthusiasms in life—steam engines.

In 1967, David impulsively bought two steam engines from British Rail. 'You see I'm like that. I act first and worry afterwards—and I've never stopped worrying ever since. But I'm still glad I bought them.' Purchasing engines is one thing, housing them is another. After temporary lodgings in sidings all over Great Britain, David's two engines finally came to rest in Cranmore, Somerset. Here David lovingly created an exact replica of a Victorian locomotive shed and an inspection pit and restored the station to its former glory. The East

Somerset Railway was opened by Prince Bernhard of the Netherlands on 20 June 1975. But amid the excitement generated by the realization of this dream, David was on the brink of finanacial disaster. 'The Inland Revenue caught up with me one night and in a state of panic I wrote them a cheque for thousands when I already owed the bank a considerable sum for the railway venture. I remember walking down to the bottom of the garden and crying my eyes out. Then I came back and painted the greatest painting I've ever done in my life (Cheetah). With the help of a good accountant I crawled back up by my boot straps. Now I'm so careful, I've gone to the other extreme!'

At the time of this crisis, Pluto, the planet of death and rebirth, transformation was much in evidence in David's chart. Yet the whole incident serves as an illustration of David's astrological make-up. While David's Taurean Sun may have seen a potential wise investment in the purchase of his two engines (at a cost of £5,000 in 1967—worth £80,000 today) behind the collector's 'eye' was the burning desire to preserve an aspect of the steam era (prompted by his strong Saturn—'the preserver'); his great love of the engines themselves and his impulsive decision to buy them is typical of the Aries-Uranus content in his chart.* 'The excitement of steam railways came to me through the eyes of an artist. If Rembrandt had lived in the railway age, he would have been a railway enthusiast revelling deeply as I have done in the smoky cathedral interiors of steam sheds.' That at the time of the crisis he was able to summon up the emotional-creative energy to produce a great work rather than hurl himself into the lake is no doubt a reflection of his strong Jupiter-Pluto combination. His wife, Avril, was tremendously supportive during this crisis—as on many other occasions: with harmony-loving Libra placed on the cusp of his relationship 'house', and Venus its ruler in soft, compliant and compassionate Pisces, the indications are indeed that he would derive much support and love from his partner. Of course, David expresses these 'energies' himself; and gentle Venus together with his sensitive Moon in Cancer are much in evidence in his own deeply emotional response to experience and his care and concern for God's creatures—those who cannot help themselves. Conversely, with Saturn contacting his Moon he has a tendency to blow hot and cold and to keep those he loves at an emotional distance at times.

David is fundamentally a traditionalist. 'I'm very conservative in my painting. I don't experiment—sometimes I get very daring and use

*The quintile aspect between the Sun and Jupiter, and the square aspect between the Sun and Mars tend to increase David's Arian impulsiveness and emphasize his single-minded determination to get what he wants.

water colours! . . . I love this country. I wouldn't dream of living
anywhere else. It incenses me that England struggles along as a fifth-
rate nation when if we pulled our fingers out . . . we need a Falklands
or a Dunkirk before anything happens.' But despite his fixed
principles in regard to his art and his country, David would be lost
without a challenge. 'My latest venture is the David Shepherd
Charitable Foundation. It's an attempt to control my charitable
activities. I do quite a few paintings for charity, but instead of
donating the entire "fee" to one body, only some will go to that
charity while the rest can build up in a capital fund—and so create
more.' Also looming tantalizingly over the horizon is a television
series to be made in America about wildlife. Not a picturesque nature
study, but the stark and shocking facts about the destruction of
wildlife. 'Did you know two hundred acres a minute of tropical rain
forest are being stripped. In forty years we'll have wiped out the
entire tropical rain forest belt. It's already affecting the world climate
patterns . . . no longer is it raining in Zambia, Kenya, Ethiopia. It's not
a natural disaster, it's our own bloody fault. Four Belgiums a year are
becoming desert. Man is far more likely to self-destruct by his
murder of the environment than by a nuclear holocaust. By the end
of this century, Ethiopia will seem like a Sunday picnic.'

I'm not the first person to recognize that David could well be an
endangered species himself. He is a man who refuses to bask
comfortably in the luxury his talent affords but consistently ploughs
back into humanity the fruits of his success. David has a fiery furnace
within him to preserve the beauty of Earth and all her creatures. Not
just a self-indulgent fantasy but a solid Taurean quest. And for all his
spectacular Martian feats he is a Taurean son at heart.

Note for Astrologers: (1) David's exact time of birth is unknown; his mother
once told his wife that he was born in the early hours of the morning. There
is little doubt in my mind that David has Aries rising; his appearance and his
modus operandi are typical of this sign. Futhermore, the progressions and
transits, and the synastry between himself, Avril, and the other members of
the family, work well with this degree of Aries on the Ascendant and
Capricorn on the Midheaven.

(2) In 1960 when David's career took off, progressed Venus (using secondary
progressions) was conjunct the Sun, and the progressed Ascendant (by 1°)
was also conjunct the Sun. Transiting Jupiter was in Capricorn (conjunct the
Midheaven twice—April-May and November—and simultaneously trining
Neptune. Transiting Neptune squared Mars, and transiting Pluto trined the
Midheaven.

(3) In 1975, when David came near to financial collapse, transiting Pluto was
hovering around the Descendant, transiting Uranus opposed the Sun,
transiting Saturn opposed radical Saturn then went on to square the Sun.
Fortunately, protective Jupiter was in the first house.

GEMINI

21 May – 21 June

TWO-TIMING TRICK CYCLISTS AND PETER PAN'S PEOPLE

GEMINI
TWO-TIMING TRICK CYCLISTS AND PETER PAN'S PEOPLE

GE M I N I people are always busy, busy, busy. They have people to see, places to go and not nearly enough time to fully assimilate anything they encounter. It must surely have been a Gemini who uttered the immortal words, 'If it's Tuesday, it must be Belgium.' Geminis are the zodiac's grasshoppers and mayflies—and sometimes even the wasps! These individuals rarely explore anything in depth since one-track pursuits place severe limitations on their insatiable appetite for manifold intellectual and social stimulation.

Geminis are popular members of the Zodiac. They usually have a lively intelligence and a biting sense of humour put together in a warm and approachable personality package. Of course this sign has its drawbacks, largely in the area of lack of commitment and a short-fall in sincerity: issues we shall encounter periodically through these pages.

The most recognizable Gemini characteristic is constant movement. These airy people are dreadful fidgets and can only remain still if their mental zones are thoroughly occupied. In conversation, Geminis are great flag-wavers: they paint beautiful pictures with words and whatever utensil happens to be in their hands at the time. They are often highly strung, if not downright neurotic, and tend to live permanently on their nerves. This is not a sign that usually suffers from obesity and Geminis rarely run to fat as they grow older (unless there's a family disposition to do so). Like their thought processes Geminis favour a clean-cut, precise outline.

Geminis tend to be such communicative individuals that many people make the mistake of assuming this sign is easy to understand. It is not. The archetypal Gemini could be likened to an alien from outer space who takes on human form. This rarefied being functions superbly well on every level but one: he cannot successfully integrate the peculiarly human quality of emotion. Emotion foxes him completely. Indeed, from his point of view the feelings that everyone else professes to be so important seem only to interfere with the smooth running of practically every item of life. Thus many people find the Geminian fascinating but rather unreachable. They can talk to him, but never really know who he is. His avenues of communication all seem to be one way and never lead to the heart of the matter. And sometimes there is an unnerving feeling that behind the bright and informed chatter, nobody's home.

These individuals are never easy to take apart. Like one of those Russian dolls, there's more than one of them (and in Gemini's case, all entirely different) encased within the original mould. The sheer variety and diversity that Geminis are capable of is part of their appeal, yet the split personality syndrome also poses a considerable problem for them. Certainly, taking apart Gemini and its ruling planet Mercury, through myth and symbol reveals many interesting and variegated facets to this elusive, lighter than air, air sign.

The Heavenly Twins are Gemini's familiar symbol. Myths of every culture contain a twin-motif, from Egyptian Set and Osiris to the Vedic Asvins. The theme of dualism is clearly at the base of all twin myths, and since each two represent opposing principles they are often portrayed as 'mortal' enemies, like Romulus and Remus or Bielborg and Chernabog. However, where Gemini is concerned, Greek Castor and his twin Polydeuces (Pollux) seem most appropriate.

Castor and Polydeuces were twin sons of Leda; but Castor's father was the mortal, Tyndareus, whereas Polydeuces was fathered by the great god Zeus. In myth the couple were usually depicted as young athletes (Polydeuces was an adept boxer) travelling the world on horseback. However, fate had a nasty trick in store for the twins. As a typically Geminian jolly jape, Castor and Polydeuces abducted the Leucippides sisters on their wedding day. (Even the roots of Gemini's aversion to marriage can be found in myth!) Naturally the bridegrooms, Idas and Lyceus, were somewhat annoyed by the ruse, and after a bloody skirmish Idas killed Castor. In return Polydeuces slew Lyceus. Zeus seemed highly delighted with the resultant state of affairs and offered his son immortal life. Polydeuces, however, being of a fair and just airy temperament, refused unless Castor was allowed to leave the Underworld and join him on Olympus. As a compromise (yet another airy solution) each twin spent alternate days with the other until they were both deified and became the constellation, the Twins. This myth provides a perfect allegory of union through interchange—a central and recurring theme for Gemini.

Gemini is the third sign of the Zodiac. In fiery Aries and earthy Taurus the focus centres on the individual, who he is, and what he has. In Gemini the idea of communion is forged. The individual looks beyond himself. He seeks information from others and knowledge about the world he lives in. He needs to stretch his wings before he can look within his emotional depths in the following water sign, Cancer. In this way, the first four-fold cycle of the Zodiac is complete. In the northern hemisphere late May and June are the months of early summer when a sense of expectancy and hopefulness hovers in the fresh green and newly opening blooms of the countryside. In the southern hemisphere harsh winds carry the remaining leaves off the trees—Nature's growth process continues busily underground. Clearly the underground, or rather the Underworld, seems a strange location for anything to do with Gemini. After all, this is Scorpio-Pluto land and surely utterly remote from Gemini's airy regions. Yet time and time again, links are forged between those two extremes.

Greek Hermes, like Roman Mercury, was the winged-heeled and helmeted messenger of the gods. He was, above all, a communicator and an interpreter. He spread the word through his literary abilities, by his talent for oration, and by darting from place to place and person to person. Mercury/Hermes was also frequently painted as a mischievous god—a bit of a trickster. And because he loved stealth and darkness, Zeus made him messenger of the gods to Hades. Indeed, Hermes' role as the guide to souls (Psychopompus), which he shares with Mercury, ranks as one of his most significant. For in this role Hermes not only performed a service for Pluto, the Lord of the Underworld, but provided a unique link between Heaven, Earth, and Hell.

Mercurial/Geminian people certainly dart from one thing to the next, grasping information quickly, filtering out any interesting ideas and passing them on. Many of these individuals have a childish love of pranks and take a delight in leading others up the proverbial garden path—largely to observe their reactions. The quintessential Gemini is a playful but detached observer, and to a certain extent most Geminis identify with this lighter aspect of Mercury than its more obscure side.

Gemini is not the only sign to be ruled by Mercury. Virgo too shares this planetary ruler. While Virgo is also a sign associated with the intellect, its nature is vastly different from Gemini. Indeed, this pragmatic earth sign relates far more readily to Mercury's underworld affiliations. And for this reason Thoth, scribe to the Lord of the Underworld, Osiris, is a better Mercury figure for Virgo (see Virgo pp. 235–6). Thoth, whose was frequently represented as a baboon, was the Egyptian god of wisdom. He was sometimes portrayed holding a scientific instrument or 'pen' and paper in hand. Thus, on one level Thoth represents a mentality that apes and mimics, yet on another he stands for precise, analytical, scientific investigation. (Or perhaps there is a double symbolic pun intended here, that science is a baboon!) This 'silent notator' emerges in a few Geminian individuals who control and focus their quicksilver mentality. And it is worth remembering that even though Gemini has a reputation for being unable to concentrate all his energies at any one time on a single objective, most Geminians have the capacity to do so should they wish to.

Scandinavian myth provides a fascinating Mercury figure in the form of Loki, who was the foster-brother of Odin, god of death, wisdom, and magic. Indeed Odin himself has a Mercurial dimension in that he was revered for his intellect. (Odin's equivalent in German myth was Wodan, from which we derive Woden's day—Wednesday; in French, this day of the week is Mercredi—Mercury's day.)

Loki is a curious figure in many ways. He is half divine and half demonic. He is also both male and female (a familiar theme for Mercury figures). He (or she) assists the gods, for which they are eternally grateful, yet they also hate him because he betrays them. Two stories illustrate Loki's ambivalent, paradoxical nature.

Odin had a son called Balder (the Beautiful and the Good). So beloved of the gods was Balder that when he dreamed of his own death, they commanded the goddess, Frigg, to make him invulnerable to any hurt. This she did by taking an oath from all things of the earth not to harm him. However, she omitted one plant—the mistiltienn. In an act of devilment and treachery, Loki disguised himself as an old woman and wheedled the truth out of Frigg. Whereupon he plucked the mistiltienn out of the ground, gave it to Hother, the blind god, who threw it at Balder and killed him—a deed for which the gods never forgave him.

In a second story, when the gods had found their home, Asgard, they asked a giant to build a wall around it for protection. For payment, the giant requested the goddess Freya and the sun and the moon. To this the gods agreed, but with a proviso: that the wall was to be completed before the end of winter, a task they knew was impossible. However, unbeknown to the gods, the giant had a magic stallion to help him and three days before the winter's end, the wall was practically finished. In desperation, the gods called upon Loki for help: in fact they threatened him with death unless he did so! Loki turned himself into a mare and lured the stallion away, thus rendering the giant helpless and the wall incomplete. Thor then killed the giant. Later, Loki gave birth to a grey foal with eight legs that became Odin's charger.

Both these tales illustrate the capacity of Loki as a mediator and as a valuable but dangerous ally.

The first story is considered by many sources to be variation on the theme of the dying god of vegetation—the symbolic death of nature in winter. The mistiltienn, or mistletoe, was used by the Druids in their fertility rites, and in the Middle Ages the same plant was thought to have the power to discover buried treasure. All these themes are essentially Scorpionic and Plutonic.

Loki's paradoxical nature is typical of all things Mercurial. Although he was instrumental in the killing of Balder, he himself did not actually wield the murder weapon. He set about finding the 'Achilles Heel' of the matter, and let fate do the rest. His seduction of the stallion not only preserved Freya and the sun and the moon, but also paved the way for Thor to slaughter the giant. Loki is only as good or as evil as those who use him. This kind of detached stance is a familiar one to many Mercury/Gemini individuals. Part of them delights in playing the devil's advocate: they cannot resist putting a chain of events into process, then withdrawing to watch the outcome. They rub shoulders with dark shadows, yet remain untouched by them. While Mercury figures like Loki, Hermes, and Thoth lead to the dark environs of the Underworld, unlike those souls they accompany or take account of they are at liberty to come and go.

The caduceus, Mercury's staff, is a fascinating piece of symbolism in itself. In esoteric Buddhism, the wand was considered to represent the axis of the world, the two snakes standing for Kundalini, the sleeping serpent who lies at the base of the backbone, who when aroused —through powerful psycho-sexual stimulation—rushes up the spinal column and brings enlightenment. In astrological terms, Kundalini is the essence of Mercury and Pluto. A more traditional view of the caduceus suggests that the staff represents power (earth), the serpents wisdom (fire and water), and the wings diligence (air). In the present day, the medical profession also uses Mercury's staff as its symbol, perhaps following the example of the ancient Mesopotamians who thought the intertwining serpents represented a god who could cure all. In many ways the caduceus could be seen as a symbol of a supreme state of health—the balance of mind, body, and spirit.

This theme of union and balance is taken up by the Tarot card of the World/Adept. The sex of the figure is ambiguous. He-she is surrounded by a serpent swallowing its tail, and placed in each corner are the fixed signs of the Zodiac representing the four elements. This card is thought to symbolize the ideal state from which humanity came and to which it returns. (It may not escape notice that this is the general theme of Adam and Eve in the Garden of Eden, which came equipped with a serpent and a Tree of Knowledge.) This ideal state is achieved through the merging of the self-conscious with the sub-conscious, and the blending of these with the super-conscious—the final state of cosmic consciousness.

Carl Jung developed much of his work with archetypes from studying alchemy!* 'When the alchemist speaks of Mercurius, on the face of it he means quick-silver, but inwardly he means the world-creating spirit concealed or imprisoned in matter . . . Mercurius is the divine winged Hermes manifest in matter, the god of revelation, lord of thought and sovereign psychopomp.' In Jungian terms, Mercury symbolizes the union of the unconscious with the conscious, and as such, plays a pivotal part in the process of individuation (be-coming an individual), a process that is ultimately the province of Leo (see Leo, pp.192–3).

In astrological terms, Mercury's position as the first planet out from the Sun can be seen as the vital two-way link between the solar force (self) and all the other planetary bodies. As such, Mercury becomes the messenger of the ego and takes on his familiar role as mediator.

So far, much of the symbolism discussed has involved Plutonic/Scorpionic themes as well as Mercurial ones. And even astronomically there are some curious parallels between these two planets. Since Mercury is placed so close to the sun, most of the time it is completely obscured by the sun's glare. From our point of view on Earth, it seems as though Mercury only presents one side of itself to the sun, the other remaining in total darkness. Only comparatively recently have scientists discovered that this planet does in fact spin on its axis. Pluto is also quite obscure from Earth, giving rise to many hypotheses including the idea that its surface is covered with ice which reflects the sun, thus rendering most of it invisible.

At this point I would like to return to Loki and the idea of his being a valuable but dangerous ally since 'he' brings to mind the role of an ally figure in Shamanism. In the **Teachings of Don Juan** and subsequent books, Carlos Castaneda tells of his experiences as an initiate. In order to progress along the precarious and immensely dangerous route to becoming a 'warrior', the initiate must first locate his Ally. An Ally is an entity capable of leading a man beyond the boundaries of himself. The Ally can be either masculine or feminine, depending upon the initiate's perception and predisposition, and he can be used as a force for good or evil. The initiate must, however, 'conquer' the Ally when he is first confronted by him, otherwise the 'giver of secrets' will turn on him. In effect, the Ally is a guide on a visionary journey through the inner universe. 'He' must be mastered in order not to lead the traveller astray. If this is not accomplished, complete unconscious chaos will overpower the individual and drive him to madness, if not death. Indeed where the psyche is concerned, the borderline between the harnessing of shamanistic power and lunacy is a very fine one indeed.

Mercury as the shaman's Ally comes the nearest to establishing why underworld symbolism of the Scorpio/Pluto variety permeates all myths and symbols associated with Mercury. While Mercury (and thus Gemini) has a darker shadow side which to a certain extent reflects its underworld associations, Scorpio-Pluto themes in regard to Mercury primarily illustrate the importance of Mercury as a guide to the underworld of the unconscious, of all things hidden, powerful and ultimately transformative. The mind is the channel through which the unconscious can speak. The harnessing of the

---

*In alchemy, one of the most important processes is the sublimation of quicksilver (Mercury), which represents the enoblement of thought.

mind (Mercury) to the will (Pluto) are the magician's and the yogi's route to power and enlightenment.

So, what conclusions can we draw from these mythical and symbolic highways and byways. (Incidentally, Mercury was also the Lord of Roads!) On a mundane level, Gemini-Mercury folk are not only the Zodiac's thinkers and communicators, but also the zodiac's plotters, planners, and schemers. They flirt with treachery occasionally, yet with eloquent skill rarely leave their fingerprints behind. Their curiosity and thirst for information draws them into all manner of diverse areas, yet they hardly ever drink deeply from any one 'well'. Mercury's capacity as a metal displays a unique ability to run around uncontrollably when let loose, yet its fluidity, its sensitivity to atmospheric changes makes it a fine instrument for calculation and assessment. Its dynamic, amorphous character also provides it with unlimited potential for transformation. Thus, on a more subtle level the Gemini individual has the capacity for transformation at his fingertips—where he invariably keeps it. Unlike the Scorpio (unless he has a strong water or Scorpio/Pluto content in his chart) he lacks the emotional wherewithal to immerse himself totally in the watery depths that makes for personal transformation. He is instead the agent of change. An interpreter, a mediator, and an observer.

In keeping with this magical, transformative theme, many Gemini individuals become fascinated by magic. Some of them make brilliant sleight of hand artists, and so find their way into the entertainment business as conjurers and mentalists. Others follow the magic path of inner space instead, but invariably forsake it when it threatens to become an obsession. Many Geminis take up careers as psychologists and therapists, thereby leading others to their unconscious depths and vicariously experiencing some of their own. One Geminian business tycoon spends most of his time acting as a counsellor/therapist to his highly-paid, highly-stressed personnel!

The Gemini gift for detached observation makes these individuals excellent journalists and writers. Ian Fleming, the author of the James Bond books and one-time foreign correspondent (Sun and Mercury in Gemini), Sir Arthur Conan Doyle, creator of Sherlock Holmes and a keen spiritualist (Sun, Mars, and Ascendant in Gemini), and Jean-Paul Sartre, writer, leader of the French intelligentsia in the 1940s, and the founder of existentialism are all notably articulate Geminis. And on the female front, Gemini communicators include the novelist Françoise Sagan (Sun, Mercury, and MC in Gemini), the writer and occultist Alice Bailey (Sun and Venus in Gemini), and the doomed Anna Frank whose diary paints a vivid and moving picture of the Nazi holocaust (Sun and Mercury in Gemini).

Geminis are also the zodiac's best salesmen. Most of them can size up a situation and a person quicker than most people can blink their eyes—a knack that gives them a distinct advantage in the market place. (Yet another of Mercury's roles was the Lord of Trade.) Mercurial men and women are often extremely good with money—not through any innate thrift, nor through clever budgeting (for this sign can be a reckless spender at times). No, Gemini's financial skills lie in juggling other people's money via, for instance, the Stock Exchange, the Commodity Market, or Insurance brokerage. Gemini individuals thrive on the mental challenge of being one jump ahead of the game, which is why they also flock into the advertising business or any kind of media work.

Indeed, there are few areas of life where Geminis cannot find a niche for themselves. They slip into every kind of role and find something to interest them whatever they do and wherever they go. Geminians will carry on an animated discussion with a Jehovah's Witness, the newspaper boy, the visiting MP, or the person next to them in the check-out queue. They love to know what makes people 'tick'. But like the Arians, they hardly ever show the same intense interest on a second meeting: a shortcoming that makes them seem two-faced, shallow, and insincere.

Gemini is not an ambitious sign. Mercurial types lack the tenacity and sense of purpose to aim singlemindedly for fame, riches, and glory. Yet many of them do reach important positions in life. Since the Gemini man or woman has little use for power, others rarely find them threatening. Thus they frequently reach the pinnacle of success by accident rather than design, and hardly ever by clawing their way up or riding roughshod over others. Of course, Gemini finds little trouble in winning friends and influencing people, which also helps his upward mobility. Sadly, some Geminis never fully realize their bright potential and move from job to job in the dwindling hopes of finding a suitable vehicle for their multiple talents. One of Gemini's major problems is focusing his abilities in any one direction long enough for it to bear fruit.

Gemini has been described as the Jekyll and Hyde of the zodiac. By and large, Geminis circulate in their loftier regions along with Dr Jekyll, but they cannot altogether lose sight of Mr Hyde. As I discussed earlier, Mercury people are often fascinated by the mysterious and the obscure, yet they often fail to recognize the hidden motives behind their actions, or indeed their 'shadow' side. On the one hand Geminis can be some of the most intelligent, objective, and adaptable people in the Zodiac, but on the other, some of the most cunning and manipulative. Many Geminis sail criminally close to the wind at times: they are not opposed to underhand tactics. And for many of them the ends frequently justify the means. However, Gemini is not an immoral sign, but rather an amoral one. Vitriol, sarcasm, and the bitter, crushing repost also belong to the Mr Hyde in Gemini. Since this sign is not primarily a physical or an emotional one, its most deadly weapons are words. Geminis, like their Virgoan cousins, are past masters at the intellectual put down. On another level, the darker Gemini twin emerges in some as childish and irresponsible behaviour. While members of this sign tend to retain their youthful looks until middle age, sometimes an equally youthful lack of responsibility and emotional immaturity is part of the package, an issue that will be taken up in later sections.

Although one would hardly associate this light and airy sign with paranoia, this phenomenon lies at the root of many Geminis' ducking and diving tactics, especially where their personal life is concerned. Geminis do not like to be probed at depth by anyone—not even a psychiatrist. They wonder what motives lie behind anyone's interest in their affairs. Thus they'll change the subject, make a flippant remark, or turn the question round should anyone threaten to penetrate the surface skin. (I should add that this tendency is far more marked in the Geminian man than in Geminian females.)

Geminians make some of the most interesting, amusing, and versatile individuals in the Zodiac, yet they're not the best people to trust with any privileged information. Their open minds allow for a constant two-way stream of ideas and information, and if a few of your secrets slip out along with the flow, well—it's not the end of the world, is it? Also, don't worry if you've lost the thread of your argument, or even paused for breath, the Gemini is guaranteed to finish off your sentence for you and neatly encapsulate your ideas. Then demolish them. He may even pick up your mannerisms and your accent at the same time.

Gemini men and women rarely carry the burden of humanity's suffering on their shoulders—they're not the guilt-laden, emotional soaks of the zodiac. But at times, when life seems depressingly full of drudgery and strife, the Geminian can be counted on to cut your problems down to size (probably along with the rest of you) and help you see the funny side of things. And even if the Peter Pan you thought you knew turns into Captain Hook every so often, it's reassuring to know you can always find the Real Thing in Never Never Land!

RELATIONSHIPS

Love and marriage don't always go together for Gemini. Like their Sagittarian opposites, Gemini men and women tend to suffer from emotional and psychological claustrophobia when confined to a lifelong sentence of matrimony. And while most Geminis hate to be alone, they find a daily regime of the same person and the routine pedestrian aspects of a long-term relationship a poor alternative. Geminis of both sexes need a certain amount of freedom and independence in their relationships and some extra-mural activities to help them tolerate the responsibility and commitment of marriage. Yet given their thirst for diversity in all things (including love) Geminis still manage to tie the knot like any other sign. But again . . . and again . . . and again! Multiple marriages are not unfamiliar to this sign.

However, their frequently disastrous track record for relationships has little to do with any awkward or bloody-minded behaviour on their part, for these are some of the most genial and easy-going people in the Zodiac. No, the unstable nature of their love lives stems from their inability to handle and relate to their delicate and often immature emotional systems. Like any of the signs who need to protect their vulnerable emotions, Gemini men and women tend to marry with their heads, then spend much of their marital existence with severe 'heart-burn'!

THE FEMALE GEMINI

Is there a Gemini woman in your life? If there is, you'll probably need to read the whole of this book to come to grips with her. Ms Gemini is more moody and more changeable than the Cancerian female, except that in Ms Gemini's case her temperamental swings are rarely the result of any hypersensitive emotions, but simply a response to her grasshopper mind. The Gemini woman doesn't try to please all of the people all of the time, she just has an innate knack of tuning into the mood of the moment and moulding her multi-faceted persona to fit any situation or individual. From her point of view she is anything but inconsistent: she merely allows herself to be borne along in life's slip-stream, enjoying and adapting to each twist and turn of the route.

Deciding what she wants to be when she grows up (a problem that invariably still haunts her in middle age) is a major preoccupation for the Gemini little girl. Her ambitions change from ballet-dancer to show-jumper, then from concert pianist to athlete, novelist, actress, or TV presenter. Anything, in fact, that seems out of the ordinary. Different. The Gemini child has a vivid imagination in which she frequently lives, along with her storybook companions, in preference to the real world. She may alternately enchant and exasperate her parents with her apparent lack of direction, her endless chatter and curiosity, and her innocent capriciousness—qualities she never loses. As she outgrows her short socks and has the braces removed from her teeth, she may look in the mirror one day and see to her amazement the woman in herself emerging. This realization may prompt her first (age) panic attack. Even Gemini little girls have to grow up. Or do they?

The Gemini adolescent solves the problem of advancing adulthood by acquiescing only to the parts she likes most—like the attractive curves, and the freedom to do as she likes without the restraint of a paternal guiding hand forever holding her back. Yet she usually retains the inner little girl with her emotional whimsicality and her refreshing candour—along with a degree of impracticality and a certain lack of responsibility for herself.

Marilyn Monroe personified the Geminian woman with all her vicissitudes. This beautiful, intelligent, immensely vulnerable sex-goddess was the product of a broken home. She had a deeply unhappy childhood with (according to her) several sexual assaults by one of her guardians. This hardly helped her weak psychological structure. (There was a history of mental illness in the family.) Marilyn longed for fame and the bright lights, but she was intelligent enough to realize that her career as a sex symbol was to be a short one unless she developed her acting skills. This she did to her credit, although not all her colleagues considered her acting talent equal to her stunning bodily proportions. And many openly decried her chronic lateness and her deep insecurity as an actress. But Marilyn was not an ordinary star. She had a unique combination of playful innocence and lush sexuality.

Despite the success her career brought her, she never found the sense of peace, fulfilment and real happiness that she craved. Marilyn married three times (some say four): first, the 'boy next door', then a famous baseball star, and third, an intellectual/playwright. She moved from man to man, hoping that each one would provide the emotional oasis she sought. But as each relationship collapsed, she became ever more inwardly demoralized and lost until towards the end of her life, living on a diet of pills and alcohol, she hovered on the brink of complete mental breakdown.

If Marilyn herself never really knew who she was, certainly no one else did. Friends and colleagues variously describe her as 'quiet', 'someone who liked to read and write poetry', 'a little girl lost', but also (as an assistant director on the film **Something's Got to Give** said about her) 'Next to her, Lucretia Borgia was a pussy-cat!' Even the nature of her sexuality was open to opinion. The **Life** photographer, Philippe Halsam, said of her, 'When she faced a man she didn't know, she felt safe and secure only when she knew the man desired her; so everything in her life was geared to provoke this feeling. Her talent in this respect was very great.' Of herself Marilyn admitted, 'The first effect marriage had on me was to increase my lack of interest in sex.' Indeed, one of Marilyn's psychiatrists, Dr Ralph Greenson, considered her to be a woman who found little satisfaction in sex. Whatever her real feelings about her sexuality, Marilyn clearly craved love and affection, but since she had such a weak grasp on her own identity and such poor self-esteem, she was unable to accept love, even when it was offered. Also, Marilyn suffered from the typically Geminian 'grass is greener . . .' syndrome and a low boredom threshold. And even if she had had a stronger psychological structure, no doubt she would still have needed much more from a man than he alone could hope to offer.

Regarding Marilyn's psychiatric problems, few people, apart from those closest to her, realized how emotionally and psychologically damaged she was. In letters to a colleague, Dr Greenson mentioned that Marilyn had 'a tendency to paranoid reactions . . .' and after her death, he commented that she was a woman who had 'ego weakness and certain psychotic manifestations including those of schizophrenia.' Had she not been the star she was, he would have institutionalized her the year of her death.

Her tragic and untimely 'suicide' seemed almost inevitable. She was for all her womanly appearance a 'lost and lonely child' at heart. And at 36, the prospect of a loveless, childless, and ageing future seemed intolerably bleak and meaningless.

Of course not all Gemini women are manic depressives or suicidal schizophrenics. Nor do they necessarily have a weak hold on reality and their self-esteem. But they often do not know who they are.

Paradoxically, the Geminian woman, like the Virgoan and the Libran, usually spends much of her time analysing Life. Yet even though she may reason things out well, she still doesn't know why she encounters confusion and instability in her life and her relationships.

Establishing what she truly wants is probably the basis of the Geminian lady's dissatisfaction and instability in life and love. After all, what can you expect if you initially set your sights on a macho-man, then once you've found him discover that you need someone with whom you can communicate. As soon as you have replaced Mr Beefcake with Mr Sensitive and Intellectual, excrutiating boredom sets in, so it's off to pastures new with the **enfant terrible** from the trendy ad agency. And so on.

One Geminian woman gave herself away with the following comments in my questionnaire. I quote verbatim: 'My ideal man is very intellectual and powerful with a great sense of humour. He must be well-read, knowledgeable about the arts and love music. He should be devoted to me, but not dote on me. He should be appreciative of female beauty but absolutely faithful. He would have to love sports, horses, cars, skiing, fencing, water-sports, evenings out, dining, theatre, ballet . . .' I have my doubts that she will ever find this dream-boat!

The Gemini woman, unlike the watery or earthy type, needs something more in her life than a husband and 2.8 children. This woman is a thinker. She also needs lots of adult company and penning her into a domestic cage is tantamount to 'Gemicide'. Yet if Ms Gemini only has a career (or two) she yearns for the permanence and the deep and meaningful content an intimate relationship could bring. It could be argued that this is a predicament may women find themselves in whether or not they're Geminian. But while other women resolve the conflict by marrying, mothering, and maintaining a career, even if the Geminian accomplishes all these things, she still feels vaguely unfulfilled and discontented.

The Gemini woman, like the Gemini man, prefers to paddle in the waters of life rather than submerge herself. This she does, partly because she needs to keep her head above water in order to see what boats are coming over the horizon, and partly because she is terrified of 'drowning'. Yet it is precisely this stance as an onlooker and dabbler, rather than a wholehearted participant, that leads to this sense of incompletion.

Although it is difficult to place the Geminian woman into only two types, there are two broad categories into which she falls. I'll call them (somewhat tongue in cheek) the **Butterfly** and the **Thoth-Fairy**.

The **Butterfly** is the more familiar Geminian woman. This Mercurial lady loves socializing and entertainment. She is usually intelligent and quick-thinking, although she may fail to fulfil her bright potential through over-diversification. The Butterfly's daily timetable is packed with activities from dawn till dusk. And even if she finds the odd moment to relax, she'll be checking her diary, writing a list, or making one or two telephone calls. This lady places meditation classes at the top of her running list, but somehow she never manages to enrol, let alone find the twenty minutes to meditate! Like the Aries woman, this kind of Gemini thrives on finding interesting people to talk to and bring together at dinner parties. She usually knows the in-crowd and is an avid reader of gossip columns. She likes to be fashionably dressed (whatever her income) and she loves to try anything new and different in the cookery or interior decorating line. She'd hate to be classed as dowdy, dull, or ignorant. And to her credit, she's usually well-informed on most subjects, from the Egyptian Mystery teachings to growing grapes. She has a score of friends, acquaintances, and hangers-on to defray any threat of loneliness or boredom. But since she never has time for a self-reflective moment, she has no idea that many of them consider her frivolous and superficial. This kind of Gemini is not the sort others rely on for emotional support in times of deep personal crisis.

Where love and relationships are concerned, the Butterfly flits from one person to another, often keeping two (or more) relationships going at the same time. One Geminian friend of mine had a lover whom she referred to as her 'mistress'. She used to secretly visit her 'mistress' (another Gemini) in the middle of the night, returning at dawn to the flat she shared with her live-in lover. In typically Butterfly fashion, she eventually left home and married her 'mistress'! Now even they are divorced.

The Butterfly finds it enormously difficult to 'settle down'. Initially she may take a delight in playing the loving wife, the perfect hostess, and the doting mother. But, like an actress in a long-running play, no matter how many angles she takes on the role, eventually her enthusiasm is exhausted. In the marriage stakes, Butterflies make good 100-metre sprinters, but poor marathon runners. Marilyn Monroe (clearly a Butterfly) apparently telephoned a friend the day she married Joe DiMaggio and said that she wanted a divorce.

To a certain extent, maintaining an interesting job and an active social life can help the Butterfly sustain a long-term relationship. But it takes a very special man indeed to clip the Butterfly's wings.

There are, however, a breed of Gemini females who are far more serious minded and responsible than their fly-by-night sisters. And in my experience, this is quite independent of any more sobering horoscopic factors. (Queen Victoria is a case in point: Sun, Moon, and Ascendant in Gemini; Venus and Mars in Aries.) These women would seem to resonate with Thoth, and so I'll call them **Thoth-Fairies**. They are often extremely articulate and able to concentrate and focus their energies better than the Butterfly. They like to put their minds to deep and penetrating subjects and frequently have an excellent grasp of political issues. These Thoth-Fairies make good investigative journalists, teachers of obscure or 'diffcult' subjects, healers, and accountants; indeed anything that demands mental stamina and good concentration. This type of Geminian also takes her duties more seriously and tends to keep her wandering eye and itchy feet under control. In many ways, this lady takes after her more Saturnine Aquarian cousin. Once she has made her marriage vows, she intends to stick to them and makes a thoroughly efficient job of wife and motherhood. Like the Aquarian, provided she has some watery content in her chart, she no doubt gains tremendous satisfaction in her domestic role, and may never give a second thought to any career aspirations. But the Thoth type of Geminian who doesn't have her Moon or Venus in a water sign nearly always needs some outlet for her mental abilities. While this kind of Gemini hardly ever flits from man to man, she nevertheless usually experiences some dissatisfaction in her relationships.

Although these two categories of Gemini women appear to be at opposite ends of Mercury's staff, they are united by a common emotional factor. Gemini females tend not to relate well to their emotions, which is not to say they cannot feel. While some maintain control of their emotions by disassociating themselves from irrational feelings of anger, hurt, and despair, others respond to such feelings with the emotional control of a little girl. On the one hand, the most sophisticated and articulate Geminian is capable of huge emotional storms and irrational outbursts. On the other, those Gemini women who appear calm may pay the price with a nervous breakdown at a later stage in their lives. The Gemini lady doesn't trust easily. She finds it difficult to give of herself totally to anyone. Thus the root of many Gemini lady's leap-frogging antics lies in an inability to commit herself to any one man—a familiar tendency for all the mutable women. As this is often unconscious, Ms Gemini, like the Virgoan, the Piscean, and the Sagittarian, often bemoans the fact that she cannot find permanence, security, and happiness in relationships. While some Geminis (more usually the Butterfly type) exhibit their emotional capriciousness by moving from man to man, others (more often the Thoth-Fairies) either seal off their emotions, or live in an emotional fog with their partner.

Gemini women suffer from the classic problem of all dual signs: seeking their other twin in a partner. Time and time again, Ms Gemini becomes involved with an emotionally complex man (usually of the watery variety). The Geminian can be attracted to down-to-earth men, materially successful men, or passive, gentle, artisitic dreamers. But whatever their outer 'garb', under the surface they amount to an emotional maze. Since attraction is a two-way affair, the man is normally drawn to the Geminian because he feels she will release him from his emotional swamp. Occasionally a 'translation of energies' occurs and the Gemini female responds to her partner by 'feeling' him rather than by questioning and analysing him. She learns to trust and to give of herself. In return, the partner finds security with Ms Gemini and learns to verbalize and rationalize his feelings. In other relationships, after the initial (sexual) attraction has worn off, the Gemini woman finds her partner moody, remote, and difficult, while he finds Ms Gemini unfeeling and insensitive. Sadly, the more the partner retreats behind a wall of silence, the more the Geminian resorts to her most lethal weapons: vitriol and sarcasm. Not a pretty sight.

Of course, not all Geminian women will fit neatly into either category: often there's a little bit of both in every Geminian female. Also, many Mercurial ladies manage to find lasting happiness in relationships. As with everything in astrology, much depends on the chart as a whole and the way the individual reacts to and develops through her experience.

The Geminian woman is usually extremely romantic. Like her male counterpart she may have a talent for writing poems and love letters. Sometimes she enjoys a love affair through correspondence, the telephone, and her imagination far more than in the flesh! Even when she's married, the Geminian woman endeavours to keep the romance alive by leaving little love-notes around the house or in her husband's brief-case. She also likes to buy spontaneous and thoughtful gifts. Since she's on the flirtatious side herself, she tends to be suspicious about her partner's real activities when he's 'late at the office'. But a partner's infidelity can be forgiven and forgotten by this woman (unless, of course, she has some Cancer or Scorpio in her chart).

Gemini women make good mothers once their children can talk to them and accompany them on outings. The Mercurial lady is not in her element with nappies, bottles, and prams. And although Geminians enjoy young minds and the company of youngsters, it's not the end of the world for women of this sign if they find they cannot have children. Indeed, whether by choice or not, Geminis rarely have large families.

Of course, if you want your Gemini to be a doting mother, she'll gladly immerse herself in the part. Then she'll need some leave of absence to join the 'Freedom for Caged Animals' movement . . . and the operatic society . . . and the ski-club . . . It's not that she doesn't love you or the children; it's just that it's awfully difficult for an airy woman to stay in one place when all those winds of change and opportunity are blowing. And remember, although Ms Gemini may discuss your relationship rather a lot, and analyse you, your friends, and the children (usually while she's making lasagnas for the freezer and writing her thesis on extinct dialects), she really doesn't understand herself at all. Yet if you handle her firmly but with a loose grasp, appear strong but not dominant, gentle but never weak; if you have a serious outlook on life but flaunt convention every so often, debate matters frequently but let her do all the talking, she'll never move an inch from your side. And if all this sounds quite impossible, simply love her. She's worth her weight in Mercury!

THE MALE GEMINI

Don't blink your eyes or you may miss him. Mr Gemini is a fast mover—usually in the opposite direction if he suspects you want to begin a deep and meaningful relationship with him. There are ways, of course, of catching Mr Mercury, but a full frontal assault on his emotions is not one of them. Not that the Gemini man doesn't find women attractive: nor is he backward in coming forward when he sees something he wants. And he could never be classed as a loner. But Mr Gemini feels distinctly uneasy when a relationship threatens to become heavy. Ideally, the Geminian would like to have friends who just happen to be lovers rather than the other way round.

Indeed friends are a very important part of Mr Gemini's existence, and if you intend to team up with this character then you must be prepared to share him with his scores of friends from the office, the squash club, his philosophy classes . . . And if that isn't enough, there are the ten Mr Geminis you'll share your bed with! The Gemini man, unless he has plenty of earth or water in his chart, needs constant social stimulation—his mind is the most overactive 'organ' in his body. If there's nothing planned in the way of people for his entertainment after work or over the weekend, he'll restlessly scour the papers for a good show, an art gallery, or a sport's event. A cosy evening by the fireside just for the two of you is likely to be a mere annual event. And even then he'll have to check that the telephone is working every now and again.

Clearly if you want a deeply intimate and exclusive relationship with a lover, Mr Gemini isn't your man, but a partnership with this airy individual can have its compensations.

For a start, boredom will be a thing of the past. The typically Geminian male is fun to be with. He's usually witty and game for anything new. And even if he doesn't have a Master's degree he's normally intelligent, well read, and well informed. He'll have an answer for any question you care to throw at him. He'll know all the in-places, and wherever you go interesting snippets of information will pour effortlessly from his lips. In fact Gemini is probably the most streetwise sign in the zodiac. Mr Gemini is also a generous man: generous with his time and generous with his worldly goods. He's hardly ever aggressive or unkind, at least not unless you've made him look stupid or he's been proved wrong. He's also immensely easy going and he's not the sort to make a huge fuss if you've burnt his birthday dinner—or even if you've forgotten it was his birthday! He is, however, extremely evasive and fights shy of committing himself to anything of a too permanent nature—which may include you. But he's very understanding. And if you dissolve into tears for no discernible reason—perhaps in the church as yet another of your friends gets married—he'll do his best to translate your incoherent mutterings between the sobs and help you rationalize matters.

Like Mr Leo and Mr Libra, the Gemini man never feels his age. Regardless of his greying temples he'll still consider himself a young man on the threshold of life. And fortunately for him, men of this sign usually retain their youthful appearance well into middle age. As a child, the Geminian views the adult world as an even more exciting adventure playground than the one he's in. And he cannot understand why adults have such little apparent fun in it. As he grows into manhood he cannot altogether lose his childish love of pranks, and he usually finds it very difficult to take authority figures and bureaucracy seriously. His disregard for red tape and stuffy rules and regulations is refreshing to say the least: like the Aries man he cannot stand unnecessary impediments in his path. This man prefers to take a short cut to the main chance. While he's not exactly dishonest, if he can get away with a devious move or two he will—and with the innocence of a small boy, charming but cute. However, while this kind of attitude and behaviour may be mildly (or greatly) annoying to others in his professional life, it does a great deal of damage in his private life, or more specifically his one-to-one relationships. The Gemini man, like his airy brothers, has little time for sentiment in his career: how others may feel about his actions is of little import to him. Sadly, this abnegation of emotional values is not exclusive to his professional life.

At this point it might be advisable to place the Geminian man into two camps—Before and After (before the great love affair and after). For love is the transforming agent for this sign. Until the Geminian has felt the fire of his emotions and until he has related to another individual from his heart rather than his head, while he may seem entirely sane and rational to others, he also appears extremely insubstantial and immature. Some Geminians never make the transition.

To other men, the 'before' Gemini leads an apparently enviable life. He usually has a large pool of girlfriends to draw from (none of whom get to meet mother, unless it's by accident). Friends learn not to expect to see any one girl on more than a few occasions (and certainly not consecutively). They also learn not to probe him about any of his women, (a) because he only makes quips about his love life, and (b) because he can become rather rude when prodded too much or too often. Whenever he's with a girl, he's always attentive and seems genuinely happy in her company. Why, his friends and family wonder, doesn't he settle down with one of them? From the Geminian's point of view, he may choose to use his women like library books, because he has no intention of being limited only to one volume, and certainly not for life. He probably openly admits that he hates heavy scenes, and the moment one of his girlfriends pauses in front of the ring display at the jewellers, he drops her like a hot potato! At the outset of a relationship, he may make it quite clear that he's not the marrying kind. However, sometimes the Geminian wishes that he could find the right person, so he keeps on trying out new models in the hopes that he might find one that suits him.

At the basis of the Geminian's undulating romantic path is the fear of commitment. The Geminian prefers to be non-committal in most areas of his life, and the thought of binding himself to one person for the duration is quite appalling. Not only does he see marriage as a threat to his freedom, but deep down he doubts whether he's made of the 'right stuff'. In times past (most notably the Victorian and Edwardian era), when marriage was largely a contractual arrangement in which love and romance had no part, the Gemini was happy to 'bind' himself to another on paper, in the knowledge that he was emotionally and sexually off the hook. Then it was the norm to seek pleasure outside marriage. But since the 1920s, romantic love has been an essential prerequisite of marriage, and infidelity frowned upon. Thus the Geminian frequently sees marriage as a trap. Not only is he expected to bestow his worldly goods on a wife, but also marry her for love and remain faithful to her!

Like all airy men, the Gemini tends to view emotions as inferior. Although he will admit he has them, he prefers that they maintain a low profile. He, like the Aquarian, thinks falling in love is only a temporary hormonal imbalance brought on by lust. He has a sneaking disregard for those who make such a song and dance about love. The 'before' Gemini has never made the transition from erotic love to the deeper all-involving variety. As soon as his initial sexual fever has died down, he snaps out of the unnatural romantic haze. Once this has happened, either he leaves the relationship and moves on, or for all sorts of more practical and cerebral reasons he may decide to live with her or even marry her—provided she puts no great emotional pressure on him. And because he has established that falling in love is an illusion, induced by sexual enthralment that *always* evaporates, he sees no point in being anything other than monogamous. On the other hand, he may become hooked on the sexual high new relationships provide, and thus finds fidelity a super-human task.

Despite the polarity of this sign, Geminians are not extremists. Their airy, detached nature is ill suited to radical behaviour of any sort. Geminis never lose their heads. Clarity and reason are their gods. While in some areas of life their dispassion is admirable, it nevertheless acts as a barrier to their deeper feelings. Rather like the individual who takes tranquillizers to prevent him from feeling pain or deep anxiety, while he is able to cope with life he is simultaneously cut off from any gloriously happy feelings. In many ways the archetypal Gemini lives a kind of valiumed existence: isolated from the unpleasant dark side of his nature where anger and hate lie, but also from its refulgent aspects. While anger bears no resemblance to love, the ability to give full rein to both stems from the same emotional source. Although it would be a gross generality to say that all individuals who are incapable of giving vent to their anger (whether or not they're Geminian) are also incapable of demonstrating or feeling deep love, it is nevertheless extremely unlikely for an individual to rise to one but not the other. Thus the Geminian who is able to become demonstrably angry is one who is also capable of expressing his feelings of love to the same degree. And vice versa. In his defence, the Gemini man who cushions himself from violent emotional expression is probably hypersensitive. As a child, he may have been terrified of emotional displays and therefore learned to seal himself off from such experiences.

Clearly, there are Geminian men who are much more tuned-in to their feelings. And although I would suggest that the more emotionally oriented Gemini is one who has his Mars, Venus, or the Moon in a water sign, it is not impossible for the extremely airy man to look into his deeper emotional depths. How and when he does so is in many ways a bit of a 'chicken and egg' situation.

Which leads us to the 'after' Gemini.

The 'after' Gemini is one who has been struck by the thunderbolt of love, and instead of finding himself burnt to a crisp is transformed by the experience. Whereas before he believed, somewhat cynically, that love was lust under a pen-name, suddenly he finds another person means more to him, and in a peculiar indefinable way, than anyone else—or his independence come to that. Not only do these feelings retain their sharpness beyond the nine-days wonder of sexual enthralment, but they gain in depth and magnitude. Why I say a 'chicken and egg' situation is that it is uncertain whether it is the partner who inspires the Gemini to previously unscaled heights of emotional expression, or the Gemini who has to be open to receive such a catalyst in the first place. I tend to favour the latter view. But either way, after the great love affair, the Gemini is irrevocably changed. He cannot go back to emotional obscurity.

The 'after' Gemini is a much more substantial figure. While he may retain some of his cynicism, his tendency to quip, and his devil's advocate stance, he's no longer on the outside looking in. He no longer has to ask how something feels to know if he is feeling it or not! He's more likely to hold his partner in his arms when she's awash with misery than cross-question and analyse her. And he's not so embarrassed or ill at ease when confronted by another's distress, or his own. He's also far more likely to lose his temper!

The 'after' Gemini is not so afraid of commitment. Since his emotional growth has caught up with the rest of him, he's better able to cope with the (emotional) pressures of a wife and children. He may still need a degree of independence and plenty of extra-mural activities in his life, but marriage doesn't represent such a trap for him. And like the Saturnine Aquarian, he's usually very good at dealing with the practical and financial side of marriage.

Geminian men are often immensely drawn to watery women. In the 'before' Gemini's case, because his emotions are stuck in a time warp he seeks a feeling type of woman in order to vicariously experience emotion. This kind of supply/demand relationship works well if the Gemini man learns to relate more through his feelings than his intellect. But if he constantly rationalizes or retreats every time he is confronted by an emotional issue, the relationship will come to a sticky end. While he finds the partner increasingly tiresome, over demanding, and irrational, she will feel the Gemini is cold, indifferent, and unfeeling.

Two friends of mine, Harry and Lisa, are a case in point. Harry, a Geminian divorcee, had just surfaced in emotional tatters from a traumatic encounter of the Scorpionic kind when out of the blue he married Lisa, an exceptionally attractive, if rather capricious, Cancerian. The relationship glittered with potential. Lisa also had some planets in Gemini so a good intellectual rapport was part of their mutual attraction. They also loved socializing and shared an interest in esoterica. Sadly, and this is not a weakness related to their Sun signs, neither saw the other person for what he or she truly was. To Lisa, Harry was a sophisticated man about town, and to Harry, Lisa was a sweet, funny 'kook'. However, so busy was Harry keeping up with appearances and the hectic pace of life, that he failed to see he was standing on emotional quicksand.

Problems initially started in the sexual arena. Lisa was highly sexed while

Harry could 'take it or leave it': the more Lisa clamoured for love, the less able Harry was to function. She felt unattractive and rejected. He felt got at. If Lisa could have surfaced above her emotional chaos she might have been able to back off and wait for Harry to chip himself out of his emotional prison. As it was, her frustration and hurt compelled her to hurl accusation after accusation at him. And her Geminian articulation turned into vitriol and abuse. Harry felt like a helpless child since his fragile emotional structure hindered his ability to retaliate forcibly. Ultimately, divorce was the only solution.

Ideally, Harry needed a companion to share his life and his interests: someone who wouldn't stifle his need for air by heavy emotional demands. Yet time and time again, he became hooked by just such women. Although he could relate to women on a mental level, he was unable to be emotionally at ease with them since he didn't trust them. How could he when his own emotions were so delicate that they threatened to snap at the first onslaught. Yet because the psyche demands wholeness, he was continually driven to develop the one part of his 'anatomy' that was weak, through relationships with emotionally overpowering women.

Harry, like all 'before' Gemini men, was looking for the true 'princess' to awaken his inner sleeping prince. But unless there is an open gate, she won't be able to find him!

Strangely enough for a sign that has so much difficulty with emotional intimacy, Geminian men often have a talent for writing about love—even if it's just a simple love letter. Gemini is happier in the realm of words than he is in the flesh. Since the Geminian invariably experiences some grievous emotional harm in at least one relationship, unrequited love is a theme close to his heart. W.B. Yeats,* the poet (Sun, Mercury, and Uranus in Gemini), unsuccessfully wooed the beautiful revolutionary Maud Gonne for sixteen years. After constant proposals of marriage and constant refusals, he turned his attentions to her adopted daughter, Iseult, with equal lack of success. In many of his love poems his Geminian spirit is quite evident, especially in the following extract from a poem written after Iseult had rejected him.

> I can exchange opinion with any neighbouring mind,
> I have as healthy flesh and blood as any rhymer's had,
> But O! my Heart could bear no more when the upland caught the wind:
> I ran, I ran from my love's side because my Heart went mad.

Gemini men are not the jealous and possessive type. In fact, this is the one sign of the Zodiac that can tolerate an open marriage—and make it work. But Geminians do like intrigue. A certain amount of cloak and dagger tactics—secret telephone calls and assignations—feeds their active imaginations and staves off boredom. They also find that enforced separations allow them a necessary breathing space. If Mr Gemini discovers

---

*Yeats had a great interest in many areas of life including the mystical. He explored Christianity, Neoplatonism, Theosophy, Spiritualism, even magic, and he was a great admirer of Blake. But as one biographer, Professor A. Norman Jeffares, said of him, 'even in the midst of this search for belief, his mind remained partially sceptical, ironic, even potentially mocking'.

that his lover has been unfaithful, the wind may temporarily disappear from his sails, but he's not the type to bear long and silent grudges. Besides, it gives him a tactical advantage!

Since, in the main, Gemini men are still 'children at heart' they tend to take to fatherhood like a duck to ice—not at all sure of their footing. Small babies with wrinkly, red faces are not Mr Mercury's favourite 'things'. He has little motherly instinct. And he'd prefer to ignore them until they're at least six years old (if not 23). Once his children become interesting, however, his relationship with them improves. And the children of a Geminian father often find him their biggest pal as they grow older. He cares that they do well at school, simply because he can't abide dullards, but he's not overly ambitious or domineering. Also, like Mr Leo, he's not the greatest disciplinarian—he'd rather reason things out with them than wield the whip hand.

Mr Gemini is number one on every hostess's party list. This man can talk to anybody about anything. He has almost as much charm as Mr Libra and he can make the dreariest wallflower feel like Brooke Shields. That is, unless she's affected his heart. The Geminian man tends to become rather rude and quite distant—he may shoot off in the opposite direction—if he's smitten. Like Yeats, his heart cannot take the strain! Because Mr Gemini is a bit of a showman (not so much a double act, more a one-man band) he needs a strong and practical woman, or a soft and sensitive one, to act as a homing device.

Mr Gemini may have some difficulty learning to trust you enough to let his feelings speak rather than his intellect. But despite his ironic stance where love and romance are concerned, he does have feelings. And when he's found that a meeting of hearts as well as minds has its compensations, he'll transform himself into a model husband. But remember, the secret of keeping him by your side is never to tie him to your apron strings. This man needs freedom to circulate beyond the boundaries of home—and without a timetable and a rule book. And if sometimes you wish your Geminian could look into your eyes without informing you that there are some funny black spots on them, at least by the time your friends are nodding off by the fireside and turning up their deaf-aids, he'll still be finding something new and interesting to fascinate you.

SUMMARY

Geminians are not the most consistent members of the Zodiac. Their attention spans are short and their boredom thresholds low. Commitment to one individual with all the incumbent burdens of emotional intimacy and responsibility is not their strongest suit. Thus some of them move restlessly from one partner to the next avoiding the demands of a long-term relationship while others marry but keep their partners at a safe emotional distance. Although Geminians are adaptable and stimulating partners their tendency to guard their feelings through lack of trust makes them elusive and difficult to feel close to. On the plus side, those Geminian men and women who develop their emotional muscles as well as their cerebral cortex make understanding, open, and giving partners.

GEMINI PARTNERSHIPS

Geminis are easy-going individuals—they can get along with almost anyone. However, where relationships of the intimate kind are concerned, fiery and airy partners provide them with the freedom they require and are less likely to emotionally swamp them.

Aries

Geminis and **Aries** have much in common. Both love new challenges and a stimulating social life, and neither enjoys long drawn-out hostilities. However, while these two often find each other mentally stimulating, they can irritate each other. Mr and Ms Aries get far too steamed up about everything for the Geminian's liking, while the Arian feels the Geminian never puts his heart and soul into his arguments—or his actions. This relationship rarely encounters sexual problems—they can be quite a swinging couple—although Mr and Ms Aries can be a little too emotionally intense and demanding for Gemini. A shortfall on responsibility can lead this couple into financial difficulties.

Taurus

Taurus is the great stablizer in Gemini's life and sometimes the great obstacle! Unless these two have personal planets in each other's Sun sign and/or some harmonious planetary links, they have little in common. Gemini is usually far too changeable and difficult to pin down for the Taurean, while the Bull seems much too security-oriented and cautious for Gemini. However, the Taurean is also very patient (and slow to anger), so it's only a question of time before the Gemini dances to the Bull's tune! Sexually, this can be a good combination: Taurus lends sensuousness to Gemini's versatility.

Gemini

Lack of communication is hardly a problem two **Geminis** encounter in their relationship. However, although these two may talk to each other they don't always hear each other. Depending on the watery content of both charts, this couple either distance themselves totally from their emotions or become 'drowned' by them. Extra-curricular activities are a major feature of this partnership. Both individuals like to have a constant stream of activities, friends, and entertainment in their lives. After a stimulating sexual start, sex may become low key. Fortunately, since these two are likely to lead very busy lives, they may never notice any cracks in their relationship.

Cancer

Although the signs of Gemini and **Cancer** sit side by side, temperamentally they are poles apart. Cancerians are deeply emotional and highly self-protective individuals, and unlike Geminis, they hardly ever place reason and rationale above feelings and instinct. Yet they are invariably attracted to one another. If each partner has personal planets in the other's Sun sign their chances for compatibility are higher, otherwise plenty of harmonious links are needed between the charts for this relationship to stand the test of time. The Geminian usually cannot cope too well with the Cancerian's moods and silences, while the Cancerian cannot communicate his feelings through words to the Geminian. If the Geminian is in touch with his feelings and the

Cancerian less inhibited, sex can be marvellous between these two.

Leo

Gemini usually finds the **Leo** individual fun to be with. Leos love socialising as much as Geminis although these fiery types can be too interested in upward-mobility for Geminis' liking. Since Leo tends to be a possessive sort, a Gemini partner can make him feel very insecure at times. And the Geminian can become extremely bored by his Leo partner's endless need for praise and reassurance. This couple are often as happy as they appear to outsiders, but sometimes the strong (and stubborn) Leonine partner is rather overpowering for the Geminian. Sex is usually good and problem-free for these two.

Virgo

Although Gemini and **Virgo** both have good minds and enjoy using them, they have entirely different modes of thinking. The Virgoan is more practical and tidy-minded than the Geminian, while Mr and Ms Gemini jump from one idea to the next. Thus, each tend to irritate the other. However, these two are often highly attracted to one another. At first their relationship works well on all levels, but in the long term, unless there are many good planetary links between the charts, they will be pushed further and further apart by their incompatible temperaments.

Libra

Libra is one of Gemini's ideal partners. Mr or Ms Libra is just as keen as the Geminian to keep conflict at bay and both partners find little difficulty in accommodating each other. This relationship is often extremely cultured and refined. It is also usually high on romance but weak on real emotional depth. Provided this suits them both, harmony will reign. Sometimes the Libran feels the Geminian takes him (or her) for granted, especially as the Venusian allows Mr or Ms Gemini such freedom and independence. On the other hand, the Geminian thinks the Libran spends too much time analysing their relationship and pointing out his lack of commitment!

Scorpio

Gemini and **Scorpio** make strange bed-fellows. The Scorpion is deeply fascinating to Gemini—a mystery he cannot resist. But once the relationship has begun, the Geminian invariably finds he is 'in over his head'. Mr and Ms Scorpio need deep emotional exchange before the mental variety, so after the first flush of romance and the initial sexual thrill, they find the Geminian rather cold and passionless. On the other hand, the Geminian discovers his magical mystery tour with the Scorpion has lead him into the centre of an emotional volcano! With harmonious links elsewhere in the charts this relationship can lead to mutual understanding and the development of love and trust. But this relationship always demands a lot from both individuals.

Sagittarius

Sagittarius is Gemini's opposite number, and like most opposites they attract each other, yet also repel! These two like to be on the move. They rarely have time to sit and ponder about anything—including their relationship—so on the surface they lead an easy life together. The Sagittarian is a happy-go-lucky sort and provided the Gemini partner goes along with everything he wants, any thunder clouds stay away. Lack of commitment is a mutual problem for these two. On the plus side, their loose grasp on each other can help their relationship withstand the years. But on the other, the relationship's weak emotional foundations may collapse with the stress of a major crisis or two.

Capricorn

Capricorn is one of the most difficult partners for Gemini. Neither seems able to appreciate each other's qualities—except in the early stages of their relationship. The Goat is much too serious, practical, and 'long-sighted' for Gemini. He tends to criticize and trivialize Mr or Ms Mercury's offerings. And worse, never have the time for fun. Yet Capricorn can provide the Geminian with the structure and direction he needs in his life while Mr or Ms Gemini can inspire the Goat and lift his plans and projects off the drawing board. Initially there can be strong sexual attraction between these two.

Aquarius

Friendship is the most important factor in a Gemini-Aquarius relationship. These two often consider themselves 'best friends' first and lovers afterwards. And sometimes sex takes a back seat (after an exciting start) for these two. The Aquarian partner is a good mental match for Gemini, and their relationship is never dull or uninteresting. The Uranian is the easier type of Aquarian for Gemini, since he is just as keen on his freedom and independence, even though he's rather unpredictable. The Saturnine is too dictatorial and stubborn for Gemini, although with this Aquarian Gemini's life runs like clockwork!

Pisces

Pisces is enormously attractive to the Geminian. Pisces' brand of sensitivity and gentleness is very appealing to Gemini—he thinks he can lead the Fish out of his troubled waters but inevitably finds he has joined him instead. Both these signs lack direction! Sometimes these two drift apart through lack of commitment and failure to communicate their needs. Both signs also find it difficult to trust. But if both work their way through their problems instead of running away from them, they can build a mutually rewarding relationship. Sex can reach some special heights for these two—especially if they are emotionally in tune.

SEXUALITY

Far from being their whole existence, sex is usually a thing apart for Geminians. These individuals are not the most passionate in the Zodiac. Like all the air signs they tend to spend rather more time thinking and talking about sex than actually getting down to the nitty-gritty. Yet, despite their easy-going personalities, Geminians are usually sexually complex creatures.

Of course, one cannot judge anyone's sexuality from his or her Sun sign alone: many factors, not all of them astrological, go towards an individual's sexual make-up. Thus the themes that follow will apply to a greater or lesser extent to those men who have their Sun or Mars in Gemini and those women who have their Moon, Mars, or Venus in this sign.

Mercury people tend to be sexually precocious. Because these individuals are naturally curious about everything in life, they often experience a deep fascination about what goes on behind their parents' bedroom door. Sometimes their curiosity leads to a very early sexual awakening indeed! Geminian children are highly aware of the anatomical differences between the sexes and they tend to enjoy games where these differences can be explored—like 'Doctors and Nurses'. This same curiosity invariably makes for early teenage sexual experimentation. And because Geminians thrive on change and novelty, it is entirely possible for some of them to become sexually jaded by their mid-twenties!

The truly Geminian man or woman is eminently capable of having sexual relationships without any emotional involvement whatsoever. 'I love the eyes-meeting-across-a-crowded-room thing,' wrote one man with his Sun and Venus in Gemini. 'You know, finding someone really attractive and going off with them. There's something about the anonymity and the unknown that makes for real excitement. Somehow when you try to make something out of it—a real emotional number—it [the relationship] loses its specialness.' Although a total disregard for the emotional content of a relationship is more a tendency of the Geminian male than the female, the Geminian woman with her Venus in this sign and the Moon in another air or earth sign (or vice versa) is equally capable of indulging her sexual appetite without any emotional accompaniment. Indeed, the strongly Geminian woman often appears to take her pleasure like a man, and moves from partner to partner with no apparent emotional 'conscience' whatsoever.

In many ways, the typically Geminian woman has a neurotic sex drive, since there is a complex interplay between her mental and sexual needs. On the one hand, her changeable nature and her restless mentality require much variety and stimulation which urge her to explore different sexual relationships, yet because she is not really a creature of the flesh, the physical side of sex is almost always a disappointment. Sometimes this can lead to out and out promiscuity as the Geminian woman tries to resolve her sexual dissatisfaction by moving from lover to lover in the hopes that one will provide her with the satisfaction she needs.

The Geminian woman will often say that she falls in love easily and often. While this may be true in some cases, more usually, the Geminian woman just thinks she is in love. The Gemini female responds quickly to people. If she meets someone she 'clicks' with it seems only natural to want to explore the meeting of minds further—in the bedroom. Sometimes, the sexual exchange lives up to the promise of the mental one, in which case Ms Gemini will want to pursue the relationship. But often, even with a promising sexual start, the Geminian loses interest quickly. Thus, she falls out of love as quickly as she fell in.

In effect this is a two-tiered issue. On the one hand, sexual boredom tends to set in early with Ms Gemini—even if she is emotionally involved and happy with her lover. She is easily discontented. On the other, the Geminian female may tire of a partner because once she has explored the physical and sensual perimeters of a relationship, there is nothing left to hold her interest. The emotional bond is lacking—perhaps because she is incapable of deep emotional involvement in the first place, or unprepared to take the risk.

The Geminian woman's mind is her most vital sexual 'organ'. Since this woman bores easily a rich and changeable fantasy life is essential to her survival in a long-term relationship. It is very unusual for women of this sign (unless there is plenty of earth in the chart) to be aroused by the sight of bare essentials basking in the light of a naked light bulb. This woman likes to be mentally tantalized before she is visually assaulted by the real thing. Erotic imagery, suggestion, and her imagination work far better than her optic nerves. The Geminian woman is attracted to a man first through his intellect and his image, then by his body. Indeed, this preoccupation with the image of a man can lead to some problems in relationships. And like other mutable women (the Virgos, the Sagittarians, and the Pisceans) the Geminian often falls in love and into bed with an illusion and thus experiences a very rude awakening—sometimes weeks or months later.

From the response to my questionnaire and the various comments I have gleaned from Geminian women over the years, it would appear that of all the zodiac signs, this is the one with the widest range of sexual possibilities. Some Geminian women maintained that sex was very important to them in their relationships while others placed sex last on their list of priorities. Some strongly Geminian women admitted to leading a promiscuous existence (married or not), whereas others were completely monogamous. However, one theme did seem central to almost all Geminian women I spoke to: the need for change, growth, and expansion in a sexual relationship. Gemini women do not like routine and ritual. Sex to them is an organic process that should enrich the relationship and reflect its changing nature.

The Gemini woman changes her identity like her underwear—daily. Likewise the type of sexual experience she wants at any one time differs greatly. Sometimes she may feel withdrawn and reticent so she needs a lover to gently coax her into bed: sometimes she may want to play 'prostitute' and use the full gamut of her sexual skill to turn on her lover and herself: sometimes she was to 'talk dirty' and at others only bill and coo. Sometimes she likes to live dangerously by making love in the car, a plane, or in the bathroom during a dinner party. And then again she may delight in creating an evening of sexual magic—dinner, candlelight, soft music—the works. If sex can become a voyage of discovery opening up new areas of herself and her partner, the Geminian feels fulfilled. Sex to this sign involves the mind first, the emotions second, and the body last of all.

Romance, too, appeared immensely important to the Geminian woman. While her varying sexual stance can confuse a more consistent lover, who is never sure whether he's coming home to Madame Sin or the Ice Maiden, if he arrives clutching a bunch of pink roses he'll always be welcome. The more intellectual kind of Geminian may maintain she's a realist through and through—she doesn't need a man to make her life complete—but she's a romantic at heart. And like most Geminian ladies, she wants to experience a superior type of love, one that encompasses the physical, the emotional, and the cerebral—if not the spiritual.

There is a certain trend in some Geminian women to follow the route of the Virgo Siren (see pp.241–2). This kind of Geminian is highly sexually attractive to men. However, her sexuality is rarely instinctive. She has learned the value of sex appeal and found out how to 'sell' herself. She knows how to please men and, like Marilyn Monroe, only feels 'safe and secure' if she knows a man desires her. This kind of Gemini lady often has a coolness and sophistication about her that suggests there is a volcano waiting to erupt under the hands of the right man. But her passion is invariably only skin deep. Because this lady doesn't really trust men, she rarely lets then 'get to her'. While she may do very well for herself by marrying for money, power, and fame—sometimes all three—her heart is as hard as platinum. Indeed, the Geminian and her Virgoan cousin make some of the best call-girls in the Zodiac, and some of the greatest sex-symbols (Sophia Loren, Joan Collins, Raquel Welch, and Bo Derek are all Gemini-Virgo types).

Of course it is entirely possible for women of this sign to have a tender heart as well as abundant sex appeal. Yet there is a tendency for Geminians, like many airy women, to have a kind of contrived sexuality. And after making love many a Geminian female is left with a nagging feeling that there ought to be something more. Sometimes this is because the anticipation of sex is greater than the experience itself. But also because the Gemini tends to guard her deepest feelings: she never fully lets herself go. Sometimes lack of trust is combined with a feeling of guilt about sex—sex is 'dirty', not very nice—and this too prevents full union. Mercurial little girls are prone to picking up their mothers' attitudes to sex, and if these were negative, they invariably encounter inhibitions and problems in their adult sex lives. Fortunately, nowadays with the more open forum for sex, the Geminian has the opportunity to sort out any deeply-rooted problems.

The Gemini man is also prone to feeling guilty about his sexual feelings—no matter how 'normal' they may be. This sign, like Virgo, has a tendency to have a 'hole in the corner' attitude to sex. If the Mercurial little boy receives a reprimand for exploring his sexuality as a child, unlike the fiery or earthy child who might pass off the incident lightly, the idea that he has done something naughty remains ingrained on his psyche. Sometimes, in adult life, the Geminian man cannot feel free and easy about sex, especially with his long-term partner, because of his guilt feelings. Thus he may gain far more sexual satisfaction outside the marriage, sometimes through brief affairs and sometimes through call girls and prostitutes.

Like their female counterpart, the sexual range for the Gemini man is vast. Some lead very active sexual lives with one partner (or more) while others feel the 'whole thing' is extremely overrated. Also, like many Geminian women, Mr Gemini often finds sex in the mind works a great deal better than in the raw. 'I can make love 20 times a day in my head,' admitted one man with his Sun and Mercury in Gemini, 'but I have considerable difficulty raising the enthusiasm (or anything else) when the opportunity actually arises!'

The uninhibted Gemini man is usually sexually adventurous. His curiosity encourages him to try almost anything. This kind of Gemini is often an avid reader of 'girly' magazines at school, and with his Mercurial skills he may well have a 'little business' in the senior common room, selling prophylactics! While he may decline from indulging in any really kinky behaviour, 'straight' sex tends to become rather boring for this man. While he's unattached he'll probably sow his wild oats very liberally indeed. Threesomes and group sex often appeal to Geminians, as do voyeurism, the use of mirrors, and all types of pornography. The anonymous one-night stand is also tailor-made for Geminians.

Yet despite their need for novel experiences in all areas of life—including sex—most Geminians marry and become fathers, sometimes more than once. As I discussed earlier, some Geminian men adapt themselves well to long term relationships and remain entirely faithful, while others find monogamy impossible.

Like the Geminian female, if Mr Gemini's long-term partner is as open-minded and adventurous as he is, he is unlikely to get bored with her or his sex life. But if his lady is the type who lies on her back (and only on her back) the Geminian man is likely to take off after his roving eye. Indeed this man, like his Sagittarian opposite number, has a reputation for being a bit of a Don Juan. The source of the Geminian's lady-killing behaviour frequently lies in his restless desire for change and his dislike of commitment. But, the Geminian, like the Sagittarian, also relishes youth. And one of the ways he convinces himself that he is still young and attractive is by making conquest after conquest. Sometimes the older he gets, the worse he becomes. Just how sexually satisfied he is by his bed-hopping antics is debatable. And one wonders what he is trying to prove, and to whom.

Apart from the continual novelty the Geminian finds by changing partners frequently, he also escapes any of the deep emotional exchange that inevitably accompanies a sexual relationship of long standing. The Geminian not only fears the constraint of emotional commitment, but also what he will unleash if he opens up his emotional store-house. Sex and emotions do not go hand in glove with the Gemini man. Indeed sometimes he can be completely put off his sexual stroke by heavy emotional demands. Feeling sexually excited by a partner and attending to the physical demands of sex are quite enough for Mr Gemini without having to worry about whether he's being loving as well. And many a Geminian, even if he does love his partner, is quite mystified as to how men can combine the two in the sexual act. He often thinks those who say they do must be lying.

Mr Gemini can be a rather inconsistent lover. His appetite for sex varies considerably since he is more responsive to his mental senses than his physical ones. Mr Gemini can be aroused to greater sexual peaks by the accompaniment of erotic suggestion and fantasy than the mere sight of a nipple or two. Yet because the Geminian's mind is the centre of sexual activity, he is much more vulnerable to problems with his sexual mechanism. Communication breakdowns from the mind to the machinery happen far more to Mercurial individuals than to many other zodiac types.

If Mr Gemini has any doubts about his ability to perform, if he feels any pressure from his partner or guilt about his sexual needs, or even if he feels emotionally overpowered by his partner, his ability to function will be impaired. And no amount of physical stimulation will arouse him! Although the causes for impotence vary greatly from individual to individual, it is worth bearing in mind that the demise of sexual drive can be a form of passive anger. And since the Geminian man dislikes emotional excesses of any kind he may be more prone to impotence for this reason than any other. If he cannot bring himself to express his hostile feelings for his partner verbally he will communicate them instead by rejecting her sexually.

In keeping with the hermaphroditic theme of Gemini, a few Geminian men and women experience some ambiguity over their sexual identity. In some this manifests as bisexuality, in others as homosexuality, and in a few as transexuality or transvestisism. As with impotence, there are many possible causes for homosexuality or any other sexual aberration. But where Gemini is concerned, the curious nature of this sign, its tendency to play both actor and observer, the desire to explore all forms of communication including sexual—and from both sides—could well be contributory factors. One man with Mars in Gemini told me, 'I find sex the most powerful form of communication. In fact I can't really talk to a woman until I've made love to her. Although I prefer women, I have had [sexual] relationships with men.' Another with Sun in Gemini admitted, 'I have an inclination towards many sexual partners and bisexuality. Physically, I like rather boyish women.'

The Geminian prefers sex of the 'running buffet' variety rather than a four-course sit-down meal: the advantages being, that Mr and Ms Gemini are free to circulate and take a little bit of this and that (preferably nothing too indigestible) without being committed to the full menu. Fantasy, risk, and the unusual put the spice into sex that they crave; routine and the familiar depress their sexual taste buds. A tendency to opt for quantity rather than quality is a failing many of them share with the fire signs. And like the Arian and the Sagittarian, they need to develop their sensitivity to another's needs—emotional as well as sensory—to make for two-way gratification. Most Geminians also need to trust a little more to allow for emotional exchange as well as sexual. In this way the Geminians' gift for spontaneity, versatility, and experimentation can be enriched by tenderness, gentleness, and most important of all, love.

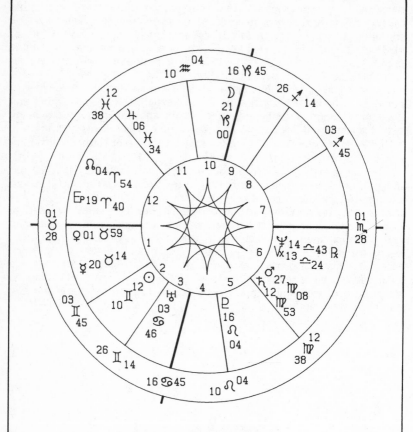

SUZI QUATRO

3 6 1950   3h 0 m 0s EST

PLACIDUS 42N20 83W3

PROFILE OF A GEMINI WOMAN
SUZI QUATRO

Observing Suzi Quatro emerge from the rehearsal room, it was difficult to associate this petite, fresh-faced, self-assured lady with the black leather-clad rock and roll singer renowned for her aggressive, raunchy performances. But then, she's a Gemini woman, and used to slipping in and out of different roles with the dexterity of a salamander. And in keeping with the Geminian thirst for change and diversity, Suzi was in the throes of a new career venture—taking the leading role of Annie Oakley in the stage musical **Annie Get Your Gun**.

Curiously, Suzi and the real Annie Oakley have several parallels in their lives. Like Annie, Suzi's life has been dominated by men, she has spent much of her time on the road, and despite her gutsy, no-holds-barred persona, she has a butter-soft centre. Also, like Annie, Suzi has three sisters and one brother.

Suzi was born and raised in Detroit, USA. Her (Italian) father was a professional musician and her (Hungarian) mother was a singer: 'Everybody plays an instrument in the family. We were all involved in bands together. I remember having music around right from when I was teeny.' At school, music was her best subject, and she was good at English. ('I have a love of words'); she also excelled at gym and enjoyed business courses. 'I wasn't really a great student—I was on the road by the time I was fifteen. I made a point of educating myself later on.' Suzi knew from the start that she wanted to be an entertainer: 'I didn't mind what, just as long as I was an entertainer . . . put me on stage and just try to get me back off again! That's the way I've always been. In my family everyone used to get up and do a song at each family gathering. We had a costume for every number . . . we were all hams. I guess that's where it all came from.'

In Suzi's chart the Moon rules the fourth 'house' of family-life, suggesting that she felt a great sense of belonging and connectedness to the family, and found home a secure and comfortable bastion against the outside world. The Moon itself is placed in Capricorn at the very top of the chart (on the Midheaven) indicating her mother was an important influence on Suzi's direction in life: her sense of values and her demeanour imprinted themselves firmly in Suzi's mind. But since the Moon forms a square 90° aspect to Neptune, and the Sun (a symbol, among many ideas, of the father) is square to Saturn (and Jupiter), some shadows are cast over Suzi's experience of 'mum' and 'dad'. Since Suzi came from a good Catholic background, the sense of discipline and the sound moral values she received are certainly expressions of the Sun-Saturn square: yet this aspect can also indicate over strictness and a subsequent feeling of inadequacy. The Moon-Neptune square can 'create' some fog over mother as a real individual as opposed to her image, and may 'cause' emotional miscommunications between mother and daughter. However, both these aspects have their positive side in that Sun-Saturn squares have a reputation for 'giving' the individual plenty of staying power and 'backbone' while the Moon-Neptune square boosts any artistic potential and indicates heightened sensitivity and receptivity to the aesthetic and the spiritual.

While Suzi maintains she was not an exceptional student, with Mercury rising to the Ascendant* she looks far from unintelligent. No doubt lack of motivation and a preference for music and entertaining combined to produce an academic shortfall. Also, by the time Suzi was fifteen, she was on the road with 'The Pleasure Seekers'. 'We started the band when I was fourteen—originally we were going to call it 'The Hedonist'. It wasn't the happiest of bands since we had the wrong mixture of people.' Amongst the group were two of Suzi's sisters (a Pisces and a Virgo) and another Gemini. 'It was Patty (the Pisces) who wanted an all-girl band—I didn't mind. We used to talk at cross purposes a lot of the time.' It is not unusual to find members of a family belonging to the same astrological Quality:† in Suzi's family, her two sisters, her father, and herself are all mutable signs, but different elements. While Suzi is a breezy Gemini, Patty and her father are hypersensitive Pisceans, and her other sister a finicky Virgo. Thus although they all share the mutable tendency to scatter and diversify, they each have a different perspective on the world and so tend to operate at cross purposes. Right from the start Suzi loved living out of a suitcase—a Utopian existence for a Geminian: 'I always wanted to be on the road and playing. To me performing was my life's blood. I never wanted to

*Mercury is also quintile Jupiter, and trine Mars and Saturn.

†Cardinal, fixed and mutable.

come home to Detroit. In many ways, the band was just like another family—a cocoon.' Many people with the Moon on the Midheaven work from home. In Suzi's case she not only worked with three members of her own family, but felt that the band was in itself another family—a cocoon. The presence of the Moon on the career point of the chart often indicates an individual who will come into contact with the public—someone who has a sense of what the people want, both of which are true of Suzi. Also her choice of 'Cradle' as a name for one of her groups is a highly Moony idea. Suzi spent seven years with 'The Pleasure Seekers'* playing all over the United States. Then in 1971, she was 'spotted' by the entrepreneur Mickey Most, who brought her over to England. 'I was very homesick at first since I had none of my family or any of my friends around, though I never thought of going back. I was determined to make it.' By the time she was twenty-three she had her first number one hit, 'Can the Can'. She had also met the man she was eventually to marry.

'I formed a band about a month before the record came out. I auditioned for players and all these men turned up—not a single woman. So I chose the best players—one of whom was Lennie. We certainly made a great impression on each other when we met. We started talking and talked for hours, and played music into the night. I fell in love with his guitar playing and he fell in love with my bass playing. He decided it was the band he wanted to work with—immediately—and I decided he was the guitar player I wanted in my band. Within two weeks were were in love.' Since neither Suzi nor Len (a fiery Sagittarian and another mutable type) are the sort to 'hang around' once they've made a decision, marriage was the next step. But they had counted without Suzi's image as a rock star; and the powers that be considered marriage would hamper her growing popularity. 'Yes, it was disappointing—we'd even bought the ring and got the papers—but we lived together instead, and when it was OK all round, we got married [1976].'

Suzi and Len have a strong, immensely happy marriage. They work together and live almost 'in each other's pockets'. Ironically, Sagittarius and Gemini jointly carry the worst reputation in the zodiac for durability in relationships. But then, Sun signs are only part of the whole astrological picture. Though Suzi has her Sun in Gemini, her Mercury, Venus and Ascendant are all placed in the 'fixed' and eminently stable sign of Taurus, and her Moon is in yet another sober and practical sign, Capricorn. Len is less earthed than Suzi, having only the Moon in Taurus, and he is extremely fiery; thus they provide a good balance for one another. 'I think Geminis find

*'The Pleasure Seekers' and 'The Hedonist' have a distinctly Taurean flavour about them.

tremendous fascination for Sagittarians. I love Lennie's verve for life, his passion, his sense of humour and his sense of right and wrong. We complement each other. He has things I don't, and vice versa.' Suzi, with her Moon and Venus in earth signs, clearly wants security and stability in a relationship. Since her own family had been close and enjoyed a strong sense of unity, she sought a similar experience in her own marriage. 'We've never had a year when I thought we'd split up. We don't argue much. But I'd say you have to work at a marriage.' One of the classic problems with marriages in which the husband apparently takes the back seat is that he often grows to resent his position and feels his masculinity threatened. Not so with Len. While he may not be the household name that Suzi is, in the music business Len is highly regarded. 'Len is very sure of himself—that's one of the things I really admire and love about him. He lets me be the star, but he's always the man. When we met I could see my many changes fitting nicely under his wing.' With Scorpio on the cusp of her seventh 'house' of relationships, a tendency to attract powerful partners and experience tremendous highs and lows in relationships is suggested. In many ways the partner becomes the agent of psychological and emotional growth—a process that is rarely achieved without some pain and difficulty. Suzi's seventh 'house' also describes her ideal partner as a Scorpio-Pluto type. While Len is a Sun Sagittarian, he has his Mars conjunct Pluto. Although Suzi considers Len and herself to be a 'superb match', like any couple their life together is not entirely free from problems.

When Suzi was twenty-nine, she and Len decided to start a family. While the sceptic might view the thirty borderline to be a natural time for life assessment, astrologers look to the return of Saturn to its original place (at around twenty-nine) to be a period of reflection and readjustment. The year of the Saturn return can be one of great achievement or great difficulty—sometimes both. Twenty-nine proved a difficult year for Suzi because she failed to become pregnant—a situation that remained unchanged throughout 1980. Conversely, her career was soaring: her concerts were sell outs, she had another hit song, and she was much in demand for acting roles after her success in the American TV series **Happy Days**—a show for which she had been booked two weeks and remained for fifteen episodes.

Finally, in early 1981, Suzi became pregnant. Yet the happiness was short lived. 'At the stroke of midnight on New Year's Eve [1980/81] we heard a huge crash. The Christmas tree had fallen down. It seemed like an omen. And it was. I had a miscarriage the following May when I was three months pregnant. I was absolutely devastated. I went through hell.' Like most women who lose a baby during pregnancy, the emotional trauma that follows is truly dreadful; a crisis for which one is entirely unprepared. For Suzi, the blow was that much more cruel, having waited so long to become pregnant in the first place. To make matters worse, the emotional roller-coaster, anger, and sense of let down that follow a miscarriage nearly always rebounds onto the partner, regardless how understanding he is or how much love exists between them. Thus Suzi and Len both underwent a considerable emotional crisis and much strain at this time. Happily, Suzi became pregnant again the following December and she gave birth to their daughter, Laura, in September of 1982.

Astrologically, problems regarding children and pregnancy are principally the province of the fifth 'house', and stressful angles between Pluto and the Moon or Venus. In Suzi's chart, Pluto is placed in the fifth house, suggesting (among many ideas) that this planet's life and death properties and its process of transformation are linked to childbirth and child-rearing. Suzi also has Saturn placed in this area of the horoscope, which further indicates difficulties and delay in the creative process—especially since the Sun forms a 90° square to Saturn. Of course, Suzi did achieve a second successful pregnancy, and two years later her son, Richard, was born.

Suzi's fifth 'house' Pluto also has much to do with her sexy rock and roll image. The fifth 'house' covers creativity as a whole, and thus involves the creative aspect of love and sex that can ultimately engender new life as well as creative self-expression. For almost twenty years of her professional life Suzi has expressed herself on stage in an overtly sexual manner. Her tight-fitting black leather gear and her gravelly voice are hallmarks of her style. In a sense, Suzi has found an ideal channel for Pluto's sexual energy here, since an undirected fifth 'house' Pluto can emerge as sexual repression or sexual compulsiveness!

Pluto's transformative nature can also be seen in the way Suzi has developed her talents, moving from hard rock to straight acting roles. As a Sun Gemini, changing images is second nature to Suzi, but the process of becoming, of increasing in 'stature', is Plutonic in essence. Suzi's part in **Happy Days** led to many other acting offers, but since she was heavily committed to bookings as a rock star she was unable to accept most of them. One role she did manage to fit in, between 'gigs' and babies, was as a murderess in the TV series **Dempsey and Makepeace**—another piece of Plutonic type-casting.

Although Suzi is Geminian enough to have lots of strings to her bow—or rather her guitar—she hasn't fallen into the Mercurial trap of dissipating her talents. Suzi has her strongly earthy content to thank for this. Her Taurus Ascendant, Mercury, and Venus show a level-headed, security-oriented approach to life, as well as artistic sensibility. Suzi certainly has the Taurean vocal chords and the musicality associated with this sign. Yet she can also draw and paint: 'I design my own greeting cards. They're usually done on a childhood theme. I love to say my thoughts through a child's mouth'—echoes of the Geminian Peter Pan! 'Then again there's a very serious side to my nature. Lennie sometimes calls me "the hanging judge" because I've got such a strong moral streak. Almost unrelenting.' This tendency can be related to Suzi's Capricorn Moon on the Midheaven—a sign of strong moral principles and sometimes a distinct lack of mercy—and the Sun-Saturn square. Suzi also holds a down-to-earth but far-seeing attitude to her career. 'I've never been out of work. I've always wanted to branch out by you have to do it at the right time in your career. When the rock and roll thing is happening you want to take it for all it's worth. You don't just stop and say, "Why don't I do this instead?" because that's really dumb!'

Suzi's Virgoan Mars adds even more weight to the earthy content of her chart. Not only is her Mars in this fussy, perfectionist sign, but also in the Virgoan sixth 'house' of work. 'Yes, I'm an obsessively hard-worker. An absolute perfectionist. I want everyone to think that I'm good at whatever I'm doing—always. I want the applause but I can take criticism, as long as its valid and constructive.' Suzi displays many of the qualities of the Virgoan workaholic (she even went back to work ten days after her son was born, despite having undergone major surgery! 'I'd say I was determined, but not ruthless. If someone asks me to climb a mountain, I'll say yes. Then when I'm half-way up I'll think what the hell am I doing up here?' While she loves being a wife and mother ('I want to have another baby before I'm forty') Suzi would never give up work to become a full-time **haus-frau**. Unlike many Geminian women, she is very clear about her needs and desires. While she may want to do 'everything', she could never be a wife and mother at the expense of her career.

Despite the bubbly, confident exterior, Suzi has plenty of sensitivity* some of which is expressed through her writing and music. (Both she and Lennie work on all their music and lyrics together; they've also written a screen-play.) 'I write a lot of poetry. There's a very soft, vulnerable side to my nature, but I wear my vulnerability inside. It's not good to show it to the world because people stamp on you though I'm told it comes through anyway.' While her inner vulnerability is undoubtedly there, I wouldn't like to be at the receiving end of Suzi's wrath or indignation—'No one will ever step on me.' Small is beautiful and all too easy to underestimate in Suzi's case!

1986 provided Suzi with the opportunity to combine her singing

*Venus rising in Taurus. Moon square Neptune; Sun trine Neptune.

and acting talents in the role of 'sharp-shootin'', tough but tender, Annie Oakley. Her success in this stage musical could well be a watershed in her career. With transiting Pluto trining Jupiter* a metamorphosis on both a career and personal level is indicated. It may well be that Suzi's hard rock image will totally fade away to be replaced with a more mature, far softer one; and while she may continue to perform as a singer, she will find the pull of her career as an actress far greater.

Suzi is far from being the typical Geminian discontent. She might enjoy the sight of a rainbow but she'll never expect to find a crock of gold at the end of it. This Geminian butterfly wears a pair of sturdy Taurean boots: boots that were made for walking firmly to their destination. And sometimes for stamping!

Note for Astrologers: (1) Suzi's birth time was given between 3 and 7 a.m. After seeing Suzi, comparing her chart with others' in her family and relevant transits and progressions, roughly 2 Taurus rising worked best.

(2) In 1973, when Suzi had her first hit and she met Len, progressed Sun was conjunct Uranus, progressed Venus was sextile Mars; transiting Saturn was conjunct the Sun, transiting Jupiter was square the Ascendant and transiting Pluto was square Uranus. In 1976—the year of marriage—transiting Neptune opposed the Sun (!), transiting Uranus squared Venus, transiting Saturn was in the fifth house while Jupiter transited Taurus. In 1981, when Suzi had a miscarriage, progressed MC opposed Pluto, progressed Ascendant squared Saturn and transiting Saturn squared Uranus. In 1986 (**Annie Get Your Gun**) progressed Sun was conjunct the IC, Jupiter returned to its original position, transiting Neptune opposed Uranus and transiting Pluto trined Jupiter.

*Jupiter is involved in a 'T'-square with the Sun and Saturn, thus when one 'leg' of the 'T'-square is triggered off, the others are also drawn in.

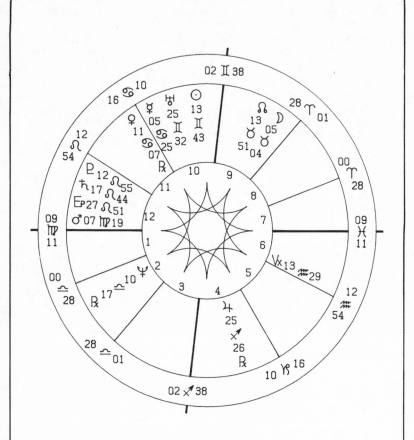

BOB CHAMPION

4 6 1948   11h 10m Os GMT

PLACIDUS 51N7 OE16

PROFILE OF A GEMINI MAN

BOB CHAMPION

Bob Champion was born with a
name he was destined to live up
to: Robert, or Hreodboarht, is
derived from two Old English
words—**hrothi**, 'fame', and
berhta, 'bright'. Champion, of
course, speaks for itself. Indeed,
there have been few stories over
the past decade—possibly
longer—to rival Bob's chronicle of
heroism. As both a sportsman—one of the world's top
jump jockeys—and an individual,
he has triumphed over cancer
against considerable odds, and
few will forget that remarkable

day in April 1981 when he and his equally courageous mount,
Aldaniti, won one of the world's most dangerous races, The Grand
National.

Horses were in the Champion blood: seven generations of Bob's
family had been professional huntsmen, including his father.
However, initially Bob was frightened of horses and preferred
exercising the hounds. As a child he spent most of his time on and
around the neighbourhood farms, often in the company of his
younger sister, Mary. He and Mary had, and still have, 'a volatile
relationship': Bob would tease her dreadfully and they fought like
tigers at times. Bob's early life was 'ordinary' and uneventful. His
father was the more dominant parent, although his mother 'was
pretty strong too'. Bob was 'average' at school, but clearly not cut out
for the academic life. After a reluctant start, by the time he was nine
Bob had decided he wanted to become a jockey. However, he was
still unconfident when it came to jumping and had to resort to a few
underhand tactics at times. On hunts, a family friend used to take his
horse over the hedges and ditches for him. Eventually he gained the
confidence to mount the obstacles himself. Not that Bob was a
coward. Friends and family considered him a stubborn, determined
little boy, quiet but spunky. The television sports commentator
Derek Thompson, who was a childhood friend of Bob's, said of him:

'He was very shy, but he had a killer streak in him and a hell of a temper at times.' While his parents supported his wish to become a jockey, they felt he should have a trade to fall back on in case he didn't make it. Since Bob had a flair for mechanics it was decided he should study engineering; so at the age of fifteen he entered Trowbridge College, Wiltshire, and a year later he left with a diploma in engineering.

Bob's chart contains some classic aspects for a sportsman. Mars, the planet of action, had just risen at birth and occupies the favoured Gauquelin position for sportsmen.* Mars forms a strong and even more energizing square 90° aspect to the Sun and a harmonious sextile 60° aspect to Mercury—the planet of travel and communication. It is Bob's strong Mars that 'gives' him a hell of a temper and plenty of spunk! The Sun is also powerful in the chart: it is situated in the tenth 'house' of the horoscope conjunct the Midheaven—a placing that shows great vitality and strength. The Sun and Moon, as major masculine and feminine symbols, represent (among several ideas) mother and father. Bob's Sun, with its square to Mars, suggests he found his father a forceful, possibly domineering man while his Moon in Taurus, with its more harmonious aspects, indicates he had an easier relationship with his mother and saw her as the typical earth-mother. However, since there are four planets altogether (Sun, Uranus, Mercury, and Jupiter) in the fourth and tenth 'houses' the parental picture is multi-coloured and confusing to say the least. Suffice to say that both parents emerge as strong characters in Bob's life, although I expect his mother's influence was more covert and ultimately more powerful.†

It would be difficult for an astrologer to pinpoint horse-riding **per se** in Bob's chart. Sagittarius is the sign traditionally associated with horses and sport in general, and though Bob does have his Jupiter in this fire sign this factor alone is not enough. There is certainly a feeling of action, speed, and good-sportsmanship in his chart, and by applying a finer astrological technique Jupiter becomes part of a powerful configuration with the Moon, Mercury, and Uranus, thus uniting the principle of action and daring with all things Jupiterian—including horses.§ However, I suspect that since riding was a family pursuit it provided the most natural avenue for Bob's

*Michel Gauquelin in his extensive research of astrology (thirty years) found the diurnal positions of some planets (i.e. their placing in the 'houses') to be of significance. In the case of great sportsmen, Mars predominated just above the horizon (in the 12th 'house') and just past the MC (the 9th 'house').

†See **Notes for Astrologers** (1).

§See **Note for Astrologers** (2).

sporty talents: he was an excellent pole-vaulter and cross-country-runner at school, and at the age of twelve he took part in (and completed) a forty-mile hike across the Yorkshire moors. Uranus in the tenth 'house' of profession shows that he could have made a living out of his engineering abilties, and his Virgoan Mars would certainly come in handy for any fiddly wire work. In keeping with the precise and fussy nature of Virgo, Bob is a perfectionist; however, he is not infallible. A few years ago, impatient to have his Ansafone installed, he preempted the telephone engineer and wired it up himself; but instead of recording any messages for him, the machine picked up half the village's telephone conversations!

One of the main attractions of going to Trowbridge was that Bob could stay on his Uncle Arthur's farm; and Uncle Arthur kept point-to-point horses. 'Every morning I rode out before going to college. I'd only been there a few months when I entered for my first point-to-point. It was a bit of a disaster as I fell off at the last fence.' By the age of nineteen it was clear that Bob was far too good for point-to-points, so with some encouragement from a friend in August 1967 he became an amateur jockey with Toby Balding's team at Fyfield, Hampshire. Six years later, after a year's freelancing, he became stable jockey to Josh Gifford. This was to prove a long, happy, and fruitful association. One of Gifford's most prized horses was Aldaniti, which Bob rode on his (Aldaniti's) racecourse debut at Ascot and many more races besides. Bob was impressed with Aldaniti and was convinced he would one day win the Grand National. Yet despite being one of the most promising chasers in the country, Aldaniti was accident prone and was all too often being sent back to the stud for rest. Throughout the 1970s Bob steadfastly built up his reputation as one of Britain's top jockeys, and despite some severe problems with his weight, his future looked secure. Then in 1979 his career as a jockey and his life hung in the balance.

On 11 May 1979 Bob was kicked by a horse he was riding at Stratford. 'Fury Boy didn't make the last fence . . . I was thrown, and just as I was about to get the reins he kicked out with his hind legs and got me right in the balls.' Although in considerable pain, Bob managed to remount Fury Boy and finish the race. While he anticipated some discomfort and swelling after the accident, Bob was a little concerned when two months later one of his testicles still remained numb and swollen ('not that it interfered with any of my activities!'). He might have continued to ignore this longer had he not been prompted by a passing romantic encounter with a vet to seek immediate medical advice. A few days later a tumour was diagnosed. The prospect of cancer was dreadful to Bob. He assumed all cancers were fatal. Thus some hours after hearing his 'death sentence' he considered suicide. 'You don't hear about too many people recovering from cancer and that [suicide] seemed the quickest way out. I thought I would jump out of the window but every time I looked out and saw how far it was to the ground I changed my mind.' Bob went into the Royal Marsden hospital the next day for the first of two operations and the beginning of an ordeal that was to last many months. Having come to terms with the removal of one testicle, Bob was faced with the news that the tumour was malignant; worse still the cancer had spread into his lymph glands. The prognosis was grim. Untreated, he had eight to twelve months left to live, with chemotherapy he had a 75 per cent chance of survival—but he would be unable to ride. Considering the odds sounded 'pretty hopeful' Bob agreed to go ahead with the treatment, although the prospect of losing all his hair and being unable to have children was a 'cruel blow'.

Bob spent five months in and out of hospital from August 1979 to January 1980. They were the most gruelling months of his life. He underwent six painful, humiliating, and extremely unpleasant courses of chemotherapy and at one point he almost died of septicaemia (7 October). Throughout this period one thought sustained him: 'I had an obsession about winning the Grand National on Aldaniti in March 1980. I would lie in bed night after night believing he would win and the thought of anyone else riding him was too painful to consider. He was my ride and I was going to be there to ride him.' But those hopes seemed dashed to pieces when, at the end of November, Bob 'on leave' from hospital saw Aldaniti almost crippled in a race at Sandown. It looked as though he would never race again. Back once more in hospital, Bob came near to giving up. He refused his drugs and, free from his drip, wandered down to the children's ward. 'It was a very important lesson in my life. There was I moaning and groaning ... thinking only of myself, and downstairs those poor little kids were going through the same thing without complaining. Seeing them was the turning point for me. If they could take the treatment then so could I.'

On 31 January 1980 tests showed that the malignant tumour in his chest had gone. He was free to leave. The only clouds ahead lay in the stress attached to the monthly check-ups. By February he started to train again and three months later he was steeple-chasing in America.

Cancer remains one of the most baffling of diseases. There is no one definite cause for the various forms the disease takes, although its emergence (in some forms) seems linked to stress—Cancer is often diagnosed after an individual has experienced emotional or psychological crises. Astrologically, Pluto has most in common with the idea of cancer. This planet is associated with all things underground especially the subconscious; its effects only become manifest after some considerable time. Individuals with Pluto linked to the personal planets have a tendency to repress emotions—particularly anger—which can cause blockages in the psyche. Sometimes these blocks can work their way out through physical illness—like cancer. As a sprightly Sun Gemini, Bob would not seem to be the ideal candidate for stress-related conditions, especially since he is renowned for his hot temper. But both Gemini and Virgo (his rising sign) are highly-strung signs and prone to worry. More to the point is the placing of Pluto in the hidden twelfth 'house' of Bob's horoscope.* This combination suggests that whenever Bob encountered emotions or urges he couldn't understand, deal with, or express, he would throw them into his twelfth 'house' dustbin where they built up and 'fermented'. But instead of turning into good compost, which they might have done had they been consciously recognized, accepted, and integrated, they leaked out undetected and turned his system into a time bomb. Pluto, of course, also represents death and rebirth; and in the process of fighting cancer, and literally coming to death's door, Bob came through a renewed man. Here the helpful contact from the Sun to Pluto and Saturn would have provided him with as much inner resolution as outer strength.

Bob knew he had won his long and arduous fight against cancer by February of 1981 when three days of extensive tests proved he was all-clear. During the same month he rode Aldaniti to victory in the Whitbread Handicap—it was Aldaniti's first race after his year long recuperation period. Bob's cherished hopes of riding Aldaniti in the Grand National looked attainable, if only Aldaniti could remain accident free. On 4 April what in 1979 had seemed such an impossible dream became a sensational reality as Bob romped home in the Grand National on Aldaniti—clear winners by a good two lengths. It was a dramatic and emotional victory, the triumphant seal on a courageous and incredible battle by both man and beast.

Bob and Aldaniti shared a common destiny in the Grand National, and both clearly had a tremendous struggle to get there. With such links in real life there should also be some astrological connections. And there are. Aldaniti's Ascendant-Descendant axis—the most sensitive and 'personal' in the chart—falls exactly on Bob's Jupiter-Uranus opposition. This is a highly-charged and successful link between them. And there are many more.† Aldaniti also had his own

---

*Pluto is also conjunct Saturn, suggesting even more of a tendency to suppression.

†Aldaniti's Sun is conjunct Bob's Mercury. Aldaniti's Jupiter is sextile Bob's Jupiter and trine his Uranus. Bob's Saturn and Pluto are conjunct Aldaniti's IC. Bob's vertex is conjunct Aldaniti's MC.

Plutonic 'cross' to bear,* and with the Sun in square 90° aspect to volatile Uranus it is no wonder he was accident prone!

While Aldaniti and Bob seemed made for each other, the same cannot be said for Bob's partners in romance. Bob is and always has been an extremely popular man—especially with women. With his Geminian Sun and his Cancerian Mercury he has an irresistible combination of Puckish charm and bashful naïvety. Also, with Mars on his Ascendant in 60° sextile aspect to Venus and square the Sun, he's a physically ardent man! But Bob, like any plain-speaking Yorkshire lad, cannot afford to go soft and mushy-eyed over women. (Apparently one of his favourite sayings was, 'Women ain't people'!) His chart, however, tells a different story. With Pisces on the cusp of his relationship 'house' and Venus contacting Neptune, Bob is clearly one of the great romantics at heart and tremendously idealistic about women. He adores them but cannot deal with them as real people. From his late teens he had a constant stream of willing and beautiful ladies in attendance, but his relationships were notoriously tempestuous. He locked one of his girlfriends in the car boot during an argument. When she was eventually released she chased him round the stable yard with a pitchfork.

Six months after his Grand National win, Bob married a girl he'd known 'off and on for some time'—Jo (a Sun Libran). Within sixteen months Bob discovered he was going to be a father. He and Jo were jubilant. The discovery put pay to the doctor's gloomy predictions that he would never have his own child. But when Michael was born (3 November 1983) it looked as though fate had dealt them a cruel blow. 'When Michael was born, the only way I can put it is that he was wired up wrong. The valves to his heart and lungs weren't going where they should. It's very rare. He had a long operation and we went through a very worrying three weeks. The main problem was getting his body to work on its own once he was taken off the life-support system.' But Michael, like his father, was a plucky little chap and pulled through his ordeal. Now he's a healthy active five-year-old—and he loves horses!

Crises do curious things for relationships: they either draw the couple closer or drive them apart. Within seven months of Michael's birth Jo left Bob. 'I tried to get her back, but it was no good—she had another feller.' Divorce followed two years later in the early summer of 1986, and after a lengthy legal tussle Bob was allowed access to Michael for four days a month. Clearly the divorce and the separation from his son affected him deeply; but as with everything else in his life, he fought the situation with courage and stoic resolve.

*Pluto is square Aldaniti's Ascendant-Descendant axis.

Neptune is rarely the best of planets to have involved with the relationship 'house', especially when it is linked by a 'hard' angle to Venus. Over-expectation is one manifestation of this combination; disappointment, deception, and betrayal are others. It is also possible that with perfectionist Virgo rising, Bob is over critical of others, especially the women in his life, which they find difficult to put up with in the long term. Jonathan Powell commented in the book he co-wrote with Bob (**Champions Story**, Gollancz, 1981), 'At home Bob was fanatical about tidiness. He would insist that his girl-friends kept his rooms immaculate and spotless at all times . . . One newspaper thrown carelessly on the floor was enough to annoy him. Sometimes, at dinner parties, he would polish the table between courses and usually he ensured that all the washing up was completed before coffee was served.' Of course, Sun Gemini men do not have the best of long-distance records where marriage is concered, and I suspect, in keeping with his restless, mutable nature and his optimistic Jupiter, he'll take the plunge again. But hopefully not again and again . . . !

While Bob has achieved much in his life, like many Geminians he is not an ambitious man and is remarkably fluid about his future direction. While he 'works twenty-four hours a day at being a trainer' (he has his own stables) he also manages to attend many functions for his cancer fund and he travels abroad frequently. When asked what he'd most like to do now, he replied somewhat dourly: 'I'd like to go to a desert island where there isn't a soul and get thoroughly bored for a week!' Somehow I don't think being bored to death is the answer to Bob's musings, especially after he's shown such a redoubtable grasp on life. True Champions always live to fight another day.

Note for Astrologers: (1) The tenth 'house' is usually where mother is located. While Bob's father would seem to be the ideal candidate for the Sun-Mars square and the Uranus-Jupiter opposition, mother cannot be entirely ruled out. Her influence was likely to be covert because the Moon forms a square aspect to Pluto hidden away in the twelfth.

(2) In Bob's ninth harmonic chart, there is a powerful grand cross with the Moon in opposition to Mercury exactly squared by a tight Jupiter-Uranus opposition from the 9th to 3rd 'houses' respectively. The ninth harmonic is sometimes referred to as 'the fruit to the tree'—the 'fruit' represents the completion of what the 'tree' has to offer. In other words this harmonic chart shows the life's purpose. In Bob's case the dramatic and challenging combination of these four planets describe speed of movement, inspired leaps of faith and tremendous effort and will. Also interesting in the ninth harmonic is Mars in Pisces opposition Saturn in Virgo from the twelfth to sixth 'houses' respectively.

(3) Relevant progressions and transits are as follows. In 1979, the year his

fight against cancer began, the progressed Ascendant conjoined the 2nd 'house' cusp, the MC squared the 2nd-8th axis, and the vertex conjoined the 8th 'house' cusp; transiting Saturn in Virgo was conjunct his Mars on the day cancer was confirmed and proceeded to transit his Ascendant and square his other mutable planets (including the Sun) over the following eighteen months. On the day of the Grand National the Sun, Moon, Venus, and Mars closely sextiled his Sun, transiting Neptune conjoined his Jupiter and opposed Uranus. His son's birth coincided with Uranus squaring Bob's Mars-Ascendant and Jupiter opposing his Sun. When Bob's wife left him in 1984, transiting Uranus opposed his Sun.

CANCER

22 June – 22 July

LOONY LOVERS AND MELANCHOLY MOON BABES

CANCER
LOONY LOVERS AND MELANCHOLY
MOON BABES

IMAGINE yourself on a deserted sea-shore: above, the night sky is blue-black; clouds scud across the face of the moon, which at one moment appears as an elusive, ghostly spectre, then all at once as a vivid, luminescent sphere. We are in Cancer territory: an intensely private haven where experience and feelings, the ephemeral and the transcendent eclipse the mundane and the gross. This potent imagery of the sea and the mysterious, commanding presence of the moon is peculiar to Cancer, a sign of strange inconsistencies, rich imagination and deep, often inexplicable, yearnings.

Like all the water signs, Cancerians are experts at camouflage. Their sensitive natures are usually well hidden behind a bravado front, or at least an impenetrable one; indeed, the more buoyant and tough a Crab's façade, invariably the softer and more vulnerable his inner core. This sign, like Pisces, finds the world a hard and unremitting place; but unlike the Fish, who cannot survive out of his watery depths, the Crab has adapted himself to the rigours and demands of terra firma. Yet he remains essentially a creature of the sea and as such is attuned to the ever-changing currents of his feelings and the cyclical nature of his psychological depths.

Cancer is often considered a delicate sign: the female is thought to be fragile and helpless, and the male anything but robust or resilient. However, one look at tennis star Virginia Wade or five times Mr Universe Arnold Schwarzenegger (Mercury, Venus, and Ascendant in Cancer) soon puts pay to this idea. Cancerians come in all shapes and sizes and varying degrees of physical fitness and strength. Yet behind the myth of Cancers' weakness there is a grain of truth. Cancerians are emotionally and psychologically super-sensitive creatures, and if their emotional equilibrium is upset, their health tends to suffer—they're great ones for eating for comfort. But as far as their actual physique is concerned, Cancerians are usually remarkably tough.

Crabs of both sexes can be extremely attractive and sensual—if a little on the voluptuous side. They often have expressive, limpid eyes (which can be highly sensitive to strong sunlight) and a luminous quality about the skin. Round faces and large heads are further common features of this sign, characteristics which can make many Cancerians appear rather out of proportion. Crabs are also some of the most ungainly movers in the Zodiac, and only a minority scale the sartorial heights!

In many ways Cancerians are more unfathomable and enigmatic than Scorpios. Since Scorpio is an extreme sign—these individuals love and hate with a vengeance that is only too apparent—even if you don't know why you're in their bad books, at least you know you are: Cancerians, on the other hand, disguise their feelings and motives like chameleons change their colours (and for the same reason), and they rarely allow anyone access to their real opinions and perceptions.

One gets a small insight into Cancer's nature from the behaviour and habitat of the crab, their crustaceous symbol. Spider crabs, for instance, are covered in hook-like projections which pick up bits of sea weed and shore-life, so they scuttle around in camouflage like mishapen heaps of sea-side flotsam. The hermit crab has no shell of his own, but hides in old shells of other crustacea and even bits of old boxes! Cancerians often feel safer and more secure in 'borrowed plumes'; consequently, this sign is noted for its tendency to adapt other people's ideas, habits and life styles for their own. The need for a protective shelter to retreat into in times of danger is not only a characteristic of the crab, but also the tortoise, which was a symbol for Cancer in ancient Babylon.

Crabs have no skeleton: with the exception of the hermit variety, their soft, immensely vulnerable body is protected by its own shell. The shell cannot grow along with the crab so every so often it is discarded to reveal another, larger one. When the time comes for the old 'skin' to be shed, the crab retires to a dark hole. Under the protection of the dark, the crab takes in water to expand the new shell before it hardens, and only when he is fully 'armour-plated' does he return to sea life. The Cancerian, like the crab, is constantly modifying and reshaping himself and his world view; yet this is not an abstract process, but one (in keeping with the symbolism of water) aided by his feelings and senses. Periods of quiet, a retreat from the dissonant world outside, is essential for Cancerians' psychological health. And if they cannot find the time and space to be apart, they bury themselves in a black mood instead!

Although without their shells crabs make easy prey, if one of their limbs is damaged or lost it invariably grows again—often larger than before. Aside from evoking thoughts of the many-headed Hydra—who grew three heads for every one she lost—which has a small place in the mythological roots of Cancer, the analogy here is that little of Cancer's experience is lost or rendered useless: he uses every situation, especially the most painful ones, to develop and strengthen himself.

In a similar vein, the pearl—a Cancerian precious stone—is made up of layer upon layer of pearl that the oyster creates in order to soothe the pain of the foreign object in his shell. Suffering produces valuable growth for Cancer.

One last point before dispensing with crabs. Baby crabs, or zoea as they are known, do not resemble the adult at all: they look like tiny number 6s. Placed on their sides, one on top of the other, two little zoea accurately resemble Cancer's glyph ♋.

The sphinx is one of the less familiar, ancient symbols for Cancer. The Egyptian sphinx, the crumbling remains of which can still be seen on the banks of the River Nile, is, like many a Cancerian, a complete enigma. Although it is the Egyptian sphinx that is associated with this sign, in a roundabout way, the Greek sphinx also has connections with Cancer. In Greek legend, the sphinx was a monster with the head and breasts of a woman and the body of a lion who had been sent to plague the city of Thebes. The sphinx devoured any passers-by who failed to answer two cryptic riddles. Oedipus answered them both, upon which the sphinx committed suicide. Oedipus couldn't be a more appropriate figure for Cancer, since he married his mother (and killed his father!). And, of course, an aspect of Freud's psychoanalytic theory, the oedipal complex (the desire to remove one's father and appropriate one's mother), takes its name from this legend.

Sadly, the constellation of the Crab is the most inconspicuous in the heavens and contains only a few stars. However, in keeping with Cancer's secretive nature, astronomers have hypothesized that a number of the Crab's stars could well have been swallowed up in the seas of space. Yet Cancer is by no means inconspicuous from other astronomic viewpoints. The summer solstice in the northern hemisphere occurs when the sun reaches 0° Cancer. For three days after this, the sun remains at maximum latitudinal elevation. To ancient cultures this cosmic standstill was one of the most significant and magical occasions of the year; consequently, many religious festivals were celebrated at this time. Indeed, the ancient Akkadians named this position 'The Northern Gate of the Sun', whilst to the Chaldeans it was 'The Gate of Men'.

But by far the most illuminating symbol for Cancer is its ruling planet, the Moon. There is a direct link between the Moon and this sign since many sea creatures (including crabs) reflect the lunar cycle in their sexual behaviour and their procreative process, and of course the moon affects the ebb and flow of the tides. In ancient cultures the moon was seen as the instrument of fertilization of the earth and of women—not just because the female's menstrual cycle mirrored that of the moon. In some societies a man was considered entirely superfluous for making babies, his only function being to rupture the hymen to allow a moonbeam to enter. It was thought that all a woman had to do to become pregnant was to bare her belly to the full moon. Thus it's not surprising that moon cults dominated primitive societies. The moon was felt to be fundamental to man's survival and the continuation of life.

Cancer is full of maternal symbolism—some even consider Cancer's glyph to represent the breasts themselves—so perhaps an excursion into lunar myths and symbols is justified.

In ancient times both the moon and the sun were seen as the most important cosmic influences on man, and their respective gods and goddesses reflected the powerful life-giving properties of these bodies. In the zodiac, the Moon and Sun rule consecutive signs of Cancer and Leo—the latter exemplifying solar (masculine) principles of strength, leadership, organization, and autocracy, and the former the lunar (feminine) themes of reflection, sensibility, fecundity, and nurture. For some thousands of years now, societies the world over have largely followed solar principles and in the process suppressed feminine ideas—sometimes to the point of extinction: the infamous witch hunts of the Middle Ages, when an estimated 9 million 'witches' were murdered is a case in point. Our current Gregorian calendar is based on the solar year which replaced one formed from lunar months. Consequently, a return to lunar values has been long overdue and this century has seen the beginning of an upswing to the feminine.

But back in the proverbial mists of time, the cult of the Moon Goddess and her role as the Great Mother held sway. However, since nothing in myth ever seems straightforward, the moon deity was not always a woman. In the most ancient cultures of all it was the moon god who took precedence over all others and it was only with the rise of solar worship and the transference of some aspects of fertilization to a sun god that the transition to moon goddess

took place. The solar myth of death and resurrection (see Leo pp.192–3),
which mirrored the disappearance of the sun each day, was originally related
to the moon's three-day evanescence every month. During the transition
from moon god to goddess, many of the moon deities like Ishtar, Isis-Net,
and Artemis were thought to be both male and female. Gradually, the moon
goddess became more identified with fecundity and motherhood rather than
fertilization **per se**, although in later religions an offshoot of her original all-
powerful self resurfaced with the concept of the moon goddess and her
consort/son. The goddess' consort, like earlier moon gods and later solar
heroes, died and was reborn. With her son now taking over aspects of death
and resurrection, the moon goddess became immortal: she was the heavenly
representative of all women, the eternal feminine. She was Magna Mater,
Mara, Mary, mother of God. Although it might be viewed as heretical by
some, the Virgin Mary is a direct link with the moon goddess: her son, Jesus
Christ, like all solar heroes, died, was buried and rose again on the third day.
The Catholic Church—or Mother Church as she is more familiarly known—is
built on Mount Vaticanus in Rome, an ancient shrine to the mother goddess.

The withdrawal of the moon's light for three days held great significance
for lunar societies. Many cultures believed that after death souls journeyed to
the moon before eventually returning to Earth. In hermetic doctrine, 'return
to the mother' was the equivalent of dying. That the life-giving moon should
hide her face from the Earth suggested to many ancient societies that she was
not only a nurturing goddess but also a cruel and destructive one. (For the
Egyptians, the vulture—a distinctly 'dark' and forbidding creature—was a
mother symbol.) To the Greeks, Hecate represented the dark power of the
moon while Artemis (in her role as midwife) reflected its bright aspect.
Hecate was associated with metamorphosis, but her curative powers could
both heal and destroy. Hecate was not the only moon goddess to cast an
ambivalent shadow on the moon. Demeter, Hestia, and Isis are further
representatives of the moon goddess: they were 'virgin' and pure, yet also
mothers and prostitutes.* In Christianity the Virgin Mary and Mary
Magdalene could be seen as two faces of the same woman. Indeed, the few
remaining statues of the Black Virgin probably relate to this idea of the dark
side of the moon/mother. Curiously enough, many shrines to the Black Virgin
were reputed to have great healing powers.

The relationship between the lunar cycle and the menstrual cycle (which
means moon-change) remains one of the most fundamental links between
women and the moon. Yet fear and superstition have been the handmaidens
of menstruation since the very earliest times. Centuries ago women were
frequently outcast at their 'time of the month', although in some societies a
woman was considered to be at the height of her 'powers' at this time and
treated with reverence. However, the ostracization of women during their
menstrual period was originally for the woman's benefit herself. Seclusion
and quiet suits the psychic state of a woman at such a time—a time when she
should choose to be alone to commune with the goddess and relate to her
femininity at its deepest level.

Although these latter ideas may be easy for the Cancerian female to relate

*For a fuller explanation of the Virgin Goddess, see Virgo (pp.234–5)

to, Cancerian men find the idea of psychically getting in touch with their femininity rather difficult to swallow. The point about Cancer, and the reason why this sign presents such a quandary for men is that these archetypal themes, these lunar rhythms and responses, have to find expression through the male psyche. Both Cancerian men and women are hypersensitive individuals, they need regular periods of peace and privacy to provide a balance between the demands of the outer world and their important inner space.

'O! Swear not by the moon, the inconstant moon, that nightly changes in her circled orb, lest that thy love prove likewise variable,' cried Shakespeare's Juliet. In this, she expressed a commonly felt fear in less sophisticated times, that there was something unreliable about the moon. In the Tarot pack, the Moon, among other ideas, is a symbol of treachery, deception, and illusion—hardly a card to 'bank on'. The tendency for women to behave more irrationally than men was attributed, at least in earlier times, to the moon's changing faces and inconsistent appearance. (The moon rises 58 minutes later each day, and at certain times of the month can be seen rising during the daylight hours: the moon's size also varies considerably depending on its proximity to the Earth.) Words such as lunacy are derived from the moon (**luna, la lune**) and originated at a time when madness was attributed almost entirely to the moon. To be illuminated by the moon (**mens**) produces mind, whereas to be struck by the moon is to become a lunatic. In astrology, inspiration, imagination, and the creative mind come under the Moon's 'influence', while Neptune (in esoteric teachings, the higher octave of the Moon) not only represents 'higher' qualities of the mind such as prophecy and clairvoyance, but also folly, illusion, and even, perhaps, madness.

With its links to both the Moon and Neptune, Cancer is a sign that is highly receptive to higher states of feeling and mystical experience. The Cancerian individual is one who empathizes with the suffering of others and cares enormously about helping his fellow man in an active way. Thus many Cancerians are drawn to the healing and helping professions. Women like Elisabeth Kübler-Ross who has devoted her life to the study and care of the dying—she prepares terminally ill patients for the experience of death and beyond—exemplify this aspect of Cancer. Dr Ross has also written of her profound mystical experiences.

Cancer, like all water signs, is motivated by the feelings. That his opinions change from month to month, or even day to day, is not through some perverse whim, but through his sensitivity and instinctive adaptation to the changing emotional currents within him, which in turn affect everything in his life. In essence this is a feminine quality and perhaps to some degree less potent in the male Cancerian than the female. A man's nature is far more rigid and less fluid than a woman's: for a man, if something is right today it should still be right tomorrow; yet for a woman, what is right today may not *feel* right tomorrow—her subjective view has altered the appearance of things. Cancerians find it enormously difficult to be objective about life and this, combined with their self-protective instincts, produces a chronic evasiveness. Thus, male Crabs more than any other men in the zodiac, with perhaps the exception of the Fish and the Archer, are extremely difficult to pin down and display a remarkable talent for U-turns.

The Crab is a great believer in self-defence, so his shifting stance is not only a result of the changes in his subjective inner world, but a deliberate ploy to camouflage his motives and wishes. Crabs never move from A to B: they do a grand tour around the object of their desires, hoping to lead everyone else off the scent; then they reach out from the point of maximum safety. Crabs also hate to make fools of themselves and their sense of humour rarely stretches as far as their idiosyncrasies or imperfections.

Black moods and swampy silences, more typical of the pre-menstrual female, descend on Cancerians suddenly and inexplicably. An unintentionally hurtful remark may have triggered the descent—Crabs take things very personally—but more often than not it's nothing in particular. Like crabs, Cancerians are best left alone to bury themselves when this happens. At these times, they are definitely not amused. The male Cancer is just as prone to mood swings as the female and when something is wrong or they feel offended they tend to become snappy and bitchy.

British politician Edward Heath, who was replaced as leader of the Tory party by Margaret Thatcher, cannot refrain from getting back at her at every opportunity—attacking her and her policies from the safety of his 'wet' position on the back benches. In true Cancerian style, he can't forget, can't give up, and will needle her relentlessly even when she's no longer Prime Minister. Once Crabs get their clutches into something, or someone, they'll never let go. Tenacity, determination, and a degree of pig-headedness (or perhaps crabs-clawsity) are hallmarks of Cancerian individuals.

By and large, astrology books emphasize the protective, cherishing, and sensitive qualities of this water sign, qualities that reflect the 'bright' moon. But what about Hecate? Where does the dark side of the Moon emerge in Cancerians. In a nutshell, through the less desirable characteristics of their opposite number, Capricorn. Some Cancerians display a calculating, ruthless streak every bit as dehumanizing and insensitive as the cruelest kind of Saturnian.

One of the dilemmas astrologers face with Cancer is that although it is a sensitive, yielding water sign, it is also a 'cardinal' one. Thus, characteristics of initiative, ambition, and drive also belong to this sign. Such qualities find a greater ease of expression in a forceful fire sign like Aries or a cool down-to-earth one like Capricorn; but Cancer's watery depths are antithetical to the intense heat of burning ambition. Few Cancerians admit to or recognize an ambitious, competitive streak—they may have ideals and yearnings instead. Part of them craves for positions of power and the trappings of success, yet their gentle, sympathetic natures are ill suited to such solar ideas. On the plus side, Cancerians who make it to the top of their particular tree frequently find their caring, understanding personalities are a positive bonus. On the other, the one step forward and two back syndrome is a major obstacle to many a Cancerian's progress. Sometimes, because Cancerians tend to be too self-protective and too cautious to head straight towards their goals, they get beaten to the post by others. When this happens some Crabs build up huge stores of resentment and bitterness. The dark side of Cancer can also be a revengeful and jealous one.

The sea usually provides a source of fascination and pleasure for Cancerians; some people like Jacques Cousteau (MC, Mars, and Neptune in Cancer), or

Edward Heath, become well-known for their watery skills. Music and the arts in general are also Cancerian/lunar gifts, as exemplified by Hector Berlioz (Asc. Cancer), Debussy (Moon Cancer)—two of whose most popular works are **La Mer** and **Claire de Lune**—Degas, and Modigliani. Connections between the Moon's position and writers have been demonstrated by French statistician Michel Gauquelin, and indeed, many famous writers have a strong Cancerian theme in their charts: Iris Murdoch (who won the Booker Prize for her novel, **The Sea, The Sea**), George Sand, Pearl Buck, Jean Anouilh, and Antoine de Saint-Exupéry, among many.

Cancerians are also prodigious collectors. They love the past, which in some emerges as a deep interest in history, but more often a preoccupation with their old memories. Cancerians hoard everything from old school reports, baby mugs, sealing wax, even handle-less spoons and engine-less motor-bikes—perhaps because such things may come in useful some day, but more often because Crabs cannot bear to be parted from anything that has once belonged to them. Yes, Cancer is a possessive, acquisitive sign; however, possessions often mean more to them in terms of security or sentimental value than anything else.

Cancer is considered to be the most domesticated sign of the zodiac. While many Cancerians make wonderful cooks, interior decorators, do-it-yourself buffs, and gardeners, their skills are not born out of a fundamental need to serve, like Virgo, but a deep attachment to the home and the comfort and security it provides. The first time I entered my brother-in-law's flat there was little doubt in my mind that the owner was a Crab. Evidence of crustacea was everywhere from the moment the ancient velvet drape across the door was pulled aside to reveal a cornucopia of bric-à-brac in the lambent light—a proverbial womb with a view. Home, a place to hang their hat and their trunkfuls of memorabilia is fundamental for Cancer—like crabs, their shell, small or large, keeps the world at bay.

Family, or more specifically mother, is the linchpin of a Cancerian's life, in keeping with the lunar-feminine-maternal symbolism of this sign. Cancers of both sexes are deeply affected by the experience of mother and early family life, on which I shall expand later. Many Crabs are exceptionally close to their parents and siblings and go on to create a huge family of their own, while others do their best to put as much distance between themselves and their roots as possible. Extending the theme of 'mother' a little further afield, the United States is a Sun Cancer country: on the one hand, it is an extremely female-dominated society; on the other, its effusive hospitality, its excessive appetite for food, and its creature comforts are supremely characteristic of this sign.

Money is also something Cancerians like to have in abundance. While this is hardly the most profligate sign of the zodiac, Cancerians, especially the female, find it hard to resist spoiling themselves—often. A Cancerian tends to feel very insecure without sufficient supplies (whether it's food, drink, or money). Going away for a weekend can seem like army manoeuvres for Cancer, but when a 'rainy day' arrives, they can hardly bear to break into their reserves. This lunar sign is considered thrifty—some might say downright stingy—and many Cancerians make excellent businessmen, financiers, and accountants. Occasional (financial) binges followed by stringent cutbacks are characteristic of this sign. Crabs also tend to moan about their lack of funds even when they're financially solvent.

Cancer Crabs are complex creatures and like their Scorpio 'brothers' they're often as much a mystery to themselves as to everyone else. This is a deeply sensitive, private, and introspective sign that nevertheless feels the cardinal impulse to extend and prove itself in its sphere of influence. The Cancerian needs to tap the strength and potency of his feelings and find expression for them out in the world. Like the moon who has no light of her own, Cancerian people need plenty of emotional feedback and reassurance to project themselves on the world at large.

One night, when you're quite alone, gaze upon the moon's enigmatic form; consider its rhythms and its elusive nature, and you may just catch a glimpse of Cancer's reflective, fluctuating, richly textured inner world.

RELATIONSHIPS

The Cancerian man or woman is one of the zodiac's best marriage prospects. Crabs are usually caring and considerate, loving and demonstrative. Life without love, tenderness, and security is practically unthinkable to this sign, yet alone liveable, so most of them tend to marry (or form long-term relationships) early in life. Children are normally a top priority and follow as soon as Crabs feel emotionally and financially secure—or sometimes before. The urge to have a large and happy family life is a strong one for lunar types.

Cancer is not a sign to treat relationships lightly; once Crabs have made a commitment, they'll stand by their partners until the seas run dry. Divorce is anathema to them. However, Cancerians, like anyone else, are capable of landing themselves with incompatible partners. Yet all too often, because this sign cannot face the trauma of breaking up the home, they cling to the security of their marriage, and thus exist in an emotional wasteland.

THE FEMALE CANCER

The Cancerian female invariably possesses a bright, welcoming veneer, but she always sports a 'trespassers will be prosecuted' sign across her heart. These sensitive water-lilies need to be treated with great care. They suspect that hurt and rejection are looming around every romantic corner; consequently, they buttress their emotions against every eventuality. Of course, what makes the Cancerian woman such a conundrum is that she, like her male counterpart, is a master of disguise. She is often extremely giggly and school-girlish, giving the impression that life is just a jolly jape; but rest assured, behind every front, be it gauche and bubbly, or cool and distant, there hides a gentle, tremulous maiden.

The Cancerian little girl is probably the most innocent in the zodiac. To her the magical realm of fairy tales and make-believe is startlingly vivid, and her awakening to the real world is a slow and painful process. As an adult she still remembers the day she discovered that Santa Claus did not exist, and the time her elder brother threw her favourite doll into the dustbin. And it still hurts. From these early days the female Crab salvages her shaken dreams and deposits them carefully in her inner vault. She learns to cope with life by pretending she doesn't care and sealing off her emotions along with her memory in her safety deposit box. Later on, part of her enchantment as a female is that she combines a sense of womanly wisdom with a sense of wonder and innocence.

Like most children, and certainly most Crabs, the Cancerian female's formative years with her parents and siblings are crucial to her later ability to handle her relationships and do well in life. The Cancerian female who is loved, cherished, and protected by her parents enters the adult world emotionally intact and open hearted—if somewhat ill-equipped to meet such hazards in life as rejection and failure. On the other hand, the Cancerian little girl who encounters harshness and difficulty, and who feels misunderstood and unloved, emerges from childhood emotionally at sea, although she probably handles the adult world with reasonable assurance.

The Cancerian female does not experience quite the same dilemma over mother and mothering as her male counterpart. Unlike the Cancer man who has to adapt his maternal impulse to a male psyche, the female Cancerian is at liberty to mother to her heart's content. Yet even for Ms Cancer, coming to terms with the experience of mother—good or bad—is essential to the success of her adult relationships. The Cancerian woman who allows herself to be dominated by her mother may never feel free to make her own choices or decisions without the maternal seal of approval. Since women are more prone to feeling guilty and becoming duty bound, the Cancerian woman, like the Virgoan, is often the sort to put parental obligations before her own fulfilment. Thus, some Cancerian women never marry or raise a family. Others do, but remain at the constant beck and call of their parents and are permanently worried about offending them or not paying them enough attention. As a result, their own relationships suffer: the partner is relegated to second place and/or bored rigid with her endless agonizing over her inadequacies as a daughter.

Cancerian women easily feel inadequate. No matter how lovely, talented, or clever they may be, they invariably consider themselves lacking in some department. If Ms Cancer had plenty of encouragement and confidence-boosting as a child, the tendency to feel inadequate is mitigated. But since this is such an impressionable sign, one that relies on other people's views to catch sight of its own identity, negative opinions remain deeply ingrained on Cancerians' psyches. Regardless of the sort of feedback Ms Cancer received as a child, she needs repeated assurances about her abilities. Since she doesn't like to fish for compliments, hoping that they'll arise spontaneously, one of the reasons why she disappears into a heavy silence is that she feels worthless and needs a booster injection of self-worth.

Astrologically, the Cancerian woman is the quintessential female: nurturing and yielding, changeable and irrational. She is the dutiful daughter, the compliant wife and the loving mother. All over the world there are Cancerian paragons of femininity like the Princess of Wales; and then there are some who seem patently at odds with this stereotype, like Emmaline Pankhurst. Yet even if Mrs Pankhurst used violent methods to put her message across, she was, after all, fighting for women's rights. And aside from her trail-blazing activities on the suffragette front, Mrs Pankhurst was also a wife and mother.

Ms Cancer usually loves her home. She will tend and care for it like one of her precious plants or pet creations—not that she is manically tidy or obsessive about dust. No, the Cancerian woman's home is a reflection of her sensuous and unpretentious nature. She tends to favour the cluttered look—lots of paintings on the walls and objets d'art on every available surface; large, comfortable armchairs and sofas, soft fabrics, old lace and furniture from all cultures and periods. She often has bits and pieces from the family home—old carpets or drapes—partly for sentimental reasons and partly for thrift. The Cancer woman is a great 'squirrel'. She is also wonderfully resourceful. I once knew a Cancerian lady who made a dress and shirt out of some old curtains; later these items became a couple of cushions and a stuffed toy, until finally, the remaining good bits were put into a patchwork quilt. And every patch could tell a story . . .

Ms Cancer is normally an excellent cook, and even if she maintains that she can only boil an egg, she cares enormously about good food. As a hostess, she may not dazzle her guests with her sparkling intellectual delivery, nor her brilliantly funny anecdotes, but a warm and interested glow circulates about her as she attends to everyone's needs and gently plies them with food and wine.

Almost all Cancerian women, whether they're the active-striving sort or the passive-resistant variety, will express their nurturing abilities in one way or another—not that they all have to produce ten children to do so. Of course, having babies is perhaps the most tangible way of giving vent to any cherishing, protective instincts, but some Cancerian females opt for a fulfilling career instead. Indeed, this concept of the Cancerian woman as the zodiac's prize domestic cow tends to obscure her diverse and manifold gifts. The Cancer female, in keeping with her cardinal sisters, the Arians, the Capricorns, and the Librans, is not an entirely passive creature: she has goals and plenty of determination and tenacity to achieve them. But since she is a water sign, her striving personality is concealed, or only to be glimpsed at, in the soft focus of her femininity. Occasionally, the Cancerian woman will harness her ambition to a successful career in business, or more likely a creative, artistic one. But sadly, because of the sensitivity and introspective nature of this sign, the Cancerian woman lacks confidence in her abilities and as soon as marriage and the children arrive, she tends to let her talents retreat into the background. Thus the Cancerian wife and mother, like the Capricornian, often expresses her ambition vicariously through her husband and children.

However, the importance of being a wife and mother should not be thought demeaning for the Cancer female. Most women reach a point in their lives when they want a child: it becomes an emotional, psychological, and sometimes a biological craving. Yet feeling broody can turn into an occupational hazard for the Cancerian woman! Once the babies have arrived and passed through childhood, the majority of the zodiac's mothers breathe a sigh of relief and get on with the pleasant task of being themselves. Not so the Crab. Women who have a strong Cancerian theme in their charts (particularly the Moon in this sign) often become completely 'hooked' on being pregnant and having small, helpless babies to care for. Unlike some women, who resent their bloated shape and the discomfort of pregnancy, not to mention the rigours of labour, the pregnant Cancerian is in her element and her glory—the process of giving birth is probably the most supremely creative thing she will ever do. The Cancerian woman is acutely responsive to her lunar rhythms and her emotional cycles: in the pregnant state she is closely in touch with the core of her femininity, and giving birth provides her with a sense of completion and fulfilment at a deeply psychic level. During her years as a mother, she explores all dimensions of her being: she is alternately nurse, cook, teacher, and counsellor (all good Cancerian professions) and consequently feels thoroughly replete. Naturally, when the children wish to stretch their wings and—horror of horrors—leave home, she feels bereft and empty. Unfortunately, many Cancerian mothers are dreadfully possessive and try all sorts of manipulative ploys to keep their children tied to their apron strings. Others, who no doubt benefit from some airy, fiery, or earthy personal planets, successfully wean themselves from their offspring, with perhaps some help from a menagerie of pets and projects.

But what about Ms Cancer's lover or husband? Has he disappeared under a pile of nappies and toy trucks? To be honest, Ms Cancer's partners are likely to come poor seconds to her children once they've arrived, although like the Librans, women of this sign try enormously hard to please all of the people all of the time. However, BC (Before Children) all Ms Cancer's cherishing gifts are bestowed on the man in her life. The Cancerian woman is romantic and sentimental. She's also very good at getting her man—not that you'd notice: she moves in discreet circles, and like her male counterpart she's as obvious as a chalk mark on a white wall when it comes to showing her feelings. The Cancerian woman needs a dependable, sensitive, considerate partner, preferably of the earth sign variety. But since opposites attract, she often falls for an extrovert, freedom-loving rogue of the airy or fiery type. If the relationship enters deep and choppy waters, she'll cling to her man like a sea anemone—regardless of how miserable he makes her, or whether he wants her or not. If he manages to shake her off, she'll retreat into her shell for a while to nurse her emotional wounds and file the experience in her memory bank. Then very cautiously indeed, she'll set about finding Mr Safe and Secure. Ms Cancer never makes the same mistake twice.

This innate ability of the female Crab to hang onto relationships whatever the content stems from her need for security at all costs. The Cancerian is not the only woman in the zodiac to do so, of course, but because she is an emotionally giving type, she tends to suffer more than most when her love is not reciprocated or when her relationships lack deep emotional content. Because she puts up with the slings and arrows of discontent and hardship, the Cancerian woman, like Ms Pisces and Ms Virgo, can become a dreadful martyr to her relationships.

Ms Cancer also runs the danger of marrying the first person with whom she becomes involved—any port is better than none in the dangerous and unpredictable waters of life for this woman! Cancerian females often move straight from the parental nest into nuptial security. Sometimes these early marriages are tremendously successful—and if there's one woman in the zodiac determined to make her relationships last, it's the Crab; but sometimes they prove disastrous. Ms Cancer frequently expects to find the same unconditional love and indulgence from her husband that she encountered with her parents. Consequently, she feels hurt and disillusioned when she discovers adult relationships are far more demanding on all fronts. Also, like many women who marry too young, her 'Sir Galahad' at 18 may turn into 'Quasimodo' by the time she's 29.

Nevertheless, Ms Cancer will only resort to divorce as a last recourse, and usually years after she should have done. Many of my Cancerian clients have experienced years of relentless hostility with their partners because life as a single woman held more horror for them than any amount of marital misery.

Ms Cancer is an extremely possessive lady. Her life is thickly entwined with those she loves. She fears that if they leave her, part of herself will also be lost. Indeed, Ms Cancer is probably more incapable of letting go than the Scorpio female. Ms Scorpio will detach herself from painful situations—and take her revenge as well—whereas the Cancerian woman believes that persistence will wear down any amount of resistance and that her patience will be rewarded—eventually. Although the Cancerian woman may have to face an unwelcome parting, she rarely lets go of her emotional and psychological attachment. Thus, her inability to accept the finality of a relationship not only causes her months, if not years, of despair but also hampers her ability to get on with the rest of her life.

Extra-marital affairs also pose a considerable problem for the Cancerian woman. If she is unhappy in her marriage she'll respond to another man who offers her love and affection. But Ms Cancer isn't made for liaisons dangereuses. Although she finds no difficulty in keeping an affair secret, she cannot stand the impermanence and precariousness of such a relationship. She wants security and commitment from her lover. If he is unprepared to take her on permanently, she'll have no alternative but to retreat into the hollow shell of her marriage. If, on the other hand, Ms Cancer suspects her partner of being unfaithful, she'll do her best to talk herself out of her fears. She's extremely unlikely to risk a confrontation since that might place her relationship in jeopardy. She'll probably drop a few loaded comments that **could** imply she knows **something** in the hopes that he'll get cold feet and end the affair. As a last resort (after she's tried spoiling him with all his favourite meals and dressing to 'kill') she'll employ a tearful appeal, reminding him of all she's done for him, their happy times, the children . . . But leave him? Not likely!

Most of the time, the Cancerian female is a sweet-natured, patient soul. She hates rows, especially if anyone shouts at her. She's hopeless at arguing adroitly since her emotions erupt like a storm at sea and destroy her capacity to reason. Sometimes, however, the Cancerian woman's anger, resentment, and hurt bubble over so that she acts like a raving banshee. Like the Scorpio woman, after the emotional tidal wave has subsided she feels purged and extremely remorseful. And in typical Crab style, any of the headway she made by voicing her grievances is immediately given up by her tearful retractions.

The Hecate creator-destroyer principle lies potentially within every Cancerian female. In some this manifests as occasional bouts of verbal, psychological or even physical cruelty. At these times, the Cancerian female feels alienated from those she is closest to: she seems only to see their inadequacies and feel burdened by them. Thus she strikes out ferociously at those she loves most, and will not cease until she receives an equally powerful response. Emotional tension builds up in the lunar female in the same way as premenstrual tension does in many women, but for Cancer these dark periods are not necessarily linked to her menstrual cycle. Another way in which the Cancer female acts as a destroyer rather than a creator-nurturer is through the unleashing of her stores of resentment and bitterness. Since the female Crab tends to live her life through others, and sacrifice her own abilities in the process, she sometimes feels tremendous resentment when others find happiness or success. Instead of rejoicing in their achievements she feels bound to criticize or demean them. Not overtly, of course. It is also the dark side of the moon that reveals itself in those Cancerian women who display little of the genuine feeling ability of this sign and quite coldly and ruthlessly exploit men for their own (usually materialistic) ends. In this respect, Ms Cancer bears a marked resemblance to the Virgoan 'Siren' (see pp.241–2).

If you want an open, easy, uncomplicated sort of woman, stay away from Ms Cancer. Of couse, if she's set her sights on you, you might just as well give in gracefully and save yourself the bother of running after all those flipperty-jibbits and good-time girls. It's only a matter of time before you find her patiently waiting at the top of a dead-end street. But take heart, it won't be long before the delights of those other women pale in comparison with her delicate but rich brand of femininity.

Please take great care of this woman. Like a sensitive plant she needs daily nourishment (in the form of love and reassurance) to bloom and thrive. Treat her harshly, trample on her feelings, and she'll quietly waste away. You need have no fears about the Cancerian's mothering qualifications. She will wrap your children in cotton wool, together with their first lock of baby hair, and attend each and every sports and prize-giving—on crutches if necessary.

Ms Cancer may not be the wittiest lady in the zodiac, nor the most adventurous, but she'll always laugh at your jokes (at least in public) and follow you to Timbuktu if necessary. Yes, she is a hyper-sensitive soul and maddeningly changeable. One moment she'll perch herself adoringly on your knee, then the next rail at you like a fishwife for throwing out an empty box. But could she be less emotional and more consistent? Not really. Her emotional vicissitudes are an essential part of her magic. And anyway, why ask for the stars when you have the moon?

THE MALE CANCER

Even a smattering of astrological know-how is better than none when you meet a Cancer man. Embarking on a relationship with a Crab can be likened to a journey down the densely forested Amazon—mysterious, tantalizing, obscure, wonderful, and perhaps rather alarming. At least if you have a map, you lessen your chances of running round in ever expanding circles. This man is about as understandable as Sanskrit to the average Westerner. He can rarely be reached by an intellectual route since it is his powerful feelings and his need to protect them that have placed him behind his smokescreen in the first place. Ironically, most Cancerian men consider themselves utterly straightforward and uncomplicated. It's only other people who don't understand them!

Like the other two water signs, Scorpio and Pisces, the Cancerian man tends to soft-pedal his gentler qualities in order not to be considered weak or lily-livered. Consequently, some Crabs have an even heartier, huskier front than the most self-confident fire sign. Fortunately, with the clear-cut divisions between masculine and feminine roles disintegrating, the Cancer man can now express his sensitive nature without feeling like a whimp. Nevertheless, when they were little boys, Crabs invariably found it very difficult to 'pull themselves together' when they were in a distraught state after their pet fish had died or the boy next door had massacred their butterfly collection. From the earliest days, these sensitive little chaps have needed a tender touch and love of the unconditional variety. Dependent upon the type of mothering they received and the sense of security they derived from family life, Cancerian men grow up to be stable, confident, and loving individuals themselves. But if the Crab felt unloved as a child and his family experience was unsettled, he is likely to desensitize himself over the years and adopt a rather cool and aloof exterior. And while he may handle the outer world reasonably well, his emotional life is somewhat stunted.

It is said that Cancerians have memories like elephants, which means that every small incident that has made an emotional impression on the Crab is stored in his memory bank and drawn out to be re-examined periodically throughout his life. An accusing look will occasionally appear on my nine-year-old Cancerian's face when, apropos of nothing, he'll remind me of the time I threw his grey Range Rover across the room and broke its wheel. The incident remains vivid in his mind, not because he liked the toy, but because he remembers the outrage and hurt he felt at my display of anger. Cancerians never forget an injury. Of course, not all memories that Cancerians regurgitate are sad ones. But by and large, the Crab, like the Scorpion, often takes a kind of masochistic pleasure out of feeling sorry for himself. Certainly, Cancer's ability to recall feelings and impressions with great clarity is one of the reasons why they make such marvellous writers and artists.

The Cancerian man treasures his early years when as a baby and toddler he was cosseted, cuddled, and indulged. Indeed sometimes he never progresses emotionally from these times, which makes him a very awkward Crab to deal with since he can be as rational as a two-year old when he's upset. Cancerian men often like to be babied by their partners, even if they're stalwart breadwinners and fathers. Conversely, many Cancerians are apt to mollycoddle their wives or girlfriends.

The whole experience of mother and being in the bosom of their family creates an indelible imprint on Cancer men's psyches which they must come to terms with to enjoy fulfilling one-to-one relationships as adults.

There is a tendency for many Cancerian men to elevate the importance of mother in their lives, so that she assumes superhuman proportions. They are consumed by her being. As Oscar Wilde said, 'All women become like their mothers. That is their tragedy. No man does. That's his.' The Cancerian man who idolizes his mother may never find another woman who can rise to her exalted status in his eyes, so he never marries and may well live with his mother, or close by, until she dies. Other Cancerian mother's boys marry, but constantly compare their wives, often disparagingly, with mother. And even those Crabs who don't have a mother complex invariably find themselves wishing that their wives were more nurturing/capable/efficient/or loving—in fact, just how they fondly recall their mother was.

Most people are familiar with the idea that mother is the model upon which all little boys base their concept of womanhood. A positive and warm relationship between a boy and his mother enhances his appreciation of her qualities, which he later seeks in a wife. Even if he has a difficult relationship with his mother he will nevertheless (unconsciously) look for a woman with her characteristics. Thus he continues his unfinished business with mother in his marriage.

At some point in their lives, perhaps around adolescence or in their late twenties,* Cancerian men (like any others) must deal with their image of mother, accept her for what she truly is, and free themselves of her psychic conditioning. The Cancerian man's future relationships stand or fall on his ability to resolve this issue. Like the Capricorn woman who must come to terms with her image of father and find fatherly qualities in herself, the Cancerian man needs to locate his own motherly characteristics so that he neither projects them onto a partner nor directly seeks to repeat his mother/child relationship. Although men of any sign are capable of becoming mother-fixated, Cancerian men, by dint of the powerful emotional thrust and emotional reactivity of this sign, are generally more prone to such a tendency. As I mentioned earlier, Cancerians tend to feel unsure of themselves and need plenty of feedback and reassurance to gain self-confidence; they are immensely impressionable and vulnerable to other people's opinions and feelings. Thus, the sensitive Cancer boy is highly susceptible to mother domination—after all, mother knows best . . . Doesn't she?

Not all Cancerian men love their mother, however. Some of them despise her. Yet like the mother-worshippers, they find it terribly hard to rid themselves of her influence and are in effect, just as mother-possessed. The Cancerian man who hates his mother may do so because she was unsympathetic, inadequate, or unloving, or because she let him down in some way—perhaps by leaving his father and the home. The Crab who feels his mother has failed him often gains the impression that because the most important woman in his life let him down, all women are unreliable and to be mistrusted—even feared. Consequently, instead of rushing into matrimony as soon as legally possible, he will avoid it like the plague.

Clearly, many Cancerian men avoid marriage for reasons other than a deep-seated hatred of their mother or an all-consuming love of her. This sign is highly self-protective and therefore cautious in the extreme. Many Crabs keep marriage at bay through sheer fear that it might end in divorce! But by and large, most Cancerian men need the security structure of marriage and the routine of the domestic sphere. When Mr Cancer remains on his own, nine times out of ten there is some unresolved emotional issue—particularly over mother—at the root of it.

Even though many Cancerian men emerge through childhood and adolescence without a maternal albatross on their psyches, any woman planning to catch a Crab is well advised to ingratiate herself with his mother—at least until she can establish the state of play.

*Progressed Lunar Return around age 27; Saturn Return around age 29.

Putting mother on one side for the moment, the majority of Cancerian men are sentimental and gentle. These individuals usually understand women very well, which makes them enormously sensitive and sympathetic partners—the sort who will take over the domestic helm if their wife is laid low with 'flu. Indeed, many Cancerian men are adept and extremely imaginative cooks, and don an apron with as much enthusiasm as some men do their rugby boots. The Cancerian man normally enjoys the company of women. He likes listening to gossip, although he prefers not to add any comments of his own, just in case matters rebound on him later. He is fascinated by women's physiology, especially anything related to childbirth. It is often the Cancerian husband who emerges exhausted but exhilarated from the delivery room!

Donald Sutherland is typically Cancerian. He delivered his last three sons himself, and while studying for a role as a heart specialist he helped sew a plastic valve into a real-life patient. (Not surprisingly for such a caring sign, many Cancerian men join the medical profession, especially as obstetricians.) Like many Crabs, Sutherland's home and family are supremely important to him; so much so, that he has dragged them all in and out of hotel suites and rented houses the world over, and in between times has kept in touch with them by telephone (regardless of distance or the time of day or night). Sutherland also admits that he is a hypochondriac. He discusses his illnesses and injuries to anyone who cares to listen; even illustrious stars like Donald Sutherland have a touch of the Cancerian old woman about them.

Despite, or perhaps because of, the deeply emotional nature of this sign, many Cancer men find difficulty in playing 'love's young dream'. When they are attracted to someone they tread extremely cautiously. They don't want to risk making fools of themselves by any over-extravagent romantic gestures. Sometimes they're also rather on the mean side. It may take the Crab many months to summon up the courage to tell a lady that he loves her; even then his declamations may be so heavily disguised as to be completely obscure. Mr Cancer would rather his partner made the first move in a relationship, although he sometimes makes this extremely difficult since his evasive, indifferent stance may convince her that he cares not one iota. This can lead to a romantic stalemate. Sometimes, even when the woman makes the opening gambit, matters do not proceed very rapidly. Mr Cancer can get an attack of chauvinist indignity. After all, real men chase the woman, don't they? Thus he waits (now with success virtually guaranteed) until he can initiate the full romantic opener.

Like their opposite number, Capricorn, Cancerian men like long-term guarantees and a no-risk policy in their relationships. However, unlike the Goat, Mr Cancer normally expresses his feelings and shows sensitivity and considerable tenderness once he's assured himself that his affections will be returned. The Crab cannot face rejection; he'd rather not have loved at all, than to have loved and lost.

Once Mr Cancer has found Ms Right—or rather the other way round—he will scuttle off to nest in comfort and seclusion. He is, of course, extremely possessive, and although he does his best to conceal it (often by appearing indifferent) he is really rather clingy. If the relationship thrives, he will happily entwine himself around his partner for life—this man means what he says when he promises to have and to hold. If the relationship founders, he will still be unable to prise himself away from his partner, but he will slip into his moody, remote shell instead—the Crab is as adept as the Scorpion at the icy emotional cut-off. While part of him hopes that his partner or events will bring about an end to his connubial misery, should a parting appear imminent, he will try to stave it off, even temporarily showing renewed interest in his partner.

Mr Cancer is a reluctant divorcee. He also hates paying alimony. While he is prepared to put his every last penny (well, almost) toward the welfare of his children from a previous marriage, he resents having to support a wife who turned out to be a poor emotional investment. Even if a Crab remarries, he cannot altogether leave his burden of bitterness behind him. He is often torn between what he knows his obligations to be and how he feels about them.

Fatherhood supplies an all-important chance for Mr Cancer to exorcise his motherly skills and feelings. The whole process of pregnancy and childbirth involves and touches the Crab at his deepest emotional roots. Unlike many fathers who only relate to their offspring when they can talk to them, the Cancer man cossets and cares for his little ones from their earliest days. As they pass through childhood he is never too busy to listen to their problems, help with their homework, or pick them up from parties (even when they're 18). Indeed, his major trouble as a parent is letting go of them when they reach adulthood. Occasionally, of course, the Cancer man balks at fatherhood, usually because he himself has misgivings and deep reservations about his own childhood.

The Cancer man is not noted for his aggressive behaviour: he side-steps as much as possible and, like the Scorpion, only attacks when he or those he loves are in danger, or he has been deeply hurt. Yet every so often there can be a cold and seemingly unfeeling side to these men. Since this sign is emotionally vulnerable, the ability to isolate themselves from their emotions is almost a necessity at times. While brief periods of detachment, accompanied by a snappish manner, is par for the course for most Cancerians, some Crabs seem perennially unapproachable, even callous and cruel. Like the female Crab, the dark side of the moon has a ruthless and unrelenting face.

Normally, however, the Cancer man is a warmly sensuous individual. He is extremely tactile too, and once he feels liked and loved he reciprocates with obvious affection. This man makes a marvellous host—welcoming, considerate, and immensely generous with the food and wine. In the company of good friends, the Cancerian comes out of his shell—he may even run the risk of becoming thoroughly sozzled and telling everyone how much he loves them all! Indeed, when the Crab releases himself from his armour-plating, he is one of the most entertaining and garrulous men in the zodiac.

If your idea of Mr Right is the archetypal hero—a composite SAS -Action Man - Sir Lancelot figure—forget the Cancer man. Even if he's wearing battle fatigues, underneath he's a reticent, tender-hearted sort of chap. The Cancerian man is never a stock character. He's immensely changeable and fluid: his moods ebb and flow like the tides and his opinions change like the face of the moon, sometimes coming full circle. He can be as loony as Spike Milligan one moment, then as brooding as Proust the next. He can seem as impenetrable as Fort Knox and as secretive as the KGB, then suddenly as innocently beguiling as a child. He will probably take it in turns to play 'mother' or 'baby', depending on his frame of mind and his huge emotional needs; but indulge him, otherwise he'll be hurt and become very prickly and distant. Yet for all his crabby, awkward ways, he is one of the most caring men in the zodiac.

Do not expect this man to proclaim his love for you loudly and often. He is much too subtle and shy for such behaviour; he also tends to think he's devaluing something rather special if he keeps bringing it into the light. Develop your ESP powers, take a course in Transactional Analysis, and you're half-way to understanding a Crab; let him know that you care, show him your savings account and your Nursery Care certificate and you're home and dry. One more thing: make absolutely certain of the strength of your feelings and the depth of your commitment before saying 'yes' to the Crab. Once this man has you in his clutches, HE'LL NEVER LET YOU GO!

SUMMARY

Courtship can be a shifty business for Cancer: one step forward, two steps back, tweak your partner, and a do-see-do . . . Yet once a relationship looks like a long-term proposition, Cancerian men and women put aside their circumnavigation techniques and attach themselves like limpets to their partners. These individuals believe in sticking by their loved ones and protecting their interests come what may. Yet their security needs often prevent then from exploring their full and diverse emotional range. Cancerians do not like brief encounters; they move cautiously from one long relationship to the next. Above all, they want to establish a close and loving bond with a partner. Yet, their practically impregnable self-defence structure frequently hinders a smooth emotional dialogue and makes them extremely evasive people to deal with. Their family, or more specifically mother, is the linchpin to their ability to handle and sustain adult relationships. Emotionally disparate Cancerians experience difficulty in relating happily to their partners and frequently feel rejected and misunderstood, while those who are emotionally whole achieve fulfilling relationships where they can express love, tenderness and affection, and cherish to their heart's content.

CANCER PARTNERSHIPS

Cancerians need sympathetic, strong and supportive partners, preferably of the earth or water element, yet they invariably team up with the more extrovert, less emotionally consumed fire or air signs.

Aries

Cancer and **Aries** are the most unlikely match, yet initially they are often extremely attracted to one another. The Aries partner loves Cancer's romantic, sensual nature, and his mystery, while the Crab admires Aries' forthright, fun-loving attitude to life. However, the Ram cannot cope with Cancer's changing moods and his need for privacy, while the Cancerian tires of the endless activity and attention-seeking behaviour of Aries. These two often do well materially out of life, although emotionally they may find each other very hard going. These two are entirely different sexual 'animals', thus problems are sometimes encountered in this area.

Taurus

Of the earth signs, **Taurus** is probably the most ideal mate for the Crab. Taurus is another extremely security-oriented sign, yet it is also highly practical and very sensual indeed. Thus the Bull provides the Crab with a solid foundation for their love and plenty of delights along the way. Cancer and Taurus appreciate the good things of life, like food and wine, painting and music. Sex between these two is often marvellous and lasts well into old age. However, this partnership is inclined to be safe but rather unthrilling.

Gemini

The **Gemini** man or woman is by no means the ideal partner for Cancer. Geminis hate to submerge themselves in deep emotional waters, which is the Crab's natural habitat. Thus despite the communicative, sociable nature of Gemini, Cancer often feels rather lonely with this airy individual. However, if either partner has planets in the other's Sun sign, many of their emotional differences can be bridged. On the plus side, the Geminian can 'take' Cancer out of himself and help distance him from his emotions, while the Crab can encourage the Geminian to place more value and trust on his feelings. If the Geminian has some watery planets in his chart, sex between these two can be excellent.

Cancer

When two **Cancers** get together (usually after much shilly-shallying) they stick to one another like Siamese Twins. These two understand each other extremely well, which means that when they are both happy they move along in blissful symbiosis; yet when things go wrong they know exactly how to hurt and manipulate each other. A flourishing sexual relationship and the 'joys' of parenthood are crucial to their success and happiness. This partnership is extremely difficult to dissolve. Neither will want to be the one to leave; thus, this couple can exist in mutual unhappiness for years.

Leo

The Cancer-**Leo** couple can provide an excellent balance for each other, especially if the Cancerian is the woman. The Cancer partner is drawn to the warm and demonstrative nature of the Leonine, while the Lion feels appreciated and needed by the Crab. Problems set in with this relationship when the Lion begins to treat the Crab like a servant. Honesty is very important between these two: the Cancerian must learn to stand up to Leo from time to time, and not resort to devious manoeuvres to achieve his ends. Provided there is emotional harmony between this couple, their sex life can be superb.

Virgo

Virgo is another supportive, practical partner for Cancer. These two work hard at their relationship yet they both have a tendency to suffer painfully in silence rather than air their grievances! Sometimes the Virgoan lacks the drive and ambition Cancer seeks in a partner. Also, the Crab often wants more material things out of life than the Virgoan and feels frustrated if he cannot satisfy his acquisitive instincts. On the plus side, the Crab can encourage the Virgoan to relate to his feelings, while the Corn Bearer can help the Cancerian to rationalize his emotions. This combination is a highly durable one, if a little dull.

Libra

Libra is often the most attractive airy partner for Cancer. The Libran is usually a gentle, considerate individual, although in time the Cancerian may find that he cannot reach deep below the surface with this airy partner. As a couple, these two can achieve great things on a material level, and their home and children are normally treasured and beautiful assets. Sex is an important outlet for their love and can reach splendid heights. The Libran usually tries hard to understand the Crab's feelings and moods, but spends too much time analysing them and not enough relating to them. This couple often like to write each other little notes and exchange 'special' and thoughtful gifts.

Scorpio

Cancer and Scorpio relationships are intensely meaningful, intensely emotional, and intensely private. The Scorpio is just as passionate as Cancer and just as security-oriented. Indeed, these two have much in common, but often their mutually strong self-defence mechanisms drive them apart. Sometimes power struggles get in the way of their love, and both are capable of making each other very angry indeed. Yet the making-up is always wonderful. (Sex plays a very important part in a Crab/Scorpion relationship.)

Sagittarius

Sagittarius and Cancer have little in common, yet this never seems to prevent them falling madly in love with each other. In the long term, however, their relationship demands much work and some good Moon and Venus links. The Sagittarian is far too ephemeral for the Crab and seems only to fan his insecurity, while Cancer's motherly and hypersensitive nature is far too complex for the Archer to cope with. These two can learn and gain a lot from each other, but it takes much love and patience.

Capricorn

Cancer-Capricorn couples are polar opposites, yet both have strong similarities in their natures. Both signs look for security and durability in relationships and sometimes jettison emotional fulfilment in the process. The Goat can be a little on the stern and critical side for the Crab, while Cancer can seem over sentimental and weak to Capricorn. These two provide a perfect balance for each other as parents although the Goat invariably has to wield the rod. Sex can be a powerful plus for this couple, but problems set in when the Goat puts his schedule first and lust afterwards, while the Crab feels spurned and hurt if his more spontaneous advances are rejected.

Aquarius

Aquarius and Cancer are an astrological mis-match, yet like most antipathies they are often fatally attracted to each other. Cancer loves the unusual, amusing, and bright side of Aquarius, while the Waterbearer is compellingly drawn to Cancer's gentle sensibility. Both these signs are complex, and tend to find each other's emotions totally foxing. Initially, both will try hard to accommodate each other's idiosyncrasies, but in the long run the Aquarian tends to find the Crab impossibly moody, and Cancer sees the Aquarian as an insensitive 'brute'. Sex can be a problem area for this couple unless there are good Venus-Mars links.

Pisces

Cancer and **Pisces** are usually a very loving and caring couple. Both take it in turns to play the comforter and the comforted, and spend much of their time debating why the world is so against them. This relationship is high on feelings but weak on practicalities. The Crab nearly always has to take on the yoke of responsibility, while the Piscean partner muddles along. Yet arguments or major showdowns rarely occur between these two. Occasionally the Piscean feels somewhat suffocated by the Crab's over-possessiveness, while Cancer wishes the Fish was more reliable and loyal.

SEXUALITY

Some astrologers maintain that Cancer, like its opposite number Capricorn, is a reluctant lover, if not a downright poor one. In truth, most Capricorns are 'horny old goats' whose over-tight working schedules aren't elastic enough to fit in all the sex they would like! And although Cancerians are cautious and hesitant about displaying their sexual interest in anyone, they're one of the most sexually active signs in the zodiac.

Clearly, to have the Sun in Cancer merely represents the tip of the iceberg where sex and astrology are concerned. An individual uses the whole of his being in his sexual life—mind, senses, and body: thus one needs to examine the whole chart to gain any real insight into sexual make-up. By and large, however, men with their Sun and Mars in Cancer, and women with their Moon, Mars, and Venus in this sign, will relate more directly to the following themes.

Cancerian men and women are motivated by their feelings. Every experience in life touches them at a deep emotional level and, in the main, they are virtually incapable of responding with dispassion to any given situation. Thus sex for both male and female Crabs is an emotional experience first and foremost and a bodily pleasure second.

Strangely enough, for a sign synonymous with caution, Cancerians usually get off to an early sexual start. On the one hand, their sensuous natures and powerful response to emotional-sexual stimulation pushes them over the sexual precipice even when they were determined to hang on until Mr or Ms Right came along. On the other, many Crabs, like many Librans, find the prospect of being prematurely seduced infinitely preferable to turning someone down and risking an ugly scene! Also, many Cancerians want to get through their sexual initiation test so that they can feel on a par with their contemporaries. A sense of inadequacy and a need to belong often forces Crabs to lose sight of their cherished principles far sooner than they had anticipated.

By and large, however, the Crab's cautious, insecure nature is present in his or her sexual behaviour as in everything else, and once deflowered the

Cancerian resorts to type and shilly-shallies and ducks and dives around every potential sexual encounter. Crabs never rush into bed. They feel their way very carefully. First Mr or Ms Cancer must establish a relationship of sorts—time spent in reconnaissance is seldom wasted on the Crab. In this way the Cancerian builds up confidence and ascertains whether or not the attraction is strong enough and worthwhile enough to risk a possible emotional hurt. Cancerians of both sexes do not like to be taken by surprise; they like to prepare themselves for seduction. Mr Cancer usually times his operation carefully, while Ms Cancer uses her excellent sixth sense to warn her of serious sexual intent.

Mr and Ms Cancer also like a slow and gradual build-up to sex—moving 'cold' into the bedroom and baring all under the glare of strip-lighting freezes their sexual taste-buds. Also, they tend to feel deeply inadequate about their bodies.

Cancerians are able to touch high peaks of emotional experience. For them, strong sexual attraction is almost always accompanied by deep and passionate feelings. Consequently, this powerful combination frequently clouds their ability to differentiate between sheer animal magnetism and real love. (Cancerians find it all too easy to become sexually enthralled with someone.) Like Pisces Fish, Cancerians on an emotional and sexual high project all sorts of non-existent qualities onto their partner and thus experience a dreadful come down as the sexual novelty wears off and the real person emerges. If indeed love has turned out to be just infatuation, many Cancerians will use the sexual cool-off to signal their general disinterest, hoping that the partner will get the hint and gently fade away. Others, however, with the decline of their previously intense romantic/sexual interest and the realization that the beloved has feet of clay, cannot accept that love was merely lust in disguise. They feel the partner has changed. Love has gone. Yet because the Cancerian cannot bear to let go of the relationship, he or she may well drift into marriage, deeply dissatisfied and vaguely resentful.

Of course, the glorious and intense sexual overture can act as a curtain-raiser to the Real Thing. And once the enchantment has lifted, Crabs can build a solid and secure relationship on their enduring love.

Cancerians rarely go in for light-hearted, non-committed relationships. They want their partnerships to be meaningful. Only if Mr and Ms Cancer are emotionally desensitized will they entertain casual sexual encounters. They need the security and continuity of a long-term relationship to allow their sexuality to bloom.

The Cancerian girl is aware of her sexuality early. She also believes in love. Since this is just about the most essentially feminine lady in the zodiac, she is not short of potential lovers in her teens (or at any other time in her life for that matter). Ms Cancer will usually choose a safe and probably older man to initiate her into the mystery of sex. He, of course, may turn out to be the one and only man she ever has. Like many women who are cautious and protective about their feelings, the Cancerian woman takes many years to develop her full sexual potential. Since she, like Ms Virgo, is vulnerable to her mother's views on sex, she may have many inhibitions to surmount before she is free to let herself go. As one woman with her Moon and Mars in

Cancer told me. 'Although my husband seemed happy enough about our love life, I felt something was missing. I loved him, but I always felt tense when we made love. I used to pretend to have orgasms. I didn't want to hurt him, so I never talked about it. Eventually I got so screwed-up—I'd got to the point that I couldn't bear to make love at all—that I went to a therapist. After several sessions, I realized just how much my mother's hatred of sex had got through to me. My husband and I went to sex therapy sessions together and now you wouldn't believe I'm the same person. He gets the headaches now!'

Certainly if the Cancerian woman is free of taboos, she is a giving, if rather reserved, lady in bed. For her, the intensity of her emotional/sexual feelings are enough. She doesn't need the embellishment of any extravagent techniques, and she's not the type to hurl herself around to the accompaniment of voluble grunts and groans. Her imagination is strong—she may have a rich fantasy life that she wouldn't dream of discussing with her partner—and she usually loves erotic literature. Ms Cancer is rarely attracted to macho-men who are 'into' weight-training and the body beautiful. She prefers a gentle, sensitive, and sensuous man, if possible, with more experience than herself. The Cancer woman normally hates a spoken dialogue in bed—she's happier with her feelings and her imagnation. But afterwards, she does like to be reassured that she was satisfying. Like Ms Libra, the Cancerian woman is happy if her lover is happy with her.

The Cancer woman is probably more susceptible than other zodiac types to a sharp drop in interest in sex after she has had a baby—especially if she is breast-feeding. Not only does Ms Cancer tend to be a mother first and a lover second, but her emotional/psychological state is so wrapped up in her small baby that she finds it extremely difficult to transfer her interest elsewhere. Although it would be wrong to suggest that the Cancerian mother is sexually aroused by her infant, because of the complex interaction between her emotions and her sexual response, her intense involvement and love of the baby is similar to that between her and her lover. Once the baby is weaned, Ms Cancer's interest in sex and her husband usually returns—but very gradually.

Sometimes the Cancer man also experiences a change in his sexual pattern and his attitude to sex after the birth of his child. He may feel displaced. Lost. Unconscious memories of his own baby/mother relationship are stirred within him. On the one hand, he feels the need for a deeper level of emotional-sexual interaction with his partner; on the other, no matter how much attention and love his wife affords him, he feels rejected and extremely insecure. Consequently, his sexual interest is stronger and more persistent than ever before. One can only imagine the dilemma this poses for a strongly Cancerian couple!

As I mentioned earlier, the Cancer man cannot bear to be laughed at or to lose face. Thus, he has much to gain or lose where sex is concerned. Unlike the Cancerian female, who prefers someone older (one who knows the ropes) to cut her sexual 'teeth' on, Mr Cancer is likely to choose an equally inexperienced partner. Yet he runs exactly the same risk as his female counterpart of remaining with his first 'love' and so missing out on untold sexual thrills with anyone else.

The Cancer man usually reads a vast amount of literature on sex before and after he reaches square one. He gets to know female anatomy through diagrams and photographs—he's nearly always a 'breast-man'—almost as well as his own, which may supply yet another reason for Cancerian men's proclivity toward careers as gynaecologists, obstetricians, and sex therapists! Mr Cancer often develops a keen interest in erotica, to the extent that he may write some (soft) pornography of his own or take some raunchy home snaps or videos. However, since he is also a romantic, hard-core porn rarely appeals to him: he prefers his erotica to be suggestive and beautiful and sensual.

Unlike Ms Cancer, who apart from her private fantasies is on the conservative side in bed, the Cancer man is a sexual hedonist. Sadly, if he lets his needs for emotional security get the better of him, he may never give rein to his full sexual potential and his over-protective attitude to his partner may prevent him from venturing further than the missionary position!

Mr Cancer is usually a very considerate lover. He cares that he is pleasing his partner and locating the right erogenous zones. Unfortunately, nerves often affect his performance and pleasure in the early stages of a relationship, although he normally camouflages his predicament well. Cancer men also tend to fall into sexual ruts—they like their familiar routes to pleasure. Provided that their partner is equally happy to progress along a predetermined course, all is well; but this safe technique can become rather boring to a more adventurous female.

Curiously enough, for a sign synonymous with gentleness and care, Cancer has a reputation for indulging in sado-masochistic sexual practices. (22° Cancer is considered by astrologers to be the degree of sadism.) The dark side of the moon has been revealed in various aspects of Cancer's life throughout these sections and its destructive and violent face is by no means exempt from the sexual arena. However, the more crude and unsavoury types of sexual practice are by no means familiar to everybody with a Cancerian theme in their charts—only a minority plummet these depths.

Sex and water seem to go together for many Cancerians. Some enjoy making love by the sea or in the undergrowth by the side of a lake or river, and if a sexual picnic cannot be arranged, the bath or shower will do. Two Cancerian friends of mine have a special little ritual they indulge in from time to time. They deck the bathroom out with candles, and accompanied by a bottle of wine and their favourite music, they spend the entire evening in the bath—and not just soaping each other's backs either!

The feel of water on the skin, of sun-tan oil or creams, acts as a sexual stimulant for many Crabs. (Oral sex is often a great favourite with this sign.) Smell, touch, and sound, in fact all sensory experience excites and stimulates Cancer's sexuality. Indeed, Cancer, like Scorpio and Pisces, is capable of achieving a transcendent level of experience through sex.

Cancer men and women have deep sexual needs. For them the sexual act is never merely a matter of two bodies coming together in the pursuit of pleasure. It is an all-pervading experience. Cancer is a discriminating, cautious sign. These individuals never bestow their sexual favours lightly—they have too much to lose on an emotional front. But you won't find many Cancerians talking about their sex lives or what sex means for them. As with all things for Cancer, sex is an intensely private affair.

PROFILE OF A CANCER WOMAN

BARBARA CARTLAND

I'm sure Barbara Cartland —writer, historian, political 'activist', and alternative health pioneer—would be the first to agree with St Matthew when he says 'A prophet is not without honour, save in his own country and in his own home': for while, in her eighty-five years. Ms Cartland's vast and diverse range of activities and her list of achievements could fill ten separate entries in **Who's Who**, she always seems to be overlooked when the honours are being bestowed: indeed, she is usually much criticized and occasionally the subject of some derision by the British media. The British aversion to overt self-promotion and unashamed success notwithstanding, the astrology does not make any easier Ms Cartland's passage to acceptance and appreciation as an individual* (which has nothing whatsoever to do with her immense popularity as a writer). Indeed, Ms Cartland's birth chart depicts an individual whose over-ebullient persona is fundamentally at odds with her gentle, compassionate inner self and an individual whose struggle for recognition is long and arduous.

Barbara Cartland was born just before midnight on a warm summer's night at the turn of the century. Thus her sensitive Cancerian Sun is found at the nadir of the chart, hidden away in the protective fourth 'house' of the horoscope. By contrast, at the moment of birth, the Moon was rising over the horizon in boisterous, pioneering, and bellicose Aries! Since the Ascendant is the area of the chart most indentifiable with the persona, it is no surprise that Miss

*See **Note for Astrologers**.

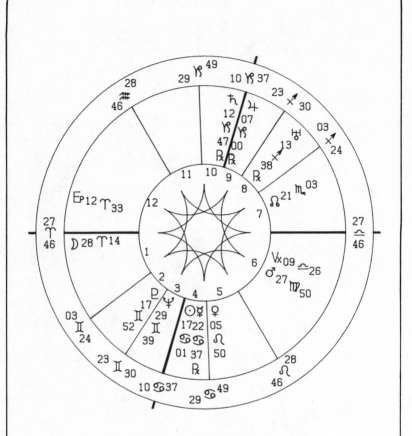

BARBARA CARTLAND

9 7 1901   23h 45 m Os GMT

PLACIDUS 52N30 1W55

Cartland comes across as a highly confident, madly enthusiastic, somewhat egotistical personality. Sadly, this is all many people ever see, since the Aries bumptious brilliance obliterates the finer, more subtle areas of her nature—although on the plus side, her Arian influence bestows her with considerable courage when she needs it.

Like many people of her generation forced to confront the horrors and tragedy of two world wars, Barbara needed to focus on the bright and positive side of her personality to ensure that she was not emotionally broken. 'I was thirteen when the First World War broke out. Every single home in the country had a casualty. My uncles were killed, my cousins were killed ... people mourned excessively. When it was over, all I wanted to do was dance. It was an expression of being alive. You put on a sort of bright armour. You didn't want anyone to see your hurt. We couldn't bear any more emotion.' The First World War not only robbed Barbara of her uncles and cousins, but also her father. 'I saw a lot of my father before he went to war, but just at the time you begin to view your parents as real people, he'd gone. The worst of it was, first we were told he was dead, then later informed he was just missing. The uncertainty was ghastly. Of course in the end he was dead—he'd been killed in the trenches with his men. There was no body—the bombs and shells had left the ground as though it had been ploughed.'

Although the loss of her father affected Barbara deeply, she had the close relationship with her eldest brother Ronald to sustain her. 'Ronald was the person who most influenced my life. My father was in politics before he went to war, and Ronald wanted to be a politician from an early age. He was an extraordinary man—a visionary. We were like twins.* My whole life was influenced by him and everything I've done for the people has been for him.' Sadly, she was to lose Ronald too in the Second World War, at Dunkirk—tragically, the day after her younger brother Tony had been killed. 'I never thought he (Ronald) would be killed. I thought he was so wanted. On his death, everyone said, on both sides of the House—even the Socialists—that he'd have been Prime Minister.'

Barbara's chart gives some indication of the loss and separation she experienced within her family. But though her adolescent years were dominated by anxiety, fear, and bereavement, her childhood was not without joy. 'I was a happy child. We lived in Pershore and I remember most vividly the plum trees in bloom. Imagine, acres of pink and white blossom. It was just like a magical fairy land—all gilly flowers with their gorgeous scent.' With her Sun in Cancer at the opposite end of the chart to Saturn, there is a suggestion of loss of

---

*Ronald's Capricorn Sun formed an exact conjunction to Barbara's Saturn on the Midheaven.

relationship with the father. In Barbara's case, not because of any emotional or psychological alienation, but the physical death of her father. Mars, her chart ruler, forms a 90° angle to Neptune, which gives a further indication of loss and suffering, although this aspect manifests in other ways in her life, as does the Sun-Saturn opposition. Also significant is the conjunction between Neptune and Pluto. Since both these planets are slow movers, they remained together in Gemini from 1890–1902. Thus they exert a generational influence. This conjunction merges two themes: erosion (Neptune) and transformation (Pluto); sacrifice and elimination; ideals/illusion and death and resurrection. A whole generation of individuals born under this conjunction were in the flower of youth when their lives were transformed by war and death.

While Ronald was the member of the family with whom Barbara felt the greatest affinity, like all Cancerians her mother was a special person to her. When Barbara wrote her mother's biography she entitled it **Polly: The Story of My Wonderful Mother**. The strength and importance of the family bond is deeply etched in Barbara's chart—the Sun in Cancer and Saturn in Capricorn stradling the parental MC-IC axis, and the Moon placed on the Ascendant and strongly aspected.

With her father gone, money was in short supply for the Cartland family. Reluctantly, her mother sold the family home, and while the boys remained at public school she and Barbara moved to London, although holidays with the boys were spent in Worcestershire. 'I had to think of some way to earn money. I thought I might become an artist since I'd made some pretty menu-holders . . . but then because I was so bored in the country during the holidays, I decided to write a novel. None of my friends believed I would. It took me a year and it (**Jigsaw**) was published in 1923.* While she was writing **Jigsaw**, Lord Beaverbrook, who'd just bought the **Daily Express**, gave her the opportunity to break into journalism: 'He said to me, "You're out on the town every night, Barbara, why don't you ring me up in the morning and if you can give me a paragraph, I'll give you five shillings." I thought, "I'm rich!" The stories were all rather feeble in those days—not the sort of nasty stuff they have now . . . Lord Beaverbrook taught me how to write—never a superfluous word and always keep to the point. He also introduced me to all the famous people in the world—his great friend was Winston Churchill. But, oh, the ignorance of the young; I used to get so bored at dinner parties with all these great statesmen, I never really listened to what they had to say. I just wanted to go off dancing with some young man!'

*Jigsaw was described as 'Mayfair with the lid off'. It ran into six editions and was translated into five languages.

Even now, at eighty-five, Ms Cartland suffers from a surfeit of energy. She writes on average twenty-two books a year, organizes countless functions and events—many for the St John Ambulance Brigade—makes various television appearances, broadcasts, lectures, and travels abroad. Perhaps the only concession she makes to her advanced years is that she no longer finds the strength to Charlston the night away. Barbara maintains that she owes her fitness and energy to a sensible diet and massive doses of vitamins—a belief she has turned into a major crusade. Her campaign for good health was inspired in 1935 when she saw the results produced by giving vitamin B (in the form of Marmite) to the starving poor. She went on to study Culpeper herbalism, and for the past three decades she has been at the front of the alternative health movement. 'I've always been linked to the medical profession. During the Second World War I was the only lady Welfare officer in Bedfordshire looking after the troops. I was terribly busy—always interfering with people—too much energy, of course. Now I do my best to avoid orthodox medicine.'

Astrologically, Barbara's sixth 'house', Mars in Virgo, can be linked to her fervent pursuit of good health. So too is her work for the the the St John Ambulance Brigade, of which she is Deputy President ('they don't have female presidents'). The Brigade also made her a Dame of Grace in 1953. 'Their work is marvellous, the St John is very close to my heart. During the Royal Wedding (1981) a hundred of them volunteered their services for free—even paid their own fares up to London. They attended to 3,200 cases along the route. Even the choirboys at St Paul's were paid £700 each!' Barbara's pioneering ruler, Mars, is also evident in her courage and daring. In 1931 she conceived the idea of an aeroplane-towed glider, and carried the first Glider Airmail from Marston to Bristol. It was a journey the BBC recreated on 'The Time of Your Life' in 1985—although they weren't prepared to put Barbara's life at risk: 'if you kill Barbara Cartland, it's the same as crashing Concorde!'

Barbara admits to being ambitious. 'I remember when I was young Ronald saying he was going to be the Prime Minister and Tony was going to be head of the army. I thought I'd just get to know everybody. When Ronald died I was offered three safe Tory seats, but I had to refuse because of the children. I was a mother first and foremost. But I did become a County Councillor (Hatfield 1955–64). I was the noisiest councillor they'd ever had. I was always making the most terrible scenes through the Press. I'm always fighting.' While Barbara recognized she had a fighting spirit that could be summoned up to attack any number of deserving causes, she never thought her own marriage would become a battleground.

Barbara's name has made frequent appearances in the **Guinness Book of Records**—usually for her phenomenal annual output of

novels—but never for having turned down forty-nine proposals of
marriage. 'I was always looking for a special man. I didn't want to be
famous myself, but I wanted to be married to someone like a Prime
Minister.' After forty-nine refusals, Barbara succumbed to the charms
of Alexander McCorquodale. She married Alexander in 1927 and her
only daughter, Raine, was born two years later. 'He was terribly nice
and terribly kind. I thought it was going to be a success but it wasn't.
I had been very spoilt . . . and then he had a slight drink problem. We
had a bitterly fought divorce . . . went on for years.' She and
Alexander were divorced in 1933 but she was left virtually penniless.
'He lived in frightful grandeur while I had nothing. But I didn't let it
get me down. I just worked very hard.' Three years later she married
Alexander's cousin, Hugh McCorquodale (a Sun Aries), a marriage
that was to prove mutually happy and fulfilling. 'It was so romantic.
Hugh fell in love with me at my wedding to Alexander as we were
signing the register in St Margaret's Westminster. After my divorce I
didn't want to get married again although I had a wonderful affair
with Nigs (Viscount Rattendon). But then I suddenly realized that
there was nobody as sweet and kind as Hugh. He was the rock to my
restless sea. It all worked beautifully. We had two marvellous sons
and twenty-seven years of perfect happiness.'

With harmonious Libra on the cusp of her relationship 'house' and
Venus, its ruler, in the exuberant fire sign Leo, the promise and
certainly the expectation of happiness and great love is portrayed. In
keeping with the motherly nature of Sun Cancer women, Barbara's
desire to have children was paramount in her life. 'The press often
ask me what was the most thrilling experience of my life. It was
when my first son, Ian, was born (October 1937). I was absolutely
hysterical with excitement. I was so keen to have a son. I had Glen
two years later, and if war hadn't broken out I'd have tried for more.'
Letting go of the children—usually a traumatic event for Cancerian
mothers—presented no problem for Barbara. While Raine is married
to Lord Spencer (the Princess of Wales' father) Barbara's two sons are
never far from her side. 'Ian is my manager and lives on the estate.
He rings me five times a day. Glen comes home every weekend and
we always go on holiday together.' While Barbara loves all her
children and grandchildren, it is clear that she has a preference for the
male sex. 'I find women very difficult to live with. You're always up
against women's emotions. They fasten their emotions on you. Men
are much easier to live and work with. They don't take umbrage like
women.'

It is unusual for Cancerian women to experience little affinity for
their own sex. Once again it is a measure of the strength of Barbara's
open and direct Aries-Mars influence that she should, against her
natural Sun Cancer inclinations, prefer the ways and company of

men. In Jungian terms she has a strong animus (the projection of the masculine). While she loves beautiful clothes and accessories and surrounds herself in glorious colour—the personification of the ideal feminine—she handles the world with the assertive style of a man. Yet the heroines in her novels are archetypically Cancerian—ultra feminine, sweet, and above all pure. Though Barbara extols the virtues of chastity and remains convinced that all men want the woman they love to be a virgin until marriage, she herself achieved an ecstatically happy marriage to a man who adored her and placed her on a pedestal in spite of her previous entanglements. One must either draw the conclusion that Barbara is preaching the philosophy of 'do as I say, not do as I do', or that she recognizes that her ideals are not practicable in the real world, although they should be aspired to in order to prevent complete moral decay. In the light of some comments she made towards the end of our conversation, I suspect the latter is true. 'My life has its complications. It never works out quite how you want it to. You always think when you're young and you read novels like mine that you're going to marry a Duke who'll absolutely adore you and have fifteen sons. It simply doesn't work out that way.' It is when Barbara Cartland moves away from her soap box that one glimpses the inner wise woman. She might weave wonderful fantasies for people to build their hopes and dreams upon, but she knows only too well that a deep and binding relationship demands far more from two individuals than just the romantic bliss they can generate.

Romantic novels are not the only books to pour forth from the Cartland fountain. She has published biographies, autobiographies, history books, cookery books, health and beauty books, and even one on the supernatural (**I Seek the Miraculous**). 'I'm not a psychic, but when I visit places to work on a plot for a book—perhaps a temple in Delphi or Sri Lanka—suddenly the inspiration is there—it all comes together, like a revelation . . . when I dictate my books, I don't go into a trance, but the words definitely flow as though they'd already been written.' One can trace Barbara's intuitive abilities, her heightened sensitivity and her interest in the spiritual to the 90° angle between Mars (her chart ruler) and Neptune. This linking of the Mars energy to the ethereal Neptunian heights, which can produce transcendant experience or sheer escapism, is also the driving force behind her writing. Barbara has experienced the power of spiritual healing at first hand and witnessed paranormal phenomena. After her husband Hugh's death in December 1963 a strong scent of carnations permeated her bedroom. 'I knew it was Hugh. You see he'd always believed death was the end of everything: there was no afterlife—although I firmly believe in the wheel of rebirth—and it was his way of telling me he'd been wrong. Every year we went to

Paris for a second honeymoon. Hugh would buy me a huge bunch of carnations, Malmaisons—you can't get them now. Each morning he'd place one in his buttonhole. When the same exotic scent kept wafting into my room after the funeral—everyone noticed it—I knew it was him.'

A mere two thousand words can hardly do justice to a life as rich and varied as Barbara Cartland's. While her role as the Queen of the romantic novel is most familiar to the public, throughout her life she has energetically fought for countless causes* and will no doubt continue to do so until she draws her last breath. When asked what she would like to be remembered for she said, 'for giving the people beauty and love ... love is the most beautiful, sacred, and Divine emotion we can experience in life. Love between a man and a woman, which is both physical and spiritual—the perfect love—is something we all yearn for and the nearest thing we get to the love of God ... we all reach for the stars and although we may not touch them, we try.'

Note for Astrologers: (1) Saturn is an extremely significant planet for Barbara Cartland. It is the most elevated planet; strong in its own house (of, among several ideas, professional standing) and in its own sign. Saturn is also conjunct the angle. While there are strong indications of the success she has achieved in her life—most notably Jupiter conjunct the Midheaven—the Sun-Saturn opposition has consistently put a spanner in the works. As Robert Hand in **Planets in Aspect** says of this aspect: 'Others feel as threatened by you as you will feel threatened by them ... Don't wait for accolades from your competitors (or your superiors)—you may wait a long time.' Barbara Cartland, like many writers, has a rising Moon. This placing also provides a strong indication of her involvement with the public.

(2) Since there are so many significant incidents in Barbara's long and multi-dimensional life, to include long lists of relevant progressions and transits was out of the question. Thus, I have left it to the zealous astrologer to work them out for him or herself!

*At her instigation, the Minister for Housing (1962) instructed local councils to provide gypsies with houses. She was also behind the Government enquiry into the housing and conditions of the elderly (1956).

PROFILE OF A CANCER MAN

COLIN WILSON

Are science and mysticism one and the same? Is optimism a form of self-deception? Where does the universe end? Why are we here anyway? And for that matter who is Colin Wilson? For answers to these (and more) simple topics of interest to everyday folk, why not, like me, drop in on Colin Wilson one afternoon for some tea and conversation. Alternatively, you could read one of his forty or so highly speculative books; or, if this still seems too daunting, simply digest this profile.

Colin Wilson is by no means your average Cancer man. He is a prolific writer, a typical obsessive intellectual, yet, paradoxically, an intuitive rather than a logical thinker. From plain working-class origins and without the benefit of a university education, he became a leading writer by the age of twenty-four. Yet in some ways he appears to have been fighting for recognition ever since!

Colin was born in Leicester in 1931. His father was in the boot and shoe trade and his mother was 'just a mum'. 'I was very much a love-child. My parents had to get married and I was born six months later!' Two brothers and a sister followed. While the family was not well off, Colin remembers his childhood as exceedingly happy. 'I was always a jolly and dominant little boy. I was lucky being the first born—I was spoilt, which was a good thing because it got me used to thinking that life was good. It gave me a great feeling of confidence.' As a child, Colin was always top of the class, but since neither of his parents had come from an academic background, and because there was no money, university—even with the aid of a scholarship—was out of the question. 'When I was a child I wanted to be a scientist. I discovered from an early age that I could easily master subjects; and I found it such fun just absorbing things that I've done it all my life.' As an example of his precosity, when Colin was thirteen, he thought it would a great idea to summarize all science in terms of simple

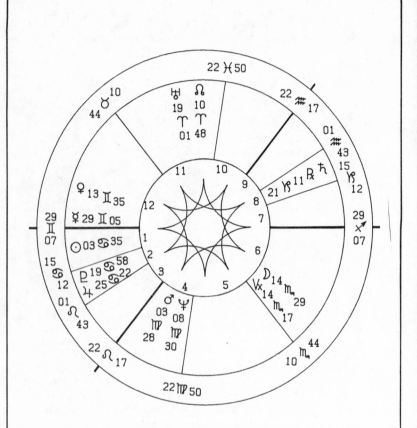

COLIN WILSON

26 6 1931   3h 30m 0s GMT

PLACIDUS 52N29 1W09

formulae so he started work on a little book called 'A Manual of General Science'. 'I got more and more absorbed and it ended up as seven volumes—full of everything I had devoured along the way, including aeronautics and philosophy! Later on I devoured everything I could find on music, art and literature.' Colin left school at sixteen, and after six months working in a factory, became a lab assistant at his old school. However, during his six months' sojourn in 'industry' he lost his interest in science. 'I'd taken to reading poetry and become very subjective and introverted, and I'd decided I wanted to become a writer. So by the time I was sixteen and a half I'd switched from science, which up until then had been a great dominating obsession, to literature.' Within seven years, on the publication of his first book, **The Outsider**, he was hailed as a major writer. And together with John Osborne (who had a similar overnight success with **Look Back in Anger**) he became one of the original 'Angry Young Men'.

Since Colin was born at sunrise, his persona (viewed astrologically through the Ascendant) reflects the Sun's forceful effulgence. The power of the Sun on the Ascendant virtually ensures that this dominant little boy would make an impact on his environment—if not the world. Closer still to the Ascendant—within two minutes—is Mercury, symbolizing communication, knowledge, and information. While the proximity of Mercury to the Ascendant by no means guarantees a giant intellect, it certainly suggests an immense curiosity and the ability to impart information well—especially since Mercury and the Ascendant are in the airy, Mercurial sign of Gemini.

With Mars and Neptune in the fourth 'house' of family, a mixed experience of early life is indicated. Neptune in this area can breed insecurity in childhood; sometimes the individual feels he lacks a strong family bond, or the home conditions are far from ideal. Neptune in this position can also indicate a blissful childhood. While Colin has happy memories of his early years and clearly relished being spoilt, the relationship with his father was far from perfect. Indeed Colin's father was a bad-tempered, frustrated man. He disliked his work and tended to take it out on the rest of the family. Although in later life his father mellowed considerably so that people thought him an amiable, charming fellow, when Colin and his brothers and sisters were young they came near to hating him at times. Mars in the fourth reinforces the idea that father was a fractious, difficult man and, with the conjunction to Neptune, it is likely that Colin never really knew him—at least as a youngster. Fortunately, his mother—an all-important figure for Cancerians—was wonderful. 'I'm very close to my mother. She isn't matriarchal, she's a rather quiet, sweet sort of person (an Aries!), though she's quite strong. As a child, I was tremendously emotionally attached to Mum, and I'd imagine that when I grew up I'd take her on a trip around the world. Unfortunately, she wasn't well enough when the opportunity arose.' With his Moon in the emotionally potent sign of Scorpio and its trine 120° aspect to Pluto, the indications are that Colin would have a deep and powerful relationship with his mother, and while mother obsession can become an occupational hazard for some Cancerians, Colin seems to have escaped this psychological impediment.

Like many a Cancerian man, Colin discovered the route to sensual experience in his teens; and by the time he was nineteen, he was reaping the harvest of some of his wild oats! His girlfriend became pregnant, thus Colin was 'pitchforked' into marriage. Predictably, the marriage failed, not because of any incompatibility, but simply through the domestic pressures placed on a young couple with a baby. After eighteen months spent in five different homes they decided to separate.

Almost a year later, in the December of 1953, he met his second wife, Joy. 'I met Joy in a big store in Leicester. I was greatly tempted by her, she was a sweet, easy-going, good-natured girl [a Sun Aquarian with Moon in Sagittarius and Venus in Pisces]. When I asked her what books she had on her shelves and she said, **Ulysses**, Yeats' poetry and Proust (in French). I thought she'd be ideal!' Although Joy was engaged to a fellow student at Trinity College, Dublin, Colin persuaded her to come down to London where he was living by then. 'Joy took a bed-sit in London. I used to spend all day writing at the British Museum, then I'd take my sleeping bag up to Hampstead Heath and sleep out under the stars. Just occasionally I'd spend the night with Joy.' Two years later, in May 1956, the pattern of their routine, gentle existence changed beyond recognition.

Over the Christmas of 1954, Colin conceived the idea of a book called **The Outsider in Literature**. He sent a draft to the publisher Victor Gollancz, who, to his surprise and delight, agreed to publish. Colin was paid £75 as an advance, and **The Outsider** came out in May 1956. 'Joy and I were living in a small flat in Chepstow Villas at the time. I went out to get the Sunday papers, and discovered **The Sunday Times** and **The Observer** had rave reviews about it. Then someone told me there had been banner headlines in the **Evening News** the day before saying, 'He's a major writer and he's only 24'! Well, by ten o'clock, the 'phone was ringing like mad . . . radio, TV, **Life** magazine, **Time** magazine—the sleeping bag story was everywhere.'

Clearly for a Cancerian the onslaught of publicity must have been alarming and invasive to say the least. 'Yes, I found it a vertiginous experience.' He became public property, and his every move worthy of journalistic copy. Unfortunately for Colin, his private life provided

the newspapers with a field day. 'We were having dinner one night
when suddenly Joy's parents burst in with a horse-whip! They'd
discovered Joy was living with me and, worse, her sister had read
some journals of mine containing notes for my novel **Ritual in the
Dark**—all about a homosexual sex-killer. They were pretty alarmed.'
In the ensuing furore, Colin was forced to summon the police, who
asked Joy's parents to leave—after all, Joy was over twenty-one! The
situation might well have been contained within the family ranks
had Colin and Joy not been entertaining a dinner guest—Gerald
Hamilton (on whom Christopher Isherwood based his Mr Norris). On
witnessing the extraordinary tableau of events, Gerald belted off and
rang all Fleet Street. 'The result was that as soon as the police and
Joy's parents had left, the doorbell rang and there was the **Daily
Mirror** with photographers and journalists.' In an effort to escape the
press, Joy and Colin fled to Devon, which only made the story more
sensational—'Runaway lovers in mad dash to Devon hideaway'. With
the help of the **Daily Express** they next found their way to Ireland,
and eventually back to London.

The constant pressures of notoriety ultimately persuaded them to
move out of London. 'The press became quite hostile—they were
sick of angry young men—so we rented a cottage in Cornwall. It was
beautiful—by the sea in a little valley with a burbling brook; it even
had roses around the door.' While this idyllic setting would appear to
be the perfect one to foster a writer's inspiration, it proved extremely
distracting, and instead of writing all day making love seemed a far
more attractive idea! 'I cheated on Joy a bit but she took it in her
stride. She tended to be not in the least suspicious or jealous unless it
presented itself under her nose, then she did her nut! The result was
that if ever I spent a couple of days away with a strange girl, it was
such a marvellous relief to get back to Joy . . . You get tremendous
charm from women. If someone has stars in their eyes about you,
well, it's a marvellous ego boost. Of course, I've grown out of all that
now.'

Cancerian men tend to be faithful: they don't like taking risks in
their relationships and are appalled at the prospect of rejection or the
severance of an emotional bond. While Colin is a committed family
man who adores his wife and his children, he is (or rather was) only
faithful in his fashion. Astrologically, this can be traced to the strong
Geminian and Jupiterian influence in his chart. Colin has his Venus
and Ascendant in Gemini, and his 'house' of relationships is ruled by
Jupiter, which is caught up in a configuration with Uranus and
Saturn.* The Geminian side of his nature is restless and variety
seeking, and not ideally suited to one permanent romantic

*See **Note for Astrologers**.

partnership. The Jupiterian influence suggests he seeks a larger-than-life experience in relationships. Since Jupiter is in a tense 90° angle to volatile Uranus he is prone to sudden romantic liaisons that provide excitement and novelty. Yet because Jupiter is held in check by the responsible hand of Saturn, he knows where his obligations lie. Colin is extremely lucky in that he found the right woman with whom he could have the security and loyalty he thrives on, yet who also gave him the romantic rope he needed. Had the astrologer lacked the benefit of this first-hand knowledge, it would have been all too easy to assume he found his marriage a restrictive factor in his life. As it was, the opportunity to pursue the occasional extra-marital liaison relieved the pressure and frustration that his Saturn in the eighth 'house' of emotional and sexual exchange might otherwise have brought to bear. Since Colin's Mars is given an idealistic colouring by the proximity of Neptune, he might well have been the type to fall in love, and certainly to nurture high expectations of women. 'No, I don't fall in love and I haven't sought that experience in relationships—I've just got a strong sex-drive . . . So few women can reach you through the intellect. Joy is different.' While Colin has not sought a transcendental level in his relationships, the ecstasy-seeking nature of this Mars-Neptune conjunction is a strong, if not overriding, influence in his life.

'My basic obsession is that feeling of ecstasy—the good beyond the present moment. We're looking at the world from a worm's eye view. It's only when suddenly you get these "peak moments" [moments where an intense feeling of elation spontaneously floods the system] that you see that the world is truly wonderful . . . When my daughter, Sally, was about two, she disappeared in the middle of Cheltenham. We spent what seemed like hours searching for her in a state of desperate anxiety. Luckily we found her. I remember as I was driving home in the car I suddenly thought, "Aren't big red buses beautiful, and isn't exhaust smoke a lovely smell." All that agony of uncertainty had gone and there was this ecstatic feeling of wonderfulness. I realized that the relief had opened me and made me see the good beyond the present moment.' Astrologically, 'peak experiences' are Neptunian in essence; Colin, with his Mars (a symbol of energy and drive) close to this planet, has turned the pursuit of ecstasy into a kind of personal crusade, or, at the very least, it has become a driving obsession. Since this duo is to be found in the pragmatic earth sign of Virgo, Colin is concerned with the nature of the experience and how it can be realistically harnessed. 'The idea of ecstasy being an illusion fascinates me—Bertrand Russell tells of a man who when he was drunk thought he knew the secret of existence and wrote it down. When he looked the next morning, he'd written, "There's a strong smell of paint." The question is, if these moments of ecstasy aren't delusions, then how can you make them come back? How can you turn them on at will? This, I suppose, has been the central question of all my work.'

The layman often assumes that mystics are people who waft around in flowing garments with an ever-present aura of peace and serenity about them. This, of course, is romantic fantasy. Mystics are human and thus just as prone as the rest of us to the pitfalls, problems, temptations, and ecstasies of the human condition. The difference with the mystic is that he has penetrated, or attempted to penetate, the veil that stands between man and truth. Thus he no longer exists in the shade: he sees the limits man imposes on himself and the infinite possibilities he can become. Colin is certainly a mystic by this definition. With his scientific, keenly analytical mind, he has steadfastly and objectively argued the case for and against each and every aspect of the paranormal, yet like the true adept his exploration and investigation has been conducted in the manner of a quest for truth and illumination. 'To me, science and mysticism are very much the same thing. Einstein once said that the motive that drives people to science is the motive that drives people out of cities at the weekend and onto high mountains where they can see wide views. And it is true that science gives you this wonderful feeling of standing on a mountain top with great views in front of you. For me, science simply meant the acquisition of knowledge. I was fascinated by what I perceived to be a circle of knowledge; that is, chemistry leads on to physics, which leads on to biology, geology, psychology and so on.'

Although Colin accepts that 'peak experiences' and the surges of inspiration he gets while writing are mystical experiences of a sort, he maintains he has never had a vision or been transported out of his body. 'What I find happening more is that I get into these states of driving optimism. At my best I'm fizzing and bubbling with a sort of optimistic energy and this is the basis of my work and my life. In my teens I went through states of tremendous depression and attempted suicide once. I actually got as far as taking the bottle of potassium cyanide off the shelf and uncorking it. Then, just as I was about to drink it, I had a clear impression of myself a few minutes hence lying on the floor with an appalling pain in the pit of my stomach. In a funny sense I'd become two people: there was this little idiot Colin Wilson feeling very sorry for himself and me looking down on him not caring whether he killed himself or not, but that if he did, he'd kill me too! So I put the cork back in the bottle and suddenly I felt all these problems dissolve away as silly and trivial.'

Colin's Cancerian Sun and Scorpio Moon show him to be a man of depth and intensity, a man capable of huge emotional ups and downs. Yet this part of his personality is balanced by his detached, rational approach to life—qualities that stem from the Geminian emphasis and his Virgoan Mars. Each time his emotions threaten to plunge him into uncertain chaos, his rational side comes to the rescue—a factor that is as evident in his personality as it is in his writing. Leaps of faith and forays into questionable and vague areas of the paranormal are balanced by clear argument and objectivity. 'I've always been an odd mixture. I'm a very intuitive person yet I'm reasonably articulate. I'm also not a quick-witted person in the sense that I can reel off brilliant answers and epigrams on the spur of the moment. I'm a slow, intuitive Crab. I'm also very persistent. I'm like Bruce and the spider.'   .

Indeed, Colin has needed his persistence over the years, for although he had a major success with his first book, and thus seemed set for life, he has never scaled those same lofty peaks with any other work. He has, of course, had several best-sellers, but he feels the critics have ignored many of his best books and even slaughtered some of them. His most recent novel, **The Personality Surgeon**—a masterpiece according to some—received only one review in the British Press. Did reviewers bracket him as quirky and consider him just a cult writer? Or is it merely a severe case of Cancerian hypersensitivity? Colin disagrees, but thinks he could well have upset the Establishment. Whatever the real reason for his 'exile', twenty-five years in the literary wilderness is a bitter pill to swallow, especially when you have been hailed as a great writer with your first book. It is tempting for an astrologer to speculate that perhaps this is Fate's way of ensuring that he continues his prodigious output, for over the years it has been the lack of necessary funds that has kept him manacled to his typewriter. 'I'm convinced that there's a definite Fate behind life. It's as though God, or Fate, keeps putting weights and loads on you until you feel you can't take any more. Then suddenly something wonderful happens, and you think, yes, life is WONDERFUL! It's the old carrot and stick: the carrot keeps you going for a while, then just as you think you have it right, back comes the stick again.' From an astrological point of view, Colin's dilemma can be related to Uranus, the ruler of his tenth house of profession and life direction, locked in the tense configuration with Jupiter, Saturn and Pluto: as much as Jupiter gives with one hand Saturn stubbornly confiscates with the other, and at the midpoint between them inspiration is born. Perhaps, like many people with a Uranian-Aquarian theme to their life direction, Colin is a man whose ideas are light years ahead of his time: the kind of man future generations will hold in high esteem and wonder at the short-sightedness of his twentieth-century contemporaries. But for a man who confesses a surfeit of optimism and an obsession about ecstasy, perhaps it is just Fate's way of awakening him to the realization that so-called success and failure are merely 'two imposters' and just another aspect of Maya!

Note for Astrologers: (1) Jupiter, Colin's 7th 'house' ruler, is in conjunction to Pluto and in opposition to Saturn (in the 8th 'house' of emotional and sexual exchange): all three planets are squared by Uranus thus forming a cardinal 'T'-square. The Moon in Scorpio is also quincunx Venus (in the secretive 12th 'house') and widely quincunx Uranus—thus forming a Finger of Fate. Both these configurations suggest tension in regard to relating and the desire for freedom versus the need for stability and security.

(2) Colin's 6th 'house' Moon in Scorpio is much in evidence in his interest in crime—strictly in the abstract sense. In 1960 he co-wrote the **Encyclopaedia of Murder**—'I suppose it was the kind of desire on my part to bring order into the world, and crime at that time had never been put into any order like a dictionary.'

(3) In 1956, when **The Outsider** was published, Colin's progressed Ascendant was conjunct Pluto and square Uranus: transiting Jupiter was conjunct the IC (month of publication). On 24 May there was a lunar eclipse at 3° Gemini—square his Neptune and semi-sextile his Sun.

LEO

23 July – 22 August

PUSSY-CATS AND
PRIMA DONNAS

LEO
PUSSY-CATS AND PRIMA DONNAS

THERE are two astrological myths that are harder to dispel than any others: first, that all Scorpios are sex-maniacs; second, that every Leo is a self-centred show-off. Leaving Scorpio on one side for the moment, while Leo is a sign synonymous with self-consciousness (in its truest sense) and creativity, it expresses itself in varying degrees of light and shade from individual to individual. Thus, for every pushy and overbearing Leo, there is a warm-hearted, humane one. Certainly, this sign has more than just a passing association with the theatre and the arts, and even those Leos who hide their sunny aura behind a big black cloud possess an in-built attraction for the limelight, and an instinct for using a situation to good dramatic effect.

Another astrologer once told me that she found Leo the easiest sign of the zodiac to spot. She explained that while all the other signs think you'll never guess which one they are, Leos assume you will. In fact, you must, otherwise they get miffed and very huffy. After all, the monarchy expects to be recognized, and Leo is a sign noted for its royal connections—mythical and otherwise—a link which Leos of every status, nationality, and creed seem to reflect. As far as their appearance goes, Leos usually have an imposing presence and a regal bearing: small or tall, slim or chubby, Leos tend to thrust back their noble shoulders—some might say, puff themselves up—and most display a proud carriage and an elegant gait. Like the other fixed signs, Scorpio, Taurus, and Aquarius, Leos often have a square jaw; also, the forehead is pronounced and invariably beautifully dome-shaped. Although physical beauty owes more to genetics than astrology, Leo can be a strikingly good-looking sign, if only because Lions know how to make the best of themselves.

Although Leos' reputation for being pompous and self-glorifying applies to some rather than all members of this sign, there is a tendency for many of them to be over confident about themselves and overrate their effect on others. At the end of her first consultation with me, one Leo lady voiced the opinion that I must have enjoyed doing her chart and was no doubt fascinated by her life story—perhaps I could use her as a case history. Much as I hated to admit it, I did, and I have. But I must add, like many other Leos, my client's warm and positive personality more than compensated for any tendency to elevate her importance.

To appreciate the drive towards self-understanding and self-mastery (which is far nearer the core of Leo than the desire to display its talents *ad nauseam*) one must look beneath the surface of this ebullient fire sign and explore its myths and ancient mysteries.

Leo, whose symbol is the Lion, is ruled by the Sun. The physical sun is, of course, at the centre of our solar system, and the star around which all of the planets, including Earth, orbit. Astrologically, the Sun symbolizes the true self, the spirit that permeates the individual's nature and his experience. Thus, it is hardly surprising that a sign linked to such a powerful planetary body should contain some equally strong and powerful themes.

In the past, every culture worshipped a sun god: he was Aten/Amen-Ra to the Egyptians, Quetzalcoatl to the Aztecs, Mithra to the Persians (Iranians), Brahma to the Hindus, and many, many others. The sun gods themselves and the tales of great mythical heroes like Osiris, Vishnu, and Hercules emphasized the importance and power of the life-giving sun and reflected its disappearance (death) and joyful reappearance (resurrection) the following day. Even now, the theme of a hero's struggle, his death and resurrection, form the basis of many of our best loved fairy tales, which in turn find their way into some of the great operas and ballets—Wagner's **The Ring** and Tchaikovsky's **Swan Lake**, for instance.

One of the fundamental mysteries contained in all religions, including Christianity, is the birth of a self-sacrificing god. This great and glorius being is almost always born of a virgin; his life involves many trials and tribulations; he dies, often at the hand of others, after which he is incarcerated and then reborn. It is the incarceration, or 'tomb' experience, however, that is crucial to all solar myths. It is at this point that the Creator/God imprisons himself in his creation in order to transform and revivify 'him'. In fairy tales the hero frequently enters a forest, or a castle, wherein he undergoes some transforming experience, often one involving a choice. In **Swan Lake**, the hero, Prince Siegfried, while walking through the forest, meets the Swan Princess Odette, and falls in love with her. She has been turned into a swan by a wicked magician and only returns to her human form at night. The spell can only be broken by one who swears his true love for her, but if he proves false she is doomed for eternity. Later, at a ball in the castle, the Swan Princess suddenly appears (dressed in black). Siegfried swears his love for her, only to find he has been tricked by the magician who has substituted his evil daughter, Odile, for Odette. Siegfried finds his way back to the forest where he is reunited with his tragic Odette. They hurl themselves into the lake, thus breaking the spell, to find everlasting life together.

This fairy tale, like many other stories and myths of a similar vein, has a weighty implication in psycho-spiritual terms: it can be seen to describe a process of the death of the conscious ego through contact with the greater self and the birth of self-realization. Surely, it can be no cosmic accident that the founder of analytical psychology, the great Carl Jung, was born with his Sun in Leo. This transformation theme is also found in ancient alchemical texts: representations of a child lying in a hollow oak (a tree ruled by the sun) symbolize the alchemical furnace, Athanor. This furnace had to be kept at a critical temperature for the formation of Philosopher's Stone, from which the alchemist could turn base metals into gold. Here, the constant heat of Athanor is reminiscent of the fixed nature of this fire sign and, of course, gold is Leo's metal.

To return to the hero-motif once more: in many heroic myths, the lion forms a central part of the action. Hercules' first labour was to kill the Lion of Nemea, which was invulnerable to wounds. Afterwards, Hercules always wore the skin around his shoulders. Vishnu was half man, half lion; Mithra was often depicted as a lion (also, incidentally, a symbol of royalty) slaying a bull—a ritual act of re-creation. Sometimes in bas-reliefs Mithra and the bull are shown with a scorpion or serpent in the background, which gave added symbolic weight to the theme of death and rebirth in solar myths.

Mithra's heroic tale follows the familiar path of decline, fall, and ultimate resurrection, yet it also provides some very interesting astrological food for thought. The central Mystery of Mithra involves the journey of the soul. It was thought that the immortal soul descended at birth through the spheres of the planets, gathering impurities along the way. During life on earth, which was considered a term of trial, the soul had the opportunity, through moral effort and revealed wisdom, to cleanse itself. After death, the spirits of good and evil fought for possession of the soul. Mithra intervened on behalf of his initiates, and those who were fortunate passed onwards and upwards, back through the spheres into the realms of light. Initiation to the cult and its mysteries were steeped in secrecy, but it appears that there were some real and bloody rites as well as the more symbolic ones. Adepts were graded according to their degree of initiation, of which there were seven—Raven, Husband, Warrior, Lion, Persian, Courier of the Sun, and Father, which related, somewhat obliquely, to the seven then-known planets.* This is one of the few 'religions' that ties in graphically with planetary symbolism. It also has shades of Edgar Cayce's concept of planetary sojourns, or the planets as dimensions of experience for the soul to pass through prior to incarnation.

Fascinating as this may be, how does it all relate to Leo? The urge for self-expression is tremendously strong in Leos, which is why so many of them tread the boards, professionally or in amateur dramatics, acting out various roles—heroic and otherwise. Yet Leo men and women are heroes and heroines in their own right, albeit on an extremely subtle level. The hero's journey is basically one of self-discovery, of seeking the centre, or of finding the light within himself. In the real world, the Leo individual feels impelled (often unconsciously) to find out who he is and his place in the scheme of things. But for Leo, this is never accomplished in a vacuum: Leo needs feedback from others; he needs an audience, some applause, approval, and appreciation to urge him on his way. How he is perceived by others acts as a mirror for self-recognition. Leo is also a tremendously creative sign: the outpouring of his talents are precious offerings of self-expression, which is why Leo, of all the signs, becomes so crushed if his gifts are rejected or criticized. At some point, however, the creative process becomes an inner journey—perhaps after some failure or setback. Like the passage of the sun, rising, peaking and sinking to do battle in the Underworld to win the right to rise again, the Leo man or woman has to fight the untamed creature—the lion—in himself in order to tap his own creative source and shine anew. It's a sort of solar cycle of becoming. Without inner reflection and its offshoot, humility, there is a certain brashness, a harsh neon-lighting to Leo's nature instead of a constant, inviting warmth that radiates everything in its path.

The Leo who has yet to make the journey is one whose ego towers over him like an unvanquished foe, one who, to everyone else, seems only a crashing, self-centred bore.

Aside from the process of transformation symbolized by the passage of the sun under the earth, the sun as both giver and withholder of light also

*Comparatively recently, mosaics were uncovered at the Mithrae at Ostia showing the symbols for the seven degrees and their connection with the planets.

presents a theme of dualism—not dissimilar from that of Scorpio and Pluto.*
In the **Rigveda** the sun was considered ambivalent, being radiant yet also
'black' and invisible. There are several implications for Leo here: on the one
hand there are Leos whose temperaments belong to the beneficent, 'light'
and outgoing 'daytime' sun, and there are those who tap its darker, more
inscrutable, occasionally tyrannical and manipulative side. On the other,
there are those Leos who are every bit as warm and affectionate as their
sunny counterparts, but who hide their light under the proverbial bushel.
Also, each and every Leo cannot maintain a permanent high of 77°
fahrenheit—there are times when the brightest Leo feels like digging a hole
for himself and climbing in. When Leos, like Scorpios and Capricorns, hit a
trough of low pressure they go down with a bang, and Leo's black clouds
have a way of enveloping everyone and everything.

Another aspect of this dualism of the sun is that many Leos undergo a
change from one extreme to the other during their lifetime. Until her mid-
twenties, Leonine Princess Margaret was a happy, carefree, ebullient
female—the darling of the Royal Family. After the Peter Townsend debacle
and the unhappiness and stress of her marriage to Lord Snowdon, her
persona—at least to the public—became obdurate and sour. Now, in middle
age, she seems, after her 'wilderness years', to be regaining her former **joie de
vivre**, though with an added, more mature glow. On the other hand, Princess
Anne, another Leo, appears to be doing the reverse. From a truculent,
abrasive, and generally lacklustre early youth, she seems in her mid-thirties to
be developing a more mellow, deliciously humorous, and benign personality!

Certainly, the concept of the **sol niger**, black sun, provides an explanation
(without looking at the deeper layers of the chart) for the many Leos who
exude a more sober and restrained aura, even if they also retain the warm
spirit of this sign. Sometimes, however, those Leos who withhold their fire,
are, in truth, repressed and embittered. Besides needing love and affection in
huge doses, the Leo man or woman also needs to succeed, and for the more
materialistically minded, to have the trappings of success. For Leo, high self-
esteem and the attainment of his goals are essential, and much is at stake
should he feel either are in doubt—especially if he sees others making the
grade. There is an unpleasant side to Leo that resents others taking centre
stage and the accompanying applause, which in turn hampers his own
progress. When resentment and envy fill Leo's heart, instead of his usual
spirit of optimism and good will, a somewhat sinister and unappealing side to
his nature emerges. While Leo pouts and froths at the mouth, there's little to
fear, but the more self-control a frustrated Leo can muster, the more likely he
is to resort to unfair and ruthless tactics. Leo can be a devious manipulator
when he wants to be, and like the Lion, once his anger or his greed is aroused
he'll go for the 'kill'.

All signs have their less attractive side and Leo's impetus to strike back

*The evolution of the atom bomb and its essential component, Plutonium, is—in
astrological terms—an entirely Plutonic idea. Yet an atomic explosion resembles the
same fusion that occurs on the surface of the sun. How appropriately symbolic,
therefore, that the dropping of the first atomic bomb on Hiroshima during the Second
World War took place with the Sun in close conjunction to Pluto in Leo.

fiercely when wounded—particularly when his pride has taken a knocking—can be devastating and irrevocable. Some Leos can also pick up the dictator syndrome and power-seeking tendencies of this sign—Napoleon was a Leo—which, combined with their drive and determination, makes them a formidable force or opponent in any walk of life. To some extent all Leos like issuing orders and having others running around after them; they also deeply resent anyone getting the better of them.

As a fire sign, Leo is motivated by his emotions, instincts, and desires; like Aries and Sagittarius, he is an 'act first, think later' individual, yet unlike the other two fire signs Leo is more reflective, often more considerate, and certainly more tenacious. He is also infinitely more stubborn. This sign hates admitting that he's wrong and most Leos can be extremely dogmatic and bloody-minded at times. Pride can be a dreadful affliction to Leo. Like King Canute, guided by the power of his cement-like convictions (and his omnipotence) the Leo individual will attempt to enforce his will on others and usually prefers to drown rather than admit he is in error.

Sometimes Leos not only attempt to foist their opinions on everybody else, but stubbornly refuse to acknowledge anything that they find unpalatable. Thus, it's only when the bailiffs arrive, the divorce petition is served, or they land up in hospital that they eventually face the truth.

While Aries and Sagittarius can shrug disaster off their shoulders like an old coat, Leos cannot accept failure at all. A Leo will put on a brave face to the rest of the world while he wrestles with the situation, but he doesn't accept defeat with a good grace. On the plus side, Leo learns from his mistakes and, of course, it is often in the face of failure that he embarks on his inner journey.

Inasmuch as Leos despise weakness in themselves, they abhor it in others. A Leo individual, by dint of his own courage and strong will, rarely empathizes with those who seem unable to cope with life and who buckle under the pressure of their problems. Thus he is often feared by others since he makes them feel even more inadequate and lacking in moral fibre. In this way Leo loses many friends and potential allies, yet, sadly, he often fails to realize why he is avoided or his invitations are declined. Indeed many Leo men and women are unaware of the forceful impact they make and cannot understand why others assume they are so strong.

To a greater or lesser extent, most Leos have an artistic streak. Some make a career of their talent while others use their flair to decorate their homes and fill them with attractive (and often expensive) furnishings. Literary talent—or perhaps just the 'gift of the gab'—is another Leonine trait which, along with their love of dramatics, propels many of them into the theatre and the music industry. Amongst many notable Leo names are Cecil B. de Mille, George Bernard Shaw, Mick Jagger, and Leonard Bernstein (Venus conjunct Neptune in Leo); and on the female front, Coco Chanel, Zelda Fitzgerald, Jackie Onassis, and Lucille Ball. Mythologically, Leo owes its musical and literary skills to its links with Apollo—god of light, intellect, and the arts. However, Apollo is also extremely apposite for Leo since he was a golden and beautiful god. Leo is the archetypal 'golden boy' (or girl) of the zodiac, full of great potential, possessed of magnanimity, grace, and charm, heir to a golden future. The individual who taps this aspect of Leo is blessed indeed. However, like the 'black' sun, there is a darker side to Apollo: he was a merciless archer who inflicted rapid death on his foes; he was also a god who revelled in adulation. This less laudable aspect of Leo can be seen in those who crave the tinsel of life and the pursuit of pleasure, perhaps most obviously demonstrated by many people involved in the theatre and film industries. The effusive life style of many stars, their exaggerated affection for all and sundry, and their need for constant attention and praise can make Leo's gold somewhat tinny and worthless.

The Royal Family is another great Leonine institution. This regal sign not only figures conspicuously in almost all the leading British Royal Family's charts, but their patronage of the arts—especially theatre—goes back many centuries. Prince Charles and Prince Edward were keen actors during their university days and the Christmas concerts held at Windsor Castle during the Second World War always featured the Queen and Princess Margaret in leading roles; Edward VII and Edward VIII were both keen on the theatre, and indeed on some actresses! Further back still, Louis XIV, the Sun King no less, virtually turned his reign into a splendid, great and glorious Leo pantomime.

Whether you like it or not, Leo is the sparkling jewel in the zodiac crown. No other sign has quite so much charisma and no other sign can glitter and dazzle as spectacularly as this resplendent fire sign. Yet, like 'fixed' Aquarius, Taurus, and Scorpio, Leo is a sign of extremes. At best, Leos are warm, beneficent, happy, spirited, generous, talented, and creative; at worst, self-indulgent, moody, obstinate, vengeful, possesive, and jealous. Leo's strength rests in his determination, his loyalty, his wisdom, his courage and the power of his love—of which we shall hear more later. His weakness lies in his pride, his susceptibility to praise and flattery, and his craving to be noticed. Self-discovery (through inner revelation) is Leo's quest, even though at times he seems merely self-centred, vain, and autocratic. Make no mistake, the Lion is metaphorically and literally the king of the jungle: his roar is just as powerful as his bite—although he's only pretending—sometimes. Treat this sign with respect; you may be glad you did one day.

RELATIONSHIPS

All the world loves a Leo . . . or so most Leos believe. How could anyone resist these gorgeous feline creatures? Presumably only those who resent permanently playing in the chorus or watching from the wings. Perhaps this is being rather hard on Leos, for even if most of them can only thrive on a constant hum of approval and appreciation from their partners, and a certain respect for their role, they are usually extremely affectionate, generous, and loyal in return. Certainly this sign is not a loner: Leos need partners like actors need audiences. Indeed, all the fire signs are a sorry sight without love in their lives; so much so, that Leos in particular are prone to illness and depression if isolated for too long or lacking in love. Only Libra can equal Leo as an ambassador of love, and although Mr and Ms Libra may have the wooing edge with their delicate brand of charm and flattery, the Leo man or woman has far more heart, passion, and constancy and is not such a familiar figure in the divorce courts. However, like all the fire signs, Leos tend to hurl themselves into romantic experience—head first, reason later—so they often collect a few emotional scars on their way to the altar.

THE FEMALE LEO

If Margaret Mitchell had given us Scarlett O'Hara's horoscope, Leo would surely have figured strongly. Scarlett was a woman of passion and courage: she was also resourceful, immensely proud, and fiercely jealous—all good Leo characteristics. Scarlett was never simpering or submissive, she was far too open and spirited for a glimmer of feminine guile to emerge. The Leo woman, like Scarlett, can dazzle and captivate almost any man she wants, but once she falls in love, she becomes totally committed—sometimes to the point of obsession—even if, like Ashley, he is patently wrong for her.

Everything about the Leo woman seems larger than life—especially her feelings. 'I express my emotions dramatically . . .' wrote one female with her Moon in Leo '. . . I like to show the world how much I love my partner. When I'm in love, the object of my affections is the most wonderful person in the world and I find it impossible to believe that anyone could dislike him. That is until I'm hurt or rejected, then he becomes the biggest blackguard in the world!'

Ms Leo, like Ms Aries and Ms Sagittarius, probably went through a tom-boy stage when she was a child—all the fiery ladies want to have a go at being one of the boys at some period of their lives—and as an adult a mischievous streak peeps out from the most sophisticated and feminine Leo veneer from time to time. But unlike the other two fire signs, who struggle awkwardly out of their adolescent cocoon into womanhood, Ms Leo usually manages the transition with great aplomb. Sagittarius and Aries find great difficulty in tailoring their strong personalities to fit a (newly) curvaceous body, but the Leo lady never forgets, even for a moment, that she is 'all woman'. Like many aspects of her life, Ms Leo can't resist play-acting at times. The Leo woman, whether she's one of the more typical extrovert, flamboyant sort or the less familiar subtle and moody variety, is highly aware of the potency and impact of her femininity. Although she is just as competitive as Ms Aries and just as autonomous as the Sagittarian, she can conceal her dominant, forceful nature behind a meltingly feminine, and often extremely decorative exterior.

The Leo lady is a fascinating mixture of fiery capriciousness and 'fixed' constancy. On the one hand, the Leo woman can pout and flounce with the best of them, yet her emotions are never superficial. Her coquettish, flirtatious behaviour belies immense loyalty and depth of feeling. In keeping with her fiery nature, Ms Leo wants excitement and challenge in her love life, yet she also needs security and consistency. Some Leo women find tremendous difficulty in establishing a balance between these extremes and lurch from a relationship that panders to the more carefree and adventurous side of their personalities to one that provides the stability and dependability they need. Occasionally, the Leo lady manages to find all these qualities in one man and one relationship, but more usually, she settles for a reliable, dependable partner while she generates all the sparks and dynamism herself—and with some to spare!

The Leo woman is never dull. Even if she has one of the more passive signs rising, which makes her appear more like a mouse than lion, once you dig beneath the surface the strong, proud—sometimes unruly—Leonine qualities are sure to be found.

Two keys open up this woman's heart: one is attention, the other is humour. The Leo lady likes to be amused. She probably romped and giggled her way through childhood, and even if times were hard she usually saw the funny side. To Ms Leo, laughter is the greatest antidote of all—it dissolves anger and tears, of which there are many in her life. Consequently, a man with a good sense of humour is absolutely essential for the Leo woman. Of course he must also make her feel loved and special.

A Leo lady is an all or nothing individual: she puts herself body, heart, ...nd soul into a relationship and naturally expects some equitable return. While at first Ms Leo's feelings are selfless—all she wants is to pour her love over her partner like a soothing unction—once the initial 'heat' has worn off, her devotional fires need some stoking. Flattery, some gentle ego-massage, a pretty 'je ne sais quoi' from the jewellers, go a long way; but best of all, and at considerable gain to her lover's bank account, the Leo woman wants to be constantly informed that she is adored and exalted above all others—even the children.

While the Leo woman is prepared to invest much, if not all, her energies into making a relationship work, she is not the sort to chain herself to the relentless demands of domesticity and the children—or the office for that matter: she needs some fun and entertainment. Most Leo ladies love going out, whether it's to a party, the theatre, or just a romantic dinner à deux. The fun of dressing-up, of getting there and of being seen, is essential to this woman's psychological well-being. Even the more introverted Leo likes to be entertained and needs the stimulation of good company. The Leo woman maintains her sanity with liberal doses of pleasure and amusement, and no matter how loyal she is, if she's bored or starved of affection and the good times, she'll turn her attentions elsewhere.

Which leads us to the subject of fidelity.

Despite Ms Leo's low boredom threshold, she basically fears change. With her 'fixed' temperament, her emotions are vulnerable to any threat to the status quo: while she loves innovation and challenge in her outer life, emotional upheaval and change are anathema to her. Consequently, the Leo woman, like the other 'fixed' ladies (Aquarius, Taurus, and Scorpio), often remains in a relationship for the security it provides even if it no longer inflames her emotionally and sexually. The Leo woman who stays in such a relationship does so under a misguided sense of loyalty. Nevertheless, the Leo woman is not a doormat. She may stick to her man like glue for fear of being lonely and impoverished, but eventually she will look for an escape hatch, usually through the love of a better man, but sometimes via the lure of a well-paid job. Once she has found a 'cushion' to soften her landing, she can wrench herself away from an unfulfilling relationship, but she doesn't sever any emotional bonds easily—they wear away gradually with age.

Ms Leo takes her marriage oaths very seriously and she is not one to leap blithely in and out of adultery, nor does she condone any such behaviour on her partner's part. This female has enormous pride: she is also extremely possessive and jealous. Ms Leo is always on the look out for any potential usurper for her husband's affections: rightly or wrongly, the Leo lady considers her man to be a much sought-after commodity—after all, if she finds him irresistible, so must every other hot-blooded female. Despite her sunny, open disposition, the Leo wife or girlfriend is on the scent immediately her suspicions are aroused: strangely enough, perhaps because of her 'fixed' mentality, her fears often lead her up the wrong track.

A client of mine was convinced that her boyfriend was having an affair with his secretary. Over a period of weeks she poured out her anxieties and her sleuthing activities—equal to any Scorpio—to her closest friend. No one was more devastated than my client when her boyfriend moved in with the bosom pal!

Even though Ms Leo presents a super-confident, highly glamorous, image she is often insecure about her looks and her ability to sustain her man's interest and affection. All of which goes a long way to explain why the Leo woman's dinner parties are often extremely thin on young, beautiful, and nubile females.

Clearly, the Leo woman who has found herself—and her man—is unlikely to feel threatened by competition, and indeed, the Leo female who can identify more with her rich inner qualities rather than her outer charms rarely experiences doubts about sustaining a relationship. Although some Leo women manage to find a quality of inner peace in their twenties and early thirties, a great many more reach this point after 40.*

Power and control, often concomitant with security needs, are also issues the Leo woman frequently faces in her relationships. Ms Leo dislikes being in a subservient or subordinate position to anyone, including her lover or husband. Even if the Leo female thinks she can be the proverbial 'little woman' her strong will and her urge to dominate suggest otherwise. This woman likes her own way and, fortunately for her, is capable of using a variety of devices, if not brute force, to get it. Even the 'little woman' will admit that no one countermands the way she runs the home. Provided a partner is prepared to acquiesce in her overriding views on home decoration/friends/his ties/next year's holidays, happiness will smile on their relationship: but given strong opposition, World War III could break out! On a more serious note, occasionally the need to control and dominate the partner emerges in the way that some Leo women browbeat, downgrade, and humiliate their partners to bolster their own position. In some ways, many Leo women like this find themselves in a Catch 22 situation: on the one hand they need a fitting consort, someone who measures up to their high standards and reflects their star quality: yet on the other, they cannot tolerate anyone who outshines them. To complicate matters further, while this kind of Leo lady seems bent on wielding the whip hand, she secretly longs to be dominated—a factor that encourages her to choose passive men as partners whom she increasingly grows to despise.

The ability to compromise is something the Leo woman needs to work towards in her relationships. While she is an enormously giving sort and has many wonderful attributes to offer her lovers, she should occasionally yield to their ideas, values, and opinions—even if she does know more and can do it

---

*The outer and inner changes that arise at the Uranus opposition—the astrological mid-life crisis which occurs between 38 and 42—are especially potent at freeing the 'fixed' individual from any inhibiting and restricting patterns and thus leading to greater self-awareness and inner strength.

better and quicker than they can. Otherwise, her partners, and perhaps everyone else, will see her only as a tiresome virago.

The fire signs are noted for their quick tempers and impetuous manner. The Leo woman is as quick to anger and provoke as Ms Aries and Ms Sagittarius, but she is far better at controlling herself. This can be both a strength and a weakness. While the Leo woman gains from counting to ten and avoiding unnecessary verbal skirmishes, she also has a tendency to block and suppress her anger, and so turn herself into an emotional pressure cooker. Thus, instead of a short, sharp burst of temper which enables her to kick over the traces easily, Ms Leo is prone to occasional major blow-outs that can be devastating both to her equilibrium and everyone else's. The Leo woman, like the Libran, hates to be unpopular, so she tends to stifle her real feelings, especially any hostile ones, to avoid any such possibility. This woman doesn't like to acknowledge any dark aspects of her nature: while Ms Leo is frank enough to tell you that she doesn't like your green hat, she'll rarely let it show that she despises you. By avoiding confronting people with her real feelings and consistently putting her best face forward, she is sometimes considered to be rather phoney and hypocritical. In an intimate relationship the Leo woman often tries hard to come to terms with irrational feelings of anger and resentment over her partner's misdeeds. Thus, she is rather prone to frigid silences, shattered only by the slamming of doors and the crashing of crockery!

Ms Leo is inclined, as the old cliché goes, to falling in love with love. She topples headlong and heart-first into romance and her love beams over her inamorato like an arc lamp. The Leo woman is particularly fascinated by strong, silent, and intellectual types—the more brooding and complicated the better. The Leo lady also likes there to be something special and important about her man—or at least something different. Status is crucial to Leo. And provided her lover can keep her interest, respect, and admiration, and demonstrate his love extravagantly and frequently, she'll make a wonderfully attentive and nurturing wife. (And wife it should be: the Leo woman is one of the least likely ladies in the zodiac to take to 'living in sin'.) What makes her romatic dreams even better, however, is enough money for life's big luxuries. Ms Leo is often clothes-mad and highly fashion-conscious: she has excellent, if expensive, taste, and prefers to keep well ahead of the Joneses. She is fond of quoting that 'money can't buy happiness', but in her case it definitely helps to minimize the misery.

Traditionally, Leo is thought to be a sign that loves children and relates well to them. Leo women are usually extremely good with young children and adolescents: they can involve themselves in play without looking or feeling foolish, and bring out the best in youngsters by responding to them with the child in themselves. These women are often natural teachers: their vivid imaginations and enthusiastic approach to learning inspires and stimulates young minds. Yet motherhood *per se* and the relentless rearing of offspring year after year is not exactly the Leo woman's idea of heaven.

Pregnancy and childbirth, while being the most creative and self-involving experience a woman can have, come with a hefty price-tag. Over the years, the Leo mother, although often a dedicated and efficient one, resents the time the children take up when she could be pursuing other avenues of creativity. This is one of the explanations why Leo women tend to have only one child and why Leo mothers favour the use of nannies and child-minders. If the Leo female cannot fulfil her goals, or at least have some outlet beyond the children, she can become bitterly resentful of her ties and take out her frustration on the rest of the family. As a fire sign, the Leo woman has definite aims in life: she also has a materialistic streak as well as an idealistic one. If she's single-minded enough, nothing will stand between her and her ambitions—not even her loved ones. But if her drives are unfulfilled or her life-style is not as she desires, she'll direct her ambition through her children and husband instead. Even less overtly ambitious Lionesses tend to make pushy and demanding parents—they're great believers in discipline and good manners too. Also, unlike the Cancerian, who tends to consider herself a mother first and a wife afterwards, the Leo female almost always puts her husband first—perhaps because, unconsciously, she fears he might love the children more.

This fiery lady was never made to be a domestic drudge. She is one of the most vital, bright, and sizzling stars in the zodiac. Of course, she can be vain, moody, cantankerous, and as stubborn as a mule on occasion. But she's never really a neurotic or complex creature. To love and to be loved is essential to her psychological survival, although she wouldn't mind money, success, and fame into the bargain. Don't be taken in by her confident manner: her ego is made of porcelain and prone to crack at the slightest tap. Indulge her frequently, support her with a firm but loving hand—she likes to feel she's not the only one in charge—and the sun will never set on your relationship.

THE MALE LEO

Consider for a moment a combination of Henry VIII and Winnie the Pooh and you have an identikit picture of the Leo man. Yes, he can be as arrogant, autocratic, pompous, and even as ruthless as Henry, but take off the fancy dress and you'll find a steadfast, soft and sentimental creature. Mick Jagger is an almost perfect Leo prototype (Sun, Mercury, Ascendant, and Jupiter in Leo). Even his facial features are 'classically' Leonine. He exudes charisma and sex appeal and has maintained his phenomenal success for over twenty years. Despite constant publicity over his dissolute pop-star existence, he is a traditionalist at heart—he believes in marriage and his children go to private school. In a characteristic Leo manner—and demonstrating the chauvinistic side of this sign—he agreed only to marry his second wife, model Jerry Hall, if she gave birth to a son. A few centuries ago, perhaps, the threat of the executioner's block would have hung over her instead.

Leo men, like their female counterparts, are often extremely attractive to the opposite sex. They normally have charm by the bushel, a wonderful sense of humour, and the ability to mix with anyone, somewhat in the style of their Aquarian opposites. However, their sense of humour frequently stops short at themselves and although their 'hail fellow, well met' ambience appears all-embracing, unwelcomed familiarity soon breeds Leo's contempt. This man cares enormously about protocol—he believes in pecking orders too—and provided he's chief rooster, he can be as magnanimous, generous and easy-going as, well, Henry VIII!

Like his fiery brothers, Mr Aries and Mr Sagittarius, the Leo man is a paladin at heart. In childhood he revelled in stories of adventure and romance, and as a grown up he continues to believe that faint heart never won fair lady, or anything else come to that. As a boy, he probably enjoyed playing fearless leaders and threw a tantrum if anyone else tried to muscle in as head-honcho. And although his friendly, giving nature won him lots of school chums, he also alienated a good many by being a thoroughly ungracious loser. (Leos sulk gloriously.) As he matures, the Leo man learns to temper his omnipotent tendencies for the sake of social and professional survival, but given the right scenario—his birthday party/a group expedition/the company's centenary—and he soon slips into his kingly garb, taking over the whole show and upstaging all-comers. Luckily for him, there are plenty of people who don't mind being told what to do and where to put themselves; and to give him his dues, he always rises splendidly to the occasion.

Of all the signs, Leo holds most true to the old cliché that all men are little boys at heart. These men often retain their boyish features well into middle age and tend to mature psychologically and emotionally rather late in life. As a fire sign, the Leo man is lead by his emotions, instincts, and enthusiasms: he is all too prone to ignoring red lights and good advice, thus landing himself in extremely hot water from time to time. He has the highest regard for his own opinions and experience, and combined with his 'fixed' nature, he frequently becomes the irresistible force and the immovable object all at the same time! Fortunately, he is immensely plucky and resourceful and usually rises to live another day even after the most ghastly catastrophes.

The little boy in Leo men can be attractive and lovable at times, yet absolutely infuriating and completely out of place at others. While his impulsive generosity and ardent declamations of his feelings will have a lady falling at his feet during the heady days of their romance, years of marital togetherness later the same ingenuous behaviour rarely has a similar effect, especially when the telephone is about to be cut off or he's just bought a Porsche with his redundancy settlement. Most Leo men nurture a childish desire to have the biggest and best out of life, which often tempts them to live beyond their means and in the style to which they'd like to become accustomed. A Leo man on the breadline can be a pitiful sight. Luckily, men of this sign are enormously determined and tenacious, and unless there are difficult Neptune contacts to the Sun or Mars, they usually manage to go far in life and stumble on a crock of gold even if they don't reach the rainbow's end.

If this fits the Leo stereotype so far, read on. In my experience, many Leo men do not altogether resonate with the sunny, outgoing nature of this sign but respond to its darker, more obscure side and its less constant, even anarchistic, tendencies.

All signs contain elements of their opposite number within them and from time to time display characteristics of the other sign. In this way, some Leos seem to pick up the volatile, unconventional qualities of Aquarius.* This sort of Leo may be strongly altruistic, and thus warm, friendly, and inviting to the

*In some esoteric teachings, Uranus (Aquarius' ruling planet) is considered to be the higher octave of the Sun—Leo's ruling planet.

world at large; but when it comes to one-to-one relationships he soon catches a cold. Freedom to be himself without constraint or criticism is essential to this man, which means that he is too self-oriented and, basically, too selfish for the symbiosis of an intimate relationship. On the one hand, this kind of Leo may be wrapped up in the single-minded pursuit of his career and/or is totally consumed by his creative muse, which leaves little time or emotional energy over for anything or anyone else. On the other, he may find it emotionally and psychologically difficult to adapt or yield to another's needs and although he may want the comfort, security, and indeed the love a marriage would provide, his relationships prove volatile and unsatisfactory. Sometimes he loses heart altogether and becomes a loner.

The sort of Leo who taps his polar opposite may not be content with a conventional marriage; he is idealistic if not rather bohemian; he wants something 'different' from his relationships and his partner and he is likely to balk at the traditional breadwinner and patriarchal roles of husband and father.

There are also some Leo men who relate to the more subtle, deeper, and perhaps murkier aspects of this sign. Such an individual exhibits little or none of the extrovert tendencies of Leo. He wants complete control of everything and everyone in his life (he is tremendously security oriented) and he can be a difficult and inscrutable man to live with. Yet his feelings usually run deep. He is capable of passion and emotional intensity (like most Leo men) but he finds it difficult to communicate his feelings verbally; thus he rarely has trouble-free relationships. Because he is a complex individual, he is not the sort to attract or indeed want a carefree, light-hearted contact with a partner; but because he controls and protects his emotions, emotional mis-communications and subsequent estrangements pepper his relationships. 'My most heart-rending relationships have been unfulfilled, including several cases where there was a commitment both ways . . .' admitted one man with Venus in Leo. '. . . Fate seemed to decree that the ideal woman was to remain only a "chaste" relationship and not lead to fulfilment.' Fate often seems the obstacle to happy relationships for this man. And perhaps, sometimes, this is indeed the case.

The darker side of Leo also gives rise to some very unsavoury characteristics indeed. Some Leo men are not only manipulative—even cruel—but are often on a proverbial power trip. This kind of Leo may or may not be overtly dictatorial, but his will is absolute and he brooks no opposition. He is more than likely to be a Right Man (see pp.460–1). This kind of Leo, like the more iconoclastic type, is self-obsessed in the extreme with little or no regard for anyone else's feelings or needs. In the immortal words of American film star/comedian Jerry Lewis* to his wife on leaving her and his six sons, 'I did it all for me and you got in the way, so now I'm releasing myself from these obstacles to see if I can enjoy my life again.'

To a certain extent, the darker aspects of this sign potentially lurk within every Leo man, and it's worth considering that it's not such a large step from wanting to be in sole charge to becoming an out and out dictator.

Certainly, there is more than one Leo man who wishes that the words to

*Neptune rising in Leo. Sun conjunct MC.

love, honour, and obey were still compulsory in the wedding ceremony, and although the rise and rise of feminism has done much to elevate the status of women in marriage, the Leo man, together with Mr Aries, Mr Taurus and Mr Capricorn, represent the zodiac's last bastion of chauvinism. Almost all Leos are possessive about their property and their loved ones (which can mean one and the same thing). They also hate to lose face and simply will not stand for any flighty—and certainly no adulterous—behaviour by their women. I have known one or two Leo men to cause a show-stopping scene in public over a suspected indiscretion. As far as he himself is concerned, Mr Leo is basically a faithful type—even if he can't resist playing Lothario in a social setting. He's also on the lazy side and once the flames of a new-found passion die down, he finds conducting an affair on the side exhausting and taxing on his memory and imagination. He's not the most adept liar in the zodiac, although he can bluff things out well.

Like the other status-consumed signs of the zodiac (Capricorn and Aries), the Leo man wants a partner who will reflect his image, but not a woman who is going to upstage him every step of the way. Unless he's very emotionally mature and his ego is thoroughly intact, he won't take to a career girl (especially if she threatens to make more money than him) nor to a 'blue stocking'. Unlike Capricorn, whose taste in wives is rather conservative, Mr Leo likes his women with a bit of colour about them—a pretty face rather than a perfect pedigree. After all, he can always pull her into line as they go along! Sometimes the Leo man, in keeping with Apollo, cares a little too much about the outer wrappings of a woman instead of her inner beauty. Thus his love may well fade along with her looks, or he may find that his swan princess was a goose after all.

Very feminine women appeal to Mr Leo. Since he cares tremendously about his masculine image he tends to suppress his gentler (feminine) and, to him, weaker side. However, the Leo man who dismisses the urge to behave like a Napoleon *manqué* and who expresses his sensitive qualities is often even more attractive to women and experiences a richer emotional dialogue in his relationships.

In keeping with the kingly nature of this sign, the Leo man's home is his castle and he enjoys being treated like the ruling monarch. This means that the family, especially his wife, must carry out their duties efficiently and uncomplainingly, and constantly remind him that he is wonderful, irreplaceable, attractive, successful etc. To be fair, when Mr Leo is truly appreciated, there is no husband or father more generous, affectionate, and indulgent. Indeed fatherhood often brings out the best in Mr Leo. He finds no difficulty in locating his inner little boy and throws himself wholeheartedly into the role of pram-pusher/doll's house builder/sportsmaster/electronics buff/Red Indian chief/and story-teller extraordinaire. He would like his children to be well behaved and shouts at them rather a lot, but since they know he's as soft as sheepskin underneath, they tend to ignore him. Naturally, the Leo father cares that his children do well in life so he can be as pushy and ambitious for them as his female counterpart; yet his love, like the Cancerian's, is often entirely unconditional. In many ways the Leo who misses out on fatherhood, or who has no youngster to relate to in a fatherly way, loses the opportunity to develop a major area of his psychological anatomy which he may increasingly regret as he grows older.

Whatever you do, don't attempt to change this man. Apart from the fact he's perfect, he won't budge an inch unless he wants to. Of course, you can always pander to his vanity and pay homage to his ego, which usually waves a magic wand for anything you want. Perhaps it's a cliché to say so, but Mr Leo is the lion-heart of the zodiac. He is immensely proud, loyal, protective, and gallant, and sometimes rather bolshie and fierce too. He's not exactly the most flexible person in the world either, but at least his feelings are never a mere flash in the pan.

Love and romance are as necessary to Mr Leo as his self-esteem and his Barclaycard, and with all these intact there is no lover more generous and indulgent. Although the pathway to connubial bliss may be bumpy and hair-raising at times, have faith; in time it should lead to a golden future.

SUMMARY

'I want to be alone' is a cry you'll hardly ever hear from a Leo. These individuals thrive on good company in general and a loving consort in particular. Yet their relationships, at least when younger, often yield much heartache and disillusionment. The Leo man or woman must allow his partners to have an equal say in the running of their relationship otherwise perpetual power struggles will ensue that eventually stifle their love—no matter how great. These solar individuals must find a way to express their strong personalities and tread the inner path of self-discovery without trampling over their partners and leaving them constantly in their shadow. Developing a gentler, more compliant attitude to people, relating to weakness, both in themselves and others, would win them many more hearts and smooth out the cracks in their relationships. Like all the fire signs, Leo men and women have strength, optimism, courage, and above all plenty of love to give their partners; but before they can find real happiness, they must acknowledge their own faults and be prepared to change themselves.

LEO PARTNERSHIPS

Few individuals hold luke warm feelings about Leos: they either love them or hate them—and vice versa. While Leo benefits enormously from a more pliable, watery partner or a supportive, earthy one, men and women of this sign find relationships with airy or fiery people less restricting and more fun.

Aries

Leo and **Aries** create great impact as a couple. They are both forceful, optimistic types and no matter how many times they come to blows—verbal and otherwise—they usually feel tremendous respect for each other. This partnership tends to be high on ideals and future possibilities, but a bit low on practical realities. Thus, as a couple they may experience some financial problems. Sometimes they have a little trouble deciding who's running the show, but provided Leo gives his Aries partner plenty of independence, the Arian is prepared to let the Lion have the upper hand. Sexually this couple make lots of sparks, although boredom can set in rather early.

Taurus

Traditionally, **Taurus** is considered to be one of Leo's antipathies. Yet these signs often experience an irresistible fascination for each other. The Bull's unflappable nature provides an excellent foil for Leo's excitability while the Lion appears invitingly warm and vivacious to the Taurean. But it doesn't take long for them to discover that they're both as stubborn as a bull! In the long term, Taurus' patience wears a little thin with Leo's continual insistence on his own way all of the time. On the bright side, however, Taurus appreciates the good things of life as much as Leo—he is often a keen patron of the arts—so these two can enjoy a cultural and gastronomic feast together—often. Taurus and Leo are also extremely sensuous signs and with or without great love, this couple usually have a splendid sexual relationship.

Gemini

The **Gemini** man or woman makes a highly compatible partner for Leo. The Geminian has little time for overblown, emotional dramas and can chivvy the Lion out of the iciest sulk. Their joint sense of humour, their love of entertainment and intellectual repartee, make their relationship mutually stimulating; emotionally, however, they are often poles apart. Gemini individuals rarely pander to Leo's super-sensitive ego, and with their mercurial temperaments invariably manage to make him feel thoroughly insecure. Leo, on the other hand, is far too emotionally demanding and stifles Gemini's need for freedom. Given that these two can compromise on their differing emotional and sexual needs, the range and liveliness of their relationship can make it a happy and durable one.

Cancer

Cancer/Leo relationships can work well, especially if they have personal planets in each other's Sun sign. Indeed, astrologically, this combination is the classic Sun/Moon dyad. The Lion provides the Crab with security, loyalty, and considerable love and affection, while the Cancerian tenderizes Leo and nurtures and sustains him. Moods and silences (invariably springing from misunderstandings) spoil this partnership. The Lion unintentionally hurts the Crab, who then pays him back by emotionally withdrawing from him. The more Leo clamours for an explanation the less inclined the Cancerian feels to give one. Although the Lion appears to run this relationship, in truth it is the Crab who holds the strings. Children are important to Cancer and Leo, and parenthood draws them closer, regardless of its problems and their temperamental differences. Sex can reach some glorious peaks for these two—otherwise it can be a total disaster.

Leo

Two **Leos** together usually understand each other very well, but wish their other half wasn't so dreadfully bossy and stubborn! Both like to hog the limelight and share a strong competitive streak, so petty jealousies and major showdowns pepper their relationship. These two also need to curb their extravagance and stop blaming the other for being the spendthrift! Certainly, insecurity and lack of loyalty are things a Leo partnership rarely suffers from and these two usually provide a mutual protective society. The physical side of their relationship should be excellent since both are keen to demonstrate their affecton for the other as much and as often as possible.

Virgo

Leo and **Virgo** can forge an extremely good relationship provided that they survive the early stages. These two have little in common temperamentally speaking, but since they are zodiac next-door-neighbours they could benefit from having personal planets in each other's Sun sign. One of the biggest drawbacks to this combination is that Leo likes to cut corners and go straight from A to B, whereas Virgo prefers to analyse the situation thoroughly before doing anything. Thus, there is a stop-go quality about their daily existence. In many ways the Virgoan makes a perfect partner for Leo since he is an industrious, behind the scenes type and provides a good base and sympathetic backcloth to Leo's strong, up front personality. However, Leo sometimes discovers a little too late (as he reads the detailed goodbye note by the first-aid kit) that he underestimated the Virgoan! This couple need some time to establish a satisfactory sex life.

Libra

Of all the air signs, Leo finds **Libra** the best balance for his indomitable personality. The Libran man or woman often measures up to Leo's high ideals in a partner: with their genial, amenable natures Librans seem to have no difficulty in tolerating Leo's childish behaviour and gently massaging his ego. The Leo/Libran couple is usually very sociable, and the more stimulating their outer life, the better, since these two sometimes strike an awkward emotional bond. Libra can be a little cool and detached for Leo's passionate depths, while the Libran finds the Lion somewhat of an emotional volcano. These two bring out the best in each other sexually.

Scorpio

Of all the water signs, **Scorpio** is the most captivating to Leo with his mysterious ways and unfathomable depths. While Leo is usually a spontaneous, frank, and open individual—he tends to wear his heart on his sleeve—the Scorpio is subtle and obscure from head to toe. Thus each find the other's approach to life enviable—at first. In the long term, however, Leo finds the Scorpion manipulative and his moods frustratingly impenetrable, whereas the Scorpion considers the Lion brash and selfish. Time, patience, and some harmonious Moon and Venus links help the survival of this partnership. Given that they can distance themselves from their emotional standpoint and learn to compromise and communicate more, both can benefit tremendously from each other and learn a lot about themselves. Sexual attraction is usually high between these two, and when it's good, it's very, very good, but when it's bad . . .

Sagittarius

Leo finds **Sagittarius** enormous fun as a partner and when things are going well with this partnership, it soars. Both these signs love doing things in style, but if funds are short and they are forced to cut back, their relationship suffers since each tends to take his frustation out on the other. This combination is a good one for friendship, but in an intimate relationship the Archer finds the Lion too possessive and jealous, while Leo feels Sagittarius lacks commitment. These two place a great deal of importance on their sex lives, but sometimes fail to reach each other's most erogenous zones!

Capricorn

The Leo/**Capricorn** couple have their time cut out trying to make their relationship run smoothly. Both signs can be arrogant and obstinate, and both think that they know best. Provided the Lion has a strongly placed Saturn in his chart and the Goat some more fiery detail, they can find some productive and harmonius common ground. Capricorn frequently complains about Leo's hasty, ill-conceived actions and his self-centred attitude, while Leo considers Capricorn selfish and slow in the extreme. There are frequent arguments over finances between these two and the Lion often feels the Goat is a perpetual damp squib. Children are an important asset to this relationship: both individuals make excellent parents (in their own way), and take much pride and pleasure in their offspring. When the physical side of their relationship works well it can offset many of their differences.

Aquarius

Aquarius and Leo are literally poles apart, yet they are often enormously attracted to each other. Intractability and selfishness mar their happiness and both frequently berate and criticize the other for exhibiting their own weaknesses! Neither partner likes the other getting the better of him so power struggles tend to erupt over the smallest issue. On the plus side, Aquarius' quirky, humorous personality provides a stimulating challenge for Leo and they hardly ever find each other boring. With good links between Moon and Venus, Aquarius and Leo can find much harmonious common ground and if both improve their tolerance quota their relationship can prove durable and even fun! Although initially good, sex can become low key between these two, unless they can bridge their emotional differences.

Pisces

The **Piscean** presents a magical conundrum to Leo. Trying to understand the Fish's ways and point him in the right direction (put his life straight) provides an irresistible challenge to the Lion. Pisces, on the other hand, wants to water down Leo's enthusiasm and drive. While Leo can inspire Pisces' confidence and enable him to put substance into his dreams, the Fish helps Leo to understand and relate to his gentler (weaker) side. Sometimes, however, the Lion fails to comprehend Pisces' motives and demeans his all-important inner world; thus he drives the Fish away. Conversely, Pisces' chaotic and impractical nature can frustrate and hinder Leo. With good lunar aspects this relationship can develop into a sensitive, loving, and mutually supportive one. And provided these two are emotionally in tune, their sex life should be excellent.

SEXUALITY

Leos are immoderate creatures: small is not necessarily beautiful to them unless it happens to be a flawless solitaire diamond or a solid band of 18-carat gold. Where love and sex are concerned, Leos want the greatest, most marvellous experience possible—a hole-in-the-corner romance or a forgettable one-night-stand is simply not their style. Yet like all the greatest romantic idealists in the zodiac, Leo men and women invariably spend half their adult lives searching for the highs in love and sex and the other half coming to terms with what they've got!

Leo · is a strong and powerful sign: thus, even though many factors—astrological and otherwise—shape an individual's sexuality, the force of the Sun in this sign can be seen 'at work' in the sexual arena whatever the gender and whatever the rest of the astrological picture.

Sexually speaking, Leos are usually early developers, although they mature emotionally comparatively late. The need to be loved and to demonstrate their passionate feelings propels them into relationships before they have had enough experience of the world to judge the outcome of their actions. Consequently, Leo men and women tend to learn about themselves and the opposite sex the hard way. Like the other fire signs, desire frequently burns away any residue of common sense and foresight. However, since Leos are more security oriented than Aries or Sagittarius, this impetuous state of affairs normally vanishes by their late twenties.

Certainly this sign has a reputation for being highly sexed: Leos fall in love at the drop of a hat and like to express their feelings as physically as possible as soon as possible. And although there are bound to be Leo men and women who choose to be celibate, this sign is probably the least likely of all to do so. Yet while Aries and Sagittarius bestow their sexual favours liberally and in a relatively guilt-free fashion, Leo is a little more selective and has infinitely more staying power.

The Leo woman is a warm, loving, sexually responsive creature. She has a strong desire nature but can be remarkably self-controlled when she wants to be. She needs to be highly attracted to someone before she commits herself sexually and she's extremely unlikely to go to bed with a man simply because he's taken her out a couple of times. Sexual intercourse is by no means an inevitable night-cap for Ms Leo. And when she says no, she means it! While the Leo woman will accept an invitation to dinner or the theatre from almost any man (remember, this woman loves socializing), she'll only sleep with someone she really wants.

Unfortunately, Ms Leo's natural flirtatiousness and sexual appeal often lead her into compromising situations. Men frequently assume that her flattering interest in them and her coquettish manner is an open invitation to bed: thus when they receive a sexual rebuff, they feel outraged and extremely frustrated. It takes the Leo woman all her time to extricate herself from the situation. Not surprisingly, many Leo ladies, especially when younger, gain a reputation as a 'prick tease'.

In many ways the Leo woman finds herself in a dilemma where sex is concerned. Presented with someone she 'fancies' her passion urges her to consummate the relationship without hesitation, yet her need for security and long-term guarantees, not to mention her self-esteem, persuade her to hold back. Sometimes the Leo woman decides to keep the seduction at arm's length for a while, which may preserve her reputation, but often also takes the zest and excitement out of the experience. On the other hand, if she yields to her desires, she worries herself sick afterwards in case she has been a 'quick lay'. Only a few Leo women become accomplished bed-hoppers: neither their security systems nor their self-esteem permit such a practice.

Ms Leo also frequently faces a choice between marrying for security as soon as possible (whether she's in love or not) or waiting for the love of her life and risk being left on the shelf. If she's brave enough, the Leo woman will wait until she has found a man who thoroughly inflames her before committing herself to a lengthy internment. Yet because of her preoccupation with her image and status, Ms Leo often marries early, and often lives to regret it.

One of the problems Ms Leo encounters if she marries too young is that she cannot have had enough emotional and sexual experience to recognize if her partner is sexually adequate or not, nor indeed can she be aware of the range of her own sexual needs. Thus she may lead a thoroughly unfulfilled sexual existence, unless and until she has an affair with someone who enlightens her. The Leo woman really needs to explore her sexuality before committing herself to marriage or a long term relationship, but sadly the risk factor often appears too great for her.

Most of the Leo women who volunteered information about their sex lives maintained that sex was an exceedingly important part of the relationship, but that they could tolerate an inferior partner in bed if they loved him enough and/or they had material compensations. It seems that, unlike Ms Aries and Ms Sagittarius, the Leo female who wishes to become Isolde to a modern-day Tristram is definitely in the minority. Indeed, of all the fiery women, it appears that Leo, Queen of Hearts, is the most calculating lady when it comes to love, sex, and marriage!

Nevertheless, the Leo woman is usually a first-class lover. She's not the type to read a how-to manual on sex, unless it's to arouse her interest—her instincts are all she needs. She gives herself joyfully to a partner and with enough enthusiasm and skill to ensure that he won't lust after anyone else. Ms Leo doesn't intend to share her lover with anyone and most Leo ladies are unreasonably jealous of their husband's past mistresses or wives. Indeed, pestering their lovers for information about previous partners is a gentle form of torture many Leo ladies indulge in: for them, comparisons may be odious, but they are also very necessary.

Making love can be quite a performance with the Leo woman. She prefers a romantic build-up—luscious, lascivious looks over the peaches, and Ravel's **Bolero** after the coffee and **crème de menthe**. The Leo female, unlike the other two fire signs, likes plenty of foreplay and she usually loves tantalizingly and sensuously peeling off her clothes (and her lover's)—the mounting excitement does wonders for her appetite. Only if she's extremely horny does Ms Leo like a hot and breathless encounter in the shower. She's also one of the more conservative women in the zodiac and she needs gentle coercing and plenty of time to get used to any of the more exotic techniques. Threesomes and group sex are completely out for this woman—she can't stand the competition—unless she has her Moon or Venus in an air sign or a strong Uranian theme in her chart. However, the Leo woman sometimes has bisexual leanings.

Women of this sign often model themselves on sultry movie stars. To this end the Leo woman will acquire decorative postures and gestures to make herself sexually appealing—like Ms Libra, the Leo lady needs to know that she's looking good to perform well! This woman will buy sexy underwear and diaphanous negligees to enhance her charms, and she likes to put plenty of perfume over herself and the sheets—preferably satin, of course. Yet, the Leo woman may play at being a sex goddess for many years without experiencing her sexual essence or even an orgasm. Since Leo is a fixed sign, the Lioness often blocks her ability to lose herself in making love and consequently never has a peak sexual experience.

While male Leos tend not to emulate famous screen lovers (although some of them can do an excellent Rambo imitation if they're not careful), they are usually attracted to glitzy, glamorous women. And although Leo men can make love without any theatrical accoutrements, most of them prefer to do it in style. High self-esteem is crucial to the success of Mr Leo's love life. He needs plenty of flattery and approbation to sustain a sexual relationship for a long period of time. While he has a strong sex drive, as far as performance goes, he's not one of the sexual marathon 'runners' in the zodiac.

The Leo man loves the company of women; he can even fall madly in love with one or two of them, but curiously enough, he often doesn't like them very much. This attitude tarnishes his relationships and confuses his women since he makes a huge production number over romancing them, but then criticizes them for the way they spend their time, demeans their endeavours, and won't tolerate their different opinions. Mr Leo likes to see women in their place, and the more assertive his women become the more emasculated he feels. Naturally this affects his sex life.

As I mentioned in the previous section, the Leo man often doesn't relate very well to his feminine side, since he equates gentleness and sexuality with weakness and assumes that his true value as a man depends on his fortitude and general superiority. Consequently his masculinity is vulnerable to the slightest dent in the form of criticism, a rebuff, or his women asserting their ascendancy. If his masculine ego feels threatened (legitimately or not) he finds it difficult to function at his sexual best with the woman in question. If and when this happens, his most likely recourse is to look for someone else to bolster up his flagging ego; if he's married or in a long-term relationship, this means the odd bit—or even bits—on the side; if he's single, he may continue to lead a sort of nomadic existence, moving from one woman to another in a rapidly expanding sexual wilderness.

But it's worth remembering that Leo is not a sign noted for philandering—these men are usually faithful types and rarely shy away from commitment. When they take to an extra-marital affair, it is almost always to boost their morale. Thus to keep the Lion happily tethered to the marital yoke, his partner must lavish him with attention, affection, and praise and never let him doubt his masculinity for a second. On a more serious note, Leo men who begin to question their sexual infallibility may not opt for an ego-boosting affair, but withdraw sexually from their partners instead.

Another problem on the sexual front that hits some Leo men is that occasionally they experience a schism in the way they perceive their partners. Mr Leo has a tendency to put his beloved on a pedestal and to extol her value as a wife and mother; yet the way he wants her sexually clashes violently with this virtuous image. The Leo man who finds himself in this dilemma experiences difficulty in telling his partner what pleases and excites him and indeed letting go when he makes love to her. Unless he can find an acceptable way of fulfilling his desires without losing his self-esteem or feeling that he is degrading his partner, he may suppress his physical appetite and forgo certain aspects of sex that would give him pleasure.

Fortunately, the majority of Leo men experience no problem in finding an outlet for their sexual drive: Leo is not the most emotionally and sexually complex sign in the zodiac. While these fiery individuals can be as romantic and courtly in love as Mr Libra, they don't lose any more time than they have to in pressing their attentions. And although the Leo man is a fairly forceful individual, he can be surprisingly sloppy and sentimental in bed. ·He is also more sensuous than the other two fire signs, although his performance, like theirs, would undoubtedly benefit from making sure his partner is as satisfied as he is! All the fire signs need to develop the art of give and take and to remember that the louder and more boisterous the sex, the better the quality, is not a sentiment shared by everybody!

Like the female Leo, Mr Leo is a conservative man at heart: he likes to think that he's ready for anything and as broadminded and adventurous as a Harold Robbins hero; but half the time his bravado is just an act and most of his talk merely fantasy and bluster. He's too lazy to bother with a lot of complicated equipment or too many people—besides, he runs the risk of being upstaged! Most of the men who replied to my questionnaire considered themselves highly-sexed but not in the least kinky. Almost all of them felt that sex was infinitely better when the heart was involved, though they wouldn't turn down a roll in the hay—provided the lady was attractive enough.

Fidelity is an important issue for Leos of both sexes. Leo men and women like to be the one and only in their partner's lives and most find it difficult not to display their possessive and jealous natures. If, and when, they discover that their partner has been unfaithful their trust, sometimes along with the love, evaporates instantly. Once respect and trust have gone for Leos, they cut off emotionally and sexually. However, like the other fixed signs, the Leo man or woman may stay in a broken marriage for the sake of security and the children, but the emotional bond is severed for ever.

The vulnerable Leonine ego often receives its severest test in the mid-40s. Both male and female Leos place great importance on youth and attractiveness: consequently, as the smile lines become crow's feet and the appealingly rounded belly a huge spare tyre, a major crisis of confidence occurs. Provided the Leo's partner is supremely supportive and tireless in his or her protestations of love and admiration during this period, Mr and Ms Leo come to terms—albeit reluctantly—with nature and their mortality. However, the male menopause sends many Leo men scuttling (temporarily) into the arms of another woman (often for a father/daughter type of relationship) and the mid-life crisis propels many a Leo lady into the amorous clutches of her hairdresser or her tennis coach!

As sexual partners Leo men and women are generous and eager to please. They like to know how they rate in bed and tend to fish for post-coital compliments rather a lot. Both sexes are sincere and demonstrative in love and need affection from their partners just as much as physical gratification.

Most of them like to be thought of as 'pretty hot stuff' between the sheets, although in their hearts they're really rather insecure about the whole business. By and large, it's unusual to find a Leo who doesn't want to be touched or to feel wanted—men and women of this sign normally lead an active and fulfilling sex life. Indeed the mood of the Lion—whether he's basking in the sunny aura of his contentment, or snarling and pacing with menace—is an excellent barometer of his sex life.

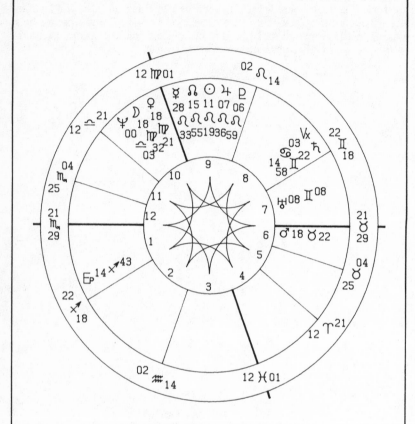

GEORGINA HALE

4 8 1943   14h 5m 0s GMT

PLACIDUS 51N33 0W6

PROFILE OF A LEO WOMAN

GEORGINA HALE

Many little girls dream of becoming famous actresses when they grow up. Some of them do. But most, even if they get one foot inside drama school, never see their name on a theatre billboard, let alone shimmer in the spotlight of stardom. To become a successful actor one needs determination, optimism, an indestructible love of 'the business', and, of course, a talent to entertain—characteristics synonymous with Leo and with Georgina Hale. Indeed Georgina, who has no less than four planets in Leo, epitomizes the virtues (and a few of the vices) of this glamorous, charismatic fire sign.

Georgina was born just outside London. Her father and mother were publicans, which meant the family (she had one younger brother) were constantly moving 'home'. Life was unsettled and noisy. 'We always seemed to live in big old pubs. I can remember going to sleep watching the illuminated beer-sign rocking to and fro in the wind . . . people would be singing—having a knees-up round the piano . . . it was all very jolly.' But there were drawbacks to the high spirits of pub life. Georgina was never able to remain at any one school long enough for her to adjust to the curriculum or make any lasting friendships. Also she felt embarrassed about her home life. 'I used to dread having to tell anyone what my father did. I could never bring any of my friends home—to begin with because of the difficulty with opening hours, but then because I felt awkward about living in a pub. I wanted to live in a house or a flat like everyone else.' Even when it came to dancing classes, Georgina seemed to miss out in comparison with other little girls. 'I used to go to tap classes every Saturday morning. All the others used to come with their mums—really pushy mums—and because mine wasn't there, I used to get left at the back.' Like many lonely children, Georgina maintained a rich fantasy life. 'I used to go to the cinema every

Monday night. I thought film stars were wonderful. so that's what I wanted to be.' Georgina was an artistic child and nurtured thoughts of going to art school when she was fifteen. But her father wasn't prepared to pay the fees. 'There I was at sixteen with no real qualifications or any direction. I thought, what am I going to do? I can't read . . . can't spell . . . can't write. So I went into hairdressing!'

While Georgina's early life was not unhappy, she herself felt rootless and lonely. In Georgina's chart, nebulous Neptune is the ruling planet of the fourth 'house' of home and family. Neptune conjures up a variety of images in connection with this area of the chart: sometimes home can be remembered as an 'out of this world' experience and the parents 'too wonderful for words'. On the other hand, family life may have been unhappy, involving the loss of relationship between the individual and one (possibly both) parents. Her mother died when Georgina was eighteen: 'I loved her but I never really knew her.' Neptune is also a symbol of the sea, the arts (especially film), and the spiritual side of life—or, as in Georgina's case, the kind of spirits that come out of a bottle! Occasionally, children who are adopted or spend some part of their childhood in an institution have Neptune in connection with the fourth 'house'. Strangely enough, Georgina was 'adopted' later on in her life (age twenty-nine) by an impressario and his wife, whom she still refers to as 'mum' and 'dad'.* Since the fourth house area of the chart is more usually associated with the father, sometimes the child grows up with an unclear picture of his or her real father, and in adult life continues to search for this ideal father figure in relationships. Certainly Georgina felt she had missed out on real family life as a child: she wanted a normal, close, and secure family bond, which sadly was lacking. And in some ways this lack still haunts her.

Apprenticeship in a large chain of hairdressers was good fun. Within a few months she was moved from the Holloway branch to the prestigious Knightsbridge shop. 'It was like another planet. I remember walking through Harrods for the first time and seeing all these formidable sales assistants dressed in black. You didn't dare pick anything up off the counter. It was the sort of place you walked through and looked. I just walked through Harrods for months!' It was while she was 'chief permanent waver' at the salon that she discovered a method acting studio behind Harrods. 'I thought it was wonderful. There I was in this other world—this Knightsbridge world. They weren't just actors who came to the studio, but business men—people who had to talk in public.' Within a matter of weeks **Vogue** magazine came to do an article on the studio, and it was a casual remark by one of the **Vogue** team that convinced her she

*See **Note for Astrologers** (2).

should go to drama school. 'The first thing I did was to go to Foyles and buy a book on audition speeches. I'd never been to Foyles and had to be shown the way by a young guy (who later became her husband). It never occurred to me to read any of the plays these speeches came from! I learned this speech and auditioned for RADA. It was the most frightening experience of my life. Someone had told me the principal liked girls who wore black and no make-up. I must have looked like a little fat ink-blot. I'd never even seen a stage before and there was this girl throwing herself about on it. I was amazed "Imagine," I thought, "being able to move and talk at the same time!"' Clearly Georgina's talent was not obliterated by her nerves or her black dress and she was awarded a place at RADA.

She spent two years at RADA, during which time her mother died and her father remarried. It was a combination of these two incidents and her general sense of insecurity that prompted her into marriage at the age of eighteen and a half.* The marriage was to prove brief but full of drama. 'I married J, another actor (and a Sun Taurus) when I was still at drama school. I was besotted with him and to begin with he was very supportive. I didn't get on with the principal too well, and he almost ruined my self-confidence. In my final term in the end of the year production, I was chosen to play Natasha in **The Three Sisters**. After the performance he (the principal) came up to me and said, "Well, I've seen some Natashas in my time, but I've never seen anything like you. You're the worst I've ever seen!" If it hadn't been for J. I would never have got up on a stage again.'

From drama school Georgina was accepted to understudy with the Royal Shakespeare Company at Stratford. She made two important discoveries at Stratford: that she should divorce her husband, and that she had severe stage fright. 'I was "thrown on" in **The Comedy of Errors** . . . I made my first entrance, said my lines, and never came back. Ian Richardson was left looking like a lemon. After I left Stratford, I didn't set foot on a stage again for nine years.' Her decision to leave her husband was triggered by his increasing dependence on alcohol, which in turn made him physically violent. 'I borrowed some money, packed a few things, and hid in the station loo until the milk train to London left.' Once back in London, she went to stay with an aunt—a stay that was to last two years. This period of Georgina's life was one of her happiest and most settled. With her aunt's support she went through with the divorce.

From the very beginning, her marriage had had its unusual moments. 'J. used to lock me in the flat when he went to the theatre in the evening. At first it never bothered me, and I really didn't think there was anything strange about it. But then it started to get me

*See **Note for Astrologers** (3).

down, so I went off and stayed with an old boyfriend. Then **he** started to lock me in too! I got pretty depressed at one point and thought about doing myself in. I remember going into the bathroom and taking this razor then all of a sudden there was all this blood . . . I rang the hospital—they stitched me up and sent me home. But I realized I wasn't any better off with the boyfriend so I decided to go back to J. I had no money and had to break open this jar of sixpences and empty them into a carrier bag. Then, carrier bag over my shoulder and my other arm in a sling, I shinned down the drainpipe. The problem was, my boyfriend lived in a flat above some shops, and I came down in the courtyard of a chemist's. So I had to walk casually through this shop as if people came down drainpipes every day with their arms in slings and a bag full of money!'

Georgina tends to become the classic 'victim' in her relationships—a distinctly Virgo-Pisces proclivity. Although she is a Sun Leo, the ruler of her 'house' of relationships, Venus, is found next to the Moon in Virgo. Thus where her emotions and her affections are concerned she is the archetypal doormat. Since Venus and the Moon also form stressful 90° aspects to unrelenting Saturn, there is a further suggestion of difficulty and hardship linked to one-to-one relationships. Saturn itself is placed in the eighth 'house' of emotional and sexual exchange, indicating much frustration and limitation in this area of life. Indeed, that two of her partners should actually lock her into the home is a direct manifestation of Saturn (sometimes referred to as the jailor) in this relationship area. The eighth 'house' of the horoscope also has much to do with financial exchange within partnerships. In Georgina's case, Saturn in this area has meant that she has been drained financially by her partners—and she certainly gets short-changed! When she is in love, her Leo influence prompts her to give generously to her beloved, while her Virgoan side cannot resist helping and 'saving' her partners. Thus when the relationship ends, she feels thoroughly used. Uranus—an unstable and highly-charged planet—is placed in the 'house' of relationships itself, with Mars poised for 'battle' on the Descendant. These two factors indicate Georgina's relationships are far from smooth and that she tends to attract unusual partners who may give her a rough time. On the other hand, Georgina herself may want more freedom than she imagines, thus she unconsciously chooses partners who rarely fit into the mould of dutiful husband and provider.

During the two-year period with her aunt, Georgina's professional life 'took off'. She appeared in several television productions and was consistently in work. Her 'big break' came in 1970 with the notorious film **The Devils**. 'Ironically, I nearly didn't go to the audition. I was meant to audition in the morning but they were running late and I had to get back to a television show I was working on. My agent rang when I got home and told me they (the director and producer) were willing to wait. If it hadn't been for a friend offering to drive me there, I'd never have gone.' **The Devils** was the beginning of a long and successful collaboration with the director, Ken Russell for whom she went on to make **The Boyfriend** (1972) and **Mahler** (1974).

Once filming on **Mahler** had been completed Georgina, in a sudden flash of self-confidence, accepted the stage role of Nina in **The Seagull** with Alan Bates. 'Since it wasn't being done in the West End, I thought I'd be able to cope. But the stage-fright was just as bad as ever. I used to stand in the wings waiting to go on, sweating and shaking. Then, horror of horrors, the play was transferred to the West End. We had rave reviews and from then on I couldn't move for offers of stage work. I've overcome my stage-fright now, although I still get very nervous. But at one time, I don't know how I walked from one side of the stage to the other.'

Stage-fright is familiar to most actors to a greater or lesser degree. And many actors believe that nerves prior to going on stage help the individual to give a better performance. As a Sun Leo Georgina isn't by nature a nervous, introverted type; but she is a perfectionist and thus highly self-critical. She has her Virgoan Moon-Venus-Midheaven to thank for her perfectionist streak and a tendency to underate her talents—unfortunately, sometimes when she needs to feel at her most confident. Her Virgoan side makes her a great stickler for detail and a tireless worker. By contrast, her powerful Sun-Jupiter conjunction in Leo makes her one of life's natural actors. On stage she has tremendous power and charisma to the extent that occasionally she overshadows some of her colleagues—a tendency some clearly consider amounts to a pathological desire to upstage! Pluto is also next to Jupiter, which increases her ability to dominate and create a powerful impact on her audience and fellow actors alike. With Scorpio rising and the Sun-Jupiter-Pluto combination, people either tend to adore Georgina or dislike her intensely. Thus she has found many loyal friends and allies in 'the business' as well as some bitter enemies. During 1984 she found herself the butt of some political in-fighting on a film she was due to make and sadly she was eventually manoeuvred out of her part. This incident marked the beginning of a two-year period of 'relative stagnation'.

In September 1983 Saturn entered the sign of Scorpio and for a two-year period, until late 1985, formed stressful angles to her Leo planets and her Scorpio Ascendant. At the same time there was a marvellous contact between her Sun and Venus.* While her career

*Secondary progressed Sun conjunct radical Venus—a progression often co-incident with marriage.

was 'uphill all the way'. she met a man she thought might change her life. At first the relationship was exciting and happy, but within a matter of months her lover (a Sagittarian-Scorpio mix) was proving unreliable and inconsiderate. While he maintained Georgina was the 'only one' she was continually finding evidence to the contrary! Their relationship lurched along for two years, then turned into an uneasy friendship. 'When I met this man I thought, "This is it! I'm going to get married and have a baby." But it just didn't work out. It nearly destroyed me. I'm a great forgiver. I forgave him so many times and in the end you realize you're being stamped into the ground . . . I think I've just got to learn to like nice men.'

Where one-to-one relationships are concerned. Georgina's chart is far from easy. However, leaving on one side the Uranian instability and the Saturnian limitation, Georgina has a tendency to underrate her self-worth. This short-fall on her value as a woman means that although she wants a kind and considerate partner, the inner woman feels she's not worthy of such a man! Her early insecurity and feeling of family inadequacy were no doubt the foundations of this 'Catch 22' situation. Of course there could be an equally strong argument for fate; and Georgina's inability to find Mr Right may have nothing whatsoever to do with the inner workings of the psyche, but plain and simple bad luck!

While the difficulties of the recent past are behind her. Georgina nonetheless feels her life is at a standstill, both professionally and privately. 'I've never really been ambitious. Each job that I've done has been the most important thing in my life at the time I've done it, and I've no great desire to play some wonderful Shakespearean heroine . . . I would like to find someone to share my life with. The important thing about a relationship is the knowing that you have another half somewhere, so that when your back is against the wall or your luck is down, or even if you're on top of the world, you can share that with someone.'

Astrologically. Georgina's life appears poised for change. Pluto, the ruling planet of the horoscope, is at the time of writing about to begin a series of challenging aspects to the Sun, Jupiter, and Pluto (culminating in 1989). This trio in Leo shows Georgina has the potential to be a great star; and with her ruler. Pluto, contacting these planets over the next three years, the time could well have arrived for this potential to be realized. Also, in 1988, with the added help of Jupiter. Georgina may find that she is no longer a solo performer in her private life. Indeed, instead of the thorns impeding her lion-like progress through life, she may well find it's roses all the way. And nobody deserves it more.

Note for Astrologers: (1) Georgina's time of birth is given as 'about tea-time. but before 5 p.m.' working with Georgina over the past seven years. late Scorpio would seem to 'turn up trumps' most consistently.

(2) At 29. when Saturn returns to its original position in the birth chart. life can be said to have come 'full circle'. The Saturn Return marks the end of one phase of life and the beginning of another. Thus it seems entirely fitting that Georgina should meet the couple who became her adopted parents at this time. Sadly. Georgina was to lose her 'adopted' mother in 1982 as transiting Neptune opposed radical Saturn.

(3) During the period in which Georgina married and her mother died the following progressions and transits occurred: progressed Mars conjunct Uranus: progressed Ascendant opposition Uranus: progressed MC conjunct Neptune—all by 1°: transiting Pluto was conjunct the MC and transiting Neptune was Square the Sun. In early 1984. when Georgina's career problems began and during the early stages of her relationship with the Scorpio-Sagittarian man. transiting Uranus opposed radical Uranus: Uranus went on to square the MC—IC axis—Moon and Venus were to follow during 1985.

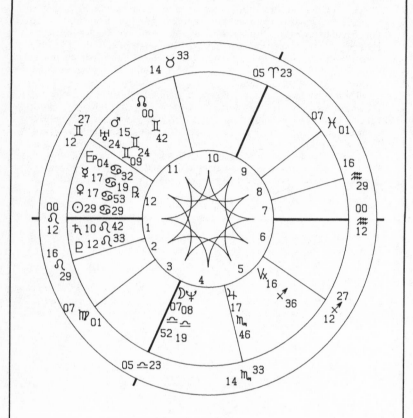

DAVID ESSEX

23 7 1947   4h 20m 0s GMT

PLACIDUS 51N32 0W8

PROFILE OF A LEO MAN

DAVID ESSEX

David Essex is an imposter! He's a Crab in Lion's clothing. He was born just as the Sun, in the last thirty minutes of Cancer, was poised to enter the sign of Leo. But because he was born at sunrise, the Sun basks in full glory on his Ascendant in Leo. To all intents and purposes, he is, astrologically speaking, a strongly Leonine character, although **technically** he is a Sun Cancer. Complicated? Not really. David is caught between two very different zodiacal 'stools': the inner man is reflective and sensitive (Cancer) while his persona—his outer image—is authoritative and strong-willed (Leo), the sort of individual who creates a powerful impact on the world at large. Before I had drawn up David's horoscope, he had no idea whether he was a Leo or a Cancer: he considered himself a 'cuspal type'. While many people who knew him well insisted he had to be a Leo, David himself felt more in sympathy with Cancer. Of course everybody was right in a way!

David was born in the East End of London. His father had a job in the docks and his mother worked in a pub—playing the piano at night and cleaning the premises the next morning. David was an only child. He remembers his childhood as happy if a little lonely at times. 'I was a "latch-key kid". I'd come home from school, slip my hand through the letterbox and find the key on a bit of string. There'd be some bread and jam waiting for me.' The East End had been badly bombed in the Second World War and for a time David and his parents lived in a council institution, 'a curtain and cubicle affair'. Eventually they were given a prefab and later still a flat. 'There was always lots of music around at home. I used to play a lot of Frankie Lane 78s. My dad was a good singer, but he never took it up professionally—couldn't face audiences. He used to sing me to sleep though—the 'Lullaby of Broadway'! My mum still plays the

piano—she can pick up any tune. She has a percussive, Winifred
Atwell style. She's great fun when she gets on the piano. You can
nearly hear the tune she's playing!. . . I got on really well with my
mum and dad—still do. Yes, I suppose my mum was an ideal mum.
She was very protective. When I was little I used to cry whenever
anyone looked at me. I had these long eyelashes, and people would
come up to me and say, "Ah, in't he lovely." And I'd bawl my eyes
out. My mum was always having to take me off buses.'

David was a naturally bright child, but never shone at school. 'The
problem with school in my area was that it wasn't done to learn. And
I was in the upper hierarchy of a gang. Although I felt for the
teachers, I ran with the crowd and disavowed any semblance of
intelligence. I could have passed the Eleven-plus [exam] but I wanted
to go to this school that had a great football team and boxing team,
so I drew Popeye all over my exam paper! I went to this really tough
Secondary Modern. It didn't inspire the best teachers, so where
learning was concerned it was a vicious circle. You had to be a base
yob to survive.'

With harmony-oriented Libra on the cusp of the fourth 'house' of
family background, and Venus, its ruler, in an easy 120° (trine) aspect
to expansive Jupiter—also in the fourth—the indications are indeed,
that David came from a happy and benevolent family background.
The Moon is also placed in the fourth 'house', suggesting that David
found home a haven away from the rough and discordant
atmosphere of his East End world. Neptune 'sits' next to the Moon,
which is not always conducive to a secure upbringing. Then again,
sometimes Neptune here creates a blissfully happy experience of
early life. Certainly the Moon (a symbol of mother) conjunct
Neptune implies mother was an 'ideal mum'; but since this
conjunction is in the area most often identified with the father, this
same idealization rubs off on dad as well. David's first home was in
an institution and he did experience some loneliness as a child—both
possible manifestations of Neptune in the fourth. Also, of course,
music was in plentiful supply in David's early life, and this too is a
Neptunian idea. The combination of the Cancerian content of the
chart and this gentle, impressionable Moon-Neptune duo on the IC
show much overall sensitivity in David—a sensitivity he protects
with his sunny Leo Ascendant and his gregarious Mars-Uranus
conjunction in Gemini.

The Leo-Gemini content of David's chart 'makes' him a natural if
rather unorthodox leader—the sort who slips easily into the upper
hierarchy of an organization (or a gang) rather than its lower echelons.
Both Leo and Cancer have strong survival instincts; thus David found
it safer to conceal his innate gentleness, along with his bright
intelligence, behind some brash Leo bravado. However, if any of his

teachers had had the benefit of some astrological know-how, they would have soon seen through his pretence of ignorance. David has a Mercury-ruled third house of communication and the intellect; and although Mercury keeps a low profile in the subdued twelfth 'house' of the horoscope, it receives a generous trine aspect from Jupiter indicating a high level of comprehension and a wide-ranging intelligence.

David's feeling for music became a passion from about the age of nine. 'And by the time I was thirteen, I used to come up to Soho to go round the jazz clubs. I eventually decided the most effective instruments to play were the drums. You bang them and they answer back—no fingering required! I had this drum teacher who used to come to the flat. And you couldn't keep that kind of thing quiet. There was a bloke in the flat below who complained bitterly about the noise—even though I used to practice with rubber pads on [the drums] after six. In the end he complained so much that he and my dad had a stand-up fight about it. My dad wasn't defending the noise I made, but my right to learn something. It was a stand for personal freedom. Luckily my dad won and I was able to carry on. The irony of it was, that my dad hated the drums more than the other bloke!' David started to work in bands semi-professionally when he was fourteen and still at school. 'Not that I went to school that much . . . GCE could have been a make of cooker from where I was at!' His ambition then was to be a jazz drummer. 'Acting, writing, being a pop star was too silly to think about . . . I didn't really identify with the Beatles or those kind of people in the sixties. The music had to be obscure and the more obscure the better. I liked black music from America. The raw energy of it . . . the personal expression of the musicians. My liking for classical music came later.' But making a living as a musician was not an option when the time actually came for him to leave school. 'I was asked what I wanted to be and I said, 'an electrical engineer'. I only said it because a cousin of mine was one. I'd no idea what it entailed. So I was sent to Plessys for an interview. I had to do an IQ test, which I passed, and I became an apprentice electrical engineer. But I only stayed at Plessys for a short while, since the band I was with—the Everons, because we were never off—went professional. We went to Germany, then Italy, then the band fell to bits. I was left in Italy playing drums for the turns in a cabaret. Some months later David returned to England and joined a blues band called Mood Indigo. He became the lead singer almost by default, since no one else in the group had a voice. 'People who came to see the band used to say, "The bloke on the drums ought to make records." And it eventually happened.'

David has great astrological potential to become an electronics engineer. The ruler of his Midheaven and 'house' of profession,

Mars, is conjunct the planet Uranus—a volatile electric-type of 'energy'. Yet this only represents one level of manifestation of this conjunction. Mars symbolizes drive, ambition, action, and desire. And with Uranus as a companion it suggests David has an impulsive, quirky streak to his nature. He resents becoming stuck in ruts, whether in a personal or a professional sense. He is progressive and iconoclastic. His early liking for the obscure in music is characteristic of the Mars-Uranus influence in his chart.

Since Uranus rules his seventh 'house' of partnerships, instability and clashes centring on issues of freedom look likely. Leaving intimate relationships aside for the moment, David admits his business partnerships have sometimes been rocky and that he has had professional bust-ups. These hiatuses have invariably occurred because he's wanted to diversify and change. 'And that sometimes means walking away from a successful formula. I want the creative fulfilment more than the outside success. First you have to satisfy yourself and then if that appeals to a wider audience, that's a bonus. . . There was a major dust-up when I wanted to change things. The set up was rolling along really well in its existing form and when I wanted to do something different, I was accused of commiting creative suicide.'

Equally as strong as his need for diversification and the liking for the new and unusual in his music—and indeed his life in general—is his desire to create beauty and harmony. David's Moon-Neptune conjunction in Libra shows an instinctive appreciation of the romantic and the poetic, and of course Libra is an extremely artistic and musical sign. So too is Cancer; and with his Cancerian Mercury and Venus in the reclusive, highly sensitive twelfth 'house' of the horoscope, there is every suggestion that David is the more inspired kind of artist rather than the relentless technician. He needs his muse. This is not to say he doesn't work immensely hard at what he does, but that his best work is done when he is inspired—even if that means getting up to compose in the middle of the night!

David's Cancerian side is much in evidence once he's taken off his assured Leonine 'armour'. Like most Crabby individuals he's keenly sensitive to emotional undercurrents. 'I have an acute sensibility about emotions, feelings, and atmospheres . . . when I'm working —writing—everything else is shut out . . . it [creativity] has to do with the way you're feeling.' How he views himself as a performer is also highly Cancerian. 'I think there are two kinds of performers: there are those who work in a huge ego way because they have huge egos, and there are those who work out of vulnerability because they want to be adopted and liked, and painfully I come into the second group . . .' David has touched the core of the Cancerian dilemma here: while his Leo side 'makes' him a natural performer with a profound urge for self-fulfilment through his creativity, he has Cancerian doubts and reservations about the whole business; he wants to be 'adopted' and 'painfully' he accepts his role.

David admits his was not an overnight success story. 'I made some terrible records in the sixties—I didn't know I was a song-writer at the time. Then after getting pneumonia—I nearly died—my manager, David Bowman, suggested I went into theatre. I'd never seen any real theatre so I went to see Sean O'Casey's **Juno and the Paycock**. I didn't understand it, but it was all so civilized. I'd been used to playing in bands with bottles whizzing over my head. Acting seemed just the thing.' This proved to be a turning point for David, since after eighteen months with a progressive repertory company, he won the role of Jesus in the American musical **Godspell** (1971). 'Godspell was the beginning of everything. In fact about three things happened at the same time. I got a part in David Puttnam's **That'll Be the Day** (co-starring with Ringo Starr) and I wrote 'Rock On' for the film which was a smash hit. So by the time the film came out (1973) I was playing Jesus Christ in a number one show, starring in a number one film, and had a number one hit on my hands!'

It was ever onward and upward for David from that point. Since 1973 he's had twenty-five Top 30 singles, he's composed the music for and starred in two major films, **Stardust** and **Silver Dream Racer**, made countless concert tours around the world, and played a straight theatre part (Byron at the Young Vic). His performance as Che Guevara in the Rice-Webber musical **Evita** won him huge acclaim, as has his most recent venture as composer of and star (playing the role of Fletcher Christian) in the musical **Mutiny**. 'Mutiny has been a hard road. At times it's been like dragging a dinosaur around. The nice part was thinking about it and writing it—except, of course, the basic undercurrent of insecurity that goes on when you're writing. The hard part was trying to get people interested in it, putting it on, casting it, then the running of it every day as an actor. I get very ambitious about projects that I'm committed to, there's a sense of going through with it at all costs.' David's Cancer-Leo combination breeds plenty of staying power, especially when the going is tough. He tends to want to move on, only when his creation is established and he's in danger of becoming artistically stagnant.

Cancer and Leo are both security-oriented, emotionally-fired signs. Thus David was not the type to delay or avoid marriage, especially since he had not suffered any emotional starvation as a child. David married a local girl (a Sun Leo) when he was twenty-one. The relationship, however, did not have a propitious start. 'The first time my wife met me I was lying drunk in a gutter. Not a thing I make a habit of! She sent me home in a taxi. When I woke up the next afternoon I found this note pinned to me with a name and a telephone number on it. It took me a week to pluck up courage to phone her and ask her out.' Although for some years, he and his wife had a happy marriage, when the 'lively' discussions became constant arguments they decided to separate (1979). Happily, they get on better now they're apart, and David sees his children—a girl and boy—regularly. With his Cancerian Venus in the secretive twelfth 'house', David keeps his present romantic interests close to his chest. And one can only speculate that his on stage affinity with a lovely member of the cast of **Mutiny** is more than just a professional one!

Astrologically, partnerships—whether they're business associations or intimate relationships—are 'located' in the same seventh 'house' area of the horoscope. Thus the urge for personal freedom of expression* hinders the symbiosis of a marriage as much as it does a long-term professional relationship. Like most individuals with Uranus linked to the partnership 'house', David is attracted to unusual people—he often finds himself drawn to women who are either much older or younger than himself, and perhaps from a vastly different background. While his Leo-Cancer side craves stability and continuity in a close relationship, his Mars-Uranus-Gemini side is susceptible to emotional claustrophobia. David needs his space in a relationship. He also tends to idealize women and place them on a pedestal,† which means his princesses have a nasty habit of turning into frogs! Nevertheless, with Venus forming a splendid trine aspect to Jupiter, in his romantic life the good times far outweigh the bad. While David is not the sort who welcomes the 'ball and chain' aspect of long-term relationships, he nonetheless needs tender loving care: thus he is the type who periodically encounters a crisis of conscience over wanting to remain faithful to the same woman or playing the field.

With diversification and creative fulfilment constant themes in his life, David, after a three-year involvement with **Mutiny**, looks set for a major change. And from an astrological viewpoint, the film world would appear to be the setting for his next challenge. David's Moon-Neptune influence and his strong twelfth 'house' show a predisposition to this field; and with transiting Neptune intersecting the point between the Midheaven§ and the Moon-Neptune conjunction, the awakening of further film potential is indicated. However, this time his involvement could well be behind the camera rather than as a performer.

Unlike many other sixties personalities whose star fizzled out as quickly as it rose, David has the talent and the courage to change and

---

*Symbolized by Uranus, the ruler of the seventh, in conjunction to Mars.

†Moon conjunct Neptune in Libra.

§Denoting among many ideas, the profession and ideals.

grow; qualities that ensure his particular star will never dwindle or fade away. Rock on, David!

Note for Astrologers: (1) David has a relatively 'easy' chart with only one square and no oppositions—except for those involving the MC–IC and the Ascendant–Descendant axes. Yet David's life has not been particularly easy. He's had legal battles (over money) and as he himself maintains his was 'no overnight success story'. He is, however, the proverbial laid-back personality; and one gains the impression that whatever life hurls at him he'll 'always come up smiling'!

(2) During the marriage year, transiting Uranus (ruler of the seventh house) was sextile the Sun and transiting Saturn was conjunct the MC and opposed his Moon-Neptune conjunction. In 1979, when he separated from his wife, progressed Venus was square the node, progressed Mars was square his Moon-Neptune conjunction; transiting Jupiter was conjunct the Ascendant, transiting Uranus was conjunct Jupiter, and transiting Pluto was square Venus-Mercury. In 1973—a peak year for his career—transiting Neptune was trine the MC and sextile Moon-Neptune, and transiting Jupiter opposed the Sun.

VIRGO

23 August—22 September

GENTLE CARE-TAKERS
AND LOVE'S LOST
LABOURERS

VIRGO
GENTLE CARE-TAKERS AND
LOVE'S LOST LABOURERS

I F Pisces is the most misunderstood sign of the Zodiac, Virgo is surely the most underestimated. Thoughtful and unobtrusive, meticulous and conscientious Virgoans may be, but in their unassuming way most of them manage to make an indelible imprint on their world; and to dismiss this sign as passive and low key is to render it a great injustice.

Certainly, Virgoans are not the types to create a song and dance about their needs, or themselves for that matter—at least not unless they're going to make a career on the stage out of it, which, curiously, many of them do. Pushing themselves forward is not a Virgoan tactic: they tend to keep themselves out of the firing line and aim for positions where they can advise, direct, and control without exposing themselves to any unnecessary flak. Virgoans, like the other two earth signs, Capricorn and Taurus, care enormously about organization and practicalities, and make a positive crusade out of forward planning and constructive thinking.

Virgoans are not the easiest people to recognize; they prefer to blend into the background rather than flaunt themselves in a blaze of colour like their next-door-neighbours the Leos. Behind their calm exteriors most of them are prone to worrying and fretting. Consequently, some become thin and angular through living off their nerves, while others become thoroughly overweight through eating for comfort! One of the most recognizable Virgoan characteristics is the careful and precise examination of each and every piece of information that comes their way. The Virgoan individual is rarely impulsive about life; he needs to absorb and synthesize whatever crosses his path. When someone gently plies you for information eliciting the minutest detail, you can be sure Virgo is prominent in the chart.

Predictably, Virgos often consider themselves utterly untypical of their Sun sign. There are two likely reasons for this: first, as I mentioned earlier, astrologers, in the main, tend to underestimate this sign and overconcentrate on its 'neat and tidy' image; and second, it is Virgo's natural inclination to dispute and question any item of information, but particularly anything that reflects on themselves.

Several years ago, I sent a friend of mine into paroxysms of delight when I calculated her chart and found her Sun to be two minutes into the sign of Libra. 'You see, I'm not at all Virgo: that's why I've never been able to relate to anything those Sun sign columns have said about me!' Newspaper generalization notwithstanding, my friend nevertheless had five other planets, including the Moon, Mercury, and Venus, in Virgo! I didn't have to wait long before her Virgoan nature got the better of her. Some weeks later I accompanied her on a shopping expedition. After traipsing round several stores, whose collections failed to meet approval, she found an ideal little number in a smart Bond Street boutique. Despite my urgent attempts to prize her away from the dressing room mirror, pay for the item and leave, my friend remained fixated on her reflection—not, I might add, in a narcissistic way, but a dispassionately critical one. After what seemed at age, her eyes lit up, 'There, you see. I knew there was something wrong!' She picked up the hem, and in the minute dog-tooth check was a tiny imperfection. Needless to say, the dress was returned to the rail in disgust. 'I don't mind paying the earth for something worthwhile; but I don't spend a penny on shoddy goods!'

Now while my friend, like many other Virgos, is quite prepared to own up to some of the 'good' Virgoan characteristics, like their infinite discrimination and outstanding good taste, few relate wholeheartedly to their antiseptic, fussy image. Ironically, Virgo is the one sign guaranteed to go to phenomenal lengths to point out *why* they aren't fussy and particular. Then again, the real reason behind their attempts to put the record straight is that although they dish out no-holds-barred criticism mercilessly on others, they simply cannot accept flaws in themselves.

Virgo, of course, is the zodiac's greatest critic. Unless you have skin as thick as a rhino's, never ask a Virgo his or her opinion over anything you care about. This sign will trample through your feelings like a combine harvester, voraciously sifting the wheat from the chaff of your endeavours and throwing most on the compost heap. Indeed, this little agricultural allegory is entirely fitting for Virgo, with its mythological connections with harvesting and fertility.

The myths associated with the zodiac provide a rich foundation for understanding the underlying themes behind the signs and planets. Far from perpetuating the somewhat sterile image of Virgo, this sign's associations with Great Mother (fertility) goddess figures show Virgo to be synonymous with nurture and sustenance.

'Season of mists and mellow fruitfulness. . .' wrote Keats, referring to the rich plenteousness of autumn. Strictly speaking, the sign of Virgo comes in a little early for the dank and decaying aspects of late autumn and actually coincides with the last resplendent days of summer when the corn is gathered, the fruit lies heavy and succulent on the trees, and the musk-sweet odour of faded roses fills the sharp evening air. Greek Demeter, with her ear of corn, and Roman Ceres are two Virgoan figures linked to agriculture and fertility. Vesta and Hestia are also Virgoan deities who were associated with the hearth, which is probably where the concepts of Virgo frantically wielding a dustpan and brush and industriously going about dreary domestic duties originated. However, 'guarding the hearth' had far more subtle and important connotations than brushing the ashes into a neat little pile. Keeping the home fires burning for the early Romans was not merely a way of maintaining heat and providing cooking facilities, but a sacred obligation. The job of the vestal virgins—all well born, discriminating 'gals'—was to nurture and sustain the royal hearth, to prepare foods (something many Virgoans do exceedingly well), and to guard sacred objects. Their duties were performed as a well-loved, highly-regarded ritual. Indeed, Virgo's need for order, and devotion to duty, even in the most mundane tasks, gives him a sense of rightness, perhaps even righteousness, and feeds his fundamental impulse to serve.

One of the strange paradoxes about great goddess figures, like Demeter, Hestia, and Egyptian Isis, is that although they are portrayed as wives and mothers and thus epitomize sexual ripeness and fecundity, they are nonetheless virgins. (Virgo, of course, is commonly known as the 'virgin'). To appreciate this anomaly, it is necessary to establish what the term virgin really means. In myth, virgin had little or nothing to do with being virgo intacta, but implied a psycho-spiritual state of pureness and wholeness. The great (fertility) goddess was an awe-inspiring figure. She represented female potency in all its aspects and she effectively held the greatest power of all—to sustain life. Her mystery and greatness lay in her supreme self-containment, which she had achieved through a sacred marriage (heiros gamos). This union with a god had brought her into possession of her own masculine soul—she was complete, one-in-herself. This process was re-enacted on earth by the virgin priestesses who attended the great goddess, whether she be Demeter, Ceres, Isis, or Cybele. These maidens were sacred prostitutes (a sharply contrasting image to supposed sexually abstinent Virgo) who gave their sexual favours as an act of sacrifice to the goddess, to ensure that she would look favourably on man and increase his lot. What is significant here in relation to Virgo, apart from its sexual ambiguity, is that this is an eminently self-contained sign, one not given to relying on others for a sense of wholeness and completeness: indeed, many Virgoan individuals are emotionally and psychologically self-sufficient. (There are other possibilities to be expanded upon along this line in connection with Virgo's emotional and sexual nature which I will discuss later.)

The concept of the sacred marriage—the union of the earthly and the divine—is a distinctly, although not uniquely, Virgoan theme: as the sixth sign of the zodiac, Virgo corresponds with the number 6—the interrelationship of the human and the divine, and the number of feminine potency in man. Virgo, as the opposite sign to the most mystical of all, Pisces, contains much of the same spiritual, devotional, and self-sacrificial qualities. But there is a sense of detachment about Virgo that radically contrasts with Pisces and its total immersion in experience. Also, while Pisces seeks to break down barriers, Virgo is busy constructing little fences around everything he encounters.

Virgo's penchant for rationalization and classification owes much to its ruler, Mercury—a planet associated with the intellect and logic. But Mercury in relation to Virgo is not the fleet-footed winged messenger, Hermes, renowned for his quicksilver temperament and lightness of touch (see Gemini pp. 102–3). Mercury's equivalent, Thoth—the ibis-headed god of wisdom, learning, and science—has more in common with this pragmatic earth sign.

Thoth was an important figure in Egyptian mythology. His principal role was to write down the testimonies, given by the goddesses Fate and Destiny, of the souls waiting to pass into the blissful after-life. He was a sort of spiritual accountant, who balanced the books in the Osirian underworld; yet his quiet and modest demeanour masked great wisdom. (Of course, Greek Hermes was no stranger to the Underworld either, since he ferried the souls of the dead over the River Styx to Pluto's kingdom.)

Thoth certainly supplies the missing link in Virgo's quest for an appropriate ruler. Many astrologers, dissatisfied with will o' the wisp Mercury (who is far better suited to Gemini), feel that the discovery of the next planet beyond

Pluto, possibily to be named Vulcan or Persephone, will provide a more fitting ruler—one that relates to the deep and enigmatic qualities of Virgo. Vulcan and Persephone are both associated with the Underworld, Vulcan the god of volcanoes and later the divine blacksmith, and Persephone, Pluto's amour and Demeter's daughter. Yet Thoth more than compensates in underworld symbolism for any missing depth and subtlety.

Thoth is sometimes portrayed weighing the soul on a scale against a feather—a symbol of truth and justice. He is a sort of silent assessor in whose hands and under whose watchful gaze truth can emerge. He is part of a process of transmutation.

It may not escape notice that these ideas of judgement, balance, and transmutation belong respectively to Virgo, Libra, and Scorpio. This is possibly a mythological attempt to interpret the astronomical tripartite relationship of these signs. (Unlike the majority of the constellations, against which the 30° segments of the zodiac roughly fit, half of the constellation Libra is taken up by the zodiac subdivision of Virgo while the rest slips into the early part of Scorpio.) Libra and Virgo certainly share the same perfectionist tendencies, while Libra and Scorpio both contain the theme of opposites—Libra, with his need to balance conflicting principles and Scorpio's tendency to swing between radical extremes (see Libra pp.275–81). As far as Virgo and Scorpio are concerned, the relationship between their respective ruling planets provides some symbolic food for thought. In myth, Hermes and Pluto, Thoth and Osiris have a special relationship with each other: Hermes and Thoth each carry out an important service for their lords of the underworld; while Thoth is a silent notator at the gates of Osiris' kingdom, Hermes takes the role of divine transporter to Hades. Astrologically, Mercury and Pluto are related in that Pluto is considered by many to be the higher octave of Mercury; also, both planets share a common quest for knowledge—while Mercury's voyages remain focused in the realm of the intellect Pluto's journeys belong to the inner world of the psyche or soul.

Virgo's association with the dense and hidden symbolism of the underworld explains much of the 'still waters run deep' syndrome about Virgo. Like Thoth, profound dignity and sometimes great power rests behind Virgo's meek and carefully tempered persona. The great recluses Greta Garbo (Sun in Virgo) and Howard Hughes (Virgo rising) both epitomize this subtle and enigmatic side of Virgo. Also, in my experience there is often something entirely destructive, certainly more in keeping with the Pluto/Scorpio principle, about the way many Virgos go about their digging and delving, pruning and sifting. Virgo is a master of the indirect insult and the intellectual put down. You can never be quite sure that there isn't a hint of maliciousness behind what is paraded as an honest, constructive, and unbiased presentation of the facts. Perhaps, secretly, many Virgos deeply resent their behind-the-scene position and gain a perverse satisfaction in pricking the bubble of those on centre stage. Virgo's eclecticism and stringent discrimination techniques can be both creative and destructive.

It is also worth remembering that it is invariably the much-put-upon, sometimes faintly ridiculed, humble little clerk who gets his own back by bringing the whole corporation to its knees one day with a well-chosen word in the right ear; or quiet 'Miss Carstairs' in accounts who sends the company a postcard from Rio de Janeiro as the receivers are called in! Very often there is an entirely praiseworthy altruism behind their efforts, but sometimes their gestures are truly vindictive.

Every student of astrology knows Virgos make good accountants, librarians, teachers, and social workers. This sign is tailor-made for jobs where order, compartmentalization and care reign supreme. They are life's indispensable cogs: they perform the functions everyone else is too busy to do and frequently the tasks that are boring, repetitive, and utterly thankless. Of course, Virgos are found in every walk of life from social services to the arts, politics, and even sports, but whatever their official position, they're to be seen cleaning up after others, reminding everyone of the essential details, and making sure that their efforts—no matter how humble—are of the highest quality and craftsmanship. Virgoan actor Sean Connery is renowned for his fussiness, fastidiousness, and stringent high standards. His private life is exactly the same, and despite his wealth and macho good looks, he is a plain-living, uxorious individual. Goethe (Sun, Venus, and MC in Virgo), in an inexhaustible quest for perfection, took sixty years to write *Faust*. Mozart, one of the most prodigious musical talents ever (he was also a fine mathematician), had Virgo rising. Not surprisingly, many writers have Virgo prominent in their charts—Christopher Isherwood (Sun and Venus in Virgo), H.G. Wells (Sun and Mercury in Virgo), William Faulkner (Moon and Mercury in Virgo), D.H. Lawrence (Sun and Mercury in Virgo), Albert Camus (Virgo rising), Agatha Christie (Sun in Virgo), and Antonia Fraser (Sun, Jupiter, and Neptune in Virgo), to name but a few.

Virgos, like Pisceans, make wonderful helpers, healers, and saviours: their analytical minds and long-suffering, caring personalities are ideally suited to the rigours and demands of the healing and caring professions. Even those who don't enter the medical profession or the Social Services frequently opt to become marriage guidance counsellors or Samaritans. Conversely, many Virgos are out and out hypochondriacs, with a well-stocked library of medical text books and an ever-ready portable medicine chest.

Astrologers often refer to Virgo and its opposite sign, Pisces, as the martyr/saviour axis, since both these signs are capable of selfless dedication to others. Sometimes of course their devotion is solely toward their vocation in a depersonalized sense, since Virgo is renowned for its workaholic tendencies. Virgo, however, is an earth sign and practical, down-to-earth values are therefore to the fore. So while Pisces may sacrifice himself for some transcendental purpose, Virgo gives of himself in a more tangible vein—although, like most polarities, each (sign) contains the seeds of the opposite. Interestingly enough, while researching the various myths and symbols for Virgo, I came across a sixteenth century engraving entitled 'The fecundity of sacrifice': the picture showed the crucifixion with the arms of the cross portrayed as branches laden with fruit—a beautiful illustration of how Virgo with its theme of fertility is interwoven with Pisces and its association with sacrifice.

While these insights are central to the idea of Virgo, in everyday life the sanctimonious and martyrish behaviour of some members of this sign seems only to infuriate others. Virgos are past masters at making others feel guilty as they nobly and uncomplainingly go about their duties, their concentrated efforts and thoroughness serving to remind others of their inadequacies. One astrologer—a doctor of science with a strong Virgoan theme in his chart, has alienated most of his colleagues, even those academics as keen as himself on objectively testing astrology, by picking apart virtually each and every statement made by those participating in his research: on many occasions his stringent analysis obfuscates any sense of the original. In true Virgo style, his passive intractibility drives others demented while he appears entirely rational and objective. Despite admiring the sheer dedication and meticulous approach to his work, one longs for him at least to admit a mistake or two—simply to make him appear human!

Although some astrologers maintain that Virgo's perfectionist tendencies are overrated and that this sign can be as sloppy as their fishy opposites, in my experience people with Virgo prominent in their charts set exceedingly high standards and apply great precision in, at the very least, one area of their lives. Many, while dressing exclusively from the 'Nearly New' shop and following Quentin Crisp's philosophy that the dust doesn't get any worse after six years, become apoplectic if one of their possessions has been moved a centimetre out of place, or Herman Hesse has been placed before Heidegger on the bookshelf. The great scientist Nikola Tesla* would only work on pristine pieces of paper; his design would occupy only a small part of the huge white surface, and if any mistake or smudge were to appear he would throw it away and begin again. Tesla was also phobic about germs; when dining, he would wipe all his utensils with a clean white table napkin taken from a pile of twenty-four that was laid beside his plate at every meal! Virgo's tolerance threshold for flaws and smut of any description is extremely low.

Cleanliness, like fastidiousness, is an essentially Virgoan trait. Of course some Virgos prefer to let their natural wholesome bodily odours shine through, regardless, but the majority find a 'good soak' excellent therapy. Indeed, meditating in the bath often acts as the only stress-reliever in Virgo's toilsome day. Why Virgos worry more than any other sign probably stems from a combination of wanting to do everything right and a tendency mentally to speculate over countless possibilities and improbabilities relating to each and every issue. Virgos have a great affinity for taking everyone else's problems upon themselves. In many ways it is Virgos' obsession with detail and the minutiae of life that often prevents them from achieving their ends—not that Virgo is an innately ambitious sign. But Virgos frequently find it as frustrating to themselves as everyone else that they are constantly sidetracked by trivia!

Virgos usually like to exercise their cerebral cortex in preference to their biceps. These logical individuals enjoy using their minds, and like their fellow mutables, the Geminians and the Sagittarians, have an insatiable curiosity about life. While some go on to collect the glittering prizes in the academic world, others excite their mental processes playing endless puzzles and word-games—punning is a great Virgoan pastime. And even the most high-minded Virgos love a good gossip, although they will no doubt hotly deny it. With their eye for detail and often wicked wit, Virgos can be hugely entertaining individuals.

*Moon in the 6th 'house'—Virgo territory.

Finally, a word about Virgo's belief in self-help. This sign has a built-in fear of becoming dependent on others. While the Virgoan individual may deluge the needy with compassion and understanding, when possible he prefers to educate others to stand on their own two feet and develop their own potential for survival and success. However, this admirable philosophy frequently backfires through Virgos' overriding sense of duty—they cannot break free (without experiencing tremendous guilt) from what they see as their obligations.

Virgos are never really the hoover and duster possessed individuals they are often painted to be. While some may indeed express their fastidious and purist ways by interminably sweeping floors and polishing surfaces, they are more likely to gather up every last piece of information and painstakingly sift through the contents, selecting and refining only that which is worthwhile and useful. Virgos may not jostle for top-dog positions in life, not because they haven't the ability to soar, but because they see too clearly the folly in empty ambition, the ugliness of greed, and the ephemeral nature of success. Take another look before you dismiss Virgo as a passive do-gooder or a niggling nit-picker; remember, Virgos are as important as the legendary Dutch boy—you know, the one with his finger in the dyke!

RELATIONSHIPS

In my experience, there seems to be a certain amount of truth in the old astrological chestnut, that those individuals with a strong Virgoan theme in their charts (not necessarily just Sun Virgos) are often latecomers to marriage, and many never marry at all. Whether this can be statistically proven, I don't know; but certainly the enormity of the emotional commitment (often camouflaged by excuses such as loyalty to dependent relatives/demanding job/or the failure to find the right person) deters many Virgos from the altar. Even those who marry young, or who move from relationship to relationship tend to marry with their heads rather than their hearts, yet nevertheless make some sad mistakes! Now, if this makes Virgo sound rather cold and heartless, read on: this sign is full of paradoxes, and like its earthy companions, Taurus and Capricorn, a tender and vulnerable heart lies behind its cool and touch-me-not exterior.

THE FEMALE VIRGO

There she is, that paragon of bright and sensible virtue, standing on her astrological pedestal—dishmop in one hand, thesaurus in the other! Having earlier dispensed with the idea of Virgo being the daily help of the zodiac, perhaps I shouldn't bring it up again; but prim and puritan, fussy and school-marmish is invariably the layman's concept of Ms Virgo. While the Virgoan female may like to know everything is in its place, because it appeals to her sense of order and completeness, she'll only become obsessive about the housework if she's inwardly unhappy and deeply unfulfilled. Certainly, this female is one of the most industrious in the zodiac and if she's not being useful, or there are no challenges for her agile mind, she'll take off on a roller-coaster of all her worries and insecurities, making Everests and Matterhorns out of each and every Primrose Hill!

Duty and responsibility to others are virtues inborn in the Virgoan woman, and even those who wish they'd never heard the words feel uncomfortably guilty if they're not putting others first and enjoying themselves as an afterthought. Often Virgoan little girls (especially those with their Moon or Venus in Virgo) sense early on that mother is a much put-upon creature who has a great burden to bear in the form of children/husband/illness—whatever—and somehow the Virgoan child feels a tinge of guilt about it all. Mother may not be a delicate flower or even a dogsbody of course, but somehow Ms Virgo perceives it thus and if she's not careful, when she's grown up, she'll follow in her mother's footsteps and become the quiet martyr to her own family. On the other hand, Virgoan little girls make wonderful mother's helps and hardly ever need an apple for the teacher since they make naturally attentive and willing students. Faced with the debris of my eldest son's seventh birthday party, it came as no real surprise to me that the small voice at my side, offering to clear it all away, came from my neighbour's Virgoan little girl. She was bright and efficient, without being cloying, so when we'd finished I gave her another party pack to take home. I'd hate to think that this might have been her intention in the first place, but her father maintained that one of her great assets was her ability to size up people very well; thus, she always got what she wanted! Virgo ladies are never stupid—even as children!

As an adult, the Virgoan female exudes sensibleness and competence from her gentle, no-nonsense exterior. She maintains that when 'everything' is done, she'll put her feet up and relax; the problem being that she never runs out of things to do! From her earliest days as a girl guide and treasurer to the Young Conservatives, Ms Virgo has been unable to sit idly by and watch anyone else labouring. First, because it makes her feel terribly twitchy, and second, because she knows she can do it so much better herself. Later on, it'll be the WI, the PTA, and the Samaritans who reap the benefits of her tireless, good-natured efficiency. Inevitably, others take her for granted and assume she actually likes her role as Super Slog, but inwardly she yearns to be as free-spirited and wayward as the most capricious fire or air sign. Of course her good nature runs out on occasion—usually when she's in danger of being proved wrong, or someone has dared to criticize her. The sparks may not fly, but the temperature plummets a good 20 degrees and icicles form from the door she firmly shuts behind her.

The hallmark of the Virgoan woman is her kindness, her thoughtfulness, and her infinite discrimination. Ms Virgo is anything but the impulsive, here-today-gone-tomorrow type; nor indeed is there anything brash or abrasive about this woman. Almost all Virgos have an extremely wise and practical head on their over-burdened shoulders; they can turn their hand to anything from unblocking the kitchen sink and erecting the garden trellis, to running the local playgroup or heading an outward-bound course. More to the point, the precision of their manoeuvres, impressive even by SAS standards, and their results are frequently accomplished without a hair out of place. (Mind you, at the end of the day, they may hit the gin and tonic rather heavily, and retire to bed with gigantic migraines!) But where, one may ask, is the real Ms Virgo, for no matter how long you may know her, she lets little of her real essence or her true feelings escape. Like her opposite number Ms Fish, or her near neighbour Ms Scorpio, the Virgoan female is fundamentally an enigma.

One of the great paradoxes within the Virgoan woman is that on the one hand she is one of the greatest realists in the zodiac, and on the other she is an out and out romantic. While she's on firm ground analysing practical situations—even abstract concepts—and separating what is true and valid from what is phoney and useless, the minute her heart is touched, she behaves like a romantic fool. While she may spend hours of her time advising others how to cope with their relationships (sometimes in an official capacity as a counsellor, at others merely as an 'Aunt Sally') in her own life she is invariably the well trampled-on doormat. A client of mine with her Moon and Venus in Virgo told me, 'I caught myself bemoaning the fact that yet again I'd loaned a boyfriend some money and I'd probably never get it back—or him for that matter. I was always doing it. What I hadn't realized was, that I **only** had relationships with these kind of men. Anyone who was reliable, unneurotic, or financially solvent, was of no interest to me!' Like the Pisces woman, the theme of suffering and sacrifice often permeates Virgos' relationships, and for many, unless there is an element of selfless hardship in a relationship, it doesn't command their interest.

While some Virgoan women become hopelessly starry-eyed about their partners and remain blind to the fact that they are being used, or that they are sacrificing themselves to their partner's autocracy or selfishness, others, like the above client, do recognize that they need to play this kind of role. Indeed, the combination of romantic idealism and practical usefulness inherent in Virgo produces an attitude in some Virgo females that they ought to experience some kind of hardship in a relationship for it to be worthwhile. And although many Virgos seem to suffer all sorts of slings and arrows in their relationships, a great many also find an extremely high level—sometimes even a transcendent quality—of love in their partnerships.

Certainly, the feeling of duty and obligation to others is at the core of many Virgos' relationships. Sometimes, of course, Ms Virgo is so devoted and duty bound to her aged and infirm parents, her cantankerous boss, her patients, or her classroom brood, that she can't marry her lover or even live with him. But by and large, when it comes to marriage, the Virgo female accepts her responsibilities without question, and can be relied upon to stick by her man though thick and thin. Indeed, the Virgo woman who remains single is usually one who recognizes (albeit unconsciously) that she cannot muster this kind of dedication to any one man.

At this point, it might be easier to place the Virgo woman in two psychological categories, the **Siren** and the **Earth Mother**, each of which reflects different aspects of the Virgo nature.

While a great many Virgoan women are naturally shy and reticent, in some this attractive reserve manifests as sheer coldness and aloofness. The Virgo woman does not give of herself easily: she tends to place a distance between herself and others, until she has weighed them up, and even then she's not the type to drape herself all over people. However, the front the Virgo female presents gives little clues as to whether she is a **Siren** in **Earth Mother's** clothing or vice versa!

The **Siren** has aspects of the Scorpio **femme fatale** and the Libran 'courtesan' about her and in my experience crops up more frequently with women who have Venus in Virgo rather than just the sun.* The **Siren** is highly attractive to certain men who sense untold delights and sensuous mysteries behind her subtle, but alluring, facade. What separates the Virgoan from her Libran and Scorpionic counterparts, however, is that this woman's fine and calculating mind is her greatest weapon—she never lets flattery get the better of her like the Libran, or allows her emotions to consume her like the Scorpion. In myth, Sirens were creatures half woman, half fish, hauntingly beautiful and fatally enticing to wayfarers. But once their prey was landed, they would devour the men mercilessly. Sirens conquered men, not for love of them, but to gain power over them.

Broadly speaking, the Virgoan **Siren** also needs to conquer men: she gains satisfaction through their enslavement to her while she remains invulnerable to them since she invests little or no emotional or psychological capital in them. This kind of woman is fatally attractive to emotionally vulnerable men. Esther Harding in **Woman's Mysteries** states that 'there are whole classes of women who even while living erotically are as cold as icebergs and as calculating as stockbrokers'. Such a woman usually displays great interest in a man, and deep concern over his welfare to the extent that

> he will feel this woman has a peculiar connection with him in things which are ordinarily secret. . . It gives him a curious feeling of warmth and closeness. . . In this way the woman finds a chink in his personal dignity and reserve through which she can enter. She touches him where it is soft and yielding, where his defences do not serve him any more. His conscious judgement of the situation and her character is nullified. . . The man feels her to represent his other self, his inevitable mate. And it does not occur to him that he has been the victim of a trick. When the woman herself is immune to love **unable to give herself totally and spontaneously to another** she plays the role of Siren to greatest advantage. The more impersonally skillful she is, the more likely it is that the man will become hopelessly enmeshed. [my emphasis]

Of course, many Virgoan women fail to recognize the **Siren** in themselves. Like the Piscean in the same boat, she may think she falls in love with men, and is as amazed as her friends when her relationships fail to last. In truth, when her love is put to the test, or real emotional demands are made on her, her instinctive coldness and self-preservation instincts rise to the surface. Indeed, taken to its extreme, this kind of woman is a dab hand at cold-blooded exploitation of a man's love, and turns her sexual response on and off like a tap.

There is often an aspect of the **Siren** in the successful Virgoan woman who is 'married' to her career, since she uses the same techniques to gain emoluments and promotion from the men with whom she works. But, of course, there are many wives who are fundamentally **Sirens** and who, while appearing to fulfil the wifely and motherly expectations of their role, nonetheless exploit their partners on all fronts and frequently emasculate them in the process.

The **Earth Mother** is certainly the more familiar Virgoan type. This is the

---

*Since Venus never moves further than 45° from the Sun, many Sun Libran and Scorpion women (as well as some Cancerians and Leos) may well have their Venus in Virgo.

sort who nurtures and nurses her pets, projects, husband, and children like the fruits of the earth themselves, and gains fulfilment and a sense of completeness through her labours. It is extremely unusual for this kind of Virgo not to take pride in her home and her produce—whether they be her distinctive tapestries, her home-made jams, her herb-garden, or her children. Like Hestia and Demeter, home is where the hearth is and she feels entirely connected to and peacefully at one with the Earth, and the goodness and vitality of its offerings. But, if this fits the Virgoan stereotype so far, remember this woman is not necessarily a pin-neat paragon of meticulousness. She may be health, hygiene and fitness-mad, but she doesn't like any artificial plastic shininess about her—it offends her instinct for all that is natural and wholesome. Also, the **Earth Mother** isn't by implication a bovine labourer; she usually has great intelligence; and while she may be resplendent in her role as homemaker extraordinaire, cradling the milk-churn in one hand and dandling a baby in the other, her book shelf is likely to be as well stocked as her pantry! The Earth Mother usually excels in the culinary department. Like the Libran female, the Virgoan is a marvellous hostess and is in her element bearing the horn of plenty for gatherings both large and small. She's also a great one for regular stocktaking in the larder! The Earth Mother is the inevitable prop around which the rest of the family circulate, the wisewoman who listens to their grief and their joy, the healer who tends their wounds—physical and emotional—and the sustainer who keeps the wheels of family life relentlessly and efficiently turning. She has no craving for power or control over her man, yet in a sense she places herself in the role of servant and in an extreme form turns her back on any of her own ambitions or individual needs.

As the **Siren** takes from life—or more especially, from men—the **Earth Mother** gives—selflessly.

Yet one must not forget that both these 'types' are united by the principle of the virgin (see pp.234–5). Virgo women, no matter how they go about forming their relationships, basically seek emotional and psychological self-sufficiency (this sign hates being dependent on anyone else). To this end, the **Siren** keeps all of herself to herself (at least all the parts that matter) and the **Earth Mother** gives herself away. In an ideal world, the ideal Virgoan is the woman who is one-in-herself; one who, in Esther Harding's words again, 'does what she does, not because of any desire to gain power over another, to catch his interest or love, but because what she does is true'. This kind of woman is not dependent on a partner for her fulfilment: she has self-contentment and therefore gives freely, sacrificing neither herself nor her needs.

Indeed the desire for this kind of psychic balance and completeness within themselves is the drive behind Virgos' quest for perfection in relationships. However, while one becomes too self-contained and self-seeking, thus rendering herself unable to participate in a (full) union, the other seeks to find herself in a partner and loses sight of her individuality in the process. Although critics may maintain that these effects can happen to an individual whatever her astrological make-up, in essence it is a peculiarly Virgoan proclivity.

Trying to accommodate both their innate realism and their romantic idealism presents quite a challenge for most Virgo women—and their partners. They veer from being sweetly understanding about their partner's appalling absent-mindedness or lack of immediate funds, to flying into a fit every time he sets a muddy wellington boot on the kitchen floor. While on the one hand Ms Virgo may rationalize that marriage is 90 per cent hard work and 10 per cent happiness, a part of her desperately yearns for her partner to fly them both away on a magic carpet to Never-Never Land. The more disappointed with the content of her relationship she becomes, the more Ms Virgo turns into a nag and a shrew. Of course, she wouldn't dream of deserting her man if he let her down—not that she'll exactly grin and bear it either. Nor will she turn into a jealous viper every time he says he has to work late at the office. The problem with the Virgoan woman is that her temperament conditions her into holding back, thus any frustration or resentment tends to emerge in subtle ways. Indeed, Ms Virgo, like Ms Pisces, is just as capable of making others feel guilty about her as she is of feeling guilty about everyone else! Often the Virgo woman who would rather have married a career than a husband makes the best martyr of all, and pours the most guilt on her husband and the family. And ironically enough, despite Virgo's Earth Mother connotations, a great many Virgoan women don't want children at all and recoil at the whole idea of childbirth and child rearing. One Virgoan mother of a friend of mine told her that she wished she'd had dogs rather than children—'far less trouble, and no arguments!'

Clearly, the Virgoan female has far more to offer a man than a can of spray polish and a pocket calculator. She is a woman of infinite resourcefulness, with great patience and gentleness. She doesn't suffer fools gladly, but unlike Ms Aries she won't inform them bluntly of the fact; instead, with laser-like precision, she'll quietly put them in their place, then graciously leave them alone. Ms Virgo may love a lame dog or two, which can make her prone to the most dreary dependents as partners, but if she successfully combines her gentle heart with her clever mind she'll find a partner who reflects her infinite good taste. It may take a partner some time to discover if there's a Siren lurking in the broom cupboard behind all the preserves, but a glance through these pages should make him pause and reflect, that his little hausfrau is by no means the 'apple dumpling' he thought she was.

THE MALE VIRGO

It's no use expecting to meet the Virgo man of your dreams at an all-night, come-as-you-are party—especially if the drinks aren't on the house. And if by any remote chance you do, he won't be the one in a puce suit and an orange tie regaling his life story—liberally laced with lewd anecdotes—while he gradually drinks himself insensible. While the Virgo man is not really anti-social, he's far more at home in the rarefied atmosphere of the 'International Computer Convention', a Third World Conference, the health club, or plain old 'home sweet home'. Mr Virgo, even if he's one of the extrovert variety, can be a bit of a hot-house plant if exposed for too long to inharmonious surroundings and unintelligent company. And while he may develop quite a knack for hiding his ascetic nature behind a bravado front, any woman planning to share his life will soon discover that he has a painfuly low tolerance threshold for the banalities of life.

Like Mr Pisces, his opposite number, the Virgoan man is never really the macho type. He may go to a lot of trouble to keep fit and trim, watching his diet, jogging every morning, and working out in the gym once a week, but any bulging biceps merely provide an excellent cover up for his sensitive and vulnerable inner core.

Master Virgo was probably unable to throw himself with sheer abandon into the joys of childhood. Both he and his female counterpart are acutely sensitive to their parents' suffering—real or imagined—and even if family life is relatively problem free, the Virgoan little boy is easily hurt and immensely sensitive to everyone and everything. Often sport is not his métier—he prefers the chess board to the football pitch any day—so he tends to have a little trouble making the running in the popularity stakes. Sometimes he becomes the school bully's favourite punching bag, which increases his sense of general alienation. Like most of the other deeply sensitive souls in the zodiac, the Virgoan boy learns early on how to hide his feelings from the world and uses his excellent mind and his gift for mimicry to win friends and influence people.

The Virgo man sets extremely high standards for himself and others, yet he is anything but the ruthlessly ambitious sort—at least not unless there's some Scorpio or Capricorn or Aries in the chart. The satisfaction of a job well done means more to Mr Virgo than a high-powered position with a fat salary. This man likes to be involved at all levels with whatever he does, checking that each part of the machinery is working well; even phenomenally wealthy and powerful tycoons, like Henry Ford II, are simple men at heart and while accepting the responsibility of their roles nevertheless rarely flaunt their wealth or power. Sometimes the lack of ambition and drive in the Virgo man frustrates their partners, but although Mr Virgo needs some encouragement not to miss the boat of opportunity, too much push and shove will send this man scuttling off into the distance. In keeping with his orderly temperament, Mr Virgo likes his women to 'run' like clockwork— ironically, of course, he invariably picks women who play havoc with his timetables and his nervous system!

I've yet to come across a man with a Virgo theme in his chart who didn't display some of the fussy and fastidious tendencies of this sign. Although it would be wrong to assume that all Virgo men are meticulous in every area of their lives, those who are generally slapdash and sloppy are certainly in the minority. A great friend of mine, who is convinced that for a Virgo he'd make a good Leo, goes to great pains to behave in a warm and extrovert fashion when we're together, but he invariably lets himself 'down' by sneaking off to the kitchen secretly to wash up between courses, and he can rarely resist discreetly wiping away any dust on the picture frames. Another becomes apoplectic if his wife fails to place his clothes in the right order in the wardrobe. Worse still, one client, married to a tyrant of a Virgo, told me she pins notes to his shirts explaining why the creases aren't sharp enough!

At the root of Mr Virgo's often obsessional fussiness is his faith that only through order can he maintain control over his life. Indeed, one of his greatest fears is that his own internal chaos—in the form of any irrational feelings—may one day take him over.

The Virgo man, like the Capricornian, rarely finds the path to true love littered with roses. Both these signs encounter major obstacles in their relationships: however, the classic Virgoan problem is one of disillusionment and let-down, rather than Capricorn's lot of relentless hardship and frustration. The Virgoan man, despite his emotional reticence, nurtures very high ideals about love in general and the right woman in particular. Perhaps because he spent a lot of time in his youth reading about love—sometimes poetry, but often erotic literature—and rather less time initiating real life relationships with the opposite sex, his expectations of women are rather unrealistic. Clearly, his ideals in this department clash violently with his down to earth, practical stance elsewhere in his life. Thus, to the outside world, Mr Virgo often comes across as a hard bitten realist in matters of the heart, while his romantic track record tells a completely different story.

Since Mr Virgo is hardly ever considered a 'ladies man', and is possibly even seen as the weak and silent type, it always comes as an enormous surprise to everyone when he makes off with the boss's daughter, or the neighbourhood's stunning blonde bombshell, especially when he does it right under the nose of charming and debonair Mr Libra, or fast and flashy Mr Leo. Besides being devious when it comes to getting what he wants, Mr Virgo is often extremely fascinating to extrovert, glamorous women. (Consider for a moment the on-screen/off-screen personality of Woody Allen and you have the quintessence of the Virgoan lover.) However, while the Virgo man may walk away with the prize bloom, he often lives to regret it.

Unlike the Virgo woman, who tends to seek out a lame dog for a partner, someone she can 'save', the Virgo man often (subconsciously) wants to be 'saved' in a relationship—although either way both sexes can become victims in their relationships. Many's the Virgo man who marries a woman who will 'front' the relationship, either through her strong personality, her charm and attractiveness, or her motherly strength and efficiency. Yet he often becomes deeply resentful and critical of the choice he has made and the position in which he finds himself.

The Virgo man, like the Capricorn, often suffers from that peculiarly English syndrome 'the stiff upper lip'. Like the typically reserved English gentleman, the Virgoan's control and rigid emotional bearing prop up his extremely insecure nature. The Virgo man hates loss of emotional control in others; it freezes him in his tracks. His own feelings are often so immature, through lack of spontaneous expression over the years, that they render him psychologically impotent in an emotionally charged situation. Ironically, the more emotionally repressed the Virgo man, the more likely he is to attract an emotionally overpowering partner.

Initially, such a relationship is fascinating for both, since Mr Virgo vicariously experiences the warmth of open feelings through his woman, while she is 'earthed' by him. But as the relationship progresses, the Virgoan man retreats behind his emotional reserve, which in turn drives his partner to more and more extreme ways of displaying her feelings. To observers, he may appear to be the proverbial henpecked husband. But behind closed doors, his emotional aloofness is as much a deadly weapon as any amount of vitriol or physical abuse that his frustrated and rejected wife can hurl.

Some Virgo men like to play Professor Higgins and set out quite deliberately to find their own Eliza Dolittle. These kind of Virgos like to work on their partners like sculptors, smoothing the odd rough edge here and there and chipping away any unacceptable flaws. While the Virgo man who tends, nurtures, and protects his fledgling wife makes a wonderfully supportive husband, his sharply critical manner can 'over the years' sap his partner's confidence, eventually rendering her unable to do anything without his blessing or approval. The Virgo man who adopts this role in a relationship sometimes (unconsciously) resents his duckling turning into a swan since she may well outgrow him in the process. Thus his cutting comments and perfectly timed put-downs are a way of binding her to him. Also, there is a certain brand of Virgo man who appears to get a sort of sadistic pleasure out of cutting his partner down to size.

Although Virgo is an earth sign, and therefore inherently dependable and practical, it is also a mutable one. The feature common to all the mutable signs is a lack of commitment—all too apparent with the flightiness of Gemini, the wanderlust of Sagittarius, and the escapist tendencies of Pisces, but far less obvious in down-to-earth Virgo. Of course Virgo's lack of commitment could well have something to do with his inherent fear that his investment may not pay off. Although the Virgo man may be entirely capable of dealing with the day-to-day running of a relationship, and while he may appreciate the security of a familiar face—one who is accustomed to his 'little ways'—psychologically, he's a bit of a loner and he doesn't take too easily to the emotional shackles of a long-term, intimate relationship. Perhaps also because Virgo is low on the initiative-taking qualities of a cardinal sign, and has none of the inflexibility of a fixed one, the Virgo man often gets swept into marriage by circumstance, or somehow marriage becomes the lesser of two evils. Although he may adapt well to his outer role, his delicate emotional constitution cannot stomach too much pressure. Like the Virgo woman of the Siren type, the moment his love is put to the test, an instinctive coldness takes over.

A Virgo man, Paul, once consulted me about his marital problems. He had been married to his second wife, Sue, for three seemingly happy years, when for no apparent reason, 'suddenly, something changed'. He had no idea what it was, but he couldn't bring himself to make love to his wife, nor really to communicate on any level with her, and he was deeply uncomfortable in her presence. When asked, he maintained that he had never actually been 'in love' with anyone, but on the other hand he had 'fancied' Sue and found her an ideal companion. He didn't know what to do: he couldn't bring himself to leave the relationship, yet he was extremely unhappy living with her.

Sue, a Sun Pisces with a passionate Aries Moon, was devastated by the demise of their relationship, since she had experienced no change of heart herself. The more Paul retreated into his shell of confusion, the more hysterical and desperate she became. Naturally, she felt rejected and wanted to know (in true Piscean style) what she had done, especially since shortly before Paul's 'retreat' they had been discussing starting a family. However, the fault, if it can be called a fault, lay not in Sue, but in Paul's need to remain emotionally and psychologically inviolate.

There had been a period, before he and Sue married, where Paul had experienced qualms and a subsequent cut-off from the relationship; but rather than lose Sue, he went ahead with the marriage. What Paul had never been able to muster, in any relationship, was a feeling of whole-hearted commitment toward a woman. There was, in effect, an element of the monk in his emotional and psychological make-up. His sudden loss of feeling for Sue was in fact a culmination of a gradual (unconscious) realization that he could not maintain indefinitely the intimacy demanded of him in his marriage. It was, of course, the prospect of fatherhood, with all its responsibilities and ties, that acted as a catalyst to his feeling of marital claustrophobia. He felt a deep sense of guilt about his inadequacy as a partner, yet was powerless to do anything about it. While his instincts urged him to put as much distance between himself and Sue as possible, his sense of responsibility and guilt demanded that he stayed. His only recourse was to withdraw psychologically from the marriage, and through his passive retreat force Sue into taking the initiative to end the marriage. In effect he was turning himself into the familiar Virgoan martyr.

The cold war dragged on for some months: initially Sue moved Paul's belongings out of the bedroom, then Paul's long weekends away turned into weeks until he no longer came home at all. Divorce proceedings (initiated by Sue) began almost a year later.

Although lack of commitment is a mutable theme, not all Virgo men are bound to suffer from the syndrome. There are plenty of Virgo men who manage to harness their self-contained personalities to relationships of the intimate kind; usually, however, these men have some personal planets, or their Ascendant, in water or fire signs.

Paul, of course, is not the only man (regardless of his astrological make-up) to experience cold feet over the idea of fatherhood. All the earth signs tend to consider the cost of children before responding to any emotional or self-gratificatory instincts. But perhaps Virgo finds parenthood more of a personal burden than either Mr Taurus or Mr Capricorn. Because children tend to upset the perfect order and stop-watch precision of his life, Mr Virgo in particular balks at such an intrusion on his time and space. Yet the prospect of physical, psychological, and emotional closeness is often a far more daunting prospect to the Virgo man than anything else. Nevertheless, once the children arrive, the Virgo man can become a caring, conscientious father; and despite his no-nonsense approach to life and the way he extols the virtue of discipline, he's rather a push-over where his offspring are concerned. In Paul's case, of course, it wasn't merely the spectre of tiny feet trampling all over his Italian-tiled kitchen that bothered him, but the recognition that children would bind him more tightly to the already constraining clutches of marriage.

The Virgo man, like the Aquarian, often assumes falling in love to be an overblown psychological disorder. He's quite happy to remain unruffled by the irrational pangs of love, which is why, when the unthinkable happens, he's completely thrown by the experience. By and large, the Virgo man is far happier walking down the aisle with his two feet firmly on the ground than he is wafting around on cloud nine. However, when Mr Virgo finds a woman worthy of his devoted attentions, he can be as delicately romantic as Mr Pisces and as ardent as Mr Scorpio. Indeed, the kind of Virgo who relates to his feelings, who doesn't view them as inferior to his intellect, is capable of finding great happiness and fulfilment in relationships.

When the Virgo man has been smitten (at last) he often finds the experience releases his normally dormant ability for extravagance and indulgence. While this sign will always keep one foot on the straight and narrow where finances are concerned—he's anything but an unreformed Mr Micawber—once he's had a taste of the good life (and provided he has the wherewithal) he'll rarely revert to his previously mean and stingy ways. As soon as the Virgo man broadens his psychological and emotional horizons (usually with the aid of a warm and feeling woman) he can become generous to a fault—at least with those he loves.

The Virgo man who relishes his position as a husband and lover usually considers no task beneath his dignity, nor any effort too great to please his loved one. He'll fuss and cluck over his wife like a mother hen, and even if he has none of the real culinary talent so often present with men of this sign, he'll rustle up a little **quelque chose** in the kitchen from time to time. Mr Virgo is also very good at remembering the little things in life. He's the sort who never forgets special occasions and the perfect gift to go with them. He's a good listener too, with an excellent memory—he likes to make mental notes of the things his partner wants, and then to surprise her with them later.

It is unusual for the Virgo man not to take his responsibilities (at least the material ones) very seriously. Even if he can't muster the emotional commitment for a long-term partnership, he is highly conscientious about his partner's welfare. Thus, if a relationship hits the rocks, his wife will hardly ever be left high and dry or cold and hungry. Of course, as I discussed earlier, it is usually very difficult for the Virgo man to end a relationship; once it's over, however, he's not the type to try to retrieve it, although the psychological and emotional scars remain with him for the rest of his life. The Virgo man isn't the sort to seethe with jealousy either. Perhaps because he's not very good at putting an authoritative foot down (at least not without sounding like a petulant schoolboy) he can seem rather too accommodating, to the point of foolishness, over any flighty behaviour by his partner. But underneath his apparent indifference, Mr Virgo is just a bit of a prude and a tinge concerned that his 'property' might be under threat. Certainly he'll never rush into the breach over a suspected peccadillo; he's more likely to sit on his suspicions for a while, then, like the Scorpio, lead his partner into a nasty little verbal trap. However, unlike the Scorpio, a dénouement is hardly ever a blood-letting experience—just a sharp rap on the knuckles and an icy (but rarely silent) cold shoulder for as long as necessary.

Despite his calm and capable exterior, reasonable and punctilious Mr Virgo is quite a melting pot of irrational neuroses—which doesn't mean he can't be thoroughly lovable as well. Dipping his toes in the uncertain waters of romance always presents a challenge to this pragmatic man, but once he's taken the plunge and allowed himself to be borne along on an infinitely beautiful experience, all his gentler, compassionate, and more giving qualities emerge. Indeed, the Virgo who considers the psychological health of his heart to be as important as its physical well being, the Virgo who places a good woman above the price of the best computer, is one who, having painstakingly searched for Mrs Right, will never give her a day's anxiety over the strength and durability of his affections.

SUMMARY

Virgos of both sexes spend a great deal of time analysing their relationships, their partners, and themselves, yet become as mystified as the most ingenuous fire sign when things go wrong. While their rational minds tell them that relationships can never be perfect, their hearts never give up hope—a factor that lures them into the most improbable liaisons at times. Like Pisces, their opposite number, Virgos' ideal relationships often turn out to have been built on sand.

The thin line between saving others and falling victim themselves is one trod by Virgoan males and females alike; likewise, Virgos need to find the middle ground between becoming a pillar of granite for their partners (and never acquiescing to their own weaknesses or needs) and depending on them for their entire security.

In essence, this sign is one of supreme self-containment, which can make Virgo men and women hold their partners at arm's length occasionally. But once their hearts are won and their trust upheld, they make some of the most dependable and considerate partners in the zodiac.

VIRGO PARTNERSHIPS

Although Virgo men and women occasionally show a passively stubborn streak, in the main, they try to accommodate their partners, whatever their astrological make-up. Ideally, however, Virgos' best partners should be drawn from the water signs.

Aries

The attraction between Virgo and **Aries** can resemble a forest fire—sudden, hot, prone to run quickly out of control, and often extremely destructive. Aries' open and ardent personality is highly appealing to the more passive Virgoan while Virgo's intelligent reticent manner is irresistible to Aries. However, headstrong Arians are difficult for Virgos to control, and their sometimes abrasive, self-willed manner deeply hurts the Virgoan and drives him to his 'den' or the drink! Given there is much love between these two and plenty of tolerance for each other's ways, both can gain enormously from their relationship. But sadly these two often throw in the towel too soon.

Taurus

Taurus makes a stable, often extremely sensuous partner for Virgo: indeed this is the sexiest earth sign for Virgo. Although the Taurean is gentle and placid, he or she is also immensely stubborn. Thus the Virgoan can become thoroughly frustrated when his every alternative is turned down or sweetly ignored. Also, Virgo can find Taurus a mite too self-indulgent and prone to excesses in the good things of life, while the Bull feels Virgo is painfully abstemious. If the Taurean is a communicative, humorous type, this relationship can happily withstand a long test of time.

Gemini

Gemini is Virgo's most attractive, yet antithetical air sign. Both share a Mercury rulership so the mental level of their relationship is usually its strongest suit. Yet Geminis invariably appear flippant and superficial to

Virgos and can't be pinned down to anything, while Virgos seem overly pragmatic and fussy to Geminis and bent on practical solutions and uses to everything. Virgo's social life sparkles with a Gemini partner, and both these two are keen on improving their minds: they often enrol at Adult Education Institutes together—different courses, naturally. Sometimes the busy pace of their lives covers up any emotional gaps in their relationship, which is fine, unless one partner has more planets in water and therefore needs a good emotional rapport as well. Both these signs dislike conflict, so that even if their relationship proves emotionally and physically cool, they tend to stay together.

Cancer

Cancer makes a good nurturing partner for the Virgoan. The Cancerian usually understands and relates to his partner's anxieties and insecurities, and soothes them away; although sometimes his gentle mothering becomes too smothering for Virgo. Problems develop between these two if the Virgoan is the husband and a reluctant father, since the Cancerian female is usually keen to have a family. However, sexually their relationship is often excellent. A tendency to allow distance to build up through hurt silences—especially if one has criticised the other—spoil this otherwise harmonious relationship.

Leo

Leo is the best fiery partner for Virgo since both may have personal planets in each other's Sun sign. Leo is the most stable and consistent of the fire signs and so provides a good balance for Virgos' highly-strung nature—although the Lion's immovable, strong-willed personality frequently presents a large obstacle to marital harmony! On the plus side, Leo's generous sensual nature warms and broadens Virgo's horizons, sexual and otherwise, while Virgo perfects and prunes Leo's enthusiasms and his life in general. On the negative side, Leo's self-indulgence and extravagant good taste is the antithesis to Virgo's modest discriminating lifestyle; consequently their relationship demands much give and take to stand the passage of time.

Virgo

When two **Virgos** get together—usually after much deliberation and shilly-shallying—they make a brisk and busy partnership. Despite their hesitant and sensible natures, however, they often bring out each other's irrational and inconsistent streak; thus, the early stages of their relationship are often prone to much coming and going. Once their relationship settles down, two Virgos work well at living together and learning to cope with each other's little neuroses. Unless there are personal planets in fire or water signs, and/or good Venus/Mars interaspects, sex frequently takes a back seat in this partnership.

Libra

Libra is the most compatible air sign for Virgo; not only are Librans perfectionists about their relationships and very accommodating to their partners, but as zodiacal next-door-neighbours, Virgo and Libra may have personal planets in each other's Sun sign. On the minus side, Libra can be too upwardly mobile, socially and professionally speaking, for Virgo, so the Corn-Bearer feels his life is increasingly weighed down by trivia, often in the form of endless, boring, but 'useful' functions. But on the other hand, Virgo finds it difficult to fault Libra's performance as a partner, especially in public, except for the occasional display of shallow thinking and too many self-indulgent excesses. Provided both partners complement each other emotionally, this can be a happy and durable partnership.

Scorpio

In Virgo and **Scorpio** partnerships appearances can be deceptive. To others this couple may seem quiet and low key, but behind closed doors their relationship can reach untold heights and depths! Sometimes the Virgoan finds the Scorpion a little oversexed and too relaxed in his approach to personal hygiene, while the Scorpion resents being criticized and feels Virgo's constant questioning amounts to an invasion of his privacy. But this relationship often stands the test of time.

Sagittarius

Traditionally, **Sagittarius**, like Gemini, is one of Virgo's antipathies, but great fascination and attraction usually exists between these two signs. One of the pluses in the Sagittarian/ Virgoan relationship is their spirited intellectual rapport. But frequently their vastly different modes of thinking penetrate the rest of their relationship as well, frustrating and irritating them both. The physical relationship between these two can be excellent and initially detracts from their mundane difficulties; but unless the Sagittarian tones down his wayward, often inconsiderate ways, and the Virgo his constant criticism and negative attitude, these two find the stress and strain of living together far too much for them in the long term.

Capricorn

Virgo and **Capricorn** plan their relationship with great care and precision. No decision is taken impulsively nor any matter brushed away lightly. Although these signs reason things out well, they can both be moody and prickly at times. Even if they have a good physical rapport, their relationship can go through periods of sexual lethargy induced by unbridged emotional problems, or simply through over-work and exhaustion. Certainly, Virgo can go places in the world with his Capricorn partner, and this couple has a good track record for marital longevity.

Aquarius

Aquarius makes an unusual but stimulating partner for Virgo. If the Aquarian partner is of the Saturine variety he can provide the Virgoan with a degree of stability as well as his bright and curious mentality. However, the more bohemian (Uranian) Aquarian is usually far too much of an extremist for Virgo, although initially there may be strong attraction between these two. (Both types of Aquarian make a good match for Virgo in debate.) Unless there is plenty of water or fire in the charts and/or compatible Moon and Venus signs, a Virgo/Aquarius relationship tends to be on the cool side emotionally and sexually.

Pisces

Where are we going? And what for? are questions hovering over the Virgo/**Pisces** partnership. In a sense they are an ideal combination: Pisces with his dreamy, malleable nature and Virgo with his practical and supportive personality. But in the long term the Virgoan can feel much put upon by the Piscean since he seems to spend his time clearing up after the Fish and constantly reminding him of the mundane details of life. Strangely enough, these parent/child roles can be reversed and then it is the Piscean who becomes the organizing, structural source in the partnership. The sexual relationship between these two can be sensitive, imaginative and fulfilling.

SEXUALITY

One of the greatest misnomers perpetuated by popular astrology over the years is that Virgos run true to their virgin symbolism and give a wide berth to love in general and sex in particular. Of course there are Virgoan individuals who find sex distasteful, or at the very least, time consuming; but there are plenty more whose earthy, sensual natures enjoy making love every bit as much as the lustiest Scorpio or Taurean.

Clearly the Sun sign only represents a part of the whole astrological picture. In order to establish an individual's sexual bias many astrological factors, as well as the individual's conditioning, need to be taken into consideration. Bearing this in mind, those men with the Sun and Mars in Virgo and those women with the Moon, Venus, and Mars in this sign will relate more directly to the following ideas.

The sexual side of Virgo is by no means a straightforward affair of requited lust: a Virgoan theme in a chart presents a wide spectrum of sexual potential and Virgoan individuals range from the chaste and the celibate to the downright promiscuous.

As a Mercury ruled sign, Virgos' mental zones take pride of place in bed before their erogenous ones. Although the tendency for sex to be more active in the mind than anywhere else is far more marked in airy Gemini, Virgo's appetite for sex is undoubtedly enhanced by erotic material. Sexual games and fantasies often provide a spicy sexual appetiser for many Virgos: some find dressing up in their partner's clothes a sexual turn on, while, according to some of my colleagues, transvestism emerges with uncanny frequency in charts where there is a Virgoan theme.

Astrologically, Mercury is considered to be an asexual planet, which may help explain some Virgos' rather detached approach to sex. This sign, like Gemini, seems entirely capable of purely mechanical sex and indifferent sexual encounters; unbridled passion is often misssing in the more cerebral Virgo. Yet somewhat paradoxically, there are plenty of Virgoan names synonymous with passion and sexual appeal – Sean Connery, Robert Redford, Sophia Loren, Raquel Welch, and the writers D. H. Lawrence and Grace Metalious (author of **Peyton Place**).

At the top end of Virgo's sexual scale, there are those lovers whose sexual skill and attunement to their partner's needs are virtually unequalled. Nine times out of ten, however, those Virgos who take the glittering prizes in bed have personal planets in water signs, or Neptune contacts to the Sun, Moon,

Venus and Mars, or the angles. Since the Virgoan feels safer in the realm of the physical and the tangible, his only access to the sublime nature of sexual love is through any Neptune aspects or the watery content of the horoscope. Yet even without the added sensitivity of water or Neptune in their charts, many Virgo men and women become sexually fulfilling partners: indeed because Virgos are, in Jungian terms, physical/sensation types, they often communicate their feelings far better with their bodies than anything else. Like the Capricorns of this world, Virgoan men and women feel that actions speak louder than words!

Regardless of the degree of their sensuality, Virgos are apt to place knowledge and experience before instinct. Because they tend also to be highly strung and nervous, letting go and simply enjoying the experience is often beyond them; they need to know that what they are doing is **right**. It is unusual for a Virgo not to have read some kind of A – Z of making love. For some, relying on technical know-how frees their sensuality, but for others, sex never really takes off from the blueprint, and their partners usually sense each and every button being pressed.

While the sexually confident and more hedonistic Virgo may lead an extremely active sex life, he or she never allows sex to become an obsession. All things in moderation for Virgo. Yet the mystery of sexual union provides a source of deep intellectual fascination for this sign. Many Virgos, men and women alike, feel sex is not an end in itself but the route to a higher relationship with another individual—the union of minds and spirits beyond the physical. On the one hand, Virgos, like many Pisceans, seek some kind of synthesis through sexual exchange, and on the other, a blissful escape from the mundaneness of life. D. H. Lawrence explored the spiritually ecstatic quality of sexual love in his writings, yet he was also preoccupied with the analysis of the sexual motives of men and women. His concept of a pure love between two individuals—regardless of gender—that could transcend the limitations of physical love was, in essence, a truly Virgoan ideal.

Virgoan women often have a natural earthy sexuality. Yet by and large this sign, like Pisces and Scorpio, gives rise to sexual extremes. Virgo women can treat sex as just another job, a duty to be performed. On the one hand this can lead to some wearily lying back and thinking what structural alterations to make to the ceiling. On the other, some women who make a living out of sex—literally bringing to life the Great Harlot—have a strong Virgo theme in their charts. The **Siren** type (see p.241) tends to use sex as a means to an end and is as cold as marble despite her alluring persona. This sort of female can turn her sexual charms on and off like a lamp and is able to manipulate a man with the skill of an inveterate Mata Hari. Virgo women of this type usually function very well on a physical level, pleasing their partners and even seeming to relish the experience themselves. However, for one reason or another (guilt, an emotional or sexual childhood scar, or fear of commitment) these women find real desire and passion elude them, often along with an orgasm! Curiously enough, the promiscuous Virgo female is often one who is anorgasmic, rather than one who cannot get enough of a good thing. The Virgo woman who sleeps around may also be one whose self-esteem is low; consequently, she finds an intimate relationship with a caring partner difficult to maintain—or even find; thus sexual interchange—regardless of who it is with—provides the only means of being close to someone and feeling wanted. On another level altogether, the Virgo female, in keeping with her fertility goddess 'roots', is one of the few females in the zodiac who suffers little or no **angst** in satisfying her large sexual appetite with a variety of lovers. This is not because she is dissolute, but because, to her, sex is both a source of profound pleasure and a gift to bestow freely (without compulsion) to whomever she chooses. To this kind of female, sex is not the binding factor in a relationship and cannot therefore place a stranglehold on the participants.

Losing one's virginity is a major stepping stone for most women, but for the Virgo female it looms like a giant and dangerous leap in the dark. With this in mind, some Virgos hang on to their virginity so that they can lose it to the right man—one who won't turn out to be a one-night-stand—whereas others leap at the first chance to be deflowered in order to remove the obstacle of fear as soon as possible. Either way, the Virgo woman's sexual relationships often have a less than auspicious beginning!

Although, from my questionnaire, it was apparent that many Virgoan women derived great pleasure from sex, others expressed deep reservations about the whole area. 'I have never liked being touched very much, and open shows of affection embarrass me,' wrote one woman with her Sun in Virgo. 'I was never interested in boys and my husband was my first and only boyfriend. I was a virgin when we married (aged 20). Sex is a disappointment and not very important to me.' Another with her Venus and Mars in Virgo said, 'I was 26 when I started my relationship with my husband—he has been the only man in my life.' However, this same female went on to say, 'once aroused, my sexual action is very strong.'

If Ms Virgo had a mother who considered sex to be **dirty**, something women had to **suffer**, the Virgoan girl, in particular, grows up with a sense of fear and guilt about her sexuality. In my experience, Virgo women, more than any other sign, unconsciously pick up and adopt their mothers' attitudes to sex—good, bad, or indifferent. If the Virgo woman has some personal planets or angles in fire, she is less likely to be sexually repressed by such conditioning. If not, the path to free and happy sexual relationships tends to be an uphill struggle.

By and large, the Virgoan woman, like Ms Taurus and Ms Capricorn, tends to place stability and security in marriage before sexual compatibility. Thus a good sexual relationship becomes a bonus rather than an essential prerequisite of marriage. Yet the Virgoan woman who manages to free herself from her weighty baggage of taboos (not just the sexual ones) releases the rich and giving sexual attributes of this sign. Indeed of all the signs, it is the fully realized Virgoan female who manages to behave like 'a lady in the parlour, a mother in the nursery and a whore in the bedroom'!

The Virgoan man is rarely culled from the Sylvester Stallone stable: he's hardly ever a precocious lover. However, while the Virgo may blanch at the thought of 'pulling' a seventeen-year-old at his sixth form college, by the time he's twenty (after some intensive research) he's usually mastered his nerves enough to put his techniques to the test. And provided by that time she's not otherwise engaged, she'll be glad she waited! Mr Virgo, like his fellow earth signs, Taurus and Capricorn, needs to be reasonably sure of success before he makes a move: he doesn't like to be ridiculed, much less criticized. Even when he has plenty of sexual experience behind him, the Virgo man tends to be an extremely subtle seducer. However, despite his diffident manner, he usually possesses a hearty sexual appetite.

Nevertheless, where marriage is concerned, sex is often last on Mr Virgo's list of priorities: consequently he's often rather disappointed and sometimes downright frustrated with his sex life. Since he's not a philanderer by nature, unless he's virtually assaulted by another woman, he'll suppress his sexual needs by working 23 hours out of 24, or pouring himself obsessively into his hobbies. Indeed, some Virgos accidentally slip into celibacy this way! On the surface many a Virgo man seems bent on perpetuating the myth that, by and large, Virgos are disinterested in sex.

I'm not the only astrologer to observe that it is a peculiarity with Mercurial individuals that being found out and subsequently punished for doing something 'naughty' and 'rude' as a child creates a barrier to ease of sexual expression as an adult. Virgo is a sign renowned for its ability to feel guilty about all manner of things, real or imagined, so it's hardly surprising that this sign should be more prone to sexual hang-ups than many of the others. Although it would be totally wrong to assume that all Virgo men are riddled with guilt over their sexual feelings, many of them do seem to hold a 'hole in the corner' attitude to sex — voyeurism is an extremely Mercurial practice: also, correction, discipline, and bondage techniques are highly Virgoan in essence.

The Virgo man is a sexually complex creature. While he is earthy by nature, and therefore in touch with his physical senses, he is often emotionally inarticulate and psychologically highly strung. 'I find great difficulty in expressing myself forcefully, which affects my ability to form good relationships', wrote one man with his Sun and Mars in Virgo. 'On top of this, I experience sexual inhibitions because of getting "too much into my head" and wanting to control.' When sexual problems occur with this sign, they are usually linked to emotional ones. Paul (see p.247) is a case in point. Virgos, like all the earth and air signs, tend to control their emotions by consistently relegating them to the back seat. Thus their emotions surface in a raw and uncoordinated state as sudden irrational outbursts, or periodic bouts of impotence. The latter, as any psychologist will concur, is a form of passive anger. Often a sexual relationship with a Virgo man will start off well but deteriorate, either through sexual difficulties or emotional hiatuses, as deeper emotional exchange is demanded. Even the Virgo man who trusts and values his emotions still needs careful handling so as not to feel emotionally suffocated in a relationship.

Clearly, many Virgo men never encounter a sexual problem in their lives. While compiling material for this section, I came across several glowing accounts of the Virgo man's sexual prowess. One close friend of mine who covered a wide, but nonetheless selective field of sexual experience, maintained that her one Virgoan lover had been the most virile and erotic of all. He never 'had a headache' and was considerate, imaginative, and highly sensual in bed—which was where they spent most of their time. What ultimately drove them apart was his lack of ambition and her desire to have children. From an astrological point of view, their relationship was typical of the strong sexual attraction between earth and fire signs. While the Virgo man is often initially fascinated by the intoxicating warmth and openness of a fiery woman, gradually he begins to feel burnt out by a daily onslaught of hectic activity and withdraws into his shell of seclusion.

Finally, a word about cleanliness and celibacy. Many Virgos (male and female alike) never have intercourse without scrubbing up first or rushing off for ablutions immediately afterwards. While this may seem a completely unexceptional practice for many Virgos, and merely a reflection of their generally fastidious natures, in some the desire to be clean reflects an (unconscious) feeling that sex is dirty. Those who find sex vaguely, or even grossly, repellent usually drop the practice altogether. While for some Virgo men and women the desire for celibacy is linked to fear and guilt about sex, others become celibate for religious reasons. But perhaps more appositely for Virgo, celibacy is linked to this sign's innate self-sufficiency, which urges some Virgoan men and women to refrain from deep intimacy of any kind—emotional, psychological, or physical.

Virgo presents a highly contrasting sexual picture. On the one hand there are Virgo men and women whose sensuality encourages them to lead rich sexual lives, sometimes to the point of rampant promiscuity. On the other, there are Virgos whose sexuality leads to diffidence, or doing without sex completely. There is a safe middle ground where, I suspect, the majority of Virgos lie. A time and place exists for everything in Virgo's life, including sex, and all things in moderation. Remember, these individuals are gluttons for self-denial.

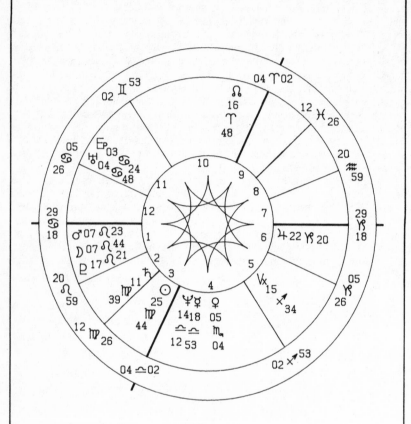

TWIGGY

19 9 1949   0h 25m 0s GMT

PLACIDUS 51N35 1W12

PROFILE OF A VIRGO WOMAN

TWIGGY

If Rubens had been alive in 1966 he would have thought that the world had gone completely mad; for here was a young girl who to all intents and purposes resembled a porcelain stick insect, an aberration of the female form, the most celebrated, the most photographed, the most imitated figure of the decade—if not the century, Woman of the Year, and only sixteen. Twiggy zoomed to fame in the summer of 1966: an overnight phenomenon whose time had come. With her fragile 87-pound frame, she embodied the spirit of the Sixties and epitomized the street consciousness of the day. Never had youth been so much in the ascendant; barriers everywhere were collapsing. It no longer mattered where you came from, just as long as you caught the mood of change, the wave of freedom. The Sixties was also a time of anarchy in all walks of life; and Twiggy almost single-handedly instigated a new direction in the world of fashion. Gone were the deb types of model and the cool, remote, sleek beauties of the Forties and Fifties—swept away by a geometric revolution in the form of an angular, gawky Cockney Sparrow. Thin was in; curves were out.

That Twiggy was a Sixties phenomenon might have guaranteed her only a short 'shelf life'; but Twiggy was more than just an enchanting face and marvellous clothes-horse; she had brains and an effervescent personality—two ingredients that were to turn her into a lasting success story.

Twiggy was born and brought up in Neasden, London—a suburban hotbed of social rest. She and her two elder sisters lived with their parents in an ordinary semi-detached house. Life was happy. The family was close. Unlike her two sisters, Twiggy was agonizingly shy. While they gaily rushed off to tap classes and enthusiastically joined the Brownies, Twiggy 'clung onto her mother's skirts', and cried: 'I was terrified of going to dance classes or anything remotely showy. I just wanted to stay at home.' School, however, was different. 'I absolutely loved school—adored it. I was pretty good at most things—not the·top of the class, but in the top few. I specially liked English and the arts.' As a teenager, she used to take a Saturday job at her local hairdressers: 'No, I didn't want to be a hairdresser, but then I hadn't had the time to give my future much thought—it all suddenly happened for me.' Indeed, even before taking her 'O' levels, Twiggy was launched on her brilliant career.

One Saturday afternoon, an East End boy with lofty aspirations called Nigel Davis spotted Lesley Hornby's marketable magic standing by the backwash at a hairdressers. He walked into her life and helped transform this waif-er thin creature into a megastar. Twiggy had arrived.

At first glance it might appear that the astrology does not support Twiggy's comments about her close and happy family life. Neptune is not the most positive influence to have in the area of family life, and this planet can indicate a weak and unsupportive family unit. Venus, however, is an extremely beneficial 'energy' to find in the same 'house'; yet since there is a tense 90° aspect from the Moon to this planet a degree of disharmony is also indicated. Thus we are left with two possibilities: either Twiggy is (consciously or unconsciously) concealing the truth with the aid of a pair of Neptunian rose-coloured glasses, or the astrology is wrong. However, there is another.

The fourth 'house' area of the chart is not simply home in the sense of four square walls and Mum and Dad, but the home of the psyche. The mid-teens is an extremely delicate time of life to experience a major change, whether through a happy set of circumstances or a traumatic event—especially if you are a sensitive 'home' bird like Twiggy. Her meteoric rise to fame with all its attendant pressures came at a time when she was psychologically and emotionally unprepared for it. And no matter how much she enjoyed the fruits of her success the price she paid was the loss of her own personal privacy. Neptune also has much to do with image, and to a certain extent Twiggy may have experienced considerable difficulty in sorting out her real self from the image. Certainly Neptune combined with her cautious Cancerian Ascendant would have made her feel very insecure about projecting herself to the world at large without some support from familiar (family) figures. This idea is given more substance by the fact that until her early thirties, Twiggy depended not only on her family for emotional support but on two men she trusted and valued—Justin de Villeneuve and Michael Witney. Also, in keeping with Neptune in the fourth, it would seem Twiggy carries around an idealized father figure in her psyche—one that has little to do with her real experience of 'Dad', since two of the most important men in her life have been considerably older than herself.

Nigel Davis, or Justin de Villeneuve as he was eventually to become, was a Sun Pisces with a strong Capricorn-Aries mix. He had all the vision plus the tactical skill and push to shape her career and ensure they both made a considerable fortune through their combined talents and labours. He was the pioneer of a new breed of promoter-managers. Under his guidance, Twiggy decorated the covers of all the top fashion magazines the world over—her every sneeze was practically a front-page story. Within months of her entrée into the big time, the market was flooded with Twiggy dolls, Twiggy clothes, and Twiggy window models. She was even moulded in wax at Madame Tussaud's. Her popularity reached such proportions that she was mobbed on the scale of the Beatles! But Justin was more than just a manager. He was very much in love with Twiggy and they had an extremely close relationship. But since Twiggy's image was one of sweetness and innocence, at first their relationship followed a strict code of conduct and Justin would dutifully bring Twiggy home to her parents every night. To say that she depended on Justin is an understatement. He was 'everything' to her, and they went everywhere together. Indeed Twiggy never attended the Woman of the Year lunch where she was guest of honour because she was paralyzed with nerves at the thought of going on her own!

It was as much Twiggy's sparkling personality as her striking looks that gave her such popular appeal. She had no airs or graces. She was simply herself—direct, funny, and ingenuous. Initially some might have winced at her vowels, but there was no mistaking the star quality that emanated from every pristine pore. And for all her humble origins, she was a professional through and through. She was (and still is) punctual. She never fussed or threw a tantrum. She worked immensely hard at what she did, and whatever she did was done to the highest standard possible—attributes only to be expected from a true daughter of Demeter. That her Sun in Virgo forms a beneficial trine aspect to a prominent Jupiter, a planet of infinite 'goodies',* indicates not only the element of good fortune that operates in her life, but also that she has an expansive, generous personality and an abundance of creative potential. Since Jupiter is placed on the cusp of the 'house' of relationships, it is no surprise that much of the good fortune she experiences in life is linked to partnerships. Justin was certainly a Jupiterian figure in her life: he fathered her potential and brought riches and increase into her life.

Virgo women are not usually noted for their outspoken, daring

---

*Jupiter is angular-conjunct the descendant; Jupiter is also the 'closing' planet in a bowl shaping.

personalities. This dimension to Twiggy's nature is to be found in her impulsive, headstrong, rising Moon-Mars conjunction in fiery Leo. Yet this extrovert coupling is not given a completely free hand, since it is restrained, to a degree, by her reticent Cancerian Ascendant. The Virgo-Cancer mix contributes to Twiggy's nervousness, and although now, in her mid-thirties, she is able to conceal this awkwardness by a supremely confident and competent persona (Moon-Mars), she admits to great apprehension when embarking on new projects and a fear that she may not fulfil expectations. Clearly Twiggy has an abundance of talents that would have ultimately got her to the top; yet without Justin's initial push, his confidence, and his entrepreneurial skills, would she have made the enormous impact she did, **when she did**? It was only her absolute trust in him that gave her the confidence to allow her gifts to blossom.* Fate and the right moment did the rest. Although Twiggy and Justin never married, their relationship lasted eight years. 'I guess we just outgrew each other, but we parted as friends.'

Uranus, the planet of change and revolution, occupies an important place in Twiggy's chart.† While this planet has wreaked havoc in her life through sudden, violent change, particularly in her relationship with Michael Witney, Uranus also inspires her to diversify in her career. Twiggy did much growing up during the three and a half years she dominated the modelling world. Yet though she had become a celebrity and made a record or two, she wanted to stretch her wings into acting and dancing. Her opportunity came with the film version of **The Boyfriend** directed by Ken Russell. Although the film itself was not a success, Twiggy's performance was stunning: she dominated the screen and she sang and danced as though she had been training half her life. Her personal triumph opened many doors, including her own television series, more recording contracts, and a film called **W**. **The Boyfriend** also forged a friendship with co-star Tommy Tune that was to prove a lasting and significant one, both professionally and personally.

W turned out to be yet another box office disaster, although during the making of this film (1973) Twiggy fell violently in love with her forty-year-old co-star, Michael Witney (a Sun Scorpio). Michael, like Justin, was to transform her life, although for very different reasons.

By nature Twiggy is more the Earth Mother type of Virgoan than the Siren. She might have the allure of the Siren but she has none of the emotional detachment and cool: peel off the professional glitter

*Justin's Pluto formed an exact conjunction to Twiggy's Ascendant; and he was indeed the agent of her transformation.

†Uranus is the leading planet in a bowl shaping. It is also exactly square on the MC.

and you'll find an 18-carat gold wife and mother. With Michael my career wasn't the important thing.' Indeed, Twiggy's career took on a low profile during most of her relationship with Michael, whom she married in 1977. A little over a year later, in December 1978, their much loved daughter Carly was born. 'My relationship with Michael was entirely different to my involvement with Justin. Justin was very protective. With Michael it was a relationship of equals.' Yet while they may have met as equals in love, they were distinctly unequal in talent and success—a factor that Michael with his sagging career found increasingly difficult to take. Throughout their relationship there had been various reports of Michael's drinking; there had been rumours of scenes and scraps in public, angry recriminations, and tearful apologies. By early 1983, they had decided to separate. Sadly, despite her desire to keep her private life out of the newspapers, the split made front-page news, and while she retained a discreet silence, he expressed his misery volubly. At the time Twiggy was involved in the smash hit stage show **My One and Only**—a part Tommy Tune had invited her to do. While her career soared to new heights (she was the proverbial toast of Broadway) her emotions were at rock bottom. Totally unfounded rumours of her romantic involvement with Tommy did little to bridge the chasm between Twiggy and Michael. Then on 30 November 1983, Michael suffered a massive and fatal heart attack.

Aside from the Virgo woman's proclivity toward dependent partners (most Virgo women cannot resist saving people from themselves) Twiggy's chart does not look overly difficult, and certainly not tragic, where love and relationships are concerned. Jupiter's influence on her partnership 'house' bodes well for enriching relationships—as Justin's proved to be. Venus in Scorpio lends a more intense and passionate tone to the picture, especially as there is an inflammatory square aspect to Venus from Mars. Pluto, a planet of transformation and violent extremes, is placed near to the Moon, which suggests some emotionally turbulent times, yet this aspect is rather wide. Perhaps the main indication of difficulty lies in the Saturn-Capricorn nature of the seventh 'house'. Saturn is a hard taskmaster to leave in charge of relationships, and it suggests that much is learned through pain and difficulty in one-to-one relationships. Twiggy, like many women with Capricorn-Saturn themes to their relationships, is drawn towards older men: Justin was ten years her senior, Michael eighteen. While the overall relationship pattern looks relatively easy, it may well be that Twiggy's emotionally volatile nature and her need for challenge and growth in all aspects of her life propel her towards men with whom she can experience an intense and powerful interaction. It is interesting to note that both Justin and Michael were water sign men

—Justin Pisces, and Michael Scorpio; signs that demand a deep emotional exchange.

It was clear when I met Twiggy in early 1985 that she was still reeling from the impact of Michael's death. And it was clear that she resents the intrusion of journalists into her private grief and her memories. 'People say we were wrong for each other. But how do they know? Michael and I both worked from our hearts not our heads . . . I think we would have got back together . . . Yes, I believe in soul mates, and I think Michael was one.'

Work was very much a healing process in the months following Michael's death. After the phenomenal success of **My One and Only**, Twiggy came over to England to make the film **The Doctors And The Devils**. 'Just resting' is not a familiar phrase to her lips! 'It's funny how everyone thinks I'm ambitious. I'm not at all. Work just happens. Really and truly I'm quite lazy!' While the Virgoan woman is far from ruthlessly ambitious, Twiggy does nevertheless have an Aries-ruled tenth 'house' of aims and direction, which suggests a certain determined pursuit of her goals—especially as Mars, the ruler of this house, is in another fiery sign, and rising. While Twiggy considers her priorities in life to be her daughter Carly and her role as mother, I think the attraction of the hearth and home, and only the hearth and home, would pale year after year. I also suspect that Twiggy has far from exploited her full potential as a performer. She is waiting for a good stage or film part—one that will stretch her abilities yet again. And even if she does find utter contentment and fulfilment in her private life, it can never be at the total expense of her talent. Perhaps like many individuals who seem to have a strong hand of destiny operating in their lives, Twiggy has to accept that she cannot have her fate and eat it! And like an obedient Virgoan 'handmaid', her calling to 'serve' in whatever capacity is greater than personal satisfaction. But then again, with Twiggy's luck, she may just manage it all.

Postscript: During 1985, while Twiggy agonized over whether to settle in Los Angeles or London, she met the actor, Leigh Lawson (a Sun Cancer). This has proved to be an immensely happy relationship, and one that may well lead to the settled family life she craves.

Note for Astrologers: (1) Twiggy is uncertain about her exact time of birth, but maintains it was in the very early hours of the morning. Working with Twiggy and going through her major life events and her family's charts, 29° Cancer seemed entirely appropriate on all levels

(2) During 1983, transiting Pluto hovered around 29° Libra, thus squaring her Ascendant/Descendant axis. Robert Hand in *Planets in Transit* comments in regard to this transit: 'A relationship that is in great difficulty or that has outlived its function in your life may end altogether, even though you don't want it to . . . Pluto is the symbol of death and resurrection, which you are experiencing through your relationships at this time.'

PROFILE OF A VIRGO MAN

JEREMY IRONS

Jeremy Irons might never have graced our cinema screens or glittered under the proscenium arch had he attained his earliest ambition —to become a vet. Although at the time his dismal 'O' level results in biology and the sciences precluded a career among the Durrellian delights of the animal world, in retrospect he is glad—even for a circumspect Virgo—that things have turned out the way they have. It is also fortunate that he learned fairly early on to put not his trust in fools: a vocational guidance counsellor informed him that he was totally unsuited to a life in the theatre since such a career lacked the stablity he required! While his parents might have quavered at the thought of their youngest son entering such a precarious profession (his father was a chartered accountant) they were relieved at least that he had managed to make a positive decision—whatever it was.

Jeremy has bitter-sweet memories of childhood. He was born on the Isle of Wight, and lived with his parents and his elder brother and sister in a house near the sea. The family kept horses and holidays were spent happily, riding and messing about on boats. Jeremy admits that the age of seven was too young to be sent away from home, but he nevertheless recalls many happy moments at his prep school and his public school. Astrologically, Jeremy's early life indeed presents a bitter-sweet picture. On the plus side, Mercury 'sits' unharassed in the fourth 'house' of home, indicating a varied and stimulating family background; but with combative Mars in Scorpio, and Neptune (a planet synonymous with mystery and the intangible*) also affecting this area, the overall pattern of Jeremy's early life looks far from plain-sailing. 'I didn't have as much security as I would have liked. My father was away a lot; I was at boarding

*This planet also symbolizes (among many ideas) the sea and the arts.

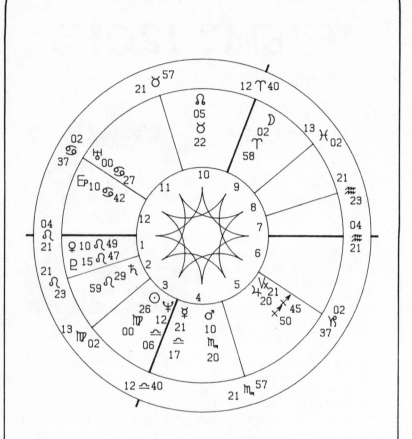

JEREMY IRONS

19 9 1948   1h 0m GMT

PLACIDUS 50N35 1W12

school; so I was unable to develop a really deep relationship with him or my mother. My parents split up when I was thirteen—just as I'd started Sherborne [public school]. A week before, my dog had died and I remember weeping all night; yet I don't recall being upset when I'd heard they'd separated. But then I know myself now—it doesn't come out for a while.' Like many an earthy Virgo (especially one with a Scorpionic Mars in a stressful 90°-angle to Venus-Pluto) Jeremy instinctively battens down the hatches on his emotions.

Jeremy may have missed out on a relationship with his father when he was a boy, but he made up for it later. 'I didn't start relating to my father until I was twenty-one, when I went to live with him and my step-mother for about a year. Then I really began to get to know him and like him enormously. I discovered I was very similar to him. I'm dogmatic like he was, and make up my mind and stick to it, just like him. We both loved boating. Our friendship continued until he died.'

Despite his obvious intelligence, Jeremy did not shine at school. 'I worked my way steadfastly to the bottom. I started in 2C, went on to 3D, and finally 4E! I think it was a combination of lack of motivation and also my reticence. I need to go over things several times to really absorb them—and I didn't have the nerve to keep asking questions.' When asked if school was competitive, he replied somewhat laconically, 'No—not at my level!' Like many Virgoans, Jeremy did not like, and certainly did not win, any bat and ball games. 'Cricket's not my bag. I used to make the sandwiches for the team. I only ever played one game of hockey. This ball came at me and hit me on the ankle. I threw down my stick and said "That's it. I'm going riding for the rest of term!"' Not that Jeremy was an entirely unenthusiastic sportsman since he was a rugger colour and led the forwards in the first XV! But although school had its enjoyable side he admits 'I think I was probably on edge a lot of the time playing a role. For many years after I'd left, whenever I'd smell the same tobacco that the headmaster had smoked, I'd tense. And there's a certain clock chime that has the same effect.'

After leaving school, Jeremy followed the well-trodden Virgoan path of the social worker (in Peckham). 'Excellent experience. It made me realize there was life outside Sherborne.' Then, after taking a job as a student ASM at the Marlowe theatre, he went on to drama school at the Bristol Old Vic. 'Bristol seemed to think I was castable. I mean I was tall. I could wear clothes and I could speak reasonably well.' A somewhat self-deprecatory comment considering he was one of only five students to be accepted into the company. From there on, he worked consistently, taking a variety of parts from Shakespearian tragedies to musicals like **Godspell**. And although he was thirty-one when he became the proverbial overnight sensation, he had never experienced a 'lean year'.

It was as Charles Ryder in the highly-praised production of Evelyn Waugh's **Brideshead Revisited** that Jeremy sky-rocketed to fame. To say that the part was tailor-made for him would be to belittle his subtle, haunting performance. Yet in many ways Jeremy is the quintessential English gentleman. He exudes a quality of smouldering detachment—very much the Lawrencian hero. Though **Brideshead** was an exciting project and a fulfilling and successful one, it had its problematic moments. 'I walked out one day. I could have been barred by the union [Equity]. The management had gone back on their word about my being able to do **The French Lieutenant's Woman**. I can remember driving back from Manchester and thinking, "What will I do if it goes the wrong way?"' Fortunately the crisis was satisfactorily resolved. But this episode demonstrates just how strongly Jeremy feels about keeping to one's word. Jeremy and his co-star, Anthony Andrews, also had their differences, although not quite to the degree the press made out. 'We had an **interesting** relationship and I think it worked on screen. We were both ambitious and competitive, and the series we both knew was to be very important to us. There were bound to be tensions . . .' Like many Virgoans, Jeremy is anything but ostentatious. He sets exacting standards for himself, and aspires to excellence as an actor rather than seeking the spoils of fame. While he used not to consider himself ambitious his wife, the actress Sinead Cusack, says he is the most ambitious man she has ever known! From an astrological point of view, that Jeremy's Mars, the ruler of the tenth 'house' of profession, is to be found in ambitious Scorpio points to a certain driving obsessiveness about his direction and aims. But his unassuming Virgo Sun extols the simple virtue of a job perfectly done. Certainly after **The French Lieutenant's Woman**, he made a career choice (the small budget film **Moonlighting**) that reflected his desire to be regarded as an actor who values quality above (financial) quantity: 'I have a good instinct for what's right.' And so far his instinct has not let him down.

Part of Jeremy's charisma as an actor is the aura of restrained sexuality that I referred to earlier: one gains the impression that behind the reserve is a veritable cauldron of sexual emotion waiting to bubble over. In his chart, this possibility is suggested by the rising Venus in Leo conjunct the planet Pluto.* However, Jeremy's image is not the only thing to be affected by this astrological combination. Venus-Pluto conjunctions do not have the best of reputations where love and romance are concerned. On the plus side, the individual

---

*Further compounded by the exact square aspect from Venus to Mars in Scorpio and the trine from Venus—Pluto to the MC.

with such a conjunction has the potential to undergo transformative experiences through relating, and so reach the very highest levels of love and sex. On the minus side, this combination can indicate trauma and upheaval in relationships and an all-or-nothing effect where sex and emotion are involved. This is a powerful and difficult 'energy' to deal with, and there is a tendency for most individuals to project their Venus-Pluto onto others; in this way their partners seem to be the source of all the trouble. Fortunately, in Jeremy's case, Venus and Pluto also form harmonious angles elsewhere in the chart, so he is more likely to tap the higher level of this conjunction, although he will not necessarily escape its more destructive dimension. Venus-Pluto would be quite enough on their own without any help from Uranus! In Jeremy's chart his Sun and Moon are placed at opposite extremes and intersected by volatile Uranus. Thus it is hardly surprising that his romantic track record resembles a roller-coaster.

Jeremy's feelings about an undeveloped relationship with his mother, and his parents' break-up, can be related to the Sun-Moon-Uranus trio. 'My mother wasn't the sort of person you could talk to about anything in depth. She wasn't overly demonstrative or very tactile, and neither was I until I went to drama school and learned about touch. It had an amazing, releasing effect on me. I remember going around hugging people—embracing my family as much as I could. They took a long while to get used to it! I realize I need an awful lot of overt affection.' Jeremy's first marriage at twenty (to a Leo) was a classic case of a young man in search of love, closeness, and affection, but without the emotional 'weight' and experience to cope with marriage. It lasted a year. He met his second wife, Sinead (a Sun Aquarian with Venus in Aries) in 1972 and married her six years later. However, this relationship too has experienced turbulent times.

Jeremy's childhood, combined with the English stiff upper lip syndrome (undoubtedly reinforced by an all-boys public school education), poured oil on the troubled emotional waters in his chart. He is the prime candidate for the 'Why are women so difficult?' school of thinking. He tends to be highly self-protective about his feelings, which causes emotional blocks and emotional miscommunications: he feels deeply, but is not always able to express those feelings easily. Where women are concerned, he wants his cake and to eat it too. His Aquarian 'house' of relationships shows he wants a free-spirited, independent sort of partner; his Moon in Aries suggests he likes a woman with spirit. However, his Venus—Pluto side desires a woman who is totally committed to him—and him only; and his Virgoan nature is more suited to the domesticated **hausfrau**! While Sinead is a demonstrative, maternal lady, she is not the type to sacrifice her career for the exclusive role of wife and mother. For Jeremy, being 'in love' is also an essential ingredient of a relationship. 'Yes, it was love at first sight with Sinead. The first time I took her out she asked me in later for coffee. I remember saying, "If I do, I'll stay forever."' He clearly adores his wife and their two sons, Sam (eight) and Max (one), and although his chart shows him to be exceedingly vulnerable to other women, he wouldn't dream of jeopardizing his marriage for an extra-marital fling. During the early 1980s, he and Sinead hit a rocky patch in their relationship that brought them to the precipice of divorce. But like a phoenix rising from the ashes, after a period of estrangement, they rebuilt their relationship. He and Sinead are both strong-minded individuals and their feelings run high: one of the most contentious issues between them centres on Sinead's need for a career versus her role as wife—an issue that reflects the severe conflict of interests where Jeremy's ideal woman is concerned. 'I think we've concentrated as much on her career as mine, within the limits of our obligations as parents—it's very important for me that I build a good relationship with the boys—I know she'll only be happy if she does have a career, but maybe, if she has more children, she'll find less need to prove herself as an actress . . . But it's important that we do nurture it (her career) . . . Yet I sort of feel that I will be quite happy when she doesn't want to do theatre . . . but then again, I know she always will.' A conflict indeed. Even without the aid of astrology, Sinead summed up his dilemma: 'Part of Jeremy wants a "little wifey" at home, but if he had one, he'd be bored to tears!'

Jeremy admits to being as demanding of the woman he loves as he is of his career. 'I think the Virgo husband and father expects too much. Virgo actors, I know, have a reputation for being difficult because they make such demands on themselves and everyone else. We're not easy-going workers.' Virgo, of course, is also an extremely practical sign. Jeremy is all too aware of the ephemeral nature of stardom: 'When I might have been chucked out of the union, it made me think what else could I do. I thought I could be an agent because I'd like to nurture other talent . . . and I might see if any writing happened. I like writing, but I've only felt "the muse" once: I began a piece at nine in the morning and worked until three the next—time just flew—and I really felt satisfied.' Photography is also a passionate interest of Jeremy's and on his return from South America, where he'd been filming **The Mission**, he considered putting together a book of his photographs.

Jeremy's practical Virgo streak emerges in most areas of his life. He's made many alterations and structural additions to the family house: 'I like building, but I'm less interested in houses now and more interested in productions. I directed a rock video in New York last year [1985] and it's something I'd like to do more of. But it made me aware just how little I know as yet, especially about getting the best out of actors.' Like most Virgoan workaholics, Jeremy isn't the type to sit listlessly by the 'phone, idly gazing through the window. Apart from his heavy workload, he finds the time to ride, ski, sail, and fly (planes, of course): 'I also like conversation—good conversation. One of the pluses about being successful is that you meet such marvellously interesting, talented people. But I do need some time on my own as well. I get claustrophobia if I'm with too many people for too long.'

Despite Jeremy's reticence about his achievements and his cautious attitude toward his future, his approach to his work, and indeed the astrology, point to success of the durable kind. In his chart, Jupiter, the planet of expansion and good fortune, is involved in an extremely harmonious Grand Trine with Pluto, the Moon, and the Midheaven. This, if wisely used, is a gift of the gods, and one that Jeremy is unlikely to squander. Since he is an individual who thrives on the stimulus of challenge, he will tend to spread his talents into new areas, always striving for excellence. While he might prefer that his private life was not quite so full of challenge as his professional one, he no doubt accepts that change and transformation are as much a process operating in his relationships as in his career. Because of the strong Scorpio-Pluto emphasis in Jeremy's chart, he is far more (emotionally) committed to his objectives. He holds life in a strong grasp. And now he's 'arrived', he's certainly here to stay.

Note for Astrologers: (1) Jeremy's fourth house is definitely 'under fire'. Although Mercury is well aspected (with the possible exception of the weak conjunction to Neptune) Mars is square Venus—Pluto and semi-square the Sun. Mars in the fourth often indicates a father who is 'a force to be reckoned with'; thus the individual has to 'fight' the father image to find his own sense of identity. The Moon—also an indicator of early life, and certainly the concept of mother—has both a square to Uranus and a quincunx to Saturn. Fortunately, the Moon is relieved by trine aspects to Venus-Ascendant, in Jeremy's case providing him with many other happier memories of childhood.

(2) Marriage to Sinead and the making of Brideshead occurred during the year of Jeremy's Saturn Return.

(3) That Jupiter is conjunct the vertex may indicate the 'hand of destiny' operating in his success.

LIBRA

23 September — 22 October

THE GOOD, THE BLAND, AND THE BEAUTIFUL

LIBRA
THE GOOD, THE BLAND,
AND THE BEAUTIFUL

FACED with a choice of where to seat their perfectly formed bottoms, Librans will always opt for the fence—one buttock delicately and evenly perched on either side. Libra, the seventh sign, is the mid-way point in the Zodiac and those born with a strong Libran theme in their charts seemed destined to balance precariously on the horns of one dilemma or another, overlooking Scylla on the one side and Charibdis on the other, rendered immobile by a crisis of indecision.

Libra, like Sagittarius, is one of the most popular signs of the zodiac. Libran individuals go out of their way to present an accommodating, agreeable, and friendly front, and it's hard to remain angry with any of them for long, even if they've stolen your boyfriend or pranged your car. My Libran clients often arrive for an appointment accompanied by little gifts; they always listen carefully and attentively, and rarely contradict or interrupt. Only later might I discover through the grapevine that they severely disagreed with, or were even angered by, some of the comments I made. One Libran client let me blithely chatter on for half an hour before she politely pointed out that she was in the minutest bit of discomfort, due to a rogue nail that was poking through the back of her chair.

Libra is a sign synonymous with beauty, grace, and charm—qualities culled from its ruling planet, Venus—and although not every Libran could win a place in the Miss World or Mr Universe contest, most are attractive and certainly know how to make the most of their assets. Occasionally they become rather plump as they get older, usually through over indulgence in the sweet things of life, and even those who are slim are rarely angular. (Extremely soft skin and dimples are also common characteristics of this sign.) However, fat or thin, dimpled or not Librans are never grossly out of proportion—balance in all things is the byword for Libra. In keeping with their attractive appearance, male and female Librans are usually extremely clothes conscious: most keep abreast of the current fashions and if they can't afford to buy anything new, they will adapt their existing wardrobe to look stylish and fashionable. The only person I know who is an exception to this rule is my Libra-rising husband, who, despite Venusian good-looks, refuses to acknowledge the value of anything as ephemeral as fashion and stubbornly persists in looking like a refugee from the Oxfam shop.

The symbol for Libra is a pair of balancing scales: the ability to hold evenly weighted opinions and to be fair and just is an outstanding characteristic of this sign. Yet, looking a little closer at Libra, some dark and conflicting shadows hover over this apparently sweeter-than-sweet sign.

To return to the idea of Libra's half-way position in the zodiac: as the Sun enters the sign of Libra on or around 23 September, day and night are of equal length. In the same way that the first degree of Aries marks the birth of spring (at least in the northern hemisphere), the start of Libra heralds in autumn—the beginning of Nature's journey underground. The first six signs of the zodiac (and Libra) are ruled by the personal planets and can be seen to represent simpler, purer ideas, whereas from Scorpio to Pisces each and every sign is ruled by one of the outer planets and so contain more complex themes. In many ways Libra acts as a melting pot, or bridge, between two spheres of experience—the personal and the collective, the subjective and the objective. In Virgo, the preceding sign, the experience of the first five signs is sifted and analysed; in Libra a new order is ushered in based on that synthesis.

What is curious about Libra is that, unlike the other **astronomical** constellations (against which the 30° equal divisions of the zodiac roughly fit), half of it is taken up by Virgo while the rest slips into the early degrees of Scorpio. In effect (astronomically) Libra is the only sign of the zodiac to share most of its territory with its next-door-neighbours—Virgo and Scorpio. No wonder Librans have an identity problem! It has also occurred to me over the years that in many ways Librans are a composite of Virgo and Scorpio, since the primary characteristics of this air sign are its abilities to apply rational thought, intellect, and rationality to life, together with its perfectionist tendencies (Virgo) and its desire to balance any extremes (Scorpio) emotionally, psychologically, or in any other area.

Even in myths pertaining to Venus or Aphrodite, Virgoan and Scorpionic themes are often present. Greek Aphrodite (born from the drops of Ouranos' blood as it fell to the oceans) was, of course, the goddess of love—or, rather of the act of love. She had many lovers, including Ares, by whom she had a son, Eros. One of the best-known stories about Aphrodite centred on her love for the beautiful child Adonis, whom she foolishly fostered out to Persephone, daughter of Demeter (Virgo) and Queen of the Underworld (Pluto/Scorpio territory). Persephone, in turn, became infatuated with Adonis and refused to give him back. To sort matters out, Zeus decided that Adonis should spend a third of the year with Persephone, another four months with Aphrodite, but he left the choice of the remaining third with Adonis himself. In the event Adonis chose to spend it with Aphrodite. The emphasis of choice is evident here—a continual Libran dilemma—and perhaps more interestingly the threefold relationship which I'll discuss shortly.

Another goddess that fits the Libran symbolism is Pallas Athena. Although Athena was a warrior-goddess she was nevertheless renowned as a deity of resolute courage and honour, guided and enlightened by *reason*. (She was also goddess of crafts—a distinctly Virgoan function.) Athena's main claim to fame was as a peace-maker, best illustrated in the story of the quarrel that arose between her and Poseidon. Since both deities claimed to be the patron of Attica, the gods as arbiters decided that the country should belong to whoever gave it the finest gift. Poseidon caused a salt spring to arise from the earth, while Athena produced and planted an olive tree. All the gods judged that the olive tree of peace and patience was by far the greater gift, so Athena became patron of Attica. Judgement, choice, and peace—all aspects of Libra—are the dominant themes in this story.

In yet another tale, Paris had to choose between Hera (goddess of women, marriage, and motherhood), Athena, and Aphrodite as to who was the most beautiful; he chose Aphrodite. Again the idea of choice is central to the story, and not between two but three. In classical mythology groups of three were believed to signify the reconciliation of opposites by a third factor that transcends them. In this latter story the three goddesses represent on one level different aspects of the feminine and, on another, Hera, Athena, and Aphrodite represent Scorpio, Virgo, and Libra respectively.

Most popular astrology books and magazines refer only to Libra's charming, harmony-loving nature, rarely to its more aggressive side, which admittedly is usually well concealed. In myth, Aphrodite is never far from strife; indeed, she could be seen as responsible for the Trojan wars since she promised the already (happily) married Helen to Paris, an act which triggered the ensuing cycle of bloody events. Ares was an important lover of Aphrodite and, of course, Athena was herself a warrior-goddess. Astrologically, Libra figures strongly in the charts of many generals and heads of state: Eisenhower, Churchill, and Margaret Thatcher are all Librans who, although charming, clearly demonstrate a gift for waging war successfully, even Adolf Hitler had Libra rising. Furthermore, the planet Venus was prominent in the charts of the start of both World Wars.

Sifting through the various myths pertaining to Libra, the themes that occur again and again are choice, love, beauty, reason, peace (and war), justice, and the reconciliation of opposites. Perhaps of all these, the reconciliation of opposites is most crucial to understanding this sign. While everyday Librans can be seen mediating between two warring factions in the office or the playground, the greater task facing each and every one of them is how to balance conflicting aspects of themselves—emotional, intellectual, or psychological. By and large, male Librans, while being entirely masculine (and the females utterly feminine), are quite able to identify with and express qualities and values more typical of the opposite sex. Most female Librans, despite looking as feminine as Brigitte Bardot or Grace Kelly, are as capable as the next man of putting aside their emotions to deal with an issue in a logical, analytical way. Margaret Thatcher is a fine example of this Libran trait: she has outstanding clarity of thought (and speech); while taking her place as an equal in a man's world (some have even suggested she is more manly than a few of her cabinet), she goes to enormous pains to look as attractive as possible. The male Libran, on the other hand, despite his articulate, rational approach to life, is often gentle and understanding. Many men of this sign are inordinately concerned with their appearance—almost dandyish on occasion—and most go out of their way to display easy charm and faultless manners; they also care tremendously about social niceties. Although both male and female Librans enjoy friends of their own sex, they often rate qualities of the opposite sex higher, identify more easily with their problems, and are altogether happier in their company.

The reconciliation of opposites has its more obvious expression in the way many Librans actively take this ability out into the world as ambassadors, diplomats, statesmen, lawyers, and counsellors. Even those who don't harness their peace-making talents to a career spend a large amount of their time offering advice to others and trying to get their friends or colleagues to see another point of view. Mohandes Gandhi, civil rights champion, lawyer and, most notably, leader of the Indian people, demonstrated the Libran desire for justice, fairness, and equality in everything he touched: he steadfastly and determinedly sought to redress the balance of the suppressed majority. Gandhi also provides an excellent example of the way many Librans get what they want without shouting and screaming about it: good argument, logical and plausible theories, and gentle but persistent persuasion are Libra's tools. Indeed, Librans really don't like losing their tempers at all: emotion clouds their judgement and reasoning ability, and upsets their equilibrium; nor does it show them in a particularly favourable light. Yet for some reason, like Aphrodite, strife of one sort or another is never very far from them.

Compromise is another characteristic of this sign. Almost every day of their lives Mr and Ms Libra, faced with the perennial problem of choice, will make a compromise. Ms Libra will spend hours debating between cooking a spicy curry that her husband likes or the mince dish her children favour, finally deciding that a chile con carne would please them all; or the Libran sales manager, torn between starting his soft soap campaign in Edinburgh in the north or Plymouth in the south, will eventually opt for Birmingham in the Midlands. While compromise is often the best answer to a sticky problem, a continual diet of half-baked solutions can make Librans seem very wishy-washy indeed. Instead of committing themselves wholeheartedly to one path, most Librans will try to cover as many choices as possible. Usually they end up frustrating themselves and everybody else. Libra's problem is not just making a choice, but the constant fear of being disliked or disapproved of in the process. Librans of both sexes care enormously about appearances, not only in the way they dress or furnish their houses, but also any action they take must be seen to be right and good in the world's eyes—an impossible task. 'You can't please all of the people all of the time', but if there's one sign who's determined to try, it's Libra.

Certainly, weighing each and every possibility and carefully balancing everything from their opinions to their diets greatly contributes to the notorious Libran indecision. Decisions of any sort always place Librans in a dilemma, especially when compromise is out of the question. Most will analyse a situation, view it from every conceivable angle, and canvas opinion before committing themselves. When they do, they frequently regret their action immediately. A friend of mine spent three agonizing weeks trying to come to a decision over which of two dresses she should buy for an important function. D-day finally arrived and after a night of troubled dreams, she decided the blue one had the edge. Just as she was about to purchase it she had second thoughts and rushed over to buy the grey one instead. On her return home she realized she had made a dreadful mistake and decided to go back and get the blue one. By the time she arrived at the shop, the blue one had been sold.

Librans find it difficult to say 'No' and hate to turn down a friend, an opportunity, or an invitation, which means that all too often they overload their already crammed social and professional schedules. They find they have to let someone down because they can't come to dinner/pick up mother-in-law/and do the promised overtime at work. If they do try to accomplish all their commitments, none are really done to the best of their ability. So, despite their desire to please anyone who makes a claim on them or their time, they manage to frustrate, disappoint, and even anger many. Fortunately, Libra's charm and generosity come to the rescue time and time again, but in the long run other people get rather tired of their frequent inability to deliver promised goods.

Another problem for many Librans is that although they may agree with one person and his ideas **while they are with him or her**, faced with another set of alternatives from another person they will find agreement there too—even if the two sets of ideas are radically opposed. Rather like Pisces, who sees something valid in almost everything, Libra finds it difficult to reject anything completely out of hand. Ultimately, this kind of behaviour makes them appear extremely two-faced, and the inability to say 'No' and failure to back any one horse give them a reputation for insincerity and unreliability.

There is also an accompanying tendency among many Librans to be fairweather friends. While Librans of both sexes may sustain some friendships over many years—even with oceans between them—like their opposite sign, Aries, Venusian types often go overboard for new friends who reflect their current interests and values. An even less desirable trait emerges in that when many Librans rekindle old friendships, it is often because that individual can provide something they need. Although this does underline a certain opportunistic streak in Libra's nature, there is nothing manipulative or devious about their behaviour.

I mentioned earlier that despite this sign's desire for peace and harmony, conflict is a regular visitor in Libra's life. Clearly the aforementioned problems of over-extending themselves and trying to embrace all available choices are two reasons why they unintentionally create conflict. But there is another. Many Librans, like some of their neighbouring Scorpions, have a problem with anger. Because this Venus-ruled sign needs to be liked and hates to appear irrationally possessed by emotions, many Librans refuse to give vent to their anger. Thus, their deliberate calm sometimes encourages others to go to greater lengths to provoke them: Libra cannot understand why people get so angry with him when he's so understanding and goes to such pains to point out the rights and wrongs of each argument. Librans' tendency to continually rationalize their arguments *and* their feelings through suppressing their emotions can ultimately present them with physical problems. Indeed, many Librans suffer from chronic headaches and other stress-related disorders. (I shall discuss this sign's tendency to rationalize emotions further in the section on relationships.)

As befits a Venus-ruled sign, most Libran individuals have an artistic streak—not that each and every one of them can paint like David Hockney, but most can decorate their home in a stylish and tasteful manner, or at least arrange a vase of flowers with some flair. Even those who are not themselves at all artistically gifted usually enjoy some kind of cultural pursuit, and certainly music and pleasing surroundings are important to almost all of them. Many Librans are also born with a set of green fingers and their homes and gardens alike tend to be festooned with abundant, lush, and trailing plant-life.

In myth Venus was portrayed as a rather lazy, self-indulgent goddess, which is why many astrologers associate Librans with indolence. While there is an extremely hedonistic side to the Libran nature, most of my Libran friends and clients are highly industrious. What is more to the point is that Librans have a knack of making their activities **seem** effortless. However, as a cardinal sign, they are both hard-working and ambitious. They are also perfectionists, and in an effort to achieve excellence in the things they care about, they will urge themselves well beyond their physical and mental limits. Like the other cardinal signs—Aries, Capricorn, and Cancer—Librans need goals, yet they rarely exhibit a strong drive, nor appear to push for positions of power or authority; in fact Librans would far rather be voted or persuaded to take on a top position. Librans achieve their ends and alight on the pinnacle of success with the apparent grace and ease of a Barishnikov **grand jeté**. While power and control are rarely Libra's **primary** objectives, it is natural for them to want to excel and receive praise and approbation for what they do. Perhaps more importantly for Libra, it is the quality of life guaranteed by adequate financial reward that spurs them to success and achievement. Although not a mercenary sign, nor really an acquisitive one, Librans will, in order to obtain the style of life they want, pull out all the stops, professionally, socially, whatever—and if all else fails they will try to marry money or do their best to inherit it!

In keeping with their symbol, the scales, Librans appear to be born with an acute sense of balance; unlike their all or nothing neighbours, Scorpio, they hate extremes of any sort. This runs across the whole spectrum of their lives, from the pathological desire to straighten every lopsided picture they see, to diluting radical opinions, or putting the pro to every con and vice versa. A Libran girlfriend of mine insists on taking an equal number of early nights to counter those spent burning the midnight oil, and one of my Libran relatives has been known to cut stewed plums in half to make sure everyone has exactly the same quantity. However, Libra's impulse to adjust the balance wherever unevenness is found can lead to some inconsistencies in their own natures. Venusian people can be, and often are, the sweetest, most obliging people in the zodiac, but at times they behave as stubbornly, argumentatively, and unpredictably as their opposite number, the Arians. It is as though the scales become weighted down with too much sugar and urgently need balancing by more acerbity. Most of the time, however, Libra's desire for peace and harmony will urge them to present their more pleasing persona, but every so often they can take you by surprise and deliver a powerful verbal punch between the eyes.

Since Libra is a sign synonymous with beauty and grace, its more cerebral attributes are frequently overlooked; yet as an air sign, Libra extols intellectual and logical values and is as keen on communication and debate as the next Aquarian or Geminian. Almost all Librans will have something to contribute to a discussion on practically any topic, and, like the other two air signs, seem to pick ideas out of thin air and latch on to the most complex theories effortlessly. What prevents many Librans from taking top honours in the scholastic stakes, however, is their frequent inability to take a hard and fast line in any one direction, which, rather like Pisces, weakens and dilutes the thrust of their efforts. Nevertheless many journalists, writers, TV presenters, and political commentators have strong Libran themes in their charts. As always, fairness, balanced opinions, and the ability to arbitrate are the keys to their success.

Regardless of how infuriating Librans can be, eternally debating on which side of the fence the grass is greener, their charm and impartiality guarantee them a soft landing when they do eventually jump. Of all the signs of the zodiac, Libra wants the world to become a better, more beautiful place to live in, and most Venusians organize their lives with these ends in mind, spreading sweetness and light, succour and love, advice and support. Sometimes, of course, rather a lot of dust gets swept under the carpet in the process. Although some accuse this sign of gross hypocrisy and two-faced opportunism, a great many more find their wisdom and gracious bounty unequalled in the zodiac.

RELATIONSHIPS

Librans are tremendously sociable creatures; most of them hate to be alone and feel incomplete without a partner. In fact Libra is the sign for relating—or rather for the art of relating. Librans of both sexes are prepared to invest plenty of time and energy on their partnerships and they are hardly ever too busy or preoccupied to discuss any difficult problems encountered within their relationships. They are enormously fair-minded and accept their share of the blame if and when things go wrong, but they will never carry all the responsibility of a relationship nor become doormats for their partners. Considering this sign is synonymous with compromise and harmony, it is singularly surprising that so many of them end up in the divorce courts. In many cases, however, the seeds of marital distress and misfortune lie in the Libran tendency to intellectualize about relationships and their frequent inability to handle deep emotional exhange.

THE FEMALE LIBRA

The females of this sign are some of the most attractive and sought-after in the zodiac. Not only can they look as delicious and sophisticated as Anna Ford or Candice Bergen, but they often have sparkling wit and bright intelligence into the bargain. Yet despite their winning ways and natural flirtatiousness, they tend not to alienate their own sex, even though they are perfectly capable of whisking a man away from the most possessive Taurean or Cancerian claws—and of dropping him with the featherlight ease of a cruising falcon.

Ms Libra's favourite play as a child was no doubt dressing up in her mother's lace petticoats with a doily perched on her head, holding a bunch of daisies in one hand and her best friend's elder brother in the other. From her earliest days Ms Libra seems to know exactly how to attract and charm the opposite sex, and perhaps less laudably to use her men as vaulting horses to professional and social success. However, her ends are never achieved in a steamy, passionate (and often destructive) way like Ms Scorpio, but with great delicacy, lightness, and finesse. In fact, everything Ms Libra does is usually in the best possible taste!

It is exceedingly rare to find a Libran lady who doesn't maximize her feminine assets to their full extent. Even if Mother Nature hasn't endowed her with perfect model features or 34-inch hips, somehow she'll have a sense of style or way of dressing that guarantees her a second glance in the street and the rapt attention of any full-blooded male at a dinner party. Unlike Ms

Aquarius, she is unlikely to fight for feminist principles strapped to the railings of the Houses of Parliament, devoid of make-up in a boiler-suit—at least not unless it was designed by Yves Saint Laurent and she's sent a calling-card..Not that the Libran lady doesn't believe in feminist principles—she's wholeheartedly in favour of equality for women—but she hates being labelled as one of a militant extremist group and believes in driving her points home in an appealing, civilized fashion with a persuasive Venusian hammer.

The Libran female is repelled by ugliness in any form. Her surroundings must reflect her taste for beauty and refinement and she becomes excruciatingly uncomfortable and depressed in dirty or unpleasant conditions. She usually needs a considerable income to support her aesthetic tastes and **Homes and Gardens** life-style and although she might prefer a wealthy partner to provide the wherewithal for her extravagant 'diet', she is quite prepared to earn her own living should he fall short. Indeed, a great many Libran women continue to work even if their husbands are substantially well-off: they like a degree of financial independence and freedom, and hate having to account for every one of life's little luxuries which they find essential for their survival. But whatever Ms Libra does for a living, it usually has to have a glamorous aura about it: if she's a humble secretary, it will be for an impressive company or somebody famous, and most Librans like jobs connected with beauty, culture, or the arts. Best of all, female Librans like to be self-employed. Libran ladies heartily dislike being pinned to the treadmill by or for anyone else, but they will put the most industrious Virgo or ambitious Capricorn to shame working for their own ends. Several of my Libran friends and clients have thriving businesses of their own—one knits and designs clothes, another restores stained glass windows, and a third (a journalist) has a successful picture syndication company; others are models, actresses, and artists. They also usually make exceedingly good employers: not only are they unfailingly understanding and fair, but extremely generous. However, in return they expect their staff to work with the same kind of commitment as themselves, and will fire anyone who fails to come up to standard. This is an enormously perfectionist sign and one that rates achievement and success highly.

Ms Libra is a very giving type of female: she loves buying spontaneous presents for her loved ones and will always search for something special and unusual to mark an anniversary or birthday. What is also admirable about this Venusian lady is that, despite her seemingly self-indulgent, sometimes profligate ways, should she fall on hard times she is capable of budgeting and economising ruthlessly until the financial crisis is over. Furthermore, if her partner should flounder financially, she's not the type to throw up her arms in distress and sink under the weight of the worry; she'll endeavour to do something constructive about the situation. One great friend of mine with four planets and her Ascendant in Libra came through with flying Libran colours when her husband was suddenly presented with a staggeringly large tax bill—and at a time when they could least afford it. She had always appeared somewhat scatty and delightfully fey, but I couldn't help but be impressed at the sight of her with furrowed brow and calculator at hand, pouring intently over sheets of figures. She eventually decided to gather together various **objets d'art**, clothes and bric-à-brac adorning her walls, chests, and cupboards, rented a stall in her local market, and sold the lot one Saturday afternoon, making the princely sum of £700.

Indeed, the Libran wife is a priceless asset to her husband. She can be wonderfully charming and decorative, draped femininely on his arm at boring official functions. She will appear endlessly interested and deeply absorbed in conversation with crusty old fogeys and tight-lipped matrons, and in her own home she can dazzle the most awesome boss or daunting client. In fact, Ms Libra is in her element as the gracious hostess: the table will be beautifully adorned, the food imaginatively prepared, and few of her guests will ever get indigestion from her **boeuf en croute**, or her conversation. All her guests will have been carefully chosen—she is a dab hand at bringing people of like and unlike minds together, often for mutual gain as well as for entertainment value—and she has a special knack of making each person feel as though they were the guest of honour. In many ways she is quite the best social stage-manageress of the zodiac.

Yes, Ms Libra is an impressive female by anyone's standards. But . . . Regardless of how caring, warm and generous the Libran female appears to almost anyone that crosses her field of vision, whether they be teachers, colleagues, her husband's old rugby mates, or the passing Jehovah's witness, she rarely allows herself to be totally involved or emotionally affected by any of them. This is a woman whose head rules her heart. Now before I alienate all my Libran friends and clients let me qualify this statement. The Libran woman with her Moon or Venus in a water sign is eminently capable of investing her relationships with true warmth and compassion, and even those who maintain a clear emotional distance from friends and acquaintances nevertheless nurture deep feelings for their children, husband and closest family. However, by and large, the truly Libran woman is prepared to be a good listener and a patient adviser, just as long as you don't make any huge emotional demands on her. Ms Libra, like the Geminian and the Aquarian, is far happier in the airy realm of logic and reason, she prefers to keep her head clear of deep emotional waters, since intense emotional exchange tends to upset the balance and harmony she craves. Thus, although the Libran female can be extremely intuitive, sentimental, and loving, she rarely acts impulsively on her emotional instincts. One of my Libran clients was completely thrown when she fell in love for the first time at thirty-eight. Despite many 'love-affairs' and a ten-year marriage, she admitted she had never known what it was like to wait in anguish for the telephone to ring or to be in any way vulnerable or emotionally dependent on someone. 'I've always had control of my love-life and been the one to initiate the breaks and maintain the tempo of the relationship . . . I absolutely hate the way I'm in the palm of someone else's hand.' In the end her emotions couldn't stand the onslaught and she returned to the sanctuary of her less emotionally demanding marriage.

Unfortunately, some Libran ladies are dreadful emotional hypocrites. They clamour about finding a special relationship or establishing within an existing one an elevated quality of love: they often appear deeply involved and committed to a partner but in truth their toes are merely dangling in the waters of romance. Librans are terrified of placing all their eggs in one basket:

should the relationship fail, they fear they will be left high and dry and alone. Consequently many of them have to have a string of admirers, suitors, or extra-marital partners as a kind of emotional insurance policy. They need to be constantly reassured of their attractiveness—a varied romantic diet dilutes the threat of emotional pain for them, although, of course, this dilettante behaviour accounts for their major dissatisfaction with the content of their relationships. Thus, despite Libra's reputation as **the** sign for love, it is worth remembering that a great many Venusian women are more concerned with the **idealized concept** of relating rather than the nitty gritty process of deep emotional exchange; and many will positively balk at the first sign of becoming emotionally vulnerable to or dependent on anyone.

Almost all Libran women, including those who are more feeling-orientated, revere emotional control. Even when the Libran woman is hurt or deeply angered she will do her best to behave in a rational manner. She hates to lose control of a situation or of herself, consequently she frequently goes to enormous lengths to avoid contentious issues and full-blown confrontations. However, it isn't altogether true to say that Ms Libra cannot show her anger: it may take some doing to push her over the edge of her rage threshold, but once reasonable argument has proved ineffective, she can shout and scream like the most dispossessed fire sign. Of course, she hates herself afterwards, and usually rushes out to buy an extravagant peace-offering as soon as she can take the tea bags off her eyes and the asprins and the gin have done their work. Ms Libra cannot bear to live in a pained silence for long and she is almost always the first to initiate apologies after a showdown. She also hates to go to sleep without settling an argument, which sometimes means she has to open up peace negotiations at three o'clock in the morning after several hours of tossing and turning.

Libra is not the most maternal sign of the zodiac; babies often prove far too noisy, smelly, and disruptive for the elegant life-style and demanding social calendar of the typical Libran lady. Often, of course, they appear the picture of perfect motherhood—especially in public—cooing and clucking contentedly over their infant. But motherhood twenty-four hours of every day of every year wears somewhat thin for the Venusian woman. She's far better handing the children's daily care over to someone else; then when she's accomplished all her various toils, especially the social ones, she can find the time to sit and communicate with them, an all-important task for this air sign. On the one hand she experiences tremendous pangs when she's away from her brood; but on the other, she hates feeling intolerant, impatient, or frustrated when she's cooped up with them day in and day out. Certainly the children of Libran mothers learn early on that unconditional love isn't part of the treaty: Libran females have high expectations of their children, socially, academically, and in they way they behave. Indeed, in many ways the Libran mother is as pushy and demanding of her children as the other cardinal signs, Cancer, Capricorn, and Aries, but she usually conceals her ambition well.

The late Diana Dors was the quintessential Libran lady—a sex goddess no less. But as she matured she proved to be a versatile actress, intelligent, articulate, humorous, and dearly loved by the British public. Diana provided plenty of juicy copy for gossip columnists during her life; she had three marriages (all to volatile men) and many well-publicized love affairs. She clearly enjoyed a rich and extravagant life-style—fast cars, swimming pools, and wild parties, although she was not without her share of personal tragedies. As with many Libran females, the men in her life came first (even before the children) and, regardless of her own personal fame and achievements, she considered her role as wife to her third husband, Alan Lake, far more important and infinitely more fulfilling. Although as a mother she was a more permanent fixture to her third son, Jason, her two sons by her second husband remained in the US with their father after the divorce and during the course of that marriage saw more of their nanny than Diana.

Yet despite her voluptuous looks and opulent, some might say irresponsible, life-style, at heart she was a resourceful and deeply courageous woman. Faced with financial difficulties that at one time brought her to bankruptcy, she worked unstintingly to return to solvency—in true Libran style often taking on far too many obligations and commitments that put her under great stress. She also stood by Alan through his alcoholic problems and his prison sentence. But perhaps her greatest struggle was a private one. During the last two years of her life, physically weakened by cancer, she continued to work voraciously, yet never let the world know of the pain she lived with constantly. Sarah Miles—who worked with her during her final film **Steaming**, made two months before she died—told me that one morning, unbeknown to Diana, she saw her doubled up in pain, gripping on to a piece of scenery. But as Diana drew towards the set, she straightened up, smiled and greeted everyone chirpily. Appearances were kept up right until the end.

The Libran woman, like her male counterpart, seems all too prone to divorce. There are a variety of reasons for this. First Ms Libra is not a loner and in many cases positively hates to do anything alone at all. Consequently, her need for a partner often prompts her to marry young before she has had time to discover who she is and whether or not her husband is a true reflection of her needs. Second, the Libran lady wants an ideal union: she is often very difficult to please and continually reappraises her relationship with her partner. She tends to compare her man to others (and often informs him how he fares), and the grass invariably seems greener on another man's patch. Many Libran females keep a kind of running tally on their marriage: 'I-did-three-hours-baby-minding-while-you-played-cricket-so-I-think-it-only -fair-that-you-look-after-little-Emily-while-I-go-off-to-my-aerobics-class!' This is the sign that gets most irate about the unfair burden carried by the woman in marriage, and the Libran female deeply resents her man if he fails to contribute to family activities or goes off to the pub with the boys when he could be whispering sweet nothings in her ear. Sometimes, despite her soft-spoken, pretty manner, she can turn into a terrible nag, which causes more friction and disharmony in the relationship.

Finally, there is the emotional issue. Ms Libra, like Ms Capricorn and Ms Aquarius, will often settle for the security and status that a marriage provides, rather than its emotional content. Thus, as the years go by and minor flaws turn into gaping holes, she may feel a compelling need for a more fulfilling union. An affair may provide a temporary solution or perhaps even lead to divorce and remarriage. Yet, all too often the lover or second husband will ultimately also be found wanting.

Ms Libra's search for harmony, balance and perfection in relationships is often an elusive one. You see, without depth of feeling and selfless love, ironically so difficult for Libra to acquire, such perfection and fulfilment in relationships is largely a question of semantics. Perfect love cannot be found in the mind, the heart must also be involved. Clearly, a Libran woman gains enormously through having her Moon, Venus, Mars, or Ascendant in a water sign. If this is the case, love becomes less an intellectualized concept and more a feeling experience, while at the same time her emotions are less likely to run away with her.

Indeed, in many ways the Libran woman has one of the best 'deals' in the zodiac. She has more than her share of feminine attributes to capture the heart of any man she chooses, yet her mind is as clear and as sharp as a glacier. She can meet a man as his equal yet she instinctively knows how to make him feel superior and distinctly unthreatened. She can be touchingly shy, delicate, and diplomatic, but when the chips are down she can wrestle with the situation as gamely as the most assertive Aries or redoubtable Scorpio. This Venusian female is all too often underestimated. Behind the fluff and dimples is a warrior maiden of the first order.

THE MALE LIBRA

The typical Libran man exudes charm and affability from every carefully attended pore in his body. He is so wonderfully considerate, so absolutely understanding, and so essentially 'gentil' that it's almost impossible to believe that he has wiped the floor with you. Like the female of the species, he is never short of admirers, from six-years-old to ninety-five, and while his rosebud lips may curl at the prospect of a morning mucking out the stables or unblocking your drains, he'll leap at the chance to advise you on interior decoration or discuss your problems about mother. Ninety per cent of the time he is the most reasonable and conciliatory man in the zodiac, but every so often the scales will tip him into outright insubordination and truculence.

Libran men are to love and romance what bees are to honey. Mr Libra usually has ladies fawning over him from his pram to his bath chair, and by the time his glands have caught up with his precocious social *élan*, he is far and away the best 'catch' on the campus. He also holds a fairly high opinion of himself and can be more vain than his female counterpart. Indeed, he is tremendously concerned about appearances of every sort. Think of Cary Grant or Roger Moore and you have a perfect Libran stereotype—smooth, sophisticated, and immensely sartorial. Mr Libra thoroughly enjoys the ritual of courtship and romance; even if he's temporarily low on funds he'll take his lady out somewhere special and make her feel that she is the most fascinating and beautiful woman he has ever met. To his credit, romance isn't short lived with this man. Most Libran husbands make every attempt to keep the romance in their marriages alive and unless they're feeling very jaded or have flipped into the more negative mean and selfish side of Libra, they rarely forget a birthday or an anniversary, and indeed love to find an excuse to buy some beautiful memento to mark the occasion.

However, appearances are often Mr Libra's biggest banana skin when it comes to the harmonious relationships he seeks. In many ways the Libran man, like the Arian, is easily taken in by a pretty face and a pert manner. He is often more concerned with the effect he is having on the object of his desires than he is assessing whether there is any depth or sincerity behind her wiles. Although he is socially and intellectually sophisticated, he tends to be emotionally naïve and thus surprisingly easy to manipulate. Conversely, the Libran man is entirely capable of his own brand of elegant manipulation, which he prefers to call persuasion and flattery. Mr Libra hates to hurt anyone or seem in any way to be a cad; if he wants to end a relationship or he develops second thoughts about a lady, he will resort to charming evasiveness to wriggle out of the situation. I always think the words of Libran Oscar Wilde are very apt in regard to the way the Venusian man is likely to behave in such a situation, '. . . each man kills the thing he loves. Some do it with a bitter look, **some with a flattering word** . . .' Needless to say, like the Arian, Mr Libra often gets embroiled in the most complicated emotional webs.

One Libran man managed to wreak havoc in two women's lives through a combination of indecision, taking the line of least resistance, and the Libran dislike of being alone. Seamus had been married for eighteen reasonably happy years to Maureen. They had two teenage sons, both at crucial stages of their academic careers. When Seamus was offered a better job with a huge salary increase 200 miles from home, rather than disrupt the boys' schooling by moving the entire family up to Glasgow, he arrived at a true Libran compromise: he would spend the week living in digs near his job, returning home for weekends. On his first day at the new job he was introduced to his secretary Angela, a divorcee, who by great coincidence turned out to live just next door to his lodgings. Poor Seamus couldn't manage to pour all his energies into his demanding new job **and** look after himself, so it seemed just as easy to let Angela take over the domestic side of his life as well as the secretarial. Eventually, it became easier not to return to his room at all, and before he knew where he was he and Angela were having a full blown affair. For eighteen months this arrangement trundled along happily, but eventually the boys' schooling was no longer an obstacle to the family's moving to Glasgow. Now Seamus found himself on the horns of a dilemma; either he had to break off the affair with Angela, causing trauma to her—not to mention the upheaval in the office—or he had to tell Maureen to remain where she was, which inevitably necessitated a confession and a subsequent legal separation or divorce. Seamus just couldn't make up his mind which path he should take, nor indeed which woman he loved more. Worse, whatever his decision, he was bound to be seen in a bad light by somebody—Angela, Maureen, his sons, the boss, the tea-lady . . .

Receiving no positive lead from Seamus, Maureen put the family house on the market and journeyed up to Glasgow to house hunt. Seamus reassured Angela of his love for her and that he would do something about the situation—right up until the day the removal van arrived at his new house. There was worse to come. Angela, madly in love with Seamus, clung to him like a limpet, meeting him furtively after work and spending extra long lunch hours with him; she even wrote him loving notes, one of which Maureen found. After the ensuring débâcle Seamus tried to end the affair with Angela, but he couldn't bear her grief, nor his guilt. He told her he still loved her. Fortunately, Angela was made of stronger stuff and, after deluging Seamus with a Niagara of emotions and accusations, she gave in her notice and applied for a job abroad! To this day, Seamus is haunted by the feeling that he made the wrong decision.

This tale provides many insights into the Libran nature. Although by no means a weak sign, in the real sense of the word, many Libran men do appear to take a remarkably passive stance at times, through their inability to make hard-line decisions. One Libran father refused to interfere in his daughter's marriage despite her obvious distress caused by her alcoholic husband's frequent assaults on her. He maintained that no one should come between man and wife, and secretly felt that it was a case of six of one and half a dozen of the other. Unfortunately, when his daughter eventually divorced her brutal husband, the father was devastated by her rejection of himself.

Also, because Libran men tend to take the line of least resistance (especially where relating is concerned), many of them simply drift into relationships. Saying 'No' is awfully difficult for this sign. Unless a relationship is causing them immense stress, they are more likely to stay than face the upheaval and disruption of a separation or divorce.

Another Libran failing is the inability to respond at a gut-level to another individual. Many Libran men, like Seamus, cannot handle powerful emotional exchange; it frightens many of them out of their wits. Ironically, strongly Libran men are often highly attracted to deeply emotional (water sign) women. Initially, Mr Libra finds watery women subtle, sensuous, mysterious, and pliable, but when they become too clinging or emotionally demanding he, like the other two air signs, Gemini and Aquarius, has to withdraw—sometimes psychologically, sometimes quite literally.

One of the many inconsistencies of Libran men is that although they crave peace, harmony, and balance in their relationships, and behave in an accommodating and understanding way to their partner, they are by no means immune to divorce. Like the Libran woman, one of the primary reasons for marital failure is that Mr Libra frequently marries too young, before he has time to sow enough wild oats or establish his own values. Another mistake many Librans make, is in marrying someone who seems just right on the surface and who everyone else approves of, but as the marriage progresses, all manner of unpleasant characteristics emerge. Although the Libran man may recoil at the idea of divorce, given that a relationship has become intolerable he will move to end it surprisingly fast. Librans have a great instinct for survival! Also, the Libran man tends to be on the promiscuous side, or at the very least is an incorrigible flirt. Thus, unless his wife is tremendously broadminded or endlessly forgiving, he is often at the receiving end of a divorce petition.

Another reason why Mr Libra's relationships sometimes fail, is that his very reasonableness and dispassion can drive his partners wild with frustration. The average Libran man will put on a pair of ten-league boots rather than enter into a slanging match. If he happens to be married to, or involved with, a woman whose emotions verge on the volcanic, he can actually make her outbursts more uncontrolled and more frequent by his apparent indifference and lack of passion. Yes, he can feel anger and even join in the fray if he's pushed hard enough, but he'll deeply resent his partner for making him do so, which ultimately makes for much hostility and distance between them.

Mr Libra can also drive his partners to distraction with his pathological indecision. Just as he has outlined why all the pros for plan A are superior and a decision seems imminent, he'll start to consider an equally plausible list of pluses for plan B. A husband and wife I know, both with Libra rising, occasionally have to abort a mission totally, whether it be a walk in the country or the purchase of a new bed, through their mutual inability to decide which, what, or who is the better alternative, without managing to offend the other partner. They are usually late for functions, having had great difficulty in deciding what to wear and how best to get there, and on one occasion arrived at a cocktail party just as the last guest was leaving. Indecision notwithstanding, Libran men usually make ideal husbands and partners. Unless there is a strong Uranian theme in the chart, most of them are prepared to adapt to their partner's needs and desires, and as long as their other half is happy, and the wheels of their domestic, professional and social lives are running smoothly, they're happy too. Also, most Libran men are ambitious and aspire to high-earning positions; fortunately for their dependents, they are hardly ever mean and tight-fisted. In fact many men of this sign thoroughly enjoy spending the fruits of their labours, particularly on life-enhancing items and activities. Sometimes, of course, the scales will tilt them into a period of extreme economic stringency, but it's usually only temporary.

Mr Libra would much prefer to avoid the darker side of life. He hates unpleasantness of any sort, which goes for spots and dandruff as much as for emotional pain and raw animal passion. Indeed, the one sure way out of your Libran man's heart would be to invite him to meet you at the local 'greasy-spoon' cafe, where the tables are liberally spattered with congealed tomato sauce bottles and corroded sugar spoons. If, to add insult to injury, you are hovering (hair in need of a wash and a dropped frayed hem) over the juke box, he'll be running in the opposie direction as fast as his elegant legs can carry him! Rather more seriously, Mr Libra's dislike of ugliness in any shape or form can make him remarkably insensitive and unsympathetic to unattractive human conditions, like some illnesses and handicaps, or any of the less pleasant emotions, like jealousy, hate, or anger. Nurturing and cherishing does not come easily to Mr Libra, at least not unless he has plenty of planets in water signs in his chart. His primary impulse is to understand things on an intellectual level since he trusts reason before feelings. Consequently, he often distresses and confuses his partners by his inability to draw close to them when they are at their lowest and most unattractive ebb. If Mr Libra finds his wife consumed with misery and a swollen jaw due to impacted wisdom teeth, he is far more likely to ask her to describe *how* the pain feels, than bring her an asprin and hold her close. Many times I've heard women married to Libran men say that although they can discuss almost anything with their husbands, they never feel really understood by them, since their husbands rarely respond to them or their plight on an instinctive level.

Although more emotionally-charged women may find the Libran man a cold fish in the long term, others find his agreeable kind of companionship adequate compensation for profound emotional interchange. Of all the signs he is the one most prepared to give precedence to his relationships, which means his wife never has to fear she will come in second place to his mother, the car, his golf clubs, or indeed his children. Like Ms Libra, he is tremendously idealistic about his partners and therefore prone to much shilly-shallying before taking the plunge, and much re-appraisal and reflection afterwards. It's far better to avoid giving this man a choice; and provided what you offer is stylish and attractive, he'll be glad you made the decision (I have known one or two Libran men admit to never having actually asked their wives to marry them: somehow they just fell in with the arrangements!) However, I think it only fair to say that Mr Libra can't be pushed into something he really doesn't want to do. Finally, a word of warning. Don't take the Venusian man for granted; like the Piscean, he may seem pliant and tolerant; but walked on and used, he'll grow icier and icier until eventually he'll freeze you out altogether.

SUMMARY

As airy people, Librans are far happier communicating and engaging in social activities with their partners than exploring the subterranean depths of their emotions. Not that they aren't warm and loving individuals, nor that they don't care enormously about their partners' needs. Indeed, Librans like to put other people first and tend to draw their own happiness through that of their partners. This is a tremendously partner-needing sign, although Venusian men and women are by no means the emotionally vulnerable or dependent sort. Librans need partners to reflect their dreams, desires, and endeavours and most are far less confident doing something off their own bat than when they have the benefit of a discussion or, perhaps more important, approval of someone else behind them. Indeed, Librans rarely make a success of their lives alone—a partner is an essential part of their psychological well being and confidence support structure.

Despite their own particular flaws and failings, Venusian men and women by and large make the best partners in the Zodiac.

LIBRA PARTNERSHIPS

It is entirely possible for Librans to make a go of a relationship with any sign of the Zodiac. Venusian people naturally bend to another persons's tastes, needs and desires, and tend to find something of value in each and every relationship. Ideally, however, Librans should find fiery or airy individuals suit them best, although many are drawn to more challenging earthy or watery partners.

Aries

Aries is Libra's opposite number, and either huge attraction or sharp alienation tends to occur between these two. Both, of course, share many of each other's characteristics, but often fail to recognize them. What may start out as a highly stimulating partnership—with the Aries partner spurring the Libran into reluctant action and the Venusian checking Mr or Ms Mars' every impulsive decision—often becomes fraught with strife over the years. However, given that Aries can develop his dormant talent for diplomacy and compromise, and Libra can raise his emotional threshold, this partnership can be enduring and fulfilling for both.

Taurus

Taurus is usually the best earthy partner for Libra, since this sign is also ruled by Venus. Both appreciate beauty in their surroundings and often share a great interest in the arts. Both like an easy life and try to be very accommodating toward each other—although the Taurean can become very resentful over Libra's extravagant tastes. Sometimes the Bull's possessiveness tends to mar the otherwise harmonious nature of their relationship, and he frequently miscontrues Libra's friendliness to all as sheer fickleness! In some relationships sex can reach sublime levels between Libra and Taurus.

Gemini

Libran/Geminian couples tend to lead very busy lives, and a constant stream of other people and social events accompany their relationship. Like Aquarius, Mr and Ms Gemini are not ones to deluge their relationships with emotional downpours, yet Libra often feels the Gemini partner is not giving enough of himself to the relationship. Sexual coolness can develop early in the relationship between these two, unless other planetary factors—particularly from Moon, Venus, or Mars—mitigate this tendency.

Cancer

Cancer is likely to be the most difficult water partner for Libra, although probably the most compelling. On the plus side these two may find much in common on the artistic and sensual side of life and much happiness in the home and with the children. The major problems with this combination are due to Cancer's hypersensitive emotions. Cancerians find it difficult to talk about their feelings, and tend to clam up when hurt; no matter how hard Libra may try to rationalize or understand the Crab, he frequently loses patience with him, especially if the moods and silences occur too often. Consequently hostile distances and dark abysses often arise between this couple.

Leo

Librans find Leos big-hearted and affectionate partners. Sometimes Leo can be too high-handed and self-indulgent for Libra's liking, while Leo feels his Libran partner is far too accomodating of others, and gets rather jealous about the Venusian's popularity! Leo also finds it difficult to apologize or back down from their rigid opinions and stances, which puts Libra's talent for compromise to severe tests. Although this can be a mutually rewarding partnership, the Libran man or woman often feels overpowered by Leo and over the years an undercurrent of hostility frequently develops between the two.

Virgo

Libra/Virgo partnerships work best when both people have planets in each other's Sun sign. Both are idealistic about their relationships and become very critical of the partner when he or she fails to come up to expectations. Virgo can find Libra a little on the sloppy and scatty side occasionally, while Libra feels Virgo is over fussy and too practical. The sexual relationship is often stimulating and fulfilling between these two, although both may fail to touch each other's deepest emotions.

Libra

Libra in a relationship with another **Libra** should be an ideal. if not perfect combination, but often it is their very similarities that drive them apart. Certainly, this couple talk about their relationship a lot, and spend much time perfecting their image as Mr and Mrs Blissfully Happy. Although they surround their homes and lives with elegance and beauty, their emotional life often lacks energy or much fiery expression.

Scorpio

Scorpio is Libra's next-door-neighbour and since they may share planets in each other's Sun signs, relationships between them can work well—sometimes. By and large, however, the Scorpion is far too emotionally extreme and much too intense about life for Libra. In the long term, Libra may find the Scorpio partner's moods difficult to live with and come to despise his secretive manipulative ways, while the Scorpio individual may find Libra somewhat shallow and inconstant for his liking. This couple often has problems over infidelity. However, like Piscean/Libran partners, the sexual side of their relationship is often excellent.

Sagittarius

Sagittarians are the sort of easy-going, optimistic individuals Mr and Ms Libra relate to well. Sagittarians and Librans enjoy the good things of life and frequently err on the side of extravagence; but as both tend to lead charmed lives they usually rise above their periodic financial crises. Although they can become irritated and frustrated by each other in the long term—Libra, because he is always having to compensate for the Archer's social gaffs, and Sagittarius, because Libra wastes so much time shilly-shallying about practically everything—their union is nevertheless usually a happy and durable one.

Capricorn

Libra is either highly attracted to **Capricorn** or distinctly hostile. Usually, however, Libra admires the Goat's authority and firmness, and relies on his decision-making abilities, while Capricorn appreciates Libra's balance and emotional control. The drawback to this combination lies in the Goat's rigid hold on the purse strings, which can interfere with Libra's need for life's little luxuries. Thus, severe arguments over money are frequent between them. Although this couple often 'go places' in the world, their different values and perspectives on life can make the domestic environment somewhat hostile. Their sexual interaction is an important and binding aspect of their relationship—if the rapport is good the relationship endures; if not, these two tend to lead thoroughly independent lives.

Aquarius

Aquarius' mind and eccentricity are initially fascinating to the Venusian, although in the long term the Water Bearer's refusal to compromise, or bend to anyone else's desires, wears down Libra's tolerance quotient. Feelings are often low key between these two, and although there may be much sexual activity at the start of the relationship. this too usually ultimately assumes a low profile.

Pisces

Pisces is likely to be the best water partner for Libra. Both people find it easier to bend to another's will than face a confrontation of any sort. Both are also dreadfully indecisive. Yet there are many pluses for their partnership: the Venusian and the Piscean appreciate romance and sentiment and both are usually affectionate and generous with each other. Problems arise in this partnership if Pisces becomes too emotionally draining on Libra. since Libra's tendency to discuss and rationalize everything only aggravates Pisces' anxieties. Sex can be extremely good between these two because they each like to imbue it with the highest artistic expression and fantasy.

SEXUALITY

It is said that thoughts of sex cross an individual's mind every ten minutes of his or her adult life. How true this is. I don't know. since I've never carried out any fieldwork on the topic! But. if I had to choose an astrological sign to whom this could well apply. Libra would be one of the front runners. Although Scorpios take top honours as the sex maniacs of the zodiac. Librans in their delicate. airy way. place great emphasis on their sex lives. and whether or not they actually engage in rampant sexual activity. they certainly **think** about it a lot. Indeed it is true to say that Librans usually consider themselves to be strongly sexed–if not downright over-sexed. However. because they. like the other two air signs. Gemini and Aquarius. are creatures more of their minds and imaginations than their physical senses. they tend to inflate the significance of sex in their lives. Clearly. as a sign ruled by Venus–goddess of love–Librans usually display some considerable talent in this area. and even if their response isn't exactly instinctive and full of feeling. most of them quickly acquire great expertise in their love making. Perhaps also because Librans spend a large amount of their time perfecting. analysing. and reflecting on their one-to-one relationships. they find the sexual arena provides one of the most potent sources of connection and interaction with another individual. Yet. in keeping with the airy nature of their sign. Librans often find the actual physicality of making love far less erotic than the anticipation and preparation for the event.

The Sun sign. of couse. is only one part–admittedly a very important part–of the birth chart as a whole: thus the astrologer aiming to appeal to a mass audience is faced with a difficult enough task to paint an accurate character portrait of each and every Libran or Taurean living on this planet: since an individual's sexuality is one of the most mysterious and complex areas of his or her life being. such a task is even greater. Broadly speaking. however. men with their Sun or Mars in Libra are likely to relate to the themes outlined in this section and those women who have their Moon. Mars. and Venus in this sign as well as their Sun.

The Libran female is usually highly attracted to the opposite sex. and vice versa. Like the Piscean woman. she is somewhat of a chameleon by nature and capable of adapting (often unconsciously) to the tastes of the man she is with at the time. However. while the Piscean female evokes a mysterious and helpless appeal, it is Ms Libra's intelligence and piquant wit that enhance her desirability.

In many ways, with both the male and female Libran, traits of the opposite sign, Aries, and its ruler Mars, emerge in their sexual behaviour. Although Ms Libra is infinitely more subtle and ingenious in her courtship tactics than the Martian female (she rarely adopts such a cavewoman approach) unlike Ms Aries, who frequently turns out to be a luxurious pussycat under the sheets, the Venusian female often takes a surprisingly assertive role. The Libran woman learns her craft like the most conscientious Virgoan, and is often keen to display her excellence and attentiveness to a partner in bed. It may well be, however, that in some cases, the Libran woman's preference to initiate much of the sexual interaction conceals a basic insecurity and fear of yielding totally to another, or being in any way submissive. This is by no means always the case of course: the Libran woman, contrary to her vacillating stance where daily decisions are concerned, usually knows what pleases and arouses her, and, as befits a love goddess, uses her powers to ensure she gets what she wants.

Most Libran women need to know they are looking attractive in order to function at their sexual best—and, indeed, to become aroused in the first place. The Libran woman tends to see herself through her partner's eyes; thus, if she feels unattractive, she assumes her partner thinks the same, and she cannot therefore respond to him. Even when making love, Ms Libra likes to arrange herself in flattering positions. This is not the best lady in the zodiac to take by surprise, and certainly never when she is scrubbing the floor with her hair in rollers and half a jar of moisturizer on her face. Unlike some of the other signs who can be aroused by touch and sight, the Libran lady's imagination must first be fired. She usually loves erotica—as long as it's in good taste—and a romantic and exciting setting is an essential curtain raiser to sexual activity. Fantasy is also an important part of Ms Libra's sexual life: indeed, I found that several Libran women from my questionnaire shared the same romantic fantasy figure: mid-nineteenth-century man, complete with sword, thigh boots, flowing shirt and waistcoat—the sort of character Douglas Fairbanks Junior immortalized in the 1930s.

Apart from Ms Libra's liking for romance and fantasy as a sexual aperitif, she is often fond of wearing no underwear beneath her outer clothing. In this way, she not only feels exciting, but also excites herself. Altogether, the Venusian woman needs plenty of mental imagery and erotic stimulation to trigger her body responses.

Like her male counterpart, Ms Libra is often a wonderfully versatile and skillful lover—inventive, unselfish and keen to please. If there is a criticism, it is her difficulty in letting go and allowing her feelings to take over, which can sometimes make her approach to making love somewhat sterile. This emotional reserve is, in turn, a block to the full union of mind, body, and spirit that makes the sexual act such a fulfilling experience. However, those Libran women who also have plenty of planets in water in their charts are far more likely to find sexual interaction, and indeed their one-to-one relationships in general, infinitely more fulfilling.

Both male and female Librans need constant boosters to their attractiveness, preferably in the form of a continual stream of admirers and lovers; even when married, Mr and Ms Libra tend to encourage new liaisons, although they are usually discreet and careful not to hurt their partners through any of their extra-curricular activity. Strangely enough for such a fair and just-minded sign, and also one that is ultra-refined, Librans can be extremely promiscuous. Both sexes, of course, find saying 'no' requires a superhuman effort; consequently if the setting is right and the opportunity presents itself, they have the utmost difficulty in turning down a romantic encounter. Fortunately, Libra is a sign not noted for carrying undue burdens of guilt—they can nearly always justify their actions and their infidelity. Also, Librans like an element of danger and intrigue in their relationships—they find the idea of secret assignations both romantically and sexually appetising. Clearly, though, the Libran man and woman who has found the perfection he or she seeks in a partner, is rarely susceptible to infidelity.

Another trait common to both male and female Librans is a liking to keep in touch with previous lovers. Since this sign likes to surface from its romantic and sexual exploits smelling like a rose, if they can continue to maintain a thread of contact—no matter how slender—they feel neither rejected nor disliked. One man with his Mars in Libra commented, 'I always care about past lovers and am reluctant to lose touch completely with them . . . I never break off a friendship, we just drift apart. I am always eager to start a new affair and have to make a conscious effort to select only suitable partners to avoid causing or receiving hurt.' Another woman, with Venus and her Ascendant in Libra, said, 'one of the saddest things about ending an affair is losing contact with the person. I can never understand why the fact that you may no longer want to sleep with somebody should stop you having dinner with them or keeping in touch. Irrevocable partings seem thoroughly uncivilized to me.'

The male Libran usually considers himself a lover to be reckoned with. Unlike his opposite number, Mr Aries, or even Mr Leo for that matter, he is not so obsessed with the idea of conquest and isn't the type to boast or notch up numbers on the bedpost. Mr Libra is a great admirer and appreciator of the female sex; flirting is second nature to this man and his conversation (preferably of the tête-à-tête variety) is liberally peppered with compliments and subtle sexual innuendo all the way from the dinner table to the bedroom. Libran men consider romance an essential ingredient of sex, and most are extremely uncomfortable with the idea of a quick lay, even one preceded by a good claret and a superlative Chateaubriand. They naturally want to please their women, and the romance and build-up to the sexual act itself is just as much for their benefit as for the lady of their desires.

As in many areas of his life, Mr Libra is an artist—and a very smooth one at that. Because he usually understands women extremely well he tailors his seductions to the way a woman likes to be wooed and won. Of course, behind the charm and decorum Mr Libra is just as capable as the next Aries or Scorpio of going off the boil once his libido is satisfied—however, he always lets his partners down with style. One client of mine told me that when she was an innocent virgin of eighteen, she fell in love with a Libran medical student. After two or three romantic dates, he suggested they made love. My client refused for fear of his losing respect for her. The following day he invited her round to his room for tea and a chat, whereupon he proposed they could remain just good friends, meeting occasionally, or, if she wished to change her mind and go to bed with him, they could begin a serious relationship. Since she still couldn't overcome the hurdle of guilt and fear over losing her virginity, she reluctantly agreed to be 'friends'. True to his word, her Libran student invited her out to drinks three days later—with him and the boys. Instead of holding her hand as on previous occasions, he slapped her heartily on the back and offered her a pint; he then talked shop to his co-students for the major part of the evening. It took only one more similar outing to drive his message home to her. 'But', she sighed, 'he was so nice with it, I never really felt rejected.'

So devoted to the female sex are some Libran men, they even make careers out of their skills. Although the word gigolo has rather decadent connotations, conjuring up vistas of 'pretty' boys playing consort to geriatric ladies in return for gifts and financial remuneration, the gigolo's ability to make a woman feel desirable, both in bed and out, is just where Libran men excel. Why such behaviour is appropriate to the Libran man more than any other sign is that such individuals are in a master class of their own when it comes to using their charm, companionship, and sexual skills to please women. One immensely Libran gigolo who appeared on BBC television in 1984, commented with obvious pride in his craftsmanship: 'I never, never fall asleep before the lady.' He was full of praise for the 'fair sex', and the courtship, attentiveness, the wine and roses appeared every bit as important to his 'career' as satisfying a woman in bed. However, despite his attractive looks and Latin charisma, a certain coldness haunted his expression, and I couldn't help feeling he might well have been a highly attractive, well-programmed robot! Although the Libran man may not be an out and out gigolo, there is often something obsequious and emotionally detached about his approach to women and sex.

Like the female Libran, Mr Libra is often a wonderful sexual technician, but with a distinct inability to invest his love making with great depth of feeling—at least not unless he has plenty of watery planets in his chart. The Venusian man, like the Geminian and the Aquarian, rarely settles for plain, straightforward sex; he likes the unusual and the exotic. Although he usually takes the initiative in bed, he is not averse to playing a passive and submissive role sometimes. Some astrologers maintain that the Libran man enjoys and practices the most extreme forms of sexual expression to gain sexual satisfaction. Whether this is true or not can be argued at length, but the implication here is that, like most airy men, Mr Libra needs rather a lot of erotic stimulation to activate the body!

Finally, a word about mirrors. Libra is often said to be the most narcissistic sign in the zodiac; thus the use of mirrors as a sexual turn on is highly apt for this sign. One Libran girlfriend of mine, engaged to a man with his Mars in Libra, told me that their mutual fondness for making love in front of the mirror almost got them arrested one night. Finding themselves alone in the dimly-lit mirrored lift of their 30-storey hotel, they couldn't resist temptation—especially at 4.30 in the morning. On their third ascent in the lift they came to a halt on the fifteenth floor and just managed to extricate themselves from their disarrayed state before the hotel security man stepped in!

In the main. Librans are natural lovers and companions. They love to be in love and/or sexually enthralled with someone. But in the long term, unless the partner reaches their lofty standards of perfection, once the initial fascination has worn off, they tend to become critical of the lover, argumentative, and emotionally and sexually restless. Some also have a tendency to keep their lovers and partners dangling on a string—Librans love playing emotional games with people. Sometimes they seem cool and uninterested in the partner, then just as she or he is about to pull away, the Libran man or woman will woo them back with gentle coaxing, flattery, and attentiveness. As a sign synonymous with love, courtship, and the art of relating, Librans have the potential to be sexual gadflies or Byronic supremos.

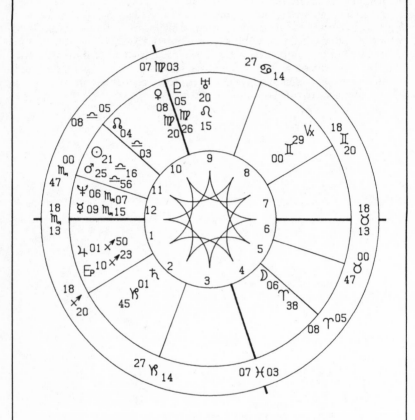

HRH THE DUCHESS OF YORK

15 10 1959   9h 3m 0s GMT

PLACIDUS 51N32 0W8

PROFILE OF A LIBRA WOMAN

HRH THE DUCHESS OF YORK

There is a little-known sign, Caucus the Cowespat (the **s** is silent) that lies in between Regulus and Pollux. The Cowespat—which rules muddy fields and turf—appears with uncanny regularity on the Ascendant whenever members of the Royal Family are about to fall in love.* Thus was the case when, in September 1985, the then Miss Sarah Ferguson placed a dainty green wellie on the mossy grounds of Balmoral and realized that she felt something more than mere friendship for HRH Prince Andrew. Destiny had struck once again. The Caucus Race had begun.

Sarah, like the Princess of Wales before her, belonged to a charmed circle of the aristocratic élite. (She shares a common ancestor with Prince Andrew, the 4th Duke of Devonshire, 1720–64.) Her father, Major Ronald Ferguson, a former commander of the Sovereign's Escort of the Household Cavalry, is the Prince of Wales' polo manager and a close friend of Prince Philip. From her earliest years Sarah mingled with members of the Royal Family although, unlike Diana, she had no presentiment that one day she might marry one of them.

Sarah was brought up with her elder sister, Jane, at her parents' home near Ascot. She was the proverbial tomboy—one of her earliest

---

*Cupid's dart struck the Princess of Wales in a ploughed field.

memories is of trying to plunge a firework down the loo—and she loved ponies and animals. From the age of eight she attended a weekly boarding school, which she loved. While Danes Hill featured ballet high on its curriculum, Sarah preferred the sports field—'I wasn't exactly built for ballet.' She went on to Hurst Lodge Girl's School, where she excelled at tennis and netball (she was games captain), and in her final year she was made Head Girl. While never an academic high-flier, Sarah was by no means unintelligent. She left Hurst Lodge with seven 'O' levels and might have done even better had she not been faced with a major crisis the year of her exams.

On Sarah's fifteenth birthday, her mother told her and Jane that she was leaving their father. The news of her mother, Susan's, affair with the Argentinian Polo player Hector Barrantes caused a huge scandal at the time. However, her parents' decision to separate came as no great surprise to Sarah since she had been aware for some time that all was not well between them, though she had chosen to keep her fears to herself. Sarah's father remarried some eighteen months later—to another Susan, by whom he has three more children. Sarah was to comment later that life was not drastically altered after her mother left. Also, her mother did not leave immediately for Argentina; she remained in London for a year and was in 'arm's reach' of her daughters. Nevertheless, fifteen is an extremely sensitive age to witness the breakdown of one's parents' marriage.

Sarah has a fascinating chart, and by no means an easy one. While her Sun occupies the harmonious, diplomatic, and charmed sign of Libra, she has indomitable Scorpio rising and Pluto, her chart ruler, on the Midheaven conjunct Venus (her Sun sign ruler). This implies that she is a lady of infinite emotional and psychological resources, an individual who has great depth and inner strength—a force to be reckoned with. While Venus and Pluto in prime position at the top of the chart speak volumes about her destiny as a public figure (which I will discuss later), the MC–IC axis also describes the parental influence. While the fourth and tenth 'houses' of the horoscope are linked to the parents as a whole, the tenth 'house' is more usually associated with mother and the fourth with father. With the Venus-Pluto colouring to the tenth 'house', there is a suggestion that Sarah experiences ambivalent feelings over 'mother'—feelings of great love and admiration, yet also some anger and resentment. Sometimes individuals with Pluto on their Midheaven feel mother was adept at emotional manipulation. That Sarah's Moon (a symbol of mother and the emotions) is caught up in a tense configuration between Neptune and Pluto* suggests that her mother was the cause of some

*A Finger of Fate: the moon is quincunx both Neptune and Pluto.

emotional stress in her life, if only through her dramatic departure from the family. Also, with the Moon in square 90° aspect to the Moon, the theme of distance—in Sarah's case a literal one—is underlined. Fortunately, Jupiter in a lovely 120° trine aspect to the Moon counterbalances much of the disharmony inherent in the other configurations and suggests there is plenty of love, support, and common ground between Sarah and her mother. Neptune, as ruler of the fourth 'house', on the one hand presents a picture of an idyllic childhood, and on the other a rather insecure one. If father is shown in the fourth 'house' then he emerges as a rather idealized figure. While Sarah's early childhood was happy and secure, the stable family boat was rocked by her parents' separation. Sarah's father, however, is anything but a Neptunian, 'unreal' figure to her. Sarah felt she might have idealized him when she was at school, but during and after the crisis she got to know him very well—she sees him 'very clearly'—and is obviously extremely close to him.

Like many strongly Scorpio-Pluto individuals, Sarah is adept at relegating her greatest anxieties to her inner vault while appearing unaffected on the surface. While she handled her mother's departure and her father's unhappiness with admirable self-possession, she was nonetheless affected by the crisis. Her inability to concentrate on academic work was one casualty of the upheaval; becoming a compulsive eater for a year was another. A stay at a health farm cut the latter problem down to size, although Sarah still worries about her weight and is 'always on a diet'. Like many Libran ladies, a return to the halcyon days of Rubens would be welcomed!

Despite her Sun-Mars conjunction in a cardinal sign—usually a forceful, driving combination—as a young girl Sarah had no great ambitions. She never gave her future serious thought and preferred to 'cruise along'. On leaving school she went to Argentina to stay with her mother and Hector—with whom she gets on extremely well—but on her return a year later the prospect of a direction in life was as elusive as ever. Learning to cook and arrange flowers were hardly the most stimulating of activities for someone with Sarah's spirited nature, but she was eventually **persuaded** to enrol at the Queen's Secretarial College. A variety of jobs followed, of which a three-year involvement with a PR company proved most successful. Indeed Sarah was able to use her trouble-shooting abilities to full effect as a PR and relished negotiating near impossible deals and tracking down elusive facts and figures. Sarah thrives on challenge and likes nothing better than a 'mission impossible'. Her employers liked her for her initiative.

Sarah's inability to find the right career niche can be related to the presence of directionless Neptune next to Mercury—the ruler of the

MC.* However, Sarah is anything but indirect as a person. With assertive Mars next to her Sun, and her Moon in the fiery, impetuous sign of Aries, she is straightforward and immediate in her actions. Hence her attraction for work that demands initiative and quick responses. In keeping with her Martian spirit she is marvellous in a crisis but abhors non-essentials: 'Crisis is easy; it's the trivial I can't deal with.' Aries and Mars are to challenge and adventure what bees are to honey; and if the future looks uncomfortably bland, Sarah will seek out a crisis or two. Like the bee she chose for her coat of arms, Sarah needs plenty of 'buzz' and 'hum' in her life!

Although something of an oversimplification, there are three main astrological themes in Sarah's chart: Libra-Venus, Scorpio-Pluto, and Aries-Mars. These three entirely different modes of expression sometimes have great difficulty working together. Sarah's Libra side can be lazy and too accommodating at times; she may rely too heavily on others seeking their opinions and reactions before making her own. Her Aries-Mars side is precisely the opposite, indicating she is too impulsive and hasty on occasion with a tendency to rush in where angels fear to tread! The Scorpio-Pluto influence adds a certain obsessiveness to her nature, even some secrecy; she can be stubborn, with a tendency to make mountains out of molehills. Sarah has the potential to be a wonderful and loyal friend but a dangerous enemy. She will fight for everything and everyone she believes in and loves, and always aims to emerge from the fray smelling like a rose! A true mission impossible at times.

Relationships are destined to play an important part in life for any female with Venus on the Midheaven and her Sun in Libra. If Venus also happens to rule the seventh 'house' of relationships and form a close conjunction to Pluto a relationship could well turn out to be a destiny in itself. Sarah is not the capricious type: where love and romance are concerned, she's an all or nothing lady. By the time she was twenty-six there had been only two serious relationships in her life: the first with skier Kim Smith-Bingham—five years—and the second with motor-racing entreprenneur Paddy MacNally—three years (both were Sun Sagittarians). Of the two it was Paddy she came closest to marrying and Paddy, with his logical approach to life, who influenced her most.

The 'gutter press' did its best to turn Sarah's romantic history into a Harold Robbins' saga; but despite a couple of ridiculous stories about her days in the 'drug dens of high society' there was nothing remotely scandalous about her past. And there would have been something very odd about her indeed had she not had a boyfriend or

*The Midheaven symbolizes, among several ideas, ambitions and life direction.

two by the time she was twenty-six! Astrologically, Sarah emerges as the type who needs security and permanence in her relationships. She is a great romantic and requires constant reassurances that she is loved and adored—above and beyond anyone else. Sarah, with her Aries Moon and Scorpio Ascendant, is not the sort to tolerate competition! That the two previous men in her life should be from the most non-committal and free-ranging sign of the zodiac is perverse, to say the least, but then Sarah does like a challenge. Paddy MacNally was, of course, considerably older than herself and well established; thus, despite his astrological bearing, he had the maturity and sophistication she liked. However, Sarah's relationship with Paddy was far from smooth.

Despite her confident, outspoken personality, Sarah is insecure and emotionally vulnerable. Once in a relationship, she becomes emotionally dependent on the partner. Yet she realizes that by becoming so dependent on anyone she increases her vulnerability: a sort of Catch 22 situation. Also in typical Libran fashion, she can't decide which is more important—her independence or a sharing-caring relationship. It is the Venus-Pluto duo that urges Sarah to seek deep and meaningful relationships, yet this combination also breeds fear of rejection. For the duration of her relationship with Paddy, onerous Saturn ploughed its way through her Sun and Ascendant sign, accentuating her insecurity and making any close partnership very hard going indeed. In her relationship with Paddy, marriage seemed the solution to the insecurity she felt with him, but once the commitment was there and the insecurity removed she realized that the relationship was not really right.

By the summer of 1985 her three-year relationship with Paddy had reached 'le crunch'. In July he asked Sarah to marry him. It was what she thought she had wanted but she found herself unable to give him a yes or no. By the end of August, on the morning she left for Balmoral—at the invitation of the Princess of Wales—she telephoned her mother and told her she was going to marry Paddy. In the late afternoon as she got off the bus at Balmoral she knew 'it was Andrew'. As the Italians say, 'the thunderbolt' had struck.

Prior to Balmoral, the press had made much of Sarah's presence in the royal box at Ascot (June 1985). But at that time, Sarah was merely one of a group of friends that circulated around Prince Andrew. From childhood Sarah had mixed with the Royal Family, and she had been a close friend and confidante of Diana's for some time. With her relationship with Paddy at the forefront of her mind during the summer months, her meetings with Andrew were strictly on a good friends basis. Nothing more. During the last few days of August and early September her feelings for Andrew 'changed from cold to hot'. But she 'hadn't a clue what to do about it. It all seemed so impossible.' By the time she arrived back in London she was in that peculiar state of 'wobbily knees' and absent-mindedness familiar to the newly in-love: two friends she drove from Heathrow vowed they'd never get in a car again, at least not one driven by Sarah! The same evening she and Paddy had a blazing row, and 'that was that'!

For the Royals, the path to true love is invariably impeded, and even accelerated, by journalists. By January 1986 the press were in a high old state: features on Sarah's clothes, her figure, her hair, her favourite food, and her impeccable pedigree appeared with growing frenzy and by the time she joined the royal skiing party at Klosters in early February, according to most of the tabloids, she and Andrew were as good as married. However, this was all news to Sarah and Andrew. Despite their mutually strong feelings, they spent little time together: Andrew, as a naval officer, was on duty on HMS **Brazen** much of the time. The separations were particularly agonizing for Sarah, whose security threshold is rather low. But by 24 February some of Sarah's doubts and uncertainties disappeared when Andrew proposed. Sarah, in characteristic fashion, offered to let him take it (the proposal) back the next day if he wanted to. Of course, he didn't. When the Queen returned from Australia she gave her permission for the marriage and was apparently 'overjoyed'. Prince Philip, however, was a little concerned that the wedding might interfere with the start of the shooting season or Cowes Week!

At the time of writing, the wedding on 23 July is still some months away. Once the hectic preparations and the day itself are behind them, Sarah and Andrew will be faced with the development of their relationship on an intimate level and the expansion of their roles as public figures. Astrologically, their relationship looks very strong indeed.* There are some spendid pointers for durability and good team-work—both of them stressed their ability to work as a team on their engagement. But like any relationship it's not perfect. In their relationship chart, like the Prince and Princess of Wales, the planet Uranus figures strongly.† On one level this suggests their interaction is a volatile one and the relationship has huge peaks and troughs: they may well encounter periods where they feel 'trapped' by the relationship, then others where they feel totally at one with each other. On another level, as a couple they may experience a sudden change in the tide of their affairs—and their outer roles could alter dramatically. The astrology paints a curious mixture of freedom and

*Composite Saturn conjunct composite Mercury (the Ascendant and MC ruler); composite Sun conjunct the IC; composite Sun in wide trine to composite Uranus; composite Mars conjunct composite Jupiter.

†Uranus is the most elevated planet in the composite chart. Composite Uranus is square composite Venus.

joie de vivre versus heavy responsibility.

Certainly Sarah's fear that a sense of complacency will develop in her marriage is singularly unlikely: neither individual is the complacent type and both seek a degree of excitement and expansion in their relationships.* Both also need security. Andrew is to Sarah a strong, calm, and very gentle man—'a woman's man'. Thus Sarah brings out the Piscean in Andrew. And, although as a Libra-Pisces couple, they may encounter many of the problems of an air-water relationship—lots of discussion but a tendency to miss the emotional point—they are both very giving individuals and neither can stand a cold war for long. Sarah finds herself in the typical Libran position of rushing off to buy peace offerings even when she may not be the one to blame!

Two of Sarah's greatest gifts are her energy and her vivacity. She has Aries true-grit and Scorpio resolve bound up in a gracious and benevolent Libran package. As she matures, her sterling qualities will be ever more evident and ever more valuable to the Royal Family. No astrologer with access to Sarah's chart prior to the engagement could have doubted her destiny to join the royal ranks. She has extremely close links with all the Royals, particularly the Queen Mother, whose chart closely resembles her own. With her Venus-Pluto conjunction on the highest point of the chart, there are indications that her role will be anything but a minor one. When Pluto, her chart ruler, crosses the Ascendant in the early 1990s some of this potential will be released. During this time almost all members of the Royal Family show change and transformation in their charts. What all this ultimately means is not for me to ponder upon and for all of us to find out as history unfolds.

Of one thing we can be sure, HRH the Duchess of York will more than make her mark in life.

Postscript: My original draft made far more of the Duchess's Finger of Fate in her horoscope. I suggested (among other possibilities) that this configuration could indicate some problems with the reproductive system. I came under pressure to remove this since it might arouse fears that Sarah would be unable to have children. Now (April 1988) the Duchess's pregnancy is in its 5th month. I feel able to elaborate on the astrology. I did not feel this astrological pattern would **deny** children but that she would experience problems in this area—fibroids or infections, perhaps—even a premature baby. There were strong rumours circulating throughout 1987 that Sarah's increased concern over her failure to conceive had urged her to take a fertility drug.

While this pregnancy may indeed result in a healthy offspring, the Duchess may be prone to subsequent miscarriages—indeed, it was alleged that she had

---

*Uranus is the ruler of Andrew's 7th 'house': Sarah's Uranus is square her Ascendant-Descendant axis.

had an early miscarriage in 1987–though she could well have other successful pregnancies.

Note for Astrologers: (1) When Sarah was fifteen and her mother left the family, relevant progressions and transits were as follows: progressed Sun and Mars were conjunct Neptune, transiting Uranus was conjunct her Sun and Mars, transiting Neptune was square the MC-IC axis, transiting Pluto opposed her Moon (and so triggered the Finger of Fate), and transiting Jupiter was conjunct the IC. The period covering the engagement and marriage (1986) progressed Sun was within one degree of the Ascendant, the progressed lunar return was imminent, progressed Venus was conjunct the north node. Transits were less significant. Transiting Saturn was within 3 degrees of the Ascendant in the September of 1985. In March 1986 transiting Jupiter conjoined the IC. On the day of the proposal, the Sun was opposing radical Pluto, transiting Venus was at 13° Pisces. On the wedding day, transiting Venus was at 13° Virgo, the north node was conjunct Andrew's MC and opposing Sarah's Sun-Mars conjunction.

(2) Aspects of the synastry between Sarah and Andrew are far too many and varied to go into here at length. Suffice to say, Sarah's Sun is conjunct Andrew's IC, while his Sun is conjunct her IC—thus each reflect the other's deepest psychological and emotional needs. The awkward Venus-Uranus square in the composite, although unsettling, does reflect the Uranian colouring to relationships in both their charts—Sarah has Uranus square the Asc-Desc axis, and the Sun and Mars are sextile Uranus; Andrew's Moon is square Uranus, and he has Uranus on his Ascendant in exact square to Sarah's Ascendant. The composite has an extremely powerful alignment involving the MC-IC axis in exact square to the nodal axis and the vertices. To me, this suggests a significant and destined partnership, especially as 29° of the mutables appears to be one of the major royal degree areas.

PROFILE OF A LIBRA MAN

CHRISTOPHER REEVE

No, it's not a bird nor a plane, it's Libra-man, Christopher Reeve! Better known to many of his fans as Superman. And in the way that truth is often stranger than fiction, Christopher Reeve himself has tapped some supernormal levels of experience that could well turn his fictional role into a reality—one day.

Christopher's biography reads like one enormous success story. He appears to have lead a charmed life with only one or two clouds to spoil its sunny horizons. Christopher was born and brought up in New York, the eldest son of two temperamentally very different parents. His mother and father split up when he was four, although his mother remarried three years later and had two more children. His father also married again and had three children by his second wife. While his mother and step-father, with whom he lived, led a comfortable, middle-class existence, his father—a poet and translator—lived a somewhat bohemian life. Where his mother was concerned, Christopher could do no wrong: he was a golden child and adored by her. With his father, however, he could do no right. Thus from an early age Christopher found himself with a Libran problem on his hands: maintaining the balance between the two very different family environments and sorting out whose opinion of him was the right one! 'Was my childhood happy? I'd say it was successful. Full of achievement and opportunity. But when I see photographs of myself as a boy, I was never smiling. I was a serious and a precocious child—older than my years.'

School was a series of glittering successes for Christopher: 'I adapted to school life very well.' He was top of his class, captain of

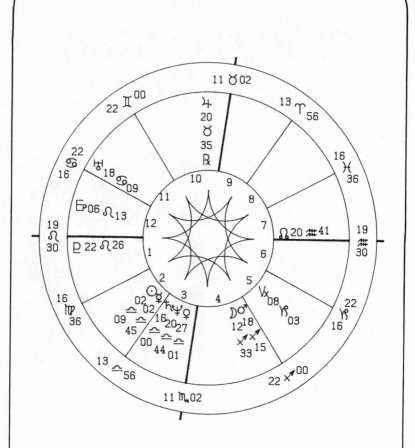

CHRISTOPHER REEVE

25 9 1952   3h 14m Os EDT

KOCH 40N45 73W57

the team, student council representative, star at ice hockey, and conductor of the school choir. Since he was a high achiever in sport, athletics, music, and drama, there were many potential avenues for him to follow as a career. But by fifteen Christopher knew that he wanted to be an actor, a decision that won the wholehearted approval of both families.

Christopher is very Libran indeed. He has five planets in this sign—the Sun, Mercury, Venus, Saturn, and Neptune. Thus from an early age he would have felt a strong desire to please—first his parents and his teachers, and last of all himself. It is usually the strongly Capricornian child who feels older than his years and has responsibility thrust upon his small shoulders at an early age. While Christopher has no Capricorn per se in his chart, Saturn (Capricorn's ruling planet) is placed in his Sun sign, although at some distance from the Sun itself. The early trauma of his parent's break-up is not immediately obvious in his chart: the Moon and Mars seem fairly innocuous in the fourth 'house' of home and family. But although Mars in this house can merely represent an energetic home life, one that is full of strenuous activity and non-stop action, it can also indicate that one parent (most usually father) was a force to be reckoned with.* Certainly with the Moon close to Mars, home and family was (and is) extremely important to Christopher. It is Pluto, the natural ruler of the fourth 'house', that suggests the upheaval and trauma in the early home life. Since Pluto contacts Jupiter in the tenth 'house' and Mars in the fourth, Pluto colours Christopher's experience of 'Mum and Dad'; thus there is an indication that he might well have felt somewhat oppressed by one or both parents. Christopher was, of course 'adored by mother'; yet she became very emotionally dependent upon him. She was only twenty when Christopher was born and in some ways was unready for motherhood. This, combined with the separation from her husband, meant that Christopher and his brother became her emotional life-line. Christopher felt that he had to take care of her. Thus for all the opportunities and benefits he received from his comfortable background there was an emotional price to pay. And indeed, this early experience of mother as a burden—no matter how much he loved her—may well have coloured, albeit unconsciously, his expectations of women in general.

Astrologically, there is every indication that Christopher would have excelled at school. Not necessarily because he was gifted intellectually, but because he was highly motivated. Christopher has Leo—a sign of leadership—rising, and the Sun, his chart ruler is placed in ambitious Libra

---

*The fourth and tenth houses of the horoscope have much to do with the parents: the 4th is usually associated with father, the tenth with mother.

together with Mercury–the planet of intellect and communication.*
This combination of Leo-Libra would have made him a popular and
strong and effective figurehead. With Leo rising and the planetary
emphasis in Libra (a sign noted for its appreciation of music and the arts)
it's no surprise that Christopher shone in these areas. His flair for
athletics and sport in general is shown by his Mars in the sporty fire
sign, Sagittarius.

From high school, Christopher went on to Cornell University,
where he majored in English and minored in music. He graduated
from Cornell at twenty-one and won a place at Juilliard, where he
studied acting. Juilliard proved to be another success story for
Christopher. He played many lead roles while he was there, from
Shakespeare to Restoration comedy. 'It was one of the happiest
periods of my life. I loved being independent in New York. I was
poor but happy.' In the autumn of 1973 he started out professionally
and was working almost immediately. His first important part was
opposite Katharine Hepburn on Broadway in **A Matter of Gravity**. It
was after **Gravity**, while he was working off Broadway, that
Christopher was offered the chance to audition for **Superman**. 'I
really wasn't interested. I thought it sounded a bit silly. So I turned
down two auditions. But it must have been fate. It was Christmas
time and I was going home. The audition happened to be at the
Sherry Netherland Hotel which was on my way to Grand Central
Station, so I decided to go. If the audition had been anywhere else I
probably wouldn't have gone. When I saw the script I realized what
I'd nearly passed up!' Out of five hundred actors he was chosen for a
screen test and immediately afterwards (January 1977) he was offered
the part. **Superman** was a turning point in Christopher's life,
although with his abilities and his success rate (only twenty-two
when he played opposite Hepburn) he would have become a star
regardless. But as it happened, **Superman** was the perfect vehicle for
his talents.

Most people associate Christopher Reeve only with **Superman**
despite the diverse range of parts he has taken on since the first film[†]
He is entirely philosophical about this and doesn't appear to mind
this symbiosis. 'Superman was (and is) a very important part of my
life. I feel he is a very special image for children and I'm committed
to Superman because of that.' Indeed, there are many qualities about
Superman that Christopher identifies with. 'Clark Kent I don't
identify with at all. He's just an affectionate gesture to the Thirties.
No, it's the romantic optimism of Superman I relate to. He's a
gentleman.'

*The Sun is virtually combust (within 30 minutes) Mercury: an indication
(according to some sources) of mental genius.

†There have been four **Superman** films to date–all blockbuster successes.

Superman couldn't have a more ideal horoscope than Christopher's; and it is uncanny how man and myth merge so beautifully in the astrology. A great leader of men, an invincible hero, a helper of mankind, should have Leo rising; and with super-human powers he ought to have Pluto in a dominant position. Superman's skills and his 'brief' to help the human race are ideally represented through the Pluto-Ascendant contact in Christopher's chart. One astrology book* goes as far as to say '(Pluto conjunct the Ascendant) gives a kind of X-ray vision that enables the native to perceive the workings of the subtle forces of the universe, unknown to other people . . . they use secretive, and even superphysical means of accomplishing their purposes.' And yet another† says about the same aspect: 'You defend those entrusted to your care, and the people you love know that you will protect their interests at all costs.' As for Superman's 'romantic optimism', Jupiter on the Midheaven and Mars and Moon in Sagittarius 'provide' huge stores of optimism—and success too. Sagittarius is a sign renowned for a love of adventure and the spirit of 'the quest'. It is also a very philosophical sign and a highly philanthropic one. And what more could a romantic hero be blessed with but a stellium of planets in the most romantic sign of all—Libra. Not only this, but Venus, the planet of love and affection, is right next to idealistic, inspirational Neptune. This latter aspect often suggests that the individual puts those he loves on a pedestal and that his expectations of love are rather unrealistic, or never to be realized. 'I don't think Superman puts Lois Lane on a pedestal, but he certainly has a problem there. He can't show he loves one human being more than any other because he's meant to love the human race as a whole. Yet he's madly attracted to her.' In real life, Christopher also feels that he doesn't place the woman in his life on a pedestal. But with Uranus ruling his house of relationships and his Moon in free-spirited Sagittarius, he certainly wants something 'different' in his relationships—a partner who is 'growth-oriented', possibly even rather unconventional. He also believes in the power of love.

1977 was important for Christopher not only because of the 'birth' of **Superman**, but because he met Gae, his girlfriend and the mother of his two children Matthew (born in December 1979) and Alexandra (born November 1983). Gae is a Sun Capricorn with her Mars in Libra, her Venus in Sagittarius, and her Moon in Leo—all of which form major and harmonious contacts to Christopher's chart. They have 'a good understanding' and their relationship grew out of warmth and friendship. However, Capricorn and Libra are two very different signs

*The Astrologer's Handbook by Sakoian and Acker.

†Planets in Aspect by Robert Hand.

temperamentally: Capricorn is enormously realistic and practical while Libra is more ephemeral. Thus no doubt there are times in their relationship when they feel poles apart. On the plus side, Libra and Capricorn usually make a good working team and neither takes their commitments or their decisions lightly. Christopher clearly adores his children and takes his responsibilities as a father seriously: 'I don't think I'm a great dad because I'm away so much. But I don't believe in uprooting my children and taking them all over the world. I think it's important they are settled and have continuity in their lives.' While his family life and his relationship provide the necessary security and stability in his life, he also needs to feel his relationships are constantly expanding and reflecting his changing attitudes and requirements.

There is a powerful spiritual theme in Christopher's chart. While such potential sometimes lies dormant in the individual's consciousness, in Christopher's case it has well and truly asserted itself. When I tentatively mentioned to Christopher the possibility of an interest in spiritual matters I anticipated that even if he were to acknowledge such a leaning he would be unprepared to discuss it. Happily he was not. 'My acting coach is a dedicated spiritual follower and this together with my own ideas filter through into my approach to my work. I do a lot of work with dreams and use visualization techniques. I practise meditation ... I've worked with spiritual healers and I'm a great believer in holistic medicine. But I have a strong intellectual and rational side too and I don't see why they should be mutually exclusive.'

Astrologically, there are several indicators of Christopher's interest in the paranormal. Moon and Mars in Sagittarius are just as much adventurers of inner space as they are of the physical world—a factor that is emphasized by Mars' 60° (sextile) aspect to Neptune.* Sometimes a Mars-Neptune contact can indicate self-delusion and a desire to avoid reality by escaping into flights of fancy—or the gin-bottle; but in Christopher's case Neptune is under the control of Saturn (which in turn sextiles Mars); thus he approaches any extrasensory experience or phenomena with caution, reason, and even a touch of healthy scepticism. Indeed, this Mars-Moon/Saturn-Neptune contact indicates a high level of mature spiritual insight based on practical experience. The Sun and Mercury and their contact to Uranus† also suggest unusual, possibly even telepathic, mental powers and certainly a well-developed intellect. But it is Pluto's

*Neptune is a planet synonymous with the arts, film, and photography: all of which have figured in Christopher's life.

†Sun and Mercury quintile Uranus.

placing on the Ascendant in Leo that provides the greatest 'food' for spiritual thought.

The transformative nature of Pluto is a powerful influence to have on what is arguably the most sensitive and personal point of the birth chart. Leaving aside the more negative properties of this planet (such as obstinacy, paranoia, and misuse of power), Pluto in its finest aspect puts the individual in touch with the highest levels of consciousness and spirituality. Sometimes, in order to reach such levels, the individual is pushed to the limits of his physical, mental, or emotional capabilities. Leo has much to do with journeys of self-discovery; thus Christopher's attitude to his life and work reflects these combined principles of transformation through development of the higher self. Like many people who have one of the outer planets rising at birth Christopher felt 'different' from other people.* 'By the age of nine or ten I knew I'd come to do something. What, was not clear but I felt it was a noble calling. Pieces of this are constantly being revealed.' Christopher has also had paranormal experiences that have convinced him of the existence of 'higher forces' and other levels of being.

That Christopher senses he has a mission in life might urge the sceptic to assume that he has over-identified with his Superman role, or at the very least is suffering from severe delusions of grandeur. But Christopher is far too intelligent and pragmatic to succumb to any such delusions. Indeed, he is one of several individuals in the arena of public life who is 'coming out of the closet' and revealing his interest in spiritual matters and their practical application in life. As such, Christopher is joining others in spearheading a spiritual upsurge in the collective unconscious.

Christopher has always been a leader in one capacity or another—as captain of his school team, as a leading man, and even portraying leaders of men on stage and screen. Thus it is tempting to speculate that he may well be a real leader of men in time to come, perhaps as a political figure. 'Politics could be a direction I might go in later. But not at the moment. There's too much that I still want to do in film and theatre. There are, I feel, certain limitations in politics and with politicians—a politician is always trying to please all of the people all of the time and can never follow his own inner direction. A really creative person looks inside himself and moves from his inner voice.'

In keeping with the transformative nature of his rising Pluto, Christopher is compelled to continually change his persona—changes that are brought about as much as a result of his outer challenges as his inner journeys. **Superman** is one such outer challenge that in some synchronous way has reflected Christopher's inner potential.

*See also profiles of Sarah Miles and Clare Francis (pp.427,37).

And I for one have a sneaking suspicion that Superman is alive and well and working for the good of mankind through the mild-mannered persona of Christopher Reeve. And I won't be in the least surprised when in real life he assumes the voice of the American people and takes up residence in a large white building in a place called Washington.

Note for Astrologers: (1) In regard to Christopher's fourth house Mars. Howard Sasportas's comments in **The Twelve Houses** make interesting and thought-provoking reading: 'Those with this placement may have to do battle with father in order to reclaim their own sense of autonomy and freedom of expression.'

(2) In 1977 when Christopher became 'Superman' and met Gae, progressions and transits of interest include: secondary progressed Ascendant trine the vertex, secondary progressed Sun conjunct Venus (Sun ruler); transiting Jupiter in Taurus—returning to its original position conjunct the MC; transiting Saturn conjunct the Ascendant-Pluto; transiting Neptune at the mid-point of Moon-Mars; transiting Pluto hovering around Saturn.

SCORPIO

23 October – 22 November

SAINTS, SINNERS, AND EMOTIONAL MEGALOMANIACS

SCORPIO
SAINTS, SINNERS, AND EMOTIONAL MEGALOMANIACS

EVEN those with a rudimentary knowledge of astrology tend to treat Scorpio with great respect, instinctively fearing its mystery, power, and strength. Scorpio is an enormously complex, some might say, fathomless sign; those individuals born with their Sun in Scorpio or who have a strong Scorpionic theme in their charts often appear enigmatic, impenetrable, and obscure.

As befits an enigma, a Scorpio individual rarely advertises his or her brooding complexity with a dark and swarthy countenance. Most are perfectly acceptable members of the human race—charming, courteous, and distinctly unthreatening. Only a few play out their archetypal image, cloaked in black, staring out at the world under hooded lids like some giant bird of prey—a cross between Theda Bara and Rasputin! But whatever front they project, it is worth remembering that it is designed (no matter how unconsciously) to mask an intense and turbulent inner nature. Of the other signs of the zodiac, only Cancer is as adept at creating such an inscrutable façade to protect its vulnerable emotional nature.

The one physical characteristic that almost all Scorpionic individuals share is a magnetic quality about the eyes; regardless of whether they are blue, brown, or indifferent, the eyes have a penetrating power, almost as if they could pierce the soul. The infamous Scorpio stare can be used to good effect in almost any situation to keep others at bay or at least on their guard; on the one hand, many Scorpios sport the best pair of 'bedroom' eyes in the zodiac; and on the other, those same eyes in anger can 'ice over' and immobilize an opponent at a glance. Small or tall, dark or fair, the typical Scorpio appears permanently poised for crisis; most are rarely at ease, unless secure among friends or family. While needing close emotional contact with others, an innate suspicion and highly efficient self-defence system frequently keeps others at arm's length.

Most Scorpios are fascinated by the mysterious and the occult—it simultaneously attracts yet alarms them. As an astrologer I am always prepared to be put through the proverbial wringer when consulted by a Scorpio client for the first time. They are rarely initially forthcoming since they want the astrologer to 'prove' herself (or himself) before revealing the slightest chink in their armour. Many are highly sceptical about astrology, but once impressed by the astrologer's accuracy, helpfulness, and, above all, confidentiality, they can become obsessively interested in the subject. Indeed, some of the best known names in serious astrology have a strongly Scorpionic theme in their charts—Liz Greene, Françoise and Michel Gauquelin, and Robert Hand.

At the risk of boring the reader with weighty symbolic insights, a brief foray into the myths behind Scorpio and its ruling planet, Pluto, may nonetheless provide some intriguing links to the inscrutable Scorpionic nature.

The symbol for Scorpio is the scorpion—a fascinating little creature, and at least in some forms, absolutely deadly. Much is made of the scorpion's ability to sting itself to death when encircled by fire, which, unfortunately is utter nonsense. I say unfortunately, because most astrologers like to allude to the scorpion's prediliction to die by its own hand, or rather its own sting, as symbolic of the way Scorpio individuals often seem hell-bent on self-destruction. Certainly, Scorpio types have a well-deserved reputation for cutting off their noses to spite their faces, but in my experience these individuals are some of life's greatest survivors, and the process of self-destruction is hardly ever a conscious or voluntary act.

Another piece of folklore that needs exploding is that the scorpion possesses an antidote to its own poison. While the scorpion may not be immune to its own poison it never, ever stings itself! Poetic licence notwithstanding, the Scorpio individual can be a pretty pugnacious and vindictive type, but, and it's a big 'but', only when attacked or hurt. The Scorpion only stings in self-defence, but when it stings it goes for the kill. Most Scorpio individuals have a strong sense of justice, but, unlike many Librans who dispassionately debate the finer aspects of just conduct and hate to get their hands dirty, Scorpio plots and plans his revenge (sometimes for years) with total destruction in mind! There are in fact only about half a dozen species of scorpion that are deadly—many are completely harmless. However, it is worth remembering that almost all, when stepped on, can give the offender a nasty twinge!

The scorpion tends to live in fairly inhospitable surroundings, often on the edge of humanity. While few Scorpio types actively seek out barely habitable or unpopulated terrains, they are often considered loners by others—or at least remote and unreachable much of the time. Again, this is not a self-imposed isolation but the result of an over-effective defence mechanism.

Perhaps one of the most interesting features about the scorpion is its ability (unrivalled in any other life form) to survive the most extreme conditions and hazards. Scorpions were found to have withstood the intense heat, blast, and radiation effects of a nuclear test site in Nevada. Yet some can equally well exist in extreme cold. As a species, they are slow to grow and mature and have an immensely long life span. What does this tell us about Scorpio? Certainly, there is no other sign capable of withstanding life's extremes, whether emotional, psychological, or physical; it is a sign of enormous tenacity, determination, and resistance. I can remember, as a child, experiencing the worst (English) Channel crossing for ten years. Waves lashed over the sides of the boat, everything that moved had to be strapped down, and everywhere you cared to look green and groaning faces bobbed up and down—that is, with the exception of my Scorpio mother. My mother, fearing that if she were to be ill she would need hospitalization—a fate worse, to her, almost than death—remained mute, statuesque, and rigid for the entire six-hour journey. It was only when she arrived home many hours later that she completely collapsed and was ill for days!

Whether Scorpios really live any longer than most other signs is difficult to prove; what is true, however, is that they have an incredible grip on life and rarely give up the ghost without an immense struggle.

There is a childhood rhyme about a little girl who had a curl and 'when she was good, she was very, very good, but when she was bad she was horrid!'

This was obviously written with Scorpio in mind. No other sign of the zodiac presents such a range of potential from the most base to the most elevated—not only from one Scorpio to another but within each individual Scorpio. The Scorpio at its highest level is symbolized by the eagle—admittedly a bird of prey, but nevertheless a magnificent specimen whose wing span averages six feet and whose powerful structure enables it to soar higher than any other winged creature. The mythological background to the eagle is literally vast, but suffice to say most cultures associated this bird with power, spiritual strength and, in some parts of the world, war. Many individuals tap this Scorpio aspect of the eagle in their life and work, particularly in the healing and the scientific professions. Marie and Pierre Curie, Alfred Nobel, Nikola Tesla, Sigmund Freud, and Dr Christian Barnard all have strong Scorpio themes in their charts.

The lower aspect of Scorpio is demonstrated by those who seem fatally attracted to an ultimately self-destructive path of ravage and debauchery. These are the individuals who experience the dark night of the soul. The Marquis de Sade (Pluto conjunct Mars with Mercury in Scorpio), Charles Manson (Sun, Mercury, Venus and Jupiter in Scorpio), and Aleister Crowley (Mercury and Jupiter in Scorpio) are three such individuals—the latter two combining the Scorpionic extremes of drugs and magical practices.

The Scorpionic individual more than any other seems compelled toward extremes of light and darkness, whether as an onlooker or through direct personal experience. It is the Scorpios of this world who, when physically, emotionally, or psychologically devastated, gain immense inner strength through their struggle and emerge out of the debris of a situation like a phoenix rising from the ashes. Allegorically this process is mirrored by nature's cycle of death and rebirth, which is at its most potent while the Sun passes through the sign of Scorpio in late October and November. During this period of the year (at least in the northern hemisphere), Nature stands bare and stark to the elements, while her energies are poured underground to rekindle the life process. Many Scorpios are intensely curious about the cycles of life and death: to some this amounts merely to a morbid fascination about death, to others a deep interest in life after death. Of course, there are many whose work involves them (daily) in life and death situations—the police and the medical profession are two strongly Scorpionic institutions. On the other hand, almost all Scorpios find the sexual, emotional, and psycho-spiritual aspects of conception and childbirth absorbing, if not obsessive. Indeed, I once spent most of a dinner party discussing aspects of the menstrual cycle and childbirth with a Sun Scorpio man to whom I had just been introduced!

Certainly many of the themes mentioned so far have their symbolic roots in the Pluto-rulership of this sign, most particularly the death of Nature, which is beautifully portrayed in the myth of Pluto and Persephone.* This Greek myth is probably the most familiar allegorical rendering of Nature's demise,

---

*Pluto abducted Persephone and held her captive in his underworld kingdom. Her mother, Demeter, deeply distressed, searched the length and breadth of the Earth for her, during which time Nature withered and died. Pluto eventually compromised and allowed Persephone to leave his kingdom and return to Earth for six months of each year—a time when the Earth became once more rich and fruitful.

but all cultures contain myths upon this theme. Scandinavian lore tells of Balder 'the Beautiful', the second son of Odin, who was inestimably kind, handsome, and good. Despite all his mother, Frigg's, efforts to ensure his safety after Balder had dreamed of his death, he was killed in an act of treachery engineered by the mischievous, Mercurial god, Loki (see Gemini p.103). Frigg was desolated at Balder's death and begged one of the gods to go down to the kingdom of Hel—the kingdom of the dead—to bring him back. (Since Balder had not died in battle, he had not gone on to glory in Valhalla.) Hermod, another of Odin's sons accepted the challenge. After a journey lasting nine days* he came to the land of the dead whereupon he found the goddess, Hel, and asked her to release Balder. She agreed to do so only if everything on earth, living and dead, mourned Balder.

On Hermod's return, messengers travelled the world commanding everything to weep for Balder. All things willingly complied with the exception of a witch—Thokk. Thus Balder could not be saved, and the world knew no more true happiness, justice, or beauty. However, the gods, assuming Thokk had been none other than Loki in one of his disguises, caught him and bound him hand and foot. In consequence, evil was not wholly triumphant and the world became a mixture of pure and impure, joy and tears, beauty and ugliness, life and death.

Scandinavian myth propounded that from the time Loki was captured the world would degenerate until its dissolution. After the great catastrophe, there would be a rebirth; the earth would emerge anew from the ocean; the sons of the gods would return to Asgard (the homeland of the gods); and the earth would be fertile and beautiful. This was to be the return of Balder.

Polarization runs rife through this myth—the struggle between good and evil, death and rebirth—although there are some more obscure insights to be gained from the tale. Loki is an entirely Mercury-Gemini figure; he is constantly skirting the edge of darkness, running the gamut between plain mischief and outright treachery. Gemini has much to do with opposites and many of the symbols and myths pertaining to this air sign have major connections with Scorpio-Pluto (see Gemini p.105). Scorpio and Gemini individuals, perhaps more than most, are propelled between opposite 'forces', both on an inner and outer level. The inescapable hand of fate is also much in evidence in this tale. And ultimately all the characters involved and their actions (for good or bad) can be seen to be working towards an immutable outcome. Astrologically, Pluto, of all the planets, has the strongest association with fate and destiny. And to a certain degree most Scorpio individuals can relate to feeling 'up against fate' periodically in their lives, when no matter how they try to block, avert or change a situation, they are compelled toward an inexorable chain of events.

Pluto, to date the outermost known planet in the Solar System, poses an enigma for astronomers. According to its size, mass, and orbit, it should not, by the laws of physics, have the apparent effect on Neptune that it does. Some have speculated that the planet's surface is covered with ice, thus all that can be seen of Pluto is the Sun's reflection on the ice—a factor that

---

*Although days are specified here, the nine-fold cycle of time possibly reflects the nine-month gestation period.

renders most of the planet invisible. In Greek myth, Pluto, God of the Underworld, was a dark and mysterious figure who frequently employed a magic helmet that made him invisible. Here, aspects of both the physical planet and the mythological god underline the smokescreen tactics of most Scorpio/Pluto natives—their ability to project an outer reticence that belies the strength and impact of their true natures. One of the most important functions of Pluto in astrology is in its effect on the unconscious, influencing the motives and impulses that lie hidden behind the individual's behaviour that, in turn, have a powerful effect on the outcome of his life.

Which leads us to another important dimension of the Pluto principle—that of transformation. Scorpionic or Plutonic individuals periodically encounter crisis points in their lives through which, as I have already discussed they usually emerge stronger and wiser. In many ways this sheds new light on the kamikaze approach to life displayed by some Scorpios, for their behaviour need not be judged as a sort of self-destructive leitmotiv, but instead a natural urge towards transformation.

Scorpios, like no other members of the zodiac, need crisis points both to charge and release their powerful emotional and psychological energy. They experience a deep and necessary satisfaction from pitting themselves against almost anything, especially if it involves championing the cause of the rejected underdog. Unfortunately, many of them fail to recognize just how many problems and dramatic situations they actually create themselves.

In many ways the late Richard Burton was a classic example of the individual whose life was a continual process of crisis, trauma, and transformation. One of eleven children from a poor Welsh family, he struggled to become one of the finest actors Britain had ever produced. At a peak in his career and after such fine performances as Becket in the film of the same name, he was lured to Hollywood by the prospect of fame, fortune, and Elizabeth Taylor. In true Scorpionic style he turned his back on everything he had built up and previously valued—his first wife, a fine theatrical career as a natural successor to Olivier, and, some would say, his senses! In the mid-1960s and early 1970s he became the highest paid film actor of his time, reflected in an extravagant and lavish life-style. He also pushed his body to its limits in a punishing regime of alcohol and high living; his work and reputation suffered tremendously in consequence. After divorcing, remarrying, and divorcing Elizabeth Taylor, he married twice more, but the cycle was downward to ever more personal excesses, depression, and disillusionment. Sad to say, at the point in his life when his phoenix was poised to rise from the ashes, with a happy and fulfilling marriage to his fourth wife, Sally, and a return to the sort of calibre role and performance he was worthy of—the film of Orwell's **Nineteen Eighty-Four**—he died suddenly and tragically.

Until the discovery of Pluto, Scorpio was ruled by the warlike planet Mars, and to a certain extent there is a bellicose element in every Scorpio individual. Of course, this aggressive streak is by no means as raw or as evident as it is in the impulsive Aries man or woman. The Scorpio is every bit as ignitable as Aries, but infinitely more subtle. Instead of rushing headfirst into action and thinking afterwards, like a Martian, Scorpio lets his anger fester and simmer until it builds to a point where its action is finite and absolute. Aries' weapons are swords, pistols, and battering rams—Scorpio's are of the nuclear variety. It is an interesting cosmic 'accident' that the evolution of the atom bomb coincided with the discovery of Pluto, and that Plutonium is central to its composition. Neither can it be merely by chance that the 'father of the atom bomb', Robert Oppenheimer, was not only a Sun Scorpio but had Pluto on his Ascendant.

Scorpio is the sort of hero and fighter that makes Aries look like a bumbling amateur—there is hardly anything Scorpio cannot do if he wants to, or in order to protect and survive. Most have a steel backbone and the women in particular, an iron hand in a velvet glove. Margaret Thatcher, dubbed by the Russians 'The Iron Lady', has Scorpio rising and Saturn in Scorpio on her Ascendant. Within minutes of the IRA assassination attempt on her life at Brighton in 1984, she picked her way through the rubble and debris of her hotel to emerge calm and serene with not a hair out of place—and at 3 a.m. Six hours later she appeared at the Party Conference and gave her speech as scheduled. To the world at large she was supremely in control, and despite coming within a hair's breadth of losing her life, she displayed no weakness whatsoever.

Akin to their fighting spirits, most Scorpions are intensely ambitious, although few will admit it and many even fail to recognize it. Some Scorpios also have a somewhat cruel and malicious streak; thus although they can be entirely selfless and altruistic, they are equally capable of ruthless behaviour on occasion especially as a defence tactic or in the pursuit of a desired objective. Sometimes the root of Scorpios' ambition lies in an early deprivation of some sort—perhaps there was little money available in their childhood, or they may have been underrated or passed over at some time. Ambition in Scorpio's case is linked to power and control, rarely to prestige. Scorpios seldom seek money for money's sake, rather for the sense of security it provides. Of course there are some Scorpios who are ambitious for their ideals and beliefs—many religious and political fanatics have Pluto or Scorpio well featured in their charts.

In order to relate to Scorpio and comprehend their all or nothing approach to life, one must understand that they are primarily and forcefully motivated by their feelings. Anger, jealousy, happiness, love, and hate are felt with seering sharpness and almost unbearable intensity, such that they are compelled to respond in kind. To make matters more complex, most Scorpios (unless they have many fiery planets in their charts) recognize the sometimes destructive power of their feelings and subsequent actions, and thus try to control and, hold them back. Scorpios, or those with a strong Pluto theme in their charts, excel at repressing and suppressing their emotions—a practice that ultimately brings them more difficulties.

Of course, emotions aren't the only things that are suppressed with Scorpios. Some act on the belief that if you refuse to acknowledge something, it cannot have any effect. With this in mind, many Scorpio men and women never consult a doctor, or a marriage counsellor, or an accountant before it is too late; in Scorpio's book, admitting something might be wrong or asking for help is tantamount to admitting defeat. Most, of course, worry frantically behind the closed doors of their minds, which has a further detrimental effect on their psychological, emotional, and physical health.

Paradoxically, once something is out in the open, Scorpios use their fighting spirits courageously to attack the situation, and most surmount their difficulties: it is a sign of enormous strength and resourcefulness, and most also have excellent recuperative powers.

While trying to keep a tight lid on their bubbling emotions, and in the process hoping they'll magically disappear, Scorpios constantly analyse and re-analyse situations and impressions. They are never content with a superficial knowledge of anything: many Scorpio/Pluto types make excellent researchers, psychologists, detectives, and undercover agents, and few skeletons remain in other people's cupboards when Scorpios are on the scent. However, with their deeply creative minds, Plutonic individuals are inclined to imagine all sorts of dastardly things being thought about or being done to them by others—consequently a great many of them live in a perpetual state of semi-paranoia!

Many astrologers have likened the Scorpio temperament to the Norwegian fjords or the Scottish lochs—depending on the weather, serene and picturesque when fine, remote and brooding when overcast. The important point about the metaphor, however, is that mountain lakes are usually immensely deep, and, particularly in the case of Loch Ness, impenetrably dense from a certain depth (due to black silt-like deposits). Of course, Loch Ness has the added bonus of a monster lurking in its depths. Perhaps it is not stretching poetic licence too far to suggest that every Scorpio carries a monster within himself, usually in the form of an emotional or psychological war wound, that surfaces from time to time to create major disruption. Needless to say, if the monster were confronted, it would no doubt turn out to be relatively harmless, since its ferociousness is considerably inflated by fear.

Never underestimate Scorpio. Members of this sign rarely make a song and dance about themselves—they move in mysterious and sometimes inexplicable ways. Make a friend of Scorpio and he or she is yours for life, but become an enemy or betray their trust and you'll need a fallout shelter for protection. As a sign of acute extremes, Scorpio individuals can provide a shining torch of insight and strength for others to follow, or a fetid well in which to fester over their turbulent thoughts and feelings.

RELATIONSHIPS

For a sign synonymous with extremes, relationships for Scorpio are either intoxicatingly wonderful or hellishly difficult: often both levels are experienced in one relationship. As I mentioned in the previous section, Scorpios rarely become loners voluntarily. Both sexes need the intimate understanding and emotional closeness provided by a secure and deep relationship. Indeed, security and depth are perhaps the most important ingredients in a relationship for this sign. However male and female Scorpios tend to be extremely self-protective, and in some cases, rather than run the risk of being hurt, they will avoid entering a relationship that will make huge emotional demands on them, or periodically cut off or distance themselves from a partner.

THE FEMALE SCORPIO

Think of Bette Davis, or rather the types of heroine she plays (especially the aptly named 'Jezebel' for which she won an Academy Award) and you have an extremely accurate portrait of the Scorpio woman in full flight. Bette Davis has her Ascendant in Scorpio and her Moon conjunct Pluto, and her intensely proud, volatile, passionate spirit is the hallmark of her personality both on screen and in real life. Ms Davis is ideal in other ways, too: she has sultry looks, not to mention a pair of extraordinary flashing eyes; in her youth, she could both seduce a man with a lingering look and a sweep of her lashes yet stop him dead in his tracks with a withering glare. She has a fearsome reputation as an actress, not only for sheer professionalism and high standards, but over the years she has fought for her rights with various film companies and in consequence been suspended sixteen times without pay. Her private life has been no less stormy; with four marriages behind her to date, she is quoted as saying 'The theatre was the one great durable romance of my life.'*

But not all Scorpio females are so easily identifiable. Many are blonde, sweet, and shy—even frothy—like the American actress/producer Goldie Hawn. However, such an outer appearance could be likened to Loch Ness on a sunny day—penetrate the surface and a miasma of bubbling emotions lurks below.

The Scorpio female is all woman—a mixture of Scarlett O'Hara, La Dame aux Camélias, and Mata Hari: she can be utterly alluring, gentle, and yielding one moment, then as wild as an alley cat on heat the next. Of all the signs of the zodiac, Ms Scorpio is potentially the most devious and the most manipulative, although she would hotly and passionately refute such labelling.

Scorpio women are often as much of a mystery to themselves as they are to everybody else—including their partners. Like the Cancerian female, Ms Scorpio picks up emotions and subtle undercurrents like a psychic sponge and becomes completely emotionally waterlogged in the process. Once she feels her intuition is right, absolutely nothing can persuade her otherwise. However, unlike some of the other signs of the zodiac, Ms Scorpio will never confront an individual with her fears or suspicions; she will weave an intricate web of verbal and emotional ploys to trap her suspect instead. Invariably, if her worst fears are founded, she wishes she hadn't found out; yet, even if they are unfounded, a vestige of suspicion will always remain. Ms Scorpio yearns to be loved and needed, yet her volatile emotional structure somehow drives her to destroy those she loves most through mistrust and frequent displays of stormy petulance.

As a child, the Scorpio female is likely to have been instinctively, but not intellectually, aware of the emotional and sexual undercurrents between her parents. Indeed, the Scorpio little girl usually manipulates her father pretty well from the age of two onward and frequently considers her mother a rival for her father's affections. Given a secure and happy family life, in adulthood the Scorpio female should be able to harness her powerful emotional energy into the sort of intense relationship she requires. But presented with a pattern

*Ms Davis is a Sun Aries with her Venus and Moon in Gemini.

of unhappiness or emotional deprivation as a child, the Scorpio tendency to repress and cut off from painful feelings will manifest instead, giving rise to stormy and unsatisfactory relationships.

As mentioned in the previous section, the Scorpio imagination is very fertile indeed; in youth, Ms Scorpio may have developed a passion for strong romantic literature and most often identified with tragic heroines—a practice that tends to imprint itself on her unconscious to the extent that in adulthood she often encounters a tragic element in her own relationships. In some cases this can be as dramatic as the death of a beloved fiancé or the prevention of marriage by parents or fateful circumstances. Princess Margaret (Moon conjunct Pluto and Venus square Pluto) is a case in point since she was pressured by the government and her family to give up the divorced Peter Townsend. Her subsequent marriage to Lord Snowdon also led to much bitterness and despair. Eva Braun (Ascendant in Scorpio and Moon square Pluto) is another: she chose to die with her lover, Adolf Hitler, rather than live without him. More usually, however, the tragedy of the Scorpio female is that she never feels loved enough or treated as she deserves to be. I must add that fated or tragic circumstances in the love-life are more likely with Pluto contacts to a woman's Moon, Venus or Descendant rather than merely the placing of the Sun, Moon, Venus or Ascendant in Scorpio.

Certainly the Scorpio female's relationships are never lightweight or superficial. Unless she has a strong Uranus or personal planets in Gemini or Sagittarius, she is psychologically and emotionally unsuited to a casual love affair; however, she can use sex to achieve her ends. She is also attracted to complex individuals who provide a constant challenge to her analytical and probing personality—and, one must remember, like attracts like! Another important commodity for the Scorpio female is security. This female cannot function when she is emotionally all at sea: like Ms Pisces and Ms Cancer she needs constant reassurance and emotional feedback to anchor and stabilize her. Unfortunately, sometimes for the sake of security, Ms Scorpio will put up with an emotionally and sexually unfulfilling relationship, becoming increasingly bitter in the process.

In keeping with the fundamental Scorpio theme of extreme feelings and actions, females who have this sign (or Pluto) prominent in their charts are capable of experiencing the very best and the very worst in relationships. At the highest level, the Scorpio female who can tap the eagle within her can scale the very peaks of romantic, sexual, and spiritual love. Indeed, many Scorpio women, like most Pisceans, want a soul mate: they are not content merely with a good emotional and sexual rapport, they seek a spiritual or psychic level of contact with a partner. If Ms Scorpio finds her soul mate, her relationship can touch some extraordinary levels of depth and sensitivity, and the shared experience of love transforms an otherwise ordinary life into something very special indeed.

Still at the upper end of the Scorpio extreme, the Plutonic female may find a man worthy enough to pour upon him her apparently inexhaustible supply of love, affection, and devotion. When this woman loves, it is a total commitment and there are no lengths to which she will not go to protect, nurture, and adore her man.

At the opposite extreme, some Scorpio females seem to attract more than their fair share of trauma in the form of emotional, psychological, and even physical violence through one-to-one relationships. The reasons why some women (regardless of Sun sign) accept such violent treatment in relationships are manifold, ranging from disturbed and aggressive childhood experiences to a deep-seated lack of self-worth. The Scorpio woman who finds such a pattern developing in her relationships may discover the problem lies in an inability to deal with her own anger. As mentioned earlier, confrontation is often avoided by Scorpios—they prefer to bring things into the open by gentle underground prodding and manipulation so that they have time to retreat if necessary. Combined with a dislike of confrontation is a fear of the effects of their anger. Many find it extremely difficult to respond immediately and honestly to a contentious issue or hurt; they block their anger, allowing it to emerge only in snide or cruel comments or icy silences. Consequently, many experience anger vicariously through their partner. Even those females who do not necessarily experience physical violence in their relationships nevertheless seem prone to a fair degree of friction and tension with their partner.

Relationships for most Scorpio women are a mixture of these two extremes. Sometimes the Scorpio female will find a partner who suits her emotionally and sexually, yet she periodically feels hard done by and unloved. Like Ms Cancer, she often recalls a previous, more glorious relationship that slipped through her fingers, or which she renounced for all sorts of reasons—very possibly her present husband! She sometimes hints to close friends, or other members of the family, that there are unmentionable things she has had to bear in secret and perhaps one day everyone will appreciate her suffering . . . A typical Scorpio marriage is likely to have many glorious ups and some calamitous downs; for a while everything runs well, then suddenly divorce seems just around the corner. Much as Ms Scorpio would like her relationships to be as smooth as silk, her intense and complex inner nature simply won't allow it. Even when things are peaceful and serene, she's poised for the next crisis!

Certainly the Scorpionic female is unfailingly loyal, and it is usually extremely difficult for her to be unfaithful—the guilt she experiences and the self-torture she goes through are unrivalled in the zodiac. She also fears getting out of her depth in an extra-marital affair. Thus, despite her ability to attract and magnetize any man she wants, while one hand beckons 'come-hither', the other carries a 'Trespassers, keep out' sign! Yet sometimes through deep emotional or sexual dissatisfaction with a partner, Ms Scorpio will succumb to an extra-marital relationship. The affair is never casual or light-hearted. The Scorpio female is incapable of half measures and once she has crossed the emotional and sexual Rubicon, there is no turning back. Furthermore, as soon as her emotional and physical allegiance has swung to a lover, she cannot respond to her husband. Thus, although Ms Scorpio may be devious and secretive enough to run a string of clandestine affairs, once her heart is captured her frigidity towards her husband inevitably gives her away.

A Scorpio client of mine, Eleanor, had been married to George for 38 years. They had two sons and three grandchildren. Their life together was secure but uneventful—that is until one afternoon she came face to face with her first love, David, in a restaurant. The impact of the meeting and the rewakening of memories and long-forgotten feelings were the spur that prompted her to consult me. Her story was an extraordinary mixture of fate and the Scorpionic obsessive self-will. She was seventeen when she fell in love with David, but, sadly he was posted overseas when the Second World War was declared. A few nights before he was due to leave, Eleanor suggested they should marry, but David, being a cautious Cancerian, preferred to wait until the war was over. Feeling rejected, desperately lonely, and not without a tinge of revenge, within a few weeks of his departure she married George. On her return from the honeymoon she found a telegram awaiting her from David: it read, 'I was wrong. Let's marry on my next leave.' Being the single-minded Scorpio lady that she was, she put David firmly out of her mind and threw herself body (but not soul) into marriage—at least for 38 years.

Eleanor's ensuing emotional crisis on seeing David again, caused reverberations not only through her own life but David's, his wife's, and George's. As an all-or-nothing Scorpio, she was prepared to walk out of her marriage and into the sunset with David, but she had reckoned without George's tenacity and David's less courageous stance. Despite her strenuous mental and emotional efforts to put back the clock and start life anew with David, it seemed that fate and everyone else had other ideas. Although David held mutually strong feelings for Eleanor, he was also immensely attached to his wife; eventually he and his wife moved hundreds of miles away, which should have brought the affair to a natural conclusion. But not for Eleanor. She sold the family home and, together with George, moved to within five miles of David.

To judge Eleanor's behaviour as ridiculous and selfish in the extreme is to forget that she is first and foremost a Scorpio lady. For 38 years she had kept the lid on her feelings tightly battened down. Yes, she loved George and the boys and her life was full. But it was only on seeing David that the tumultuous feelings of passion she was capable of were again released: the release was of atomic proportions, and, once exploded, there could be no turning back. David had become an obsession and her single-minded aim became to remain near him for the rest of her life, regardless of the disruption to George's life, not to mention the emotional turmoil for all concerned. It remains to be seen whether what would appear to be a highly self-destructive path leads to any kind of personal transformation.

Some men might consider living with a Scorpio woman necessitates a crash course in female psychology and psychic self-defence, for Plutonic ladies, by and large, need considerable understanding. Almost all are prone at times to impenetrable moods and silences. They are sensitive in the extreme and it takes only the smallest slight to trigger a spiral of mental and emotional angst. During a 'silence' most of them are frenetically trying to come to terms with their hurt and anger, and their partner needs sonar equipment to establish what is wrong: usually, of course, it's him! In many ways Ms Scorpio thrives on these kind of crises—she simultaneously revels in, yet is made distraught by, emotional scenes. Once it is over, however, she feels a tremendous emotional release: the whole process seems to recharge her emotional and psychological batteries.

The best way to deal with a Scorpionic woman in a bait is to force her to verbalize her grievances—trying to jolly her out of it is useless. Give her your point of view and allow her time to sulk and gnash her teeth! Then if you're not seething yourself, get her into bed as quickly as possible!

Ms Scorpio is also a great hoarder—not of objects, but memories and, more particularly, grievances. When a Plutonic lady says, 'I'll never forget what you've done!' she means it. What is sad, is that all too often Ms Scorpio over-reacts or misinterprets the other person's actions and, with her stubborn opinions impervious to argument, she makes an unnecessary enemy and herself thoroughly miserable in the process.

While the Scorpio female clings to her memories like a barnacle, she is also extremely adept at burying unpalatable and painful issues by emotionally detaching herself from them. Once Ms Scorpio has 'iced-over', little or nothing can be done to reverse the process.

This tendency to bury, or rather suppress, emotional hurt is something most Scorpionic women need to overcome, for repression of any sort acts like a pressure-cooker whose release valve has jammed. Ultimately the inner tempest finds its way out in a more violent and destructive way, often in physical or mental illness.

No section on the female Scorpio would be complete without a word on her notorious jealousy. The fear of losing the beloved, especially to someone else, is common to everyone who has been in love, not just Ms Scorpio. However, because the Scorpio woman's love is so deep and intense, and because her whole security system is threatened by the loss of a partner, she is possessive in the extreme. The more devious and manipulative the Scorpio (and the more colourful the background), the more paranoid she is about her loved one's potential infidelity. Equally, the more insecure she feels in a relationship, the more demanding and possessive she will behave. Nearly all Scorpio females who are betrayed wreak some sort of revenge. Most, will at the very least, pack their bags, or their lover's, and threaten never to see him again. Sometimes this is indeed the case, but more often than not, rather than risk loneliness and deeper insecurity, they will hang onto the relationship—Scorpios find change extremely threatening. Of course they never forget either, which means that once their love and trust has been betrayed, their feelings for the partner can never ever be the same. Depending upon the gravity of the partner's infidelity and the depth of Ms Scorpio's hurt, she will get her own back by rejecting him emotionally and sexually for a time whenever he tries to make amends.

Despite the difficulties the Scorpio woman often creates for herself in relationships, once she can overcome her insecurities and her fears she can be an enormously warm, loving, and compassionate creature. Unless she has a strong Uranian theme in her chart, she is one of the more conservative and traditional females of the zodiac. She is the sort who puts her all into marriage and supports and fights for her man every step of the way. She is a tireless worker, a wonderful homemaker, a protective (if rather ambitious) mother, and endlessly resourceful. Like Ms Capricorn she is always there when you need her and, provided you give her your exclusive love and affection (which means over and above the children), the tigress will behave like a perfect pussy-cat.

THE MALE SCORPIO

As the Americans would say 'Nice guys don't win ball games!'—a senti ment close to the heart of most Scorpio men, for these are not exactly the zodiac's 'good guys'. Yet despite, or maybe because of, their colourful image they hold considerable fascination for the opposite sex. Obviously not all Scorpio men are proverbial 'bastards'; like the female of the species they run to sharp extremes—some are unswervingly loyal, morally unimpeach able, and capable of giving their all to the woman they love; while others trample ruthlessly over other people's feelings and are bent only on self-gratification.

The typical Scorpio man is a curious mixture of fiery passion and icy self-control. He is capable of more emotional and sexual excesses than any other sign of the zodiac, including Pisces, yet he can turn his feelings off like a tap and become as remote and unreachable as a mountain eagle. He is enormously difficult to get to know intimately; he is likely to be charming, communicative, and friendly on the surface—even a shade boyish—but he'll give a little of his true nature or his intentions away to anyone. Remember, this man has spent many years working on his smoke-screen. Sometimes, the Scorpio man will present a truer surface reflection of himself so that he seems distant, deeply thoughtful, perhaps even troubled—a veritable Heathcliffe amongst men. Prince Charles (Sun and Mercury in Scorpio and Pluto rising) falls into this category; he is also basically a great reformer and once deeply committed to something, is not afraid to speak out and risk unpopularity because of his beliefs. However, regardless of the front a Scorpio man erects, he is never a simple, straightforward creature at heart—no matter what he says.

Like the Piscean and the Cancerian male, Mr Scorpio is emotionally vulnerable and deeply sensitive—qualities that are basically antithetical to a macho man. But unlike the other two water signs, he is more aggressive, more anxious to control, and more power oriented; thus he frequently compensates for what he views as weakness by behaving in a tough, ruthless, and sometimes utterly dissipated manner. However, regardless of how rakish he appears, the Plutonic male needs a deep, lasting, and secure relationship in his life.

The Scorpio male, like his female counterpart, is sexually and emotionally precocious. As a child he is likely to have been acutely aware of the differences between little girls and little boys, and although not so classically oedipal as Master Cancer, he is frequently emotionally consumed by his mother and learns early how to manipulate her. The Scorpio little boy usually develops an appreciation of female beauty from an early age, and while experiencing intense feelings of love for his mother, he can quite dispassionately assess her attractiveness. My eldest son, who has his Moon in Scorpio, continually compares me to other mothers and once even suggested I changed my lipstick colour to improve matters. One night—he was seven years old at the time—we were watching the Miss World contest on television when he suddenly turned to me and said, 'Don't worry, Mummy—you'll be pretty one day!'

Mr Scorpio is innately romantic and sensual and he usually encounters at least one major relationship before his teens are over. By his late twenties the typical Scorpio male has had more experience with women than most of the zodiac put together!

He is, of course, a man of extremes. Like his female counterpart he prefers a relationship of depth and intensity, but, unlike Ms Scorpio, he is able to play the field and 'love 'em and leave 'em' without experiencing paroxysms of guilt. At the outset of a relationship he is likely to be extremely ardent and insistent with his attentions; he is as extravagant in his adoration as he is with his gifts; he can turn his hand to poetry, serenade his lady with a Chopin nocturne (even if he has to hum it softly in her ear), and he'll buy out Interflora if he can afford it. (We'll come to his sexual prowess in the next section.) Like Mr Aries, he loves a challenge, but unlike his Mars-ruled brother, he won't give up and move on if she proves too difficult or unobtainable. Indeed, the more mysterious, elusive, and unreachable his women behave, the keener and more intense his ardour becomes.

If Mr Scorpio finds Ms Right, he will maintain a high level of passion and interest for her. He is not one to shirk his breadwinning duties either and he usually throws himself into the role of husband and provider with the verve of the best Capricorn and Taurus. Since most Scorpio men are ambitious and also exceedingly proud, the Scorpio husband will, if necessary, strive 23 hours out of 24 to support and sustain his wife and family.

The Scorpio male can be quite a traditionalist, too. He would prefer his wife not to work, not just because of his pride or because he dislikes the idea that she might earn more than himself, but because he fears she might become too independent. Scorpio likes to be the dominant partner in a relationship: if he has control he feels more secure. Provided there is enough money in the bank, he makes sure his wife has all she needs, but he is enormously resourceful and usually hates waste of any sort. Occasionally he can become obsessive about saving things (old clothes, records or milk bottle tops)—and if something can be recycled, he's happy.

Mr Scorpio often has extremely high expectations of the kind of woman he wants to share his life with. Like the female Scorpio, he believes in the concept of a soul mate. Ideally he needs a woman with whom he can share peak experiences in love, and a high level of emotional, psychological, and spiritual compatibility. He often has a strong sense of destiny and I've known several Scorpio men, both friends and clients, who've told me that the moment they first saw their wives, or the one great love in their lives (not necessarily the same thing!), they felt they had known them before. (The idea of reincarnation often fascinates Scorpios of both sexes.)

Perhaps because many Scorpio men do nurture such high expectations of love, and perhaps, more pertinently, because they are emotionally complex individuals, they are frequently disappointed with their partnerships. Although they accept mundane aspects of marriage as part of the course, they also need to reach intense levels of emotional and sexual experience with their partner.

At this point it might be easier to divide the Scorpio male into two categories—the emotional **dredger** and the emotional **submarine**. The **dredger** type likes to bring his emotions up to the surface and clear them out; the **submarine** prefers his feelings to remain in the depths, allowing them to surface infrequently when least expected, and preferably under cover of dark.

Both types are united by the depth of their labyrinthine emotions. The **dredger** is the more boyish Scorpio type; he doesn't hide his interest, or rather his passion, for women; he is likely to have turned the act of seduction into an art, and there isn't a ruse or a persuasive manoeuvre he cannot muster to magnetize and win over a woman. (He's not afraid to be called a ladies' man.) The **dredger** is deeply fascinated by the psychology of women and never seems to tire of exploring their psyches as well as their erogenous zones. He is not so fearful of the power of his own feelings and, like some Piscean men, is a regular emotional sponge. However, he is enormously vulnerable and doesn't react at all well to emotional hurt. One Scorpio (**dredger**) client of mine experienced such trauma when his girlfriend left him that he awoke one morning to find most of his hair lying in clumps on the pillow—possibly one of the rare cases of emotionally-induced alopecia. Unfortunately, the **dredger** all too often experiences as much disappointment and frustration in marriage as the **submarine**. He seems to have an uncanny knack of picking the 'wrong' woman—perhaps because he often marries on the rebound. Time and time again I see sensual Scorpio men married to 'not-now-George' types of wives with whom they appear to have little emotional or physical rapport. The natural outcome of their frustration is usually a series of affairs. However, Mr Scorpio (whatever emotional category he falls into) is usually enormously loyal to his wife, and the tragedy in this case is that if only she were emotionally and sexually responsive he wouldn't need to look elsewhere.

The **submarine** type of Scorpio is infinitely more inscrutable. He may well have been discouraged as a child from showing his feelings or weaknesses, and, like the Cancerian in the same boat, he has built up an impenetrable shell to protect them. The **submarine** often acts in a cool, controlled manner and is rarely emotionally demonstrative —certainly in public! He may have a well-developed intellectual front, which means he is relatively at ease—or rather safe—discussing the arts, the stock market, or the decline of moral standards with women, but is rendered completely mute in an emotionally charged exchange. He is as fascinated by women as the **dredger**, but ill at ease in their company and unable to deal with them comfortably. The **submarine** is enormously subtle, which means that much, if not almost all, of his seduction technique passes unnoticed. So careful was one Scorpio client in his choice of phrase when proposing to his girlfriend, that she had no idea he'd asked her to marry him! The **submarine** is usually extremely good at manipulating people—he has a knack of finding their Achilles' heel and needling it mercilessly. Because he is repressed himself, he gets a strange satisfaction out of making other people excruciatingly uncomfortable, if not downright miserable. Basically, he is deeply unhappy about himself and often carries an extra large chip on his shoulder.

The **submarine** not only finds it difficult to express his feelings but he usually has a major problem with anger. Like the female Scorpio with the same difficulty, his anger is rarely dealt with spontaneously and honestly; it emerges instead in snide and cruel comments, and sometimes, like Ms Scorpio, vicariously through his partner. Conversely, he may control his anger for a time until it suddenly erupts with such uncontrollable force that he becomes physically violent. Afterwards, he feels deeply remorseful but cannot come to terms with his aggressive outburst; thus he determines to control his temper even more. Consequently, he needs an extremely forthcoming, emotionally unrepressed woman to help remove his emotional barriers. When, and if, this happens he is as capable as the **dredger** of expressing his deep feelings and sensitivity, and ultimately of finding fulfilment in a one-to-one relationship.

While I have attempted to outline the basic characteristics of each Scorpio type, in some cases there is a merging of both sets of qualities. Thus, the Scorpio who is typical of the more emotionally forthcoming **dredger** type may, for instance, also have a problem with anger. On the other hand, a typically **submarine** type may well appear awkward, stilted, and reserved with women in general, but has no problem expressing his feelings and showing his love to a woman he feels close to.

Almost all Scorpio men are possessive about the woman they love—and even those they don't. Only Mr Taurus and Mr Cancer can equal Scorpio's tenacity in this regard. Because the latter considers what is his belongs to him, he is extremely jealous and continually on the alert for any interloper. Also, of course, because he is prone to the odd secret affair himself, he finds it awfully difficult to trust his partner completely! Some Scorpio men make no bones about their jealousy—these are the men whose wives frequently appear to live under semi house-arrest and, when out, in protective custody. Others are far more subtle, and give the impression that there isn't a jealous or possessive bone in their body. This is a myth: behind their cavalier attitude is the same deeply suspicious nature. The betrayed Scorpio lover is a tragic and unforgettable sight; he is awash with grief and emotional and mental torture; his pride has taken a fatal fall, his security system has been shattered, and his feelings seethe like a bubbling cauldron of hate, anger, and hurt. After the initial shock-horror reaction, he will probably turn to ice and threaten never to let the partner darken his doorstep again. But like the female of the species, his overriding need for security may prompt him to take her back—but at considerable emotional and sexual cost. Like his female counterpart, Mr Scorpio never forgets!

I read once that the Scorpio male was too practical ever to fall deeply in love. While it is plausible that Mr Scorpio might be too sceptical or too emotionally and psychologically controlled to allow such a phenomenon to happen, he is one of the signs of the zodiac most capable of experiencing love at its most profound level. Don't expect him to tell you what's bothering him when he descends into a silence and wanders about the house like a displaced ghost—he's just submerged into his depths for a while and he'll only come up when he's good and ready. He may not be the easiest sign of the zodiac to handle or to live with, but his love, once given, lasts a lifetime and, like Mr Capricorn, improves with age.

SUMMARY

Male and female Scorpios are usually their own worst enemies, rather than anyone else's. As people of radical extremes, Scorpio individuals are capable of demonstrating the most devoted and the most selfless sort of love for a partner, yet also the most cruel and callous behaviour. Almost all have a tendency to repress and control their emotions, which gives rise to moody behaviour, much frustration, and a periodic sense of isolation. Most also fear confrontation, which makes them difficult to pin down and to reason with at times. Understanding, love, and security bring out the best in Scorpios of both sexes; hurt, rejection, or betrayal, the worst. Certainly they are individuals who find little difficulty in committing themselves (body and soul) to someone they believe in and someone they love, and for their particular brand of loyalty and courage, many partners are quite prepared to put up with an emotional temperature that can vary between 120° centigrade and 30° below.

SCORPIO PARTNERSHIPS

Ideally, Scorpio's best partners should be of the earth or water temperament. Yet, like almost all individuals, Scorpios fall hook, line and sinker for their antipathies—in this case the air and fire signs.

Aries

Aries and Scorpio relationships are always passionate—at least to begin with. They can both love and hate with fierce intensity. Scorpio finds Aries stimulating but insensitive and much too impulsive. Aries is drawn to Scorpio's deep and sensual nature but hates his moods and secretiveness. This relationship works better as a brief encounter rather than a lifelong commitment. Only when there are many more harmonious links between the charts can such a relationship work in the long term.

Taurus

Taurus is Scorpio's opposite sign and both share many similar characteristics which either pull them closer together or drive them further apart. Sex is often the main attraction between these two signs, for both are sensual in the extreme; stubbornness and rigidity is their downfall! Both people place financial and emotional security high on their list of priorities, which occasionally means they remain together even as bitter enemies. Sometimes Scorpio creates emotional scenes simply to intensify their relationship and 'rattle' the Bull's placid self-complacency.

Gemini

Scorpio can find **Gemini** somewhat lightweight, yet he admires this air sign's mental dexterity and witty nature. Good communication can help this relationship enormously and Gemini is often able, like Libra, to encourage Scorpio to air his grievances and anxieties. Sometimes this couple encounter sexual problems, usually because the Gemini partner is less sexually and emotionally oriented than Scorpio, which gives rise to tensions in general and much frustration, in particular in Scorpio.

Cancer

Scorpio and **Cancer** are highly compatible water signs. Both are security-oriented but also need much emotional nurturing and cherishing. These two signs tend to be extremely defensive, which can mean that a large part of their courtship (and sometimes their marriage) is spent trying gently to wear away each other's protective screen. Much love and tenderness can be shared between this couple, but when hurt, both will scuttle into their shells to brood and sulk. The physical side of their relationship can be extremely good: the emotions play a crucial part in their sexual response and, indeed, sometimes sex becomes as much of a weapon as an olive branch.

Leo

Scorpio and Leo are traditional antipathies, but nevertheless often find each other irresistible. Sexual attraction is usually strong between these two but when angry with each other, they can fight like cat and dog! Both are extremely stubborn and like their own way: Leo tries to push (and sometimes bully) Scorpio round to his way of thinking, while Scorpio resists and manipulates the Lion to his own ends later. Both can be extremely loyal to each other, and, despite severe clashes at times, Leo is the most constant and secure fiery partner for Scorpio.

Virgo

Virgo and Scorpio often make a good partnership. Both tend to be analytical and there is usually a high degree of mental compatibility between the two. On the negative side, Virgo, like Capricorn, does not tolerate emotional extremes too well and becomes intensely frustrated when Scorpio refuses to rationalize his emotions. Scorpio finds Virgo a highly compatible bedfellow unless Mr and Ms Virgo is pernickety and over-fastidious about sex.

Libra

Libra is a giving, understanding partner and often manages (where other signs fail) to get Scorpio to voice his grievances and problems before they produce major conflicts. Also, since Scorpio and Libra are next-door-neighbours, both may have personal planets in each other's Sun sign. Sometimes Scorpio finds Libra a little too cool and sexually refined, while Libra considers Scorpio sexually excessive and wishes his emotional swings would balance themselves out more easily and more often. This partnership has a good chance of success if the Scorpio individual has some planets in air in his chart and the Libran some in water.

Scorpio

A dual Scorpio relationship veers from intensely passionate peaks to icy troughs. Like most twin combinations, the relationship either works extremely well or not at all. Both tend to be extremely jealous and suspicious of each other, but provided there are no sexual problems, they usually remain committed to one another. The drawback to this combination occurs when one partner descends into a slough of broody despond, since the other tends to take the whole thing personally and becomes angry, miserable, and just as moody as the first! However, the relationship rarely lacks depth and carries the built-in deterrent of mutually assured destruction should it fail!

Sagittarius

Sagittarius is usually far too flippant and emotionally non-committal for Scorpio; he may also lack the sexual intensity Scorpio likes. On the plus side, the Archer's optimism and enthusiasm can offset Scorpio's tendency to brood and worry, although his jolly approach to life can equally well irritate Scorpio. On the other hand, Scorpio's devious behaviour and emotional games can send the Archer strutting off to pastures new. If both people have planets in each other's Sun sign there is more chance of a smoother, more durable relationship; but by and large, the Sagittarian is far too insensitive and inconsistent for Scorpio.

Capricorn

Capricorn is probably the best partner for Scorpio. The Goat is tremendously stable, constant, and resilient, thus providing plenty of security (financial and otherwise) for Scorpio. The drawback to this relationship lies in Capricorn's emotional reticence, which can make Scorpio feel unloved and left out in the cold at times. Conversely, Mr or Ms Scorpio can alienate the Goat with his or her intense emotional highs and lows. On balance, however, this partnership is tremendously durable and resistant to the varous slings and arrows of fate.

Aquarius

Scorpio and **Aquarius** combinations frequently begin well but end acrimoniously. Aquarius is far too detached from his emotions for Scorpio, who appears irrationally consumed by them to Aquarius. Scorpio appreciates the Water Bearer's clarity and skill in argument, but after a while his inability to relate to and understand Scorpio's feelings can cause distance and much (suppressed) anger and resentment. If the Moon signs are compatible the relationship has a far better chance of survival!

Pisces

Pisces provides a loving, gentle partner for Scorpio, although the Fish sometimes lacks the commitment to the relationship Scorpio needs. Both are prone to emotional and sexual excesses (and infidelity if either partner proves physically or emotionally cool). On the other hand, Pisces can feel overpowered by Scorpio, in which case he may withdraw emotionally and sexually. However, when these two fall in love it usually lasts a lifetime.

SEXUALITY

Scorpio men and women certainly have a phenomenal reputation to live up to where sex is concerned. Even people who have never given astrology a serious thought, other than to peer absent-mindedly at the newspaper 'stars' on their way to work, seem to know that Scorpios are the sexy sirens and Casanovas of this world. However, it would be a mistake to assume that every Scorpio is seething with passion and lust and has nothing more pressing on his mind than where his or her next sexual delight is coming from. As already discussed, Scorpios are enormously complex individuals and sex for this sign is rarely a simple matter of physical gratification. While strongly fiery or earthy individuals can enjoy their love making without any huge emotional overtones, those who have a dominant Scorpionic or Plutonic theme in their charts are powerfully affected on an emotional and psychological level by the nature and experience of sex.

Astrologically, Scorpio, Pluto, and the 8th house of the horoscope are intrinsically linked to the hidden, mysterious, and taboo dimensions of life—one of which is sex. Like Cancer and Pisces, Scorpio men and women like to lose themselves in intensely sensual experience, whether in an artistic, musical, imaginative, or emotional sense. In some Scorpionic or Plutonic individuals, sex is a means not only of gaining heightened emotional and sensual experience but also a mysterious—if not mystical—process of psychic cleansing and surrender, a process that generates an enormous sense of liberation. Almost all Scorpios nurture the idea of finding someone with whom they can experience a transcendental level of emotional and sexual contact.

It is a difficult task to outline general characteristics of a sign when, as an astrologer, one knows that a multitude of diverse (astrological) factors contribute to an individual's personality and temperament; to do so for sex becomes even more of a conundrum. While many men with their Sun, Mars, or Ascendant in Scorpio (or strong aspects to the Sun, Mars, and Venus from Pluto) will relate to the sexual themes outlined below, those women with their Moon, Mars, and Venus in Scorpio (or Pluto aspects to Venus, Mars, and the Moon) will find them more applicable than those merely with their Sun or Ascendant in this sign.

Most Scorpionic women have enormous sexual magnetism; whether they accept it or not is another matter altogether. At the risk of repeating myself, Scorpio is a sign of extremes; thus some Scorpionic women live up to their Mata Hari image while others turn out to be the middle-aged puritan spinster along the road! Unlike fiery or airy women, the Scorpio lady is rarely open about her sexual life; she is a private, secretive female and sometimes thoroughly perplexed by her own sexual needs and responses. While the Mata Hari Scorpio may be alluring in her mystery and beauty, she is never flashy or keen to advertise her wares. At a social gathering she will seek out a man she wants and subtly attract him to her; there is nothing obvious or blatant about her approach. Her intuition acts like a highly sensitive radar system that tells her what move to make and when, and how to weave just the right amount of 'will she, won't she?' out of the situation. Indeed, there is a curious quality about a Scorpio woman's sexual appeal; she manages to appear distinctly hostile to some men while being magnetically attractive to others.

Almost all Scorpio women, regardless of their extreme category, extol romance. They love to be wined and dined, given red roses and expensive jewellery; somehow the romantic ritual lends a sensual spice and magic to seduction. Like their opposite sign, Taurus, many Scorpio women find the intimacy and sensual pleasure of good food and fine wine a sort of foreplay in itself. And while we are on the subject of foreplay, unlike the fiery woman, speed is not of the essence for Scorpio; the longer and more drawn out the courtship and the sexual preamble itself, the more piquant the pleasure. In fact, Ms Scorpio should never be rushed over anything.

The Scorpio woman is rarely the type to fling off all her clothes and expect the mere sight of her femaleness to excite a man. She is one of the signs of the zodiac who uses clothes as an erotic accoutrement. Ms Scorpio is often fond of beautiful silk underwear—camisoles and suspender belts—and some Scorpio women even go in for high boots and leather-wear! However, the erotic trimmings are a mere overture to the sort of sexual performance many Scorpio women are capable of. Ms Scorpio has a lush and deep sexuality which is never contrived. When she finds a man who arouses her physically and emotionally the gateway to her sexuality opens to reveal an ocean of sensitivity and responsiveness. When the Scorpio woman is in love (or at least totally infatuated), she finds a level of self-expression in sex that is not only deeply emotionally and physically fulfilling but is suffused with a transcendent quality. The Scorpio woman who is unrepressed and emotionally unblocked usually has a high libido; sexual interaction is not only a way of releasing tension but of communicating her feelings to her lover at the most profound level.

Although there may well be some Scorpio women of the Mata Hari variety who have a trail of lovers in tow and a sexual history that reads like the **Kama Sutra** or **Lady Chatterley's Lover**, the truly Plutonic lady would be happier with just one superlative relationship. In my experience of strongly Scorpionic females, whether clients or friends, while they may have encountered more than one sexual relationship (at least) by mid-life, they are by no means promiscuous. A 'quick lay' is not usually in Ms Scorpio's repertoire—a sexual relationship for her requires rapport and commitment on all levels. Only if she has personal planets in air or fire or a strong Uranus theme in her chart will she make light of a sexual encounter. Indeed, the Scorpionic female who moves from relationship to relationship (or seeks extra-marital affairs) is not a raging nymphomaniac but looking for the sort of complete union she craves.

At the opposite extreme, there are some Scorpionic women who find sex distasteful, if not downright disgusting. Such women have for some reason—most often a sexually repressed mother—grown up with the fear of their own sexual power. These women also frequently encounter great difficulty in expressing anger (which I discussed earlier). Sometimes they remain a virgin for life, often campaigning over the garden wall or in more public places—like television—for greater censorship and higher moral standards. In effect they develop an unhealthy obsession with sex and see only its dark and terrifying face. Not all Scorpio females who find sex unpleasant remain virgins of course. Many marry and have children but still retain a basic distaste for the sexual act. Others sense that sex should be a glorious experience and, though anorgasmic, keep on trying and trying (often with various partners) but never managing to achieve a climax. Again, emotional blocks and the fear of losing control (albeit unconsciously) that is synonymous with Scorpio/Pluto is at the root of the problem.

Most women's sexual response is linked to their emotions and this is almost always so for the water signs. One woman with Moon in Scorpio and a strong Venus/Pluto aspect seemed to encapsulate the Scorpio woman's ethos with this comment in my questionnaire. 'When I was younger I used to envy some of my girlfriends who went out—and usually to bed—with lots of men and didn't get hung up about it. I've never been able to be casual about a relationship, which has meant that I've been awfully hurt in the past. Now, in my thirties, I've found the most wonderful man who is just as intense and loving as myself—we have amazing sex—and for the first time in my life I feel fulfilled—complete. I'm not searching any more.'

If one is to believe astrological lore, the Scorpio man is a legend in his own bedtime. Scorpios are said to be the zodiac's lustiest, most virile, and most sex-obsessed men. Judging by various clients' and friends' experiences (and my own observations), a great many of them seem bent on perpetuating their own myth. I can remember sharing a mixed flat in my student days and being both shocked and impressed by the behaviour of one of my Scorpio flat-mates—an actor, I might add. He was the boyish **dredger** type with great charm, intelligence, and attractive looks—if a shade on the debauched side. Since he was my then boyfriend's best friend, I was both witness and confidante to his peccadilloes, while never being the object of a seduction myself. (Even the most rakish Scorpio has some scruples!) To my knowledge, in the two years that he lived at the flat, he spent, at the most, four nights in his own bed. At one point during the run of a play he was in, he was conducting affairs with two of the women in the cast, each of whom thought she was the only one. Apparently, he used to make love to them alternately in their dressing rooms. Unfortunately and inevitably, his women found out about each other and all hell broke loose—luckily just at the end of the run. Even my own friends weren't immune to his charms—despite prior warnings—and they were nearly all convinced that they were the ones who could reform him. I spent a large amount of my time acting as a kind of answering service and eventually had to keep notes on the various story lines that went with each woman!

The Scorpio man inevitably seems drawn to a certain amount of intrigue in his relationships; first, because he finds it difficult to resist temptation, which necessitates secrecy if he already has an existing partnership, and second, many Scorpio men find that cloak-and-dagger tactics and an element of danger add more than just a little spice to an affair. Also, since most Scorpio men have a high libido, if they are married to or are living with a less sexually oriented partner, or one who has many inhibitions, they will tend to seek physical satisfaction outside the relationship. Unlike the female of the species, the male Scorpio can (and often does) relish a purely sexual affair, since he can detach himself from his emotions all too easily if he wishes. However, when he falls in love and finds sexual **and** emotional fulfilment with his lady, he remains faithful. 'I knew when I married my wife that the physical side of our relationship was less than perfect', wrote one man with his Sun and Ascendant in Scorpio, '. . . but I was very much in love with her and thought in time I could get her to enjoy our love-making more. This has never happened despite being married for six years. I'm afraid I've had to resort to several one-night stands and brief affairs to help me cope with the frustration—and the rejection—I feel.'

Although the male Scorpio appears to have an insatiable sexual appetite, he is nonetheless usually an excellent lover. Even if and when the Scorpio cuts off from his emotions, he still retains his sensitivity and intuitional skills as a lover and is capable of reaching the same sexual heights as the Piscean. Mr Scorpio, like Mr Capricorn, often has great control, thus he can usually satisfy the most voracious appetite in a woman as well as those who need considerable coercing to become aroused. However, like the Goat, he sometimes controls himself so well that he can't let go at all!

Occasionally, the Scorpio man is so emotionally repressed that he encounters much difficulty in the sexual arena. On the one hand, he may refrain from sexual interaction altogether, and on the other he may be unable to function sexually without unusual or bizarre forms of erotic stimulation.

There are a few Plutonic men who can only become aroused by sado-masochism and bondage, for instance—the element of cruelty is perhaps the less acceptable side of Plutonic sexuality—although in most men these tendencies surface only rarely. The reason why some men can only find sexual satisfaction in degrading women through sado-masochistic practices is usually because they cannot integrate the feminine in themselves. These kind of men are enormously vulnerable: they fear, usually because of some traumatic past experience, that by forming an emotional attachment to a woman they risk being hurt or rejected; consequently, they despise women because they represent and continually remind them of their own weakness and can never respond to them sexually in a loving or tender fashion, only with cruelty.

Some of the heroes and heroines of the writer, D. H. Lawrence, have a thoroughly Scorpionic aura about them. Indeed, Lawrence himself had Scorpio rising and Mars conjunct Pluto. In particular, Birkin and Gerald, in **Women in Love**, and their lovers, Gudrun and Ursula, express and interact with various dimensions of Plutonic sexuality. Gerald is a character deep in conflict, consumed by his suppressed and turbulent emotions and his powerful, sometimes cruel sexuality— a combination that ultimately drives him to suicide. Birkin, on the other hand, is a more cerebral, less sexually and emotionally repressed individual, and it is through him that more of the elevating aspects of Scorpio love and sexuality emerge. Ken Russell's film of the book entirely captures and perhaps enhances through visual imagery and music the suppressed, lush, deep, turbulent sexual tones of Lawrence's writing—perhaps most effectively in two particular scenes; one where Birkin and Gerald consummate their friendship spiritually, mentally, and physically by pitting themselves against each other in a wrestling match, and the second, where Birkin communes with Nature, immersing himself naked amongst the rain drenched foliage. Both sequences bring out the immensely tactile and sensual quality of Scorpionic sexuality.

One of the most constant themes in Lawrence's writings is the mystical awareness operating in the sexual union that transforms the lovers' perception of themselves and each other. The following quotes from **Women in Love** emphasize Lawrence's fascination with this idea:

The body of mysterious night upon the body of mysterious night, the night masculine and feminine, never to be seen with the eye, or known with the mind, only as a palpable revelation of mystic otherness . . .

There were strange fountains of his body, more mysterious and potent than any she had imagined or known, more satisfying, ah finally mystically-physically satisfying . . .

It was a perfect passing away for both of them, and at the same time the most intolerable accession into being . . .

Both male and female Scorpios find sex the most potent and profound way of expressing themselves. A Scorpionic individual who is tense, prickly and on the attack is usually one who is sexually frustrated and emotionally unfulfilled. Although this explanation could apply to almost anyone with these symptons, regardless of their zodiac sign, Scorpios react more extremely to the ebbs and flows of their emotional and sexual equilibrium. Both sexes like power and control and many of them resort to using sex as a weapon—witholding their love as a punishment or as a means of getting what they want. Yet despite the battleground created by many Scorpios in their sexual lives, most are usually highly sensual and extremely giving partners capable of touching the most subtle, and in some cases, the most transcendent level of sexual love.

FENELLA FIELDING

Fenella Fielding is the quint-essence of the Scorpio femme-fatale. She combines the child with the sophisticate; the vulnerable with the worldly-wise. Her expression varies from the seductive to the enigmatic, and with a sweep of her black feathery lashes and a toss of her dark, wavy locks she could send shivers of expectation down the spine of any hot-blooded male. And then there's the voice. A sort of silky, fruity purr that reaches the parts to which other resonances merely aspire! Thus not surprisingly, especially during the 1960s, Fenella 'cornered the market' in sultry vamp roles—parts which brought her tremendous success yet often concealed her talent as an actress.

From the beginning Fenella's life seemed different from other girls. Her parents kept a haberdashery shop in London, and although the family was not particularly wealthy she and her elder brother were largely relegated to the care of nannies and governesses. Her parents were 'ill-matched': her father was English and her mother Romanian, and to Fenella, their marriage appeared 'noisy and volatile'. 'I don't remember my childhood as being happy. I remember it as being a strain. Behaviour mattered but the person inside didn't.' Though her relationship with her mother was strained they drew closer in the last few years of her life: 'Her death was a dreadful wrench'. Fenella adored her father, although he had a violent temper, 'he could be jolly frightening', and while her parents were concerned for her welfare, Fenella never felt as though they really loved her.

Astrologically, the pattern to Fenella's early life is complex. There are four planets to consider in the fourth 'house' of home and family:

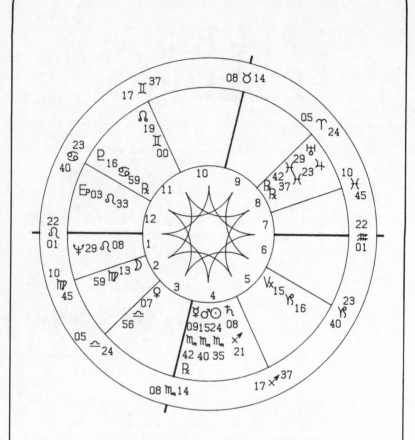

FENELLA FIELDING

11 7 1927   22h 44m 0s GMT

PLACIDUS 51N32 0W8

Mercury, Mars, the Sun, and Saturn—each one implying something different. Mercury is the strongest resident in this 'house' since it is placed almost exactly on the IC angle. Mercury suggests that the home was a sphere where communication and reason came before emotional closeness. Mars describes the friction Fenella experienced at home and also suggests that she considered her father somewhat of an authority figure. The Sun in the fourth certainly emphasizes the importance home and family have played in her life, but although the Sun forms a helpful trine aspect to Jupiter and Uranus, which would lead one to believe that family life was fortunate and happy, the Sun is also 90° away from Neptune. This latter aspect implies home was anything but a positive experience and that Fenalla felt 'lost' within the family—misunderstood, even rootless. Finally, Saturn in the fourth rarely corresponds to a jubilant experience of family, and separation from one or both parents is often coincident with this placement. In Fenella's case, while neither parent left the family circle, she felt quite cut off from them emotionally. Indeed all these astrological factors combine to support Fenella's feelings that her childhood was 'a strain' and not very happy. As far as Fenella's experience of mother goes, the Moon is placed in Virgo and forms a 90° square aspect to Saturn. Children with their Moon in Virgo frequently see their mother as a problem. They worry about her. She may seem nervous, neurotic, overburdened, and difficult to please. When Saturn adds 'his' Draconian hand, the picture becomes even more one of emotional distance and conditional love.

As a child, Fenella remembers always wanting to be on the stage when she grew up. But although she clearly showed some theatrical talent, her parents were none too keen on her taking up the stage as a career and in order to get to drama school she had to take an entrance exam in secret. Not only was she successful but was awarded a scholarship. 'My parents were thrilled—it was a **scholarship**, after all, and they thought it would be some kind of fabulous finishing school! But very soon they went off the idea because it meant I would probably become an actress.' Sadly, Fenella's parents were to make life so difficult for her at drama school that in the end her scholarship was removed. Her withdrawal from the school affected her deeply. She lost a tremendous amount of confidence and felt she didn't want to act any more. Thus a series of 'dead-end' jobs followed. Gradually, however, she regained some of her former confidence and enthusiasm for the stage and was given the chance to sing a number in an amateur show. 'Amateurs often bring in professionals to see their shows. The professional who came along criticized the whole thing, but for some reason he was highly flattering about me!' After that, Fenella did several more amateur shows and was constantly urged to take up theatre professionally. 'Eventually I considered I might have a go, but I was still held back by the thought that my parents would stop me. Then a friend wisely observed, "If you were really serious about your acting, if you really wanted to do it, you would." And of course he was right.'

Fenella's big break came when she was offered the part in a Sandy Wilson musical. 'It was an extraordinary show, very outré, very decadent. They needed "someone with her own aura" and in a way it was **force majeure**. My part was an aristocratic nymphomaniac—only I didn't know it was that until I read the papers. I just thought she was sexy.' The show, which ultimately moved to the West End, proved to have a considerable cult following, as did Fenella. Indeed, though she took on a diverse range of parts, for many years following she had an exclusive claim on all aristocratic vamp roles.

Fenella's chart is tailor-made for an upper crust sex-pot. She has three planets in the smouldering seductive sign Scorpio, including her chart ruler, the Sun. Venus is placed in its own sign of Libra—the sign synonymous with relating and eroticism: Venus rules Fenella's tenth 'house' of profession, so it is more than likely she would have taken her Venusian abilities, whether as an artist or a sex-goddess, out into the world. Fenella also has Leo on her Ascendant—a sign noted for its regal qualities as much as its dramatic abilities—and with Neptune rising to the Ascendant and contacting the Scorpio Sun, her image as a delectable siren is practicably inseparable from her real self. of course Fenella has taken on a wide range of parts during her career, yet I think even she would agree that it is difficult perhaps well nigh impossible, for her to escape entirely from her seductive image.

There are plenty of indicators for success in Fenella's chart. The Sun and Mars both form harmonious 120° trine aspects to Jupiter and Pluto, thus creating a grand trine. This configuration indicates marvellous creative talent and the ability to use that creativity in a personally transformative way. On the one hand, Fenella may find that playing a part opens up new and challenging avenues within herself: on the other, she can powerfully affect those with whom she comes into contact. While Fenella can use this talent on stage and screen to captivate an audience, there are other possible outlets for this almost magical ability. One of these outlets is through spiritual, healing work.

During 1985, at a party, Fenella was speaking to a man who clearly had mediumistic powers. 'His voice suddenly changed, and he started telling me things that had happened in my past—absolutely correct—then he ended by saying, "What are you doing about **your** psychic development?" Well, I was staggered and a shade embarrassed since he'd said so many personal things within earshot of other people. I then forgot about the whole thing until a couple of months later when I had this feeling that I **ought** to do something about what he said.' She got in touch with an organization that teaches psychic development, and when I spoke to her she was already in her second term of training. Like most Scorpios, Fenella has one foot firmly on the sceptical ground while the other hovers uncertainly yet compellingly in the mists of the mysterious. While it is comparatively early days to ascertain whether her sharp intuition will develop into clairvoyance or inform her she's in no-man's land, astrologically the grand trine and her rising Neptune point to genuine psychic and healing ability.

Neptune's presence on the Ascendant occurs with uncanny frequency in the charts of artists, mystics, and psychics. Yet Neptune has a reputation in astrology for causing as much confusion, escapism and self-delusion as it does artistic or spiritual genius. The Ascendant is arguably the most sensitive angle in the chart. (This point is most usually identified with the persona—the image the individual projects to the world.) Thus Fenella's Neptune 'endows' her with a glamorous, unreal aura, and great psychic sensibility. Yet this aura of unreality and overall suggestibility permeates many areas of her life, most notably her partnerships.*

Strongly Neptunian individuals, like Fenella, are not always best suited to the world of business. Fenella, sensing this, has preferred in the past to let other people handle her financial affairs, leaving her free to pursue her creative endeavours—a solution that has not always proved to be in her best interests!† In the mid-seventies, she embarked on an uncertain financial venture. Since disclosing essential facts might prove libellous, the nature of the business and the transactions must remain unspecified. Suffice to say Fenella unwittingly put her trust in a valued friend and left him to his own devices and her business. When she came to claim her dues, she found the profits from the business had been ploughed elsewhere and the 'cupboard' was bare. And since she was seemingly responsible for the business, she was left with all the debts. This propelled her almost to the point of bankruptcy and left her no option but to sell up 'everything', including her house. To make matters worse, at this low point in her life, her mother died (September 1977).

Fenella admits that she has periodically suffered from 'bad guidance'. Despite the toughness of her Scorpionic Sun, Mars, and Mercury, time and again she is made vulnerable by Neptunian suggestibility and inertia. Some of this adverse guidance has come not only from those who should have had her best career interests at heart, but from her 'close friends'. Fenella has not yet married. As a true Scorpio, she has had some intense and wonderful affairs, but none of them have led to marriage. 'I have almost married once or twice, but never actually got there. In my thirties I had a passionate relationship with a truly remarkable man, but it was very stormy. It lasted a year, and the aftermath was everlasting. It was like an explosion when we met—a volcano. The effect was lingering

*See Note for Astrologers.

†Neptune rules her eighth house of joint finances.

because I could feel him still there, somehow observing–judging my life. There isn't any great reason why I haven't got married. I'm not against marriage. I suppose it's just happened. Although if I'm honest, deep down, even in a very long relationship, I must have known it wasn't right. I think early on in my twenties I made some kind of decision about marriage. I was in a relationship that was looking like marriage. But I thought I ought to give myself two years to find out if I was any good [on stage]. I thought "If I am any good I've established myself. Then I'll get married." You see, I reasoned that if I was established as an actress when I met someone, it would be an essential part of me–no one could take it away. But, of course it doesn't always work out like that. And you can't always arrange these things.'

With Aquarius ruling Fenella's 'house' of partnerships, there is a suggestion that she needs plenty of 'space' in one-to-one relationships, and she is certainly looking for something 'different' in a partner. Since Venus is in an air sign (Libra) and her Moon in the cerebral sign of Virgo, there is an indication that she needs a mentally stimulating partner. 'I think "the like mind" is what is important to me in a relationship.' Yet with her strong Scorpio emphasis–a water sign and therefore synonymous with feeling and the emotions–she also needs security combined with passion and love. Uranus, the ruling planet of the relationship house, is placed next to 'good times' Jupiter and both are harmoniously linked to the Sun, so she should find at least one partner who represents the extraordinary 'white knight' she seeks. Yet because both the Moon and Venus have stressful aspects from Saturn and Pluto respectively, she has experienced much difficulty and heartache in relationships–even some physical violence. 'Yes, I recognize I need space in a relationship–privacy when you want it and company when you want it. I find it easier to explain what I mean by an analogy. It's like being in a teeny-weeny dressing room. You want your dresser to be there, but you don't want her there until you **actually** want her! . . . At the time my mother died this marvellous man came into my life. It was such a lift. He said, "I'll take care of you. I won't interfere with your career. All your worries are going to disappear into the background." In the event, he lost me a lot of friends and he kept deterring me from doing various parts. He was definitely not an asset to my professional life.'

I put it to Fenella that, with the links between Moon and Saturn, and Venus and Pluto, she might hold back emotionally in an intimate relationship. 'I feel I'm very open, but other people do say I'm difficult to get to know . . . if you've got very difficult parents, and I would say mine were both difficult in their own way, you tend to get brain-washed. If there's been a constant repetition of "this is what you're like", you begin to think, "this is what I'm like." It makes you prey to people brain-washing you. I think I'm more easily influenced than I would like to be.'

There's certainly more than a grain of truth in Fenella's comments about brain-washing. If enough people tell you you're a bumbling idiot or a superstar, eventually you'll fit comfortably into the role. Thus Fenella's receptivity to her parents' opinions about her (real or imagined) have become absorbed into her self-image. Her reliance on her parents' permission and approval for her every important action has led to a simlar reliance on partners and associates in adult life. It is the strong Neptunian influence that 'makes' her susceptible to 'brain-washing' and clouds her self-image, and it is the Moon-Saturn link that makes her a virtual prisoner of her emotional conditioning.

Few Scorpios find life smooth and uneventful. It is the nature of the 'beast' to experience peaks and troughs in life—sometimes only emotionally and psychology. During the mid to late seventies Fenella underwent a series of deeply upsetting and traumatic events, a time which she refers to as 'the crash'. She was financially ruined and emotionally torn apart by these events. Only towards the end of 1985, as Saturn moved out of Scorpio, did she begin to feel she was emerging out of a long tunnel. With only a few more Saturnian 'ashes' to form, Fenella's phoenix is poised for take-off—although I suspect she might be quite surprised at the direction it takes. It may well be that over the next few years Fenella will find new avenues, both in career and personal life, open up leading to greater success and fulfilment. And in her own inimitable words, 'Dahling, I can hardly wait!'

Note for Astrologers: (1) Like many individuals in public life, especially when they are strongly Scorpionic, Fenella does not wish to divulge her age. Thus I have avoided any mention of dates and ages when particular events in her life occurred. With one exception, the death of her mother, which revealed the following transits: the Sun, 29° Virgo, Mercury, 14° Virgo, Satum 25° Leo, Uranus 9° Scorpio, Neptune 13° Sagittarius, the north node 13° Libra.

(2) Neptune can be seen both as a conjunction to the Ascendant and an opposition to the Descendant: thus Neptune is definitely a factor colouring her relationships and suggests deception, and over-expectation in relationships—the rose-tinted glasses syndrome.

(3) Robert Hand's comments in **Planets in Aspect** are particularly apt in regard to Fenella's Moon-Satum square. 'Your parents were especially responsible for your feeling of dependence and your inability to stand alone. Unfortunately parents sometimes don't realize how damaging it is for their children to be dependent on them.'

*Transiting Pluto (her Sun ruler) conjunct the IC 1987–8.

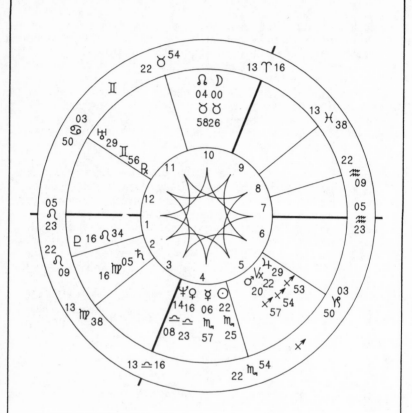

HRH PRINCE CHARLES

14 11 1948   21h 14m 0s GMT

PLACIDUS 51N30 0W10

PROFILE OF A SCORPIO MAN

HRH THE PRINCE OF WALES

To the royal House of Windsor, on 14 November 1948 at 9.14pm, was born Charles Philip Arthur George, first child of the Duke and Duchess of Edinburgh, and the future King of England. It was an auspicious and keenly awaited event not only for the Family itself, but for the hundreds of people gathered that night outside Buckingham Palace and indeed for the millions of Royal watchers and loyal subjects scattered throughout Britain and the world. Even with the most unpretentious and down-to-earth parents he was destined for a life

of almost unparalleled privilege. There was, and is, a proportionally high cost to pay—constant media scrutiny of his public and private life which has in turn cast a shadow over his destiny.

Photographs of the young Charles capture a questioning, not exactly hostile but mistrustful little boy—'The generalized perception of Prince Charles was of a lonely child with large ears and unflattering grey trousers'. By the time he went to Cambridge University everyone had woken up to the fact he was the world's most eligible bachelor and his image vastly improved. Throughout the 1970s he became increasingly admired and his romantic exploits were eagerly consumed by the media and public alike. Nevertheless, the child, as father to the man, had left a legacy of the sometimes hard and lonely moments of his childhood.

During the 1950s when Charles was growing up, it was unthinkable for him (or his sister, Anne) to accompany the Queen and Prince Philip on their foreign tours. Thus from a young age he had to endure long absences from his parents. By the time he was eight he had left the comparative safety and familiarity of his day school in London's Knightsbridge for the unfamiliar rigours and demands of boarding school—Cheam. Not only did he encounter the perennial problem of any young boy—home-sickness—but also the added difficulty of forging genuine friendships,a situation that was to dog him through his years at spartan but 'character-building' Gordonstoun and later at Cambridge.

Charles has an impressive chart. His Sun in Scorpio falls on the cusp of the fifth house of creativity and self-expression (Leo's natural house) while the regal sign of Leo rises, with Pluto dominating the first house—the area of the chart directly concerned with the persona. This combination reveals an intense, uncompromising individual, one who through his passionate, highly-committed and determined nature is likely to encounter much turbulence, both on an inner and outer level.

As a child Charles would have needed much demonstrable love and lots of encouragement for his efforts. His mother, Her Majesty the Queen, is easily identified in the horoscope: Charles' Moon in the 10th house at 0° Taurus falls exactly on the Queen's Sun. The Moon forms 120° aspects to both Saturn and Jupiter making a powerful Grand Trine configuration. All this conspires to show not only the supreme importance of his mother in his life, but the immense support he receives from her and the admiration he holds for her—a hard act for any future wife to follow.* With three planets in the 4th house, father emerges as a more complex figure. The Venus-Neptune conjunction suggests a fabulous, but possibly unreal, image of his father. Mercury also paints a contrasting picture of an expressive, articulate individual, yet also a somewhat tricky and even critical and elusive one. Sometimes Mercury here indicates more than one father: in Charles' case the Mercury factor could well represent his Honorary Grand-father, the late Earl Mountbatten, who was not just a much loved uncle but a great mentor.

Certainly Charles' chart in regard to the fourth house** is far from straightforward, and the accompanying Sun-Pluto square does little to allay rumours that he and his father have a difficult relationship. Apparently, though Charles virtually hero-worshipped his dashing father when he was young, his more introvert personality and his lack of enthusiasm for rough sports initially disappointed Philip and began to drive a wedge between them. The long separations from his parents no doubt added to the emotional distance between Charles and his father; thus from an early age he acquired the Pluto/Scorpio skill of supressing his real and painful feelings behind a stiff upper lip.

While rugby may not have been Charles' forte, he soon developed skills in other directions, sailing, flying and horsemanship—he is a world class polo player. His artistic talents have lent themselves to writing, not only

*Charles has always been exceedingly close to the Queen Mother who must also have been a wonderfully loving and supportive mother-figure for him.

**See Note for Astrologers (1).

most of his countless speeches but a children's story, **The Old Man of Lochnagar**, originally created to amuse his younger brother, Andrew, and he paints with considerable craftsmanship—one small water-colour making it to the prestigious Summer Exhibition at London's Royal Academy in 1987. Opera is another great passion and, like many members of the Royal Family, he has a brilliant talent to amuse.

His love of gardening and conservation (no doubt initially fostered by his father's involvement with the World-Wide Fund for Nature) has led to the creation of a magnificent wild flower garden at his country home, Highgrove. When asked what he would like to have been had he not been born the Prince of Wales, he declared 'a farmer!'. And why not with an elevated Moon in Taurus, **the** sign for agriculture, in the 10th house of profession.

To this already formidable list can be added a thirst for adventure and exploration—the quintessence of Operation Drake, a scheme whereby 400 young people were able to sail around the world partaking of a variety of scientific and community projects. Indeed his concern and identification with young people has become one of the hallmarks of his role as the Prince of Wales. In 1978, he succeeded Lord Mountbatten as the President of the United World College, an institution where students the world over can combine two years of academic study with physically demanding activities and community service thereby promoting not only racial harmony but a spirit of human fellowship.

It is these latter qualities—his concern for conservation and the ecology and the fellowship of man—that have gradually formed the basis of a spiritual quest which at one level is a deeply personal path and on another his future manifesto as King of England.

As an astrologer, all too often one sees little of a natal chart's potential fulfilled by an individual; in Charles' case—in spite of the pressures and privileges of his role, or conversely because of them—he has expressed his talents and his individuality through many and varied avenues. Like so many of the celebrities featured in this book, by strange synchronicity he has an angular Pluto.* A characteristic of such a strong Pluto is a compelling drive to pit oneself against the extremes of life, whether in Clare Francis' case as a lone yachtswoman facing nature's elements, or Jeffrey Archer's phoenix-like resurrections from bankruptcy and political disgrace to ever more successes, or transcending the boundaries of the physical into the supernatural like Christopher Reeve.

Aside from the compelling nature of Pluto, Charles' propensity for living on the knife edge is to be found in his Mars-Jupiter conjunction (Sagittarius) which opposes Uranus. Thrills, excitement and inventiveness are the flavours of this planetary set-up, so too are irrationality, perversity and recklessness. By contrast, Charles' Venus-

*Pluto conjunct the Ascendant.

Neptune conjunction in Libra shows his artistic, gentle and caring qualities; it also speaks volumes about his relationships.

Charles is enormously idealistic about women; he has two models of perfection (his mother and grandmother) on which to base his expectations of a wife. In keeping with Venus and Neptune, he seeks glamour, sensitivity and grace in a woman—a companion who will be there whenever he needs her and compliant enough to disappear when he doesn't; a soul-mate. With his Scorpio-Pluto, Moon-Taurus side he wants an all-consuming relationship in love—he's not a man for half measures. His Uranus-ruled 7th house of partnerships shows he also has an unorthodox streak: on the one hand an attraction towards forbidden fruit and novel experience and on the other a difficulty in finding stability and durability in long-term relationships.

Prior to Diana, there had been several female companions in Charles' life. But for one reason or another, including religion or the fact they had a 'past', marriage remained elusive as ever. Diana couldn't have been more perfect—beautiful, titled, young, innocent and, most important of all, madly in love with him. She was also astrologically practically perfect with her Uranian-Aquarian Moon reflecting Charles' 7th house, her Taurean Venus mirroring his Moon and her Libran Midheaven close to his Venus-Neptune conjunction and on the Ascendant of the Great Britain (1066) chart. Their marriage in 1981 was the wedding of the century and millions the world over celebrated the glittering climax of a modern-day fairy tale. But eight years on the fairy-tale is looking slightly moth-eaten, if not seriously moribund.

Despite the euphoria around the happy couple in the summer of 1981, at the time I voiced my misgivings about certain elements in their relationship in my book **Synastry**: 'Inevitably stressful factors emerge in the synastry . . . there are some incredibly powerful cross-currents between them (which may result in 'block-busting' rows) . . . Charles' innate self-control may give the appearance of abject coldness on occasion; he may feel compelled to pull Diana into line which may crush her expansive and freedom-loving personality . . . each of them will have to watch the tendency to blow hot and cold and 'freeze' each other out when hurt. Both Scorpio (Charles) and Cancer (Diana) have a tendency to detach themselves from painful situations whilst internally brooding about them, so from time to time there will be marathon icy silences at Highgrove . . . The Moons fall in square signs (Aquarius, Diana; Taurus, Charles) which can amplify the emotional coldness and distance caused through the Moon-Saturn link . . . Their dislike of the rigidly conventional and staid bureaucracy will bring fresh air to the established view of the monarchy and they will emerge as two separate individuals within the relationship and not solely as a symbiotic unit. Unfortunately, the Mars-Uranus square is not the best aspect to have for a long-term relationship . . .'

Astrologers initially made much of the fact that the Princess of Wales was the archetypal Sun Cancer—motherly, gentle, sweet-natured and demure. It's easy to forget that this sign can also be an emotional vortex and crabby in the extreme. Add to this Diana's complex Moon-Venus-Uranus link, her Mars-Pluto-Uranus conjunction (in the 8th house of emotional and sexual exchange) and the swan-princess soon develops webbed feet! She is, like most women, a creature of her emotions. She needs love and affection in abundance and considerable support and encouragement to fulfil her duties and responsibilities—not to mention the expectations of the nation, if not the world. She may personify a much-needed myth, but she is none the less human—and still very young.

One doesn't need to be the greatest astrologer in the world to see that Diana, with her fascinating but volatile chart, was at 19 (with all the youthful values and tastes of her generation of 'Sloaney' aristocrats) hardly going to walk down the aisle and into the pressures and constraints of the Royal Family without some difficulties, regrets and even U-turns along the way. Into this scenario place a Prince 13 years older (who has the tastes and intellectual values of a sophisticated man years his senior), a man who is also complex and emotionally needy yet brought up to expect women to rise serenely above their own emotions, and a sea of marital troubles potentially looms ahead.

It is highly possible with their different ways of dealing with emotions (he suppressing his feeling in order to remain in control and she needing to give voice to her feelings in order to gain reassurance) that they would continually set off each other's insecurity systems while being unable to respond to them appropriately. As Diana grew more desperate for love and attention, and therefore more demanding, Charles would be less and less able to respond and thus distance himself from her. If this were to continue unresolved week after week, year after year, the times of togetherness and harmony would be replaced by increasing periods of hostility and alienation.

I am certainly not saying that Charles' and Diana's relationship was destined to become an emotionally arid desert with no happy and fulfilling moments. They have many lovely astrological links between them which have been apparent in their camaraderie and their teasingly affectionate manner in public; their passionate care and enjoyment of their children is clearly another area of mutual delight, and there are many more lines of harmony drawing them together. However, given that the rumblings of discontent have reached enough of a crescendo to alert the media to their trying to lead separate lives, I have for the main part looked at the reasons (astrological and otherwise) for any marital problems. It's also worth mentioning that marriage, by and large, is an institution fraught with potential hazards and difficulties. No two people, especially if they are strong and dynamic characters, are going to exist permanently in blissful symbiosis. Almost all marriages have peaks and troughs. Charles and Diana's overriding problem is not that they have to cope with their differing personalities and priorities but that they must work through their personal dramas within a high-profile goldfish bowl. And as much as the media has in the past accelerated the path of romance, it could well now be impeding the natural process of a marriage that is simply changing gear and pitchforking it towards a much more dramatic and irrevocable conclusion.

Over the past decade, Charles has become increasingly absorbed in the inner life. What started initially as a passionate concern for ecology and the human condition has led to a spiritual search. Since the death of his much-loved mentor, Mountbatten, the distinguished writer-philosopher Sir Laurens van der Post has become a close friend and advisor. Increasingly, Charles' speeches reflect his personal philosophy; while in the main these ideas are laudable by anyone's standards, his apparently radical views have inspired murmurings of disapproval among the powers that be.

Circles close to the Royal Family maintain Charles is becoming increasingly frustrated by the non-committal stance he is pressured to take on issues that he cares deeply about: he feels ineffective—a man with a leading role on the world's stage but no real power. Astrologically, this dilemma is portrayed by the 90° square aspect from the Sun to Pluto—no one feels the pressures and frustrations of life, or indeed fate, as the individual with a Sun-Pluto square. Ironically, the very inspirations that make him potentially a great leader are the forces that could conspire against him fulfilling such a destiny.

Astrologically, 1988 looks to be a watershed for Charles. As transiting Saturn and Uranus oppose Uranus in his birth chart, the desire to be free to say and do as he wishes has never been stronger: so too are the burdens, responsibilities and restrictions of his position. That he rubbed shoulders with death on the ski slopes of Klosters and carried the blame for his friend's death is the outer manifestation of an inner process depicted by these aspects. Breaking the rules (Uranus) comes with a heavy Saturnian cost. As a future monarch, will he really be free to carry out the things that he most wants to do; will he be allowed to challenge the status quo which, as an uncompromising Scorpio, he will have to do if he is to help Britain and the world become a better, more caring society? And even if he feels he can, will the powers that be permit such radical interference from a figurehead?

As an astrologer viewing the current planetary picture, one is tempted to speculate that Charles is finding increasing difficulty in blending his spiritual inner values with his outer role. In the process he is retreating further and further into himself thereby widening the already large gulf between himself and Diana.

While, in times past, a Royal wife would be expected simply to put up with a situation no matter how desperate, the Princess of Wales belongs to a generation that has come to expect greater things from life and certainly from relationships. Whereas Charles may suffer in silence and put up with an unsatisfactory relationship, Diana's chart shows she cannot live without love.* The all-or-nothing flavour to her emotional life suggests that if she were seriously unhappy in her marriage she would have the courage and determination to end it; she would also be extremely vulnerable to falling in love with a man who could demonstrate the affection and empathy she needs. As I said in **Synastry** seven years ago, 'The "T"-square involving both feminine planets (Moon and Venus), desirous Mars and unpredictable, 'revolutionary' Uranus . . . implies that she requires great freedom of self-expression, and despite her desire for security she needs plenty of stimulation in the way of exciting and novel experiences. On the one hand she may bring a breath of fresh air into her relationships by the sheer force of her personality, never letting them stagnate or fall into dull routine. On the other hand, if her marriage becomes too restrictive, she will break out and seek new and more exciting horizons. As future Queen of England, the latter possibility is unthinkable let alone practicable – but then twenty years ago divorce for any member of the Royal Family was undreamed of!'

While the Princess of Wales is an extremely responsible and duty-born individual and would never put her own needs before those of her children, if she were to fall head over heels in love with someone who was prepared to go through proverbial hell, fire and water, not to mention the wall of Royal opposition and the British Government, she might well attempt to sunder the marital knot. Of course, the Royal Family would do everything in their power to prevent such a course of action, but faced with a truly determined Diana, nothing short of brute force would prevent her from leaving.

The twist in the tail of my hypothesis is that a legal separation or a divorce might become the very lever that would permit Charles to free himself in an entirely honourable fashion from the shackles and responsibilities of a role he does not in his heart of hearts want. After all, as King he would be the head of the Church of England–a position even in these enlightened times incompatible with being a divorced man. However, I believe that at this point in time Charles would reject out of hand the thought of marital separation and especially removing himself from the running of the monarchy. But give the simmering situation enough time it will surely bubble to the surface–and as far as the astrology is concerned we would be looking toward the early 1990s.

Charles has been preparing to become King all his life, but like the Prince of Wales before him, Edward VIII, he may believe he can have his cake

---

*Sun in Cancer in the 7th house trine elevated Neptune in Scorpio; Venus (ruler of the Midheaven) in its own sign of Taurus square the Moon (in the 2nd house of feelings) and Mars (in the 8th house of emotional and sexual exchange).

and eat it. In Charles' case it not the woman of his choice who is unacceptable, but the very things he stands for and the things he cares about. Paradoxically, free of Kingly office he may ultimately be the effective force he truly wants to be.

Several astrologers, both past and present, have suggested that Charles may not become King. While in these uncertain and violent times accident or assassination cannot be ruled out of such forecasts, I consider the above scenario the most plausible. But I must emphasize that this is just a scenario. I am not speaking from a godlike position of absolute knowledge. I'm like a weather forecaster, putting two and two together in an attempt to make four! It is also interesting and reassuring to note that Prince William's chart shows every indication that he will make it to the throne, thus any such crisis involving Charles will not jeopardize the entire future of the monarchy.

With the strong Pluto-Scorpio themes in his chart, the Prince of Wales has a powerful destiny to fulfil. It just may not happen quite the way the world expects.

Note for Astrologers: (1) The 4th house represents the foundation of the horoscope—not just home and family but the ancestral roots.

(2) By the end of 1991 and throughout 1992, transiting Pluto will reach Charles' Sun bringing out natal Sun-Pluto square. (Pluto will have squared its natal position in late 1989 and 1990.) In 1993 Pluto will conjoin the Queen's Midheaven at 25° Scorpio; Saturn transits the 3rd decanate of Aquarius on and off throughout 1993. 21°-25° of the fixed signs picks up Prince William's Venus, Prince Harry's Moon, Princess Diana's Venus, Moon and Uranus, the Queen's Mars, Saturn, Neptune and Jupiter and the Queen Mother's and Prince Andrew's Moon. In fact this degree area is significant in the charts of virtually all the leading members of the Royal Family and all three of the Great Britain charts. Also in 1993, transiting Uranus and Neptune will conjoin Charles and Diana's composite IC and the Queen's Ascendant. By progression around this time, Charles' progressed Ascendant will conjunct Saturn, while the Queen's progressed Venus (her Sun-ruler) will oppose her Saturn and Midheaven.

SAGITTARIUS

23 November–23 December

GYPSIES, ADVENTURERS, AND THE DON JUAN SYNDROME

SAGITTARIUS
GYPSIES, ADVENTURERS,
AND THE DON JUAN SYNDROME

SAGITTARIUS is as different from his next-door-neighbours, Scorpio and Capricorn, as day is from night. While the latter two signs identify with the serious side of life and tend to encounter major difficulties and setbacks along the way, Sagittarians seem positively to jaunt through life—irrepressible, ebullient, and vibrant. However, it is possible to have too much of a good thing: 'Nothing in excess' quoth the ancient Delphic Oracle—a motto that should be written in large red letters and pinned inside every Sagittarian's wallet or handbag, or stuck on the 'fridge or the drinks cabinet; for this sign, unrestrained and unchecked, can wreak havoc not only in its own life but in those of others.

Occasionally when teaching astrology I have asked people to choose the sign of the zodiac they would most like to have been born under, and by far the most popular choice is Sagittarius. Jupiter-ruled, this sign is famed for its *bonhomie*, optimism, and happy-go-lucky nature; while some signs seem synonymous with struggle and difficulty, Sagittarians often appear to live charmed lives.

My Sagittarian clients are also some of my most affable and amenable. They have the same huge sense of humour and friendly ease common to all the fire signs, yet will never argue as much as the Arian or try to protect or augment their ego every step of the way like Leo. They enjoy learning about the symbolism and enter the consultation in the spirit of an adventure. One or two of my Sagittarian clients have become keen astrologers themselves and often drop by unexpectedly with antiquarian astrology books or tales of astrological delight.

Sagittarians of both sexes are usually tall and even those born to small-statured families are taller than expected. One of the major characteristics of those with their Ascendant or Sun in Sagittarius is their lolloping gait which, combined with their fiery speed, makes them awfully clumsy. (My brother-in-law with Sagittarius rising once managed to break three chairs in one afternoon merely by sitting down in them!) They are usually long in the leg, particularly from the knees upwards, and some have problems with over-padded thighs! Another characteristic that seems very common with Sagittarian individuals is that no matter how new or well-made their clothes may be, they still manage to appear slightly dishevelled, perhaps with a safety pin concealed in a hem or a torn sleeve lining. Like their Aries and Leo brothers and sisters, their features are strong and well defined, and their hair abundant. However, out of the three fire signs, male Sagittarians seem most prone to baldness.

Sagittarians' good fortune and benign and expansive natures owe much to their ruling planet, Jupiter—the largest and most impressive planet in our solar system. In Roman myth Jupiter was a sky god and his presence was associated with thunderbolts and flashes of lightning; he was concerned with oaths, treaties, and alliances and was the guardian of public morality. (This

latter aspect is perhaps not so easily identifiable with many Sagittarian souls!)
The same idea of sky and thunderbolts is repeated in the Greek myth of Zeus,
king of the gods, and astrologically a Jupiterian or Sagittarian theme in a chart
is usually related to the loftier side of life—philosophy, religion, metaphysics,
and law. Jupiter/Zeus also had a fearsome temper and, when displeased,
would hurl deadly and destructive thunderbolts at his offenders. This is fairly
classic behaviour in some Sagittarian or Jupiterian individuals: when they are
happy, content, and life is running to their liking, peace, harmony, and
generosity reign supreme; but hurt, angered, or their actions blocked, the
temperature soars, plates fly, and vitriol and shattered glass rain down
mercilessly on their opponent. Fortunately their anger is short lived, like the
Aries variety; they forgive and forget easily and hardly ever bear grudges.

Zeus was the son of Cronos (Saturn) and in the same way that Cronos came
to power after murdering his father Ouranos, Zeus became king after a
successful struggle between Cronos and the Titans. (I particularly like the
idea that here jolly, roll-on-the-good-times Jupiter triumphed over miserable,
wet-blanket Saturn.) Indeed, in many ways these two planets seem pitted
against each other in astrology since they represent opposite characteristics of
expansion and limitation, joy and sadness, happiness and pain. In everyday
life one comes across individuals who seem to achieve all (and more) out of
life with apparent lack of effort and ease of manner; others, however, appear
dogged by misfortune and setbacks, and although they may well get there in
the end, there is often a price to pay. The former (Jupiterian) individuals have
an apparently in-born expectation that life will unfold well for them and
their optimism and good humour open doors of opportunity and possibility
for them. Other, more Saturnine individuals, seem to expect difficulties as
par for the course and consequently have a natural mistrust of life that in turn
appears to dog their tracks with disappointment and failure.

The symbol for Sagittarius is the Centaur—half man, half horse—whose bow
and arrow is aimed forcefully upwards into the distance beyond. The
Archer/Centaur is a divine questor; his bow and arrow is not aimed to kill nor,
indeed, aimed at any fixed objective; his fiery arrows are released to
illuminate a path. The Sagittarian individual is not one for fixed goals in life;
he wants to see and do many things, some of which evolve out of one
experience into the next without any apparent forethought. Consequently,
the Sagittarian hates to be limited by anything so mundane as a rigid
ambition. The Archer is an enormously open-minded individual; he has the
enthusiasm and wonder of a child and sees possibilities and glorious vistas in
the most unexpected quarters. He is often deeply interested in spiritual
philosophy, which, like his divine optimism, bolsters him against the darker
aspects of life. The poet and mystic William Blake, was a strongly Sagittarian
individual, as was the writer and supporter of parapsychology, Arthur
Koestler.

One of my clients with several planets in Sagittarius had a series of mystical
experiences that profoundly altered his life. At thirty, he was a successful
businessman, married with two children, yet he had the usual Sagittarian's
pair of itchy feet and longed to spend more of his time travelling and soaking
up foreign cultures. At the time he first consulted me his marriage was falling
apart and divorce was imminent—his wife had met someone else and

although the affair was a fleeting one, the trust had gone out of their relationship. He was extremely upset at the thought of losing his children and was also deeply affected by the break-up of the marriage itself. Driving home late one afternoon along a quiet country road, all at once he was overwhelmed by the colour and beauty of the countryside that seemed not only to surround him but also to be within him. He got out of the car and walked into the woods, where the sounds of the birds and the rustling of the foliage heightened and intensified the visual experience to a point where he seemed to leave his body. Gradually the effects faded but he was left with a profound sense of wonder and peace. This was the first of several such experiences.* During the course of the following year, he sorted out his business affairs, found a girlfriend who shared his interest in the mystical and the metaphysical, and went off to India, where I believe he is happily ensconced in an ashram.

In myth, however, Centaurs (or Satyrs) were invidious creatures renowned for violence and lust. They were the product of a strange union between the Thessalian hero, Ixion, and a cloud. Ixion had murdered his father-in-law over an argument about his wife's dowry. For some reason Zeus took a shine to Ixion and purified him of his sin. In return Ixion became infatuated with Zeus's wife, Hera, and planned to seduce her! Zeus heard of his intentions and fashioned a cloud (Nephele) into the likeness of his wife. Ixion was decieved and after mating with the cloud, the Centaurs were born—all except one, whom I shall discuss shortly.

Many of the tales in which Centaurs play a part contain a Sagittarian motif; the following myth involving Nessus is a case in point. The Centaur, Nessus, earned his living ferrying travellers across a mountain torrent, the Evenus. One day, the great Heracles—a solar hero in the Leo mould, famed for his twelve labours—hired him to carry over his new bride, Deianeira. Half-way across, Nessus was overcome with lust for Deianeira—an occupational hazard for most Centaurs—but was thwarted in his efforts by her loud screams which alerted Heracles. Heracles took his great bow and sent a poisoned arrow through the Centaur's side. As he lay dying, Nessus begged Deianeira to take his blood-soaked robe, informing her that were Heracles to wear it, he would never love another woman. Deianeira took the robe and stored it away, never for a moment doubting Heracles' love for her. Many years later, however, Heracles became infatuated with the king of Oechalia's daughter, Iole, and stormed and sacked Oechalia for the love of her. In an effort to win him back, Deianeira sent a messenger to him with the robe. As soon as Heracles put it on, it began to burn him, for the robe was impregnated with Nessus' deadly poisonous blood. Deianeira, overcome with grief, killed herself. Somehow, presumably through his superhuman strength, Heracles managed to climb Mount Oeta and build a high pyre for his body: only Philoctetes would agree to light the pyre, and in return he received Heracles' bow and arrows. As the pyre burned Heracles' body, suddenly there was a violent thunderclap: Heracles was freed from his mortal bonds and his spirit caught by Zeus and carried to Olympus. Zeus' wife, Hera (amongst other attributes, the goddess

---

*Astrologers please note that during this time my client had Neptune transiting his Sun and Mercury.

of wives) forgave Heracles; she accepted him as a god and gave him her daughter, Hebe—the goddess of youth—as his wife.

Both Ixion and Heracles were great heroes, but they had flaws. While Heracles was famed for his strength and valorous deeds, he was nevertheless unfaithful to his wife. Poor Deianeira unwittingly became the agent of his death and so killed herself, but Heracles had a noble death; he was made immortal and taken up to Olympus. Certainly the gods do seem to smile on Jupiterian folk; and though the Sagittarian individual frequently takes the most dreadful liberties in life, he or she usually manages to come out on top. That Heracles should find immortality through burning to 'death' on a pyre can be seen to illustrate the tapping of the spiritual fire that courses through Sagittarius. Clearly, not all Sagittarians respond to the spiritual side of this sign, and then the fiery drive finds other outlets of expression. Yet often the restlessness of the Sagittarian individual is quelled once he or she has begun to pursue an inner quest and embrace a spiritual or philosophical path.

Some sources maintain that the mating of Ixion with Nephele produced the Centaur, Cheiron, but in later myths Cheiron is said to be the son of Cronos. Cronos (Zeus' father) took a lusty liking to the nymph Philyra. In order to escape him she took the form of a mare, but Cronos turned himself into a stallion and caught up with her. The result of their union was Cheiron. Unlike the other Centaurs, Cheiron was a noble figure who lived a peaceful existence in a cave with his mother and his wife, Chariclo. He was a healer, teacher and a prophet and in many ways something of a maverick. His abilities were revered by the gods and men alike, and many young heroes were brought to Cheiron by their fathers to be trained by him, in particular Achilles (whom he fostered), Jason and Aristaeus. Heracles was also a great friend of Cheiron's—some even say he was guided by the Centaur—but sadly, Heracles was to play a part in Cheiron's tragedy. One evening, Heracles visited the Centaur; while they were talking Cheiron accidentally dropped one of Heracles' poisoned arrows on his foot. From that moment he was in dreadful agony, but since he was immortal, he knew he must forever bear the pain. However, Heracles found a solution. Prometheus (who had incurred Zeus' wrath by stealing fire from the gods, and for his punishment had been chained to a rock where an eagle came every day to eat his liver) could only be released if an immortal was prepared to give up his immortality. Thus Prometheus was delivered from his fate by Cheiron. An ironical, sad and painful ending for such a noble figure.

Cheiron shows a very different side to Sagittarius. He was part animal, and therefore in touch with the earthy, 'human' aspect of mankind, but was also a god with divine gifts. (The Sagittarian, while partaking of the good things of life, often voraciously, is frequently blessed with great wisdom and beneficence.) The pain Cheiron had to bear was accidentally self-inflicted; and in a sense Heracles also suffered a self-inflicted death since the blood concealed in Nessus' robe had been poisoned by his own arrow. Leaving on one side the clumsy tendencies of Sagittarius, there is often an aspect of the teacher and healer in Jupiterian individuals. Indeed, on a more profound level, it could be said that the Sagittarian who experiences pain in his life—often through his own actions—and who subsequently taps this healing potential of his own nature, has found the essence of the Sagittarian myth and brought it into living expression.

There appears to be a link between both mythological figures, Cheiron and Zeus, in that Zeus seduced Cheiron's mother, and when caught **in flagrante delicto**, turned himself into a horse and galloped off. Which leads us to yet another dimension of the Sagittarian nature—the Don Juan syndrome (which I shall discuss later) and the Jupiterian predeliction for disguise. Many Sagittarians can out-perform the grandest Leo thespian, not only on stage but in real life. The Sagittarian, like the Aquarian, dislikes being cast in one role: he's a nomadic rover at heart and prefers the repertory theatre existence of a new role every week—and a new town. This need for change is not only part of his restless roving nature, but an instinctive dislike of being scrutinized, or of people trying to classify him. As consummate actors, Sagittarian men and women can turn a run-of-the-mill story into a riot of ridiculousness and laughter. In essence they are the zodiac's entertainers and clowns, although in true Pagliaci style, many an Archer hides his sadness under his buffooning mask. Bette Midler is, in many ways, the quintessential Sagittarian: a buoyant, zestful performer with a raucous 'camp' sense of humour, yet able to invest immense pathos and poignancy into her acting and singing when required.

Zeus was an enormously powerful god; and in keeping with this idea, some Sagittarian-Jupiterian types can be 'power-hungry'. All the fire signs like to run the show and while Sagittarius is often apparently more easy-going than the other two, he doesn't like being overshadowed. While there is nothing essentially wrong in developing a taste for power—after all somebody has to take on the principal role in every walk of life—how that power is wielded matters tremendously. Several astrologers have noted the presence of Jupiter in key positions in the birth charts of many of the leading Nazis during the Second World War. Certainly there was nothing beneficent about any of these men except in the way they looked after themselves. Most of them ordered or took part in actions of unspeakable horror, presumably in the belief that the ends justified the means. For these Jupiterian individuals, power corrupted absolutely. While the Nazis might provide a rather extreme example of Jupiterian excess, it is worth bearing in mind that power, once held, is always difficult to relinquish—for even the most idealistic of Jupiterian hands.

All the fire signs are unfailingly honest and open. Little flames of truth burst from their lips before they have time to consider the consequences of their words. Many are the friends, family, and opponents of Sagittarians who have been on the receiving end of the disturbingly candid, but usually malice-free opinions and thoughts. Aries is famed for his chronic foot and mouth disease, and although Sagittarius is every bit as undiplomatic, he has more charm than his Mars-ruled brother and people seem better able to swallow Jupiter's medicine than Mars'. A one-time Sagittarian neighbour of mine is a case in point. I had for some time coveted what I thought to be the most beautiful kitchen table that stood in expensive glory in a trendy high-street shop. To my delight, it was reduced to half-price in the January sales and, being a cheerful spendthrift fire sign myself, I shot in and bought it. The table was delivered the same afternoon and, as I had anticipated, was far too large for our tiny cottage kitchen. Fortunately, my next door neighbour's sitting-room was temporarily doubling for the junk-room. so I was able to deposit the table among his stacks of books and various orange boxes. When I heard my neighbour returning from work later that afternoon I called him in to explain what this wonderful table was doing in his house. Before I could tell the tale my neighbour silenced me with his immediate perception of my plight. 'No—I know what you're going to say . . . I've seen it . . . Not to worry, it can stay there until you move. I'm not surprised you don't want it in your house. Heap of old junk isn't it!'

Given that Sagittarians have a penchant for speaking first and considering the impact of their words later (usually as they see the recipient's stricken expression), this same verbal frankness often proves to be at their own expense. Sagittarians receive inspired ideas like radar traps and sail into God-given opportunities with the ease of a hang-glider. Yet, rather than keep these ideas to themselves, they seem hell-bent on letting the world and his wife know about them first. Consequently the Archer is often pipped at the post by one of the more calculating signs who got to work on his ideas before he had time to finish his pint and cigar! When the Sagittarian has been out-manoeuvred or sees his ideas in print before he has time to utilize them himself, he may hurl a few Jupiterian thunderbolts about the place, but once his anger has subsided he'll shrug his shoulders and optimistically turn his attention to a new horizon. John De Lorean may be a Sun Capricorn but he has several planets in Sagittarius. His entrepreneurial skills certainly suffered from all kinds of Jupiterian excesses, including a £77 million loan from the British Government. How the Court found him not guilty of dealing in drugs when he had been videoed passing cocaine over to the CIA may also owe much to Jupiter's divine providence.

Paradoxically for a sign synonymous with truth, there are a great many Sagittarian individuals capable of fabricating the most marvellous stories to disguise the real facts of a situation. Part of the reason may be the Archer's delight in fantasy and story-telling and his preference for embellishment rather than understatement; another may be a childish horror of being found out, or shown up in a bad light. Indeed, there seem to be two kinds of truth for Sagittarius, or perhaps three. First, the quest for truth—spiritual truth—and the meaning of life. Second, truth in terms of an honest opinion, whether voiced about Aunt Mabel's ghastly hat, an author's prized manuscript, or even a friend's table! But, thirdly, for the Sagittarian truth depends on the angle and motive he cares to take. One boyfriend of a client of mine was apparently unable to tell the truth—even to help himself. On one occasion my client rang her lover's office to see if he had returned from Portsmouth. 'Yes,' came the reply, 'he popped in an hour ago and went off to lunch.' Two hours later the lover phoned my client, '. . . can't speak for long, I'm in a pay phone on the motorway . . . been terribly delayed in Portsmouth.' When confronted by my client that she knew he was back he explained, 'when I got to the office I realized I'd left some papers in Portsmouth so I had to go back and get them.'

Fortunately, or unfortunately depending on your angle, Sagittarians are thoroughly likeable and all too easy to forgive. Most are also enormously generous and capable of bringing happiness and glad tidings with them wherever they go. Perhaps because Archers are so easy to get on with, they are welcomed by any group or organization and are first on the list for prospective party-givers. It is also worth noting that Sagittarians actually like to be invited to the right places, and to be seen mixing with the right people. Although the Centaur may seem above such things as class or following a particular stream, most of them are enormous intellectual and cultural snobs. They have some of the Geminian's curiosity about them and, while displaying casual indifference, will sniff out the 'in' rock group or author and adopt the trendiest fashion or life-style. In some cases this can amount to downright one-up-manship, so that however casually a name is dropped, whatever sounds emanate from the hi-fi or exotic travel documents drop out of the **Spectator** and the current exhibition programme at the Tate, there is an unsubtle innuendo that they are ever so slightly superior.

The Sagittarian, although vastly different from his Capricorn neighbour in most areas of life, likes to show evidence of a 'good background' every bit as much as the Goat. Most Jupiterian homes sport some relic of ancestral delight, even if it has to be bought—threadbare Persian rugs are a particular favourite. By and large, Sagittarians like to do things in style, which often necessitates living above their means in order to accommodate their image. One Sagittarian girlfriend of mine, although forced to earn a menial living (temporarily) as a clerk in an insurance company, used to pick up a taxi from work just to go one block. She felt better in the knowledge that she was keeping up appearances. The interior of my friend's 'fridge also had much to say about its owner—empty except for a bottle of Bollinger and some Camembert!

Another point about Sagittarian individuals is that most of them tend to be extremely gullible. Rather like the Aquarian (another great truth seeker), Archers' trusting, accommodating natures often mean they can be led astray by dubious financial schemes, persuasive con-men, or out and out charlatans. The Jupiterian soul is also a soft touch where money is concerned; he positively enjoys being magnanimous (on occasion), although he likes spending money on himself best of all. Since the Sagittarian is often somewhat absent-minded, he may actually forget to whom he has loaned money (and sometimes borrowed from) and, combined with his tendency to over-extend himself, he often has to wear dark glasses when he enters his bank!

The theme that unites all Sagittarians, male and female, young and old, is a thirst for distant horizons. In keeping with the Archer's questing nature, Sagittarians need freedom to explore their world, either with their itchy feet or their expansive minds. The Sagittarian is often a great thinker, though not in the logical, quicksilver way of the Geminian or the practical, detailed manner of the Virgoan—indeed he can sometimes seem absent-minded and forgetful in the extreme. However, his range of perception is vast and his perspective acute; he grasps complex thought structures instinctively without necessarily following their processes. The Sagittarian is often an artist at heart and his brilliant visions emerge through music, painting, or writing. Winston Churchill was the quintessential Sagittarian in many respects, as were Mark Twain, Maria Callas, and Edith Piaf.

The typical Sagittarian hates restraints of any sort, either mentally or physically, and male and female Centaurs are destined to cross frontiers of one sort or another. Most have a tendency to roam through life with their heads in the clouds, which can make for some nasty tumbles on occasion, but the air is always sharper and the sky a perennial blue thousands of feet above Earth!

My mother-in-law, who is a strongly Jupiterian individual, has a framed photograph of a speeding horse in her bedroom. Underneath the picture is a little motto which epitomizes the Sagittarian outlook:

> Three things come not back,
> The sped arrow,
> the spoken word
> and the neglected opportunity.

RELATIONSHIPS

The Sagittarian, like his fiery team-mates Leo and Aries, loves being in love. Male and female Sagittarians adore the opposite sex and are rarely short of suitors and admirers. But—and it's a big but—when it comes to marriage their previously sunny horizons are filled with threatening thunder clouds, making them some of the most reluctant husbands and wives in the zodiac. The Sagittarian finds the ties and commitments of marriage as difficult to accommodate as the Geminian and the Aquarian. However, unlike Gemini or Aquarius, who have difficulty in getting to the altar at all, the Archer usually rushes into marriage with high hopes and blind optimism, only to realize later it isn't quite as much fun as he thought it would be. Consequently, strongly Sagittarian individuals are not strangers to the divorce courts. Sagittarians, like their fiery compatriot Arians, sometimes experience a temporary aversion to marriage after an acrimonious divorce, but when once again spiked by Cupid's dart, most will canter enthusiastically to the Registry Office again . . . and again . . . and again! (Once bitten twice shy is not a maxim they appreciate.) Of all the signs of the zodiac, Sagittarius seems most prone to multiple marriages. However, despite the generally poor track record of many Sagittarians regarding marriage, some manage very durable, long-term relationships *provided* they have plenty of scope, mental and social stimulation, and above all freedom.

THE FEMALE SAGITTARIUS

The female Archer has much of the adventurous, happy-go-lucky qualities of the male about her. She may be as feminine to look at as Princess Diana (Sagittarius rising) or Jane Fonda (Sun Sagittarius), but she's a tomboy at heart. She is also a much better marriage prospect than her male counterpart. One of the explanations is that, like almost all women, Ms Sagittarius operates through her Moon, Venus, and Ascending sign when it comes to love and relationships, rather than her Sun sign. Thus, if her Moon or Venus is in a gentle water sign, or a steadfast, reliable earth sign, she is likely to bring a far more stable and consistent quality into her relationships. However, regardless of the watery or earthy content of the chart, the spritely, forthright nature of Sagittarius will also be much in evidence.

The Sagittarian woman is extremely idealistic about her relationships. She is likely to have read avidly from an early age and identified strongly with heroines like Mary Queen of Scots and Edith Cavel. As captain of the hockey team, she probably spent many afternoons leggily leaping across the sports field, eye on the ball but heart pounding for the art master. Every so often she may have slipped away from the hurly-burly of common-room debates to do hip and thigh exercises in the bathroom, perhaps also anxiously to tweeze her eyebrows. (Sagittarian ladies' hair usually comes in large quantities—sometimes where they wish it didn't!) Hoping, yet not daring to hope too much, that the art master might smile at her, she would serenely, yet forcefully stride into morning assembly—only to catch her shoulder bag on the door handle and shatter her sophisticated image.

Ms Sagittarius is exceedingly romantic and longs to be the cool, unreachable siren of her romantic novels, brave and daring yet meltingly feminine. But in real life she's far too honest to place her fire behind an icy mask and nine times out of ten she'll initiate a date and even do the proposing.

Certainly the Sagittarian female wants something different out of her life and marriage than she thinks her mother settled for. She may not know exactly what or who, but she feels her senses ought to be assaulted by love and her life enriched (sometimes quite literally) by the experience. Some Sagittarian women determinedly avoid the nuptial knot—at least until their thirties—preferring to explore their fun-loving formative years unhampered by domesticity and the marital treadmill. Others marry the first person they fall in love with, then spend most of their time trying to stretch their bonds to accommodate their need for independence and freedom. However, despite the prevailing astrological view that Sagittarian women invariably flounder in marital waters, I have found that Jupiter-ruled ladies are just as ready to fall in love and waltz romantically down the aisle as the next Cancerian or Piscean. What is different is their attitude to relationships and how they see their role.

Unlike the more pliable water signs or duty-bound earth variety, Ms Sagittarius is not prepared to act as a doormat for her partner nor become an efficient charlady/cook/nanny either. She has ideals beyond the kitchen sink and fails to see the point in becoming a skivvy when she could be out seeing LIFE or doing something life-enhancing. Nearly all Sagittarian women have a restless, creative streak within them that demands an outlet beyond the home. For some this means a new adult education course every year; for others it's the membership of the amateur dramatic society or the gliding club; many more have a novel on the go in the attic, or a printing press going full tilt in the basement. The Sagittarian woman who is content solely to spend her time in the home nurturing and cherishing the children is one with a strong watery or earthy element in her chart: in this case the husband is usually the one displaying all the freedom-loving, adventurous qualities of this sign.

This is not to say that the Sagittarian woman cannot handle the home and the children well if she has to. I must make it clear that this sign is as capable as the next Virgo of good house management; and she can make an excellent job of bringing up the children too, once they've gone beyond the nappy stage and can talk to her, visit the museums, or go roller-skating. It's just that the female Archer's arrows were made to fly further afield than the home and become severely blunted aimed at four square walls all the time. While Ms Sagittarius likes a home she can be proud of, she'd far rather someone else cleaned it. Although she has bags of energy and enthusiasm she resents wasting time on dusting and polishing; thus housework tends to be done in fits and starts—a major blitz every so often, rather than a sensible daily dose. Ms Sagittarius likes casual elegance and detests apple pie order, which is a good thing as Jupiter-ruled ladies become completely neurotic trying to win the housewife of the year award.

In many way her culinary skills mirror her approach to life. Ms Sagittarius hates following a recipe and frequently finds difficulty in organizing her cooking so that the oven reaches the right temperature (or has even been turned on) before she puts the cake in. She would much prefer to throw in handfuls of this and that; and indeed when she does, what usually emerges is an exotic and wonderful creation.

In keeping with her spontaneous approach to the culinary arts, the female Archer rarely attaches much forethought to entering a relationship, nor indeed much patience to running one. Like all the fire signs, she acts on impulse and instinct. However, it is unusual to find the Jupiter-ruled lady married to the humble bank clerk, at least not unless he's captain of the local rugby team or a student of philosophy in his spare time. Regardless of financial restraints, Ms Sagittarius will invest plenty of style in her marriage, and on her partner. However, fierce and proud though her love may be, loyalty is not her strongest suit; if she falls out of love with her man or he fails to live up to expectations, she will have no hestiation in moving on.

Some Sagittarian women, expecially those with no earthy planets in their charts, have great trouble in keeping their relationships on an even keel and often become down-right neurotic about their partners. Sagittarius is a highly-strung fire sign and also a 'mutable' one; while fiery Leo sticks by a relationship through the good times and the bad, and fiery Aries positively relishes the challenge of a difficult partner, some Sagittarian women seem unable to take the ebbs and flows of relationships in their stride. Small incidents, which might pass by unnoticed by another sign, are magnified ten fold by Ms Sagittarius. She can blow up like an inflatable dinghy when upset or outraged, and instead of waiting for her feelings to subside and for the natural course of time to sort things out, she will take immediate action, which she invariably regrets later. Needless to say, unless her partner is cast out of granite, few lovers can tolerate the severe rises and falls in emotional temperature over a long period of time.

A great friend of mine—Amanda—has her Sun, Ascendant, and Venus in Sagittarius, and her Moon in fiery Aries; she has no planets in earth signs, so in many aspects of her emotional life she exemplifies the more unstable kind of Sagittarian—emotions running on all four cylinders with the brakes and suspension needing considerable attention. Amanda yo-yoed in and out of relationships like a punch-drunk boxer. Although each relationship may have spanned a year or two it would be peppered with many breaks and separations. During one particular relationship, every month or so I'd receive a frantic telephone call from her telling me it was over and she was returning to her own flat. Thus, once a month she'd pour all her belongings into giant dustbin liners and rush tearfully home. These sojourns were usually precipitated by her lover's equally unstable and volatile behaviour. On one occasion, during a traumatic row in the car, matters became so heated that she made a hasty exit (not exactly unaided by her lover), which might have been all right had the car not been moving at the time, *and* along a hot and dusty Spanish road miles from the nearest town! Amusing as this may sound, to my friend her life, at least as far as her relationships were concerned, was far from happy.

Amanda's career as a model had opened the door to a jet-set world of fun, wealth, and the good times. She hob-nobbed with the famous, made trips to exotic parts, and took her choice from a gaggle of sports stars, entertainers, and playboys. (A Sagittarian lady's Utopia!) Unfortunately, a large part of her glamorous image was good old Jupiter's dab hand with disguise, and although outwardly she could cope with her jet-set existence, inwardly she was a little girl lost in a world of sharks and barracudas. With regard to love and romance her Jupiterian quest for larger than life experiences propelled her into the arms of the requisite Don Juans that inundated her high-gloss world—men that her emotionally vulnerable nature really couldn't cope with. Had her Sagittarian, neon-lit personality been underpinned by some stabilizing earthy planets, she would no doubt have been able to steer a firmer course through the mine-laden waters of romance. As it was, her insecurity continually interfered with her independent, free-spirited personality, swinging her from one emotional stance to another.

Once a relationship (usually with a highly attractive, don't-fence-me-in type) had gone beyond the first stage of passionate romance, Amanda would become neurotic and dependent on the partner, regardless of whether he was right for her or even if he made her happy. Unsure whether or not to become wholly committed to the relationship, yet not wanting to make her dependence obvious, she would seek reassurance from the partner, who usually couldn't commit himself either—a state of play that naturally produced deep insecurity in Amanda. On the one hand she would insist on her independence and freedom, yet when her partner offered no resistance, her dependence and need would leap to the fore urging her to make emotional demands on him. Every time a major impasse arose in the relationship she would, in true Jupiterian style, erupt like a hot water geyser, then cut and run, only to return to her lover a week or so later.

This kind of see-saw pattern, admittedly compounded by a lack of down-to-earth qualities in the chart, is not untypical of strongly Sagittarian ladies. Some, instead of lurching from a freedom stance to a dependent one *within* a relationship, move from partner to partner. In many ways, rather like some Pisceans and Geminians, a great many Jupiterian ladies have a problem with commitment, yet they fail to see that the lack of commitment is a fault in themselves, not in their partner.

This clash between freedom and dependence was voiced by several Sagittarian ladies who responded to my questionnaire. One wrote, 'Whether I am conscious of it or not, I miss my freedom when I'm in a relationship. Perhaps that is why I end them. I certainly notice my overriding need for freedom clashes with my security needs.' Another female put the dilemma in this way, 'There is a total conflict between my needing stability and security on the one hand and freedom and excitement on the other.'

This difficulty in establishing a happy balance between these two warring factions in the female Archer's personality stems not only from an inability to become totally committed to another individual, but also from a fear of emotional pain. However, the Sagittarian who encounters pain in her life and faces it instead of running from it, is one who should be able to find peace of mind and relief from her inner restlessness. Amanda is typical of the Sagittarian female who wants the world to be sunny and glorious—a kind of never-ending Disneyland. In this state of mind, problems and responsibilities become something to be feared instead of acknowledged and dealt with before they become overpowering. Amanda's flights with dustbin liners represents fruitless attempts to remove herself from the scene of the pain without attempting to solve the underlying issues.

However, there is more to Amanda's story. Amanda's thirtieth birthday ushered a major crisis. Gone were the halcyon days of her twenties when all things were possible. Somehow she'd reached the end of the rainbow and there was no pot of gold. With middle age (according to Amanda) just around the corner, great haste had to be made in order to put her life straight. Although transformation was unfortunately impossible overnight, she made an important discovery that the problems she experienced with men had something to do with her own inconsistencies. Presented with this new awareness she began to take a more adult and responsible attitude to her existing relationship, which in turn produced a much more tolerant attitude in her lover. Although she still felt the impluse to leave after every blazing row, she began instead to wait for the dust to settle and to search for solutions in the debris. Hopefully, in time, she will bridge the chasm between her desire for independence and her security needs so that her spirit of adventure and love of excitement will neither be crushed by the responsibility of a long-term relationship, nor a stable, committed relationship be constantly undermined through her fiery restlessness.

Many Sagittarian women never experience such conflict in their partnerships. Because the Jupiter-ruled female is frank and direct (and absolutely hopeless at playing emotional games) she is usually able to prevent her relationships from becoming a soup of emotional chaos by voicing her opinions and feelings every step of the way. Indeed, like Ms Aries, who also insists on her own way most of the time, Ms Sagittarius is no stranger to the use of airborne missiles to drive her argument home. The Sagittarian lady is also enormously philosophical and optimistic about life and she usually manages to make the best of any given situation; should any great obstacle arise she can usually find a way round it. Although not an overly jealous or possessive type, should she suspect or discover her lover is unfaithful she will confront him immediately. If she loves him enough, she'll remain after the firework display has died down—if not she'll leave without hesitation.

Ms Sagittarius in incapable of living a lie where her emotions are concerned and many a suitor has limped away with third-degree burns from her candid assessments of her feelings for him. Because the female Archer is capable of the most insistent sort of love, she is rarely prepared to settle for a luke-warm response from her man. While some may accuse her of inconsistency and fecklessness, others see only her warm spirit and enormous generosity. The Jupiterian female may never become a fully-fledged housefrau, nor a gentle, yielding support for her man—she'll never be content to take a back seat to him either.—She's an adventurer and a philosopher at heart, never too busy to learn something new or embark on a voyage of discovery, physical or mental. She may suffer periodic bouts of foot and mouth disease but at least her heart is in the right place and she's never lost for words to tell you how much she loves you.

THE MALE SAGITTARIUS

The Sagittarian man, like the Aquarian and the Geminian, has a dubious reputation when it comes to love, romance, and marriage. Although he is in his Archer's element, ardently pursuing amorous adventures, he enters marriage like the preoccupied hunter falling into an elephant trap. As with the Aquarian and the Geminian, Mr Sagittarius has an almost drug-like dependency on freedom, a state totally antithetical to marriage. Unfortunately, the male Sagittarian, like some female Centaurs, has a major problem with commitment and responsibility; thus until these requirements are acknowledged and assimilated by his 6-cylinder, 6½ litre personality, Mr Sagittarius should be given a wide berth by any aspiring wife.

Of course the Archer is not without his assets, nor, indeed, a trail of willing women to shower them on. He is usually extremely charming and debonair; he has friends everywhere—a great many of them old girlfriends—and no matter how many times he treads on people's toes and ruffles their feathers, he is unfailingly popular and often dearly loved. Even the sixty-year-old Centaur has something of the mischievous schoolboy about him and certainly a flirtatious twinkle in his eye. Irresistible and funny but elusive and with just a hint of danger, he is indeed a formidably attractive package for most women.

The male Sagittarian, like his female counterpart, enjoys the good things of life. He never does things by half and on occasion his indulgences verge on the excessive. He is enormously hedonistic, but fortunately capable of working hard enough and becoming successful enough to accommodate his expansive life-style. He dislikes being pinned down to appointments or long-term plans—a factor he struggles with at work but rarely bothers with in private life, much to the annoyance of his nearest and dearest. One friend of mine drives his family to distraction with his non-committal approach to arrangements. Every Christmas he waits until the family have sorted out who is going where and when before deciding which gathering looks the most fun. No matter how infuriating and inconvenient this is for the rest of his family, when he does appear his bravado and high spirits guarantee that he is immediately forgiven.

While friends and relatives may suffer only periodically from the Centaur's aversion to commitment, his girlfriend or wife has a full-time struggle on her hands. Time and time again I listen to the anguished wails of my female clients hitched up to Sagittarian's rambling wagon—how do they cope with his almost pathological inability to commit himself?!

One client of mine, Nikki, endured a typically casual but frustrating relationship with a Sagittarian, Sam, for two years. Although Sam appeared to adore her when he was with her, he would always leave without indicating when, or even if, there would be a next time. He would drop in and out of her life like an overgrown Tigger descending on a confused

Christopher Robin. No matter how Nikki tried to explain that, although **he** found the casual nature of their relationship entirely satisfactory she did not, his attitude was that she could take it or leave it! During the course of one long weekend together he suddenly announced on the Sunday morning that he was off to spend the rest of the day with his friend, Bill. No, she hadn't been invited. Not only did this come as the proverbial bolt from the blue to Nikki, especially as she was looking forward to a cosy Sunday together, but Bill was in fact **her** friend! With true Sagittarian thoughtlessness, it hadn't occurred to him that the acceptance of the invitation and his subsequent departure would in any way upset Nikki. On another occasion, Sam threw a large dinner party to celebrate his birthday—except that Nikki was left out. Nevertheless, he turned up a week later to see if she would go sailing with him!

Although Sam had some complex patterns in his chart that made his Sagittarian nature even more elusive and foot-loose, he serves to illustrate that, by and large, Sagittarian men are often extremely reluctant to become deeply involved in a relationship, with all its inherent responsibilities, commitments, and restrictions. Like some female Centaurs, the male Sagittarian wants life to be fun, with the horizon of possibilities constantly expanding in front of him; thus, to be tied down by anything as cloying as the love of a good woman is anathema to him.

There is another aspect to the male Centaur's reluctance to tie the nuptial knot. Strangely enough, Mr Sagittarius is extremely idealistic, if not something of a perfectionist, about love. He needs a woman who can respond to him on a higher, possibly spiritual level, someone to whom he can relay his visions, his dreams, and his beliefs. For many years he may search for this quality in his relationships without finding it, thus becoming the perennial bachelor—always the best man, never the groom! (Even my typist says she knows more Sagittarian bachelors of an indeterminate age than any other sign.) Sometimes the Sagittarian may marry without finding the special something he is seeking in a woman, in which case, unless he has many earthy planets in his chart, he will continue looking for her during his marriage. Sagittarian men are often extremely promiscuous and all too prone to the casual affair. Unfortunately, because they are usually persuasive and charming, many women are completely taken in by their earnest ingenuousness; however, the relationship rarely leads to a graceful glide down the aisle, but to a series of frustrations and disappointments instead.

Of all the signs, the Sagittarian man is probably the least 'understood by his wife'—according to him. Over pâté and a good claret in the wine bar he will pour out his unhappiness on the bosom of 'the one woman who could rescue him from this quagmire of wretchedness'. The poor unsuspecting 'mistress' frequently forms the picture of a veritable harridan waiting for him at home. Of course she is utterly floored when she sees his charming, attractive wife at the Christmas party, upon whom the Archer clearly dances much attendance. Despite their yearnings and longings, Sagittarian men are rarely the partner to walk out of a marriage. Nine time out of ten it is the wife who becomes tired of watching her husband being charming and witty to all and sundry yet skating free of emotional and sometimes financial responsibility to her and the family.

Another point worth noting about the Archer's wanderlust: although he may behave like an oversexed teenager, the physical side of a relationship is not really the most important thing for him and, indeed, his performance in this department may be less than wonderful. (I cover this in more detail in the section on sexuality.) The Archer wants his relationships perpetually to expand and enlarge, and if he feels emotional claustrophobia setting in, he may seek the excitement of untrammelled territory in a new (often clandestine) relationship.

The Sagittarian man is often very attracted to earthy or watery women (especially Virgos or Pisceans). He needs a partner who will clear up after him, someone who will apologize for him and be there to support or nurture him when his plans misfire. All too often, however, after a period of time he finds his wife becomes critical, negative, and even worse—emotionally dependent on him, and a continual reminder that he cannot take off just when he feels like it. It strikes me as both amusing and uncanny how many Sagittarian men appear to follow the path of their mythological ruler, Zeus, when it comes to romance and relationships. Zeus was bound—and I choose the word carefully—by marriage to the goddess Hera. Hera was pathologically jealous, and gave Zeus an extremely hard time. They quarrelled constantly, almost always over Zeus' indiscretions. Yet try as he might, he could never be free of her. Nor, if the truth were told, did he really want to be. He needed her. Zeus thrived on Hera's shrewish nature—her continual harassment provided the spur for his forbidden love affairs and, while he complained bitterly about her, she was exactly what he required. Given total freedom and released from his marriage bonds he would surely have found another Hera before too long.

Many Sagittarian men follow in Zeus' footsteps. They become involved with women who are 'mother earth' or the 'ice-maiden'. While it may appear to outsiders that the Sagittarian runs the relationship, in reality it is his more circumspect partner. The Sagittarian's partner is usually an ideal feminine figure, which does not necessarily mean she wears pretty dresses and has nothing but recipes and washing powder on her mind. No, she is the nurturer and sustainer, she has an air of mystery and a kind of 'dark power' that fascinates the Sagittarian male and draws him to her. These qualities, of course, belong to all women on an archetypal level; thus in principle it is possible for the Sagittarian to find them in any woman. However, more usually the Sagittarian will opt for a woman who provides a contrast to his free-ranging personality, a female who is sensible, cautious, reflective and restraining. Yet because of his frequent bouts of insensitive and self-willed behaviour she becomes shrewish, demanding and over-restraining. In other words she has become his Hera. Or perhaps the Sagittarian has actually turned her into Hera!

Sagittarius, like the other two fire signs, Aries and Leo, is usually strong on machismo and weak on sensitivity. Like the textbook Aries and Leo he relates more easily to masculine ideals of strength, fortitude and authority, and avoids prolonged contact with his gentler more vulnerable qualities. Yet without recognition of his feminine side he is unbalanced. Thus the most obvious (and usually unconscious) course of action is for him to find a woman who will supply the missing (or rather unintegrated) qualities for him. Wherein lies a problem: because he doesn't understand the feminine at all well, and in the confines of long term relationships he feels overpowered by women with their (to him) excessive emotional demands. What he needs both attracts and repels him.

In a strange way, almost all Sagittarian men find someone or something to run from in their lives; their freedom is relative to their 'earthly' chains of responsibility. Without a binding factor 'flight' becomes pointless and the Sagittarian merely an aimless wanderer. I must emphasize that I am talking in general terms here, and while a strong Sagittarian theme in a man's chart shows a tendency to run away from emotional demands and responsibilities, not all Sagittarian men will do so.

Since the Sagittarian man has difficulty in understanding the feminine, he is usually oblivious of any subtle tactics and manoeuvres performed by women in his life. Like the female of the species, he is frank and open in the extreme, although he is not incapable of some fairly artful dodging when necessary. A Sagittarian friend of mine was having an affair with an intense Scorpio lady. She lived with him only periodically since her home was abroad (the ideal Sagittarian situation). In true Scorpio style she was forever manipulating him and playing emotional and psychological games that unfortunately (for her) always flew over his head. One morning his girlfriend icily informed me that she was off to London for a couple of days. She mentioned some scene there had been over his usual lack of consideration and she was leaving, without letting him know where, in order to pay him back. Later that night my Sagittarian friend dropped in, and, **en passant**, I asked after his girlfriend. A look of surprise mingled with perplexity flooded his face. 'Come to think of it I haven't seen her since last night. Oh well, I expect she's just popped off somewhere. I meant to ask, do you have any . . .?' It clearly hadn't occurred to him for one moment that his girlfriend was making a statement by her absence, nor indeed had her disappearance registered on him.

Obviously, the male Sagittarian has something to offer in long-term one-to-one relationships even if fidelity and constancy aren't at the top of the list. The Sagittarian male, like the Aquarian, is a great 'pal'—full of advice and good cheer when someone is down, just as long as he's not expected to hang around for long to help pick up the pieces. He is likely to take his lady out often for celebrations—even if it's only because it's Friday—and he's normally extremely generous, unless the bank have asked him to return his cheque card. He has enormous enthusiasm and great zest for life, and even when things look their blackest he'll find something optimistic to say. He may behave like an overgrown schoolboy at times, but at least he's never boring. And with his uncanny lucky streak he'll usually fall on his feet and find goodies of one sort or another to enrich both his and his partner's lives.

SUMMARY

Sagittarians of both sexes tend to enter into relationships with little care or consideration; consequently many of them really do 'marry in haste and repent at leisure'—often more than once! Like all the fire signs they are as subtle as sledgehammers about their feelings, and their attraction for someone is immediate and obvious. When in love they charge in like a fire engine on call, only to have to reverse out of the situation somewhat awkwardly and abruptly when they realize it was a false alarm. Consistency and loyalty are not their strongest suits, although they have much to offer a partner with their generosity, warm-heartedness, and optimism. Their weakest point is their reluctance to take on emotional responsibilities and commitments, largely because of their overriding need for freedom. Once Sagittarians have discovered that committing themselves to one partner can be an exciting and fulfilling experience in its own way, and that caring and sharing need not necessarily place a stranglehold on their desire for space, their partners can look forward to a rich and continually expanding relationship. Like good thoroughbreds, Sagittarians need plenty of exercise, both mental and physical, in 'wide open spaces,' and, given enough rope they rarely hang themselves, but become, instead, exemplary husbands and wives.

SAGITTARIUS PARTNERSHIPS

Sagittarians can find something positive and good from a relationship with virtually every sign of the zodiac. But, like most signs, their antipathetic qualities—reflected, in Sagittarius' case, in the earth and water signs—are by far the most attractive.

Aries

Aries is a good combination for Sagittarius, having an equally jolly approach to life and not being one to bear grudges—even after the most fearful fights. The drawback with this combination is that both signs have difficulty in self-restraint, thus they often encounter major financial problems in marriage. Also, despite Aries' natural independence, the Ram frequently resents his Sagittarian partner's freedom and lack of commitment, which can give rise to unfamiliar feelings of insecurity. The Archer, on the other hand, can find his Aries partner a little too selfish and bossy for his liking and a trifle too jealous and intense.

Taurus

Sagittarius and Taurus is one of those all or nothing combinations—it either works extremely well, or not at all. Taurus is a placid, gentle kind of partner and he is initially fairly tolerant of the Archer's free-spirited, somewhat insensitive behaviour. However, Taurus is a mite too stubborn and unadaptable for Sagittarius in the long run and far too resistant to change. Taurus is also extremely security oriented and usually finds the Archer aggravates his neurotic tendencies. Sagittarius, in turn, resents the Bull's continual pressure to conform and tow the line.

Gemini

Sagittarius and Gemini are opposite signs, and rather like two Archers in a relationship, they often see their negative characteristics mirrored in the partner. Certainly this couple likes to be on the move and is rarely housebound. They usually have an active social life and think little of travelling hundreds of miles for an evening's entertainment. Emotional closeness and depth is sometimes difficult to achieve with this partnership, especially if one partner has more watery planets than the other. More often than not it is the Archer who is more emotionally demanding than the Gemini and also more sexually oriented. Both prefer to avoid powerful emotional confrontations, however, and, provided there is plenty of external stimulation in their lives, the relationship works well for both.

Cancer

Sagittarius and **Cancer** relationships are rarely easy to handle unless there are many compatible planetary links between the charts. The Crab is possessive and insecure and cannot tolerate the Archer's footloose and fancy-free behaviour. Initially, the Archer finds the Crab mysterious and fascinating, but in the long term he cannot deal with Cancer's oversensitive and moody behaviour. Sexual difficulties are frequently experienced between these two signs, often because of the Archer's insensitivity and impatience; Cancer, if emotionally bruised, rather than vent his feelings will shut off sexually, which angers and frustrates Sagittarius.

Leo

Sagittarians find **Leos** warm-hearted and generous. This is usually a very stylish partnership, and as a couple they exude success and confidence. Sometimes Leo's oversized ego grates on the Archer, who is less self-obsessed, so the Sagittarian spends much of his time cutting Leo down to size. One of the problems with two fire signs in a relationship is that each person likes his own way and assumes his ideas and feelings should take priority. Consequently power struggles tend to erupt periodically between them.

Virgo

Virgos are immensely attractive to Sagittarius, and vice versa. At first both partners appreciate each other's way of thinking and there is usually much spirited and stimulating communication. Unless there are many harmonious contacts between their charts, however, once the initial attraction (sexual and otherwise) has worn off, a severe clash of temperaments emerges. Virgo is enormously practical and organized, but somehow the Archer manages to get him so agitated and uncertain that his neat little world threatens to crumble. On the other hand, Sagittarius becomes increasingly frustrated by Virgo's insistence on duty first and fun later, and his tendency to shut off completely when the emotional temperature rises. But if the Archer can develop more patience, and the Corn Bearer more plasticity, the relationship can provide many happy and stimulating years for both of them.

Libra

Sagittarius and **Libra** is perhaps the best of all combinations: Venus-ruled Libra manages to tame the Archer's restless spirit without making him feel trapped, and also kerbs his inconsiderate manner. Sagittarius encourages Libra to be more spontaneous and open about his feelings, and, generally speaking, excellent communication exists between these two individuals. Both signs are socially oriented and, like the Gemini/Sagittarius couple, they have a constant influx of friends and invitations. Sometimes Libra is a little too refined for the Archer's liking, but overall they share many similar outlooks and values, making this a sympathetic and durable partnership. Sex for this couple can be excellent, since both are attuned to 'pleasure-seeking', although fidelity is neither individual's strongest suit.

Scorpio

Although Sagittarius and **Scorpio** are Zodiac neighbours and may therefore share Mercury or Venus in each other's Sun sign, they make awkward 'bedfellows'. Scorpio is intense and secretive while Sagittarius is open and easy-going. While there may be much initial attraction between the two, in a long-term relationship they may fail to fulfil each other's needs. Both usually experience strong sexual feelings for each other at first, but after the initial passion has worn off, huge emotional differences emerge. The Archer often finds Scorpio too possessive and manipulative for his taste, while Scorpio finds the Archer insincere and unfeeling.

Sagittarius

Two **Sagittarians** in a relationship together either works extremely well or not at all. Like most dual combinations, each partner tends to see the negative aspects of the sign in the other, which can lead to arguments and tensions. Like the Sagittarius/Aries partnership, extravagance is natural to both, and unless one partner is more earthy, and therefore more financially restrained, critical money problems can arise. Also, one Archer is likely to be more insistent on freedom than the other, which can build up resentment and hurt in the more rooted partner: many of the underlying tensions in their relationship hinge on this issue. On the plus side, their strong bond of friendship carries them through most difficulties.

Capricorn

Sagittarius is immensely attracted to the stable, practical and consistent qualities of **Capricorn**, indeed the Goat is usually the best earthy partner for the Archer: probably because as zodiac next-door-neighbours they may well have personal planets in each other's Sun sign. Sagittarius admires Capricorn's stalwart personality, while Capricorn receives a good shot in the arm from the Archer's forceful exuberance. In many ways Sagittarius and Capricorn are exact opposites, for while the Archer is a divine optimist, the Goat is a perennial pessimist. Ultimately, Capricorn may prove too negative and critical for Sagittarius to live with year after year while Capricorn may tire of the Archer's inconsiderate, irresponsible and profligate ways. Sexual attraction is usually strong between these two.

Aquarius

Sagittarius and **Aquarius** have some of the same problems as the dual Sagittarian couple—one will tend to be more freedom-oriented than the other. If both people have personal planets in water and harmonious contacts between respective Moons, this combination can be sensitive and emotionally tuned to one another, otherwise the Archer will feel the Waterbearer is a mite too cool for his liking. On the plus side, both people enjoy new and exciting experiences, and find much stimulation in each other's company.

Pisces

Sagittarius finds **Pisces** romantic, sensitive, and adaptable while Pisces is impressed, if not a little in awe, of the Archer's confidence, optimism, and enthusiasm for life. Once the honeymoon is over, however, both people may feel they cannot come to grips with each other and many misunderstandings arise between them. Pisces needs a very supportive partner, which Sagittarius hardly ever is, so the Fish feels dreadfully insecure unless he can overcome his neuroses. Both signs find responsibility and commitment difficult, so this combination either marries immediately or after years of running around each other in ever-decreasing circles.

SEXUALITY

Despite the Archer's attraction and appeal to the opposite sex, he is, of all the fire signs, the least in touch with his physical senses. This may sound like a paradox given Sagittarius' enviable sexual popularity; indeed, observing the Archer flirting audaciously at a social gathering, it would seem implausible that he or she could in any way be sexually indifferent or inadequate. However, Sagittarians (particularly the males) can be remarkably insensitive to the subtle nuances of lovemaking and, despite their enthusiasm, often leave much to be desired as lovers.

As with all the signs of the zodiac, it is extremely difficult to discuss an individual's sexuality based on one sign factor alone; the individual's sexual nature is made up of many components that are related to the horoscope as a whole. In attempting to outline certain sexual characteristics, in the case of the Sagittarian, many influences, such as the Mars and Venus placing and aspects from the outer planets to the personal ones, will add considerable light and shade to the overall Sagittarian theme.

Because female sexuality as a whole is intrinsically linked to the emotions, the Moon, Venus, and Mars signs are often more indicative of how a woman will respond sexually than her Sun sign. Thus, the following characteristics will tend to apply more to those women with Venus, Moon, or Mars in Sagittarius than those with just the Sun or Ascendant in this sign.

A strongly Sagittarian female is enormously keen on sexual conquest. The female Archer loves being in the company of men, and her humour and attractive personality make a tempting prize which she is not slow to capitalize upon. Rather like the Aries woman, it is extremely important for Ms Sagittarius to strike while the iron of passion is hot. The Sagittarian female feels instantaneous attraction for someone but, given too long to think about it or too many obstacles, she'll soon lose interest. Likewise, once 'under the sheets' she is intensely irritated by laborious foreplay. Ms Sagittarius needs to be 'taken' while her passion is at a peak. If the initiative is not seized at the crucial moment, the quality of the sexual encounter loses its intensity and therefore much of its satisfaction—at least for her. She also frequently interprets any holding back on the man's behalf as implying that he does not find her attractive or exciting enough, which quickly deflates her confidence and dampens her ardour.

The Jupiterian female is an extremely giving sort and her generosity of spirit rarely stops at the bedroom door. Indeed, Ms Sagittarius frequently suffers from the same problem as Ms Libra in that she finds it awfully difficult to say 'no' (unless she is physically repulsed by her prospective seducer). However, Ms Libra's inability to say 'no' stems from her overall indecisiveness and a basic dislike of hurting people's feelings, whereas the female Archer is at the mercy of her impulsive, fiery desires. Freud might have said that she has a problem with delaying her gratification, or a strong id and weak superego! Clearly, those Sagittarian women with plenty of earthy or watery planets in their charts are going to be more cautious about bestowing their favours liberally, but by and large, most Sagittarian females make warm, responsive, and eager sexual partners.

Of all the fire signs, Sagittarius is the least constant. In regard to sex, the Sagittarian female's passion can vanish as quickly as it ignited; this female needs more than physical pleasure to keep her sexual flame alight. Although she appreciates a good physique and dashing looks in a man, he must also appeal to her on a mental level—she adores a man who is witty and bright. While a lover or husband commands her respect and admiration she will continue to find him sexually attractive (provided she did in the first place, of course), but if he falls in her estimation she will be unable to respond to him physically. One Sagittarian client of mine had an extremely good physical relationship with her husband for twelve years when, almost overnight, she could hardly bear him to touch her. It was only after their divorce that she traced her sudden loss of desire to the time she suspected he had begun to fiddle his company's books!

This sudden loss of desire can occur without such dramatic causes as this and after a far shorter time span than twelve years. Remember, Sagittarius is anything but constant or consistent! In keeping with Jupiter's thunderbolts, the Sagittarian woman can seem almost excessive in her desires at times yet once the hurricane is over, she can be quite cool and sexually uninterested. Rather like Jupiter's anger, her passion flares up powerfully and quickly, but once over, it is as though nothing had happened. This blowing hot and cold behaviour vis-à-vis sex is more pronounced in some Sagittarian women than others and although some Capricorn females are also prone to sudden sexual cut-off, the Sagittarian experience is more ephemeral and not so deep rooted, and certainly not irreversible!

As a lover, Ms Sagittarius is also unfailingly honest. Unless there is much water in the chart, she will make no bones about the situation if she is dissatisfied with her lover's performance. She is not the kind of lady who murmurs ecstatically 'You're wonderful . . .' if she doesn't mean it. After a disappointing lovemaking session she may disappear into an angry silence, but it won't be long before she pours out her complaints and grievances. Of course, there are some Jupiterian ladies who can act up a storm under the sheets—even if the earth hasn't moved a single inch—but it is usually only a temporary measure. In the same spirit of truthfulness and honesty, once Ms Sagittarius has found her feet in the sexual department, she is rarely coy about informing her lover or husband (sometimes both!) what 'turns her on'. Like all the fire signs the female Archer finds erotica fascinating and she usually loves to discuss her fantasies with her partner to mutually heighten sexual excitement.

Sagittarius is an adventurous sign, and the female Archer, like her male counterpart, hardly ever fights shy of a novel experience in bed or out of it!. On the one hand Ms Sagittarius is ready to try all sorts of exotic sexual techniques, and on the other she enjoys the sheer thrill and excitement of a new partner. Loyalty, as we have discussed earlier, is not the female Archer's strongest suit and she is one of the few signs of the zodiac to experience little guilt or angst when unfaithful. Although intrigue is something usually associated with a sign like Scorpio, Ms Sagittarius often likes a dangerous aspect in her sexual encounters. One female with her Moon and Mars in Sagittarius wrote, 'I enjoy taking risks in sexual relationships. I mean, I really enjoy taking the risk of being raped!' Another said, 'I adore intrigue. It is wonderful to have a secret liaison with a man. I love getting into a situation unexpectedly—this is terribly exciting ... Sometimes I do unpredictable things like chatting someone up in a pub, then going off with them ... but it has to feel right at the time. Usually things work out well, because I'm very optimistic.'

Which brings us to another feature of this sign. Although Ms Sagittarius reveres truthfulness and fair play, despite her high principles, she is frequently not strong enough to keep away from married men. Fortunately, unless she falls into the category of the extremely insecure Sagittarian woman, she will not expect a great emotional commitment from her married lover. Like Ms Aquarius, the female Archer is capable of enjoying a good 'roll in the hay' without any emotional overtones.

Theoretically, the Sagittarian female is not a complex creature where sex is concerned. She has a healthy, enthusiastic approach to making love and is not likely to suffer from emotional repression or severe sexual hang-ups. I say theoretically, because some Sagittarian women may have difficult Mars and Venus aspects to complicate matters, in which case the usual Jupiterian relish for sex will be considerably muted.

Finally, a word about love and sex. Although the Jupiterian female can enjoy sex without emotional commitment, when the two combine, sex becomes a celebration. Ms Sagittarius is not a selfish lover; she will go to immoderate lengths to please and excite her partner, which in turn increases her own passion. Although she may be on the promiscuous side, Ms Sagittarius is not the type to enter into a sexual relationship with anyone who doesn't wholeheartedly inspire her. She is honest about her feelings and rarely manipulates her lover emotionally or sexually. Indeed, she brings much humour, warmth, and spirit into her lovemaking.

The male Sagittarian, like the female of the species, is keen on sexual conquest. Yet, strangely enough, Mr Sagittarius often finds sex somewhat overrated, and once he has 'proved his manhood' he is happy to pursue other dimensions of experience. Clearly, the Sagittarian man with plenty of earthy planets in his chart is going to be more obsessed with the physical aspect of making love than the Archer who is predominantly fire and air, but there seem to be many inconsistencies (sexual and otherwise) with this sign.

Many Sagittarian men take their Centaur symbolism rather too literally: they find the opposite sex irresistible and flirt outrageously at every available opportunity—the types who disappear in the middle of parties to return later with their shirt buttons on the wrong fastener. There are several reasons for the Archer's womanizing ways. First, he frequently treats his sex life as a kind of sport: the thrill of the chase and skill of the game often providing more of the excitement he craves than the 'kill' itself. He may even seem to need his sexual skirmish like some men require their regular round of golf! The second reason has much to do with Sagittarius' preoccupation with youth. This sign is often obsessed with physical fitness and sets immense store by looking trim and bouncing with health. (Youth is also a time when it is acceptable to be relatively responsibility-free, and excessive behaviour can be tolerated as youthful exuberance.) While the Centaur is in peak physical condition and free of responsibilities, his sexual life soars happily. However, once he marries and responsibilities begin to weigh on his reluctant shoulders, the less satisfied he becomes with his existing sexual relations and the more he looks to pastures new to spice things up. Consequently, his apparent compulsion for sexual conquest has its roots in a desire to retain the vividness of youth.

Although the sexual shenanigans of some Sagittarian Don Juans can be attributed to their sporty natures or their need to feel youthful and therefore desirable, in many the reasons are deeper and more complex. The subject of the Archer's lack of commitment has been mentioned several times in this chapter and, again this failing frequently lies at the root of his restless bed-hopping. It is not simply the prospect of a more exciting partner or a greater sexual thrill that keeps a certain type of Archer questing ever more sexual experiences, but an unconscious feeling that he may actually be unable to sustain (sexually or otherwise) the rigours and demands of a long-term relationship. He may even suspect he is somewhat shallow. The Sagittarian Don Juan never allows himself to become too deeply involved in a sexual relationship. Although he may be intensely keen in the early stages when he is sexually infatuated with someone, as the relationship progresses he will aim to put plenty of time and space between meetings. Often another reason behind this syndrome is subconscious doubts over his manliness—fears assuaged by ever more sexual conquests.

Sagittarian Don Juans come in all shapes and sizes, married or single, but it is the married Don Juan who poses the greater threat both to himself and others.

To illustrate, I'll recount the imagined case of a Sagittarian bachelor in his mid-twenties who marries an immensely stable (earthy) woman. For a few years he remains faithful; he enjoys the security of his relationship and the way his life runs smoothly and efficiently. Everyone assumes he has settled down happily. Around the age of 29 he feels the first pangs of constraint and boredom; his future seems predictable and unexciting—he is also no longer so youthful. Thus he embarks on an affair. The affair brings his marriage to an end, and before he knows where he is, he's married to his mistress. Within the space of two years he finds the relationship restricting and difficult (and no improvement on his first), so he embarks on another affair. This time he sees the red light of emotional commitment well in the distance and he exits from the relationship in good time, with the excuse that his wife is too ill/threatening suicide/or he can't afford another divorce. From this point he goes on to have several more affairs, but only when his second wife throws down the gauntlet of divorce does he really consider leaving her. By this time a secondary problem has hit our Archer; he finds his periodic bouts of impotence that peppered his first and second marriage becoming an ever-present hazard in his casual affairs. It is at this stage that he seeks professional help.

Now, as this is a kind of fairy story, it should have a happy ending. In an ideal world, with the aid of therapy, our Archer should be able to see his problem with responsibility and commitment is not only at the root of his bed-hopping antics but also the prime cause of his impotence. Unconscious feelings of guilt over his lack of commitment to his first wife, then his second, have built up to a point where they interfere with his conscious actions. While consciously wanting to make love to another woman, his unconscious, overloaded with guilt, prevents him. Obviously there are many other reasons behind impotence in men—ranging from the purely physical to fear of failure—but this cause suits our imaginary Archer. Through these revelations he should realize that his restless quest from woman to woman is merely an attempt to run away from himself. Alas, there is no guarantee that such a realization will make him alter his escapist behaviour.

I must make it absolutely clear that not all Sagittarian men are Don Juans, any more than all Aquarian men are Right Men (see pp.460–1). Many factors, astrological and otherwise, lead to the manifestation of this syndrome. Indeed, some Sagittarian men (and there were several in my questionnaire) did not rate sex particularly highly at all; and a few by their fifties had only experienced one or two sexual affairs. Although the Sagittarian man who has few sexual relationships in his life, or who relegates sex to every other Sunday, may be in the minority, he does serve to illustrate the point that the Sagittarian's physical senses (like the Geminian's and the Aquarian's) are less important to him than his intuitive and intellectual faculties. This certainly provides an explanation as to why many Sagittarian men find sex, although necessary, ultimately disappointing: somehow they never achieve the highs they anticipate.

By and large the Sagittarian man is far from conservative in bed. He is usually open-minded and experimental, if not downright exhibitionist on occasion. Like the female Archer, he enjoys erotica and, given the opportunity, is likely to accept an invitation to an orgy or a wife-swapping party.

The Centaur is also a firm believer in the joy of sex—in more ways than one. Even if making love has been an unmitigated disaster, his sense of humour will provide an effective antidote. One Sagittarian lover of a friend of mine decided to perform a Woody Allanesque stunt on their first night together. After a hot and passionate encounter on the sofa, they moved to the further expanses of the bedroom. She slipped between the sheets and waited expectantly while he disappeared into the bathroom. Some minutes later she was aghast to see him hurtle through the door, stark naked, launch himself horizontally into orbit and crash-land on top of her and the bed, which collapsed on impact!

Sagittarius is also a sign that likes talking about sex. On the one hand many Archers like to talk while making love—suggesting this position or that, or generally enhancing the procedure with colourful sexual dialogue. On the other hand many enjoy a good discussion about sexual experiences any time, anywhere. In some this amounts to downright indiscretion, with raunchy stories of how and what happened with this or that person. (While on the subject of indiscretion, the Sagittarian husband is not the most subtle of individuals when engaged in an extra-marital affair: he often takes unprecedented risks and frequently returns home minus his tie or his briefcase!)

Like his fiery brothers, Mr Aries and Mr Leo, the Archer's ability to perform well in bed is immensely important to his self-esteem. However, he is also too prone to the fire sign fault of placing quantity before quality, which often prevents him from becoming a truly satisfying lover. If the Archer can apply tenderness, consideration, and sensitivity to his lovemaking rather than concentrating on his technique, he can become a superlative lover. Like Mr Aries, the Sagittarian male would benefit from a relationship with an older more experienced female who could introduce him to the delicate art of seduction and show him how to truly please a woman.

Sagittarians of both sexes tend to rush their lovemaking. On the one hand their forceful personalities propel them far too quickly into a sexual encounter, thus often landing themselves with an unwanted partner. On the other, many Sagittarians tend to be too hurried about the sexual act itself, which means they lose out on the more subtle levels of emotional and sensual contact. The Sagittarian man or woman who has learned to be more selective and curb his or her impetuous ways is one who can bring the best qualities to lovemaking and attain a supremely high level of sexual experience.

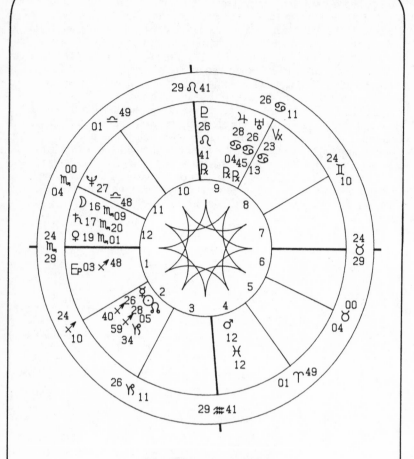

CHRIS EVERT

21 12 1954   4h 30m 0s EST

PLACIDUS 26N7 80W8

PROFILE OF A SAGITTARIAN WOMAN

CHRIS
EVERT

If horoscopes were paintings—and some astrologers might argue they are—Chris Evert's chart could be entitled 'The Ice maiden cometh in a chariot of fire'. For while her horoscope sports an energetic Sun and Mercury in fiery Sagittarius (which in turn forms a beautiful trine aspect to the Midheaven and Pluto in Leo) the moon, Venus, and Saturn are clustered just behind the Ascendant in icy-controlled Scorpio. It is undoubtedly this combination of cold steel and fiery passion that has helped her become one of the greatest tennis players of this century.

Chris was born in Fort Lauderdale, Florida, USA. The family was staunchly Catholic and close-knit. Her father was a tennis pro, thus the whole family took a keen interest in the sport; and although Chris became the star, four of her siblings were national junior champions. Chris took her first tennis lessons at the age of five and a half, under the guiding but disciplined hand of her father. Indeed the whole family ethos was one of hard work and little play. It was her father who instilled in her the concentration and discipline that has proved to be the foundation of her considerable success. 'I heard the same phrases—"racket back, turn sideways, watch the ball, follow through"—over and over again.' Even though the Evert family lived within a mile of the sun-drenched Florida coast, a trip to the beach was a mere annual event. Nor was Chris allowed to spend the night at any of her friends' houses, in the certain knowledge that she would be up until all hours! 'Life revolved around school, mass, tennis practice and home.' Not that Chris resented the restrictions imposed upon her, even when it meant giving up her cherished wish to become a cheer-leader. From an early age she seemed able to accept that everything in life comes at a price—especially success.

Curiously enough, her father, while considering her a good player, never thought of her as world champion material! To begin with, she was on the small side and in order to hit a reasonable backhand she had to hold the racket with two hands—a technique that has since set a trend.

Action-packed Mars in the fourth 'house' of home and family ensures that there was never an idle moment during her formative years. Yet sometimes Mars in this area indicates friction in the home. Since volatile Uranus is also connected with this area* and the Moon (a symbol of mother and childhood) is close to restrictive Saturn, there is more than just a hint of difficulty linked to Chris's childhood years. Chris was (and is) deeply attached to her family; but while her disciplined upbringing has proved invaluable to her career, she may have missed out on a sense of freedom and irresponsibility as a child. While Chris's father would appear to be the one who wielded the rod, astrologically, mother emerges as the dominant character in Chris's life.† And indeed when Chris did rebel and make her bid for freedom, her mother bore the brunt of her resentment.

Chris was only fifteen when she achieved her first big breakthrough. In 1970 in a tournament in Charlotte, North Carolina, Chris beat Margaret Court, the Australian number one. 'I always felt sick in my stomach when I had to play girls my own age, but when I played someone ten years older I thought that if I didn't win I still had ten more years, and that made me feel much better . . . I had nerves of steel that day and beat her 7–6, 7–6. It was a hell of a match.' The world was made increasingly aware of the sixteen-year-old sensation during 1971 as Chris demolished players years her senior, like Virginia Wade and Françoise Durr. She even came within a whisker of winning the US Open but fell to the cunning and superior skill of one of her idols, Billie Jean King. Chris was a phenomenon and a crowd puller; first, because she was so young (although by the late Seventies, teeny-bopper champions were to become almost commonplace), and second, because she was eye-catching and very feminine indeed. The Press and the public loved her. Her colleagues did not.

Despite Chris's attractiveness, her killer instinct was unmistakable once she got on the courts. Since she had beaten many first-class players she was feared and resented by the 'old hands'. They considered her an unwelcome outsider. In the summer of 1972, she played her first Wimbledon and reached the semi-finals, losing to Evonne Goolagong. But to reach the semi-finals at such a prestigious

---

*Uranus is the ruling planet of the fourth house.

†See Note for Astrologers.

event was no mean feat for an eighteen-year-old. Chris has never considered herself a gifted player in the sense that there is an indefinable magic about her game. 'Most of my success has been because I worked at the game . . . I practised so much that I was very accurate. I outsteadied everybody, and always managed to hit one back . . . I have a good frame for tennis. I'm built well, I have good balance . . . my style of play isn't to throw myself all over the court but is based on consistency and accuracy rather than acrobatics.' Chris was also fortunate in that she did not have too much too soon. She was able to take on the best players in the world when she was capable of doing so—capable of winning. Also helpful was Chris's strong base line—her strict and sheltered upbringing in a close family circle. Her parents spared no effort to keep Chris's life as normal as possible within the bounds of her burgeoning tennis career: 'I took my homework to tournaments until I was eighteen.'

Chris's 'killer instinct' can be traced astrologically to the concentration of planets in Scorpio. Scorpio is known to be a ruthless sign, and certainly one capable of emotional detachment. Both the Moon and Venus (primary female symbols) are placed in this 'fixed' water sign bracketing cold and clinical Saturn. Since Venus is conjunct the Ascendant in Scorpio this whole cluster of planets gains in importance. The Ascendant is the individual's window on the world; thus the determined, single-minded, almost robotic image we have of Chris on court stems from this Scorpio emphasis. (Intriguingly, one of Chris's other nicknames is the iron-lady—a title she shares with Margaret Thatcher who has Saturn at the same degree on her Scorpionic Ascendant!) Since the Ascendant, Venus (and by association Saturn and the Moon) form an exciting trine aspect to Uranus, Chris clearly underrates the element of inspired play that permeates her game. Chris, of course, is a Sun Sagittarian (a sign considered to be sporty) and since her Sun forms a helpful trine aspect to the MC and Pluto there is every indication of the fame and success she has achieved through her work. Her success has made her a multi-millionairess, and this too is indicated by the Sun's aspects to Pluto and the Midheaven. Furthermore, the Sun is placed in the 'house' of money and possessions.

While her steely determination and cool mechanical play has become the hallmark of her game, off the courts Chris is a warm, lively, and extremely witty lady. She is also unfailingly generous, although in no way self-indulgent. It is her Sagittarian side that encourages her spontaneity, enthusiasm, and frankness. She has become well known for her direct one liners; and although her early years in big-time tennis were peppered with some unpleasant bitchiness from other players, she is now one of the most popular players on the circuit.

1972 was not only significant for Chris because she had made the semi-finals at Wimbledon; she had also fallen in love with Jimmy Connors: indeed her emotional high helped ease the pain of her defeat to Evonne Goolagong. (Chris is always a gracious loser in public, but in private she takes it very hard—like many Americans Chris is conditioned to be a winner.) As far as temperaments were concerned, there was an attraction of opposites between Chris and Jimmy, but they also shared a mutual intensity over tennis and an equally strong desire to be successful. Chris 'wore her heart on her sleeve' over Jimmy, which astounded those who knew her well since, in keeping with her Scorpionic Moon and Venus, she was normally emotionally highly controlled. But the affair was a difficult one to stage manage. Not only did they have to cope with separations, but when they were in the same place they were constantly chaperoned by their mothers. 'It got to the point where I wouldn't talk to my mother. I ignored her and cut her out of the conversation.' (No one can do this as well as someone with a strong Scorpio streak.) Her intense but frustrated love for Jimmy propelled her into running away from home (1973), although the situation resolved itself not long after. Considering the Sagittarian-Uranian content of her chart, it was a rebellion long overdue. Despite making wedding plans for November (1974), the marriage was postponed and their relationship petered out. Chris was to comment some eleven years later: 'I don't think it would have worked . . . perhaps (because) two people who are so intense would just kill each other in a marriage.' During the course of her romance with Jimmy, her emotions never interfered with her tennis and she was formidably successful during the entire span of the relationship—a feat she was not able to repeat some years later.

The next four years were to see Chris making conquest after conquest on the courts, taking the Wimbledon championship twice and the US Open four times. She was as single-minded as ever about her tennis and there was no major romance in her life, although she was seen in the company of eligible men like Burt Reynolds and Jack Ford (son of Gerald Ford). All this was to change in the summer of 1978 when she met the 'Adonis' of English tennis, John Lloyd. Chris and John had admired each other from afar for some time, without either of them taking any kind of initiative to get to know each other. But thanks to a match-making friend of Chris's, a meeting was engineered. Their relationship began tentatively, and with only a few days in hand before Chris was due to return to the US, they had little time to establish their mutually strong feelings. Ultimately it was up to Chris with her Sagittarian spark to get things off the ground. 'After our third date I was disappointed that John hadn't even tried to kiss me. So when we said goodbye I went up to him and hugged him . . . I knew it was up to me to make a move.' Four months later they decided to marry and announced their engagement on Chris's birthday on 21 December 1978.

John Lloyd, one of England's most talented but ill-fated players, is a Sun Virgo with his Moon in the fiery sign of Leo. He is very much the soft-spoken Englishman—perhaps a little too nice to nurture the ruthless streak necessary for men at the very top of their profession. Chris has no planets in earth signs so it is likely that she would find John's earthy Virgo nature a steadying and reassuring influence—and a highly attractive one. John, on the other hand, has little fire in his chart, thus Chris with her vibrant drive and her clearly expressed ambition (typical of her Sagittarius-Leo combination) was someone he found highly appealing.

Chris and John married on 4 April 1979. Whereas before, when Chris was in an emotionally charged state, her tennis suffered not one iota, prior to her marriage she experienced several major defeats. Banner headlines screamed 'Ice-maiden turns to slush'! However, once the wedding was over her game picked up. A marriage between two world-class tennis players is no easy match. Depending on tournaments, the couple is either on top of each other twenty-four hours a day, or separated by continents! There are also the psychological pressures such a relationship must stand. It is never easy for a man to take a back seat to his more successful wife, especially when both are involved in the same career. Initially it seemed that John could accept such a position if anyone could. 'I had often thought it would be very difficult for someone to marry me unless they were as famous or more famous than me. John is a quality guy . . . he doesn't have a big ego and I saw that he wouldn't feel threatened either by my money or my fame.' To begin with Chris and John coped well with their differing schedules and John's less spectacular success, and they were clearly very much in love.

Certainly Chris needed John's support in 1980 when she reached an all-time low in her career. At one point she came close to giving up. A sabbatical seemed the ideal solution; it offered Chris the time to recharge her batteries away from the pressures of full-time tennis. In this, Chris set a trend, and it is now common for players to take breaks away from the game. John gave Chris badly needed encouragement and strength during this period and by May of that year she was back on court with a vengeance. Throughout the first half of 1980, Saturn was much in evidence in Chris's chart; so too was Uranus.* While Saturn indicated a period of poor spirits and low energy, Uranus promised a change of direction. In the event Chris did not give up, but this period gave her the opportunity to consider what she might do when she retires.

*Transiting Saturn squared her Sun; transiting Uranus conjuncted her Ascendant.

Throughout 1982, while her career continued on the up and up her marriage began to show signs of severe strain, and by December 1983 Chris and John made a formal announcement of their separation. Clearly, the relative states of their careers had much to do with their marital problems. While John was quite able to accept Chris's star status, he was deeply depressed over his own game, a depression that gave the outward appearance of abject apathy. As a Sun Virgo, John is more likely to keep his fears, his worries, and his disappointments to himself. When he fails to reach his own high standards his anger turns in on itself and emerges as a sort of terminal inertia: 'Respect is very important in a marriage and I started losing respect for John.' Instead of displaying a positive attitude to getting his game back (which of course was impossible in his state of mind), John spent increasing amounts of time slumped in front of the television. 'After a while, I just got angry because he is a great athlete and he was just wasting his potential.'

While both of them recognized the time had come for them to part, it was Chris who opted for a separation rather than a divorce. John felt a separation was merely postponing the inevitable; but he was proved wrong, and by Wimbledon of 1984 they had agreed on a reconciliation. 'I felt determined to make it work, and if you put a lot of effort into something it works more easily ... I wanted to go back to being a wife, and to be with John, but I didn't want to make too many promises because I thought actions speak louder than words.'

With the two planets most associated with love and affection held in the iron grip of Saturn, it would have been exceedingly unlikely for Chris to have found her way to rose-strewn marital happiness. On the one hand, the Moon-Venus-Saturn combination in Scorpio suggests she needs plenty of security and a close emotional bond with a partner—a repeat of her family experience; yet her Sagittarian side demands freedom and independence: almost a case of 'hold me close, but don't fence me in'! While this combination in itself suggests that it would take some time for Chris to acclimatize herself to marriage, her protected upbringing and the constraints imposed upon her by her career meant that in early youth she had never fully exploited her need for diversity and romantic adventure. Consequently, prior to the official separation she became involved in a relationship with Adam Faith. During much of 1983 Neptune was contacting her Sun, 'producing' a state of confusion and uncertainty in her life. By 1984, as Saturn returned to its original place in the horoscope, major decisions of a long term nature were due to be made. It was a time of endings and beginnings.*

---

*The 'Saturn Return' happens to everyone around the age of twenty-nine. It is the astrological 'coming of age'.

December 1984 marked Chris's thirtieth birthday—a time when the prospect of retirement inevitably percolates every athlete's thoughts. 'Age has never scared me, the only thing which does is that my tunnel vision isn't as strong as it used to be. I don't have the motivation and that worries me ... the reason I'm still playing at thirty is because I feel deep inside that although it's going to be hard work for me I can still improve.' Chris is a far-sighted, highly intelligent person and some consider that since 1984 she has been easing herself into a transitional period. She already has some involvement in the business side of the companies whose products she endorses, and with her televisual talents she has more than one string to her 'racket'. 'I don't think I'll miss the pressure or the charge of adrenalin ... I'll miss making a 100 per cent commitment to something, but maybe I'll commit myself to other things instead like a family.'

With Saturn now moving through Sagittarius shortly to conjunct her Sun in 1988, yet another period of endings and beginnings is indicated. And perhaps this will indeed mark the point where she leaves the intensely competitive arena of professional tennis, but with the prospect of new horizons still to conquer. Of one thing she is sure: 'Personal relationships are more important to me now than they were before ... it's really a myth about being happy when you're at the top and it's only afterwards that you realize what life is all about.'

Postscript: Sadly, but perhaps almost inevitably, Chris and John were divorced in April 1987. In March 1988, John remarried and Chris attended his wedding with her newly revealed husband-to-be, ex-Olympic skier Andy Mill. She and Andy postponed their own wedding to attend John's. In the original text in order to avoid possible upset to Chris and even influence the outcome, I only hinted at divorce with the phrase, 'endings and beginnings'.

Note for Astrologers: (1) Regarding mother: the MC/10th house can, among many ideas, represent mother. Chris has Pluto conjunct the MC which suggests mother was a powerful figure in her life, and that she might well experience ambivalent feelings over her mother.

(2) In the April of 1987, at the time of her divorce, transiting Uranus was conjunct radical Mercury (co-ruler of her 7th and 8th houses). At the time of writing (April 1988) Chris is planning to remarry, Andy, in the Autumn of this same year. If they do marry, say in September 1988, with transiting Saturn conjunct her radical Mercury and transiting Uranus conjunct her Sun, the chances of a trouble-free, long-term union with Andy are very slim indeed.

(3) References **Lloyd on Lloyd** by Chris and John Lloyd with Carol Thatcher, published by Willow Books, Collins (1985).

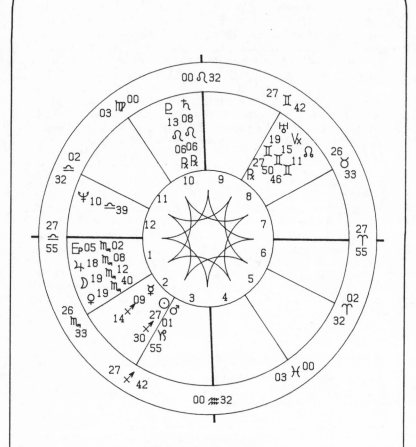

URI GELLER

20 12 1946   2h 0m 0s EET

PLACIDUS 32N4 34E46

PROFILE OF A SAGITTARIAN MAN

URI GELLER

Some fourteen years ago, I remember sitting riveted to my television set watching a tall, dark and handsome Israeli bending keys and making watches stop, and performing a variety of telepathic wonders before my very eyes and those of two million other viewers besides. Thus it was with great trepidation, and not a small amount of awe, that I presented myself at his doorstep in the April of 1986. Would objects hurl themselves around the room? Was my every thought vulnerable to his piercing third eye? (I carefully left all my keys hidden in the car!) But my fears were to prove groundless and Mr Geller turned out to be charming, diffident, humorous, accommodating—and ever so slightly out of the ordinary. A singular man. And if that sounds like a paradox, read on.

Uri Geller was born in Tel Aviv some months prior to Israel's independence. He was an only child and extremely close to his mother—a distant relative of Sigmund Freud. His parents separated when Uri was eleven and he and his mother went to live in Cyprus where she later remarried. Thus Uri saw little of his father (a professional soldier) while he was growing up. 'The divorce didn't really affect me. I understood it. Pehaps it was a shock for the first few days. I didn't miss Tel Aviv; on the contrary Cyprus was a whole new experience. I learned different languages . . . I witnessed a war first hand, the Turks and the Greeks; the Greeks and the British. It was an education for me, a lesson in terrorism and warfare. Because of my father my mind was militaristic. I understood the whys and wherefores of war.' Uri hated school. He was bad at maths and only liked art and physical training. But he had ambitions. 'I always dreamed of becoming a movie star. I admired Lon Chaney and Boris Karlov. I wanted to be the monster—the Dracula figure—in films. But I went into the army as a paratrooper.' It was while in the army that

Uri was wounded in the Six-Day War: 'A sniper opened fire on a group of us and a bullet went through my arm.' After his term in the Israeli army Uri became a photographic model. 'I was money-hungry then. Being very poor as a child made me want to be very rich. Then I saw spoon-bending was very profitable. People were astonished at my abilities and I became very much in demand. That's what made me begin to use my powers professionally.'

Uri's chart shows the pattern of change and upheaval in his early years, as well as the exposure to stimulating and novel experience, since Uranus—a volatile, revolutionary planet—is linked to the fourth 'house' of home and family. While Uri in philosophical Sagittarian fashion dismissed his parents' divorce as 'no big deal', with Uranus itself in the eighth 'house' (one of the more unconscious areas of the chart) and the presence of Saturn and Pluto (two astrological 'heavies') close to the parental MC/IC axis, one suspects much of the trauma was internalized or quickly relegated to the mists of time. Saturn and Pluto add some colour, or rather some shades of grey, to Uri's perception of mother—especially as the Moon (a symbol of mother) is aspected by Pluto. On the one hand the tenth 'house' Saturn-Pluto conjunction suggests his mother has been a formidable influence on his life, if only because at one time she had to be both mother and father to him and was thus faced with the difficult task of combining a nurturing role with an authoritative one. Yet this planetary duo are not the easiest of 'energies' to deal with in an angular house; and there is a suggestion either that Uri felt his mother was his responsibility even as a young child, or that he unconsciously picked up any unexpressed frustration or anger she may have felt. The tenth house is more familiarly seen as the area of profession. Saturn and Pluto seen in this context indicate Uri's terrific drive for recognition accompanied by commensurate financial reward: this conjunction also describes the ambivalent way the world at large views Uri and his abilities. Pluto, of course, has much to do with the hidden and mysterious in life, which aptly depicts the use of unseen, non-understood forces in Uri's line of work.

Uri was four years old when his metal-bending abilities manifested themselves. 'I was eating some soup and suddenly the spoon curled up in my hand ... There was also strong telepathy between my mother and I. I knew what she was thinking. I knew if she was going to win or lose at cards. I didn't think there was anything special about it. I thought everyone could do it. But by the time I went to school I realized it was unique. I used to mend a lot of watches.' But although Uri astonished many friends with his spoon-bending it wasn't until he was twenty-two that the Press 'discovered him'. 'Golda Meier saw me at a small party doing telepathy. She was interviewed the following day and the journalist asked her what she was predicting for Israel, and she said, almost jokingly, "Well, I saw Uri Geller yesterday, maybe he can tell you." And that started it.'

In 1972 Uri left Israel for Europe and the United States. While as an entertainer he was a show-business sensation, the scientific fraternity was more interested to discover whether there was anything other than clever conjuring to his psychokinetic and telepathic stunts. Uri had been invited to the States by the astronaut Edgar Mitchell (of the Apollo 14 mission) and the scientist Dr Andrija Puharich. While Uri was tested by many scientists throughout the world—most of who could find no proof of trickery, but in the way of all scientists faced with phenomena they cannot understand, could not wholeheartedly support the idea of paranormal forces either*—it was Puharich who took him under his wing but, sadly, who also damaged his credibility.

In 1974 Puharich published a book, **Uri: A Journal of the Mystery of Uri Geller**, based on his three-year investigation of Uri. Unfortunately, instead of keeping to the plausible reportage of Uri's feats, Puharich added information about Uri's contacts with extra-terrestrial beings: space intelligences who had apparently been 'programming' him (Uri) since 1952. Not surprisingly the public's reaction to the book was one of almost total disbelief. 'I think Puharich misinterpreted my powers. He wanted to believe that my powers came from extra-terrestrial beings. People thought we were lying, or just plain crazy. But although a lot of what he wrote was misinterpreted, I cannot say, even today, where these powers come from. For all I know, there could be other beings, other intelligences behind what I do. But I've never been visited by little green men from Mars!' Uri broke away from Puharich after the book was published. 'I was very naïve when I met Puharich. I also had no money and I lived in his house. There were all these scientists, all these tests ... I hated the whole thing. And that's when I broke away from him and started doing things by myself. My really big success happened in England on the Dimbleby Talk-in [BBC TV, December 1973]. That show made me world famous and I began getting invitations from all over the world to do TV. That's what I did for the next four years.'

Controversy still hovers over Uri's powers. Are they real; or is he simply a marvellous conjurer? I am entirely convinced that Uri's

*The prestigious British scientific magazine **Nature** was the first to present a report on the investigation of Uri's abilities. The scientists Russell Targ and Dr Harold Puthoff concluded that Uri did indeed possess telepathic powers. But the overview of the researchers regarding his psychokinetic abilities was that 'they were unable to confirm the authenticity of such feats under conditions that eliminated the possibility of deception'.

telepathic abilities are genuine. During our time together, he asked me to draw a simple sketch (on my note-pad) while he looked away (at a blank wall). There was no other person present in the room and since the room was entirely devoid of furniture bar the window seat we were perched upon, there was no question of any reflection or collusion. I drew a baby's toy, shaped like a dumb-bell with a cord dangling from one end. I had shaded in the sides with lines on one end and dots on the other. Uri reproduced it exactly—and to scale. I cannot personally vouch for any of the psychokinetic phenomena, since nothing bent or flew around the room while I was with Uri; but there have been many reports of objects hurling themselves against walls or mysteriously appearing out of thin air in his presence.

Extraordinary mental powers do not immediately leap out of Uri's chart at the astrologer. One has to search for them. Mercury and the Moon are most associated with the mentality. Both these planetary bodies link to Uranus—the most discernibly telepathic of the planets.* Thus there is a suggestion on the one hand of quick thinking, a certain instability in both temperament and mentality, and on the other, razor-sharp intelligence, a high level of intuitive thought, and, yes, telepathic abilities. Uranus' position in the hidden 'ground' of the eighth 'house' also points to psychic and telepathic experience; and since Uranus is linked to the MC† there is an indication that such experience could be used out in the world as a profession. As I have already discussed, Pluto's position in the tenth 'house' of career indicates working with unseen forces—the supernatural, the psychic, and the occult; it also suggests working in such areas as psychology, politics, the police, intelligence and mining—of which we shall read more later. There is also plenty of sensitivity in Uri's chart: Neptune in the spiritual twelfth 'house' emphasizes his links with the mysterious world of inner and outer space, although this area of the horoscope can be an escapist's haven! Venus, Uri's chart ruler, is placed in the deep and probing sign of Scorpio, which in turn forms a challenging aspect to Pluto—further evidence of his attraction toward paranormal phenomena. (Spoon-bending **per se** has no known astrological correlation!) Uri's Sun and Mercury are both in Sagittarius, a sign that often treats life as a quest. Like most Sagittarians, Uri feels the urge to travel unknown territory; he has something of the spirit of the natural explorer and adventurer. As it happens, Uri's wanderlust has more to do with mental travel than the physical variety, although he does a considerable amount of 'globe trotting' as well. By and large the astrological picture is one of

*The Moon is quincunx Uranus; Uranus is the mid-point of the Sun and Mercury; the Sun is the mid-point of Mars and Uranus.

†Uranus is novile (40°) the Midheaven. See **Note for Astrologers** (2).

somebody with a high degree of sensitivity and receptivity towards psychic or telepathic phenomena; someone whose natural curiosity, enthusiasm, and drive have pushed him beyond the frontiers of the mind's 'normal' range. Yet Uri is also something else. He is a showman. And it is this awkward coupling of staggering paranormal ability with the entertainer's gift for good effect and self-promotion that have made him such a conundrum to both the public and the scientific fraternity alike.

In many ways Uri seems bent on perpetuating his ambiguous image, half showman, half parapsychic. While seeming open and easy-going he is almost impossible to penetrate at depth. He claims he and his powers are straightforward, then hints that he is in touch with secret and special things. 'I don't have any great secrets. There could be some spiritual secrets, some Qabalistic secrets, deep powers—positive powers—that maybe I'm not allowed to reveal—even if I knew about them ... When I'm not flying off to take up a contract and I'm at home, it gets a bit boring, so I write and do certain things I don't talk about, time-consuming stuff, secret stuff. I won't talk about it.' One or two articles on Uri have hinted at his involvement with intelligence operations and he even told one journalist that he had survived an assassination attempt.

Certainly with the strong Scorpio-Pluto emphasis in his chart it is highly likely that at some point in his life, and with his abilities, he would be involved in some cloak and dagger work and he has almost certainly been scrutinized by Western military intelligence and possibly Soviet intelligence too. But Uri has a Sagittarian propensity for exaggeration, an ability to bend the truth as easily as a fork; and I suspect he gains a certain humorous satisfaction from leading people up the proverbial garden path. However, while this ambiguity suspends some doubt over his psychic abilities, the uncertainty may also provide a safety valve for Uri. After all, he could be a dangerous man to have on the wrong side of the cold war!

One aspect of his more secret work Uri was prepared to discuss were his mining activities. In 1978, he met the chairman of Rio Tinto Zinc, the late Sir Val Duncan. Duncan, who was an amateur dowser, helped Uri to develop his dowsing powers to locate minerals underground. 'That's when I saw we were no longer talking about £1,000,000, but £50,000,000! The mining industry is worth billions, which is why I diverted from show business and went into secretive work for large conglomerates. Most of the companies want my work kept secret because they didn't want their names linked with this kind of thing!' Uri is able to locate the presence of minerals or gold initially by dowsing over maps. Once he has roughly located the area, whether it's Indo-China or the Solomon Islands, he flies out with some of the company for a more detailed search. In this way he has become very rich indeed. While he has not had a 100 per cent success rate in locating minerals, gold, or diamonds, companies like Zanex, an Australian minerals and exploration company, are more than pleased with their investment in Uri.

In the same year that Uri left show-business and began his involvement with big mining conglomerates, he married Hannah (a Sun Aries with Moon and Venus in Pisces). Although he'd known Hannah since he was twenty-two, Uri, like most Sun Sagittarian men, wanted 'to play the field' a little before he committed himself to marriage. Indeed if one believes all one reads in newspapers Uri was quite the 'Don Juan' in his youth! 'My relationship with my wife is very easy. We know how to enjoy ourselves. The things that make her happy make me happy. We don't have much of a social life—a few close friends. We never find each other boring.' Uri's Moon-Venus-Jupiter conjunction does indeed suggest he is a **bon viveur** where love and romance are concerned; yet this trio also describes the type of woman to whom he is attracted. Thus his experience of Hannah is one of great love and mutual happiness. Nevertheless, with Pluto aspecting this trio and Uranus also associated with partnerships,* he may find a snake or two lurking underfoot in his marital paradise. Indeed this combination is hardly one of emotional calm, and suggests the feelings are deep but not always easy to express. Thus few individuals with such planetary linkings experience trouble-free relationships. Sagittarian men, especially those who have a strong Uranian influence in their chart, need plenty of 'rope' to withstand the constraints and responsibilities of marriage. Fortunately, Hannah as an independent, spirited Sun Aries should be able to provide him with stimulating companionship and the space he requires, yet she can also instinctively respond to his emotional needs. Certainly Uri exudes domestic contentment and happiness, and he obviously dotes on his young son and daughter.

While Uri may have 'settled down' in an emotional sense, physically he acts like a wound-up spring. He can only sit still for a short space of time and his concentration span is brief. He runs ten miles a day and leaps onto his exercise bicycle if ever there's a dull or free moment. 'About eight years ago I changed the way I lived—we're now total vegetarians, no flesh, no preservatives, no colour, no additives. I'm also on the aerobic trip. Of course I don't totally enjoy running. I do it because it's good for me!' Sagittarians can be sporty types and certainly restless. But in Uri's case, with Mars placed next to his Sun, there is even more emphasis on action. Since Mars is also known as the planet of war, Uri's early experiences of war and his

*Uranus is quincunx the Moon and Venus, and placed in the eighth 'house' of emotional and sexual exchange.

'militaristic mind' can be related to this conjunction. To a certain extent he seems obsessed with fitness and youth (not an uncommon theme for Sagittarians). 'I believe in the power of the mind. If I can bend metal, which must mean I change the molecular structure of metal, then why not be able to affect the molecular structure of other things? If you are young in your mind and healthy, then you look young and healthy. I may be almost forty but I think I'm twenty-five. I live the life of a twenty-five-year-old—not because of how I think, but my outlook on life.'

In keeping with the philosophical, expansive nature of his Sagittarian Sun and Mercury, Uri has no fixed ideas and sees 'life' as a series of limitless possibilities. 'I believe in everything. If you tell me you're going to turn yourself into a puddle of water on the count of five, I'll believe you. I might smile, but I'd believe it was possible . . . I believe in God. I believe things are changing. I see it [collective destiny] like a river. We're all in a boat moving down the river. We're free to move around in the boat, but the boat itself has its own impetus and is being borne along by the current. God is taking us.'

Within an hour or so of our meeting, it was quite obvious that Uri was itching to get on his bike. He did, however, have time for a moment of contemplative thought before he sprinted into the April sunshine. 'I suppose what I want most of all out of life now is peace of mind. Money brings a big calm in your life. But that's for now, I have things to do, things that I want to do, but peace of mind is most important. But maybe I'll change. I'll believe anything.'

Postscript: Although Uri, in easy-going Sagittarian fashion, maintains a diffident attitude toward ambition, his output tells a different story. 1986 saw both the publication of his book **The Geller Effect** which tells of the past ten years of his life, and a new game for Matchbox Toys. 'Strike'—a game of chance and skill that enables the players to find treasures of the world—the archetypal Sagittarian game!

Note for Astrologers: (1) Uri's Sun is placed within a degree and a half of the Galactic Centre—in his year of birth, 26° Sagittarius. The vertex in Uri's chart is found on the Galactic point (the point where the plane of the solar system cuts the plane of the galaxy) at 15° Gemini. Twelve days prior to his birth there was a solar eclipse at 15° Gemini. Since the vertex is considered by most astrologers to be linked to fateful events, it is interesting to note in the December of 1974 when Uri 'hit the big time', there were two eclipses, one close to his vertex and the other close to his Mars.

(2) Regarding the novile aspect between Uri's Midheaven and Uranus: the novile 40° aspect is one ninth of the 360° circle of the horoscope and thus relates to the ninth harmonic. In Uri's ninth harmonic chart, Saturn and Jupiter flank the Ascendant-Descendant axis respectively, the Moon opposes Mercury, and Uranus sits apart from the rest of the planets near the

Midheaven. David Hamblin in **Harmonic Charts** comments that: 'it is certainly remarkable how religious leaders and visionaries, and people with clairvoyant, healing, or other types of psychic power, tend to have very strong ninth harmonic charts.' Hamblin also considers that the strong oppositions (mentioned above) in Uri's H9 describe the nature of his psychic powers having much to do with the control and focusing of thought.

(3) In December 1973 the following progressions and transits were operating in Uri's chart: secondary progressed Venus (the chart ruler) conjunct radical Mercury, progressed Mars (by 1°) conjunct the IC; transiting Uranus conjunct the Ascendant, transiting Jupiter opposition Saturn and Pluto, transiting Neptune conjunct Mercury. In 1978—year of marriage and career and personal change—secondary progressed Sun and Mercury conjunct the IC, secondary progressed Mars square the Ascendant-Descendant; transiting Uranus conjunct Moon-Venus (December), transiting Neptune opposing Uranus and transiting Jupiter conjunct the MC (September), conjunct Saturn (November).

CAPRICORN
23 December–20 January

THE TRIED, THE TRUSTED, AND THE FAITHFUL

CAPRICORN
THE TRIED, THE TRUSTED, AND THE FAITHFUL

A STROLOGERS vary in their opinions as to which sign of the zodiac is the strongest and the most powerful; most, however, tend to opt for either Scorpio or Capricorn. Both these signs are powerful, but draw their strength from different sources—Scorpio from a bottomless emotional reservoir and Capricorn from a granite-like determination and indomitable hold on reality. However, Scorpio's Achilles' heel lies in the tendency toward irrational extremism and self-destruction, a factor that ultimately gives Capricorn the edge; for this sign is eminently in control of the emotions and, intent on self-preservation, will never allow feelings to override reason or practical considerations. Although sometimes dogmatic but rarely extremists, Capricorn individuals combine the potential for the wisest, most honourable behaviour in the zodiac, and also the most domineering and self-centred.

Capricorn is an earth sign and, true to this element's function, Capricorn Goats place their trust in the solid ground beneath their feet and extol the virtues of realistic thinking and the practical facts of life. Capricorn is also an innately suspicious and self-protective sign and believes in letting the other fellow show his cards before playing his own hand. Yet, like all individuals, the Goat has his human failings and despite his caution and reserve he can be misled and emotionally hoodwinked on occasion. However, Capricorn is a dutiful and attentive student of life and once 'bitten' takes every measure—even a vindictive one—to ensure nothing like it ever happens again!

Capricorn is ruled by the planet Saturn, a planet whose mysterious majesty fascinates astronomers and astrologers alike. Traditionally, astrologers thought Saturn exerted a malefic influence and attributed all manner of humanity's ills to its evil nature. Modern astrological thought considers Saturn to represent the necessary restrictions and structures individuals must encounter to gain greater self-awareness and mastery. Nevertheless, glancing through the astrological columns in newspapers and magazines, the reader is usually informed that difficulties and problems are imminent when Saturn passes through this sign or that. Thus, even the layman begins to build up a picture of Saturn-ruled Capricorn as a sign synonymous with struggle and difficulty.

If we look a little deeper into the myths behind Saturn a slightly broader perspective emerges. In Greek myth Saturn, or rather Cronos, was one of the Titans, a son of Ouranos (god of Heaven) and Gaea (Earth). Of all her children Gaea sought Cronos' help in ending the tyranny of her husband's reign and releasing those of her children Ouranos had imprisoned on Earth. Saturn duly castrated and murdered his father, but instead of releasing his brothers kept them in their prison and took over his father's throne. What does this tell us about Capricorn? First, Capricorn can be relied upon to carry out his duties, particularly those of a filial nature; yet there is an immensely opportunistic side to Capricorn that will seize a chance, especially to gain a sought-after position or career objective. Capricorn also relishes positions of authority and, with goat-like determination, plods relentlessly and strategically to the top of his own mountain. Due to their belief that they are nearly always right and know what's right for everybody else there is also a cruel streak in many Capricorn individuals.

Saturn showed a slightly different face in Roman mythology. Saturn was the Roman god of agriculture and his annual December festival was an absolute riot of feasting and debauchery! In Rome his temple, which contained the treasury, stood on the Capitoline Hill. Solvency and financial security are always close to Capricorn's heart; indeed, to some, money could be said to be a veritable temple! The lusty, sometimes decadent, side of Capricorn is usually more concealed, but frequently emerges in an enormously strong sexual drive. Also one only has to consider the behaviour and life-styles of some Capricorn figures like Rod Stewart, Elvis Presley, Janis Joplin, and the zany English comedian, Freddie Starr, to see the raunchier and more intemperate side of Capricorn at work and play.

Both Greek and Roman myths about Saturn contain a theme of fate and time. Roman Saturn was associated with the sowing of the seed and the reaping of the harvest, and Greek Cronos set in motion the Fates—he was also known as Lord of Time. And, of course, words like chronology, chronometer and chronic are derived from the Greek word **chronos**, meaning time. Cronos, the god, was much concerned with his own fate, too. Since Gaea had wanted Ouranus overthrown in order to secure the release of her children, she was less than pleased when Cronos continued to keep them imprisoned. In her fury she put a curse on him, that he in turn would be dethroned by one of his own children. In an attempt to escape his fate, Cronos devoured every child his wife, Rhea, bore him. However, when she was due to give birth to Zeus, she enlisted the help of her mother-in-law and delivered him safely in a cave. Rhea then wrapped a stone in some swaddling clothes and handed the bundle to Cronos, informing him that it was their new-born son. Cronos swallowed the stone and thus sealed his own fate.

Astrologically Saturn is considered to have much to do with fate, or rather with coming to terms with one's actions past and present. Since the planet Saturn takes approximately 29 years to orbit the Sun (thus completing a full circle around the zodiac and, in turn, the birth-chart), the 29th and 58th year of life (or thereabouts) have particular significance for Capricorns, as do each of the seven-year subdivisions. Indeed, some clearly recognize that their lives seem to move in seven-year cycles.

But back to the story.

As soon as Zeus was born, his mother took him to the divine goat, Amaltheia, who nursed him in the safety and seclusion of a cave high up on Mount Dicte. When Zeus grew to manhood and acquired all his divine powers he fulfilled Gaea's prophecy and after a ten-year battle overthrew his father, Cronos. Cronos was sent to the underworld, while Zeus became king of the gods.

The divine goat Amaltheia provides some interesting mythological links for Capricorn (whose symbol is, of course, the Goat). Amaltheia was the mother of Aigokeres—the Greek word for Capricorn; he, like his father Pan, was half man, half goat (though he is frequently portrayed with a fish's tail). Pan, the Goat-foot god, was the great deity of nature, and a rampant hedonist in the vein of Dionysus. Indeed, many cultures had a horned deity they associated with nature; the Gauls worshipped an antler-headed god, Cernunnos, who was no doubt the forerunner of Herne the hunter, a medieval English figure—also antler-headed—who seemed to have been a cross between a nature god and the devil. Interestingly, Cernunnos was often depicted with a purse full of grain or coins. Over the centuries aspects of Pan and Saturn have become intermingled so that we find Satan, the Devil, bearing some characteristics of Pan—particularly the aspect of lust and debauchery—and celebrating his major festival, the Saturnalia, in December as the Sun moves into Capricorn. The tarot card of the Devil is considered to be a Capricorn-Saturn card, and depicts the baser aspects of the sign and its ruler—lust and the craving for material power and mastery over the world.

Old Father Time with his sickle is yet another representation of Saturn; so too is 'The Grim Reaper'. However, there is more to the symbolism of the old man's scythe than merely the idea of reaping the harvest. The curved shape of the sickle, like the curves of the goat's horns, are reminiscent of the horned moon and thus become symbols of the feminine. While Capricorn embodies the father principle, 'he' acknowledges his ancient links with the feminine by carrying his sickle. The glyph for Capricorn ♑ also depicts the curve of the half-moon. Some few thousands of years BC, in primitive societies, the moon was considered to be a Great Man; later this idea was modified and the reigning king or tribal leader became a representative of the moon or a descendant of the moon. The waxing and the waning of the moon were once thought to describe the cycle of a great, heroic moon king; but as these societies gradually became more solar oriented, the hero became identified with the sun and the moon became the province of a goddess. Esther Harding in **Woman's Mysteries** describes some of these lunar legends, and it is uncanny how they mirror the myth and symbolism of Cronos-Saturn.

> The typical story is that the moonman begins his career when the waxing crescent first appears, by fighting the devil of darkness who has eaten his father, the old moon . . . The hero overcomes the devil and as the moon comes to fullness, he reigns triumphant on earth. He is a wise and great king. **He creates order in the tribe and establishes agriculture, teaching his people when to sow and when to reap. He is also a maker of laws and the judge of men whose hidden motives he is able to bring into the light** . . . [my emphasis] He has no sooner reached the zenith of his power, however, than the old enemy who conquered his father begins to attack and pursue him. He is finally overcome, and the devil eats him up also . . . After his death the moonman goes to the underworld . . . where he exercises his old function of judge.

Ms Harding goes on to discuss that the myth does not only mirror the phases of the moon, but describes the inner life of the psyche—an inner life primitive man unconsciously projected onto the moon king.

> This moonman, who represents an unrecognized part of the human psyche, does for the primitive tribe what the tribesman of that age was unable to accomplish by his own intelligence. He establishes order, teaches the art of agriculture, is judge and giver of laws.

What is interesting here in regard to astrology and Jungian psychology, is that Saturn in the birth chart is thought to depict the 'shadow'—those aspects of our individual or collective psyche that we find difficult to accept or take responsibility for, which are thus projected onto others or society in general. Bearing this in mind, it is easy to see how the negative side of Saturn came to be associated with people's concept of the devil/Satan (who is usually depicted as half-man, half goat). On the positive side, Saturn also represents structure and order which are essential for our psychological well-being and for a stable and thriving society.

The psychologists and astrologers, Bruno and Louise Huber, associate Saturn with mother since it is usually the mother who takes the nurturing, teaching and disciplinary role in a child's life and thus sets the stage for his or her participation in society. Traditional astrologers have always considered the Moon to be a symbol of mother; yet there is much to be said for the Hubers' point of view and, indeed, in light of the symbolic connections between Saturn and the feminine (lunar) principle, perhaps they are not such poles apart. Also worthy of note is that the cycles of these two planetary bodies are linked. While Saturn takes 29 years (approximately) to come full circle, the moon's phase cycle is 29½ days. Also, astrologers use a method of symbolically progressing the birth chart—a day for a year—whereby the Moon takes nearly 28 'years' to return to its original place in the birth chart. While the Saturn Return is coincident with the formation of the individual's relationship with the **outer** world, the 28-year lunar cycle depicts the maturity of the **inner** realm of the psyche and the emotions.

While these mythical and symbolic highways and byways appear to have lead us up the mountain path and far away from the Capricorn in the street, these themes have a bearing on each and every Capricorn—albeit on an archetypal level.

The Capricorn type, particularly the male, is often on the small side, although the physique is athletic and the bone structure good. Most have a reserved and cautious air about them which should never be confused with timidity. Although Libra usually rates as the most attractive and physically appealing sign of the zodiac, Capricorn frequently rivals this Venus-ruled sign with its elegance, fine features, and imposing presence. Most retain their handsome looks into old age mainly because of their excellent bone structure. It is also an interesting feature of this sign that Capricorn individuals seem to be older than their years when young and vice versa. A Capricorn's lot frequently improves with age.

Life tends to be a serious business for Capricorn. These are not the here today, gone tomorrow Peter Pans of the zodiac. As children they have more understanding of the adult world than their contemporaries and enjoy mixing with their seniors and adopting their attitudes. I was both amused and impressed by this adult approach to life when taking a five-year-old (strongly Saturnian) friend of my son's home from school one day. I mentioned casually that perhaps he would like to come over for tea soon. Anticipating the usual grunt of approval, I was amazed to receive the following (verbatim) reply: 'Well, thank you. . . but I'm fwightfully buthy at the moment and only weally have time for important friends.' There was a pause, then he added somewhat condescendingly to my son, 'Do you have any Leggo, Jamie? . . . Then I might come.' This same little boy used to wander down the path to his home burdened with all manner of flotsam and jetsam, to all intents as though he carried the weight of the world on his small shoulders!

Younger Capricorns often make extremely good prefects and house captains; yet perhaps because they never thoroughly indulge in childish behaviour as children, they long to feel carefree and irresponsible when adult and to a certain extent there is a frustrated escapist in all of them.

Most Capricorns are conscientious and responsible; those who display reckless and anarchistic behaviour usually have a strong Uranian, Neptunian, or Plutonic theme in their charts. Both sexes seem to have an inborn sense of duty and purpose, and of the twelve signs, Capricorn can be relied upon to struggle his way to the top, even if he's ninety by the time he does! Unlike Aries, whose ambitions must be fulfilled early in life or else he loses heart, Capricorn expects things to be difficult and to take their time, and usually the more setbacks, difficulties, and hardships he encounters on his way, the more resolute he becomes. Both male and female Goats have a strongly ambitious streak, although sometimes the Capricorn woman will channel all her drive vicariously through her husband and children.

Not all Goats are of the mountain-hopping variety, however; some remain tethered to a post in some remote pasture, rarely attempting anything more ambitious than the occasional butt! In keeping with this symbolism, there are some Capricorn individuals who appear to lack the direction and the drive to reach a pinnacle of any sort and consequently feel embittered and frustrated by their often self-imposed limiations.

At social events the Goat may appear to stand on the outside of a group, apart and pensive. While his natural reserve may initially place him in this position, it is also part of a definite strategy. The Goat is listening to others and assessing who, if anyone, is worth his time. By the end of the evening Capricorn has usually found his way to the most interesting or influential group or person and may well be the centre of attention himself. While never the Court Jester, Capricorn has a wonderfully dry sense of humour and among close friends and family often becomes the life and soul of the gathering.

Small talk, naturally, is something all Goats abhor. I once spent an entire lunch frenetically effervescing and being incredibly interesting and animated to compensate for my mute Capricorn husband. At one point in what was rapidly becoming an interminable event, his next-door-neighbour asked him a question point-blank that warranted the sort of weighty reply of which he was eminently suited and which everyone keenly awaited. He answered in a monosyllable, after which a pin could have been heard to drop. I knew without the post mortem in the car later he had been bored beyond desperation, but when asked why he couldn't bring himself to respond even to a direct question, he replied, 'I had nothing to say that anybody there would have either appreciated or understood'!

The Goat is not a self-indulgent, profligate creature. To Capricorn, sufficiency—if not frugality and thrift—is next to godliness. Neither male nor female Capricorns like to splash their money about, although I have known some to buy up box-loads of loo rolls or discontinued lines in paint—and to drive miles to obtain them into the bargain. Others may view such behaviour as a ridiculous waste of time, but Capricorns spare no expense in pursuit of a real bargain.

Combined with their thriftiness and insistence on value for money the

Capricorn nutures an intense dislike for anything flashy. I once tried to assess the Sun sign of a doctor I had been consulting for some time. I eventually narrowed the field down to Capricorn, or its opposite sign, Cancer—the overriding clue lying in his choice of car. While other consultants of his ilk tended to opt for impressive Mercedes, or Porsches, he drove an unostentatious, extremely reliable and safe Volvo—and three years old to boot. This suggested the owner put practical consideration before style, yet was reasonably status-conscious. In the event he turned out to be a Sun Capricorn. However, I suspect that beneath his practical sensible choice lies a secret craving for a sports car, like a Lotus or Morgan (highest quality but fast!).

While still on the subject of money, it has to be said that as a general rule of thumb, the Goat tends to be on the mean side, although he usually insists that he is only being careful. If Capricorn can find a way to save money rather than spend it he's happy, although he builds up a certain degree of resentment in others and an unfortunate reputation for himself in the process. It always amuses me to find that those show business personalities often the butt of jokes about their meanness frequently have a strong Capricorn element in their charts—the late Jack Benny for instance (Ascendant and Mars in Capricorn), Ernie Wise (Venus and Jupiter in Capricorn), and Des O'Connor (Sun Capricorn).

In many ways Capricorn's penchant for economy runs through most areas of their lives, not merely the financial. Capricorn is economical with praise, speech, clothes, and time. One Capricorn I know will never visit distant relatives unless he can combine two or three appointments on the way; another telephones only to impart specific information, eliminating such niceties as 'How are you?' or even who is calling. I've also noticed that Capricorn editors like to be extremely economical in style!

Positions of authority appeal to most Capricorns. They are natural leaders and like Aries or Leo never take easily to subservient roles. However, they differ from these fire signs in that they are prepared to endure a menial situation for as long as necessary in the interests of eventually getting to where they want to be. Thus it is hardly surprising that some of the most notable leaders and influential figures have a strong Capricorn theme in their charts. Martin Luther King, Joseph Smith (founder of the Mormon faith), Richard Nixon, and Mao Tse Tung were all Sun Capricorns. As far as Capricorn females are concerned, they, too, are well represented by Joan of Arc, Indhira Ghandi (Moon and Venus in Capricorn), and Queen Elizabeth II (Capricorn rising and Saturn conjunct the Midheaven).

Unfortunately, Richard Nixon and Mao Tse Tung are names one associates with the less laudible and more tyrannical face of Capricorn, and to this list we could add Joseph Stalin, Colonel Nasser, and Al Capone! Although a leader, whether of a country, a small business or a family, must set firm standards and provide a strong lead for his 'people', a one-man dictatorship is intolerable. One of the failings from which many Capricorns seem to suffer is a tendency to try to bend other people's wills to their own, and insist that everyone's desires, needs and life-styles should reflect their own views. Capricorn is usually an exceedingly wise sign but occasionally these Saturn souls can become carried away by their own infallibility. Someone who always turns out to be right and rarely acknowledges any failing can be awfully difficult to live with.

A great many Capricorns of both sexes become workaholics. As a Saturn-ruled sign, Capricorn could never be happy living a life of idleness, dabbling his toes in the waters off some tropical paradise—at least not unles he has a lazy Libran influence in his chart. No matter how much these Saturnian men and women complain of being overrun with work, deep in their hearts and souls they love it—it makes them feel worthwhile and fulfilled. Even on vacation the Capricorn male or female will, after the first few days of utter collapse, organize a routine of sightseeing and, if things get really desperate, sneak off to make a telephone call to the 'office'. Some even take their work with them or have to return early. Not only does this sign relish his work, but most make themselves virtually indispensable to their companies, clients or their patients. To Capricorn, no one can do the job quite as well as himself, and, like an anxious parent, the Goat will be seen hovering around anything he has passed over to someone else.

Although Capricorn is considered by most to be so down to earth that his leaden boots never allow him to be carried away by the intangible or the ephemeral, somewhere deep in his soul is a yearning to do exactly that. Symbolically, the Capricorn Goat is not just a simple, straightforward, cloven-hoofed mountain climber; only half his body is goat, the rest is a fish-like tail. Thus, allegorically, only one half of the Goat is orientated to the Earth with all its practical, materialistic associations, while the other rests in the watery depths of the mystical and the divine. Of course, not all Capricorns realize they have a fish's tail and many plod steadfastly up the materialistic mountain, ignoring any remotely spiritual signposts their inner voice may try to point out. Many, however, develop an enormous appetite for spiritual sustenance of one form or another, but usually not until the second half of life. I have had more than one successful client who has experienced an almost overpowering wave of disillusionment with their material lot and sought a spiritual solution; one became a born-again Christian, another a Buddhist, while others have dramatically changed their life-styles to incorporate a more spiritual approach. (This happened to Sarah Miles and is discussed in the profile on page 427.) In some, this so overwhelms them that they totally renounce the material and the worldly and move wholeheartedly into the spiritual life. John Lilly, for example (Sun, Ascendant, Mars, and Mercury in Capricorn), the scientist best known for his work with dolphins, has become a pioneer of inner space since his mystical experiences in the 1960s. Another, Carlos Castaneda, (Sun and Ascendant in Capricorn), spent several years in Mexico as an apprentice to a Yaqui Indian sorcerer observing and experiencing magical and mystical techniques which eventually became a way of life to him.

Although spiritual leaders can be found born under almost every Sun sign, Capricorn has some impressive names to its credit—Krishnamurti, Yogananda, and Gurdjieff. Furthermore, regardless of the controversy over the actual date of Christ's birth, it seems symbolically fitting that in the Christian world his nativity is celebrated when the Sun is in the early degrees of Capricorn, a sign that uniquely combines the earthly and the divine.

The fish's tail aspect of Capricorn also emerges in the artistic potential many Goats nurture. Capricorn is sometimes called the architect, or builder, of the zodiac. In the Middle Ages this propensity, combined with their spiritual inclinations, would have made Capricorn the ideal mason, applying sacred geometry to express the spiritual principles underlying Nature and the cosmos in physical form, as for example, in Chartres Cathedral. While today many graphic designers, structural engineers, and architects have a strong Saturn theme in their charts, a great many other Capricorns bring a more obviously artistic slant to their constructive talents. Many find an outlet for this potential, either professionally or as a hobby, in music, painting, and sculpture. Thus the Goat is not without aesthetic qualities and appreciation; however, wherever he directs his talents, it is usually with considerable effort and painstaking precision.

Capricorn individuals may not appear to be among the happiest and chirpiest members of the zodiac, perhaps because they tend to carry the problems of the world on their backs—it is perhaps the only sign that actually worries when things are going well! Goats really need a staple diet of problems and challenges to guard against complacency; and fortunately for everyone else, in the event of a disaster these individuals can be virtually guaranteed to save the day. But despite their stolid, unflappable, sometimes gruff exteriors, they have some of the softest hearts in the zodiac.

RELATIONSHIPS

In keeping with most aspects of their lives, Capricorn finds the path to love and marriage somewhat stoney with many hairpin bends, dreary tunnels, and major cross-roads. As befits a Saturn-ruled sign, practical considerations come first and wild, unbridled passion tends to be tucked away in the file marked 'pending'! However, it would be wrong to assume that because the Goat is more confident in the world of the rational and the tangible, he cannot or will not bend to any romantic or passionate feelings that bubble up from time to time—after all this is one of the most, if not the most, highly-sexed signs of the zodiac.

Relationships are enormously important for Capricorns of both sexes, though perhaps not in the same way as for the fire and water signs, who thrive on the highs and lows of the intense emotional content of a relationship. For Capricorn a relationship is rarely a light-hearted affair—the feelings are tender and to be protected at all costs—so male and female Goats tend to take their time before committing themselves to another person. They feel a certain responsibility to marry and procreate; there is a sense of order and rightness in what they are doing and it's not the end of the world if tumultuous feelings of love are missing. After all, security and stability are far more reliable long-term investments.

Obviously, not every single Capricorn will echo quite these sentiments, but almost all enter a long-term relationship, like marriage, with a great sense of responsibility, often placing suitability above passion, and respect and trust beyond emotional satisfaction. Male Goats make excellent husbands and providers, and the females wonderful wives and sustainers. Fidelity, loyalty and reliability are Capricornian assets, although unfortunately there is often an accompanying lack of emotional sensitivity and understanding.

THE FEMALE CAPRICORN

The Capricorn woman, like the Aquarian female, shares only a few of the typically Saturnian qualities of the male Goat. This may well be because the structured, cold, and sometimes ruthless qualities of Saturn (which rules Capricorn and co-rules Aquarius) are far less at home in the female psyche. In keeping with most women, regardless of their Sun sign, the Capricorn female tends to express the qualities of her Moon and Venus far more than those of the Sun. Nevertheless, Saturn's presence can be found lurking in various guises in all Capricorn women.

Capricorn is a sign synonymous with father, which is why it is often considered 'difficult' for a woman to be born when the Sun is in this area of the zodiac. After all, women are meant to be mothers not fathers! The unconscious dilemma that the Capricorn female faces is that although she is biologically and physiologically 'all woman', like Ms Aries she often thinks and reacts like a man. Of course, the Capricorn woman is far more subtle than the Aries female, but like her Mars-ruled sister, she has a sneaking disregard for her own sex, whom she often finds wishy-washy and over-emotional. However, the Capricorn female is far from unfeminine, and indeed often extremely beautiful and serene—Marlene Dietrich, Ingrid Bergman, and Ava Gardner are Capricorn names synonymous with beauty and allure. It is also interesting to note that both Elizabeth Arden and Helena Rubenstein, whose names live on as queens of the beauty industry, were Sun Capricorns!

The typical Ms Capricorn is a highly capable and self-sufficient lady; she is reliable, extremely protective of those she loves, honest, and conscientious; she has an iron will and steely determination that gets her places, and if she cannot do it for herself, she will become the driving force behind her husband and children. It is exceedingly important, however, for the Capricorn or Saturnian female to achieve something in her own right. To some this means clawing their way to the top of the professional tree, in anything from banking to market gardening or the theatre. On the other hand, Ms Capricorn's objectives may not be of a career variety at all, but to own a great house in the country or produce the best marrow at the local flower show. Indeed, the Capricorn lady who recognizes she has goals and sets about achieving them for herself is usually on the road to happiness and fulfilment; those who abdicate their responsibilities to their own ambitions and devote themselves exclusively to pushing their husbands and children instead ultimately feel frustrated and unfulfilled. Worse still, those they push so hard frequently resent such pressure and often end up by rejecting them.

The Capricorn woman applies great managerial skills to her efforts whether in a career or the home. Mrs Capricorn is usually the busiest and most useful member of the PTA, along with Mrs Cancer and Virgo, and whenever her talents are called upon she can be guaranteed to fulfil expectations with flying colours. Her endeavours, like her children, are well-disciplined, thoroughly organized, and useful. Yet, at the end of the day, surrounded by a life of order and sufficiency, Ms Capricorn often feels she has missed out on something—an uneasy feeling gnaws at her lunar plexus.

You see, what is often missing from Ms Capricorn's life (although not always) is love and support—not only from her husband, but also from others. Because she is such a paragon of efficient virtue, she hardly ever allows her weaknesses and sensitivity to show. She spends her time doling out help and advice to all and sundry and no one ever seems to think she may also need some sometimes. Like the redoubtable Virgo female, the moment she sends out distress signals everyone disappears—after all, rocks simply cannot be seen to crumble. This also tends to happen with women who have their Moon, Venus or the Ascendant in Capricorn, not just those with the Sun in these positions.

In many ways the Capricorn female only has herself to blame for her sense of isolation. She often places such importance on the control of her emotions, and indeed of her whole life, that when finally a situation arises that she really cannot cope with, her feelings well up like a tidal wave and threaten to overpower her. The Capricorn woman is basically afraid of the irrational, unstable world of her deep feelings, which she perceives make her vulnerable; she places security before emotional satisfaction and puts her trust in the real and the practical. Thus Ms Capricorn often maks a conscious decision to form long-term relationships, like marriage, with individuals who can supply stability and security before unbridled passion. Sometimes this works well for the Capricorn woman, especially if she has the Moon and Venus in an earth sign since she basks in the safe harbour of a stable—if rather boring marriage—frequently with all the material comforts of life.

However, there are a great many Capricorn women who marry with their heads, for which their hearts repent at leisure. It may gradually dawn upon the Capricorn female who has put her emotional needs in second place that the marriage is not so much of a haven of security as a prison in which she is somewhat lonely and unfulfilled. This realization often emerges around the 29th or 58th year of life (at Saturn's return to its natal position) or between 38 and 42 (at the Uranus opposition to its birth position). Sometimes the Capricorn woman settles for her chains and becomes resigned to an emotionally bland relationship. Others fall desperately in love with someone else and are plunged into a well of confusion—hopelessly torn between their sense of duty and obligation to their partner and their equally strong desire for emotional satisfaction. Either way, the Capricorn woman who has recognized her marriage is emotionally vapid will feel guilty about the choice she makes.

Obviously this doesn't happen to all Capricorn women, much depends on the overall content of the chart. But, broadly speaking, the Capricorn female is not the sort to take her relationships lightly and, in consequence, she tends to suffer much agony through them if they go wrong. In many ways the Capricorn female wants her marriage to have a built-in guarantee of success and she feels dreadfully pulled apart when either she, or her partner, seems to have failed.

There is another pattern that tends to occur with Capricorn women and their relationships which can be directly related to the influence of Saturn. Father is a terribly important person for all little girls, but particularly the Capricorn female. He may adore her to the extent that she places him on an unrealistically high pedestal—a man against whom all others must be measured. Conversely, her father may be remote and difficult, yet even then his image has a powerful effect on her. Consequently, when Ms Capricorn forms relationships in adult life, her men often have many of her father's qualities about them. (This tends to happen not only to women who have their Sun, Moon, Venus, or Ascendant in Capricorn, but those who have Saturn linked to the seventh house of relationships or their Moon and Venus in aspect of Saturn.) Some Capricorn women find older men extremely attractive—and safe—and of course they are much more likely to have reached a successful position in life! The point about this tendency to recreate father in romantic relationships is that, like the male Goat, Ms Capricorn needs to find fatherly qualities of strength, resilience, and determination in herself. At the risk of repeating myself, the Capricorn woman who channels her drive into her own pursuits, rather than vicariously through her partner, has less danger of becoming disillusioned with her relationships.

Another curious quality about Capricorn women is that despite their practical commonsense approach to life and their need for stability and security, time and time again Ms Capricorn becomes involved with Mr Unsuitable, Mr Weak, and Mr Cruel. Regardless of how difficult the relationship may be the Saturn-dominated woman rarely walks out: she puts on a brave face for the world and copes with her misery in private. In my experience there are two reasons for this. First of all, as I have said, the Capricorn woman is often out of touch with her emotions, which therefore makes her vulnerable to a man who is equally out of touch with his. Because she lacks the ability to perceive this, she puts up with a weak, cruel, or emotionally crippled partner by continually rationalizing his difficult behaviour and convincing herself that she can live with a minimum of emotional intimacy. The second reason, however, may owe less to the fact that her Sun is in Capricorn and more to her Moon and Venus placing or her Descendant sign and aspects. Clearly the Capricorn woman with her Venus in Aquarius or Sagittarius is a vastly different kettle of fish from another with Venus in Capricorn or the Moon in an earth sign. One of my clients with her Sun and Mercury in Capricorn, has her Venus in Aquarius. Until the age of 29 she was apparently 'quite wild'. At this age she fell in love with a most unsuitable man. They had a whirlwind affair, married, and produced a son in the space of a year. Unfortunately her husband (a Sun Aquarius) found himself in extremely treacherous, if not criminal, financial waters and reluctantly, for the sake of the child, they parted and subsequently divorced. A year or so later another man (a Sun Pisces) swept her off her feet and for five years they lived happily, if somewhat spasmodically, together. In typical Piscean style, her lover had a problem with commitment and for eight years he made various excuses as to why they should not marry—'Why sully romance with a legal tie?' 'His Aunt Cicely wouldn't like it.' She found herself in the typical Capricornian role of parent in the relationship: she managed his domestic and professional affairs for him, even helped him to buy a house and then decorated it throughout single-handed. She consulted me at a time when the relationship was in its death throes. Despite holding down an immensely responsible job and organizing numerous people's lives for them, she was completely unable to break away from a relationship that was causing her deep unhappiness. One day her Piscean lover would urge her to find someone else, then as soon as she packed her bags and returned to her own flat, he would ring her night and day. Eventually he found someone else and managed to humiliate her professionally in the process. Now, a year later, she is still trying to come to terms with it all.

The Capricorn woman is not a romantic dreamer; she had her ideals and her desires but she intends to bring them into reality. She also has great expectations which filter through all aspects of her life, including relationships. She wants the very best from her man and once she finds him she is prepared to give him unstinting loyalty and love. Indeed, once she has committed and bonded herself to a partner, only reluctantly will she sever the connection. Neither is this a lady who indulges in emotional tear-jerking displays of anger and jealousy. If she discovers her partner has been unfaithful she will consider the situation carefully and plan a suitable strategy. If discussion, patience, and time cannot resolve the situation she will handle a separation with a dignity and calm that belies her hurt and desolation. Not that she is to be underestimated. Ms Capricorn does not like to be made a fool of, and even though she may have been let down and betrayed in a relationship she will leave no stone unturned to secure a financially stable future for herself and her children.

Never expect the Capricorn woman to jump into the arms of Don Juan—at least not without a parachute. In her soul she may crave romance and excitement, but she is far too tied to practical reality to put her trust in a romantic gambol. There are plenty of other signs that will provide adventure and excitement. These are not Ms Capricorn's assets; her talents are sound, reliable, and practical to the core. Her loyalty and sense of duty are almost unrivalled in the zodiac, and although she may pour cold water on her loved one's highest hopes and dreams, he will never lack for support when things go wrong. Ms Capricorn is at her best in times of greatest difficulty and when she says 'for richer, for poorer, for better or worse', she means it!

THE MALE CAPRICORN

I may well be a little biased toward Capricorn men, having so many of them in my family; however, this has allowed me to make some excellent first-hand observations, and despite their occasional flaws and imperfections, they remain some of the finest and most honourable men in the zodiac.

The Capricorn man frequently falls into the strong and silent category; his reserve provides a natural armour plating for his feelings to hide behind. Male Goats are extremely self-protective but innately aware of their vulnerability to the female sex; consequently they tend to adopt a rather aloof and stern exterior. Almost all Capricorn men keep a tight rein on their feelings, which means that, like the Aquarian, a volcano of emotion bubbles under the surface.

As I discussed in the opening section, the myth of the son usurping his father's throne is an underlying theme of Capricorn. While the Capricorn man does not literally have to murder his father in order to establish his own identity, like the Aquarian he invariably encounters a struggle—on both an inner and outer level—in freeing himself from his father's imprint and becoming his own man. As the Capricorn female tends to recreate her experience of father in her later choice of partner(s), the male Goat finds his early relationship with his father central to his grasp of the adult world. All boys, consciously or unconsciously, see their father as a model by which their own manhood stands or falls. Thus their image of him is one they either struggle to emulate or to reject. With Capricorn this is even more marked.

Father's praise and approval is sought constantly; if he displays a positive and encouraging attitude to his son's endeavours he helps supply the building bricks of the Goat's self-esteem. Conversely a weak, critical, or harsh father can hinder his self-expression and induce a lack of self-confidence. Coming to terms with and developing fatherly qualities in himself is a major psychological issue for Capricorn. In relationships, the Goat who has learnt to accept his strength, authority, and power is likely to hold a responsible, caring attitude toward his partner; those who fail to recognize the fatherly qualities in themselves tend to seek them vicariously in a strong, supportive, and capable partner.

Obviously much depends on the overall content of the chart as to how demonstrative and affectionate the Capricorn male can be. By and large, however, Capricorn is not a sign that goes in for huge emotional displays and lavish gestures of affection. Clearly if the Goat has had an upbringing where there was little demonstrable love from the rest of the family, he is likely to be even more reserved and uneasy about showing his feelings. There is a certain similarity between the typical Capricorn male and some Aquarian men, in that the awkward handling of their emotions and feelings stems from a deep insecurity and fear of being rejected. Some Capricorn men, particularly if the Moon or Venus is in tense aspect to Pluto or Saturn, find it enormously difficult to discuss their feelings at all, even to the person they love most; it is as though the words literally stick in their throats. Consequently this kind of Capricorn frequently feels very cut off and misunderstood in one-to-one relationships. Others become so used to controlling their behaviour and emotions in the world at large that when they try to relate on a feeling level to anyone the effort can seem like chipping ice from a glacier. Again, like some Aquarian men, this is bound to cause problems in relationships, since the Goat is likely to be attracted to an expressive, emotional partner who becomes increasingly frustrated by what she interprets as coldness and distance, and therefore extremely demanding.

Clearly there are many Capricorn men who begin to flex their emotional muscles with a warm and loving partner. Indeed, once the Goat discovers his feelings *add* an extra dimension to his world rather than cripple and weaken him, he can tap great emotional depths that in turn bring more warmth and fulfilment into his life.

In keeping with their acceptance that obstacles and problems are par for the course in their life, Capricorn men often attract difficult partners. Even if they find a partner to whom they are emotionally, sexually, and temperamentally suited, she often brings some difficulties with her, perhaps in the form of stepchildren, dependants, or overdrafts! And jointly they usually encounter more struggle than, for instance, Mr and Mrs Sagittarius or Libra. Whether this is just the Capricorn's lot or whether he unconsciously draws these kinds of experiences into his life depends on one's point of view. But whatever the underlying cause, it is a familiar story.

Certainly the Goat is rarely lucky in love, at least not at first. If he marries young (late teens or early twenties) the marriage frequently encounters problems around his 28th or 29th birthday and sometimes divorce is the reluctant solution. Others tend to meet or marry around this age, although the mid-thirties is another boom time for Capricorn nuptials. If the Goat marries after his 29th birthday, he stands a much better chance of success with the relationship, although this is by no means guaranteed. The major problem with Capricorn in marriage is that by and large he is rather selfish. He tends to think his own views, whether they be domestic, financial, or paternal, are best, and his overly rigid and intolerant behaviour frequently sours the most promising relationships. Besides his natural Saturnian characteristics, this may be due to spending so many years either living on his own or in a situation where he could live more or less by his own rules. Thus, if by the age of 30 he has failed to learn the gentle art of give and take, or to appreciate that other people aren't wrong just because they differ from him, he is unlikely to be able to change easily and thus to find the domestic harmony and marital happiness he seeks. Fortunately, many Goats mellow with age, and once the pressures of breadwinning, the rat-race, and raising and educating the children are off he has more time for personal relationships and therefore finds more happiness and contentment in his marriage and life in general.

A word of warning here about the retired Goat. Many Capricorn men live to work; their self-esteem, status, and well-being is intrinsically linked to their role out in the world. Thus when they retire from their jobs, they experience a loss of identity that is psychologically very threatening. Of course this can happen to any man regardless of his Sun sign, but in my experience, men with a strongly Capricornian or Saturnine theme in their charts are particularly prone to such an identity crisis on retirement. As a secondary problem to their loss of power and prestige, their marriage, which may have been tolerable for both while he was away most of the day, may soon start to show stress fractures due to round-the-clock togetherness.

Like the female of the species, the Capricorn male expects his marriage, like his possessions, to last a lifetime. He likes the security and stability of marriage and will remain steadfast to his wife and family through thick and thin. The idea of divorce repels him, although once convinced that nothing more can be done to salvage the reltionship he adapts to the situation with a stoic resolve. Even after a divorce, when he may well have remarried, Mr Capricorn may still feel bonded to his ex-wife by an emotional umbilical cord. In his mind he may go over aspects of their relationship again and again, trying to work out what went wrong or how much he was to blame—not that anyone else would notice of course.

One Capricorn client who consulted me for two years after his divorce used to spend at least an hour of every session complaining about his wife's irresponsible attitude towards his children, what a spendthrift she was, and how unutterably selfish. He moaned about every aspect of her personality, yet it was patently obvious he was as linked to her out of marriage as he had been during it. Over the period of time he consulted me I became increasingly aware of his own mean, selfish, and autocratic behaviour—a situation hardly remedied by his continual 'forgotten' cheque book and wallet—despite running a thriving building business! By the time we discontinued the sessions by mutual agreement, I was completely in sympathy with his wife!

Considering his sentiments about separation and divorce, the Goat will usually choose a partner only after a great deal of deliberation. Her social standing, her demeanour, her procreative abilities, and her attitude to family matters are all carefully weighed in the balance. Let us take these issues one by one.

The Goat is an immensely status-conscious individual. While his animal instincts may urge him toward an encounter with an obviously sexy-looking female, when it comes to marriage, his choice is usually ultra-conservative. The Capricorn male has high standards, he dislikes anything loud and flashy—which goes for his women as well as his cars! The middle-class Capricorn will keep an eye out for a wife among the aristocracy; the working-class Goat usually sets his sights higher up the social ladder, where he considers he truly belongs anyway; the aristrocratic Capricorn only marries within his own class (unless he has a strongly Uranian or Neptunian streak), and the wealthier and more titled his wife the better.

Aristotle Onassis had several planets in Capricorn,* including the Sun and Venus. His rise from an impoverished peasant background to become one of the richest and most powerful men in the world is a Capricorn legend in itself. But his relationships also reflect a Capricorn theme. He first married the daughter of another wealthy Greek shipping owner and during the marriage became involved with the world-renowned opera singer Maria Callas. Then, in 1968 he astounded the world—and Maria—by marrying President Kennedy's widow, Jackie. Maria Callas' husband, Giovanni Meneghini, commented in his autobiography that Ari's main attraction for Maria lay in the fact that although he had money and great riches, he lacked culture—a quality synonymous with Maria. Once he had acquired culture he realized he craved class, and thus who more fitting than Jackie Kennedy. Of course Onassis' relationships and, indeed, his life were dogged with trauma and tragedy. All his women were volatile and temperamental and eventually found him very difficult to live with.

Social standing is one thing, demeanour quite another. The male Capricorn tends to be somewhat chauvinistic at heart and likes to see his woman as a foil to his strongly masculine image. Consequently, it is a rare Goat who chooses a 'career first—family second' type of wife, or a woman who paints the town red—or herself for that matter. The Capricorn man may relish competition and challenge in his career but hardly ever chooses to repeat the experience in his marriage. He likes to provide for his wife and family and play a thoroughly patriarchal role; thus he rarely stands for a woman who insists on her independence and argues with his every decision. Only very occasionally does this Saturnine male voluntarily accept the less dominant role in a relationship, since he is neither emotionally nor psychologically conditioned to it.

The male Capricorn often nurtures a secret urge to found a dynasty. Thus his desire to have children—particularly sons—does not only stem from an emotional source but from a sense of heritage and blood preservation. It is therefore an extremely bitter blow for the Goat who finds he cannot have children or whose wife is a reluctant mother. One woman who became the second wife of a wealthy Capricorn man, told me that one of the stipulations she had to accept before he would go ahead with the marriage was that she

*A variety of birth dates and times exist for Aristotle Onassis but most astrologers favour 20 January 1906.

was prepared to have children although he already had three from his first marriage.

Which brings us to another important feature of Capricorn's life—his family. Unless the Goat has had a traumatic and unhappy family background he is usually enormously loyal and absolutely devoted to his nearest and dearest. He has a strong sense of family unity which he tries to preserve at all costs. As far as the Capricorn individual is concerned, when he marries, the approval of his family is of paramount importance, and in many ways the lady who marries the Goat must be prepared also to marry his family. In my own case, I was hardly surprised, although perhaps a little miffed, when my strongly Capricorn husband took me to spend a night with one of his relatives on our honeymoon!

One of the most common complaints voiced by the women in Capricorn's life is that there is a time and place for everything—including her! Work and his endeavours come first and only when the various items on his extensive list of 'things to be done' have been accomplished can he turn to more trivial matters. Naturally this creates a certain hostility, if not downright anger in his women. One close friend of mine travelled all the way from her home in England to Australia to spend a month with her Capricorn lover. Within twenty-four hours of her arrival she found herself hard at work with him in his office, a pattern that was to repeat itself virtually for the entire month. Only when each day's work was accomplished did he have time for her and, even then, much of that was spent visiting or on the telephone to his ex-wife! Sad to say, the relationship ended with her return home.

One of Capricorn's greatest assests is his rock-like strength: in times of stress and difficulty he remains firm and sure, and unless there is a strongly Uranian or Neptunian pattern in his chart, the Capricorn lover or husband will never desert his lady when she needs him. Even when a relationship has 'died' he will hang on until it is well and truly buried, and, although reluctant to part with his money or possessions he will always accept his financial obligations in the event of divorce.

In keeping with his loyalty and devotion, the Goat is usually extremely possessive about his partner. He may never show his jealousy on the surface but at heart he feels that what is his belongs only to him. While the Capricorn man can be as easily emotionally deceived as anyone else, he is unlikely to handle the situation in an emotionally-charged way, like a hot-headed Leo or Aries. Although he will fight for the woman he loves, once he has lost his respect for her he is unlikely to want her back. However, because he is a great believer in family life, the Capricorn man may go on with the marriage 'for the sake of the children', but his relationship with his wife will have altered irrevocably. Capricorn men are entirely capable of existing in a relationship where there is no emotional communication and little love or affection.

While the Capricorn man is unlikely to say 'I love you' twenty times a day—or even a year for that matter—his love is never a nine-days' wonder. Once he has said those 'three little words', unless he informs you otherwise, you can rest assured he hasn't changed his mind. Likewise, the Goat does not go in for showering his loved one with expensive gifts: he is a practical, cautious man at heart. My mother still recalls the Christmas Day my

Capricorn father proudly presented her with a pressure cooker; it was immediately relegated to the broom cupboard until the festivities were over, where, from my mother's icy countenance, my father ought to have retired as well! In keeping with his tendency to be a late bloomer, Capricorn marriage prospects often flower later in life—like all sound long-term investments! Although, when young, the Capricorn's wife feels other couples have much more fun, by the time those same couples have retired to a bungalow by the sea, Mr Capricorn is planning a trip for them both to the Azores. All things improve with time for Capricorn.

SUMMARY

Although relationships play a leading part for Capricorn, their importance must never be allowed to overshadow other aspects of their lives. This is especially true for male Goats. One Capricorn man made this abundantly clear to me at the outset of our relationship when he quoted these well-known words in my ear one starry night, 'Love to a man, 'tis a thing apart, to a woman her whole existence. . .' The stars temporarily lost their lustre and I was brought down to earth with a bump! Even Capricorn women take a less romantic and more realistic view of relationships than most of the other signs, although they are much more responsive to the ebbs and flows of their emotions than their male counterparts. However, once Capricorns have found Mr or Mrs Right, they work enormously hard at the relationship, and even if the ship of romance sinks without trace, they are bound to have made a raft to carry both passengers to the nearest piece of dry land.

If there is a drawback (or two) to Capricorn individuals, it is their tendency to be somewhat selfish and consider themselves always to be in the right—qualities that rarely make for domestic harmony. The Goat's insistence on accepting the reality of a situation and of facing facts rather than feelings often means he or she is immune to the more subtle, but equally important pulses of life. To find more fulfilment and happiness in relationships Capricorns need to listen, to understand and, occasionally, to acquiesce in another's needs—in fact to learn that people, no matter how irrational their needs may seem, sometimes come before the practicalities of life. Given that Capricorns can find their tender hearts and learn to share their feelings, they have an abundance of fine qualities to offer a partner. Forget adventure, excitement and other such transitory stuff of life, what the typical Capricorn has to offer is sound financial security, steadfast love, and years of loyalty and fidelity.

CAPRICORN PARTNERSHIPS

With an eye to a wise investment and long-term potential, Capricorn's most durable relationships lie with the other two earth signs, Virgo and Taurus, or the water signs, Cancer, Scorpio, and Pisces.

Aries
There is usually strong sexual attraction between Capricorn and **Aries**: Capricorn personifies the strong and silent type that Aries adores, while Aries presents a carefree, adventurous spirit that appeals to Capricorn. In the long term, however, these two experience much conflict over finances: Capricorn

is a strictly pay now, live later sign, while Aries is just the reverse. Both are also dreadfully bossy so that the domestic scene often resembles a kind of Mad Hatter's tea party. On the plus side Aries, like Leo, is a marvellous sign to bring Capricorn out of one of his black holes of gloom and despondency, and given that they have some harmonious Moon and Venus contacts their relationship can prosper and flower into old age, despite its bumpy start.

Taurus

Taurus is one of Capricorn's best partners, for Taurus has a wonderfully earthy sensuousness to offer Capricorn and the physical side of their relationship usually improves, like a good wine, with age. Taurus is just as keen as Capricorn on security and financial solvency and this Venus-ruled sign often brings peace, harmony, and beauty into Capricorn's life. The drawback to this relationship lies in their equally stubborn natures, and agreeing on important issues can somtimes seem like a Mexican stand-off! Also their relationship can suffer from a lack of stimulation at times.

Gemini

Capricorn and Gemini have little in common, although they often experience a sort of ambivalent attraction for each other. Gemini appears far too superficial and inconsistent for Capricorn, while Capricorn seems too boring and earth-bound for Gemini. Nevertheless, when this relationship works—usually if there are harmonious Moon and/or Venus links—both people benefit tremendously from each other's qualities. This combination works best if the female is Gemini and the male Capricorn, thus allowing them to revert to the traditional roles of the stable provider (Capricorn) and the inconsistent social butterfly (Gemini).

Cancer

Capricorn and Cancer are opposite signs and encounter the usual problems all individuals do when confronted by a mirror image—they either like what they see or loathe it! Both signs are moody, but Capricorn can get on with his life when an emotional impasse arises whereas Cancer simply cannot. Thus Cancer often accuses Capricorn of being unfeeling. This is usually an extremely conservative couple—security comes first, and with careful and thrifty planning, they usually enter a rich old-age. Earth and water combinations have a good reputation for durability.

Leo

Capricorn and Leo encounter struggles over power and dominance in their relationship. Capricorn is initially highly attracted to Leo's sunny, generous personality, but as the relationship progresses, he tires of Leo's self-oriented behaviour and grandiose manner. Leo, on the other hand, finds in Capricorn someone he can admire and look up to, though in time he feels Capricorn is too critical and reclusive. Both these signs tend to consider themselves permanently in the right, thus their refusal to back down on issues great and small causes much friction in their relationship. Yet, with a little more give and take, these two should find they have much to offer one another.

Virgo

Capricorn and **Virgo** partnerships trundle along steadfastly and surely. Again, this is a security-oriented partnership, and one often destined to fall into a cosy rut of routine. There is usually good communication between these two signs, although the domestic harmony often owes much to Virgo becoming a doormat for Capricorn. Sometimes Capricorn finds Virgo too neurotic and pernickety for his liking, while Virgo thinks Capricorn a bit of a stick-in-the-mud. Both also tend to become bogged down and side-tracked by details and thus lose grasp of a situation.

Libra

Capricorn is often highly attracted to **Libra**—and vice-versa. Both signs are ambitious and, in a relationship, aim for and achieve a successful, comfortable life together. Libra brings a lot of style into Capricorn's life and because Libra is on the lazy side, Capricorn urges him to make use of his talents. Sometimes, however, Libra, like Gemini, finds Capricorn dull and leaden and a reluctant socialite, while Capricorn feels Libra is too emotionally bland and socially promiscuous.

Scorpio

A Capricorn/**Scorpio** relationship is usually a serious affair. Both these signs have a tendency to brood, and long silences and hurt feelings pepper the otherwise stable nature of their partnership. Capricorn and Scorpio are strongly sexed signs, but if the couple are physically incompatible, much of their sexual and emotional frustration is vented on each other in acrimonious scenes over material issues. On the plus side, there is hardly anything these two cannot achieve together, or any difficulties they cannot surmount.

Sagittarius

Of Capricorn's relationships with the fire signs, one with **Sagittarius** has the greatest potential for harmony simply because both may have their Venus or Mercury in each other's Sun sign. However, Sagittarius is ruled by Jupiter—a planet whose expansive, joyful nature is the antithesis to serious, structured Saturn. On the plus side, Capricorn can tone down Sagittarius' jubilant excesses, while Sagittarius can bolster Capricorn's sagging spirits and urge him to become more optimistic about life. The Sagittarian partner hates to be restrained or have his movements checked; he is a free spirit, so finds Capricorn a trifle too rigid and possessive. In turn Capricorn finds Sagittarius much too irresponsible, careless, and extravagant and feels he is doing all the hard work in the relationship.

Capricorn

Two **Capricorns** together support and sustain each other through thick and thin, or resist and argue between themselves every step of the way. In either case the relationship is a hard-working one. Some couples work hard to achieve a very successful, affluent life-style, but lose out emotionally in the process; others have huge obstacles to contend with in the outer world, yet become closer and stronger through their experiences—sometimes a combination of all these things. Whatever their problems, however, this couple hardly ever throw in the towel, and providing the sexual side of their relationship is good, this is an almost unbreakable combination.

Aquarius

Aquarius is the best air partner for Capricorn, largely because they both have affiliations with Saturn. Given the more stable type of Aquarian, the partnership is reminiscent of the dual Capricorn couple (see above). However, the more unconventional, unpredictable Aquarian presents the antithesis of the stable, secure partner Capricorn seeks. Feelings are usually low key in this relationship (unless there are harmonious Moon signs and contacts) and both frequently pursue independent life-styles. Sexually, this is an all or nothing combination; some have an extremely active physical relationship while others appear to be able to take it or leave it.

Pisces

Capricorn and **Pisces** have much to offer one another. Capricorn's strong and stable personality provides the ideal rock on which the insecure Pisces Fish can bask. With a Pisces partner, Capricorn individuals learn to develop their sensitivity and flex their emotional Goat's tails. One of the major problems that can emerge with this combination, however, is that Capricorn may attempt to stifle or crush Pisces' dreams while maintaining he is only trying to be practical. Conversely, Pisces can make a tremendous muddle out of Capricorn's life and even unconsciously undermine his actions.

SEXUALITY

Capricorns are late bloomers in most areas of their lives and sex is no exception. Indeed, sex for or with Capricorn, like everything else, is worth waiting for.

Most astrology books infer that Capricorn is not as interested in this area of life as some of the other signs of the zodiac, which, by implication, suggest they must therefore be poor lovers. In my experience as an astrologer, nothing could be further from the truth. Capricorn is a sign synonymous with understatement—their appearance and manner frequently disguise unsuspected potential—and in the sexual arena male and female Goats usually make highly skilled and deeply satisfying partners.

Capricorn's ruling planet, Saturn, holds the key to the powerful sexual nature of this sign*. In chart comparison, when there are many Saturn contacts between a couple, especially those involving each person's Sun, Venus, and Mars, instead of initially giving rise to a coldness and fear of intimacy, just the reverse seems to happen and the two individuals experience intensely passionate feelings for one another. Astrological tradition even states that the planet Mars is 'exalted' in Capricorn: in some mysterious way, the crystallizing action of Saturn controls and defines the desire aspect of Mars, allowing its action to be prolonged and more effective. Indeed, as a Saturn-ruled sign, Capricorn can be a truly 'horny' Goat!

---

*Remember that in Ancient Rome the feast of Saturn entailed a week of debauchery and revelry and the god, Saturn, was associated with fertility.

There is another facet of Capricorn's sexual nature that can be directly linked to Saturn: the tendency to experience a sudden cut-off from a previously strong sexual feeling and response to a partner.* Capricornian or Saturnian individuals seem to blow hot and cold sexually, behaviour that seems as mystifying to themselves as to their partners. Part of the reason may well be the Saturnian dislike of excess, or the fear that things may become out of control; whatever the case it is usually unconscious. However, sometimes an unfortunate spin-off from this sudden sexual cut-off is an intense criticism or verbal cruelty that is levelled at the partner—Saturn in its more unpleasant aspect.

The Capricorn man or woman prefers the subtle approach to love and sex: Goats rarely make a great show of their feelings for anyone—often through lack of confidence or a fear of losing face. They will move in on the object of their desires cautiously but persistently; they must first ascertain the competition and the likelihood of success before wasting unnecessary energy on a fruitless mission! Because Capricorn is a sign synonymous with fidelity, almost all Goats will steer clear of an affair with someone who is already married; likewise, once married themselves they tend to remain faithful to their partner. Obviously there are some promiscuous Capricorns, male and female alike, but they are in the minority and their behaviour is usually related to more extremist Uranian aspects in their charts or to a deep frustration or unhappiness in their marriage. This remark, by a male with his Sun in Capricorn, is fairly typical: 'I certainly sowed my wild oats when I was younger, although I held (and still do) a fairly moralistic view about fidelity in marriage. I guess I'm lucky to have found a wife who fulfils me sexually, so I don't feel tempted to stray.'

In many ways the Capricorn female is the quintessential Englishwoman—icecool and apparently untouchable on the surface but passionate and sexy once the ice melts. Although usually sexual late-starters, once into the swing of things many Capricorn women manage to encounter a wealth of sexual experience before marriage. The more secure Capricorn woman can be quite objective about sex and she doesn't necessarily expect a long-term emotional commitment from a partner—nor indeed wishes to make one herself until she is absolutely sure it's right. She knows a good marriage does not rest wholly on a sexual foundation. the more insecure Capricorn woman may use her body in the hope of eliciting a long-term emotional commitment from a partner which is usually doomed from the outset. This kind of Capricorn, while appearing in control and detached, craves love and affection rather than sex; consequently when the relationship runs out of steam and passion and the partner wishes to depart she is rendered even more insecure. Since this type of Capricorn is usually low on self-esteem, she frequently becomes involved with men who use her. However, both types of Capricorn female can tolerate a sexually unsatisfactory marriage for the sake of material security.

The Capricorn woman is often an excellent lover. Like the male Goat she is

* Many of these tendencies will be experienced by those who have Saturn in hard aspect to Mars in their birth charts, as well as those who have Venus or Mars in Capricorn.

acutely aware of the physical senses and is far more aroused by touch and sight than any amount of erotic images or fantasy. She likes her men to be in good physical shape, although like many of the stronger zodiac women, she rates power and intellect higher than a pair of bulging biceps! Once she has learned the ropes and found the key to her own and her partner's erogenous zones, she is a veritable fountain of pleasure and sensuousness. Linda Lovelace, star of the pornographic film, **Deep Throat**, and author of an explicitly sexual, apparently autobiographical book, is a Sun Capricorn, and although most female Goats would rather die than appear naked on celluloid or come out in print about their sex lives, the majority are no strangers to many unusual and certainly interesting practices. I have a Capricorn friend whose sexual history sounds like the **Kama Sutra**; however, in true Capricorn style she married for security, and from what I can gather the **Kama Sutra** is definitely a thing of the past.

Although, like the Aquarian woman, Ms Capricorn can gain a certain physical satisfaction out of a purely sexual encounter, she is nevertheless aware that sex combined with love is infinitely superior. With her ability to make a long-term commitment to one man and her enjoyment and appreciation of sexual subtlety, Ms Capricorn is an enviable wife and lover. Of course, there are some female Goats who are rather frigid emotionally or sexually. In this case the Capricorn woman's ice is almost impossible to melt and once the children have all arrived sex is relegated to Christmas and Bank Holidays. The more typical Capricorn female has a strong sex drive, and one that increases the older she becomes. One woman with Venus in Capricorn wrote on my questionnaire. 'I was a virgin until my mid-twenties as I was saving myself for the right person. In fact, my husband was my first lover, but now in my early forties I find my sexual needs keep on growing and unfortunately my husband does not fulfil me. The trouble is I can't bring myself to be unfaithful although I have plenty of opportunity.' And another with her Sun and Moon in Capricorn commented, 'My sex drive has always been stronger than my partners' which has caused me lots of problems in relationships. I would like to find **one** man who can meet my sexual needs as basically I am the monogamous sort.'

Like the other two earthy women, Ms Taurus and Ms Virgo, there is something of the earth goddess in the Capricorn woman. Unrepressed and unhindered by her mother's attitudes to sex, she has a storehouse of sensuality to offer a partner. She may have a voracious sexual appetite, and because her sensuality is an integral part of her nature, being neither contrived nor forced, she is tremendously attractive to men—even if she lacks cover-girl looks and an hour-glass figure. The Capricorn earth goddess is never coy about her sexuality: as she matures she becomes increasingly comfortable with her body and her femininity and is thus able to gain more enjoyment from sex. In developing the confidence to show her lover what she needs, she encourages greater openness in their sexual interaction. Indeed, while the Capricorn woman, like any female, is capable of being passive, once she has found her sexual confidence, she is able to give full vent to her assertive tendencies. Thus, the mature earth goddess is frequently the dominant sexual partner and tends to be the one to initiate love-making.

As I said earlier, the male Goat is also usually a late starter where sex is concerned—not because he isn't interested. He is often so intent on making sure that it's right first time, that he keeps on missing the boat of opportunity. But like Ms Capricorn, once he's found his feet there's no stopping him! Contrary to his conservative and perfectionist streak where a wife is concerned, the male Capricorn does not need to consult **Debrett** before taking a woman to bed. He likes his females to be on the voluptuous side—large breasted and wide-hipped, but never fat, or perhaps worse, too thin. One client of mine with his Mars in Capricorn was extremely upset about the failure of a sexual encounter with a woman he had found highly attractive. Unfortunately once undressed, he found she was verging on the anorexic and despite every effort he failed to achieve a full-blown erection. 'I think it would have been all right if she'd have kept her clothes on,' he said. Unlike some of the other airy or fiery signs of the zodiac, the Capricorn man cannot get on by erotic images alone; his physical senses of touch and sight are far too dominant.

Sometimes the Capricorn man enjoys the forbidden dimension to sex. While he may not feel exactly guilty about sex, he cannot altogether rid himself of the idea that it is something dark and mysterious. While he may be able to function entirely well in a 'normal' sexual relationship, he becomes extremely aroused when there is an accompanying element of danger—or rather the risk of discovery. Considering the Capricorn man often chooses a wife who is an 'upright pillar' of womanhood—the proverbial good wife and mother—he may secretly want to go to bed with a 'loose woman'. Either this craving remains a fantasy or Mr Capricorn will seek out the odd illicit sexual encounter. Very occasionally the Capricorn man will crave more than this; he may find himself aroused by some light sado-masochistic interplay. However, an individual's attraction toward the more violent aspects of sexuality is never simply a matter of the Sun-sign alone.

Contrary to his somewhat selfish stance within relationships, where sex is concerned the Capricorn man can be very giving indeed. He usually has a tremendous amount of control, which means he can provide his partner with endless pleasure while restraining his. Sometimes, of course, this goes to the opposite extremes and he has difficulty in finally unrestraining himself! Unlike Mr Aries, Leo or Sagittarius, Mr Capricorn is not so obsessed with his own performance and will go on. . . and on. . . and on to make sure that he has satisifed his partner. Capricorn men do not like to leave a job half done!

Most Capricorns (men and women alike) usually purchase a manual on sex and pleasure in the early days of their erotic adventures. Capricorn is a sign that likes maps, and although this may not be true of all of them, before many get into their stride they will have learned the major erogenous zones and recommended positions like the Highway Code. The male Capricorn, like many men, regardless of their Sun sign, may have a certain curiosity about the more unorthodox sexual practices, but he is not one who usually needs a regular diet of mirrors, chandeliers, or threesomes to keep him satisfied.

Clearly, sex is not as important for some Goats as others and from my questionnaire it was apparent that some Capricorn men were anything but strongly sexed; however they would seem to be in the minority. Certainly, there is a tendency for many Capricorn men (and some women) to slot sex in where convenient or to relegate making love to a ritualistic Saturday night or

Sunday morning. Goats aren't the types to be overpowered by lust in the middle of a working afternoon. Capricorns are industrious, conscientious creatures and like to put work before pleasure. Once their itinerary for the day, the week, or the month is accomplished, then they will allow themselves to indulge in the pleasures of the senses. Naturally, this makes for some friction in their relationships and frustration in their partners, especially those of the more impulsive variety. However, those partners with any sense come to terms with Capricorn's obsession for order and self-imposed limits, and learn to appreciate the occasional vintage champagne of sex rather than a daily dose of **vin ordinaire!**

Because Capricorn is a sign that identifies strongly with the male (or father) principle, sexual conquest and mastery is a vital pillar of their masculinity. If the Capricorn man has any doubts about his malehood or his ability to achieve success and status, he will either become a sexual recluse or act like a veritable Don Juan. His general sexual behaviour is an accurate barometer of his self-esteem, and extremes are always a danger sign for Capricorn.

Goats are not ones for embellishment in any area of their lives. Where lovemaking is concerned, Capricorns of both sexes believe actions speak louder than words and most heartily dislike—and disdain—a post-coital exchange of the 'was it good for you' variety. They are primarily creatures of the physical senses and thus gauge a partner's satisfaction through their physical reaction. They encounter great difficulties in verbalizing feelings, sensations, and emotions, and are also often extremely shy. Although the Piscean wins the Masters and Johnson Award for the most intuitive sexual partner in the zodiac, Capricorn surely takes the honours for the most dextrous. While some of the other signs reach their sexual peak in their late teens and early twenties, Capricorn individuals are likely to be still in their prime in the old people's home! All things improve with age for Capricorn.

PROFILE OF A CAPRICORN WOMAN

SARAH MILES

Sarah Miles might not at first seem the ideal choice for a Capricorn profile considering this is one of the most down-to-earth and conservative signs in the zodiac, whilst Sarah's life reads like the proverbial magical mystery tour. But underneath the unconventional, zany—some might say, utterly mad —spirit of her Aquarian Venus and Geminian Moon, there is a highly principled, serious-minded, and extremely responsible woman.

Sarah had a conventional, happy childhood. Her parents were an 'ideal couple', and the family lived an almost idyllic existence deep in the countryside. She, her two elder brothers, and her younger sister were, and still are, very close and their interrelationship strong enough for Sarah to comment 'I haven't had the necessity to look elsewhere for friendship.' Like all Capricorn females, Sarah's father has been a strong influence on her life: he was a brilliant man, highly competitive, with an overwhelming belief that everyone must achieve their potential. Thus he brought much pressure to bear on his children to develop their gifts to the best of their ability. Although all four children have opted for artistic-creative careers, neither parent was artistically inclined. While Sarah eulogizes her family life*—her love of walking in the woods and meadows where she could talk to the animals and be at one with nature, especially the trees: 'trees are the caretakers of the world and we're just camping here for a while . . .'—her experiences of boarding school were less than ecstatic. She was expelled from three schools (her only son, Tom, later bettered this by being expelled from eight!) and she was labelled an 'inciter'. Although extremely bright, Sarah suffers from Dyslexia, a virtually unrecognized condition in the 1950s which was no doubt a contributory factor to her rebellious conduct.

*Jupiter, ruler of the fourth 'house', conjunct the Moon on the MC trine Venus.

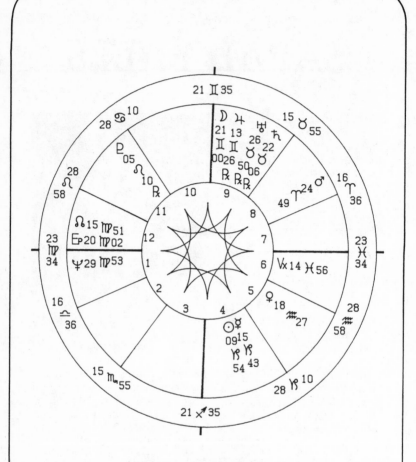

SARAH MILES

31 12 1941   22h 45m 0s GMT

PLACIDUS 51N41 0W22

However, she was athletic and excelled on the games field. Sarah compensated for the academic frustration she experienced by becoming the archetypal 'Daring Daphne of the Fourth', engaging in outrageous activities that guaranteed her the centre of attention. This, combined with her powerful fantasy world, paved the way for the actress within her to develop.

Sarah began her career as an actress at seventeen. Her first film, **Term of Trial**, opposite Laurence Olivier, brought her instant acclaim. She conveyed a fragile innocence yet with all the sensuality of a thirty-year-old—qualities that were to become hallmarks of her personality both on and off screen. Her third film, **The Servant**, with Dirk Bogarde and James Fox, established her not only as a gifted actress but a star. Throughout the 1960s and early 1970s she made many films, some of them blockbuster successes like **Ryan's Daughter** and **Lady Caroline Lamb**, films that were to place her among the most sought-after actresses of her generation.

Despite the normality of her early life, Sarah was not an ordinary child. 'I was growing up during the war and I liked to hear the doodle-bugs on their way to London. Doodle-bugs were most certainly my friends, and I couldn't understand why everyone wanted to rush down to the cellar to get away from them. I was sure they [the doodle-bugs] had come to collect me. And if only I could squeeze through the bars of my cot I could get back to where I came from.' Sarah is not the only person to feel that she belonged elsewhere in the universe. Clare Francis (see p.37) also felt like an alien and had difficulty in learning the rules of the world. Sarah, like Clare, has an outer planet rising in her birth chart—Neptune: a planet that has made a major impact on her life.

Although Sarah's Capricorn Sun and Mercury 'speak' through many of her opinions and attitudes, it is Neptune that 'exerts' an overriding influence time and time again. Neptune is a planet associated with mysticism, artistry, the watery depths of the sea, and the unconscious. Photography and the film business embody the principle of Neptune: images on celluloid and the glamorous unreal aura that surround those involved in the industry. As a highly-photogenic film actress, Sarah has captured the essence of Neptune. Her love of writing poetry and lyrics also stems from this inspiring planet. Yet Sarah has also encountered some of its less desirable facets, of which we shall hear more later.

Like many children who come from a secure and happy family, Sarah expected to find similar emotional support and unconditional love in her adult relationships. She met her husband, the playwright Robert Bolt, when she was twenty-two and married him when she was twenty-five. Four years and one son later their marriage was to end in a set of extraordinary circumstances and a fever of publicity.

Sarah commented that her life seemed to go in seven-year cycles—a phenomenon often experienced by Capricornian individuals linked to the 28/29 year cycle of Saturn (Capricorn's ruling planet). Robert was fifteen years Sarah's senior: with her Capricorn Sun, and her Aquarian Venus in a 90° angle to Saturn, an attraction towards older men is indicated, not to mention some considerable difficulties in relationships. 'I've always liked older men: in fact older people generally. I revere the old because they have the wisdom the young lack . . . I've always had an inkling for the order of things: that's why I love the Third World—people like the Nepalese who find such strength in family order.' Here speaks a true Capricorn woman, a female who extols the virtue of the family bond and reveres tradition. But Sarah's Venus also forms a 90° angle to Uranus, the personification of unconventionality! Hard Venus—Uranus contacts indicate a personality who balks at convention and the formal structure of relationships. Consequently, these two conflicting 'energies' vie for supremacy in her chart. True to her Aquarian—Uranian side, Sarah admits to a hatred of being 'suffocated' in a relationship: but in keeping with the Pisces-Neptune colouring to her house of relationships she has found that people become 'endlessly dependent' on her. Robert was the only man who did not stifle her, and the first man who left her alone. 'No, it wasn't love at first sight,' admitted Sarah, 'but I knew I'd marry him. I fell down the stairs at his home one day—landed in a noisy heap on the floor, screaming blue murder. And he never looked up from his typing! I thought, well, this bloke's going to leave me alone. So that's alright.' Of course there was far more that appealed to her about Robert than his ability to keep himself to himself. Since her own education had been an unmitigated disaster, Sarah learned much from Robert about art and literature. They had the proverbial teacher-pupil relationship. And rather than 'ten-foot high feelings of love' it was 'a total respect for his wisdom' that drew Sarah to Robert. The desire for knowledge and the admiration for intellectual brilliance emerges from Sarah's Moon-Jupiter conjunction in Gemini right at the top of her chart. This conjunction also has much to do with her high-profile public image.

Twenty-nine is a significant age for most people, but particularly those with a strong Capricorn theme in their charts. At this point, when Saturn returns to its original position in the birth chart, the individual truly comes of age: ideally, a new order should be ushered in and the old and outworn discarded. For Sarah, twenty-nine proved significant enough to leave scars that will last a lifetime.

When Sarah was twenty-nine her business manager, David Whiting, died under extremely suspicious circumstances. David had originally come to stay with Sarah and Robert while he was writing a cover story about them for **Time** magazine. His ten-day stay turned into two and a half years. From the moment David arrived it was as if all three of them were held under a spell, a triangle of disparate energies, mutually attracting and repelling. Ultimately, Sarah and David became lovers. David was a brilliant journalist and an extraordinary man. He was also a manic-depressive and attempted suicide twice before his death. 'He was as much a mystery in life as he was in death.' Initially it was presumed he had died by his own hand, but three autopsies later, Sarah became murder suspect number 1. The press had a field day and although the inquest recorded an open verdict, innuendo hung over Sarah like a Los Angeles' smog. David was not the only victim in the affair: Sarah's parents had to move from their much-loved home and Sarah and Robert's marriage collapsed under the strain. Sarah never responded to her accusers and retreated into silence, a silence she still maintains. While Sarah's rising Neptune has a silence a prime mover in her filming career it has also wreaked havoc in her life through deception and the erosion of truth—as in the Whiting affair: 'I was a total victim ... a pawn in the middle of a weird game'—heartfelt utterances from an individual with Neptune rising in Virgo.

Neptune has also been instrumental in Sarah's search for the spiritual. After her divorce from Robert, she went to live on the West coast of the United States. She found she could lead an entirely anonymous life in Los Angeles since she was 'just one of the herd'. It was during the filming of **The Sailor Who Fell From Grace From the Sea** that she experienced her first powerful encounter with the paranormal: a vision that imbued her with a sense of eternity; of simultaneously melting into nature and being at one with the universe. From then and for two years subsequently she was 'bombarded' by supernatural experience; at times there was only a hair's breadth between revelation and total insanity. While cynics might assume the latter had taken over, no one could doubt the transformative effect these experiences had on Sarah's life and her life direction.

As an astrologer might well anticipate, with helping, healing, saving Virgo on her Ascendant, Sarah feels that the paranormal episodes she went through and the information she gleaned from them had a purpose and was certainly an all-important part of her psychological and spiritual growth. 'Any growth is fraught with pain, but perhaps a glimmer of enlightenment can compensate. All I want to be now is of service. My own needs are immaterial. A lot of people need to serve out of a lack in themselves and not out of strength. You can only be of service when you are in total order yourself. I've been spending these past few years getting myself in balance so that I can serve correctly. And I still have a deal of growing to do before I can truly serve others.' While these statements could sound pompous and somewhat vague, there is no doubting Sarah's sincerity. Also, underneath the Neptunian desire to offer herself up to spiritual service, there is some sound Capricornian common sense, and perhaps just an echo of the formative influence of her father. 'One of the things I care about most is that I should fulfil my potential. Potential is limitless and boundless; and I want other people to know that too.'

Another important issue to emerge from of Sarah's exposure to the supernatural elements was a three-year period of celibacy. 'It wasn't a decision. It just happened naturally.' By her own admission, Sarah had been a sexually liberated young woman: a combination no doubt of her Mars in pioneering Aries in the eighth 'house' of sex and transformation, and her experimental Aquarian Venus.* 'In my youth, I overdosed on sex. While I wouldn't say I was promiscuous—I don't like short-term relationships—I did used to go at it a bit like a rabbit. But I've got it all out of my system now. Sex is no longer the great thing for me in a relationship. I think it's a false attraction and certainly the wrong reason for getting involved with someone.'

Some fifteen years after her divorce, Sarah still sustains loyal feelings for Robert. 'Robert is my one marriage. I don't envisage another. Perhaps because I'm quite self-contained. But I do believe in marriage—woman alone is not what woman was meant to be: man is man. Woman is woman; only side by side do they make a whole entity. Also, I don't think men and women are equal—we're equally different; and that's the magic.' As an observer, it would seem that the conflict between Sarah's Aquarian-Uranian and Capricorn-Saturn sides is still unresolved. On the one hand she espouses freedom and the value of self-containment; on the other the virtue of family order. 'I had always imagined I would live in a big rambling house with lots of children—you know, all the wellington boots lined up in order in the hall. But it hasn't happened. And I won't force it.'

There is an astrological adage that the older you get, the more like your sun sign you become. In Sarah's case, this would seem to hold true. In her twenties and early thirties she exploited the liberty, liberality, and licentiousness inherent in the Aquarian-Uranian content of her chart and the ebullience of the Moon-Jupiter conjunction in Gemini. From her mid-thirties, and after some extraordinary encounters of the Neptunian kind, a return to the more stringent, sober values of Capricorn began. 'People always go on about me being a free spirit. Alright, I was free-spirited in youth, but I now believe that you can only be truly free within discipline.' Like many Capricorn women, she has encountered various obstacles in

---

*Sarah's Venus is 60° (sextile) Mars and 90° (square) Uranus.

her path, both professionally and personally; but she believes all her experiences have been both valid and valuable. And in true Capricorn spirit she considers a hard-won success more valuable than one won easily. Clearly, part of her survival kit is her sense of humour and her sense of the ridiculous: 'Even in the most desperate situations, the worst, most dreadful moments of fear, I've been able to see the funny side. In fact, cliché or not, I hope I die laughing!' Knowing Sarah, there is little in life she cannot aspire to. And perhaps when the doodle-bugs do come to take her home, she'll wave a cheery goodbye to Earth ... but not for a long time yet, I hope!

Postscript: I interviewed Sarah in the spring of 1984. Later that year she and Robert returned to each other. They are now [Spring 1986] happily living together in London. Robert suffered a stroke in 1980 that left him almost a vegetable. But over the past six years he has made a miraculous recovery; and although he is still paralysed on one side, he can move around and, perhaps more importantly, still write. He has just finished his first novel. Sarah commented, 'I wish I could say it was all because of me, but if the truth be known, it's really thanks to the arrival of his word processor! For the first time in my life I'm jealous, and it's over a computer!'

Note for Astrologers: (1) Initially, Sarah gave her time of birth (according to her mother) as around 9.30 p.m. (D.S.T.). But since she was born at home during a New Year's Eve party, there was some confusion over the precise time. The nurse who delivered Sarah, however, maintains she was born between 11.30 p.m. and midnight. Considering the uncertainty over the time, the nature of the celebration, and the subsequent events in Sarah's life, the latter time, which places Neptune within 4 degrees of the Ascendant, would seem far more appropriate.

(2) Neptune is given more prominence in Sarah's chart by being on the exact midpoint of the Sun and Moon.

(3) Venus in square to Saturn and Uranus emerges frequently in charts of those who lead unusual sexual lives—sometimes there are inhibitions, frigidity, and abstinence themes (Venus-Saturn), and/or unconventional, occasionally bizarre approaches to love and sex (Venus—Uranus). Combined with the Moon-Jupiter conjunction, the overall picture of Sarah's love life is one of variety, yet one of extremes, from the rampantly experimental to the totally celibate.

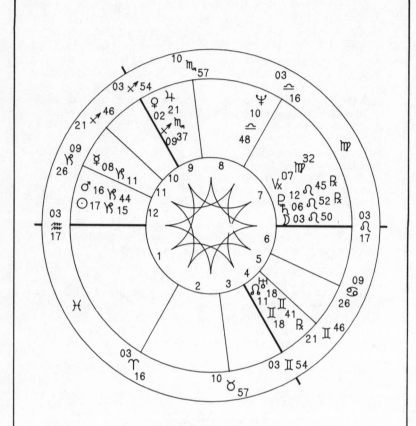

DAVID BOWIE

8 1 1947   9h 0m 0s GMT

PLACIDUS 51N30 0W10

PROFILE OF A CAPRICORN MAN

DAVID BOWIE

I must have been one of the few individuals of my generation to escape Bowie-fever. In the 1970s as I clumped around on my platform soles I remained entirely ignorant that I owed this phenomenon of fashion to an androgynous rock star. Later, my distant impressions of Bowie were brought into sharper focus through my children's addiction to the evocative music and charming film of 'The Snowman'. But he still left me cold! Then I read his life story.* So fascinated did I become with this extraordinary man that I obtained videos of his films and many of his albums—all in the pursuit of research, you understand . . .

A traumatic background of unresolved family conflicts often feed the artist's inspirations. This is surely the case with David Bowie. The family, going back to the late 1800s, was peppered with eccentric and unstable individuals, and to protect and bolster its fragile structure elaborate myths were woven; in the process, a massive amount of dust was swept under the carpet. Indeed, David's maternal grandmother—an introverted but articulate and literary woman—convinced herself that there was a curse on the family that would not be laid to rest until the last member had died.

David was nine months old when his parents married; he already had two illegitimate siblings (from different fathers)—a brother, Terry (born 1937) and a sister, Myra (born 1943 and adopted a year later). His father, John Jones, was a insular, saturnine man, whose passion for show business had led to several unsuccessful ventures as a producer. David's mother, Peggy, was a beautiful but emotionally withdrawn woman. She, like her four sisters and brother, had experienced little affection from her mother and in turn found it difficult to display love to her own children. David, with his golden looks and appealing personality, was

*__Alias David Bowie__ by Peter and Leni Gillman (Hodder and Stoughton, 1986).

the undisputed centre of attention within the family. Yet this advantageous position brought more than its share of problems. While idolizing David, his father was overtly cruel to David's half-brother, Terry, and 'in consequence, David learned to supress all signs of his own feelings, and to retreat within a protective mental shell'. Indeed, despite the outer 'normality' of David's family life, there were deep divisions between its members. David's father was never able to accept Terry as a son in any way; he was rejected and passed on to various relatives and foster-parents. Even his own mother, though he was her first-born and a love-child, rejected him. Over the years Terry became increasingly unstable and spent long periods in a mental institution. He, like two of David's aunts, became a victim of schizophrenia, a condition that eventually led to his committing suicide in 1985. David loved Terry, but the fear of his schizophrenia ultimately put a gulf between them. In consequence, David's anguished feelings of guilt bubbled away in his unconscious, emerging from time to time in his enigmatic lyrics.

The complexity and instability of David's background can be seen mainly from the 4th house and the Moon's aspects. Home and family, as portrayed by the 4th house, is ruled by a tensely aspected Mercury and occupied by volatile Uranus. Sometimes the individual with Uranus in the 4th experiences the breakdown of the family unit, perhaps because the parents divorce or one parent—usually father—is physically absent or psychologically 'out to lunch'; in some rare cases, a parent—again more usually the father—suffers some kind of breakdown or a major accident of fate. In David's case, his parents did not divorce though there were undoubted tensions between them, and their cruel and unloving treatment of Terry (whom David adored as a child) made a deep and lasting impression on him. It is also possible to see the mental problems that dogged the family through the Gemini-Mercury colouring to the fourth house.*

While the 4th house provides a graphic illustration of the family pressures and difficulties, the 10th house, where mother is invariably located, presents a much jollier picture. Grand and beneficent Jupiter rules this part of David's horoscope, and lovely Venus is also to be found here. Certainly David's mother was beautiful, and she also had grandiose ideas about life, but Peggy was anything but a jolly and extravagant individual. None the less, whatever David's biographers say about Peggy's lack of warmth, David must have experienced some positive factors about his mother; he was, after all, her favourite child and as his fame increased she became almost embarrassingly proud of him, decorating her home floor-to-ceiling with covers of his albums. The

*Gemini, of course, is the most archetypally dualist sign of the zodiac—not that everyone with a Gemini IC will hail from a schizophrenic family! See **Note for Astrologers** (1).

Moon-Venus MC trine reinforces the positive side of early life; however the Moon's other aspects tell rather a different story.

The Moon–the primary symbol of mother–is of immense importance in David's chart;* though it is placed in the bright and charismatic sign of Leo it forms a conjunction to cold and remorseless Saturn which in turn is conjunct all-powerful Pluto. This combination indicates mother was far from sweetness and light; not only is the cold emotional temperature symbolized here, but the suppressed fears and ambivalent feelings that carved their unconscious imprint on David as well. Mother, as seen through the Moon, emerges as a responsibility and the archetypal creator-destroyer figure.

The family struggle against the taint and fear of madness has in many ways found a therapeutic outlet for David through his work. In the lyrics of his many albums the themes of madness, lost childhood, ambivalent relationships, death, destruction and rebirth are worked through–he even called one of his albums **Aladdin Sane**–a lad insane. In David's first album (**David Bowie: Deram,** ** June 1967) many of the songs evoke yearnings of childhood and the search for affection. Indeed this album with its counter themes of homosexuality and sexual ambiguity was to prove seminal. But perhaps the most recurrent and poignant motif in David's lyrics is his angst about his half-brother Terry: 'Screw up your brother or he'll get you in the end . . .' (**David Bowie**, November 1969); 'Man would tear his brother's flesh . . . We passed upon the stair, we spoke of was and when. Although I wasn't there, he said I was his friend . . .' (**The Man Who Sold the World,** April 1971). Commenting on this latter album, David said 'The subject matter was very telling for me–it was all the family problems and analogies, put into science-fiction form.'

According to his cousin, Kristina, David's ambition to become a star was born at Christmas 1956 when he was taken to see Tommy Steele perform at Catford Town Hall. The seed of ambition must surely have been a strong one, since David's climb to success was as far removed from overnight stardom as Saturn is from the Sun. But then difficulty and struggle are par for the course for the Capricorn man.

Indeed, so convoluted and protracted was David's progress from **The Kon-rads** ((his first band, 1962) to **Ziggy Stardust** (1972) that it would be impossible here to catalogue it.

David was always a little different from everyone else. He had a precocious sense of the camera lens and was a pioneer of fashion by his Bromley Tech. school days. Few of his contemporaries or his teachers, however, noticed any musical talent, though he was a keen and innovative art student. Apparently he showed most talent for stretching

*Conjunct the Descendant.

**Presumably an anagram of dream.

438

Romancing the Stars

the rules. He left school with one O-level (art) and the verdict of the staff was that he was 'a complete exhibitionist—if he was capable of continuous effort his ability would have been put to better use'.

Fortunately, the views of one's teachers often prove severely short-sighted, and while David has continued to make an outrageous and glorious spectacle of himself, he has also doggedly pursued his star.

While 1972 stands out as the year that made David Bowie an international star, 1970 provided the springboard. In his memorable song, **Space Oddity**—'this is Major Tom to ground control . . .'—David's preoccupation with aliens in the family and society had clearly progressed to the far reaches of outer space. Throughout the latter part of 1969 the record see-sawed its way through the outer reaches of the charts and narrowly missed disappearing into a black hole. Faith, grit, and rather a lot of sales promotion prevailed, and Major Tom finally made it to number 5—much to the relief not only of David, but also Philips's marketing manager, Olav Wyper, who practically put his job and his company on the line to make the record a hit. The success of **Oditty** raised David's stock and three months later in February 1970 he gave a performance with his new group **Hype** at the prestigious Round House in London. The concert was not a great success, but it was to represent a watershed in David's career. The group's widely exotic costumes and over-the-top perfomance effectively marked not only the birth of glam and glitter rock but the flamboyant style that became Bowie's hallmark throughout the 'Seventies.

1970 also marked the beginning of a long—at least by rock world standards—and fruitful relationship with his fourth manager, Tony Defries. Tony approached his management of David with the verve of an evangelist. His unstinting efforts to push David to the top enabled them both to live in the style they wished to become accustomed to. With the financial pressures eased by Tony, David was able to concentrate his full energies on his music. By 1972 the album **The Rise and Fall of Ziggy Stardust and the Spiders from Mars** was released. 'It was a work of breathtaking scope . . . The character [Ziggy Stardust] was an alien from outer space who is received on earth as a rock and roll star . . . it was also an intensely personal work, a tour d'horizon of the principal themes of David's career, flowing and merging among the lyrics while also offering the latest installment of his striving for stardom. It was a work of astonishing courage, too, in which David renewed his vertiginous dance with madness and death, embracing them more intimately than ever and then attempting to break free.' The subsequent British tour was a sensational success and Defries, with virtually no remaining capital—merely a wing and a prayer, took the show to the States.

Fortunately, the big gamble paid off. But while David made a personal success, by the end of the tour the company that managed him

(MainMan) was in a serious debit situation. David and the Ziggy company, not to mention all the flocks of groupies, had taken to stardom to the manor born and in a **folie de grandeur** had spent thousands of pounds on hotel bills, champagne, hired limousines and the like. It was a severe case of the ends justifying the means: David's star had to rise–whatever the price.

But the cost was not just a financial one. The trappings and responsibilities of fame, together with the difficulty David found in separating his on stage personna–Ziggy–with the real David Bowie became increasingly difficult. 'I fell for Ziggy . . . It was quite easy to become obsessed night and day with the character. I became Ziggy Stardust . . . Everybody was convincing me I was a Messiah, especially on that first American tour. I got hopelessly lost in fantasy . . . I think I put myself dangerously near the line.' Two years later he had touched that line.

By 1974, David's gradual addiction to cocaine had put even greater pressure on the delicate fabric of his chameleon personality. He became a Jekyll and Hyde figure, charming one moment, evil the next. A colleague recalls 'being struck by the idea that I was actually working with someone who under any other circumstances would be under lock and key. The fact that he was generating all these millions of dollars for people kept him out.' Another commented, 'It was self-destruct time.'

The measure of David's stellium in Capricorn* can be seen in his steadfast grip on the ladder of success. Despite serious set-backs, he soldiered on. David's goals, however, were not money and power, but fame. These goals are shown most clearly by the Sagittarian Midheaven and the conjunction of Venus to this sensitive point. Jupiter is also well placed.** As Howard Sasportas says† of a Jupiter/Sagittarius influence on the MC. 'It is through career, status and recognition that [such individuals] seek meaning and fulfilment in life. In some cases fame itself is worshipped as something numinous and divine.' It is also fascinating that Bowie identified so strongly with a Messiah figure, like Ziggy–a trait familiar to both Capricorn and Sagittarius.†† Intriguingly,

*Sun, Mercury and Mars.

** Jupiter is situated in a peak Gauquelin position having just culminated. It is also sextile both the Sun and Mars and quincunx Uranus thus forming a 'leg' of the Finger of Fate–a configuration that reflects Bowie's extraordinary, out-of-this world gifts and his unorthodox personality. As he says of himself, 'I cannot breathe in the atmosphere of convention . . . I can find freedom only in the realms of my own eccentricity.'

†**The Twelve Houses** (The Aquarian Press, 1985).

†† Reinforced and restated by the 12th house-Neptune content of the chart.

David has personified his saviour-victim myth repeatedly on stage and film and come close to believing he was truly divine. It is also clear from the effect that he has on associates, lovers and audiences alike that he has charisma of fantastic proportions—an unearthly gift perhaps.

The twelfth house of the horoscope is a mysterious, nebulous area, known sometimes as 'the house of self undoing' or the 'house of secret enemies'. Fundamentally it is the area of the chart where the focus is on the collective as opposed to the individual; the place where the individual gives himself up to a greater force. Thus it is not so strange that both David's Sun (self-expression) and Mars (energies and drive) are to be found here. Certainly in the 'Seventies Bowie was a profound symbol of the collective climate of the supernormal and the bizarre. The boundaries between the self and the non-self are indefinite to the 12th house individual, thus it is easy to see how David nearly lost himself in his role-playing and found himself on the borderline of schizophrenia. All these 12th house factors are amplified by the Sun's square aspect to Neptune—on the one hand here we find David's muse and on the other his hyper-sensitivity and his weak hold on reality.*

Fascinating too is the way the prominence of the two leading feminine planets, Moon and Venus, have worked in David's life. Not only has he always been a fashion trend-setter, but he was one of the first men to wear make-up—he also wore dresses on stage long before the advent of Boy George. But David's identification with his anima has not remained merely an on-stage pursuit. He has never hidden his attraction for both men and women nor retained exclusive relationships with either sex.

The vicissitudes of David's love-life are as many and varied as those of his career and thus present an equally impossible task for the brief biographer to document. As always a style leader, his announcement that he was gay 'forged a landmark in the erosion of sexual stereotypes' and made enormously popular high camp in rock. While he has formed loving sexual relationships with men, he has tended to make 'long-term' live-in commitments mainly with women. However, fidelity was simply not on the menu. Most of his relationships dove-tailed with each other: indeed, he met his wife-to-be, Angela Barnett, because she was sexually involved with a man David was also bedding!

Angie was tailor-made for David—attractive, slim, boyish and outrageous. She made herself indispensible to him and, despite the pressures and excesses of their extraordinary life together, their relationship produced a son, Zowie,* and lasted 11 years—though admittedly the last four were a prelude to their divorce in 1980. The

*The search for transcendence, whether through music, art, mystical pursuits or drugs is also a reflection of the Sun-Neptune/12th house influence.

*Born 28 May 1971.

eve of their wedding in March 1970 provided a foretaste of their life together—they spent it in bed with a mutual female friend. Both of them continued to tolerate each other's peccadilloes until the advent of Ava Cherry—the black singer. While initially this **ménage-a-trois** worked well, jealousies between the women forced Ava to New York; thus David divided his time between the two. Then in 1975 this uneasy tripartate was shattered by a formidably sharp lady with a cosmopolitan background, Corrine Schwab. Her influence over David gradually became supreme. While some have called her his 'devil in disguise' others have suggested she is exactly what he needs, and certainly she was a pivotal part of his rehabilitation.

Homosexuality or bisexuality is difficult to pin-point in a chart largely because the source of such a tendency is invariably unknown. My own feelings about David's sexual shenanigans are that he is simply a voracious sexual hedonist. The Sun-Mars conjunction in lusty Capricorn suggests a powerful libido, and in the 12th house, the tendency to see no sexual boundaries. The square of both these planets to Neptune in the 8th house of sex (among several other themes) reinforces the possibility of some kind of sexual deviation. Then again, it is just as easy to see here the desire to transcend physical boundaries by intense and meaningful sexual exchange. From the comments of many of his ex-lovers it is clear David was an expert and sensitive sexual partner. The elevated Venus in Sagittarius suggests an adventurous spirit where love and affection are concerned and a liking for fiery women. The Moon-Saturn-Pluto combination supplies the reason for his poor ability to make long-term emotional commitments to others—the pain of rejection and suffering being too much to risk. This triple conjunction also suggests that he is desperately seeking some kind of maternal response from his partners, which makes Corrine, with her nun-like devotion to his care and protection, a likely long-distance runner in the relationship stakes. And with the comparitively recent hazard of AIDS, David may well have to curtail his extra-mural activities!

Business relationships are also to be found under similar planetary influences as the intimate variety. And in keeping with the frenetic activity in this area, David has had several managers. And like his private life, these relationships have had their intrigues, complexities, break-ups and dramas. But perhaps none so dramatic and transformational as his relationship with Tony Defries. Though Tony had undoubtedly helped Bowie become a great star, he himself had also become very rich indeed in the process. Understandably David resented Tony taking such a huge percentage of his earnings and speculating with it all. When the end inevitably came (March 1975) it resulted in the most massive legal suit in the history of showbusiness. And though David was able to extricate himself from Tony's clutches, he is still bounden 'in perpetuity' to pay Defries and his heirs percentages on his earnings.

One of David's greatest mistakes, and entirely uncharacteristic of a Sun Capricorn, was to sign his name, without checking even the large print, on virtually everything Defries put in front of him. He also turned a blind idea to MainMan's extravagancies. His greatest folly was to let fame stand in the way of common sense. In such a way it could be said he committed hubris. Astrologically, the potential for this folly is contained in the Sun-Mars square to Neptune in the 8th* and the Moon-Saturn-Pluto conjunction in the 7th.

The process of David's decline took roughly two years, the split from Defries in early 1975 marking its nadir. Throughout the **Diamond Dogs** concert tour in 1974 David pushed himself to his limits physically, emotionally and psychologically; the punishing schedule, the intense pitch of his performances together with his excessive life-style and cocaine addiction took an enormous toll. At times he skirted the edge of a full blown schizophrenic episode claiming at one point he was a messiah, at another he was a future Prime Minister. The apocalyptic theme of **Diamond Dogs** paralleled David's disintegrating personality. Yet his strong inner reserves prevailed. 'Always before, when he wished to break with the past, David had searched for a new muscial idiom with which to make a fresh start . . . the idiom he chose this time was black . . . "I stripped myself down, chucked things out, and replaced them with a completely new personality".'

During the **Diamond Dogs** tour BBC television was simultaneously making a documentary on David as a star. What eventually emerged on film was a disturbing portrait of a man cracking up. It was suitably entitled **Cracked Actor**. By strange coincidence the film director, Nicolas Roeg, was looking for the lead in a film **The Man Who Fell to Earth**. One look at David's emaciated form and his haunted appearance and he needed to look no further. The film's story centred on the familiar Bowie theme of an alien who came to Earth equipped with knowledge that could help mankind; instead he was rejected and turned to drink to drown his despair. Though David was by no means well throughout the filming he nevertheless acted and behaved with great professionalism, amazing Roeg with his acute awareness of the camera and his 'extraordinary sixth sense' for film-making. Through the medium of film, the strong Neptunian content of David's chart had found an ideal outlet.

On his return from filming, David found his old friend, the musician Iggy Pop, in hospital on the verge of a complete mental breakdown. Iggy's recovery and Corrine's support provided the catalyst for David's own rehabilitation. 'As David helped nurse Iggy back to health, through

*The 8th house represents what one receives from relationships. Leaving on one side the sublime aspect of Neptune, the spectre of betrayal, (self) deception and loss remains.

his loyalty and diligent steering of Iggy's career, it was as if he was vicariously solving his own problems (and assuaging his guilt over Terry). Iggy helped David directly in turn, showing by his example that a body racked by drugs could recover his vitality and physique.'

From his lowest personal point in 1975, professionally David has never looked back. Over the years he has developed into one of the great artists of our time: his work as an actor has won him considerable praise, and his innovative style, whether through videos, concerts or albums, is admired world-wide. He seems also to have overcome the family curse and instead turned it into a blessing. Through his music and lyrics he has been able to transmute the family myths and daimons, and through his many 'on-stage' characters and alter-egos he has been able to live out his inner life which has in turn struck a chord with the collective spirit of his time.

Messiah or pretender, genius or lunatic, David Bowie, may the force be with you—always.

Bibliography: All quotes are taken from **Alias David Bowie** by Peter and Leni Gillman (Hodder and Stoughton, 1986).

Note for Astrologers: (1) Re: the family tendency towards mental illness. Mercury (ruler of the 4th) on the cusp of the 12th indicates at best, inspired thinking, even visionary powers or perhaps woolly-thinking, and at worst mental confusion and instability.

(2) During the period 1970-71 when David's star rose, progressed Sun was trine Neptune (1970), progressed Sun opposed Pluto (1972), progressed Mars conjuncted the Ascendant and opposed the Moon (1970-71). In 1970 transiting Uranus conjuncted Neptune transiting Saturn trined the Sun and Mars, and transiting Neptune conjuncted Venus. In 1972, transiting Neptune conjuncted Venus and the MC, transiting Uranus squared Sun and Mars, and transiting Pluto sextiled Venus.

(3) During his years of 'self-destruction' (1974-75) there was a progressed full Moon (1975) and the MC moved from Sagittarius to Capricorn. In March 1970 during the Defries farrago, transiting Pluto cojuncted Neptune (in the 8th), transiting Neptune trined Pluto and transiting Uranus squared the Moon (and by implication Saturn-Pluto) in the 7th.

AQUARIUS
21 January–19 February

DREAM-MAKERS AND
HEART-BREAKERS

AQUARIUS
DREAM-MAKERS AND HEART-BREAKERS

A QUARIUS is often mistakenly thought to be a water sign since its symbol is the Waterbearer. However, the 'waters' that pour from the Aquarian urn are not of the wet and soggy variety but pure uncontainable ether. The **Oxford English Dictionary** defines ether as: 'clear sky, upper regions beyond clouds; medium in which electro-magnetic waves are transmitted', and ethereal as 'light, airy, heavenly, of unearthly delicacy of substance, character or appearance'. Aquarius represents all these ideas (and more) and as the most mental—in every sense of the word—of the air signs, it is the antithesis of a nurturing water sign. Indeed, of all the air signs Aquarius is the most detached, the most intellectually orientated, and the least emotionally centred; it is a sign that is long on theories but short on the practical application of its brilliant conceptions. It could be said that the cross the Aquarian must bear is that the human element he cares about so much invariably interferes with his inspired intellectual creations.

Sun Aquarians, or those with Aquarius rising, are often easy to recognize. Their faces are large with expressive, dare I say 'electric-blue' eyes, and their foreheads are strong, often giving rise to difficult-to-manage hair. Their manner can be extremely offhand, and although friendly and apparently easygoing, they are enormously difficult to get to know intimately. The more extrovert Aquarians frequently wear bizarre and zany clothes which mirror their unconventional, uncompromising spirit.

Never expect an Aquarian to agree with you. This sign loves argument and will argue simply for the sake of doing so and relish making everyone else feel uncomfortable and on edge. In one of my astrology classes I had a bright and curious Aquarian student. Each class, without fail, she would launch a series of assaults on my theories and, while her arguments were stimulating, her constant interruptions thoroughly annoyed the rest of the class and interfered with their concentration. By the end of twenty classes she was the only one who was still unable to cast an astrological chart. All the air signs have a tendency to skate on the surface of things and prefer to circulate ideas and concepts without actually getting their hands dirty with their practical implications.

As befits a complex sign with two vastly different ruling planets to choose from, Saturn and Uranus, the mythological figures and legends linked to Aquarius tend to be obscure and extremely diverse. While Greek Ouranus and Cronos have much to say about the Aquarian temperament and its mystical roots, Scandinavian and Celtic myths also provide much insightful detail.

Some astrologers might question the use of the tarot card of the Magician for Aquarius, since Temperance, the Tower and the Star clearly depict the Aquarian glyph. To my mind the Magician is the embodiment of Aquarius: he stands by a table on which are placed symbols of the four elements—fire, earth, air and water. With one hand holding a magic wand (wisdom) he points up to the heavens while the other points down to earth. In this way the

Magician connects Uranus (the upper reaches of the celestial regions, and the principle of limitless freedom of thought and spirit) with Saturn (the earth and the physical realm, and the principle of order and form). The Magician can also be seen to be harnessing the earth forces to the divine. In true Aquarian style, he is a kind of 'electrical' junction box. In keeping with the idea of the new Age of Aquarius (which I shall discuss shortly), ancient power sites in the earth—i.e. stone circles and earth works—are being re-discovered in this century. These power centres are considered to be channels to draw the Light energy to the physical plane. In the same way, the healing power of stones and the use of crystals to transmit 'energies' across vast distances is being explored. Thus the Magician as the activator of spiritual power and Light energies portrays the higher dimension of Aquarius.

Aquarian Magicians are prevalent in myths of many cultures: Britain has one of the most celebrated and best loved, Merlin (or Myrddin), the Scandinavian Odin is another. Odin and his German counterpart, Wodan/Woten, are often interwoven as gods yet there are some important differences between them. Like Odin, Wodan was king of the gods but he was much more of a warrior—he was famed for his Wild Hunt across the stormy skies. Odin, on the other hand, was the most knowledgeable of the gods: he was gifted with powers that surpassed all others, the fullest initiate into the mysteries, the master of magic, of supreme science and poetry. Interestingly, Odin was not supplied with his knowledge by divine right, he acquired it by asking questions of everyone he met on his travels (an extremely Aquarian proclivity). Odin's uncle, Mimir—whose name means 'he who thinks'—guarded a fountain that harboured intelligence and wisdom. In order to drink from the waters and thus know everything, Odin had to give Mimir one of his eyes. After drinking from the fountain Odin received the powers of prophecy. (The Aquarian individual is often gifted with great foresight.)

One of the strangest tales about Odin involves his voluntary self-sacrifice. As part of a magic rite, Odin pierced himself with his own lance, then hung himself from a tree for nine days and nine nights. After the ninth night he noticed some runes below him on the ground: with agonizing difficulty he picked up the runes which released him from his bonds. When he fell to the ground he was completely rejuvenated. The voluntary sacrifice restored him to his prime and increased his powers. Symbolically speaking, sacrifice is an integral part of creativity: and while self-sacrifice per se is not exactly an Aquarian cause célèbre, this sign does reflect some of the creative power of its opposite number Leo. Leo, like the other fixed signs of the zodiac, Taurus and Scorpio, contains a strong death and rebirth theme: in regard to Aquarius, this transformational idea could apply to the way the Aquarian sacrifices his own needs for the benefit of the group, or rather, humanity.

In Odin's story, the emphasis on nine days and nights is a reference to the power and meaning of the number nine. In many cultures, an initiate to the Mysteries would have to pass through nine degrees (or stages). According to the Rosicrucians, nine is the number 'by which man comes into contact with his inner self, unfolds his latent divinity, and attains to that state of interior illumination which is known by the name of Initiation.'

King Arthur and his knights provide a positive feast of astrological goodies—the round table, the quest of the Holy Grail and the Circle of Logres—but nothing is quite so quintessentially Aquarian as Merlin/Myrddin. Myrddin was known as both the 'King-maker' and the 'Holder of all Knowledge'. It was through his magic that Arthur was conceived and brought to Camelot. While Arthur is portrayed as 'the chosen one', it is Merlin who appears to be the ringmaster. At his last meeting with Arthur, Merlin urges him and his knights always to follow the chivalric code; he then leaves them with a cryptic message, 'But now I must depart . . . to sleep my long sleep until the time appointed when the next Circle of Logres [Arthur's kingdom] shall again be formed upon the earth'. After the enchantress, Nimue, has woven her magic around him in nine circles and so drained his powers, Merlin descends into the earth, lays himself on a stone slab and begins his sleep.

Merlin has forged an even stronger link with Aquarius in recent times. Over the past thirteen years, various groups and individuals claim to have contacted the Merlin 'energy'. Merlin has apparently appeared in many guises—as a child, as a brilliant light—and he has a remarkable gift for sky-writing and sculpting clouds (Ouranus was a sky-god). His 'appearance' has coincided with the awakening of New Age consciousness, an awakening expressed vividly in the lyrics 'This is the dawning of the Age of Aquarius.' The concept of Great Ages—long cycles of time, each with their own 'signature'—is one held by almost all cultures. The Age of Pisces, ushered in with the birth of Christ some 2000 years ago, is considered by many to be giving away to that of Aquarius, and the belief in the 'Second Coming' and the return of Arthur are rooted in this idea. Aquarius, however, is a rather impersonal sign, thus the spiritual awakening for this new Age is more likely to manifest spontaneously in the collective unconscious than through the example and leadership of a single individual in the solar-hero mould.

Those who have contacted the 'Merlin energy' say he has 'talked' of the end of 'the reign of the great patriach', but has warned that 'the pendulum cannot swing back to matriachy': a new state of balance, or perhaps equality, must exist. The late Robert Graves, the poet, talked of the same thing but went on to say we were moving into the age of magic! Over the past few years, the Alternative movement has been gaining ground on all fronts, and the idea of the Earth as a living organism, part of humanity with a life and spirit of its own, is being firmly rooted in the individual consciousness.

Balance is a quality more associated with Libra, another air sign, but equality is a distinctly Aquarian theme—consider for a moment the original theory behind Communism. Aquarius is by no means all Love, Light and Brotherhood. Aquarius represents the group and humanity as a whole; it reveres social order which by necessity takes no account of individual preferences or differences. George Orwell's **1984** painted a frightening picture of an individual's fight against state control and provided a grave warning for the future of mankind.

The concept of the New Age of Aquarius being neither matriachal nor patriachal is an interesting one. Aquarius is not only a 'masculine' sign but, in keeping with its Saturn rulership, it can be very patriachal indeed. Aquarius and the feminine have little in common; and the Aquarian man usually finds the most difficulty of all relating to his feminine side and his emotions! On the other hand, Aquarius linked to Uranus could be seen to be above sex, and of all the signs, it is Aquarius that extols the union of mind and spirit: a union that transcends both masculine and feminine.

Given that Saturn and Uranus both have affiliations with Aquarius, it is no surprise that in myth these two planet-gods are inextricably linked. Ouranus (Uranus), god of heaven, and Gaea (a sort of Mother Earth) were a husband and wife team who brought forth many scores of children. Unfortunately, Ouranus, who was fundamentally a tyrannical god primarily concerned with his own unquestionable omnipotence, hated some of his children so much that he kept them buried in the earth, denying them any light. (Aquarians tend to know what is best for others.) Gaea clearly disapproved of this action and begged another of her sons, Cronos (Saturn), to do away with his father. Cronos, being a dutiful son, carried out his mother's wishes and castrated and murdered Ouranus. He then usurped his throne and carried on a thoroughly autocratic rulership of his own which included reinforcing the imprisonment of his brothers. This myth describes the dogmatic and tyrannical aspect of Aquarius and, to a certain extent, its revolutionary side—the predilection of Aquarius for toppling established orders and replacing them with different but equally rigid regimes. Despite the progressive and humanitarian principles this sign personifies, behind its altruistic face lies a dominance and rigidity second to none—facets I shall explore later.

A major characteristic of most Aquarians is their ability to form ideas and concepts light years ahead of anyone else. Ouranus as god of heaven and the 'awakener' has much to offer the human race in urging its members ever onward and upward to states of greater intellectual awareness and higher consciousness. This theme is symbolically reinforced by the wavy line glyph for Aquarius, which can be seen as representing waves of electro-magnetic energy.

In keeping with the two very different planetary associations of this sign there seem to be two opposite types of Aquarian, the progressive unpredictable iconoclast and the rigid disciplinarian. Sometimes, to make matters worse, both qualities are found in one individual, presenting a curious mixture of cold, calculating detachment and unstable eccentricity.

One characteristic that unites both the Saturnian and Uranian Aquarian, and male and female Waterbearer alike is the quest for truth. Aquarians hate pretence and artifice and see through a sham façade like a plate-glass window. As honest and truthful individuals themselves, they expect to be treated in the same spirit of openness by others. An Aquarian would prefer to be told by an individual himself that he had a police record or a spate of bankruptcies behind him **before** he had to dig up the truth for himself or hear it from someone else. The Aquarian employer has fewer qualms than most over employing an individual with a colourful past, providing he is informed in the first place: he likes to judge people on their own merits. Aquarians are also never social snobs, merely intellectual ones, and they are equally at home with the high born as the lowly. An Aquarian husband of a friend of mine, himself of good English stock, preferred to spend his leisure hours drinking in the company of the criminal element of London's East End than with his own smart Chelsea set. He also frequently referred to my friend somewhat derogatorily as, 'my wife, a refugee from the Royal Enclosure'!

Ask an astrologer for the main characteristics of Aquarius and humanitarianism will be one of the first adjectives on his list. The feeling of brotherhood for his fellow-man is one of the key components of the Aquarian nature. It is the Aquarians of this world who care about the injustices and ills of society and who are vehement opponents of a system whereby the few who hold the financial strings, and therefore all the power, exploit the rest of society. My husband has a strong Uranian theme in his chart and gets most upset when the 'wrong people' win huge amounts of money in lotteries or he reads about the enormous salaries for figureheads of organizations. 'What on earth do they *do* to justify such a salary?' he froths. 'If they have it why don't they do something useful with it!' His one great fantasy is that some day he'll have the money to found an institution where research into alternative technologies can be carried out in conjunction with spiritual and metaphysical studies—a truly Aquarian, or rather Uranian, dream.

In fairness, the Aquarian does tend to practise what he preaches in his daily life by giving his time and money to organizations and individuals he considers worthwhile—unfortunately often in preference to those to whom he has an obligation. This sign cares enormously for the group as a whole, in a rather idealized fashion, rather than the individual himself. This naturally causes some friction in personal relationships as those who have to rely on the Aquarian for financial or moral support are frequently left to fend for themselves while 'their leader' finds the 'Society For Those Financially Ruined By Solicitors' or the local hobo a more worthy cause.

Both male and female Aquarians nurture a strong political or social conscience. It is therefore hardly surprising to find a large number of prominent political leaders and intellectual and philosophical giants (past and present) with strong Aquarian or Uranian themes in their charts: Abraham Lincoln, Adlai Stevenson, Valéry Giscard d'Estaing, Harold Macmillan, and Ronald Reagan, to name but five. Perhaps, more pertinently, Karl Marx was a strongly Uranian individual with Aquarius rising and Uranus on his Midheaven. There could hardly be a more ideal example of pure Aquarian thought than true Marxist philosophy. As far as politically minded women are concerned, the actress Vanessa Redgrave, whose involvement with the Workers Revolutionary Party has split the Actors' Union, Equity, on more than one occasion, comes to mind, and also the late Emma Goldman (Moon in Aquarius), who practised and advocated personal and political freedom and edited a New York magazine called **Mother Earth** that preached and promoted free love.*

Aquarians of both sexes are the proverbial rugged individualists. They detest petty bureaucracy and adapt their own rules for the game as they go along. The one characteristic they share with their following sign, Pisces, is a dislike of boundaries, the difference being that Pisces is motivated by his feelings so that it is the power of his emotions that pushes him to exceed any limits, whereas the Aquarian believes in freedom of expression and abhors any blocks that stand in the way of this ideal—blocks prevent growth and progression. Again this is a paradox, for although most Aquarians preach the

*Ms Goldman also had Cancer rising!

gospel of freedom, only in theory is freedom for everybody; in practice it is usually just for themselves. In much the same way, the Aquarian presents a very open-minded attitude towards world progress and change, but when it comes to himself he is frequently very closed and indeed reluctant to change either his behaviour or his attitudes.

Aquarians dislike being limited by time almost as much as they do by rules and regulations. Rather like the Sagittarian, the Waterbearer prefers to be lead by the moment and fears if he commits himself to an arrangement days or weeks in advance he may have to forgo something better that could present itself in the interim. Even in business the Aquarian is likely to be extremely loose in his plans and his schedule. A friend of mine was once employed by an Aquarian; he took pity on her jobless situation after meeting her at a party and offered her a post as his personal assistant. When she arrived at his office at the appointed time, he was nowhere to be seen and none of the staff had been told to expect her. Somewhat perplexed she returned home to be telephoned by him later that morning. On returning to his office he took her out for a huge lunch then on to the zoo. For the rest of the week she arrived at the office at 9 a.m. and having no instructions to carry out, tidied his office and watered the plants. He would arrive at noon, make a few telephone calls, then take her out to lunch, which usually lasted most of the afternoon. At the end of the week she was duly presented with a large pay packet and feeling somewhat guilty at having done nothing to earn it, my friend asked him to redefine her job situation. 'Well,' he volunteered, 'I'm planning to expand the business abroad soon and I'll need you to carry on while I'm away—just watch what I do and you'll soon pick things up. . . let's play it by ear, eh?'

The same employer was Uranian from head to toe. While retaining a seemingly easy going attitude to his operations and staff alike, every so often he would fly into a fit over some innocuous triviality. Sometimes an employee would be explosively and loudly dismissed, then have to be asked back a few days later when the dust had settled. Despite the bizarre way he ran his business, those who worked for him stuck by him through thick and thin, virtually perjuring themselves for him on occasion. Eccentricity and unpredictability are essential aspects of the Aquarian character.

Which brings me to another point—Aquarius and money. The Saturnine Aquarian can be extremely good with his finances—cautious, thrifty if not down-right mean on occasion; but the Uranian, like the proverbial fool and his money, are soon parted. The Uranian loves to gamble: the element of risk combined with his belief in his expert intuition make him a con man's dream and a gift to the bookie and the roulette table. It is a curious anomaly that a sign synonymous with truth-seeking is surprisingly easy to fool, especially where money is concerned. Aquarians more tuned to Uranus will be the first to jump into a get-rich-quick scheme and the first to respond to a hard luck story. When this type of Aquarian loses his investment he may become temporarily unhinged, but he is usually resourceful in finding a new source of funds or persuading others to await his financial recovery. However, if anyone asks to **borrow** money from the Aquarian and fails to repay the loan, the Waterbearer is outraged: friendship and trust have been betrayed!

Another point worth bearing in mind in regard to the Uranian is that although he upholds truth and honesty, in business especially he is not beyond resorting to a few 'dirty tricks'. Like his Mercurial brother, the Geminian, with his quick far-seeing mind, the Aquarian is eminently capable of out-manoeuvering a competitor or an opponent by sailing criminally close to the wind. After all, if the other person is incapable of spotting a devious move they deserve to be hoodwinked. The Aquarian, you see, is a law unto himself.

Male and female Aquarians prefer to detach themselves from emotionally-charged situations. Logic and rationale to the fore, they will dispassionately walk away from a situation that threatens to overpower them, even if they have generated matters in the first place. In argument or debate they will frequently accuse the other person of over-emotional behaviour and two of their favourite tactics are to refuse to listen to the other argument or turn the whole thing round. If really in danger of losing face and the argument, the Aquarian will leave, usually with the last word trailing off his lips as he walks out the door. The major problem with this loquacious but articulate air sign is that he cannot deal with his emotions—a crucial factor in his topsy-turvy relationships which I shall cover later.

Despite their altruistic bent, Aquarians rarely fight shy of the limelight. Male and female Aquarians are natural performers and able to command the attention of a political rally every bit as well as the Women's Institute. Indeed it is often far easier to lure an Aquarian with the prospect of fame and notoriety than a five-figure salary. One of the most Uranian figures on British television today is Patrick Moore (the amateur astronomer as he is always keen to stress). Although a Pisces, Mr Moore has his Sun in close conjunction to Uranus and his eccentric behaviour on television is entirely characteristic of this planet. Patrick manages to combine his scientific background and love of astronomy with a brilliant sense of performance. His enthusiastic expositions about the cosmos clash dreadfully with his odd-ball persona. While delivering a knowledgeable discourse on Orion or the Pleiades, one is constantly distracted by his expression and an appearance looking to all intents as though he has just lost a battle with a tumble dryer. Although considered a lovable personality by the general public, his opponents and critics—especially all astrologers, whom he denounces—find him prejudiced and dogmatic in the extreme. (In fact, Mr Moore is an ideal example of The Right Man, whom I shall discuss later.)

Aquarians of both sexes tend to veer to extremes. Some are conservative, dependable, and loyal while others are as unpredictable as the British weather—all four seasons in one day. Rather like Scorpio and Aries, Waterbearers are capable of arousing strong feelings in others; some like them enormously while others find them deeply disturbing. Certainly it is a sign that makes its presence felt wherever it may be; indeed, without the Aquarians of this world there would be fewer incandescent storms and magical rainbows to liven things up.

RELATIONSHIPS

Of all the signs of the zodiac Aquarius seems to have the most difficulty is establishing harmonious, long-term relationships. The Aquarian is first and foremost a friend and second a lover and a spouse. This does not mean, however, that strongly Aquarian individuals cannot experience happiness and durability in one-to-one relationships, but because, in the main, they find it extremely difficult to adapt to traditional roles and expectations in marriage, they frequently encounter problems with partners who don't! Obviously this tendency is much more marked with the Uranian type of Aquarian than those who are tuned to Saturn's more conventional code, but by and large the Waterbearer gets dreadfully cold feet when it comes to giving himself up to the rigours and demands of an emotional relationship.

Friendship is practically a pilgrimage for Aquarians of both sexes yet although they find it easy to make chums and acquaintances (often in all four corners of the globe), establishing a relationship of the intimate and emotional kind with any one of them can be a superhuman feat. As I mentioned briefly in the previous section, Aquarius is a sign that is happiest in the realm of ideas, where reason and logic can be relied upon to reign supreme; it is in the foggy world of emotions that this sign seems lost and apprehensive. Although the Saturnine Aquarian can deal successfully with the more 'material' dimensions of relationships—mortgages, bills, housekeeping, and the in-laws—he nevertheless finds it difficult to give himself totally to another person; to share his fears, his desires and his needs, or, indeed, to involve himself in those of his partner. The Uranian, on the other hand, finds the mundane financial and legal aspects of marriage impinge on his almost pathological need for freedom. Combined with his awkward emotional constitution he makes an extremely rebellious inmate of the marriage institution.

THE FEMALE AQUARIUS

Before I go any further, a sharp distinction must be made between the male and female Aquarian. In my experience, out of the twelve signs of the zodiac, the Aquarian female and the Capricorn woman bear the least resemblance to their male counterparts. Although they undoubtedly share the same freedom of spirit and independence of thought as the male Waterbearer, female Aquarians' emotional response and behaviour in relationships are entirely different. The obvious conclusion to draw here is that—as some astrologers, including myself, have observed—women are more naturally tuned to their Moon and Venus signs. Thus the characteristics of their Sun sign tend to be considerably underplayed, although by no means obliterated. Why this should be so strong with Aquarius and Capricorn is probably because of the close association of both signs with Saturn, a planet whose qualities are more naturally attuned to the male psyche. Women with their Moon, Venus or Ascendant in Aquarius (or strong Uranus and Saturn contacts to these planets) will tend to display more overt Aquarian characteristics than those with just their Sun in this sign.

In order to appreciate the Aquarian woman and begin to understand her approach to relationships perhaps we should start with an ideal example—Germaine Greer. Ms Greer has both her Ascendant and Sun in Aquarius and her Moon conjunct the planet Uranus, so her chart exudes a strong Aquarian/Uranian theme. Ms Greer is perhaps best known for her book **The Female Eunuch,** which created a sensation in the early 1970s; through its publication she effectively became one of the midwives to a new birth of feminism. In keeping with her strong Uranian influence, Germaine is primarily an intellectually motivated sort of woman—a quality she combines with a persuasive, articulate persona. Like many Aquarian women, she has no airs and graces: she says what she thinks and expects people to take her as they find her.

Germaine was born and brought up in Australia—a cultural and intellectual wilderness in her eyes—and she found a retreat away from her conservative and repressive background in the world of books. In keeping with the Aquarian woman's fear of stagnation and intellectual atrophy, she felt 'the grey beast of boredom lurked around every corner'. So she determind to dig a tunnel out of Australia with the aid of her intellect, devouring everything she could in the way of learning.

Women's role in society is the perfect bandwagon for the Aquarian woman and such strong opinions as 'society symbolically castrated women by foisting on them a passive, insipid role they must renounce to regain their sexuality and natural energies' is an articulate though rather extreme way of putting across the frustration many Aquarian women feel about their lot.

Marriage is clearly not one of Ms Greer's strongest suits. She said of her one marriage. 'I discovered I was in the biggest mess of my life. . . my husband was so much in love with me, he despised me. . . I wrote *The Female Eunuch* when going through the purdah of marriage.'*

Despite these rather jaundiced comments, Ms Greer seems to have mellowed along with her attitudes over the past fifteen years, and recently, with the publication of **Sex and Destiny**, appears not only to have abandonded her strident, overtly feminist stance but to have done a philosophical U-turn. While she could hardly be seen as the 'thinking man's crumpet' she has a feline attractiveness and ease of manner that is entirely sexy and 'feminine' without being in any way contrived. Like many Aquarian females she is more truly a woman than the painted beauty queen. Asked by fellow Australian Clive James on British television if she thought she would ever find Mr Right she quipped. 'Why should I want to. . . Mr Wrong is much more fun!'

The Aquarian woman is rarely a little decorative plaything: even those who are not academically gifted have minds of their own and tend to use them. They are easily bored and like to feel their lives, and indeed their relationships, are of the growing kind and contain plenty of scope and novelty. While the Aries woman will stand up and fight for what she wants, Ms Aquarius will stand up and argue. Even the gentle and feminine Princess of Wales† has been known to voice her opinions strongly on occasion, and no royal lady has made such an impact on royalty and implemented so many changes in her short 'reign'.

The Saturnine Aquarian female is a more conventional sort. Although she still has a mind of her own and a will to go with it, she accepts duty and responsibility as a necessary part of life and makes a thoroughly good job of wife and motherhood (at least on the surface). That she also makes a

---

*Astrologers may like to note Ms Greer married on her Saturn return and began to write **The Female Eunuch** during the same year.

†Moon in Aquarius opposing Uranus.

thoroughly good job of a career goes without saying, but many Aquarian women of this variety make a conscious decision to invest energies that might otherwise have been channelled into a career into husband and family—and without any feeling of sacrifice and martyrdom. If these kind of Aquarian women have plenty of water in their charts they manage to combine their homely career with a good degree of warmth, affection, and emotional satisfaction, although this may not be displayed overtly to the rest of the world. But if there is little water in the charts the cool, controlled, and capable exterior masks an emotional volcano. This type of Aquarian is prone to powerful emotional outbursts that she rarely understands yet finds completely overwhelming. It is as though the emotions have not developed as easily and well as the rest of her being (a factor often present in the charts of women who have the Moon in difficult aspect to Saturn or Uranus). In effect the emotions are in a childlike state and erupt with all the force of the infant's uncontrolled frustration and desperation. This kind of Aquarian woman, like some Capricorns, can put up with emotionally vapid relationships, in which emotional rapport is jettisoned for material comfort and security. Perhaps because this type of Aquarian woman frequently attracts a watery partner, if he has an affair, or walks out of the relationship, she is utterly perplexed; after all she has run his life with conveyor-belt efficiency. In failing to acknowledge the importance of emotional closeness, usually through fear of rejection, her attempt to remain emotionally invulnerable backfires when the partner realizes he needs a warm, emotional interchange every bit as much as an expert housewife and manager.

Some of my clients married to, or involved with, Aquarian women often describe them as cold or unfeeling. Nine times out of ten, however when checking the women's charts in question, not only do I find the Sun, Ascendant, Moon, or Venus in Aquarius, but difficult, stressful contacts to these points (particularly the Moon or Venus) from Saturn, Uranus, or Pluto. In other words, the Aquarian tendency to control the emotions, and therefore appear cold, is compounded by these aspects rather than being the sole cause.

The more typical Aquarian female is the Uranian. She is the truly bohemian and unconventional wife and mother. As a child she was unlikely to have been as involved in playing 'house' or with dolls as other little girls; she may well have felt 'different' from other children—even apart—and as she matures her life becomes full of originality and experimentation. The Uranian woman is elusive, yet loyal, romantic but never sentimental; above all she needs freedom and tends to hold others in a loose emotional grasp. A female with her Sun and Moon in Aquarius responded to my questionnaire in this way: 'One of my chief problems is my friendliness, which is far too welcoming and encouraging. People cling to me or trap me with arrangements or limitations to my need for movement and space.' She went on to articulate another typically Aquarian characteristic: 'I am totally spontaneous and like to do things only when I feel like it!'

One lovely lady I know with a strong Uranian element in her chart, although an heiress, spent several months of her life living in a Rolls Royce. While never actively drawing attention to herself, her striking looks and extraordinary clothes guarantee an audience wherever she goes. Whenever we meet our conversation revolves around concepts and ideas, never personal issues, thus I know little about her private life. Fascinating and friendly, but aloof and essentially private.

People often assume the Aquarian female is a 'woman of the world'; however, her cool exterior frequently conceals an individual who is unsure of herself and exceedingly emotionally vulnerable. 'I often feel very unsure of myself when I'm falling for somebody; the usual sophistication covers up, but underneath I feel like a little girl', wrote one female with her Sun and Venus in Aquarius. She continued 'I find it difficult to talk about my feelings and tend to put on a good face, although I'm trying to change that now. In some ways I would rather be "just good friends", and have quite a few men who take me for lunch—we have a friendship. I feel OK with them because we aren't lovers. . . I really don't have any confidence in my ability to keep a man's affections—I just can't handle it.'

The Aquarian woman is a strange mixture of airy capriciousness and earthy practicality. She is both an idealist and a realist. She is pulled one way by sudden romantic impulses then the other by reason and common sense. For Ms Aquarius, falling in love happens quickly. The attraction for the new and the unknown, with its aura of excitement and danger, is irresistible. Yet before she has begun to enjoy the experience she is invariably fuelled with doubts and insecurities. The Aquarian woman tends to be attracted to men who are different in some way, maybe because they are much older or younger than herself, perhaps because they belong to another culture. They might even be married to someone else! Even if Ms Aquarius presents a conventional, Saturnine front, or even if her security system has urged her to marry Mr Safe-and-Secure, she is nonetheless likely to be drawn to unusual men. Whether or not she follows her romantic instincts very much depends on the rest of her chart.

Since the Aquarian woman is overtly or covertly different, she holds a fascination for many men; she can be as mysteriously alluring as the Scorpio femme fatale and as enigmatic as the Virgoan Siren. She can also use her men just as well as these two females. Like all the air sign women she manages to be both welcoming and detached at the same time, which gives her a head start when it comes to playing emotional games. The Aquarian woman understands men very well; and she often has a greater liking for and empathy with the male sex than her own. Sometimes, but not always, this is because she fears—or at least does not understand—her own femininity. Of course, this has little to do with the way she dresses or how she behaves, but with the deeper layers of femininity—feeling, nurture and responsiveness. Thus her feminine power becomes an unconsciously destructive force. In order not to become emotionally dependent on a man, she must render him weaker than her, and her most effective method is subtly to emasculate him. I must stress, however, that this is an Aquarian theme; not every Sun Aquarian woman is a 'man-eater'!

Aquarius, like Capricorn, has much to do with 'father'. While the relationship between all women and their father or father figure has important repercussions in their later choice of a partner and their interaction with him, for the woman with a strong Aquarian theme in her chart it is crucial. The Aquarian woman often has some difficulty in marrying up her inner image of 'father' with the real individual, and by the time she has reached early womanhood she may still not have succeeded. Thus she has some unfinished business with him. But because of the sexual barriers that now exist between them she must take her unresolved conflict into her relationships. The battle between Cronos (the son) and Ouranus (the father) is just as much an issue for the Aquarian woman as it is for the man. While the Aquarian man has to 'do battle' with his father to find his own sense of manhood, the Aquarian woman has to free herself from her father image.

Aquarian Lucy Irvine, in her book **Runaway** makes many powerful references to her father, Richard. He emerges as a strong, dashing and ruthless figure, whom she clearly adores. She describes one lover as 'a Richard with whom I could make love'. In a **Sunday Times** article, Lucy admitted that she had 'embraced [her] father's code of behaviour . . . I've found it necessary to be ruthless. I've such a fear of weakness, I really have.' Ms Irvine's life has the Aquarian stamp on it throughout. She spent several months on a desert island with Gerald Kingsland after responding to his advertisement in a newspaper. The purpose of the exercise was to see just how and if two people could survive in the 'wild' with nothing but the raw materials of nature and each other. It proved a gruelling test of endurance on all fronts. In Lucy's 'search for identity', she has taken jobs as varied as a life-model, a nurse for the disabled and a stonemason; she has slept out in the Sinai desert and experimented with prostitution. Presently, she lives alone with her young son—she refuses to name the father—in a sparsely furnished cottage amidst a Scottish forest. Aside from her son, writing provides the structure and control in her life: '. . . every time I've got emotionally involved with anybody I've felt the loss of self-control, and it hasn't worked, has it?'

Many astrologers consider the Aquarian woman to be above jealousy and possessiveness in relationships. While some Aquarian women remain true to this ideal, in my experience a great many more are capable of as much jealousy and possessiveness as the next Scorpio! It must be remembered that Aquarius is a fixed sign and therefore finds emotional change extremely threatening. This, combined with their emotional vulnerability, frequently gives rise to deeply possessive feelings about a partner. The Aquarian female presents a paradox here, as she does in other areas of her life; while she may **theoretically** support freedom and independence in a partnership, inwardly she is deeply possessive and highly insecure.

Perhaps because this sign is synonymous with truth-seeking, while the female Waterbearer respects her partner's need for privacy and rarely keeps him on a tight rein of domestic deadlines, if she finds him out in a lie or discovers he has betrayed her, she will never trust him again. Although the Aquarian woman continues to remain friends with her lovers once the relationship is over, if she has been deeply committed yet ultimately betrayed or rejected, the separation is irrevocable: a seal descends on the contact like a slab of granite across a tomb.

The Aquarian woman is a fascinating combination of indomitable strength and featherlight inconsistency; she is impossible to place in a neat psychological box. Just when you think you know her, she will display a hitherto unseen characteristic. In some areas and on some occasions she can be judgemental and moralistic in the extreme, then again she can behave with the innocent lawlessness of a child. She can be articulate, witty, stylish sociable but there is always a certain distance about her. In some ways she is rather like Lewis Carroll's Cheshire cat, a smiling enigma that appears unpredictably and never reveals the whole of herself but fascinates and mesmerizes you.

THE MALE AQUARIUS

Sophisticated and articulate he may be among friends, colleagues, and the 'world and his wife', but the Aquarian male becomes desperately naïve and emotionally tongue-tied with someone to whom he is attracted. Both the Saturnine Aquarian and the Uranian frequently display a resolute indifference to affection: some even profess 'falling in love' to be an overblown psychological disturbance! Yet a pressure coooker of feelings and strong emotions lurks under their detached and rational exteriors.

Aquarian men need love and affection like all human beings: their problem lies in the clash between their theories and ideals of what relationships **should** be and the actual experience of intimate partnerships in the raw. The Aquarian man simply cannot understand why the women in his life become 'all emotional' and refuse to discuss things rationally. Worse, when he tells them to calm down and control themselves he is dismayed to find they become even more irate. He just has to leave them to get over it! By and large the Aquarian is terrified of emotional scenes: he likes to have control of his life, and the moment his own feelings threaten to invade his organized view of things he really cannot cope. In many ways he perpetuates his own Aquarian myth of detachment by appearing unaffected by others while his own emotional volcano rumbles and roars within.

The Saturnine Aquarian is slightly better at formal courtship than his Uranian brother, whose relationships proceed in fits and starts: yet both have great difficulty in demonstrating their feelings and playing love's romantic dream. Both nurture a natural distaste for overt displays of emotion in public. To my amazement I found my eldest son, who has Aquarius rising and his Moon conjunct Uranus, showing this aversion at the tender age of six when he was aghast to see tears cascading down his mother's face at the end of the film **E.T.** He abandonded me immediately and the expression written all over his face read, 'Pull yourself together woman!'

The Aquarian's dislike of open displays of affection leads him to behave in an extremely off-hand manner with his partner while privately regarding her as irreplaceable and very special. Indeed, some Aquarian men seem to go out of their way to treat the object of their affections in such a casual fashion and with such indifference that the partner almost needs psychic abilities to sense that he truly cares. In some cases it is a major indication that an Aquarian feels deeply about someone when he appears difficult and rude or goes out of his way to ignore the person concerned. Besides the fear and difficulty the Aquarian encounters when confronted by his feelings, he hates to lose face or be laughed at by others.

Some Aquarians, of course, are better than others at demonstrating affection—usually those who have personal planets in water (or fire) signs. Ronald Reagan,* despite being a Sun Aquarian, seems to go out of his way to

*Venus in Pisces

show the depth of feeling and regard he has for his wife, Nancy; he even created a major gaffe by publicly embracing the British Prime Minister, Margaret Thatcher—not at all the thing to do in Britain! Had he not been trained as an actor, however, I suspect Mr Reagan would have found it extremely difficult to behave in such a cavalier and affectionate fashion in public.

The Aquarian tends to be something of an extremist; he shares an all-or-nothing quality about his behaviour with the other fixed signs Scorpio, Taurus, and Leo. Thus when smitten by someone, he frequently goes well and truly overboard—the experience literally overwhelms him. Indeed, I have known some Aquarian men make absolute fools of themselves when in love. My first husband amazed his friends when, after years of night-clubbing and revelling in the bachelor life, he was seen almost overnight gazing misty-eyed at churches and spending his free time choosing china and bed linen and discussing the merits of owning your own home. Of course, like many Uranians, the thunder-flash of 'in-loveness' was indeed just that and unfortunately by the time mortgages, the in-laws, and parenthood had set in the marital bonds became extremely strained and eventually snapped.

The Uranian Aquarian needs freedom with a capital F. While part of him enjoys company and needs some kind of emotional security, like the Sagittarian he cannot bear to feel fenced in. A close friend of mine, although a Sun Cancer, has his Mars conjunct Uranus. While basically a soft-centred and caring sort, he displays an almost phobic dislike for the confines and formalized structure of marriage. He tends to see friends who have succumbed to the institution as not only settling down and out but embarked on the road to social fossilization! Each bastion of his bachelor existence has had to be painfully wrenched from him and although now living in apparent domestic bliss with his wonderfully tolerant girlfriend, the final walk to the altar seems as far away as the planet Uranus itself.

Several years ago I came across a section in a book by Colin Wilson that discussed a psychological type called 'the Right Man'.* What so impressed me were that the qualities allotted to the Right Man had a distinctly Aquarian ring to them. As the name implies, the Right Man needs to be right all the time, and in many ways he is the archetypal male chauvinist pig. He is frequently bad tempered, occasionally brutal and completely oblivious to anyone's feelings but his own. Although he seems thoroughly rational to the outer world he behaves like a martinet in the home and sometimes at the office. Of course, this kind of behaviour could be found in any individual regardless of his astrological typing. But, more specifically, the Right Man is usually prone to ruthless attempts to force other people to adopt his own mental modes—a typically Aquarian proclivity. As I cannot improve on Colin Wilson, the following description from **Mysteries** is worth quoting in full:

'He has a strong desire for truth, but the story of his life is an unconsciously distorted version, which shows him to have been a hundred per cent right and everyone else to

---

*In his book **Mysteries** Colin Wilson refers to Van Voigt, a science fiction writer, who discovered an aspect of human nature previously overlooked by orthodox psychology—a type he named the Right Man.

have been wrong.' And, paradoxically enough, this 'strong desire for truth' may make the Right Man a good scientist or philosopher. It is only where he is concerned that his perception of truth is distorted; besides which, the pursuit of abstract knowledge provides a welcome relief from his obsession with himself.

In many ways the brilliant American tennis star, John McEnroe—a Sun Aquarian—displays overtly Right Man behaviour on the court. He disputes the linesmen's calls and the umpires' verdicts time and time again, and his ridiculous temper tantrums, histrionics, and abusive language exasperate and embarrass his opponents as well as the spectators. And where his private life is concerned, his volatile relationship with actress Tatum O'Neal has provided journalists with plenty of juicy copy!

In his relationships the Right Man can be exceedingly jealous while often a philanderer himself; he may have a puritanical streak yet sexual conquest is extremely important to him. It is also essential for the Right Man to gain total submission from his partner. At home he acts like the school bully, and while he insists on freedom for himself, his wife must display a slave-like devotion to him.

Newspapers frequently carry stories that depict Right Man behaviour involving all types of individuals from politicians, footballers to the man-in-the-street. The following extract from the **Daily Mail** (27 July 1984) is a typical example:

'He was selfish as far as money was concerned' said the Judge. 'His wife did not have any to spend on herself; but he did not go short. When Mr B. wanted a video recorder from their joint account he stood over his wife and threatened her until she signed the cheque. He on the other hand would not even let her buy her own underwear! Mrs B. claimed that she had been treated like a slave. . . **Mr B. always thought he was right.** He would shout and swear if anyone disagreed with him and would not allow his wife her own opinions on how the house should be decorated.'

We are not told if Mr B. was a strongly Aquarian individual but he was certainly a Right Man. Thankfully Mrs B. was granted a divorce on the grounds of his unreasonable behaviour! All too often in a marriage, the Right Man's wife bends over backwards to accommodate him, sometimes through loyalty and love, but often through fear, which in effect makes matters worse. The Right Man, unlike others, actually acts out his self-indulgent fantasies and because they form the foundations of his self-image, he must force others continually to bolster the charade. Thus the wife unwittingly becomes a kind of accomplice. Confrontation is the best way to handle the Right Man; rather than give in to his demands and submit to his tyranny, his wife should stand up for herself, and if matters become intolerable, leave. When, and if, this happens, the Right Man usually collapses like a pack of cards.

Obviously not all Aquarian men are also Right Men; I am merely suggesting that when this type of behaviour occurs one can often find an accompanying Aquarian theme in a chart. I have heard similar stories from several of my clients about their Aquarian partners and indeed I experienced these extraordinary paradoxes for myself first hand. Both the Saturnine Aquarian and the Uranian are capable of the Right Man syndrome as are the other fixed signs Taurus, Scorpio, and Leo; but Aquarius is the most typical.

Clearly there are many thoroughly agreeable Aquarians who handle people with a great degree of fairness and treat their partners with tremendous consideration. It may be that the Aquarian who falls into the Right Man category is one whose extreme behaviour is protecting an excessive emotional vulnerability and in the process his sense of identity becomes distorted. Thus a vicious circle is created, for in order to preserve his self-esteem, he has to resort to more and more overt displays of tyranny.

Tyranny, or rather the tyrannical father, is a theme encountered in the Aquarius–Capricorn myth of Ouranus and Cronos. Like the Capricorn man, the Aquarian male has to 'wrestle' with father to become his own man. The Aquarian's father need not be a tyrant in the literal sense at all—the implication here is that the Aquarian male often feels himself to be very different from his father yet he experiences some difficulty in establishing his independence. Sometimes the Aquarian man has an underlying feeling that he is too much under the control and influence of his father; he is torn between respect for him and the paternal role and the need to rebel against his father's example. Even if the Aquarian man has a wonderful father, there is still a fundamental urge for him to break away from his conditioning.

Edward VIII had the Sun in Cancer and Aquarius rising. He also had an elevated Uranus in square to the Ascendant. Thus potentially he had both a mother problem and a father problem! Edward was in fact, terrified of his father. King George V had deliberately tried to generate respect in his sons, thus there was great distance and much hostility between him and Edward. Edward was, of course, entirely different from his father. While George was a rigid, self-disciplined, deeply conservative man—utterly committed to preserving the status quo—Edward was a free spirit and felt all too keenly the restrictions imposed upon him as an individual by his Royal position in general and his father in particular.

While Edward was enormously popular as the Prince of Wales, there was much public criticism over his unorthodox choice of female companions—he liked older and invariably married women—and his preference for social duties rather than his royal ones. That he abdicated the throne of England to marry a twice-divorced American could be seen as the ultimate Aquarian-Uranian gesture! In renouncing the throne, Edward appeared to have placed personal happiness above Saturnian duty—an act that many considered selfish and irresponsible in the extreme. Some sources suggest that Edward never wanted to be king and that his love for Wallis Simpson was an unconscious 'escape hatch'; others maintain that he firmly believed he could have both, and that when he abdicated he expected to return to England and assume suitable royal duties. But the Saturnian monarchy never truly forgave their Uranian son, and he was ignominiously left to enjoy his exile and his freedom with the woman he loved.

At the time of the abdication crisis, it was feared in some quarters that Edward's actions might have damaged the monarchy irrevocably. While he did not consciously seek to destabilize the throne, one might speculate as an astrologer that in his efforts to break away from the rigid encrusted aura of his father and the monarchy and to bring in his more informal, highly individualistic style, despite a struggle, he was defeated.

In keeping with his individualistic stance in most areas of his life, the

Aquarian man likes a woman who is a little different from the rest. Like the Aries male he likes a spark in his relationships. He admires a partner who can stand up to him, argue well, and with whom he can attain a good intellectual rapport. He also has a great appetite for forbidden fruit! The Waterbearer is often attracted to partners of different nationalities, background, religions, or ages, and sometimes to those who 'belong' to someone else. While he is unlikely actively to pursue a married woman, her unavailability often has him distractedly mooning around and writing poetry deep into the night. Love affairs in the mind, over the telephone, or on paper carry a certain piquancy for the Aquarian.

An Aquarian friend of mine has solved the problem of his insatiable appetite for brief and exciting romantic encounters by living with a woman fifteen years older than himself who treats his behaviour as that of a rather naughty child. They have one of the few successful open 'marriages' I have come across—even if it is a rather one-sided affair. There is no doubt about his love for her, nor any question that he might ever leave her; but this arrangement is the only way he can tolerate a long-term union. Rather selfish perhaps; but then the Aquarian man sometimes is.

My advice to any woman hoping to 'land' an Aquarian is to play it cool. An Aquarian hates to be deluged with emotion and the more unobtainable and disinterested a woman behaves the more his interest is aroused. Also, despite his free and easy attitude, Mr Aquarius can become terribly jealous. He is, of course, unlikely to say anything about the way he feels, but the writing is on the wall when he becomes very angry about nothing in particular and extremely peevish.

The Waterbearer is always full of surprises. If he usually treats you like a distant aunt in public and suffers from birthday and anniversary amnesia, be prepared, because one night he's likely to come bursting in with a bunch of red roses, take you out for a sumptuous meal and shower you with devoted and tactile attention. On the other hand, if he has always praised your **rognons flambés,** don't be aghast when he pushes them away one night and announces he's decided to become a vegetarian. Even the more predictable Saturnine Aquarian has a way of turning your world upside down when you are least prepared. Anticipate the unexpected, provide him with a good argument and never question his actions. The Waterbearer has a unique moral code, which can make marriage to him a little uncertain and precarious at times. Despite his detached manner, however, he is not without feelings; but frequently they are so deep they are practically out of reach.

SUMMARY

Aquarians of both sexes find long-term relationships like marriage a weighty matter. Saturnine Aquarians fulfil their duties and obligations to the letter, but often with a feeling that 'something is missing'. The Uranians on the other hand jump in and out of relationships like pogo-sticks, regarding the obligations as millstones to their freedom and independence. Obviously the key to the success of their intimate one-to-one relationships depends on whether their partners are equally emotionally undemanding or if they themselves are more in touch and at ease with their emotions. Perhaps, most importantly, Aquarians like to feel their partners are their best friends and provided that the spirit of camaraderie is shared by both, marriage need neither be a millstone nor a necessary obligation, but a constantly expanding panorama.

AQUARIUS PARTNERSHIPS

Intimate one-to-one relationships are never easy for Aquarians, which is why they are more suited to airy or fiery partners. Yet these Uranian individuals are not immune to the attract-repel mechanism operating between them and their antipathies in the earth and water signs.

Aries

Aquarius/**Aries** combinations have a warmth and electric excitement about them. Both love novelty and argument and find plenty of stimulation in each other's company. Occasionally this partnership has to watch the finances as both hate to feel limited in any way! One of the great pluses with these two is their sense of fun and love of the ridiculous; and in times of crisis, one of them at least can always see the funny side. Boredom rarely sullies the relationship, though they can tire of each other sexually rather soon.

Taurus

Aquarius and **Taurus** are not the easiest of partnerships to deal with, yet they attract each other like magnets. Taurus, another 'fixed' sign, is terribly stubborn and becomes even more intractable faced with Aquarius' penchant for argument. There is often strong sexual attraction between these two yet their differing temperaments can give rise to ambivalent feelings towards each other. Both really and truly dislike change, but Aquarius refuses to admit this and tends to feel Taurus is always holding him back. Taurus, on the other hand, considers Aquarius to be all talk and no action! Given much time, effort and good will, this can become an enormously rewarding partnership, for Taurus provides the stability, security, and patience Aquarius needs, while Aquarius provides much experimentation, intellectual stimulation and fun for Taurus.

Gemini

Aquarius finds **Gemini** an enormously mentally stimulating partner; both revere logic and tend not to become weighed down by petty domestic grievances. Occasionally the Waterbearer considers the Geminian a little too insubstantial and unchallenging for his probing mentality but this is usually counter-balanced by the freedom and independence he feels in a relationship with him. The emotional and sexual side of this relationship veers to extremes: there is either a surfeit of both or a relative shortfall!

Cancer

Cancer and Aquarius rarely understand each other: Cancer is moody and inconsistent, and powerfully motivated by his feelings which he tries to keep safely hidden behind a tough exterior. Aquarius is inconsistent in his own way and fails to recognize when he has deeply hurt or offended Cancer. Strangely enough, Cancer seems to be the best sign to put Aquarius in touch with his feelings, perhaps because Cancer is a wonderful emotional receiver and transmitter. While intitially the Waterbearer may try to analyse the Crab's curious ups and downs, and urges him to articulate his grievances, unless the Cancerian makes an equal effort to be forthcoming the relationship will suffer—especially on the sexual front. Unbridgeable distances can arise quickly with this couple.

Leo

Leo and Aquarius are opposite signs and both 'fixed', thus major emotional and psychological blocks occur periodically between them. Leo is a strongly egotistical sign and hates the way Aquarius tends to override his authority. The Waterbearer on the other hand frequently finds the Lion bossy and all too ready to turn a small misdemeanor into a major drama. Both signs, of course, see much of themselves mirrored in each other but with love and patience such a combination can bring both to greater self-awareness, which in turn provides richness and depth in their relationship.

Virgo

Aquarius and **Virgo** are both mentally oriented signs so there is plenty of common ground here. Aquarius admires Virgo's sense of order and precision but wishes Virgo wouldn't fuss so much and try to organize him all the time. Virgo considers Aquarius to be a bit of an extremist and wishes the Waterbearer would do as he says and keep to a timetable of any sort. These two signs can encounter sexual difficulties with each other but are unlikely to admit it or to seek help.

Libra

Aquarius and **Libra** make the best of the air combinations; Libra is fair-minded and gives plenty of concessions to Aquarius' paradoxical and unpredictable behaviour. In return Aquarius admires Libra's balanced temperament and feels understood but never smothered by him. A rich and varied social and/or cultural life is essential for this couple; and while they may lack the passion and angst of some of the other combinations, they have companionship and mutual appreciation. After an exciting sexual start, the physical relationship between these two can become rather thin. Shared Moon signs or energizing Venus and Mars inter-aspects mitigate this tendency.

Scorpio

Of all the water signs, **Scorpio** presents the most tantalizing and irresistible partner for Aquarius. As in the case of Taurus, Aquarians are magnetically attracted to Scorpio, and if any sign is capable of arousing passion in Aquarius it is this Pluto-ruled sign. Both Aquarius and Scorpio are exceedingly powerful and tend to bring out extremes in each other—for good or bad! Both are also capable of displaying emotional detachment and burying their feelings, the difference being that with Scorpio the feelings are never truly buried so he manipulates and plays emotional games with Aquarius. There are some Aquarius/Scorpio couples that develop the most splendid relationships, probably because there are many more harmonious links between their charts; for although this combination may have its initial fascination, ultimately it can be mutually very destructive.

Sagittarius

Aquarius and **Sagittarius** partnerships can work very well. This is usually a get-up-and-go combination as these two love travel, both physically and mentally. Great friendship invariably exists between Aquarius/Sagittarius partners and both see freedom and independence as an essential part of their relationship. Occasionally, unconscious power struggles undermine these relationships but both individuals are very good at ignoring threatening issues. The Waterbearer and the Archer are often highly sexually attuned to each other although for some reason they tend to encounter huge peaks and troughs in their physical relationships.

Capricorn

Aquarius and **Capricorn** is the easiest air-earth combination, perhaps because both share some Saturnine traits. Both signs are extremely determined, but as neither lets their feelings obliterate reason, agreement can usually be reached. In some ways this can be a rather cool partnership, which may mean that both feel somewhat lonely at times and that the other is remote and unreachable. However, neither are likely to show the world their difficulties, and to others they seem a solid and unbreakable couple.

Aquarius

Aquarius/**Aquarius** combinations present both good and bad qualities. Rather like Leo/Aquarius combinations, two Aquarians together continually reflect each other—emotional warts and all! There is a tendency for one partner to take the more freedom-orientated stance while the other becomes more rigid and resentful of his liberation. Friendship is enormously important for two Aquarians and, given they can sort out their emotional and sexual needs, the partnership can be strong and binding. This is very much an all or nothing combination.

Pisces

Aquarius usually finds **Pisces** the easiest water-sign to handle, perhaps because Pisces is Everyman and tries to accommodate all and sundry. Also, because Pisces follows Aquarius in the zodiac, both partners may have personal planets in the other's Sun sign. Aquarius often behaves in a very protective way towards Pisces, and because Pisces is such a mystifying, ever-changing sign, Aquarius finds him compelling and fascinating. However, Aquarius may be extremely hurt when he returns home one day to find Pisces has disappeared! These two are often strongly sexually attracted to each other; if they have problems with their physical relationship, emotional miscommunications are usually the cause.

SEXUALITY

The sexual arena is where the individual is usually at his most vulnerable: not only is he frequently bare of clothes but his deepest psychological areas are also exposed. In many ways sex opens a Pandora's Box of emotional and psychological Furies for everybody, but perhaps more particularly for the emotionally complex individual, like Aquarius. As I discussed earlier in the chapter, Aquarians find difficulty in dealing with their feelings, and sometimes this spins off into their sexual lives.

To Aquarius, not all emotional relationships need to be sexual, nor do sexual relationships necessarily involve the emotions. Many Aquarians of both sexes are eminently capable of entering into a relationship based purely on sex without any emotional content whatsoever. Also, despite Aquarius' reputation for being the least sexually oriented sign in the zodiac, his list of erotic techniques and variety of sexual partners can read like a telephone directory.

From my questionnaire it was interesting to find that, out of all the signs of the zodiac, those individuals with the Sun, Moon, Venus, or Mars in Aquarius were the most experimental and held the most unorthodox attitudes about sex. The ability to experience sex without any emotional involvement was also mentioned far more frequently by those with planets in Aquarius than in any other sign. One male with his Moon and Venus in Aquarius wrote, 'I have no emotional needs and have done without them in regard to sex for most of my life...' And another male with his Moon in Aquarius volunteered, 'I am emotionally somewhat cold so that "love" in the romantic sense seems almost non-existent...' Aquarian women also expressed similar attitudes: in the words of one female with her Sun and Venus in Aquarius, 'I really can enjoy sex for sex's sake and don't necessarily need to be in love, but I must be attracted to the man: then sex can be a good physical release—almost a sport—enjoyable and good fun.'

While there may be nothing wrong with sex for sex's sake, nor in preferring to avoid emotional entanglements, the Aquarian often finds his sexual relationships cause him problems because his partners cannot so easily divorce the two! Also, the Aquarian can encounter problems with sex if he senses (or is told) that he ought to be feeling something he's not: his concern can interfere with his sexual functioning, causing him periodic bouts in impotence, or in the female's case, frigidity.

Another core issue that surrounds sex for Aquarius is that of intimacy. To most people the sexual act is the greatest intimacy one can experience and share with another, and, of course, it is with this sort of close contact that the Aquarian is most uncomfortable. Because sexual exchange frequently involves exposure of the individual's most tender and private emotional and psychological parts, the Aquarian either has to allow his feelings to show, and therefore risk being made vulnerable by them, or has to develop a technique to seal them off. Of course, this is usually an entirely unconscious dilemma. While the Aquarian can thoroughly enjoy sexual stimulation and release, what he will try to avoid at all costs is a post-coital exchange of aural sweet-nothings.

Aquarians are far less at ease with their bodies and their physical senses than their minds. Thus, in keeping with the idea that the 'mind is the most potent sexual organ in the body', Aquarians of both sexes tend to find erotic imagery, fantasy, and pornography essential accompaniments to their arousal and enjoyment of sex. Again in my questionnaire, far more Aquarian men and women mentioned a liking for pornography than any other sign.

A further by-product of this Aquarian tendency (both male and female) to be more oriented towards the mind than the body, is that if in childhood there was little closeness or demonstrable affection between themselves and their parents and siblings, they will in adult life continue to be undemonstrative and to keep their emotions in check. In a group session some years ago, the issue of physical and emotional closeness was raised. One female with her Moon in Aquarius was puzzled to find that so many of the group seemed to set so much store by this. She considered she had had an ideally happy family life, yet she could never remember being cuddled or even wanting to be cuddled as a child; indeed none of the family ever openly demonstrated affection towards one another. To her this was completely normal and caused her no emotional angst. However she did appear somewhat concerned that at twenty-nine she was still single.

The Aquarian woman, like her male counterpart, tends to run to extremes in the sexual area. Some have a very weak sex drive and can 'take it or leave it', while others consider the whole thing a sort of duty and lie back and think of tomorrow's lunch.

Yet there are plenty of strongly Aquarian females who are highly-sexed and need more than one partner to stimulate and satisfy them. One mature female with her Mars in Aquarius wrote, 'I can't say my physical needs have ever been met by my husband. . . during the years when I needed physical gratification I attracted men who gave me this, and now the comfortable relationship with my husband suits us both to some degree.'

Two factors regarding sex that seem to surface more frequently with Aquarian women than any other sign are first, their open attitudes to sexual experimentation, and second, the ability to do without sex at all! One female with the Sun and Venus in Aquarius encapsulates more than one Aquarian quality with this statement: 'If a man doesn't consider me and my sexual needs then I wouldn't bother to see him again. Also, I have been involved in a threesome on a few occasions and it feels quite natural for me to make love with another woman. However, I would only have a threesome with good friends'! Feelings here form no part of the dialogue. A friend of mine who has her Venus in Aquarius (in tense aspect to Uranus and Saturn) has run the Aquarian gamut as far as sex is concerned. During the Swinging Sixties she had a sexual 'ball', experiencing practically everything one could imagine. Like the female above, she has had bisexual experiences, and considers there should be no hard and fast rules where sex is concerned—it is entirely up to the individual. Since her mid-thirties she has been celibate and for the past two years of her life has lived without any emotional or sexual relationship of any sort.

It would appear that Aquarian women, like Pisceans, Geminians, and Librans, tend to be more attracted to their own sex, or at least willing to entertain a sexual relationship with another woman, than the other signs of the zodiac. There could be several explanations for this, but perhaps the most likely are her desire to experiment, and also her emotional make-up. Some Aquarian women feel less threatened by the emotional content of a sexual relationship with another woman; thus they feel freer, happier, and more fulfilled in such a relationship.

Regardless of her sexual drive, the Aquarian woman is frequently highly attractive to others. The cool and detached exterior acts like a magnet to those who long to break down the ice and hopefully discover a searing hot passion within. Sometimes this is indeed the case but often the Aquarian woman is as reluctant to loose her emotional control as the male; and a good many partners may spend a life time trying to chip away the ice. In many Aquarian women a certain ambiguity exists because although they may hold broad-minded sexual attitudes, a constant underlying fear of rejection works within, rendering them in fact sexually frigid.

In sexual matters, as in many areas of his life, the Aquarian man runs to extremes. Some feel sex is highly overrated and once a relationship, like marriage, is established they are content to let the physical side of things take a back seat, if not lapse altogether. Others have a strong sex drive and need a variety of sexual partners to satisfy them. However, even the Aquarian man who has sexual partners outside the marriage tends to remain loyal emotionally to his wife. Some male Aquarians, by dint of experimentation and sheer variety of partners, develop highly skilled sexual techniques, yet unless the Waterbearer is equally emotionally developed there is rather a mechanical feel to his lovemaking. Unlike the Pisces man who becomes practically psychically in tune with his partner during sex and elevates the experience emotionally, Mr Aquarius applies some clever and imaginative techniques but fails to sense his way emotionally. Thus, despite all the excitement, the Aquarian's partner often feels she has just received a one-to-one demonstration in the technology of lovemaking.

Some astrologers maintain that Aquarius is more prone to suffer from a variety of sexual disorders, from premature ejaculation to chronic impotence. This, I'm sure, is untrue. However, because the Aquarian man is vulnerable emotionally and has a basic fear of rejection, like his female counterpart he may develop problems if at any stage he encounters an emotional or psychological set-back.

A friend of mine was once engaged to an Aquarian man who refused to make love to her until they were married. After several frustrating weeks my friend threw down the gauntlet and insisted they found out if they were sexually compatible **before** they were married rather than after. With his back against the wall, her fiancé arranged a weekend away in a magnificent hotel. On the first evening he proceeded to drink himself into unconsciousness so that the following day he was in no fit condition to do anything at all, let alone consummate the relationship. On the journey home, after a celibate weekend, her Aquarian fiancé confessed that he'd been so hurt by a previous girlfriend who had left him, that he had been impotent ever since. He was, of course, convinced that my friend would refuse to marry him if he failed to make love to her. Fortunately, love triumphed and because my friend, much to her own surprise, handled the situation with compassion and understanding, and contrary to his expectations did not throw her engagement ring in his face, he suddenly found he was no longer impotent!

One of the characteristics of the Right Man, discussed earlier, is his usually strong sex drive—strong because it is linked to his self-esteem. This kind of Aquarian needs to feel he is sexually competent otherwise the central fabric of his self-image is threatened. Whether or not he satisfies his partner or gives her any pleasure is neither here nor there—it is the acknowledgement that he has proved his 'manhood' that is at stake.

By and large the Aquarian man is not a sensuous type: his mind is his major erogenous zone, and he can be aroused far quicker by an erotic idea than the sight of a nude body. Like the female Waterbearer, he is sexually broad-minded and tolerant of threesomes, group sex, and bisexuality. Some Aquarian men even prefer spectator sport and there is an element of voyeurism in almost all of them. However, paradoxical as always, the Aquarian male holds some highly puritanical attitudes when it comes to his wife. Although prior to marriage (and sometimes outside it) he may enjoy some sexually avant-garde practices, he tends to be extremely conventional where his wife is concerned.

True to their unpredictable natures, Aquarians of both sexes present a variety of possibilities in their sexual behaviour. However, in the main, sex is not high on their list of priorities. Aquarius is not a sign synonymous with passion and the pleasures of the senses, and although many of them make excellent technical lovers they rarely allow the luxury of a full-blown sexual and emotional involvement to detach them from their ice-cool intellect.

PROFILE OF AN AQUARIAN WOMAN

KATHY FORD

In 1979 I was asked to do a 'blind' astro-analysis for an anonymous American lady. It was to be a present for her fortieth birthday. The only details given other than the birth data were that she had been married and had two children. A few weeks after I had despatched the analysis the intermediary told me who my mystery client was—Kathy DuRoss. Unfortunately, being a parochial Englishwoman, I was none the wiser. It was only when Mrs DuRoss herself contacted me that, reading between the lines, I established that she was the extremely close friend of Henry Ford II. It was the beginning of a productive working relationship and a firm friendship.

Kathy was born in Belding, Michigan, not a million miles away from the hub of the American motor industry, Detroit. Her father was a tool and die worker and her mother a nurse. Her early life was happy but unsettled since the family seemed to be forever on the move, and constantly changing homes. Kathy was a bright child who loved music and the arts. A fortune-teller told her mother that she should take Kathy to dancing lessons since her daughter had the potential to become a great star. But her mother, in her infinite wisdom, thought Kathy should play the violin instead. It was as she was on her way, violin in hand, to a TV talent contest—'Aunty Dee' —that Kathy was stopped dead in her tracks by a premonition that one day she would be famous: 'I knew it without any shadow of doubt.' About the same time, her grade 2 teacher, Miss Henry, imparted a piece of information that was to make a profound impression on Kathy's young mind: 'What you are now, you always will be.' 'It really stuck with me—everything about me was there at seven. It was unchangeable.' But when fame and fortune did alight on Kathy's shoulders, it was not as she had anticipated through any talent to entertain but through her meeting with a remarkable man.

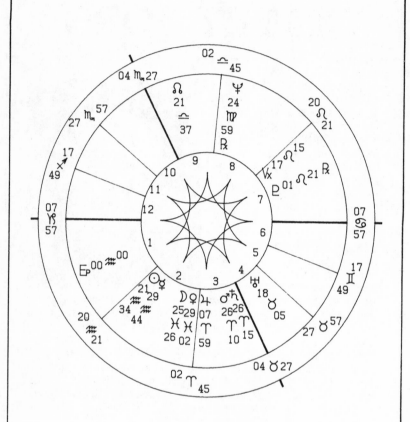

KATHY FORD

11 2 1940   5h 30m 0s EST

PLACIDUS 42N58 85W40

By her mid-teens, Kathy's uncomplicated life took a radical and unexpected turn. With practical, forward-thinking Capricorn rising, Kathy had made plans to go to university after high school. But she had reckoned without her impressionable Piscean Moon and Venus. When she was a mere fourteen years old, just as the floodgates of rising passion are beginning to open, she fell head-over-heels in love with a seventeen-year old music student, David. 'We planned on getting married when I graduated, but our calendar was shunted forward when I became a bouncing four-month pregnant cheer-leader!' David (an Aquarian-Aries mix) and Kathy were married in October 1955 when she was only fifteen, and her elder daughter, Debbie, was born in April 1956; seventeen months later, baby Kimberley arrived.

Since the income of a struggling musician was hardly enough to support a wife and two young daughters, David took a 'day job' at the Chrysler car company. Although the early months of their marriage were dominated by economic survival and interminable piles of nappies, Kathy and David were nonetheless happy and very much in love. But at nineteen years of age, Kathy's life was suddenly shattered. 'I'll never forget that night (12 December 1959). I'd gone to bed early—David was at a band rehearsal. I woke up suddenly. It was as though I had been given an almighty jolt. I looked at the clock—it was eleven forty-five. I knew when the 'phone rang later and it was the hospital, David was dead. He'd been killed in a car crash at exactly eleven forty-five.' David's death was, of course, a major trauma for Kathy: like most widows, not only did she have to come to terms with the loss of a beloved partner, she also had to cope with the day to day demands of two small children. Fortunately, Kathy's parents were very supportive during this period, and after the initial shock of David's death they urged Kathy to go to university while they looked after the children. 'It seemed an ideal solution. Somehow I was going to get back onto the tracks of my life. I thought I might become a teacher. But, I guess, I wasn't really over David . . . the pressures caught up on me and I had a breakdown.' Recovery took many months, after which Kathy decided to go into modelling. While she realized posing in front of a camera looking amorously at a vacuum cleaner, or reclining seductively on the bonnet of a car wasn't exactly taxing her brain, at least it offered her freedom and independence—an absolute must for Aquarian women. Her modelling career not only provided her with a reasonable income; it also brought her into contact with the rich and famous.

Like many Aquarian women, Kathy is a 'no holds barred' individual—'I practise right and wrong daily.' Both as a little girl and as an adult, she felt special and was determined to carve a different path for herself than that of her parents. In Kathy's chart, Uranus

(Aquarius' ruling planet) is placed in the fourth 'house' of home and roots; this planet's volatile, changeable nature is reflected in the many home changes she experienced as a child. Saturn is also a significant planet in Kathy's life.* Women with Capricorn rising are usually immensely determined and capable, and although life can appear to be a perennial uphill struggle, they accept their difficulties philosophically—often with a faintly ironical attitude. Both Capricorn and Aquarius are strong, if rather inflexible, ideas, and certainly it was the combination of these two signs and their respective ruling planets that enabled Kathy to come to grips with her early responsibilties and the trauma of losing the man she loved. Her appreciation of music and the arts, and the tendency to be lead by the heart rather than the head, are typical of her Moon-Venus conjunction in dreamy artistic Pisces—a sign that is also said to be synonymous with suffering.

Fate seems to have dealt Kathy a heavy hand at an early age. The death of a partner is a tragedy in itself, but to experience such a blow at so early an age makes the tragedy that much more cruel. There are some indications of trauma linked to relationships in Kathy's chart. First, the Moon—the ruler of her 'house' of partnerships—is placed next to Venus at the opposite end of the chart to nebulous Neptune. While on one level, this aspect indicates heightened sensitivity and compassion, it is also suggestive of romantic illusion, deception, betrayal, and loss. More significantly, Pluto, the planet of death and rebirth, is to be found in the 'house' of relationships itself. Planets, of course, are symbols of many ideas, and Pluto plays more than one part in Kathy's partnerships. But as a general rule of thumb, when Pluto is located in this area of the chart, relationships tend to bring upheaval of one sort or another into the individual's life. All too often it seems fate has played a less than accidental role in the state of affairs. Neptune's and Pluto's connections are enough on their own to account for Kathy's early unhappy experience in love without any 'flak' from Saturn. But with Saturn's conjunction to Mars—the planet of desire—the message is well and truly driven home. Thus it is singularly unlikely that Kathy would find a trouble-free route to marital harmony.

Once over her breakdown, Kathy took up the reins of her life with renewed optimism. On the surface, like all Aquarian women, she appeared 'together' and in control, but emotionally she was still enormously vulnerable. Her modelling career was 'modestly successful' and in her free time she 'dated occasionally'. 'I came close to marrying when I was about twenty-eight—a Piscean. He had many fine qualities, but I felt I had two children already and didn't need a

*Saturn rules her Capricorn Ascendant and is close to the I.C.

third!' Two years later she was to meet the man who was to change her life beyond all recognition.

'When I was thirty I met a man who was married. I was taken to a dinner party at his home. Our paths crossed at another function a month later. After that he 'phoned me but I refused to meet him as I didn't want a married man in my life. Fate had different ideas, I guess, because at the beginning of November we met at another dinner party—this time he was alone. We started seeing each other occasionally after that, and our relationship grew from there.' The man in question was none other than Henry Ford II.

These words were written by Kathy in a letter to me shortly after she had received the chart analysis and before she disclosed the identity of the man in her life. In one of those strange synchronicities I had used the phrase 'a powerful motor mechanic with political aspirations or an empire builder' in an attempt to describe the type of man she was likely to be drawn to as a partner.* At the time of this correspondence, Henry had been divorced from his second wife, Christina, for just two months. On 14 October 1980, Kathy became the third Mrs Henry Ford II at a wedding ceremony at Lake Tahoe. Ten years had elapsed since Kathy and Henry had first met, and for most of those years intrigue and acrimony had run in tandem with their love affair. 'We spent the first five years of our relationship "underground". I never went to one function with him.' But that all changed dramatically one February evening in 1975. 'We'd been to a restaurant and as we approached the car, we saw the police waiting. Henry had parked the wrong way round in a one-way street. The police gave him a breath test and that was it. He had his driver's licence taken away and the story was front page news all over the world.' 'Never explain; never complain' were Henry's laconic comments on the incident. Ten months later, after a determined attempt to reconcile his marital differences with Christina, he left her.

Henry was a Sun Virgo with Uranus rising in Aquarius. While much has been written in recent years exposing the alleged ruthless, insensitive, and devious way he handled his business affairs, his colleagues and his relations, to those he was closest to and those who knew him best he was a kind, generous, and diffident man — on one occasion mistaking Prince Andrew for a photographic assistant! In keeping with his Virgoan Sun, he was a discriminating individual who set high standards for himself and those around him; and in keeping with his Aquarian-Uranian side, once someone betrayed his trust the contact was irrevocably severed.

*Planets in the seventh house describe the nature of the individual's relationships and also qualities sought in the partner.

Mr and Mrs Ford had a strong and binding relationship: they recognized and respected each other for their differences, which made for some mammoth showdowns on occasion! During the span of their relationship they had enormous stresses placed on them by family in-fighting and unpleasant scandal. On their wedding day Henry's children refused to attend the ceremony and intimated that Kathy was nothing less than a shameless 'gold-digger'. Ironically, these pressures united them rather than alienated them.

With the Aquarius-Capricorn flavour in her chart, combined with the Pisces-Neptune content, there could be a tendency for Kathy to attract dependent partners; yet with Pluto linked to her relationship 'house' she more than meets her match with her men. 'David was a strong character—a good man. So was Henry; and he certainly didn't depend on me any more than David did. Nor do I depend on them. But I'm a sucker for a hard luck story. I'll always lend a helping hand to friends, and, of course, I've been taken advantage of.' A case in point was the discotheque 'L'esprit' that she and a partner started up in Detroit in 1975. 'I'd known the guy for five years. I trusted him and so never bothered with any partnership papers.' Her trusty partner squeezed her out of the business and took all the profits! Kathy's initial reaction was to 'get on with life and forget the whole business', but since it was the principle that mattered more than anything else, she decided to take her ex-partner through the courts. At the time of writing, some eleven years later (!) her fight continues—persistence and tenacity through adversity being hallmarks of her Capricorn-Mars-Saturn influence.*

Despite her fiercely independent Aquarian spirit, Kathy has taken on the role of Mrs Henry Ford II to the manner born. In this she reflects the subtle difference between American wives of influential, wealthy men and their British counterparts. American high-profile socialite wives know how to pamper their men: they turn being a wife into a Hollywood production! The British woman is not made of the same stuff. She sees something vaguely insidious in pandering to a man, no matter how much to her advantage it might prove. 'I can't stand the idea of women being chattels. But looking at marriage realistically, to make a marriage work, the man has to be number 1. There's nothing remotely demeaning about this. It's just common sense. If you make them feel great, then the happiness spins off on to you.' Of course, theory is one thing, practice another. And just occasionally Mrs Ford forgot who was number 1. 'Arguments and discussion', she says were very much a part of our marriage.'

Inasmuch as Kathy found her early years unsettling, her life as Mrs

*Perhaps, too, with Neptune in the area of the chart associated with legal matters, she has a tendency to fight for lost causes!

Ford II was (and still is) diverse, hectic, and full. She and Henry travelled constantly—mostly around Europe and the States—thus she longs to put down some roots and devote more time to her hobby, photography. In the mid-1970s Henry gave her a camera: to begin with, she photographed pheasant shoots and the like, but as her pictures improved she decided to develop and print her own (she now has dark rooms in all her homes). Ultimately she hopes to work as a professional. Astrologically, Kathy's love of photography is yet another reflection of the strong Pisces-Neptune flavour to her chart, as is her interest in the spiritual and the mystical.

Kathy has always been a highly intuitive individual; but her fascination with the paranormal did not develop until she was in her thirties when she discovered a ouija board in her basement. Although experimenting with the ouija is a distinctly dangerous business, Kathy has never suffered any ill effects from its influence. Indeed, the ouija has been a catalyst to a serious search for 'truth and meaning' in her life. Astrology is another of Kathy's interests. While she does not calculate or interpret birth-charts, she is familiar with astrological symbolism and finds it enormously helpful. Like many Aquarians, astrology appeals both to the pragmatic and intuitive side of her nature. Indeed, Kathy asked me to find an appropriate day (and time) for her wedding to Henry, "after all, he'd had two mistakes, he didn't want a third!" And while Henry was mildly amused about getting married at a rather inconvenient early hour of the morning, he went along with Kathy's beliefs in full faith.

With her firm belief that nothing in life is ever accidental and that every experience, no matter how small, serves a greater purpose, Kathy is 'ready for anything life can throw at her'. A few years ago, Henry was almost persuaded to enter politics and become a senator. And who knows, perhaps if he had, the White House might now be occupied by a 'powerful motor mechanic' and a glamorous First Lady of distinctly unusual gifts. And while Henry might consult his advisors about 'Star Wars', Kathy would no doubt consult the stars about his advisors! And that would certainly give the Russians something to worry about! Possibilities are infinite for the Aquarian woman . . .

Postscript: Tragically, Henry died on 29 September 1987 after a short illness. At the time of writing (April 1988) Kathy still feels his loss intensely, and despite being left enormously wealthy she is anything but a merry widow. Family politics surrounding Henry's estate occupy much of her time, and these pressures and strains on top of her grief have taken their toll on her health, bringing her to the verge of a nervous breakdown in March 1988. Fortunately, she is surrounded by loyal helpers and friends.

Kathy has been told by several psychics (including myself) that she will marry a third time. This she vehemently disputes, partly because she now longs for her 'own space' and also because 'I've been damned lucky to have been married to two wonderful men. Lightning never strikes thrice!'

Note for Astrologers: (1) The Neptunian and Plutonic influence is particularly strong in Kathy's chart since these two planets are the only ones above the horizon and set apart from the remainder.

(2) At the time of David's death, transiting Saturn was conjunct Kathy's Ascendant; transiting Uranus was opposing both her's and her husband's Sun, and transiting Venus was conjunct the MC squaring Neptune.

(3) At the time of Kathy's wedding to Henry, transiting Pluto was trining her Sun and transiting Jupiter was opposing her Moon and Venus.

(4) Henry died just hours after a Sun-Neptune square; transiting Venus was conjunct his radical Venus in the 8th house; transiting Jupiter was conjunct his radical Moon in the 2nd. In Kathy's chart, transiting Neptune was applying to a conjunction of her Ascendant; the Moon-Uranus conjunction at the moment of death fell in her 12th house and squared her radical Neptune in the 8th house.

PROFILE OF AN AQUARIAN MAN

MARTIN SHAW

Like many an actor with a list of remarkable stage and film performances to his credit, Martin Shaw is better known to the British public for his role as Doyle—one of the tough-guy team in the highly successful television series **The Professionals**. However, macho Doyle is anything but an example of perfect type-casting since Martin Shaw is a complex, highly sensitive, perceptive man.

Martin was born in Birmingham in 1945 and lived there with his parents and his younger brother until he was eighteen. His father had his own business, having started out as an draughtsman then a sales engineer. 'You could say we were working class with middle-class aspirations!' The first few years of his life were unsettled. The family moved home several times, alternating between his grandmother's house and lodgings. Other than the unsettled home conditions, Martin's early life appears distinctly uneventful. He did, however, hate school. 'I was terrible at school—loathed every second of it.' While Martin was bullied at school, some of the teachers appeared to provide just as much of a threat. 'I was advanced enough intuitively to know what real intelligence was. I could see clearly that these teachers couldn't spot genuine intelligence. Intelligence to them amounted to having a good memory—they knew nothing about intuition. So I was frustrated, angry, and frightened at the way schools were run. I didn't work. And not working got me into trouble and, although I was terrified, that made me more stubborn! It would have been much worse had it not been for a few teachers who were inspired and marvellous.' While, with the exception of English, Martin kept a low profile at school he was good at gymnastics and played cricket well. 'I wasn't good at football. Although I could run very fast, I'm a peculiar sort of "psychopathic" shape in that I'm broad-shouldered, broad-chested, then everything suddenly collapses—narrow hips and tiny, thin legs, so I was very easy to knock over!'

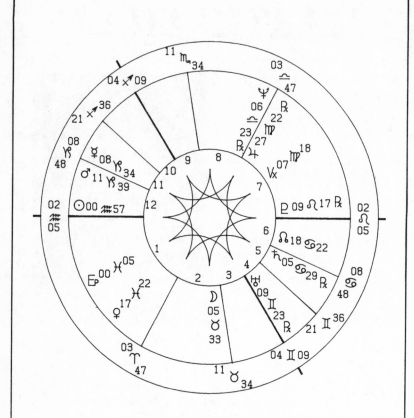

MARTIN SHAW

21 1 1945   8h 15m 0s GMT

PLACIDUS 52N30 1W55

Martin is a strongly Aquarian character. He was born just as the Sun was rising, so both the Sun and the Ascendant are found in Aquarius. Individuals with the Sun on the Ascendant almost always have a powerful sense of identity; they are usually strong-willed, determined, and able to inspire confidence in others. Since Martin's Sun is also trine Jupiter, there is an even stronger larger-than-life feel to his personality. Yet he seems to have kept his light hidden under the proverbial bushel as a child, especially at school. 'At the time, my subjective feeling about childhood was that it was happy, but as I learn more about myself in later life I get the impression it wasn't and that it was a determination to be happy.' Volatile Uranus in the fourth 'house' of family reflects the upheaval of the many home-moves in his early life. Uranus also suggests—though this was strongly disputed by Martin—that one parent (more often father) was unusual in some way—perhaps somewhat erratic and difficult to draw close to emotionally. By contrast, expansive Jupiter rules the other parental 'house'—the tenth—indicating one of the parents (possibly mother) was a benign and positive influence on his life. However, the parental picture is not entirely clear since Martin's Sun (a symbol, amongst many ideas, of father) forms harmonious contacts to other planets in the chart, suggesting a positive relationship with Dad, while the Moon (associated with mother) makes a difficult and tense angle to Pluto, implying that Mum was the source of some conflict and turmoil—this is an aspect **par excellence** for emotional manipulation and over-possessiveness. It is just possible that Martin perceived his parents as two very different and perhaps ill-matched people and that their discord, consciously or unconsciously, filtered through to him.

Martin's experience of school and his attitude toward education is in many ways typical of a strongly Aquarian or Uranian individual. As a general rule of thumb, Aquarian children do no cope as well with a set school syllabus as some of the other zodiac types: they need to be inspired by a teacher and to work within a creative framework. Martin, like many Aquarian youngsters, was under-stretched for his abilities, and with the fixity of Aquarius, he simply dug his toes in! To compound the situation, Martin's Capricorn Mercury—the zodiac's great communicator and dispenser of knowledge and information—is caught up in a tense configuration with Saturn and Neptune.* The Mercury-Saturn contact can indicate a high degree of intelligence, while the Mercury-Neptune aspect shows intuitive, artistic, and even spiritual gifts. These three combined suggest Martin has a fertile intellect and a rich imagination, but that great effort will be required to produced the fruit of his mental labours. Mercury is also the apex

*A 'T'-square involving Mars opposition Saturn square Neptune.

of another configuration known as a 'Finger of Fate'.* While this combination also suggests that his communication skills are achieved with much effort, there is a feeling for the unusual here—an attraction toward metaphysical studies and unorthodox subjects and methods of communication.

Needless to say, with an inadequate (for him) teaching system, Martin left school with 'about one O Level. I didn't work for the exams. I didn't understand the purpose of exams.' On leaving school he was offered a scholarship to drama school in Birmingham. 'I'd done some plays at school when I was about fourteen and I think people thought I showed some talent. When I got this scholarship it was the first time in my life I had been seen to be good at anything. Everybody had told me I was useless. Apart from English, which I was very good at, everything else was appalling!' His parents, however, considered he was too young at sixteen to know if acting was a suitable career avenue. Had they been aware of Martin's Jupiter-ruled Midheaven—tailor-made for the acting profession—they might have had more confidence! As it was, Martin was persuaded to spend two years working in the sale offices of a chemical firm, then a brass foundry. Ultimately, Martin was extremely grateful for his parents' wise decision since by turning down the Birmingham drama school's scholarship two years later he was able to audition for LAMDA (at the time arguably the best drama school in the UK). He was accepted and moved down to London. What followed were two of the happiest years of my life. I was with Stacey Keach, Michael Moriarty, Maureen Lipman and Anna Caulder Marshall—it was a vintage year.' Martin was fortunate to be accepted by 'a wonderful agent, Ann Hutton', whom he has been with for twenty-two years. No mean achievement for an Aquarian man!

Martin worked consistently from the time he left drama school. 'I did an apprenticeship as it were at Hornchurch Rep. For two years I did everything from the menial upwards. I made the tea, was the ASM [Assistant Stage Manager]. By the time I left I'd covered almost every aspect of theatre.' After Hornchurch, Martin went to the Bristol Old Vic and from there started to play some good parts on TV and in theatre. The years 1969 and 1970 were to launch him into the big time. He took the lead in a play by Mike Weller at the Royal Court, then followed it immediately with Peter Shaffer's **Battle of Shrivings**, in which he starred with John Gielgud. Later in 1970 he made **Hamlet** for American TV with Richard Chamberlain, Michael Redgrave, and John Gielgud (again). Also in 1970, he played Banquo in Polanski's highly acclaimed film of **Macbeth**. Thus, by the age of twenty-six he was one of Britain's brightest young actors. In the latter

*Mercury quincunx Pluto and quincunx Uranus.

part of the 1970s, he was able to reach an even wider audience with Thames Television's popular series **The Professionals**. 'The **Professionals** was a lateral step. It was good from the point of view of public awareness, but bad for professional progress. Luckily, it didn't type-cast me. I took a gamble when I accepted the job that I'd done enough classy work before and I expected people to remember that. It was a risk, but it turned out OK.'

Martin has several planets in earth signs in his chart,* thus he is able to balance the more desultory Aquarian side of his nature with some steady, cautious, and down-to-earth characteristics. Like Virgoan Jeremy Irons, he is a craftsman first and a star afterwards. Martin is extremely fortunate in having a grand trine in his chart: a configuaration that is made even more powerful because the Sun and Uranus are both on the angles.† The grand trine shows Martin has great versatility as an actor; he experiences sudden leaps of inspiration and has a remarkable gift for sensing the current of the moment. This intuitive spark would give him a definite edge in theatre work, since he can 'feel' the audience and temper his performance accordingly—his timing is therefore excellent. 'I don't care about my image—it's not a static thing. Whatever you're working on at the time is the image you're concerned with . . . Yes, I'm very much prepared to take a risk and I haven't made a bad move yet—of course, Ann's [his agent's] advice is unswervingly excellent.'

While his airy grand trine might allow him to coast along with his natural talent, other factors in his chart indicate he is a phenomenally hard worker with a strong desire for success. Martin's Mars (a symbol of drive) is placed in the industrious, ambitious sign of Capricorn; this planet, like Mercury, is bound up in the same configuration with Saturn and Neptune. Where his work is concerned, while the ability to immerse himself in a role working to the point of exhaustion at times is indicated, he may well never feel satisfied with the results. Also, despite the confidence and strength the Sun's placing inspires, he could occasionally have serious doubts about his abilities, and may even feel he is not given due recognition for his achievements.

The inherent struggle depicted by the 'T'-square is likely to surface in other areas of his life, most notably in his relationships. As I discussed in the section on the Aquarian man, this individual tends to steer well clear of intimate, long-term relationships for fear of emotional claustrophobia. Martin, of course, has plenty of earth in his chart and a romantic idealistic Venus in Pisces; thus he is by no means the elusive bachelor type. However, he still finds himself up

*The Moon, Mercury, Mars and Jupiter.

†The Sun is conjunct the Ascendant, trine Uranus conjunct the I.C., trine Neptune.

against the familiar Aquarian problem of locating his deeply buried feelings and sharing them with another person. Martin married his first wife in 1968 when he was twenty-three and they have three children. But like many early marriages, their relationship did not stand the test of time. In 1982, Martin married his second wife, Maggie (another Aquarian with Capricorn rising and Moon in Libra). Maggie is a psychotherapist specializing in core energy. 'She suits me perfectly,' he said, although he added that they had some 'amazing fights'! Before discussing the Mars-Saturn-Neptune trio in regard to relationships, it is worth commenting on Martin's seventh 'house' of partnerships, since there is more than one theme to this area.

The Sun rules Martin's seventh house, and with this 'planet' involved in the harmonious grand trine and forming another trine to big-hearted Jupiter there are plenty of indications that Martin can find happiness in marriage. But—and there always seems to be a but—Pluto is also to be found in the seventh 'house', and on the Descendant angle. On the one hand, Pluto suggests Martin is looking for the proverbial 'deep and meaningful' in relationships, and that he is attracted to strong and complex women—perhaps with a Scorpio-Pluto theme to their charts. That Maggie is a therapist—a distinctly Plutonic profession—can be seen as a positive expression of Pluto's placing. On the other hand, he may meet the less attractive side of this planet in his relationships, which could mean power struggles, even some strongly fateful circumstances. Martin does not appear to have experienced any tragedy in his partnerships, but he has certainly encountered some struggles. Since the Moon forms a square 90° angle to Pluto, any of Martin's 'unfinished business' with mother is likely to be carried on with the partner. This aspect has a reputation for emotional suppression; the individual usually has very deep feelings but they tend to be over-protected, which can manifest as an apparent lack of emotion. Martin may be typical of the kind of man who always seems to be coming up against women's overpowering emotions and their possessiveness. On top of this, with his Mars in the twelfth 'house' of the horoscope in opposition to Saturn, Martin may alternate between periods of intense frustration and anger with his partner and periods of calm and happiness. One astrologer* says of Mars in the twelfth, 'the natural aggression of Mars may sometimes be disguised as a vague and passive dissatisfaction with life: nothing feels right but he can't put his finger on what's wrong . . . having driven everyone around the bend, he miraculously snaps out of it [his sulk] as soon as he has managed to make someone else express his rage for him . . . hidden somewhere in his psyche is an incendiary device which can flare up in sudden episodes of

*Howard Sasportas **The Twelve Houses.**

uncontrolled behaviour. To complicate matters, Mars in the 12th may be the one to act out the unexpressed stirrings and anger of those around him: the battles he ends up fighting may not even be his own.' Martin agrees that his relationships have sometimes been the arena for the exorcism of some buried, but not dead, emotions. 'Whenever any feeling comes up, the first four or five layers are anger, and underneath is always sadness.' However, it would be wrong of me to imply that Martin's relationships are a constant battle ground. With his Venus in romantic, gentle, and sensitive Pisces, there is an exceedingly soft and compliant side to his nature. While he needs a partner with whom he can have a good intellectual rapport, he wouldn't dream of marrying for anything less than love. Also, Martin has confronted much of the inner struggle inherent in these configurations so they are not busily 'fermenting' in the unconscious! He is open to such areas as astrology as a route to self-awareness, which has doubtless enabled him to relate to the positive aspects of his personality as well as those in the shadow. In this way, through effort, acceptance, and understanding he can reach the highest levels of love, and find true fulfilment in his relationships.

With his Venus in the aesthetic and sensitive sign of Pisces and his Moon in artistic and sensual Taurus, Martin emerges not only as a romantic 'leading man' and a connoisseur of women, but something of an artist and a poet—not that Martin spends every spare minute jotting down rhyming couplets! 'I never had any formal music lessons—I just used to mess around on the piano at home when I was a kid . . . I'm not very good at painting or drawing, I prefer three-dimensional stuff—working in clay or wood.' Martin has used his natural musical talents in many of the parts he has played, but his performance as the aging Elvis Presley in **Are You Lonesome Tonight?** has won him considerable critical acclaim. It is evident that the musical side of theatre appeals to him greatly, but with the Aquarian-Uranian thrust to his chart he doesn't want to become involved with musical after musical: 'I love diversity.' With his Piscean Venus and his strong Neptune, it is surprising that he hasn't done more film work. 'You can't plan things really. Your career depends on what's offered.' I put it to Martin that his chart showed the potential for directing films as well as appearing in them.* 'After five years of doing **The Professionals** and working intensively with cameras, it became second nature to me . . . I would like to get in on the making of films, it's what I want, but I don't know whether I

*Leadership and good organizational skills are shown by the Sun conjunct the Ascendant, and Mercury-Mars in Capricorn. While the latter are square Neptune, in this case the aspect can be expressed positively through the creative-artistic medium of film and TV.

will.' Over the next few years Neptune, the planet synonymous with film and photography, will make several important contacts to his chart. While it is not clear whether these imply working in front of or behind the camera, major film projects are likely.

Martin has a gift of a chart for anyone working in a creative world like the theatre. He has versatility plus vision and commitment —ingredients that have already made him a fine actor. But in keeping with the delayed action Saturnian content of his chart, the best is yet to come.

Note for Astrologers: (1) During 1969/70—the years that launched him into the 'big time'—significant progressions and transits were as follows: secondary progressed Mars was conjunct the Sun, progressed Ascendant was opposition Jupiter. 1969 saw Martin's second Jupiter return, this planet went on to trine the Sun-Ascendant and Uranus; transiting Saturn was square the Sun then conjunct the Moon. By the end of 1969, transiting Pluto was conjunct Jupiter and transiting Neptune was sextile his Sun. These latter aspects were sustained during 1970 when Jupiter also squared his Sun and Ascendant.

(2) I asked Martin what effects he had noticed during 1983/4 when transiting Pluto squared his Sun, and Uranus opposed Uranus. He replied, 'Yes, it was a period of many changes. I moved house, but more importantly, there was a change in consciousness—although it started back in 1977 . . . a sort of inner quest—a search for self-knowledge in a mental area.'

PISCES
20 February – 20 March

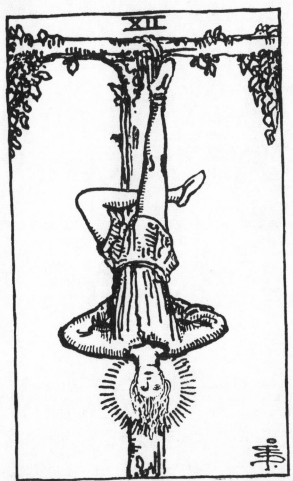

VICTIMS AND SAVIOURS:
THE GREAT PRETENDERS

PISCES
VICTIMS AND SAVIOURS: THE GREAT PRETENDERS

PISCES are a curious kettle of fish. In the jungle of human relationships they lurk like chameleons. They continually change ideas, feelings, and direction according to the climate, surroundings, and people they reflect. While the rest of the zodiac may be hopelessly confused and utterly at sea dealing with the elusive Piscean temperament, the Piscean himself appears contented to flow with the current of the moment, oblivious to any whirlpool or rapids he may be approaching. Or is he? Over my period of time as a consultant astrologer I have learned to hold no preconceptions about my Pisces clientele. Most of them will fail to agree with either my expectations or my assessments which all goes to further the myth that Pisces people are the most misunderstood members of the zodiac. However, I have found it worth bearing in mind that Pisceans are as deceptive to themselves as they are to others. They have a penchant for being extremely non-committal, and will frequently respond to a direct question with yet another, disappearing behind an eloquent masquerade. Or perhaps in truth they really have no idea where they stand. One can never be sure. The simplest discussion can turn into a maze of one-way dialogues and emotional culs-de-sacs with Pisces. They may start on one premise, change their minds half way through, and whilst everyone else is busily trying to assimilate the new stream of consciousness they will have slipped into yet another by-water. One Pisces client began by informing me that her marriage to an alcoholic had been volatile and unstable and would never have stayed the course had her husband not died unexpectedly. When I returned to this area later to comment on the unstable pattern of her partnerships she insisted that she and her late husband had been ideally happy, the relationship exceedingly special, and she doubted she would ever find anyone like him ever again! Pisces, you see, is a limitless experience and Pisceans have no fixed boundaries. But we will return to this later.

Much can be understood about the Pisces individual by considering the myths and symbols associated with this mysterious and complex sign. While the fish itself is rich in symbolism, the myths associated with the two fishes are few and far between—the Syrians providing the most appropriate. Syrian myth tells of two fishes who found in the Euphrates a giant egg. They propelled the egg to land where a dove settled upon it. A few days later Atargatis (the Syrian equivalent of Aphrodite) emerged. The goddess honoured the fishes by placing them in the heavens. She also named her son, Ichthys (Fish).

Many cultures held the fish to be sacred, usually because of the close symbolic relationship of the sea with the Great Mother. The fish was both a symbol of fertility (by dint of the massive number of its eggs) yet because of its shape and movement it was considered a sort of 'bird of the nether regions' and thus associated with sacrifice. The fish, of course, was an early Christian symbol, and indeed Jesus Christ was synonymous with the Piscean themes of sacrifice and the spiritual—a point I shall take up later.

Western myth tells of a mysterious figure known as the Fisher King. He was inextricably linked to the Holy Grail, since he was keeper of the Grail secret. The Fisher King was mortally ill and his domain, the Wastelands, was barren and dried up. The King could only be restored to health and his lands made fertile again if a mortal, through courage, endurance and illumination, could ask the right question, 'Where is the Grail?'. The Grail (an extremely complex symbol) is an integral part of the Christian Mysteries and central to the Arthurian legend. The Grail is often considered to be the cup in which Joseph of Arimathea caught the blood of Christ: he is then supposed to have brought the Grail to Britain where it is said to be buried in Glastonbury. Here again Pisces-Christian themes of suffering, sacrifice and (spiritual) resurrection are interwoven. While many believe the Grail cup really exists, it may seem more appropriate to consider the Grail as a symbol of the source of inner, spiritual illumination.

Certainly, the legend of the mortally ill Fisher King bears a strong resemblance to the myths of the dying god of Nature and his rebirth in the spring. In the Celtic version of the story, the Fisher King and his lands were said to be barren because the Moon god and his moisture had disappeared into the underworld. Indeed, fertility linked to sacrifice is a recurrent theme in Pisces, a theme most often associated with the lunar goddess, wherein lies a conundrum. For while Pisces lends itself to the feminine, it is ruled by a masculine deity, Neptune. However, prior to Poseidon (Neptune's Greek equivalent) the goddess Thetis ruled the waves. Thetis bore her husband, Oceanus, 3000 children—'all the waves in the sea'—and she personified the feminine attribute of fertility in regard to the sea. It could be argued that all goddesses arise from the one Great Goddess, Magna Mater, and thus reflect her creator-destroyer principle (aspects of which we encounter through all the 'feminine' signs of the zodiac). But while in Pisces the fertile dimension of the Great Goddess can be found along with her creative-destroying properties, this water sign personifies the highest manifestation of the feminine principle—spirit, Divine knowledge. The Great Goddess, in this aspect, becomes the Divine Sophia. And wisdom is synonymous with Pisces. Perhaps here we can also find a symbolic reason for Neptune representing the 'higher octave' of the Moon.

Wisdom and knowledge are not one and the same. It could be said that wisdom is the understanding of the heart, while knowledge is that of the mind. Wisdom has much to do with the attainment of enlightenment through inner experience and belongs to the realm of the psyche, whereas knowledge is an intellectual function. Pisces, as the last sign of the zodiac and the last of the three water signs, encapsulates and synthesizes the experience of the eleven preceding signs; Pisces is both the end and the beginning—the end of a cycle of evolution and the beginning of a cycle of involution. This sign is synonymous with the mystical and the Divine; it is the realm where the individual loses himself to be united with his Source.

In the past, and indeed in some present day religions, the meeting with the Source, or the uniting with the god was an important and immensely significant ritual. Usually, an intoxicating liquor or hallucinogenic drug would be used to transport the individual into an ecstatic state where union could be achieved. Esther Harding in **Woman's Mysteries** goes into some detail about these rituals, and she is worth quoting in full, since she describes so eloquently an entirely Piscean experience:

... In drinking the soma* the initiant gave himself up to be filled with the god. He knew that he would lose his personal conscious control. He would become the prey of whatever thoughts or inspirations came to him out of the unknown. His mind would be the playground of strange thoughts, of inexplicable feelings and impulses ... How much greater a sacrifice was demanded of those worshippers who believed that God, like the moon, was black as well as white, destructive as well as creative, cruel as well as kind. How great an act of devotion was needed can be sensed only when we contemplate giving ourselves up to the daemonic influence which arises within our own psyches.

These comments are central to the whole idea of Pisces and its connection with Neptune and the twelfth 'house of the horoscope. It is often the individual with a Piscean theme in his chart who devotes himself to the service of God or to good works—an expression of giving himself up to the god within, which in turn may lead to a process of awakening and inner communion.

Clearly, the idea of communion with the god is tailor-made for psychological interpretation, and who better to provide it than the great Carl Jung.

To dare to listen to that inspiration from within which voice the ultimate reality of one's own being requires an act of faith which is rare indeed. When the conviction is borne in upon one that anything which is put together, or made up, has no ultimate reality and so is certain to disintegrate, one turns to one's own final reality in the faith that it and it alone can have any virtue or value ... It [acquiessing to the inner 'god'] is the faith in, or devotion to, the rightness, the wisdom of that inner spark which speaks and functions of itself, quite apart from our conscious control.[†]

To those unfamiliar with Jung, the profundity contained in these comments may be somewhat obscure. What relates to Pisces here is that through Piscean experience (astrologically offered through the twelfth house and Neptune as well as the sign itself) the individual can be released from his earthly bonds and limitations. He can also, in the truest sense, meet God—a God who does not reside in the big beyond, outside himself, but within—the ever-present spark of divinity. Whether one sees this as a strictly religious experience or a psychological one—discovering the higher self—depends upon the individual's philosophical standpoint. However, the process, like the quest for the Grail, is an arduous one fraught with danger—the boundaries between enlightenment and unconscious chaos are narrow.

Along these same lines, there is a passage in one of the Hermetic texts called The Veil. 'The Veil signified the Veil of the Universe studded with stars ... that no mortal ... has raised, for that veil was the spiritual nature of the man himself, and to raise it he had to transcend the limits of individuality,

---

*The gods drank soma—a drink brewed from the Moon tree; thus in rituals to invoke the god, initiants would drink a concoction they called soma.

[†]Esther Harding, **Woman's Mysteries**.

break the bonds of death, and so become consciously immortal . . .'* 'To raise the Veil of Isis must mean to see nature as she really is, to understand what it is that underlies the manifestations of this world and of the emotions which so move us, to see them in their ultimate reality, not veiled any longer by custom, convention, by rationalization or illusion.'†

In many ways Pisces represents the Veil: it is both truth and illusion, man and God, salvation and self-undoing.

But what of Pisces' ruler Neptune? For this powerful deity plays an important part in the understanding of Pisces. In primitive societies Neptune was the deity of the Upper Waters of Heaven—the god of clouds and rain. Later he became the god of streams, rivers, and lakes, and finally king of the underwater world. Two thirds of the globe is covered by sea so the far-reaching influence of this realm on a mythical and a psycho-spiritual level cannot be underestimated. Neptune's kingdom provides many fascinating insights for astrologers, Pisceans, and their partners alike. Among the inmates were some very unsavoury characters indeed, notably the three Graiae who resided in a misty land at the end of the world where the sun never shone. They had one eye and one tooth between them—Pisceans frequently have to make do without life-enhancing utensils! Three more undesirable residents appeared in the form of the hideous Gorgon sisters who had the distinctly nasty habit of turning men into stone. While few mortal Pisceans display this knack many are quite adept at rendering others immobile by devastating emotional outpourings. Fortunately there were some more appealing inhabitants in Neptune's realm, namely the nereids, one of whom was a wife of Poseidon, Amphitrite. The nereids spent their time spinning and singing and provided a beautiful chorus of compassionate witnesses to the mysteries and dramas of sea life. Pisces is a sign noted for its compassion and sensitivity to others and the healing and counselling professions are ankle-deep in people with Neptune or this watery sign well featured in their birthchart. However, it is this same impulse to help, heal, and save that makes Pisces the emotional dustbins of the zodiac.

Astrologically, Neptune is regarded as the great deceiver, the creator of unrealizable dreams and purveyor of powerful illusions. In myth Neptune, like his brother Jupiter, enjoyed changing his identity (especially into a horse) and his usual mode of transport was a chariot pulled by creatures who were half horse and half serpent. (Links are to be found here with the planet Jupiter who ruled the sign of Pisces until Neptune's discovery in 1846.) Pisces is an extremely impressionable sign and highly adept at soaking up other people's habits and mannerisms. In fact the only other contenders for this almost magical ability to take on a new identity before your very eyes are Gemini, some of whom have made a career out of impersonation.

Finally the association of the ocean as a symbol of the unconscious is well established in depth psychology. This forges a direct link between the hidden layers of the individual and Neptune, which in astrology symbolizes the deeper levels of the psyche—particularly the collective psyche and self-perpetuated (and often distorted) perceptions and impressions.

---

*G.R.S. Mead, **Thrice-Greatest Hermes**.

*Esther Harding **Woman's Mysteries**.

Is this all really necessary, you may well ask, and where is it leading us? These mythical titbits are bound up in various guises in every Piscean and to come to grips with this elusive sign, particularly in a relationship, one must first relinquish one's foothold on the tangible, the material, the consistent, and tune into the subliminal and the sublime. Think of the sea and its characteristics of ceaseless movement and formless water—at times calm and tranquil, at others tempestuous and destructive—and you have the perfect allegory of the Piscean nature, one most often found influencing visionaries, mystics, and prophets. Thus, individuals who have a prominent Pisces or Neptune theme in their chart are in good company with Einstein, Nijinski, Michelangelo, Meher Baba, and Leonardo da Vinci. But before we get carried away by the illustriousness of such remarkable individuals it must be noted that these represent the best and most glorious aspect of Neptunian potential. There is another side. In almost equal proportion to those who use Neptune's muse creatively are those who encounter its less acceptable face—chaos and escapism. Pisceans all too often resort to a dreamworld of limitless possibilities, a retreat away from harsh realities of life or any fact and problems they prefer not to tackle. A few, if really emotionally disturbed, can enter a psychopathic state where the fine line between living in reality or fantasy becomes irradicated. Some of the more obvious forms of escapism are drug addiction or alcoholism but the chronic malingerer and the con man are also part of the same syndrome. There are plenty of murky depths and dark places in the ocean—remember the unpleasant characters in Neptune's realm—and there is an aspect of the Piscean psyche that is very dark indeed. However, it is usually well hidden and often never ever manifests. The seed of this darkness lies in Pisces' association with the mystical and the divine, for in a few individuals this inner perception emerges as a kind of messianic belief in their own divine power. Three individuals who berthed on the misty land where the Sun never shone and wreaked havoc on humanity on a massive scale were Adolph Eichmann, Attaturk, and Machiavelli.

In keeping with its escapist tendencies Pisces is the sign par excellence for burying its head in the sand, refusing to pay heed to such mundane aspects of life as tax, bills, or insurance. Of all the mutable signs Pisceans are the least concerned with the material aspects of life. But unlike their fellow mutables, Pisceans will allow themselves to be victimized by their own lack of self-discipline and control. We shall speak more of this victim syndrome shortly.

It would appear that Pisces have enormous stores of wisdom and intuition yet fall short in the common sense department. A friend and one-time neighbour of mine who has Neptune rising holds a Cambridge degree in maths and physics. Whilst in his element coping with charm particles and red dwarfs he has an almost pathalogical inability to deal with basic practicalities of life, like turning the water supply off when the pipes are frozen. I know this to my cost as one freezing January day I found myself wading through his house in wellington boots, summoning emergency plumbers and electricians, while a veritable waterfall cascaded from his loft literally washing him out of house and home. Perhaps Confucius would have said—he who has his head in the clouds should not forget where his feet are standing.

Only a moment's reflection reveals how mistaken are those who consider

Pisces to be a mild and gentle sign. On the contrary, it is enormously powerful. A student of mine once wrote that what she disliked most about Neptune was its insidious quality, best symbolized by the relentless advance and retreat of the tides that gradually but inevitably erode away the land. Whilst Pisceans never deliberately challenge anyone or take the offensive they have, like Cancer, perfected the art of passive resistance. Stubborn is also an unfamiliar adjective to use in describing Pisces, but these individuals have a unique ability to seem compliant and acquiescent while persistently doing exactly as they choose. In this way Pisceans continually frustrate and wear down any opposition, and this factor combined with their hatred of confrontation causes major problems in relationships.

I mentioned earlier that Pisces was a limitless sign. In this lies not only their salvation but also their undoing. While Pisces' pliable nature is able to accommodate any environment, the boundaries of his own identity are fairly shaky and poorly defined. Pisces is a multi-faceted and multi-talented sign but all too often their qualities and endeavours, like so many tributaries, pour into a vast ocean of possibilities and are lost. On the plus side the sheer volume and pressure of water can force back limiting barriers so that it is the Piscean who frequently makes quantum jumps in creative intellect, artistic sensitivity, and spiritual vision and has endless compassion for humanity's suffering. Yet it is this same inability to accept restraint that makes Pisces a sign least able to affect self-control or acknowledge the importance of a moral code. Pisces, like its preceding sign, Aquarius, is a law unto itself. But true to its reputation as a sign of self undoing, Pisces usually does more harm to itself than anyone else.

The limitless and formless quality of this sign and its difficulty in dealing with boundaries has a further and deeper effect in making Pisces extremely insecure. To use an analogy, one of the first things I learned about bringing up children was that their need for rules and discipline was every bit as vital as three square meals a day. Children need to have the edges of their world defined to actually feel secure and enable them to enter the real world with confidence. Unless these edges are provided they will behave in more and more extreme ways. The net result is either a child who is unable to conform to activities where mutual cooperation, team work and rules are essential or a child who is too withdrawn or frightened to mix with others or deal successfully with challenging activities. Virtually every Piscean at some point in life becomes acutely aware of his own weakness and vulnerability. He deals with this in one of two ways. In keeping with the two fish swimming in opposite directions Pisceans seem to fall into two camps: those who cling desperately to the safety of any available rock, never daring to venture forth for fear of failure, and those who offer themselves up blindly to the endless vicissitudes of life. Of course these are extremes, but in all walks of life you will find the Piscean dreamers who for varying reasons have fulfilled little of their potential and are frequently disillusioned or embittered by their circumstances.

The victim/saviour syndrome is another theme familiar to Pisces and Neptune. Astrologers often use the phrase 'Pisces are born to suffer'. Although initially this may strike one as a completely wrong assumption considering the millions of enormously happy and successful Pisceans living on this planet, it nevertheless contains a rich grain of truth. Many astrology books, serious and popular alike, discuss the Great Age of Pisces that began at the time of Christ and is presently, after some 2000 years, giving way to that of Aquarius. Christianity is the belief and devotional aspect of Pisces. Indeed the suffering and sacrifice of Christ on the Cross is the supreme Piscean statement. If we acknowledge that these archetypal themes have a bearing on individual lives, albeit on an unconscious level, it is not such a giant leap to consider that all Pisceans are stirred by a strong impulse to experience suffering, primarily for the sake of others. This urge is expressed perhaps in its most tangible form by those Pisceans who flock towards careers in the healing and helping professions. However, this syndrome is also frequently present (as we shall see later) in other aspects of their lives, particularly relationships.

Pisceans are some of the most idealistic people in the zodiac and also some of the most excessive. Despite their limitless horizons they love to pursue a cause or a mission almost as much as a good bottle of wine. However, as we have seen, Pisceans are anything but single-minded and are eminently capable of taking up the gauntlet of one cause and dropping it in favour of another, often diametrically opposed to the first. Unfortunately—or fortunately, depending on your point of view—Pisceans tend to see something of value in everything, a factor which has greatly contributed to their reputation of being indecisive and unreliable and somewhat two-faced. Yet one must never forget that it is through Pisces one catches a glimpse of Heaven; and there are no other individuals in the zodiac quite so sensitive as the Neptunians to the agony and ecstasy of this vale of tears.

RELATIONSHIPS

Pisceans are not natural loners; theoretically they need to anchor their emotions to a good, sustaining relationship. I say theoretically because in practice they have, for a variety of reasons, an awful lot of difficulty in finding or sustaining a relationship. First, Pisces is a highly romantic sign: Pisceans and Neptunians are never without their rose-coloured glasses—they even carry repeat prescriptions for them in case they break! Male and female Fish want not merely a perfect relationship but a divine one, the only problem with the latter being that they hardly ever work on Earth. Above and beyond companionship and sex, Pisceans of both sexes seek a spiritual link with their partners, and many are consciously or unconsciously looking for their soul mate. Only rarely, of course, are soul mates to be found, and even when they are they have forgotten to wear their anti-gravity boots.

THE FEMALE PISCES

Of all the females in the zodiac, the Piscean presents the greatest conundrum. She is in effect Everywoman, capable of climbing Mount Everest if she wants to, or putting her degree in social sciences on one side and staying at home to nurse her aged parents. She is perhaps not the best sign to lead a group of militant feminists, but then again it's not impossible for her to abandon husband and children temporarily to camp in the rough outside a nuclear missile base for months on end to protest. Her main problem is that she is enormously impressionable and easily influenced; consequently she gets caught up like a piece of flotsam on the swell of a cause—sometimes in the shape of a lover or husband.

Certainly Ms Pisces is hardly ever a dominating, aggressive sort of female: she is capable of getting her own way without resorting to firearms, like Ms Aries and Ms Sagittarius, or sulks and threats like Ms Scorpio and Ms Cancer. The Piscean female is usually sweet and gentle, caring and compassionate, if a little mixed-up and neurotic into the bargain. As a child she may have finished last in the hurdle race (because she didn't want to beat her best friend), or come bottom of the arithmetic test (because she couldn't help worrying about one of her pet rabbits). No doubt her name featured regularly on the lost property list read out by the headmistress in morning assembly, and during adolescence she may have worked her way through pots of green face powder to camouflage her easy blushes. But by her twenties she was probably the most sought-after female in the neighbourhood.

In many ways the Pisces lady is the most archetypally feminine in the zodiac next to Ms Cancer. She is enormously changeable, maddeningly inconsistent, subtle, mysterious, childish, yet worldly-wise. She can get into the most dreadful muddles, often financial, but more usually emotional, since she is an extravagant creature at heart. Like Ms Libra, she finds it difficult to say No in case she hurts someone's feelings, which means that she lands herself with all manner of tasks, problems, and people she never really wanted at all. Ms Pisces is also not the most jealous of females to deal with—she just gets awfully hurt when betrayed or rejected (which unfortunately seems to happen all too often). She is endlessly supportive and extremely protective of those she loves, but easily disappointed and let down by them. Occasionally, life becomes too difficult and complicated for her to bear, even if most of the problems were created by her own indecision and gullibility. She rarely asks directly for help but somehow friends and family rally round to bail her out. However, in the long run many of them grow tired and frustrated by her inability to apply practical solutions to her problems, and the way she continues to beach herself again and again.

One Neptunian friend of mine, Samantha, epitomized the kind of Piscean confusion, chaos, and helplessness I mean. From childhood she was misunderstood. Her mother had favoured her two brothers, and because financially and emotionally they came first, she was denied all the things she would have liked to have done—for instance dancing, music or riding. Her first marriage was a means of getting away from home and inevitably ended in divorce. Tragically, her second husband was killed in a car accident when she was six months pregnant with her first child. To make matters worse, he was uninsured and left her no money whatsoever—just a handful of debts. Poor Samantha was reduced to living in a caravan, desperately trying to make ends meet on a widow's pension. A story that should evoke sympathy in almost anyone . . . But . . .

Although initially Samantha's problems were enough to floor the strongest soul eight years later, despite advice, encouragement and many opportunities supplied by friends and all and sundry, her situation had changed not one iota. Every job she began or course she decided on was soon dropped, sometimes because of health problems, sometimes because of 'extenuating circumstances' or, once, because she became emotionally entangled with a rogue of a boss. Samantha wanted to be super-mum, career-girl, artist, mystic, lady bountiful, poor-little-poor-girl, victim and saviour all rolled into one. To add to the chaos she was also unfailingly generous and somewhat extravagant: every time she received a reasonable amount of money she would buy an expensive gift for her little boy, yet, of course, there was never any money in reserve when the big end went on the car or the roof needed repair. Everyone loved her and tried to help but eventually most gave up trying. Despite abilities and intelligence, Samantha was unable to focus her disparate energies in one direction long enough for them to become effective; she also lacked the self-restraint, the confidence, and the commitment to change her situation. She hoped Fate would intervene, and in the interim she suffered a lot. Perhaps the easiest and most obvious solution to her dilemma was to marry once more, but here again she ran into another Piscean problem—the difficulty in dealing with relationships honestly and realistically.

Romance is an essential part of Piscean relationships: it is the stuff of Neptune itself. It magically transports a person off the ground and up to Cloud Nine, a perch from which the fall is very hard indeed. Unfortunately, some Piscean ladies can only deal with relationships as a romance and not in reality. These types of Fish read about, dream about, and fantasize about love. If they actually get as far as entertaining the physical aspect of S.E.X. it will be couched in picturesque terms, seen in soft focus, like a romantic film—pink satin sheets and lace draperies; she will be reclining in a silk negligee and he in a flowing white shirt—somewhat reminiscent of ballet heroes like Albrecht or Siegfried. This kind of Piscean lady may find a suitable romantic mate who wines and dines her, showers her with red roses, and sends her poems and little notes which she adores. So far so good. By the time conquest and submission are due to be enacted, provided the lighting and the right setting can be arranged, romance will still have the edge. But once body contact and bare essentials are in view it's downhill all the way for this kind of Fish.

In its most extreme form this sort of Pisces turns into the 'frigid spinster'. Often this is cleverly disguised. Outwardly she may be ultra feminine, sexy, and attractive. Most likely she will bemoan the fact that she cannot seem to find a man. Her friends will be utterly perplexed. But this is the kind of Pisces who is basically clinging to the rock—the rock of her safe fantasies—far too frightened to unbatten the emotional or physical hatches. Frequently, there has been a prior long-term relationship, possibly even marriage, but often it will have dissolved. He may have been an alcoholic or disappeared in mysterious circumstances. Thus everyone assumes the previous tragedy is standing in the way of happiness and fulfilment.

Samantha resembled this kind of Fish very closely. But although she felt the failure of her first marriage and tragic death of her second husband were typical of the kind of bad luck that dogged her life, her difficulty in finding Mr Right (and thereby a solution to her problems) was not altogether another of Fate's dirty tricks. Despite her attractiveness and appeal to men, she was deeply mistrustful and frightened of them. This fundamentally undermined any one-to-one relationship she became involved in, especially when the man began to get serious about a long-term commitment.

Another factor, common to many Pisceans, is the ease with which the Fish succumbs to emotional dominance or blackmail by those dependent on her. These can range from an ageing mother to a jealous child, all of whom make the Fish feel guilty about taking any action that threatens their exclusive commitment to the dependent person. Thus, in Samantha's case, she has convinced herself that she must place her child's happiness, if not his will, above her own, blind to the fact that her own fulfilment, through remarriage, would solve many of her practical problems. Instead, partly through her own mistrust of men (and perhaps herself) and partly due to her child's displays of jealousy—which she refuses to confront properly—she has remained a single parent, despite continually talking about looking for Mr Right. In the process she is laying the foundations of future problems for herself. In years to come, as her son struggles to leave the nest, he will be made to feel deeply guilty about everything his mother has sacrificed for him, while he in his turn will probably hold her in contempt for her past weaknesses and even reject her completely. Samantha, by then no longer young and attractive, will be left with much bitterness and an increased sense of loneliness and isolation. For Pisces, the addictive quality of being treated as an emotional doormat, coupled with the inclination to suppress their own needs in the service of some, often misperceived cause or belief, is a habit that is difficult to break.

The other kind of Fish is entirely different. This Pisces lady goes from relationship to relationship. As each one starts she is convinced she has found the right man. This Fish takes no time at all to abandon herself to erotic and sensuous pursuits, taking to the delights of the flesh as a fish to water and using them as a springboard to emotional release.

More significantly, sex for this kind of Pisces provides one of the easier routes to ecstasy and transcendence—albeit momentary. While in many ways there is something admirable about the sheer spirit of generosity in which this Piscean gives of herself, this comes with its own set of problems. Because this kind of Fish is let down and disillusioned by her partners—not just once but frequently—in time she feels used and abused. While she may build up a subtle resentment toward men and attempt to pull up the emotional drawbridge, she cannot resist the need for physical gratification or entirely rid herself of the expectation that this time it will work out. Thus, the natural insecurity of Pisceans, together with mounting anxiety, all too often leads them to seek a solution at the bottom of a bottle or on the psychiatrist's couch. In truth this Fish has a problem with commitment and a deep-seated lack of self-worth.

Years ago our first kind of Pisces woman would have directed all her energies and physical and emotional drives into missionary work or teaching—sometimes both. Even now many families have a greying aunt who dedicated her life to God and the poor and the uneducated in the jungles of the East. Maybe if you press her gently she hints of a man that could have been . . . but Fate or circumstances got in the way. Barbara Bachelor—Barby in Paul Scott's **Raj Quartet**—is a wonderful example of the first type of Piscean woman—a missionary, of course. Barby is abused by people left, right, and centre. When she is eventually thrown out of the home where she has known her only happiness with her friend Mabel, she carries her head high and suffers with dignity. Even when she applies for work at her old mission station she is at first refused. Eventually the mounting hurt and disappointment take their toll and she becomes completely dotty, spending her last days as a patient in a convent unable to speak to anyone and writing abuse whenever possible. Repressed sexuality is at the core of Barby's enigmatic character and what finally triggers her mental and physical collapse is a glimpse of Mabel's niece making loud, passionate, and adulterous love to an officer.

The other type of Fish is alive and well and in plentiful supply in the theatre and film industry. Elizabeth Taylor is a classic example of the kind of excessive behaviour in which some Fish indulge. In earlier years Ms Taylor was much sought after by men the world over: she was glamorous, beautiful and ideally feminine. While in middle age she is still a stunningly attractive woman, her little-girl-lost aura seems somehow out of place. Apparently, she remains insecure about her looks and talents and veers to Piscean all-or-nothing extremes where food and alcohol are concerned. In the past, each marriage has been to the 'man of her dreams'—in photographs she is shown looking adoringly and meekly into and up to his 'strong and handsome face with its proud and jutting jaw'. Within about two years she has needed a new pair of rose-coloured glasses or a new admirer to bolster her confidence and reassure her that she is still attractive and desirable. Thus, she seems locked into an endless cycle of high hopes that fade with bitter disappointment. While she remained married to Richard Burton for many years (and even remarried him), the relationship, after a magical start, was stormy. Her third husband, Mike Todd (with whom she had a marvellous relationship), was tragically killed in an air crash. While Fate would certainly seem to have played a part in her marriages, I suspect Ms Taylor has the familiar Piscean tendency to seek herself through others—a course almost always set for disaster. It may be that Ms Taylor does indeed have an unconscious fear of commitment and that while she needs a 'rock' to cling to, she must at the same time be free to plunge herself into the waters of emotional experience and be carried along by the strongest current.

Recently, Ms Taylor seems to have done a Piscean U-turn and has immersed herself in political waters instead. In taking up the cause for research into AIDS (Acquired Immune Deficiency Syndrome), she has risked her reputation and may well have sacrificed herself on the platform of a worthy cause. However, for all her vicissitudes, she is one of life's givers; and all in all, no matter what scandals and mistakes she leaves in her wake, she has not only enriched her own life, but those of many others.

In keeping with the Pisces victim/saviour syndrome, many female Fish have a knack of picking partners who deceive or betray them, and their relationships in general seem prone to all kinds of confusion and chaos. Although it is difficult to accept that some Pisces women actually choose (albeit unconsciously) partners who disappoint them in some way, it may not be too difficult to see that Pisces' natural desire to help others unconsciously draws them to partners who present them with the requisite problems. Pisces' need for a cause or a mission is often found in the marriage partner himself; thus the Fish uses her marriage as a symbolic act of sacrifice.

One of my clients, with a strong Neptunian theme in her chart, had had ten years of supremely happy marriage to her second husband. Sadly, he had an affair with his secretary which, in effect, broke up the marriage. However, during the course of exceedingly acrimonious divorce proceedings, the husband continually berated my client and accused **her** of causing the break-up. My client was not only beside herself with misery over the rift, as she was still deeply in love with her husband, but utterly perplexed by his behaviour. Of course she continued to forgive him and wanted him back. He could not face his guilt so he had to go on blaming her. Somehow Pisces' innate ability to suffer and forgive provokes their less than perfect partners to martyr them emotionally and psychologically.

I must make it clear that not all Pisces women will encounter such graphic difficulties in their relationships. What I have outlined and illustrated are Neptunian and Piscean themes that emerge **frequently** in such relationships. Nor, indeed, will every Piscean female fall into one such category as the 'frigid spinster' or the 'profligate debauchee'; most combine some or nearly all these qualities and often without any of the severe emotional hang-ups outlined above.

By and large, the Pisces woman is the most partner-needing lady in the zodiac—perhaps with the exception of the Libran. Of course she can manage perfectly well on her own if she has to, but there is often an aura of loneliness and suffering about her when she does. She is also one of the most generous and sentimental of the signs. If Ms Pisces is short of cash she will still manage to find some tangible expression of her love, even if she has to mortgage the bicycle and trade in the cat to do it. Pisceans are wonderful givers but have difficulty in learning how to receive—at least until they are convinced of their own self-worth. They themselves are easy to please and would rather have a gift bought at the funfair from someone they love than a Cartier diamond from someone they do not. Grand gestures do not impress Pisces; they are more concerned with gifts from the heart.

THE MALE PISCES

Trying to come to grips with a Piscean male is about as difficult as trying to clasp a wriggling fish: just when you think you have him, he'll slip through your fingers and disappear. Pisces men are multi-coloured characters; they can be life's misfits, sliding from job to job, meandering from relationship to relationship, or they can surge to the highest peaks of finanacial and professional success, hand in hand with their beloved wife of 25 years! The only thread that connects them all is a gift for visions—in some this amounts to mere fantasy and illusion, but in others prophetic insights that lead to glittering prizes.

Most Piscean little boys, like most Cancerians, are sensitive and easily hurt. However, unlike the Crab, the male Pisces doesn't construct a cast-iron shell to protect his emotions; instead, he tends to run away from unhappiness or unpleasantness. Mr Pisces doesn't like the harsh realities of life and he spends much of his time escaping from those things he would rather not confront. Some may be able to cope well with financial matters, facing up to any problem and dealing effectively with it; yet these same souls when confronted by an emotional crisis will rush to the nearest whisky bottle or take the next bus out of town. In one area or other of his life, Mr Pisces is a coward and an escapist.

Direction is also something that bothers Mr Pisces. Like his inability to confront unpleasantness, there is usually one area of his life—sometimes more—where he simply cannot follow the straight and narrow track. There are Pisces men who cannot seem to find a career outlet for themselves: every job they embark upon fizzles out, or for one reason or another they have to leave. Even if they embark on a business, their partner may fiddle the accounts or the oil well they thought was gushing will turn out to be a dried up hole in the desert. Some find it difficult to reach an objective or a destination without being waylaid or sidetracked, which can involve anything from a Sunday afternoon car trip to a major personal crossroads.

A poor sense of direction is one thing Mr Pisces and his nearest and dearest have to cope with: being direct is another. The Piscean male doesn't like to hurt people: he's basically a tender, sympathetic creature at heart. He's also, as I've mentioned, a bit of a coward, so by and large he finds it awfully difficult to tell the pure, undiluted truth—at least not without coating the pill with a lot of sugar. In many ways, rather like the Archer, truth to Mr Pisces depends upon the angle you view it from!

One of my friends spent two confused years living with a Piscean man whom she adored, but who nearly drove her to a nervous breakdown. 'Victor' had more than just a little problem with the truth: he also had the added Piscean burden of being unable to say No. He was a racing driver (Pisces men can live as dangerously as some Arians if they want to) and prey to countless numbers of attractive and highly available women. My friend never knew from day to day or moment to moment what his true intentions were about anything. One night she was preparing supper for them both when she realized they'd run out of milk. 'Don't worry, darling . . . I'll pop round the corner and get some more.' She next saw him at ten o'clock the following morning. According to Victor he'd had to drive some way out of London to find any milk; sadly the car had broken down, but luckily near some friends who put him up for the night. Unfortunately their 'phone was out of order. While his tale was just plausible, the scratch marks on his back conjured up an entirely different scenario.

Pisces men are usually sensitive and caring individuals, which is why so many of them find their way into artistic careers and the medical and helping professions. Yet, while their female counterparts are often awash with feelings, by dint of their physiological and psychological make-up, male Pisces' emotions are never so bound up with the rest of their being. However, Pisces men are never really and truly the machos of the zodiac, even though upbringing and social conditioning can work wonders—at least on the outside. Remember, Pisces and Neptune are masters of disguise and illusion. If the Pisces boy has been encouraged to express his feelings and regard his sensitivity as a natural part of his being and not something to be afraid of, he is more likely to grow into the sort of adult who is warm, demonstrative, and affectionate, if a little shy and hesitant at first. If he has been taught to suppress his natural sensitivity and see it as an unacceptable, unmanly part of himself, he is likely, as an adult, to appear aloof, rather than shy, awkward, and possibly downright autocratic. This kind of Pisces man fears that unless he has absolute control not only of himself but everyone else, he will fall to pieces. These Fish often seek powerful positions in the world, yet every now and then they get up-ended by their own slipperiness. Edward Kennedy and Harold Wilson are two Pisceans who sought out the political limelight but whose manoeuvres and private lives have been a source of considerable speculation.

There are plenty of deadly Piscean piranhas in the ocean and the danger with some Piscean men of this ilk is that they resent their own weakness so much they will try to stamp it out whenever and wherever they perceive it. This kind of Fish is usually super-logical. He likes to be considered a realist and thus cannot tolerate the irrational in life, which can mean anything from falling in love to religion or the paranormal. This Piscean has picked up his Virgoan opposite number's penchant for pragmatism in all things. But like the extreme Virgoan he needs rules and structure to protect, or rather batten down, his own irrational streak. This Fish tends to be an emotional hermit. He cannot give of himself; he neither trusts his emotions nor trusts anyone else with his emotions. This, of course, may not be immediately obvious. He may have a well-developed social front which means that it is only in the confines of an intimate, long term relationship that his inability to share his life emerges. Like the female Fish of the same ilk, as soon as huge emotional demands are made of him he finds it difficult to cope. His inability to give the appropriate emotional response freezes him, and instead of the familiar Piscean warmth and understanding he presents a distinctly cold front. This kind of Fish often relates to women as prostitutes, never allowing his feelings to enter into the arrangement. If he is married he may be a good provider and father but will rarely be able to relate to his partner on a deep emotional level, preferring distance and the occasional silence laden with critical accusation. He may in fact also turn away from his wife, physically preferring to find sexual gratification with other women who, in turn, are never allowed to come too close.

Ironically, the cold Fish is often attracted to a warm and fiery partner. In keeping with the law of supply and demand, she is drawn to his emotional reticence—fiery ladies love a mystery—while he is compelled towards her passion and generosity. However, over the years their mutual admiration for each other begins to pale; the Fish finds his fiery partner unreasonable and uncontrollable, while she finds him as welcoming and understanding as a fridge-freezer!

The other and, fortunately, more familiar Fish is the type who is sentimental, forgetful, and sloppy. This kind of Pisces knows he is an emotional sponge and, like his female counterpart, cannot give enough of himself to others. He can be an extremely difficult Fish to pin down to marriage or fidelity as he has considerable trouble with commitment and self-restraint. Pisces men of this type are a real problem to women as they are attractive, adorable, and usually very romantic, but they fall in love easily and often and hate to sully romance with talk of mortgages and hire purchase agreements. This is also why some of these Fish leave a trail of breached promises and paternity suits behind them. Another problem with this Fish is that if and when he is caught, he can become emotionally and materially dependent on the partner. Furthermore, his weak hold on reality and lack of control and direction frequently causes him to seek escape from his failures. If he cannot face up to his responsibility to himself and others he will, like his female twin, seek solace in the bottle, or even mysteriously disappear.

A friend of mine—we'll call her Fay—had a classic relationship with a Piscean man, Timothy (an actor/writer). She met him at an airport the afternoon a major love affair literally flew out of her life. She was naturally in the depths of despair and the picture of tearful desolation. This wonderful Pisces man consoled her, mopped up the tears, and persuaded her not to jump off the first available parapet. Later he gave her a wonderful meal and later still made wonderful and passionate love to her on the hearthrug. My friend, of course, is worthy of a case history in her own right. The following evening, back on the road to emotional well-being, Fay met Timothy for dinner, whereupon he confessed he was bisexual and for all sorts of reasons unable to start a relationship. (Very occasionally the Piscean dilemma is not merely finding lots of the opposite sex attractive but also their own!) Sunk once more into a pit of gloom, Fay left to fulfil a six-month contract abroad. During the next few months Fay and Timothy corresponded, their letters full of poetry and colourful prose; their letters also became increasingly loving. Shortly before the completion of the contract Timothy proposed marriage, and by the time Fay was due to return he had rented a house for them and moved in. Within three weeks Fay was out on the street, bag, baggage, and wet hanky in hand—the strain of living in close daily contact had proved too much for both of them.

For Timothy, women were beautiful and special: they never had bad breath, pimples, or untidy cupboards. After three days of living together Timothy developed an obsession over cleanliness, bathing morning and evening and taking a shower after lunch. Fay dipped only once a day and, for Timothy, all too briefly. Here, too, is a classic Pisces problem (which also affects their opposite number, Virgo). If Pisces' emotional equilbrium is upset they frequently resort to obsessive behaviour, which can mean anything from excessive tidiness and pernicketyness over tiny and unnecessary details in work and daily life to, like Timothy, a desire for almost antiseptic bodily cleanliness. Fortunately both salvaged some good out of the relationship. Fay began to write in earnest and is now a successful author and happily married, and Timothy realized he was without doubt 100 per cent homosexual.

Some Pisces men, like some female Fish, seem prone to disappointments and let-downs in relationships, if not major tragedies. Sometimes they lose the person they love to someone else, or Fate somehow drives them apart. Prince Charles, although a Sun Scorpio, has Venus conjunct Neptune and had considerable difficulty finding the right partner. If one is to believe gossip, he had to forego the marriage prospect of one major love affair as the lady in question had a rather colourful past; another apparently devastated him by turning him down and promptly marrying someone else.

One of the major problems with Piscean men in regard to romance, love and relationships is idealization. Even the super-rational Fish is prone to unrealistic expectations in this area of his life—no matter what he says! As a child, the Piscean usually has a rich inner world; he identifies with the characters in his story-books, and believes that one day his princess will come. As he grows into manhood, he will have changed his reading matter to books on fly-fishing, or photography. 'Bluff your way into quantam physics' or existentialist literature, but his princess is still alive and well in his subconscious. Thus, when he falls in love these deep yearnings and desires are projected onto the female in question. He cannot see the woman for the princess! Of course, when the romantic veil drops away (usually some months later) he feels disappointed and let down. She has changed. Dependent upon the rest of the chart, especially if there are plenty of planets in earth signs, the Piscean is able to readjust his vision and get on with the task of relating to the real person; but if he cannot accept his lady for what she is, he may continue to look for his ideal woman in other relationships.

One eminent film director with a strong Piscean theme in his chart, has a major woman problem. Since he is a sensitive, insecure individual at heart, he needs a reassuring woman in his life and the constancy and permanence of marriage to anchor him. He is also a faithful individual. His problem does not lie in any philandering tendencies, but in his perception of the women with whom he falls in love. Because he is an artist and able to develop his creative power through a rich visual medium, he has greater access to his inner world of dreams and unconscious images than most. Like the poet, Robert Graves, he is in touch with the Goddess—although unlike Graves he is unaware of her power. By his own admittance he has viewed the two women he has loved as 'goddesses' and places them on pedestals; when, like any human being, they developed flaws and failings, he felt betrayed. Now, in mature years, he realizes that his partners have borne the burden of his projected ideals. Perhaps this realization will dissipate the anger, resentment and disappointment he feels at an unconscious level, which will in turn allow for greater honesty and understanding in his relationships.

Of all the men in the zodiac, it is the Piscean who seems more sensitive to the Goddess within. Those who use 'her' in an artistic, creative capacity, or in a healing, nurturing way, or through her wisdom and vision, find her at her most benign. If unrecognized or ignored, her destructive power will erupt in full force, presenting the Piscean with chaos and lack of control—at the mercy of the irrational. On another level altogether, the search for the Goddess in his partner can urge the Piscean toward definite 'types', for instance the strong mother-figure or the child-bride. And sometimes the Goddess smiles on these unions and makes them very happy indeed. Then again she may not—the Goddess, like all women, can be perverse!

Whatever form the Pisces man adopts, he's always capable of changing yet again to suit his loved one's needs and desires. He may not be the most reliable man in the zodiac, nor the most predictable (not unless he has a strong Saturn or Capricorn influence in his chart), but when he's secure he's capable of becoming a fountain of strength to those who need him and endlessly supportive, sympathetic and understanding. Mr Pisces usually only becomes difficult and unreachable when his emotional equilibrium is upset or he has lost his faith in someone or something. He may not always say what he means or even what he means to do, and if matters become too much for him he will pull the rug out from under your feet and waft away on it to some distant shore where you will never see or hear from him again.

SUMMARY

Despite the tendency of Pisces Fish, like many Scorpios, to blame Fate for the many twists and turns in their lives and relationships, nine times out of ten they create their difficulties for themselves. Pisceans of both sexes are sensitive and vulnerable—even if many of them pretend or behave otherwise. They are also strongly idealistic. While relationships hold pitfalls for all the signs of the zodiac, because of Pisces' innate desire to scale great heights in the realms of love, their path to happiness is especially full of emotional and psychological pot-holes.

Pisces will search and search for the lover who encapsulates all the qualities they desire. Sometimes, of course, they go through a considerable array of lovers before they find him or her, and sometimes it takes longer than one lifetime. However, when they find their soul mate they will create castles in the air and live in them in connubial bliss; indeed, if they can match their abilities to their dreams and believe in themselves strongly enough, the castles may even float down to earth.

PISCES PARTNERSHIPS

True to their watery fluid natures, Pisces need a good supportive partner—preferably of the earth sign variety. The earth signs provide the common sense and practical ability Pisceans all too often lack. However, Pisceans (like most other members of the Zodiac), are unfailingly drawn to difficult relationships and therefore find the more challenging combinations with fire and air much more attractive.

Aries

Pisces and **Aries** combinations can work surprisingly well sometimes. Pisces loves Aries' courage and daring, while Aries learns much about sensitivity and sensuousness from his Pisces partner. This combination may also work well because, as zodiac next-door-neighbours, both partners may have planets in each other's Sun sign. Again, Aries, like Sagittarius, has to watch his hasty tongue with the Fish, to prevent misunderstandings and hurt ruining the relationship. Nevertheless these two often find each other greatly attractive, and certainly, to begin with, their sexual relationship can be fabulous. It is their temperamental differences that stand in the way of long term happiness.

Taurus

Taurus makes the best earthy partner for Pisces: although Taurus is an immensely practical sign, it is also highly sensuous, thus the sexual relationship between these two is usually extremely good. Both are also prone to periodic over-indulgence in the good things of life —particularly food and drink—so in later life they often have to watch their diet. Pisces usually copes with the Bull's stubbornness by ignoring contentious issues; and although the Taurean can become too set in his ways for the Piscean's liking, by and large this is a very peaceful combination.

Gemini

Pisces finds the air signs almost irresistible—particularly **Gemini**. Gemini's quicksilver, emotionally detached personality is the antithesis of Pisces' muddle-headed, strongly emotional nature. At first the Fish is dazzled by the Geminian's ability to reduce almost everything to essentials; yet after the first flush of romance, the Piscean longs for the Geminian to tell him how he feels, not just how he thinks! Both can learn much from each other, given the chance, but all too often failure to communicate **emotionally** with each other causes major problems in their relationship.

Cancer

Pisces and **Cancer** tend to generate a little too much caution and fear in each other when together, but Pisces finds much security and protection with Cancer, while the Crab feels needed and nurtured by Pisces. Both these signs are creative, and often artistic, so they have many shared interests and activities. Cancer and Pisces also make a lovely parental combination: both usually adore children and find much pleasure and happiness with their offspring. Sex, too, is usually excellent in their relationship, and a wonderful tranquillizer in times of stress.

Leo

Leo can make a secure and loving partner for Pisces, and certainly at the beginning of their relationship they encounter much sexual attraction and have a lot of fun with each other. Because the Piscean tends to put aside his needs in favour of the Lion's, in time he can come to resent Leo's rule; thus the Fish may rebel by withdrawing his compliant support. Rather like the Aries individual, Leo can ultimately overpower Pisces while the Fish can make Leo feel permanently guilty. But with good Venus/Mars links and compatible Moon signs, this can be a winning combination.

Virgo

Virgos are Pisces' opposite number and their similarities all too often breed contempt between these two. Both tend to be neurotic at times and both have a knack of increasing each other's anxieties rather than assuaging them. However, Pisces can inspire Virgo to break out of his intellectual ruts, while the Corn Bearer can encourage the Fish to add shape and form to his dreams. The sexual side of their relationship runs to extremes: it either soars gloriously or plummets disastrously. However, despite their constant criticism and moaning about each other, they often manage an exceedingly durable partnership.

Libra

Libra is a sign synonymous with relating and, despite this sign's over-refined ways and dislike of excess (in any form) he is prepared to meet Pisces half way. In turn, Pisces learns through Libra's example how to balance his life and his behaviour. One of the drawbacks to a Libra/Pisces partnership is that both people can be dreadfully indecisive; consequently, they continually prevaricate over decisions both great and small. This combination, like Gemini/Pisces, tends to have a busy social and cultural calendar; but, unlike Gemini, Libra is better able to relate to his feelings so that this couple experience less emotional and sexual difficulties.

Scorpio

Scorpio and Pisces find much depth and passion in a relationship with each other, but Scorpio has to watch his over-possessiveness and jealousy with the Fish, while Pisces has to curb his emotionally generous spirit when Scorpio is around! Scorpio is a sensuous, intensely emotional sign which complements Pisces' feeling nature; thus these two can reach some splendid heights in love and sex. However, occasionally the Fish finds Scorpio rather coarse and over-insistent sexually and tends therefore to withdraw from him.

Sagittarius

Of all the fire signs **Sagittarius** holds the greatest attraction for Pisces. The freedom and spirit of bonhomie this sign exudes encourages Pisces to widen his horizons and leave his anxieties and insecurities behind him. In turn, Pisces' enigmatic and mysterious ways fascinate Sagittarius and bring out his usually dormant sense of responsibility. The major problems with this combination is that Sagittarius' inconsiderate behaviour frequently hurts the Fish deeply, yet the more the Fish clings and whines, the less inclined the Archer feels to do anything about it—or to stay around.

Capricorn

Capricorn and Pisces form an extremely stable and loving partnership. Pisces gives Capricorn the sensitivity he so desperately needs while Capricorn provides the ultimate in financial and material security. Sometimes, however, the Goat is somewhat insensitive to Pisces' tender feelings—he tries to be too practical and crushes the Fish's generous spirit and idealistic nature. Mr or Ms Pisces can, in turn, irritate the Goat intensely by refusing to do as he suggests and continuing to muddle along, creating endless messes for him to clear up. If the sexual attraction is strong between these two, they can sustain a long and happy sex life together.

Aquarius

Aquarius, like Gemini, tends to be too emotionally detached for Pisces in the long term. Although the Fish is initially impressed, if not a little in awe, of the Waterbearer's intellectual prowess, after a while he grows tired of Aquarius continually trying to rationalize his (Pisces') feelings and, indeed, his life. Pisces needs heart-to-heart contact, not just mind to mind, thus the Fish can feel utterly emotionally unfulfilled with Aquarius. However, because of Aquarius' proximity in the zodiac, such combinations can work well—sometimes—and there is often a high degree of sexual attraction between them.

Pisces

Two **Pisceans** involved in a relationship with each other either exist in a state of mutually-generated bliss or lose each other in an emotional fog. The tendency for this sign to run to temperamental extremes is exacerbated in a joint partnership as neither individual is able to balance the other's emotional vicissitudes. Qualities of gentleness, sensitivity, and mutual understanding are found in Pisces/Pisces relationships, sometimes in equal proportion to chaos, confusion, and disappointment. Sex runs to extremes for this couple—all or nothing. Yet even without an active sex life, these two can sustain a durable relationship.

SEXUALITY

As I have said many times, sexuality involves the whole of an individual's being and cannot be pinned down to any one or two astrological factors. Broadly speaking, however, those who have a strong Piscean or Neptunian theme running through their charts will bring a dimension of the highly erotic, imaginative, and sensitive to the sexual arena.

Sex is by no means just a physical experience: at its highest level it is a gateway to the transcendent. Occasionally the level of contact between the lovers is such that they experience a heightened combination of the sensuous and the sublime that transports them beyond their physical boundaries. Pisces is acutely aware of his need to escape limiting barriers, and one of the ways he can offer himself up to experience, and in the process so lose himself, is through sex. Thus, of all the signs, Pisces is the most capable of hitting the heights in love and sexuality.

Like Cancer and Scorpio, Pisces' sexual expression is linked to the feelings and emotions, but Pisces is more giving than his fellow water signs and therefore has the most to gain and the most to lose from sexual interchange. Pisceans are highly responsive to their lovers' needs and desires; their sexual skill enables them to adapt subtly to their partner's every nuance—qualities that make them some of the best sexual partners in the zodiac. It appears to be no coincidence that several of my female friends have experienced their first orgasm (although not necessarily their first sexual encounter) with a Pisces man. When Pisceans make love, they don't just want the earth to move; they want it to disappear altogether!

The Piscean female tends to have her first sexual experience comparatively early. Sometimes this is because she cannot resist temptation and sometimes because she hasn't the courage to say no! However, her sexual flowering arrives much later—perhaps in her thirties or forties. Like her opposite number, Ms Virgo, the Piscean female often develops guilt feelings about sex. She is especially sensitive to emotional undercurrents between her parents, and more particularly in her mother. If her mother was unhappy and sexually unfulfilled, or considered sex a rather sordid affair, these attitudes consciously or unconsciously tend to filter down and in turn sully and confuse the daughter's own feelings about sex. Consequently Ms Pisces hardly ever finds sex a whale of an experience the first few times. The sad fact is that, if her initial experiences are less than satisfactory, she may block off her capacity for pleasure and sexual fulfilment, and settle down to a married life where sex becomes something to be endured rather than enjoyed.

One of the advantages for Ms Pisces, even if she suffers from a few guilt feelings about sex, is that she usually falls in love easily. It is when the Piscean woman's feelings are supercharged that her body naturally responds to making love. And unless her partner is hopeless or turns out to a sado-masochist she learns very quickly about the delights of sexual intercourse. This is a woman for whom sex and love are synonymous; it is almost impossible for her to respond physically to a man unless he has also aroused her emotions. By the same token, once she has fallen out of love, she shuts off sexually.

Sometimes the Piscean woman picks up the shadow of the Virgoan Siren.

This kind of Pisces may have great sexual allure since she knows how to use her sexuality to attract a partner. Yet because it is a contrived sexuality rather than something that involves her on all levels, she gets little sexual satisfaction out of intercourse other than that of proving that she has power over men. Sometimes, of course, this is entirely unconscious and the Piscean in this situation is just desperately seeking assurances about her attractiveness. On the other hand, a few Piscean Sirens use their sexuality to 'trap' a man; then once hooked, they turn icy cold.

Ms Pisces is rarely consistent in her choice of lovers; she veers from the mature sophisticate to the ingenuous youth; she can be attracted to power in a man as easily as she can be to sensitivity and passivity. Her capacity for multidimensional experience in life in limitless. At eighteen and somewhat prudish, I remember my amazement when a Piscean friend showed me the angry red lesions on her body inflicted by her forty-five-year-old lover (her first) whom she adored! She was the sweetest, most gentle of Pisceans yet she clearly relished this blood-letting experience. Piscean appearances are frequently deceptive.

The Pisces man often has an unexpected initiation into sex. Since he tends to be on the timid side when it comes to making sexual advances what he thought was just a 'kiss and a cuddle' can suddenly get out of hand. Once in the throes of sensual pleasure the Piscean can rarely find his self-control button. Also, it is invariably the female who urges the Piscean to lose his virginity, thus shattering his illusions about the passivity of the fairer sex, albeit in a thoroughly pleasurable fashion. Indeed Mr Pisces tends to be easily led by women, and he is often trapped into marriage with his first sexual relationship through misplaced feelings of honour. However, once he has loved and lost, his low tolerance threshold for commitment soon rids him of any guilt feelings over his conquests.

The Pisces man is not a physically oriented soul—he is a sensualist. While he can be attracted to a woman without being in love with her, he nevertheless invests some emotional as well as sexual energy in a relationship. Like his female counterpart, he may have some guilt feelings about sex, if only because he tends to idealize women—seeing them as pure and perfect creatures—which interferes with his desire for them as sexual 'equals'. As a young man, Mr Pisces is frequently drawn to older women. The mature woman has much to offer the Piscean: she tends to be more at ease with her womanhood and her sexuality, and can therefore show the Piscean the ropes, so to speak. Also, since the Piscean tends to be short on responsibility the older woman is usually able to take care of herself—and him. Since she may also be married, this reduces the Pisceans liabilities even more, although then he becomes laden with guilt!

As I discussed in the section on the Pisces Male, there are a few cold-hearted Fish about, and these types tend to regard sex as nothing more than a means for physical release. At an unconscious level they may dislike women, or fear them, thus sex becomes an act of degradation rather than a mutually pleasurable experience. In a few rare cases, the cold Fish will resort to violent and cruel sexual practices. I might add that when this happens there are likely to be many difficult links between Mars, Venus and the outer planets, not to mention a suitably traumatic or repressed background.

Predictably, the Piscean man is as difficult to categorize when it comes to sex as in any other area of his life. He can be as discriminating and fussy as his Virgoan opposite, or he can be a thorough sexual hedonist. However, almost all Piscean men are fascinated by sex—some can even become obsessed with it. The mystery of sex and the dark power of the feminine is never something they treat lightly. Yet for all their natural inclinations toward sex and the ecstasy it offers, the Piscean man is often just as fearful of rejection as his female counterpart. Thus, despite his need to explore his sexuality he may be deterred through his insecurity, yet another reason why the Piscean man (and the female) are drawn to older, more experienced partners.

The element of fantasy is an important ingredient to Neptunian and Piscean souls in many aspects of their lives. Sometimes this can be a downright hindrance but in the sexual area it is a positive bonus. Indeed some Pisceans have an uncanny ability to tune into their partner's fantasies, which can certainly electrify and intensify lovemaking. To a few, fantasy involves donning fancy dress—or at least garter belts and black stockings—but to others fantasies remain just that: they prefer to leave the earth signs to carve fantasy into reality. In emotionally healthy Pisceans, as with most individuals, sexual fantasy helps put them in touch with aspects of their psyche that need aerating. Very occasionally, however, some Piscean or Neptunian types over-indulge themselves, which either totally inhibits their sexual functioning or involves them in some very strange practices indeed!

The use of photography can be particularly stimulating to some Pisceans, although most tend to be aroused by the subtle and the erotic rather than by blatant pornography. Also submission and domination provide stimulating sexual play for Pisceans: there is an underlying impulse in most Pisceans to be possessed by their lovers and both male and female Fish enjoy being forcefully taken. Not all the time, of course; Pisces is a mutable sign and likes variety.

Pisces is also an extremely unselfish sign and this quality further enhances their lovemaking. Their fulfilment is linked to that of the partner's satisfaction and pleasure and they will go to any lengths to arouse and please a lover. Most prefer not to get involved in physical gymnastics in the bedroom but are nevertheless open to persuasion and experiment. There tend to be no hard lines to what Pisces will, won't, or cannot do.

Once or twice in earlier parts of this chapter I placed Pisceans in two categories in keeping with the symbolism of the two fishes swimming in opposite directions. This is also applicable to their sexuality. Despite the natural propensity of most Pisceans to indulge themselves thoroughly in the bedroom (the swimming pool or on the hearth rug for that matter) some Neptunian folk are capable of doing without a physical relationship at all. Pisces people are easily tuned into the cosmic and some find it a positive attribute to abstain from the weaknesses of the flesh and rise above their physical limitations. More often than not, however, abstinence is not a matter of high-minded idealism. As discussed earlier, some Pisceans cannot deal successfully with their emotions, which are inextricably interlinked with their sexual response; thus they do without sex for sheer fear of what such a relationship will unleash. Platonic relationships are frequently the order of the day for Pisceans and Neptunians in this category. Sometimes an initially sexual relationship develops into a platonic one as sexual intimacy is pushed further and further under the bed and eventually locked in the cupboard. It is not unusual either for these kind of fish to have one or more homosexual friends (of the opposite sex) with whom they form a 'quasi-sexual' relationship. Although friendship is undoubtedly part of the bond, the real attraction of such a partnership is that it presents no emotional risk as both parties' sexuality is unthreatened and their vulnerability effectively hidden behind a sexual charade. I must emphasize here that I am not referring only to Sun Pisceans nor by any means to all Sun Pisceans, but to those who have a strong Piscean or Neptunian theme regarding love, sex, and relationships.

On balance, however, those Pisceans who enjoy a fulfilling sexual life are in the majority; indeed for many the sexual act becomes a veritable art form. Perhaps the one negative factor with highly-sexed Pisceans is their ability to be attracted to countless numbers of individuals which can make their emotional lives something of a turmoil.

Pisces have their own particular brand of loyalty to a partner that does not necessarily include monogamous fidelity. Paradoxically, most of them are committed to marital fidelity as an ideal—it just seems to be difficult for many of them to put into practice. A Pisces individual finds it all too easy to become enthralled with someone, and when this happens he is not content with a superficial relationship: he must have total involvement and an intimate knowledge and experience of that person. Thus, sex is a crucial and integral part of such an encounter.

One of the most consistent factors I found from my questionnaire with individuals who had a strong Piscean element in their charts was the ability to remain deeply attached to a long-term partner while satisfying their physical and emotional needs through other relationships. One female with Venus in Pisces married for 34 years expressed this dichotomy in this way:

During my engagement I was afraid I might find someone who would sweep me off my feet as I imagined there was more exciting love than we had, and this didn't happen. But since marriage I have had a number of affairs, some lasting years, on and off, and I have known several more exciting men as far as my physical needs are concerned, but I was never tempted to leave my husband for them.

There are two more features that emerge frequently with Piscean and Neptunian individuals and both are allied to the impressionability and limitlessness of this sign.

First, Pisceans often have difficulty in differentiating between infatuation and love, even between friendship and love. Thus they are considered by others as sexual and emotional grasshoppers and, as we have seen in the preceding section, their butterfly dance from partner to partner generates many deeper emotional and psychological problems for them. Second, Pisces are attracted to people because of their whole being and not necessarily because of their gender. Thus bisexuality is not uncommon in strongly Piscean or Neptunian individuals. Pisceans have a fine appreciation of beauty which knows no sexual boundaries and both sexes tend to be more attracted by soft slender—even delicate—physiques.

To summarize, Piscean sexuality is both a blessing and a curse since most of them, if observed closely, will betray an underlying ambivalence towards sex. The source of this ambivalence rests in the fact that Pisces is a sign synonymous with the mystical, the divine, and the non-physical—the absolute antitheses of the raw physicality of sex. Yet paradoxically most Pisceans have strong physical drives. Thus even the most guilt-free Fish have occasional qualms over the nature and extent of their sexual urges. This ambivalence also provides a reason for the periods of self-imposed celibacy that many Pisceans experience and the tendency under emotional inspiration to go to extremes. Above all, Pisces seeks a mystical union in sex, which is why so many of them are drawn (or should be drawn) towards the approach to sex exemplified by the ancient Eastern Tantric tradition. Through this technique the development of at-one-ness through a combination of physical, emotional, and spiritual awareness leads to the ecstasy of ideal and actual perfect union that they crave.

PROFILE OF A PISCES WOMAN
JILLY COOPER

Jilly Cooper is the quintessential Pisces lady. She is charming, self-effacing, slightly shy, deliciously funny, and devastingly attractive. Her literary output is voluminous—if not verging on Piscean excess—and her books range from romantic novels and short stories to humorous studies of the British class system, mongrels, and horses at war. She makes frequent appearances on television where her ironic wit and schoolgirl enthusiasm are displayed to full advantage. She has been happily married to publisher Leo Cooper for 27 years and they have two children, Felix and Emily.

Writing was 'in the blood' for Jilly. Her aunt wrote poetry and novels and her grandfather, great grandfather, and great-great-grandfather had all been editors of the **Leeds Mercury**—which amalgamated with the **Yorkshire Post** this century. But while Jilly knew that she wanted to be a writer when she grew up, she remained blissfully ignorant of the self-discipline involved as she romped and skylarked her way through childhood. 'I had a buttercup childhood. We lived near the moors and I remember the days seemed full of nothing but ponies and dogs . . . I was a real tomboy, and I loved it. Once when I was in a telephone box—I must have been about eleven—there were some children outside and they were trying to work out whether I was a boy or a girl! . . . I was an unholy terror at school. But, yes, I suppose I was fairly bright.' Although most of her forebears had been editors, Jilly's father was in the army: 'He was the youngest brigadier in the war.' He and her mother were extremely happy together, and the whole family—Jilly has an elder brother—was close. 'I don't really remember any "dark" days during my childhood—though I expect there must have been some. I wasn't even aware of worrying about my father in the war—at least not for the last three years—because he was working at his UN office and

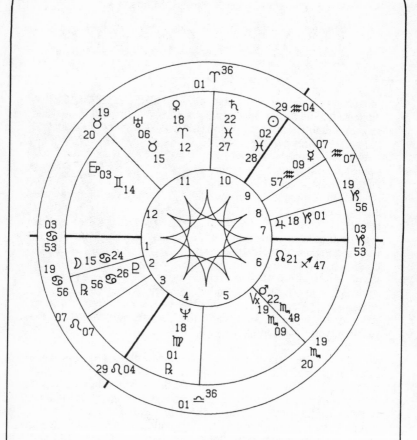

JILLY COOPER

21 2 1937   12h 0m 0s GMT

PLACIDUS 51N34 0E13

came home every night.'

The astrology bears out Jilly's 'buttercup childhood' only in part. While the Moon—a symbol of mother and childhood—is well placed in her chart, there are two difficult planets, Saturn and Neptune, involved in the area of home and family. It is possible that with fantasy-oriented Neptune in the fourth 'house' of family life, that Jilly is remembering the past in sepia-vision. On the other hand, occasionally Neptune does its inspired best in this house and 'produces' an idyllic childhood. However, with Saturn at the opposite point of the chart to Neptune the chances of a problem-free childhood are remote. Certainly Jilly was 'passionately homesick' at boarding school and nurtured plans to run away—although she never found the courage to do so—which could explain this aspect of separation and sadness in connection with her early years. Also, although Jilly had a strong relationship with both parents, there were times when her mother 'was a considerable worry'.

No doubt due to her recalcitrant manner at school, Jilly left with less than flying colours, several 'O' levels, but no 'A's'. 'I persuaded my parents that I would be happier taking Oxford and Cambridge Entrance at a crammer in Oxford. When I got there I was so pixilated with Oxford men that I went out every night and naturally ploughed my exams. After that I worked for a local paper, the **Middlesex Independent**, which I adored, and then I tried to break into Fleet Street. It proved so difficult that I insanely got diverted into PR.' By the time she was twenty-nine, Jilly was working in the PR department of a large publishing house. 'A friend asked me to find romantic stories for a teenage magazine—they were so awful I thought, "I could do better than this", so I began to write them myself and to my amazement most of them were accepted.' But it wasn't until two years later, when she was thirty-one, that she had her 'big break'. 'I was introduced to Godfrey Smith at a party and he asked me to write an article for the **Sunday Times** about being a wife. I did and when it came out I had nine jobs offered me straight away, one of them, which I took up, was as a columnist for the **Sunday Times**. I stayed there for thirteen and a half years.'

By then Jilly had been married to her childhood sweetheart, Leo, for seven years. 'Leo had always been in my life, but he married his house master's daughter when he was twenty-one, and I thought that was that. But it didn't work out. We met six years later—and were married within the year.' Leo turned out to be more than just a husband to Jilly. While not exactly in the Svengali mould, he nevertheless gently prodded and shaped Jilly's writing career, and while running his own publishing company, he is Jilly's manager—her right and left hand man!

Jilly's Piscean Sun is found near the top of the chart in the sector related to profession and life direction. Thus many of her truly Piscean qualities emerge through her writing. Jilly's romantic heroines are frequently cast in the Pisces 'victim' role: in the pursuit of love they land themselves in ghastly scrapes, increasing their dilemmas by extricating themselves from the puddle of one innocent white lie before falling into a deeper pool of confusion with yet another. Yet their muddle-headedness and soft-centred blunderings are at the core of their attractiveness and appeal. Jilly's heroines all too often have difficulties with self-restraint too—sometimes because they find gooey cakes or pasta irresistible; as ugly ducklings they rarely consider themselves worthy of the hero and often seem hell-bent in running in the opposite direction. Yet at the end of the day they are swept off their feet and into holy matrimony by the hero, who was no doubt captivated from the start by their ingenuous simplicity and vulnerability.

Jilly agrees that many of her heroines are her *alter egos;* yet in real life her gamin charm and fresh-as-a-daisy innocence camouflage a razor sharp intuition and strong personal drive. Whilst Jilly could never be considered a ruthlessly ambitious lady, with her Sun and Saturn in the tenth house of profession and status, a reclusive life on starving in the attic for her art holds little appeal either. Thus, the artistic and idealistic Piscean temperament is harnessed creatively and successfully in a career that brings her many worldly rewards. Also, although Jilly's heroines usually gleefully abandon their menial 'sekketary' jobs for love, marriage, and 2.8 children, Jilly combines her family life with an intensive and fulfilling career.

Jilly's Moon is placed in the sign of Cancer, perfectly complementing her Piscean Sun. The Cancerian theme is strong in her chart since this sign is also found on the Ascendant, and the Moon—which rules Cancer—is rising to the Ascendant degree. Cancer is another responsive, impressionable water sign; one only needs to browse through some of Jilly's books to appreciate the compassion and sensitivity that emerges through her writing. (Cancer, of course, is highly imaginative, and many writers have planets in this sign or the Moon at a significant point in the horoscopic circle.)

Cancer is also **the** sign of motherhood; people with a strong Cancerian element in their charts, like Jilly, usually nurture strong feelings and impressions about their childhood, home and family life. However, experiencing strong feelings does not necessarily imply they must be happy ones, nor that motherhood is a **raison d'être**. Cancer is a highly complex sign (see pp.147–54); all too often the myth of taking to motherhood like a duck to water is exploded and few Cancerian types find their only source of fulfilment and contentment in baking endless loaves of wholemeal bread or washing endless piles of nappies! In Jilly's case her home and family provide the anchor and security necessary to sustain her creative inspirations, but by her own admission, Jilly is not instinctively maternal. This does not imply, however, that she is a 'bad mother' or that she dislikes such a role, but that being a mother is only *part* of her life and not *all* of it. Indeed, one of the most poignant crises of her life occurred in her late twenties with the discovery that she was unable to have children. Thus her decision to adopt not one but two was anything but an impulsive, emotional gesture but a well thought-out, carefully considered yet passionately desired commitment—one typical of her strong Saturn, which I shall discuss later.

Astrologically, one of Jilly's greatest assets is the placing of her Venus in Aries, which gives the Piscean reticence and Cancerian caution a healthy blast on occasion and acts as a great confidence booster. Women with Venus in Aries have plenty of spirit; they are direct, frank, and open in the pursuit of their objectives, whether it be a new hat or a new man! In keeping with her forthright Arian Venus, Jilly informed her new mother-in-law on marrying Leo, 'I've kissed 340 men!' Whether this was a form of self-recommendation of suitability for the job, or proof that Leo had passed some sort of test, one cannot be sure, but this kind of spontaneous outburst is typical of those with Venus in Aries.

Women with Venus in Aries also admire courage and daring, if not in themselves certainly in others—Aries is, after all, a sign associated with battle and conquest! Intriguingly, Jilly first noticed her husband-to-be, Leo, at the tender age of eight when he hurled a jelly at another girl. A true hero in the making and a Sun Aries to boot! Although pugnacious Aries is not considered ideal territory for gentle, harmony-loving Venus, if, as in Jilly's case, there are plenty of planets in water signs, a fiery Venus encourages such women to leave the safety of their quiet backwaters for the romance and adventure of the high seas. Furthermore, the combination of Pisces and Aries in a woman can be formidably attractive to the opposite sex, for the gentle, dreamy, highly romantic Piscean side is given a charismatic spark and wickedly humorous edge by the Aries element. Jilly, in keeping with her Aries/Pisces mixture, acknowledges she falls in love at the drop of a hat, loves to be emotionally high, and would find life without love utterly intolerable.

Shortly after meeting Jilly I came across this opening to one of her short stories. There must have been more than just an element of personal experience behind these words as Jilly voiced this very realization about falling in love during our discussion:

One of the greatest shocks of Julia Nicholson's life was the discovery that being happily married doesn't stop one falling in love with other people. Before she was married, she was always in love—plunging into each new involvement with the alacrity of a high diver, who doesn't realise the water has been drained out of the swimming pool. After each affair, she emerged bruised and shattered, but perfectly willing, after a few weeks, to take the plunge again with someone else.

In many ways this entire paragraph encapsulates the Piscean dilemma and could surely only have been written by a Pisces.

Although the victim/saviour syndrome is another familiar Piscean theme, this tendency seems little in evidence in Jilly's life. She has never fallen for a drop-out or an alcoholic and feels the only spectrum of humanity she is capable of saving are lame dogs, cats, and horses—definitely of the four-legged variety. Here, of course, the more subtle aspects of astrology emerge. Jilly's seventh house of relationships is ruled by practical, long-term Saturn and in turn Saturn occupies a powerful position at the top of the chart in a beautiful, harmonizing grand trine with the Moon and Mars. Thus Jilly is far too sensible when it comes to a long-term relationship like marriage to settle for anything less than a Rolls Royce of husbands. Furthermore, Jupiter sits in the seventh house, indicating the likelihood of marriage to a larger-than-life individual who is benevolent and beneficial for her.

There is, of course, a less desirable side to Saturn in connection with the seventh house in that relationships can prove difficult and separation—sometimes physical, sometimes emotional and psychological—can occur. Obviously all couples experience periods when the formerly undulating path of holy matrimony appears suddenly strewn with gaping pot-holes and hills of the one-in-three variety. Certainly the following extract from **Work and Wedlock** is highly evocative of Saturn in regard to the seventh house of relationships: '. . . we've had marvellous patches and patches so bad that they rocked our marriage to its foundations, but I've come to realise that if you cling on like a barnacle during the bad patches, your marriage will survive and in all probability be strengthened.'

Another facet of Jilly's character emerges through the placing of her Mars in Scorpio. Scorpio, yet another water sign, adds depth and intensity to her emotions and endeavours and suggests a passionate, all or nothing attitude to matters of the heart. Love and sex are a serious business to people with Mars in Scorpio—a factor illustrated by Jilly's inability to fall in love and work at the same time. (A writer's block takes on a whole new meaning in Jilly's case!) Mars in Scorpio is highly sexy but can involve the individual in some cloak and dagger tactics when it comes to romance. Jilly admits to being rather wild in her youth—which is clearly the best time to exorcise such a Mars, otherwise marriage could turn into a kind of French farce with lovers hiding in cupboards or leaping out of windows, behaviour husband Leo's Aries' ego would be unlikely to tolerate!

Leo Cooper is the perfect foil for Jilly's fluid, sensitive temperament. He is a Sun Aries (Mars in the same sign) and Venus in Aquarius. He also has his Moon in Cancer, thus he and Jilly demonstrate many qualities typical of a couple who share the same Moon sign; their relationship requires little emotional effort as both are instinctively in tune and there is an underlying sense of being emotionally and psychologically 'at home' with one another. What is also astrologically significant about Jilly's choice of Leo as a husband is the strong contact Leo's Venus and Saturn make to Jilly's Midheaven (the area of life direction), significant particularly in the light of one of Jilly's comments on marriage that 'you marry where you want to go'. Certainly, Leo has been highly instrumental in helping her career and indeed providing just the sort of anchor a Pisces lady requires.

As so often happens when looking at relationships through astrology, what one individual lacks is seen to be provided by the partner—rather like a kind of planetary *paso doble*. Jilly, in keeping with her Pisces Sun, dislikes confrontation. In the event of a squall appearing over the horizon, she runs for cover to Leo, who, girding his Arian loins, launches into battle on her behalf. Thus her spunky Venus in Aries and pugilistic Mars in Scorpio tend permanently to take a back seat to her feminine and more passive Pisces side. It might be interesting to contemplate that without Leo to take the aggressive role, some of her more acerbic qualities that emerge only occasionally in her work would occupy a more dominant position, bringing her into line with the Dorothy Parkers of the literary world. Also Jilly might be surprised at her own strength and ability to fight back on her own terms without Leo's rock-like presence.

Although many facets of Jilly's character can be linked to various zodiacal and planetary patterns in her chart, with her Sun in Pisces at the highest point in the horoscope Jilly resonates most clearly with Neptune's muse. From adolescence, if not before, Jilly (in keeping with her Pisces 'sisters') embarked on a quest for the grail of the one great love affair. Whether she has found it, or ever will find it, is almost immaterial—the quest itself is the spur. Clearly Jilly's marriage to Leo is happy and fulfilling: there are few grey areas to sully its contentment. Her career and life-style are also highly fulfilling. But a Piscean woman is essentially a woman motivated by her dreams and longings such that she can never reach a point where she feels truly replete—an element of sadness and secret yearnings are an essential part of her make-up. A Pisces woman also keeps something of herself in reserve, a part completely denied to the outsider, a part an astrologer can only hint at but not unveil. Thus, when you next see Jilly grinning and effervescing on television look carefully into her eyes and you may just discern a certain dreamy detachment and sense of mystery. After all, she is first and foremost a Pisces lady.

Note for Astrologers: (1) Jilly's time of birth was given as 'just in time for lunch'. Working with various transits and progressions, around 4° Cancer rising seemed most appropriate.

(2) At age twenty-nine, as transiting Neptune conjoined Mars (in Scorpio) and transiting Saturn returned to its original position (in the tenth house and opposing her Sun-ruler, Neptune) Jilly discovered that she was unable to have children. At this point she also began her phenomenally successful writing career.

(3) Although Jilly thought August 1968 was the time her career took off, it was July that showed the most significant transits: transiting Jupiter opposed her Sun, transiting Mars and Venus crossed the Ascendant and went on to conjunct the Moon. During this year progressed Mars squared her Sun and progressed Mercury changed signs from Pisces to Aries.

PROFILE OF A PISCES MAN

HRH THE DUKE OF YORK

One of the most enduring national obsessions remains the great British love affair with the Royal Family. Since the Queen's Jubilee in 1977, the Royal Family's popularity has soared on a vast wave of enthusiasm that reached a sparkling crescendo in 1981 with the marriage of Prince Charles and Princess Diana. Now, in the mid-1980s, most of the Royals continue to command star status and constant media attention.

Prior to his marriage, Prince Charles was the front runner in the royal romantic stakes; with Charles safely ensconced in matrimony and patemity, Prince Andrew replaced him as Britain's Number One most eligible bachelor.

Charles and Andrew appear to have as little in common astrologically as they do in real life. Charles—fundamentally an ultra-sensitive Scorpio loner, highly conscious of his duties and responsibilities, and in many ways an enigmatic character—presents a vastly different image, if one not poles apart, from his charismatic, debonair brother Andrew. Yet in their inner lives they share certain themes. Obviously the eldest child in a family is bound to assume responsibility fairly early on in life (especially one in line for the throne), which may account in part for Charles' less sparkling and more sober veneer. But had their positions been reversed, Andrew would no doubt still have retained his easy-going, cavalier attitude as Heir Apparent.

Despite Andrew's court jester image, however, he is a sensitive Sun Pisces at heart and one of the great romantic heroes in embryo. While in early youth he displayed some of the more irresponsible characteristics of Pisces—though he was never without his winning

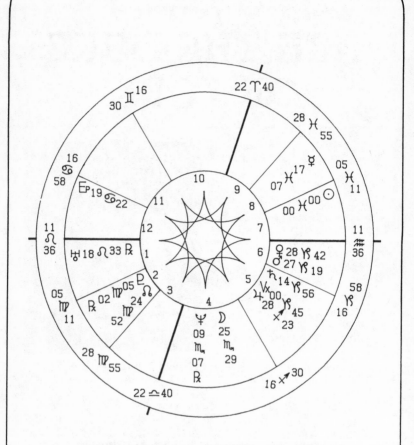

HRH THE DUKE OF YORK

19 2 1960   15h 30m Os GMT

KOCH 51N32 OW8

and beguiling charm—by his mid-20s, the beginnings of maturity and stature were clearly evident. Indeed the tendency of the Press to overplay the loutish, Hooray-Henry image prevented most of his finer qualities from seeing the light of day—at least as far as the public were concerned. Nevertheless, Andrew continued to fulfil Fleet Street's expectations of a prince who was a combination of Don Juan and Biggles, by escorting a variety of extremely attractive ladies—not all of whom met with Royal approval!

Astrologically, Andrew emerges as a complex character: his Pisces Sun in the seventh 'house' of relationships shows that he is people-oriented, and that he can relate to, understand, and empathize with others easily. Like many seventh-'house' individuals, however, he may also have a tendency to seek himself in his partners and to shape his identity through his interaction with others—a process that sometimes means he absorbs other people's ideas, habits, and even temperaments by a kind of unconscious osmosis. By contrast, Andrew's Ascendant is in flamboyant, self-confident, big-hearted Leo: this is the area of the chart most associated with the persona—the image the individual projects to the outer world—which is why the public tend only to see the gregarious, humorous, hail-fellow-well-met side of Andrew. However, Andrew also has some very down-to-earth qualities: with Venus, Mars and Saturn in Capricorn, there is an immensely practical, determined, and controlled streak. He acts swiftly and adroitly in a crisis and is a man to be relied on in times of danger when courage and the right action are essential. However, where emotional crises are concerned he is not so adept. Like many sensitive water-sign men, he was brought up to believe emotions made you weak and whimpish; thus while he has matured physically and intellectually, emotionally he tends to be rather under-developed—a factor that in the past has made him very vulnerable to, and easily duped by, the opposite sex.

Clearly Andrew has benefited from being brought up in a generation of Royals no longer isolated from the rest of society in an ivory tower of privilege. While the Queen and Prince Philip have endeavoured to uphold traditional values they have nevertheless encouraged a more informal structure in family life. Thus all their children have attended public school (and Charles and Edward university), which has allowed them to mix freely with their peers and experience their growing pains without the clutter of too much protocol. Andrew, like Charles before him, went to Gordonstoun public school in Scotland—an institution with a reputation for its spartan regime and its aims of inspiring self-reliance and initiative in its pupils. While Andrew is as circumspect as Charles over his feelings about his time at Gordonstoun, it is rumoured that he did not relish the hardy approach to life, regardless of how much character it built in him! While his Leo-Uranus side would have coped well with the challenge of Gordonstoun, as a sensitive Sun Piscean he would doubtless have longed for his home comforts and some tender loving care! Perhaps, too, his tendency to be cocky, pushy, and rather full of himself at school was a defence mechanism to protect deeper feelings of insecurity and even emotional hurt.

After Gordonstoun, Andrew signed up for twelve years in the Royal Navy as a helicopter pilot. This was to prove an extremely successful move. His abilities are ideally suited to the physical challenges and skills of such a career; he gets on well with his colleagues, and his sense of fun is shared by his fellow officers. While at school it is alleged that sometimes he clearly expected to be treated as special; in the Navy he assumes no such airs. Indeed, there is a rumour that he threatened to resign his commission had he not been allowed to serve in the Falklands War.

Broadly-speaking, Andrew falls into the category of a Pisces man who is fundamentally an emotional sponge and a romantic dreamer—the sort who expects to be forgiven for his indulgences, extravagances, and idiosyncrasies, the endearing rake who unerringly charms those he unintentionally offends. I expect, however, that Andrew will alter considerably from his late twenties and early thirties as he has the sort of chart that suggests a mildly rebellious and somewhat inconsiderate stance in youth that in maturity mellows into an uncompromising and highly committed attitude to right and truth. I also think, despite Andrew's press label as a school-boy prankster, that he has a 'kingly' chart and many of his planets occupy significant astrological degrees in Great Britain's and the Royal Family's charts. Obviously the first conclusion that leaps to mind is the dramatic and important role Andrew played in the South Atlantic war (1982), where he put his life at risk for Queen and country. However, I suspect in years to come Andrew will play yet another and somewhat unexpected leading role for his family and Great Britain.

Had Andrew been born a mere five minutes earlier his Sun would have been placed in the lattermost degree of revolutionary Aquarius. Nevertheless Aquarius, or rather its ruler Uranus, emerges as a major theme in Andrew's chart—on the Ascendant to be precise. Thus Andrew seems destined to be the most unconventional, yet ultimately fascinating, of the Queen's four children. Indeed, Uranus is the primary instigator behind his occasionally outrageous behaviour. People like Andrew who have Uranus on their Ascendants are spirited individualists from the moment they utter their first electrifying squawk and continue through life blasting huge holes in the walls of convention and bureaucracy, observing their own unique code of morality. April 1984 saw a scandalized American press recovering from the indignity of one of Andrew's jolly japes that backfired; on the spur of an unfortunate moment Prince Andrew turned a spray hose of white gloss paint over the gathered paparazzi, ruining clothes, camera equipment, and the **entente cordiale**! The following day he returned to England, tail between his legs, and disappeared conveniently to the Scottish Highlands. However, channelled in the right direction, Andrew's Uranian spark imbues him with a highly developed instinct for the right action in moments of danger and crisis. And with the Royal sign of Leo rising he is a potentially inspiring leader on the battlefield.

The Duke of York's Sun Pisces/Neptune side is a key factor in his love of photography and his ability to bring mood, atmosphere, and drama to his photographs. Andrew has already exhibited many of his photographs and clearly this is a direction he is likely to pursue throughout his life—perhaps into making and directing films. Andrew loves the glamour and exotic aura surrounding those who work in the fantasy world of film and theatre, so it is hardly surprising that the first great love of his life emerged out of celluloid in the shape of the curiously and possibly prophetically named Koo Stark. Koo—unfortunately, in the light of royal non-approval—had appeared naked in a soft-porn film (though directed by the Earl of Pembroke no less!).

In many ways Koo was perfect for Andrew—at least astrologically speaking. Indeed she herself has some grandiose, if not royal pointers in her own chart.* Koo is a Sun Taurean with her birthday falling a mere five days after the Queen's. It is difficult to resist mentioning here the theory that all men marry their mothers, or the astrological finding that many wives' and husbands' charts reflect their respective mothers and fathers-in-law! Of course, Koo in no way remotely resembles a cardboard cut-out of the Queen, but despite much pestering and haranguing from the press, especially during the death throes of the relationship, she conducted herself with dignity and aplomb and, best of all, in true Scorpio-rising style, kept her secrets to herself behind a mute silence, actually fainting from the effort during a talk show in Australia! Whether she will continue to do so in years to come remains to be seen.

Koo, like Andrew, has a Moon in Scorpio, a mere four degrees distance apart—which is a major indicator that their relationship was deeply passionate and loving. Andrew's Moon in Scorpio not only indicates his own deep and complex feelings and his tendency toward extreme emotional highs and lows, but also that he is attracted to women who are similar: ladies who are equally

*Jupiter and Pluto flanking the Midheaven in Leo.

passionate, sexy, prone to dark impenetrable moods and, at times, extremely difficult to handle! Koo definitely came up to expectations here but, though initially fascinated by her Mata-Hari persona, at the tender age of twenty-two he was too emotionally immature to handle such a relationship, and, indeed, too immature to end the relationship decisively. Ironically, had Koo met Andrew some three years later, and had she been more cautious in her earlier choice of film roles, she might well have had more chance of reaching her objective. As it was, such a destiny was not meant to be.

I had initially written Prince Andrew's profile in the Spring of 1984, when there was no sign of a future Princess Andrew. In my earlier draft I had speculated that while Andrew was attracted to rather 'exotic' women, when it came to marriage he was ultra-conservative: 'though he may flirt with the "house-maid", he'll walk down the aisle with a bride dripping in diamonds—and a pedigree to match.' This I had gleaned from Andrew's Venus-Mars conjunction in Capricorn, and the placing of Saturn (Capricorn's ruling planet) in the fifth house of creativity and love-affairs. Saturn-Capricorn themes regarding love can indicate some difficulties and obstacles to romantic bliss; they can also show an attraction to older women, or females with a strong Capricorn-Saturn theme in their own charts. Thus it came as no surprise that towards the end of 1985, a certain Miss Sarah Ferguson (whose chart has major connections with those of the Royal Family) was spending more and more time in Andrew's company. Like Koo, Sarah has a strong Scorpio theme in her own chart; but unlike Koo, she had an impeccable background; furthermore, Sarah arrived in Andrew's life just as he was astrologically primed to fall in love and consider marriage.* Thus, as far as I was concerned, Andrew's fate had been sealed.

Andrew could never have tolerated an arranged marriage. He believes in love and he was well and truly 'head over heels' by the time he proposed to Sarah just after his birthday at the end of February 1986. Not only does Sarah reflect Andrew's Scorpio need for a strong emotional bond, but her Libran Sun falls exactly on his sensitive IC point. Sarah also has an impulsive, forthright Aries Moon, which in turn reflects Andrew's Arian Midheaven. Andrew seems to seek out an Aries spark in the women he likes, since many of his friends and some of his old girlfriends have an Arian flavour to their charts. Andrew likes strong women. He doesn't seem to mind being bossed around by them and Sarah's ability to put him in his place—but nicely (!)—seems to have toned down his former rather bumptious, boisterous manner.

*Progressed Venus conjunct radical Sun; progressed Ascendant opposition (applying) radical Sun; transiting Jupiter conjunct the Sun in his 7th house of relationships (February 1986).

That Andrew has found a woman he can love, respect, and with whom he can have fun, will doubtless mature him emotionally and provide the necessary stable foundation for his life and future responsibilities. Of course, like any marriage there are bound to be some ups and downs over the years. Andrew's seventh-'house' Sun forms a close opposition to Pluto; on the one hand this aspect suggests that marriage will transform him as an individual (which is good) but that on the other, there could be some power struggles between them—each one trying to gain the upper emotional hand. Andrew's Uranus-ruled seventh 'house' also suggests that, as much as he craves security in a partner, he needs room to 'breathe' and times to be alone. He is not one to 'grin and bear' an unhappy relationship but he is gaining increasing experience in how to talk through and defuse any emotional impasses, should they arise. Andrew needs emotional highs in his life and—considering his physically active Mars in Capricorn—a fulfilling physical relationship!

Andrew expressed the idea that his and Sarah's ability to work as a team was an important component of their relationship. Since Sarah is a Sun Libra and Andrew has his Sun in the Libran seventh 'house', their mutual desire for union on all levels and working in tandem is astrologically apparent. Furthermore, they both care that their relationship works, which means that when they encounter difficulties they will work at them together rather than expecting the other person to put matters right. Andrew is a curious mix of sensitivity and detachment: he also nurtures high ideals in romance and love. While the Uranian and Capricornian side of him may present a super-rational front, faced with an emotional scene he is in turmoil. If he cannot deal with the situation, he will cut himself off. Sarah, however, will not allow that to happen; with pressure, Andrew is forced to examine his emotions, which in the process makes him a stronger and wiser man.

As a Sun Pisces, Andrew has, in essence, the whole of the zodiac's culled experience within him: he has much to draw from and much to offer. However, like any Pisces, the temptation to escape and to evade responsibilities and commitment is ever-present. Mr Pisces needs direction and firmness of purpose to realize his great potential. He also requires an anchor. Thus, marriage to Sarah, who is a woman of great strength and determination, is an important part of this process. Andrew is only twenty-eight years old; as yet we have glimpsed merely a fraction of his potential. In an ideal world, The Duke of York would no doubt use his artistic-creative skills in a professional capacity, but it may well be that the increasing pressures on him as a member of the Royal Family—some of them unexpected—will deny him this opportunity. Prince Andrew is a man destined for a remarkable future.

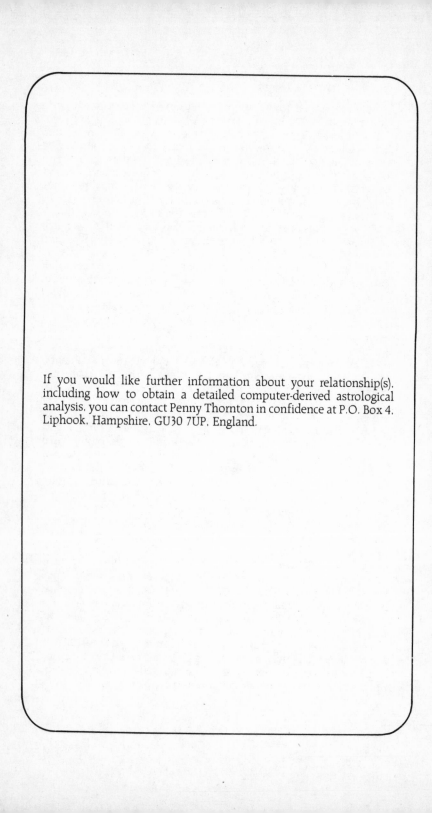

If you would like further information about your relationship(s),
including how to obtain a detailed computer-derived astrological
analysis, you can contact Penny Thornton in confidence at P.O. Box 4,
Liphook, Hampshire, GU30 7UP, England.